COLLECTED WORKS OF ERASMUS

VOLUME 9

Erasmus
Hans Holbein the Younger, 1523
Öffentliche Kunstsammlung Basel, Kunstmuseum

THE CORRESPONDENCE OF
ERASMUS

LETTERS 1252 TO 1355

1522 TO 1523

translated by R.A.B. Mynors

annotated by James M. Estes

University of Toronto Press

Toronto / Buffalo / London

The research and publication costs of the
Collected Works of Erasmus are supported by the
Social Sciences and Humanities Research Council of Canada.
The publication costs are also assisted by
University of Toronto Press.

©University of Toronto Press 1989
Toronto / Buffalo / London
Printed in Canada

ISBN 0-8020-2604-4

Printed on acid-free paper

Canadian Cataloguing in Publication Data

Erasmus, Desiderius, d. 1536.
[Works]
Collected works of Erasmus

Includes index.
Partial contents: v. 9. the correspondence of Erasmus :
letters 1252 to 1355, 1522 to 1523 / translated by R.A.B. Mynors ;
annotated by James M. Estes.
ISBN 0-8020-2604-4 (v. 9)

1. Erasmus, Desiderius, d. 1536. I. Title.

PA8500 1974   876'.04   C74-6326-X rev

Collected Works of Erasmus

The aim of the Collected Works of Erasmus
is to make available an accurate, readable English text
of Erasmus' correspondence and his
other principal writings. The edition is planned
and directed by an Editorial Board, an Executive Committee,
and an Advisory Committee.

Contents

Illustrations

Preface

When Erasmus wrote the first letter in this volume, which covers the period January 1522–March 1523, he was in the third month of a sojourn in Basel that was to last, with only brief interruptions, until April 1529. He had decided to leave Louvain and go to Basel in part because he was weary of controversy with the Louvain theologians, in part because he wanted to see the annotations to his third edition of the New Testament through Froben's press, and most of all because he feared that pressure from the imperial court, which had been back in the Netherlands since May 1521, would force him to take a public stand against Luther.[1] His original intention had apparently been to return to Brabant in the spring of 1522.[2] But it was difficult for him to leave Basel, a city with important attractions and advantages. It contained many good friends, the legacy of his earlier stay there in 1514–16. It was not involved in the war between Charles v and Francis i that had broken out in 1521. Most of all, in religious matters it had a liberal-reformist atmosphere congenial to a man of Erasmus' views and was still years away from decisive adherence to the Reformation. On the other hand, the local wine had an adverse effect on Erasmus' health,[3] and the summer of 1522 saw a prolonged uproar caused by the antics of some adherents of the Reformation.[4] So Erasmus was for a time determined to go elsewhere. But an attempted trip to Rome in the autumn had to be aborted because of a bad attack of the stone at Constance and also because of reports of the dangers of the journey.[5] Similarly, plans to migrate to France early in 1523 were abandoned partly because Erasmus' health improved with the aid of some imported Burgundy wine but mostly because his hopes for an early

* * * * *

1 See Epp 1242 introduction, 1302:11–16, 1342:57, 105–10, and Allen Ep 2792:13–23.
2 Ep 1257:12
3 Ep 1311:22, 34–5
4 See Ep 1293 n8.
5 Ep 1319:11–16

peace between the two monarchs were disappointed.[6] Meanwhile, reports of preparations for war, of religious persecution, and of the scarcity of Burgundy wine, as well as the knowledge that at least one old adversary in Louvain had become an inquisitor, made a return to the Netherlands even less attractive than it had been at the outset.[7]

Until September 1522, Erasmus lived in Froben's house, and thereafter in a house rented from him. During the period we are concerned with, he completed a number of works that were duly published by the Froben press: the third edition of the New Testament (February 1522); the paraphrase on Matthew (March), dedicated to Charles v; two new expanded editions of the *Colloquia* (March and August); the *Epistola de esu carnium* (August); two *apologiae* against his Spanish detractors, Diego López Zúñiga and Sancho Carranza, printed with the *Epistola de esu carnium*; an edition of Arnobius Junior (September), dedicated to Pope Adrian vi; the *Catalogus lucubrationum* (dated 30 January 1523, published in April); the paraphrase on John (February); and an edition of Hilary of Poitiers (February).

The works listed above certainly add up to an achievement of considerable magnitude, especially for someone who suffered more than his usual measure of poor health during the period in question.[8] Nevertheless, the predominant theme of the letters in this volume is not that of scholarly production but rather that of the serious problems posed by 'the sorry business of Luther.' By the beginning of 1522, the Reformation in Germany had entered a period of spontaneous and often disorderly growth that was to last into 1526. Even though Luther had been excommunicated and outlawed, reform erupted everywhere, especially in the towns. As the Reformation spread and gathered strength, Erasmus increasingly found himself caught uncomfortably between papalist and antipapalist zealots, each faction demanding that he publicly espouse its cause. The more Erasmus persisted in espousing 'the cause of Christ' as he understood it, and the more he tried to stand aloof from the conflict and impress on both parties the urgent need to restore 'unity and concord in the gospel,' the more he found himself 'a heretic to both sides.'[9]

Erasmus' Catholic critics were by far the more dangerous. On 19 January 1522, Juan Luis Vives wrote from Louvain that Erasmus' old adversaries among the Louvain theologians were trying to persuade the emperor that he was a supporter of Luther.[10] Erasmus believed that their

* * * * *

6 See Ep 1319 introduction.

7 Ep 1342:638–47

8 See Ep 1256 n2.

9 See especially Epp 1252, 1259, 1267–8, 1278, 1305.

10 Ep 1256:11–21

motive was the old hatred of the humanities that had made them hostile to him long before anyone had heard of Luther, and that their aim was thus not simply to destroy him personally but also to discredit those studies which had tended to undermine their authority.[11] Erasmus knew that he had other detractors at the imperial court as well. The most dangerous of these, he thought, was the papal nuncio, Girolamo Aleandro. For almost a year Erasmus had been convinced that Aleandro was bent on discrediting him at both the imperial and papal courts as a supporter of Luther.[12] Indeed, Erasmus tended to see all his detractors in the Netherlands and at Rome as agents of Aleandro.[13] Since the nuncio was himself a distinguished humanist, Erasmus attributed his hostility not to hatred of the humanities but to insatiable ambition and to a mind poisoned by the slanders of unnamed 'malicious detractors.'[14] Aleandro's supposed 'tool' in Rome was Zúñiga, who had already published an intemperate attack on the first edition of Erasmus' New Testament.[15] In mid-February, Jakob Ziegler wrote from Rome that Zúñiga had compiled a catalogue of Erasmus' allegedly heretical views (*Erasmi Roterodami blasphemiae et impietates*),[16] from which he read aloud at gatherings of influential personages. Moreover, Erasmus knew that the newly elected pope, his fellow-countryman Adrian VI, although hitherto personally well disposed toward him, was nevertheless a non-humanist and sternly anti-Lutheran.[17] So he feared that Zúñiga and others in Rome and elsewhere might succeed in turning Adrian against him.

Consequently, Erasmus undertook measures to secure his reputation and good standing with both emperor and pope. At the suggestion of Jean Glapion, the emperor's personal confessor, Erasmus attempted in April to pay a visit to Brabant in order to make his case in person at the imperial court, capitalizing on the good impression already made by the presentation copy of the paraphrase on Matthew.[18] But two days into the journey his health broke down and he had to turn back to Basel,[19] where he quickly dispatched several letters (Epp 1273–6 and doubtless several others as well) to important men at court, including Glapion. Erasmus made substantially

* * * * *

11 Epp 1263:29–34, 1268:59–66. The same point is reiterated in Epp 1273–5, 1299–1300, 1330.
12 See Ep 1256 n11.
13 Ep 1268:67–78
14 Epp 1263:1–3, 1268:70–2
15 See Ep 1260 n36.
16 Ibidem lines 167–71, 203–12
17 See Ep 1304 introduction.
18 Epp 1269–70
19 Epp 1302:51–7, 1342:333ff

the same points in all four of the surviving letters: those who call him a
supporter of Luther are either stupid or else shameless liars; he has made it
perfectly clear in his published letters (ie, those in the *Epistolae ad diversos* of
August 1521) that he has no agreement with Luther's party, whose
subversive behaviour he has always disliked and attempted to restrain;[20] he
could have done the Lutherans a great favour and caused quite an uproar in
Germany by joining their cause, but he would rather die ten times over than
start a schism; all this is well understood by the Lutherans, who hate him
and threaten him with 'vicious pamphlets'; all the ills at the root of the
current troubles can be cured peacefully 'by the emperor's authority and the
integrity of the new pope'; Erasmus will do what he can, as a humble scholar,
to advance the cause of the emperor and of the Christian faith, if only the
emperor will provide him with the necessary leisure and tranquillity by
making his imperial pension permanent and defending his reputation
against shameless falsehoods. These were, of course, conveniently one-
sided generalizations. In this context it would not have been prudent for
Erasmus to admit, for example, that he could still see some good in Luther or
that there were many 'Lutherans' who, like Zwingli[21] and Ulrich von
Hutten,[22] still thought well of him and hoped that he would be won for the
Reformation.

None of the responses to these letters survives. Erasmus informs us in
several places, however, that Glapion, Gattinara (the imperial chancellor),
and others wrote him 'letters full of sympathy,' urging him to continue his
'labours for the cause of learning,' and indicating the emperor's personal
good will.[23] Moreover, the imperial secretary, Guy Morillon, wrote to assure
Erasmus that his imperial pension (as well as the income from his benefice at
Courtrai) was safe.[24] (Given the chronic disorder of the imperial finances,
that was no guarantee of prompt or regular payment, as Erasmus was to
discover.) Unfortunately, the good will of the emperor and his entourage
did not allay the hostility of Erasmus' Louvain adversaries, who returned to
the attack after the emperor's departure for Spain in May. The Carmelite
Nicholaas Baechem (Egmondanus) found fresh evidence of Lutheran heresy
in the new edition of the *Colloquia* and denounced their author both in public
sermons and 'at drinking-parties.' Erasmus responded with letters of

* * * * *

20 After seeing the *Epistolae ad diversos*, Luther wrote: 'Erasmus at last reveals that
   he is a wholehearted enemy of Luther and his doctrine, though with deceitful
   and clever words he pretends to be a friend' (WA-Br II 527:22–4).
21 Epp 1314–15
22 See Ep 1331 n24.
23 Epp 1299:41–4, 1300:63–6, 1302:62–6, 1331:12–19, 1342:281–92
24 Ep 1287

protest (Epp 1299–1301) addressed to officials of the Netherlands government and to the theological faculty at Louvain, defending the orthodoxy of the impugned passages and once again identifying hatred of the humanities as the real motive for the attack. These letters, however, remained without effect, and the battle with the Louvain theologians was far from over. Small wonder that in the long introduction (Ep 1334) to his edition of Hilary, the scourge of Arianism, Erasmus took the opportunity to comment at length on the baleful effects of theological controversy.

Meanwhile, Erasmus was working to secure his good reputation in Rome. By mid-July he had received the good news that Zúñiga's anti-Erasmus campaign had not gone down well with the college of cardinals, tried to prevent the publication of the *Erasmi blasphemiae et impietates*.[25] But this left Erasmus in the dark and full of worry about the attitude of the new pope himself, who was still *en route* from Spain to Rome, where he arrived in late August. Erasmus first sent feelers via his old friend Pierre Barbier, who was now a member of Pope Adrian's household. The second of two surviving letters to Barbier (Epp 1294, 1302) contains a brief account of Aleandro's unsuccessful campaign against Erasmus at the imperial court and emphasizes that the emperor, the king of England, and the college of cardinals, as well as other dignitaries of church and state, were clearly Erasmus' supporters. Then, in September, Erasmus made a direct approach to Adrian himself with the dedication of the edition of Arnobius to him. In the covering letter for the presentation copy (Ep 1310), Erasmus observed that it was intended as 'a kind of antidote' against the virulence of malicious tongues, 'should any hostile report of me come to your ears,' and begged the pope either to reject such reports or at least to keep an open mind until he had had a chance to defend himself.

Four months of anxious waiting passed before Erasmus received, in January 1523, the pope's reply (Ep 1324). In it Adrian so roundly dismissed Erasmus' critics and in general displayed such obvious good will that Erasmus was overjoyed and called the letter his *Breve aureum*. It was not pure gold, however, for Adrian added his name to the long list of those who urgently pressed Erasmus to serve the church and silence his detractors by writing against Luther. Erasmus' reasons for declining to do so are most fully and frankly stated not in his reply to the pope (Ep 1352) but in his response (Ep 1313) to a similar appeal from Duke George of Saxony (Ep 1298). Some of those reasons were in fact just excuses: his age and poor health; the lack of leisure to read all that had been written on both sides; the

* * * * *

25 Ep 1302:68–91

fact that many others had already written against Luther. But the real reason was there, too: Erasmus could not honestly 'write against Luther bitterly enough to avoid seeming lukewarm to the other party' or gently enough to avoid being 'torn to pieces' by Luther's men. To Erasmus it was beyond doubt that Luther had begun in a truly Christian way with an attack on real abuses, including the worldliness of the papacy. While it is true, he said, that Luther has not done this with appropriate mildness, it is also true that 'the foolish, ignorant, and subversive clamour' of self-seeking 'monks and theologians who think like monks' have made things much worse and done great harm to the cause of both Christ and the pope. Moreover, the 'most savage' bull of excommunication against Luther and the 'even more savage' edict of outlawry have only embittered the conflict without changing anyone's mind. Meanwhile, Luther's own 'insufferable faults' have 'ruined his good things,' and many of his followers are even worse than he is. Now there is such an atmosphere of bitter hatred that if Luther is overthrown, the victorious monks will probably destroy all the good things in Luther along with the bad things, thus doing further damage to the glory of Christ and the purity of the gospel.[26] Erasmus' conclusion was that, in these circumstances, any direct move by him against Luther would only fuel an already destructive controversy and make him more unpopular than ever with the zealots on both sides. In his letter to Pope Adrian, Erasmus expressed the same view, but prudently avoided any references to 'the good things in Luther' or to the 'savagery' of the bull of excommunication and the Edict of Worms (which Adrian had just called on the German Estates to enforce vigorously[27]).

Erasmus' technique for appeasing those who pressured him to write against Luther was to offer to write instead about how to solve the Luther problem. In April 1522 he informed Glapion that he had begun 'a short treatise on how to end this business of Luther,' but that poor health had prevented its completion.[28] The work, which he later said was to have consisted of three dialogues,[29] would doubtless have had much in common with the *Axiomata*[30] of December 1520 and the *Consilium*[31] of January 1521. In December 1522, even before receiving the *Breve aureum*, Erasmus wrote to Pope Adrian (Ep 1329) offering to submit a plan for the restoration of

* * * * *

26 Cf Ep 1348.
27 See Ep 1344 n10.
28 Ep 1275:23–5
29 Ep 1341A:1338–1415
30 See Ep 1263 n10.
31 See Ep 1267 n6.

tranquillity, an offer which the pope eagerly accepted (Ep 1338). Erasmus accordingly included his plan in Ep 1352, but the surviving text breaks off just at the point at which he was getting down to specifics. The letter does include, however, Erasmus' comments on the right and the wrong way to deal with the Lutherans. The wrong way, he said, is suppression by force, which failed to extinguish the Wycliffites in England and will be even less effective against the Lutherans in Germany, where political authority is dispersed among so many princes. The right way is for the pope to investigate and to remedy the sources of the Lutheran revolt, meanwhile imitating the divine mercy by forgiving those who had 'gone astray through the persuasion or influence of others.' Pope Adrian never replied to Erasmus' letter.

Erasmus' refusal to counsel severity against the Lutherans was motivated by concern for public peace and the common good of Christendom, not by any tender regard for Luther and the other reformers. Indeed, many of the letters in this volume testify to Erasmus' growing aversion to the reformers, and one can see him moving perceptibly in the direction of his eventual public breach with them. To someone who believed that 'the sum and substance of our religion is peace and concord'[32] and could say that, if pressed, he would 'abandon some portion of the truth sooner than disturb the peace,'[33] Luther and company had to seem at least as reckless and subversive as the 'monks and theologians.' Moreover, the Lutherans were beginning to hurl a variety of accusations at Erasmus which impugned both his character and his competence as a theologian. Some, who still believed that Erasmus was at heart on Luther's side, concluded that only cowardice and the hope for gain kept him in the papal ranks. They hoped, by fair means or foul, to manoeuvre him into their camp.[34] Others, chiefly the Wittenbergers, offended Erasmus even more deeply by charging that his views on free will were false, even Pelagian.[35] (Here, of course, was the issue that Erasmus would choose when he eventually made up his mind to write against Luther.) Determined to make clear to the 'warped minds' of the Lutherans where he really stood, Erasmus included in his long letter to Marcus Laurinus (Ep 1342), published in February 1523, a catalogue of his grievances against the Lutherans. At the conclusion of the catalogue, he stated unequivocally that he would be neither leader nor colleague to those

* * * * *

32 Ep 1334:232
33 Ep 1331:24–7. Cf Johann von Botzheim's gentle reproof in the opening paragraph of Ep 1335.
34 Ep 1342:659–726
35 See Ep 1259 n5.

who preferred to 'cause universal confusion' rather than work to 'secure the victory of Christ and the establishment among all men of concord in the gospel.'[36] One partisan of Luther who had hoped to manoeuvre Erasmus into the ranks of the reformers, Ulrich von Hutten, finally realized that Erasmus was not to be so manoeuvred. It was the reading of Ep 1342 which moved Hutten to write his *Expostulatio* against Erasmus.[37] The last letter in this volume was written on the eve of the outbreak of the controversy with Hutten, which turned out to be a prelude to the more serious controversy with Luther.

Of the 107 letters presented here, 60 were written by Erasmus and 47 were written to him. These letters contain references to more than 60 other letters that are no longer extant; because so many of the references are to an unspecified number of letters, an exact figure cannot be given, but 70 to 75 would be a good guess. Only 40 of the surviving letters were published by Erasmus himself, 23 in the *Opus epistolarum* of 1529, 7 as prefaces to various works, 9 as adjuncts to other publications, and one as a separate work. Of the remaining 67 letters, one (Ep 1280A) was published by its author in 1524, while the rest were published by a variety of scholars in the more than four centuries from Erasmus' death to 1974. Fourteen of them were first published by Allen himself. To allow the reader to discover the sequence in which the letters became known, the introduction to each letter cites the place where it was first published and identifies the manuscript source if one exists.

On the whole, Allen's text and his ordering of the letters have been followed; but there are exceptions. First, Allen Ep 1280 has been redated to 1528 and will appear at the appropriate place in CWE 14. Second, Allen Ep 1412 has been redated to mid-January 1523 and appears here as Ep 1337A. Third, two letters omitted by Allen, one by Battista Casali and one by Caspar Ursinus Velius, have been included here as Epp 1270A and 1280A. Fourth, where Allen preferred the shorter of the two extant versions of Ep 1301, we have opted for the longer version, believing it to be the more interesting one historically. Fifth, Aleandro's alternative draft of Ep 1324, long excerpts from which Allen included in his footnotes to the official version of the letter, is here printed separately as Ep 1324A. Finally, the long letter to Johann von Botzheim that Erasmus published as the *Catalogus lucubrationum* and that Allen placed in his volume 1 as a preface to the correspondence is included here as Ep 1341A. Our text of the *Catalogus*, like Allen's, includes passages that Erasmus added to the second edition (September 1524) and

* * * * *

36 Ep 1342:1006–18
37 See Ep 1341A n283.

that frequently refer to events, like the controversy with Hutten, outside the chronological scope of this volume. This seemed obviously preferable to publishing the interpolations as isolated fragments in CWE 10. Textual integrity is surely preferable to chronological tidiness.

The index to this volume, prepared by Howard Hotson, contains references to the persons, places, and works mentioned in the volume, following the plan for the correspondence series. When that series of volumes is completed, the reader will also be supplied with an index of classical and scriptural references. Because the three volumes of the CEBR are now available, the biographical annotation of this volume has been kept to an absolute minimum. So has the citation of biographical sources. Wherever information is supplied without the citation of a source, the reader is tacitly referred to the appropriate article in the CEBR and to the literature there cited.

With the exception of Epp 1270A, 1280A, and 1334, the letters in this volume were translated by R.A.B. Mynors. The translation of Ep 1280A is by Ann and Alexander Dalzell; Alexander Dalzell also translated Ep 1270A and revised and completed the translations of Epp 1301 and 1324A. The translation of Ep 1334 is that by John C. Olin and James F. Brady jr, first published in slightly abbreviated form in Olin's *Six Essays on Erasmus* (Fordham University Press 1979) 93–120. For further details, see the introduction to the letter.

I should like here to record my personal debt to those colleagues who have given me the benefit of their advice and erudition. Alexander Dalzell of Trinity College, University of Toronto, provided abundant and invaluable assistance with the classical annotations. Erika Rummel of the CWE editorial staff read all the notes; her comments have led to a significant number of corrections and improvements. The following scholars generously responded to my requests for information on specific issues within their fields of competence: Leonard Boyle OP, Prefect of the Vatican Library; Rika Maniates of the Faculty of Music at the University of Toronto; Martin Lowry of the University of Warwick; Robert D. Sider of Dickinson College in Carlisle, Pennsylvania; John C. Olin of Fordham University; John J. Bateman of the University of Illinois at Urbana-Champaign; Jane E. Phillips of the University of Kentucky at Lexington; James Farge CSB of the University of St Thomas in Houston; and Peter Bietenholz of the University of Saskatchewan. The notes on currency were supplied by John H. Munro of the University of Toronto. The assistance of several other scholars has been acknowledged at the appropriate places in the notes. A special word of thanks goes to the copyeditor, Mary Baldwin, whose sharp eye caught many a petty blunder before it was too late.

Most of the work on this volume was done using materials in the library of the Centre for Reformation and Renaissance Studies at Victoria University in the University of Toronto, especially the Centre's splendid Erasmus Collection. For patristic and medieval texts I had recourse to the library of the Pontifical Institute of Mediaeval Studies on the campus of St Michael's College, University of Toronto. I am deeply grateful to both institutions and their staffs.

Finally, the editors wish to record once again their gratitude to the Social Sciences and Humanities Research Council of Canada, without whose generous assistance the Collected Works of Erasmus could not be published.

JME

Deventer

Bruges
Ghent
Antwerp
Mechelen
Brussels
Louvain
Anderlecht
Tienen
Cologne
Düren

Koblenz
Mainz
Trier
Worms
Speyer

Strasbourg
Stuttgart
Colmar
Freiburg
im Breisgau
Lauingen
Donauwörth
Breisach
Ulm
Kelheim
Landau
Dijon
Schaffhausen
Passau
Montbéliard
Langenargen
Basel
Zürich
Mauthausen
Constance
Lake
Constance

Lake
Geneva

Milan

Avignon
Noves

Bologna

Florence

Rome

Wittenberg

Dresden
Wrocław

Prague

Kroměříž

Nürnberg

Paris

Seine
Maas
Rhine
Neckar
Lech
Danube
Rhône
Elbe

N

0   100 MILES
0   100 KILOMETRES

THE CORRESPONDENCE OF ERASMUS

LETTERS 1252 TO 1355

1252 / To Udalricus Zasius   Basel, 4 January 1522

First published by Allen, this letter survived in two contemporary copies, which in 1924 (the date of Allen's volume 5) were owned privately by Dr J.F.M. Sterck of Haarlem and Dr Bruno Clausen of Rostock. No information on the subsequent fate of either manuscript is available.

On Zasius, see Ep 303.

TO ZASIUS, THRICE-GREATEST OF MEN, FROM ERASMUS
OF ROTTERDAM

Greetings, my most learned Zasius. I was delighted to hear that you are well, and in good spirits too. Ursinus[1] is as good a scholar and as open-hearted a man as any I ever saw. To him alone I almost owe my life; his   5
delightful company is so refreshing. A visit to Freiburg would not be unwelcome,[2] had I not bound myself wholly to the treadmill once again.

As for this business of Luther, I know not how it will turn out. From the start I always foresaw that it might end in civil strife, and now I fear just this. Christ take it in his keeping! I have certainly discouraged the affair, at the   10
outset and all along. For your part, if you ever supported Luther openly, I think it wiser for you to remain silent than to attack him in print. You will get no credit for it; people will think you a coward or a time-server. Leave him to his destiny.

I can write no more. Give my greetings to Latomus,[3] and thank him for   15

* * * * *

1252

1 Caspar Ursinus Velius (Ep 1280A). At this point he was visiting Basel, but by 19 January was back in Freiburg (AK Ep 835).

2 For another invitation to visit Freiburg, see Ep 1316. Erasmus made the desired visit in March 1523; see Ep 1353 introduction.

3 Bartholomaeus Latomus (Mason) of Arlon (c 1498/9–1570) studied at Freiburg, taking an MA in October 1517. He then commenced the study of law under Zasius, whose friend he became, and probably met Erasmus in nearby Basel in 1518. In November 1521, Latomus, now a lecturer in arts at Freiburg, met Erasmus in Strasbourg and accompanied him as far as Sélestat (Ep 1342:237–40). From 1522 to 1530 Latomus taught classics at the universities of Trier and Cologne. After further study (1530–1) under Goclenius (Ep 1209) at the Collegium Trilingue in Louvain, he went to Paris, where he became professor of Latin at the Schola Regia (1534–42). His reputation as one of the great Latin scholars of his day was based primarily on his work on Cicero. From 1542 until his death he was councillor to the archbishop of Trier and a champion of Catholic reform.

the elegant poem he wrote in my honour.[4] I will write at another
opportunity.

    Basel, 4 January 1522

    It is not a good plan for an old man to transplant himself.[5] Be brave;
seek comfort in liberal studies and in your old friends.[6] This storm will one   20
day turn into fine weather, and you must keep yourself for that.

1253 / From Urbanus Rhegius   Langenargen, 4 January 1522

    The autograph of this letter, which was first published in LB, is in the Rehdiger
    Collection of the University Library at Wrocław (MS Rehd 254.126).

      Urbanus Rhegius (1489–1541), whose real name was probably Urban Rieger,
    was born in Langenargen near Lindau on the northern shore of Lake
    Constance. He took his BA at Freiburg, where he lived with Zasius, and his MA
    at Ingolstadt, where Johann Eck (Ep 769) secured him a lectureship in rhetoric
    and poetry. After this he resumed the study of theology, settled in Constance,
    and was ordained in 1519. In 1520 he became preacher at the cathedral in
    Augsburg. In December 1521 he had to leave Augsburg because of his
    inclination toward Lutheranism, but by 1523 he was back. In December 1524 he
    formally adopted Lutheranism, as a consequence of which he was once more
    forced out of the city in 1530. He spent his remaining years as a reformer and
    church leader in the duchy of Braunschweig-Lüneburg.

TO THE LEARNED ERASMUS OF ROTTERDAM FROM URBANUS RHEGIUS,
AS FROM ONE THEOLOGIAN TO ANOTHER, GREETING
Your return to us, Erasmus my learned friend, is a matter for rejoicing in
Germany and indeed in all Christendom. We have waited for you as for a
sun destined to dispel the darkness of our night – that internal darkness, I   5
mean, which is the most perilous of all; for you are the prime author of the
revival of theology in our own time, and whoever does not acknowledge
that is both false and ungrateful. You were the first to recall theologians from

* * * * *

4 The poem appears not to have survived.
5 This whole postscript sounds very much like a comment on the circumstances
  mentioned in Zasius' letter of 20 March (Ep 1266:26–30): the ugly conflict
  between university and town in Freiburg (the 'storm' that Erasmus refers to in
  line 20) and Zasius' consequent determination to leave. Given the duration of
  the town-gown controversy in Freiburg (Ep 1266 n3), it is unlikely that Ep 1266
  would have been the earliest expression of Zasius' desire to 'get away from it
  all,' so Erasmus might well have known of that desire and the reason for it
  when he wrote this letter.
6 Latin and sense are uncertain.

the muddy pools of the scholastics to the sacred fount of Scripture, and that
too in such modest terms that your reproof, so salutary and so badly needed,   10
gave no offence even to your enemies, except for some few moping owls
who deserve to be ignored or pitied rather than disliked. First of all, you
urged us to study the theologians of antiquity; then led us, as it were,
upstream to the crystal springs of the original Scriptures; in a word, you
achieved so much by sleepless nights of scholarly activity that scarcely any   15
branch of learning now makes such happy progress as divine theology. It is
a wonderful sight to see humane and sacred studies so interconnected that
they can be pursued together without conflict, though previously the
machinations of the ignorant made them worse than enemies. All this we
owe to your efforts; you have left no stone unturned to secure that in place of   20
their empty philosophizing the schools of theology, at long last, should
recognize the divine philosophy of the cross. Rejoice, Erasmus, in your
victory; it begins to be recognized, not among the learned only but by
laymen too, who have been convinced by your *Paraclesis*[1] that Scripture is
the property of every Christian.   25

   The other day I heard a married woman[2] discoursing on the law and
the gospel in Paul's Epistle to the Romans with much more knowledge than
those great doctors of divinity would have shown in the old days – so much
has your clarion call roused the whole world to the philosophy of Christ. I
have no doubt at all that to breathe new life into theology is what you were   30
born to do. Fulfil your destiny: purge Augustine[3] and Hilary[4] with your
accomplished hand, until we can distinguish true from false, as you did so
successfully in years gone by with Jerome.[5]

   The church in Augsburg, where I have preached Christ now for
eighteen months, prays for you zealously; I expect to return to it shortly. The   35
man who brings you this is of good family and devoted to you for your rare
gifts of mind, although no scholar himself. Farewell, our prince of theology
and of all learning.

   From Langenargen, 4 January 1522
   Michael Hummelberg[6] my fellow-countryman sends you his greetings.   40

   * * * * *

1253
1 The *Paraclesis* was Erasmus' preface to the *Novum Testamentum* of 1516. From
   February 1519 onwards Froben reprinted the preface separately, sometimes
   combining it with the *Ratio verae theologiae*.
2 Perhaps Margarethe Peutinger; see Ep 1247.
3 See Ep 1309.
4 See Ep 1334.
5 See Epp 326, 396.
6 Michael Hummelberg (1487–1537) of Ravensburg, where he was within easy

To the honourable Master Erasmus of Rotterdam, the eminent theologian and my most respected teacher, in Basel

1254 / From Maarten Davidts   Brussels, 10 January 1522

This is the first of ten letters in this volume of which the original manuscripts were preserved in the so-called Burscher Collection (MS 0331m) at the University Library in Leipzig. The collection, whose earliest known owner was Bonifacius Amerbach (Ep 408), comprised autograph letters addressed to Erasmus. (At least one letter *by* Erasmus and in a secretary's hand, Ep 1278, was in the collection as well.) The letters found their way to the Netherlands and then to England, where they were acquired by a Württemberg diplomat whose widow gave them to a German pastor in London, who in turn gave them to Professor Johann Friedrich Burscher in Leipzig. Burscher first published many of the letters in his *Spicilegia* (1784–1802). A century later the entire collection was re-edited and published as *Briefe an Desiderius Erasmus von Rotterdam* by Joseph Förstemann and Otto Günther (Leipzig 1904; repr Wiesbaden 1968). See the introduction to that volume for the history of the Burscher Collection, which was destroyed in World War II. This letter is Ep 4 in Förstemann/Günther.

Maarten Davidts (d 1535) was a canon of Brussels with whom Erasmus usually lodged when in that city; see Ep 532:35n.

Master Erasmus, my beloved teacher, on the ninth of December[1] I received your letter[2] written from Basel on the morrow of St Thomas the Apostle. To send you a brief answer by way of acknowledgment: in the first place, as regards the money which your lordship left in my keeping for the use of Franz Birckmann,[3] I did in fact pay it over on the thirteenth of December last 5 to Franz himself, who came to Brussels then, he told me, to visit the prior of St Augustine's at Antwerp.[4] The prior, on orders it was said from the

* * * * *

reach of Rhegius at Langenargen. Hummelberg was an enthusiastic Greek scholar who had studied in Paris and Rome and then settled down in his home town as a teacher.

1254
1 A mistake for January. The feast of Thomas the Apostle falls on 21 December.
2 Not extant
3 Franz Birckmann, the Antwerp bookseller (Ep 258:14n)
4 Jacob Proost (or Probst) of Ieper (1486–1562), prior of the Augustinian convent at Antwerp, who in 1521 had become a licentiate in theology at Wittenberg; see Ep 980:62n. He was now in trouble with the Inquisition and would shortly be

emperor, had been taken from Antwerp to Brussels and at that time was
detained, as he still is, in Godshouse belonging to the Brethren of Nazareth,[5]
but the reason for this or the business in which he is concerned I do not   10
know. I have heard however that Baechem[6] and Latomus[7] and certain other
people have had discussions with him, and that the case is to be settled
soon. Some say that the prior will have to retract some things he has said in
the pulpit, and so on.

As to your things,[8] you may be sure that up to now they have been   15
faithfully and securely kept, and will be so kept for the future, as you hope
and trust they will be. On the power of attorney[9] I have spoken with Master
Guy;[10] it cannot be arranged through us unless you are present in person.
Excuse my clumsy style. No more for the moment.

From Brussels, 10 January '22 (Roman style), your humble servant   20
Maarten Davidts, at your service

To the most learned of men, Master Erasmus of Rotterdam, his most
worshipful teacher

1255 / To Charles v   Basel, 13 January 1522

This is the preface to Erasmus' paraphrase on Matthew, written in Basel in 1521
and published there by Froben in March 1522.

TO THE INVINCIBLE EMPEROR CHARLES, FIFTH OF THAT NAME,
FROM ERASMUS OF ROTTERDAM, GREETING
Right well I know, invincible Emperor Charles, the great respect and
reverence due to all the sacred literature which sainted Fathers put forth for
our benefit under the inspiration of the Holy Spirit, and especially to those   5

* * * * *

forced into a public recantation (9 February 1522); cf Epp 1256:25–8, 1258:4–5.
In June 1522 he escaped, going first to Wittenberg, and then (May 1524) to
Bremen, where he spent his remaining years as pastor and superintendent.
5 The house of the Brethren of the Common Life at Brussels, founded in 1422
6 Nicolaas Baechem of Egmond (d 1526) was prior of the Carmelites at Louvain,
where he also taught theology at the university; see Ep 878:15n. In 1520 Charles
v made him an assistant inquisitor. Baechem was one of Erasmus' most
obstinate and intemperate critics, the first two editions of the New Testament
and the March 1522 edition of the *Colloquia* being his particular targets; see
especially Epp 1299–1302, and 1341A:928–1009. Erasmus, who detested
Baechem, often made puns on 'Carmelite,' calling him 'camelus' or 'camelita.'
7 See Epp 934 introduction and 4n, 1341A:830–9.
8 Cf Epp 1258:1, 1275:11.
9 In connection with one of Erasmus' pensions; see Ep 1287:9–22, 27–8.
10 Guy Morillon, the emperor's personal secretary (Ep 1287)

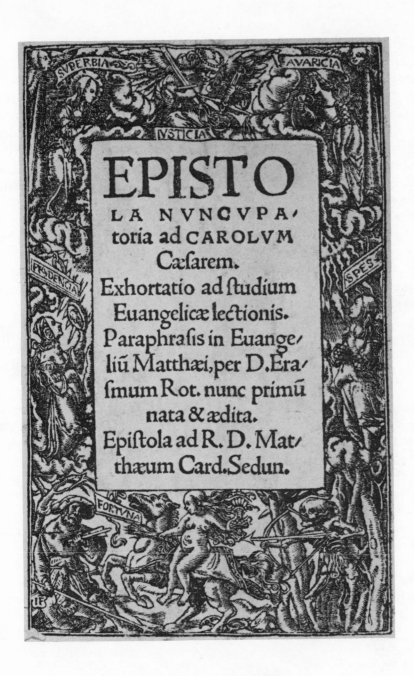

SVPERBIA

AVARICIA

IVSTICIA

PRVDENCIA

SPES

EPISTO
LA NVNCVPA-
toria ad CAROLVM
Cæsarem.
Exhortatio ad studium
Euangelicæ lectionis.
Paraphrasis in Euange-
liũ Matthæi, per D.Era-
smum Rot. nunc primũ
nata & ædita.
Epistola ad R. D. Mat-
thæum Card. Sedun.

FORTVNA

Erasmus *Paraphrasis in Mattheum* title-page
Basel: Froben 1522
Centre for Reformation and Renaissance Studies,
Victoria University, University of Toronto

which give us a faithful account of all that our heavenly Father did or uttered
in the person of his Son Jesus Christ for the salvation of the whole world; and
I am well aware of my own unworthiness. When a few years ago I first set
my hand to an exposition of the Pauline Epistles in the form of a
paraphrase[1] – it was an unprompted impulse that put the idea into my head   10
– I felt myself to be undertaking an exceedingly bold and self-confident
enterprise and one 'full of dangerous hazard' as the saying goes;[2] so much so
that after trying the experiment with two or three chapters, I was minded to
furl my sails and abandon my intended course, had not my learned friends
with surprising unanimity urged me to continue. Nor would their importu-   15
nity allow me any rest until I had finished all the apostolic Epistles that we
possess, although I had not intended to deal with any except those which
beyond all question were written by St Paul. It has not always turned out
well when I have obeyed the promptings of my friends; but in this instance I
was gratified to find the result of my rash undertaking more successful than I   20
had expected, both for its author, who earned very little unpopularity, and
for all who wish to learn the gospel authority, who vie with one another in
their gratitude, having found in my work an inspiration to pursue the
wisdom of the apostles or a great aid in its pursuit.

Having performed this task, I was not expecting thereafter to have   25
anything more to do with this type of literature. But no: I went to pay my
respects to his Eminence Matthäus, cardinal of Sion,[3] who had encouraged[4]
me to complete the canonical Epistles when he was in Brussels[5] on his way
back from the Diet of Worms, and in our very first conversation, as though
he had thought of this in advance, he began to urge me to do for St   30
Matthew's Gospel what I had done for the apostolic Epistles. I at once made
numerous excuses. I had already shown sufficient audacity, I said, in
attempting this for the letters of the apostles. The apostles were of course
inspired, but they were only human, while the majesty of Christ was too
great for the same boldness to be permissible in respect of the words he   35
uttered. If I were not deterred by the solemn nature of the task, yet the
subject-matter was unsympathetic and did not admit of paraphrase; and not
solely because in the gospel different characters appear, so that while the

*transl. corrected
in vol. 41*

* * * * *

1255
1 See Ep 710.
2 Horace *Odes* 2.1.6; cf *Adagia* I iv 32.
3 Matthäus Schiner (Ep 1295)
4 See Ep 1171:50–7.
5 Schiner spent the latter half of June 1521 in Brussels, departing for Milan on the
  thirtieth to negotiate with the Swiss on behalf of the emperor; LP III 1357, 1388.

writer adapts his style to suit them (as he has to), his pen is constrained
within very narrow limits and of course is debarred from the freedom   40
allowed to other kinds of commentary. For a paraphrase is a kind of
commentary. Besides that, since a great part of the gospel consists of a
narrative of events in a simple and straightforward style, he who seeks to
paraphrase such material will perhaps be thought to do no more than, as the
Greek proverb has it, kindle a lamp at midday.[6]   45

Then again, since the ancients in expounding the allegories show great
variation and sometimes behave, in my view, as though they were not
wholly serious, nor will it prove possible to set them down except as one
who reports the words either of Christ or of the evangelist, it is clear that I
should be facing very great difficulties. I need not add that Christ sometimes   50
spoke as though at the time he wished not to be understood, for instance
when he said, 'Destroy this temple and in three days I will raise it up,'[7] and
again when he spoke of buying a sword[8] or being wary of the leaven of the
Pharisees.[9] Again, in the discourse in which he foretells the destruction of
Jerusalem, the end of this world, and the afflictions that will befall the   55
apostles in the future,[10] Jesus so mixes and adapts what he has to say that he
seems to me to have wished to remain obscure not only to the apostles but to
us.

Again, there are some passages which in my opinion are quite
inexplicable, among them the phrase about the sin against the Holy Ghost   60
which can never be forgiven,[11] and the last day which only the Father knows
and which is unknown even to the Son.[12] Faced with such places in a
commentary, one can without peril report the differing views of different
scholars, and even confess outright that one does not understand the
passage. But the author of a paraphrase is not allowed the same freedom.   65
Furthermore, some things are expressed in such a way that they refer
equally to modern times, in which we see many things that conflict with the
institutions of the apostolic age. Granted that the evangelists knew these
things in advance by the spirit of prophecy, they cannot be recounted as if
the evangelists themselves were speaking, except in a very unnatural and   70
artificial way. My mind was influenced also by the thought that if I

* * * * *

6 See *Adagia* II v 6.
7 John 2:19
8 Luke 22:36
9 Matt 16:6–12; Mark 8:15; Luke 12:1
10 Luke 21:5–33
11 Matt 12:31–2
12 Mark 13:32

undertook this task in Matthew only, some people would demand forthwith
the same treatment for the other evangelists. If I were to comply with their
wishes, I foresaw that I should often have to repeat the same words,
wherever in fact the evangelists agree among themselves. Suppose, on the   75
other hand, I were to construct some kind of continuous narrative out of
them all;[13] since to explain the discrepancies between the evangelists is like
going round and round in some sort of maze, I could not then have
maintained the clear texture of a paraphrase.

With these arguments and many others like them I begged to be   80
excused the task that was set before me, and thought I had a good case
which must win the day. But the cardinal's eloquence and his authority were
too much for me; he took the risk and hazard of the whole business on his
own shoulders. I had not the face to stand out any longer against the advice
of a man whose wisdom your Majesty is often happy to follow in matters of   85
the greatest moment. At any rate, though I had not entirely accepted the
burden, but had only promised that I would try sometime if it could be made
to work, he went on to Milan,[14] and promised the Germans in my name that
the work would come out this winter. Consequently on my return to Basel I
was beset by my German friends, who can be very obstinate when they want   90
something, so that to fulfil the promises he and I had made I finished the
work in about a month. Thus he commanded, I obeyed, and I only wish the
result may be a happy one for us all; of which I have some hopes, if your
Majesty will accept this modest gift which is dedicated to you.

At this point, someone who knows nothing of you but your imperial   95
title will ask: What can a lay prince make of a subject that was more suitably
dedicated to abbots or bishops? In the first place, I consider that any
honourable gift made to a Christian prince is an appropriate gift. Besides
which, while no prince is such a pagan as to find the faith of the gospel
foreign to him, emperors are anointed and consecrated expressly that they   100
may either protect or amend or propagate the religion of the gospel. And so
the emperor is no teacher of the gospel, but its champion, I quite agree; yet at
the same time it is right to have some idea what it is for the defence of which
you take up arms. What is more, when I consider how devoted you are in
spirit to religion and piety, so that bishops and abbots might find in you a   105
standard or a stimulus to zeal for true religion, I think there is no one to
whom this gift might have been offered more appropriately than to your
Majesty. And so what I might fitly have dedicated to any Christian prince,

* * * * *

13 A task subsequently undertaken (but never finished) by Jakob Ziegler; see Ep
  1260:200–2, 303–4.
14 See n5 above.

and still more fitly to an emperor, I dedicate most fitly of all to Charles. Less
appropriate are the gifts offered by those who bring precious jewels,   110
high-mettled horses, hounds for the chase, or barbarous tapestries. Again,
since the evangelists wrote down the gospel to be read by all, I do not see
why all should not read it, and I have treated it in such a way that even
illiterates can understand it. But it will be read with the greatest profit, if
each person takes it up with the intention of becoming better than he was   115
before, not of adapting the gospel text to fit his own affections but of
correcting his way of life and his desires to match the rule that it lays down.
In this work I have mainly followed Origen, the most experienced
theologian of all, along with Chrysostom and Jerome, the most generally
approved among the orthodox.   120

May that heavenly prince grant you, most august Emperor, to will and
to attempt those things which are best, and may he bring your efforts to a
happy outcome, so that your great empire, which hitherto has come to you
without bloodshed, may be extended or maintained on the same terms. In
the mean while, merciful Prince, never forget that no war can be undertaken   125
for so just a cause or fought with such moderation that it will not bring with it
a vast horde of crimes and calamities, and further, that the largest share of
these evils falls upon harmless people who do not deserve them.

Basel, 13 January 1522

1256 / From Juan Luis Vives   Louvain, 19 January 1522

This is one of many letters from Vives to Erasmus (eg, Epp 1222, 1271, 1281,
1303, 1306, 1362) found in volume 2 of the first collected edition of Vives'
works, published at Basel in August 1555 by Nicolaus Episcopius the Younger.
The originals are lost. Erasmus' replies to Vives' letters, written from Basel,
have disappeared, though the dates of some of them are known. Erasmus
replied to this letter on 4 February; see Ep 1271:1.

The great Spanish humanist (Ep 927), intimate friend of Erasmus since 1518,
was at this time living at Louvain, where he had a licence to teach privately at
the university. He was also working on the edition of Augustine's *De civitate
Dei* that was to be included in Erasmus' complete edition of Augustine's works;
see lines 108–17.

VIVES TO ERASMUS
Your long-awaited letter[1] arrived a few days ago and, since it came from you,

* * * * *

1256
1 Not extant

could not fail to be most welcome; but inasmuch as it said that you are not well[2] and that things are not going as you would wish, it disturbed me, or perhaps I should say distressed me, very much, I do assure you. I wish you 5 had had a talk with me when you were here very lately.[3] I would have told you what I have heard, not that I myself think it either true or likely, but it would give you a better understanding of the attitude of certain persons, which I am sure is not unknown to you; and maybe, if you had heard this from me, you would be less troubled now by the rumours you speak of,[4] 10 which you say in your letter are rife in Germany as well. That you are thought here to be a supporter of Luther is beyond question; but by those same men who, as you well knew when you were here, have a habit of laying at your door anything loaded with envy, hatred, and malice; and they think there is no surer way to undermine your standing and reputation than 15 by coupling you with Luther. Those who make this attempt are not very numerous, but their clamour and their propaganda are unceasing, and they omit nothing that they think may help to prove their point. What they would like most is to convince the emperor and the princes, though, as far as I can make out, they do not work for this openly and directly, but in a roundabout 20 way when they see the chance. At court there are a few theologians from Paris.[5] The only thing they have against you is that they say your utterances on the subject of Luther have always been ambiguous; but they accept you without difficulty, once Luther is suppressed.

There is an Augustinian who has been haled from Antwerp to Brussels 25 these last few days to stand his trial;[6] the Cripple[7] and the Camel[8] have come post-haste to the scene. These men, I hear, have been spreading wicked falsehoods about you; but they were already doing that before Luther was born. No Orestes or Hercules ever raved like these two;[9] but the incredible case is the Stonemason:[10] in everything he says or does he is as mad as a 30

* * * * *

2 Erasmus was seriously ill throughout 1522. Cf Epp 1259, 1264–5, 1267, 1274, 1283, 1302, 1311.
3 Erasmus had last been in Louvain on the eve of his departure for Basel (28 October 1521); Epp 1242 introduction, 1342:117–28, 151–2.
4 Cf Epp 1248:54–6, 1249:23–4.
5 Eg, Luis Coronel (see Epp 1274, 1285:47) and Herman Lethmaet (Ep 1320).
6 Proost (Ep 1254 n4)
7 Jacobus Latomus (Ep 934:4n), who was lame
8 Baechem (Ep 1254 n6)
9 Orestes was driven mad by the Furies after he murdered his mother Clytemnestra. Hercules, driven mad by Hera, killed his wife Megara and their children.
10 Latomus

hatter. He would make a better tragic hero than any of the great madmen of antiquity.

Our Herald-angel[11] from Rome is an open-hearted type who keeps neither his own counsel nor other people's. He complains that he has had much to suffer from you, but maintains that all the same he has not discarded his old affection; and he has said that the duke of Alba[12] is annoyed with you because you wrote to Barbier in Spain that the Spaniards are in favour of Luther in hopes of being taken for Christians.[13] This is not credible, for I cannot think you said any such thing; and suppose you did say it as a joke, who could have passed it on to him? And then I have myself spoken to his son,[14] who told me that his father happened to speak of you

* * * * *

11 The papal nuncio, Girolamo Aleandro (1480–1542). Aleandro was a brilliant classical scholar who had taught Greek with great success at Paris (1508–13) and then embarked on an ecclesiastical career which in 1516 took him to Rome, where he entered papal service. In the summer of 1520 he was dispatched to the court of Charles v to implement the bull *Exsurge domine* (Ep 1313 n6) in Germany and the Low Countries. In October he supervised the burning of Luther's books in Louvain and Liège. He did his best to have Luther handed over to Rome and to prevent his appearance before the Diet of Worms. Failing at that, he helped the diet formulate the edict of 26 May 1521 that outlawed Luther (Ep 1313 n7). He then accompanied Charles v back to the Netherlands to continue the campaign against heresy there.
   Meanwhile, the old friendship between Erasmus and Aleandro (Ep 256) had been transformed into bitter hostility. The publication of Erasmus' very cautious letter to Luther (Ep 980) apparently aroused Aleandro's suspicions that Erasmus was a supporter of the Wittenberg heresiarch (Ep 1167:125–37), suspicions fanned by Erasmus' detractors in Louvain and elsewhere and by Erasmus' evident dislike for the harsh policy embodied in the bull against Luther. In the winter of 1520–1 Aleandro denounced Erasmus in his dispatches to Rome as a worse heretic than Luther and the agitator arousing all Germany to rebellion. Rumours of this, combined with the book burning and the denunciations of Aleandro by Hutten (Epp 1135, 1161), persuaded Erasmus that Aleandro was a very dangerous enemy indeed, bent on discrediting him at both the imperial and the papal courts (Ep 1188). In the autumn of 1521 there was a reconciliation of sorts (Epp 1342:121–66, 1271:68–70, 1281:63–5), but it did not last. By the spring of 1522 Erasmus once more believed that Aleandro was an enemy (Epp 1263:1–3, 1268:67–74), a conviction that persisted despite Aleandro's many subsequent protests that it was not so (cf Ep 1324 introduction).
12 Fadrique de Toledo (c 1460–1527), an important member of Charles' court and, since 1519, a Knight of the Golden Fleece; cf Ep 1271:140ff.
13 No letter with these words is extant.
14 The duke had five sons. The reference here is probably either to Fernando, a member of Charles' court, or Diego, prior of the Order of St John in Castile and Léon.

several times but has never made any mention of that remark; but what his father's views are, he did not know, for he never gave any indication of favouring either party. And a friend of mine who is a herald[15] is here, who would not keep it to himself if he had heard anything. For he did not conceal these two rumours: one, that you had told a bookseller in Antwerp to put Luther's books on sale and not worry about the proclamation,[16] and the other that Luther, when urged to recant,[17] replied that he was not free to do so without consulting the men who had inspired and encouraged him to launch this campaign;[18] he suspected, he said, this meant you among others, and that you alone were named among the first.

This man is the source of all the rumour spread in Germany; but you had seen right through him even while you were here. For those who thought of you in the old days as a follower of Christ owning no allegiance to any other name are still of the same opinion, and Fame, we know, 'gains in strength as she flies.'[19] This is a patch of fog which you, seeing it from a distance, think is immense; but you would change your language if it came closer and you could see and feel it. Nor is it surprising that men should tell such falsehoods about what happens a long way away, when we are told here every day of things being done at Brussels and Mechelen which have never even entered anyone's head. So you ought not to be at all upset by these reports. Those who call you a follower of Luther here and those in Germany who call you the exact opposite are the same people and pursue the same object. They play different parts to suit the theatre and the spectators, but their purpose is to make you unpopular, and as you are impregnable everywhere else, this is the point at which they try to breach your defences.

I wish you would write to your friends at court and tell them of the baseless charges being levelled against you by these men whose enmity is criminal; to Halewijn[20] for instance, and to the emperor's confessor[21] if he is at all a friend of yours, for he carries no less weight at court than Christ himself. I myself shall join them, once I am finished with Augustine,[22]and

* * * * *

15 Unidentified
16 On 20 March 1521 a proclamation ordering the burning of Luther's books was published in Charles' name in Mechelen. For Erasmus' visits to Antwerp after this proclamation, see Epp 1199, 1205, 1302, 1342.
17 Presumably at the Diet of Worms in April 1521
18 No such remark is recorded in the reports of Luther's appearance before the Diet of Worms; see WA VII 814–87.
19 Virgil *Aeneid* 4.175
20 Ep 1269
21 Jean Glapion (Ep 1275)
22 See lines 108–17, 148–62.

there I shall radiate enough heat to dissolve much of this fog; for he[23] does
not rate me the lowest of the low, and I am taking steps to join Ferdinand's
household.[24] But keep this to yourself for fear that, if it gets out, it may be   75
prevented. As for the Angel,[25] if you could at a suitable opportunity give him
an honourable mention, you would make him entirely yours; for he has
complained to me that you never thanked him for the help he gave you
against Zúñiga in that matter of the za[26] – I expect you know what I mean.
You see the sort of thing he minds about – or rather, the sort of opinion he   80
has of you, if he desires praise from you so much. But the other lot are biting
all the more viciously because death approaches, as some wild beasts do; for
there is no doubt that they will not enjoy the perennial youth which is so
entirely yours, the youth I mean that comes from the humanities, and from
Christ.   85

The Stonemason,[27] they say, is unpopular with his colleagues; he gives
himself such airs since he got the entrée to this house of the bishop of
Cambrai,[28] and they think he must be very influential because he follows
that young man around everywhere. What shadows they are frightened of!
– as though either the man he follows had any influence or any power that   90
his master might have were his to use. Your purpose is Christian, as it
always was, and beyond a doubt Christ has prepared for you a great and
plenteous reward for it, seeing what poor thanks you get from men; though,

* * * * *

23 Ie, Glapion
24 Since 1519 Vives had had hopes of becoming tutor to Archduke Ferdinand, the
   emperor's brother. Erasmus had been offered the post but declined it,
   recommending Vives instead. See Epp 917 introduction, and 1271:138–9.
25 Aleandro; see n11 above.
26 In annotating Matt 4:1, Erasmus had observed that a reading of zabulum
   instead of diabolum in a manuscript of Hilary was perhaps a copyist's error.
   Zúñiga, in his Annotationes contra Erasmum (Ep 1260 n36), pointed out that the
   form zabulum was common in Hilary and other Fathers and suggested a
   derivation from the Hebrew zebul (as in 'Beelzebul'). Aleandro then indicated
   to Erasmus that za is often used in Greek for dia. In the first edition of his reply
   to Zúñiga (Ep 1277 n1), Erasmus argued that the influence of Greek usage was
   the more probable explanation of zabulum, but did not give Aleandro credit for
   his assistance in the matter. Doubtless as a result of this hint from Vives,
   Erasmus inserted a suitable acknowledgment in the enlarged second edition of
   February 1522 (LB IX 295D). Cf Ep 1334:889.
27 Latomus; see n7 above.
28 Latomus was the teacher of Robert de Croy (1500–56), who in 1519 had
   succeeded his brother Guillaume (Ep 628:70n) as bishop of Cambrai. At the
   time of his election, Robert was not yet in higher orders and was still pursuing
   his studies at Louvain. He was ordained in 1529 and assumed his duties as
   bishop from that time. In 1546 he was a delegate at the Council of Trent.

as far as that goes, their language will moderate or grow more hostile according to the new pope's[29] attitude towards you. But tell me this: Do you wish to refute the common lot of all good men? In Christ's name, my dear Erasmus, I do beg you most urgently not to distress yourself, not to bring on old age before its time, by taking these worthless rumours so deeply to heart. A man who has Christ himself, and all men of good will, and a clear conscience so thoroughly on his side cannot easily be hurt by wicked men. You have done nothing wrong, which is the one thing a good man must achieve in life, and it is not your business what end God may appoint for you.

But why do I say this to you of all people? Warham[30] and Thale[31] and Maurice[32] attend my lectures and are my dear friends; the first two will be the more dear for what you say of them, and this last one too, if that is possible.

As for Augustine,[33] I have finished thirteen books. Seven are revised and copied out, six others have been at press for some time now; and all the time one goes on adding. It was rash of me to give myself so little time, without considering how long and diverse and recondite the work would be, so full is it of questions in history, mythology, natural and moral philosophy, and theology, as you are well aware. I would set out all the principles I am following if you were not the person I am writing to. I beg you not to take it amiss if the book reaches you later than you expected, provided that when the work appears, it is not wholly unworthy of Augustine.

You cut me to the quick with that remark of yours, 'I shall not weary you so often with my demands.' You appear to be reluctant to give me good advice in the future about the object and profit of my studies; for the

95

100

105

110

115

120

* * * * *

29 Ie, Adrian vi (Ep 1304), elected in January 1522
30 Probably Richard Warham (d 1545), who, however, did not matriculate at the University of Louvain until October 1524. Perhaps a relative of archbishop William Warham (Ep 188), he received holy orders in 1527 and held several benefices in England.
31 Probably the William Thale to whom Ep 1224 was addressed, rather than a younger kinsman as Allen suggested. Thale matriculated at Louvain in December 1522, though he had arrived earlier (cf Ep 1303:59).
32 Probably Maurice Birchinshaw (documented 1511–35), who had taught at St Paul's School, London, where one of his pupils was Thomas Winter, son of Cardinal Wolsey. In August 1518 both Winter and Birchinshaw as his tutor matriculated at Louvain. Birchinshaw subsequently pursued an ecclesiastical career in England.
33 Vives was working on an edition of the De civitate Dei, for which Erasmus wrote an introductory letter (Ep 1309).

encouragement you give me, and even what you call your demands, are simply nothing but an incentive to spur me on to do great things when otherwise I should fall behind. And do you call this making demands? What will you call the instruction a teacher gives his pupils? Do you want to be so polite to your friends and disciples that you will make them miserable, when   125
they see that you are treating them like people you hardly know or people who are as good as you are? After all I have done and said, are you still not convinced that you can do nothing I could find wearisome, except when you are afraid that you may weary me? This is like the heading of your letter: 'To my admirable friend,' and not only 'admirable' but (if you please) 'highly   130
admirable.' If in future you allow your Johannes[34] or your Lieven[35] to write like that, I shall refuse delivery of the letter; if anybody is allowed to think me admirable, it is not Erasmus. By all the laws of friendship and all the kindnesses you have done me, and anything I may have been able to do for you, I do beg you not to be so distant with me.   135

I am delighted that you had such a reception in Germany, not of course that I found anything new in that. I am glad too that you have Velius[36] with you, whose birthday poem[37] addressed to you exists (I think it's his) and is in my opinion very successful. Please give him my greetings, and Buschius[38] too, and Rhenanus,[39] if he is with you. Maurice sends his very best wishes,   140
and so does John Clement,[40] who will not go to Italy before next spring. He says he was very sorry that you set off for Basel without his knowledge; for had he known, he would have given you his company and spent the whole winter with you.

I was negotiating to hire somebody, when very conveniently Franz the   145
bookseller[41] told me that he would very shortly be sending you some books, and that if I wanted anything carried, he would add it to the rest of the parcel. So I gave instructions that he should be entrusted with the seven books[42] I have already revised. Froben can begin to print them, if you approve; and I will send ten others – as far as the seventeenth – for certain   150
before Lent.[43] The remainder by Franz himself, when he goes to the

* * * * *

34 Perhaps Hovius, Erasmus' servant. Cf Epp 867:189n, 902.
35 Lieven Algoet of Ghent (Ep 1091), another of Erasmus' servants
36 Ep 1252 n1
37 *Genethliacon Erasmi*, written in 1517; see Epp 548–9.
38 Hermannus Buschius (Ep 1291 n4)
39 Beatus Rhenanus (Ep 327)
40 Ep 388:185n. Clement was at this time studying medicine in Louvain.
41 Franz Birckmann (Ep 1254 n3)
42 Ie, of Augustine
43 5 March–19 April 1522

Frankfurt fair. From those seven you will be able to discover, if you have
time to look at anyone else's work, what principle of commentary I have
followed; though the rest, apart from the eighth, ninth, tenth, and
eighteenth, contain less matter and need less work, because they are not so   15!
diverse, and a great part of what he[44] deals with in them is obvious to
anyone. Will you please see that they print several hundred copies of this
work separate from the rest of Augustine; for there will be many studious
people who will be either unwilling or unable to buy the whole of
Augustine, either because they will not want it or because they have not   16(
enough money. For you know that the devotees of more elegant literature
read practically no other work of Augustine except this. Farewell again and
again, my best of teachers.

Louvain, 19 January 1522

1257 / To Conradus Goclenius   Basel, 6 February 1521/2

This letter was first published by Paulus Merula in his *Vita Des. Erasmi* (Leiden:
T. Basson 1607). The year-date in the text (line 21) cannot be correct, since
Erasmus had not yet moved to Basel in February 1521. Allen chose 1522
because of the resemblance of lines 6–11 to Epp 1244:41–2 and 1258:30–2 and
because of the expectation (line 12) of Erasmus' return to Louvain.

On Conradus Goclenius, professor of Latin at the Collegium Trilingue, see
Ep 1209.

ERASMUS OF ROTTERDAM TO CONRADUS GOCLENIUS, GREETING
I am very fond of Melchior,[1] and wish him all the favour of the Muses. That's
the spirit! In this way he will become known to the right people, and secure a
position for himself. He has no reason to think of retreat, but of going
forward. Only he should be careful not to give malice any foothold. With   5
Ludwig[2] you should keep up your friendship on courteous terms. If you

* * * * *

44 Ie, Augustine

1257
1 Melchior Vianden, of Vianden near Luxembourg (d 1535), was a teacher at the
  College of the Castle. The reference here is apparently to a call to teach
  elsewhere, perhaps at Tournai. Not until 1525, however, did Vianden move to
  Tournai to teach at the new, and short-lived, trilingual college.
2 Probably Ludovicus Carinus (Ep 920), who lived with Erasmus as his *famulus* at
  this time

write to Nesen,[3] write with some caution. He has been certainly the most
unfortunate of my friends.[4] He keeps nothing to himself, and cannot discern
what to say, and when.[5] He is no benefit to the humanities, nor to the
Lutheran cause, nor to his own pupils. The only wise man is he who can   10
match his wisdom to the times we live in. One can hardly trust oneself.

I hope to be with you in Lent,[6] unless prevented by disorders here
which seem imminent.[7] I was delighted with Verdun's[8] letter, if only he has
sufficient influence. I thought of adding it to my book, but there were
reasons against it.[9] I wonder that you gave Hilarius[10] a gold piece; he had   15
enough journey-money from me, and from Pieter Gillis[11] on my account.

I would have written more, but felt I knew too little about the man who
brings you this. Good news about Campen.[12] It would be fair if now in my
old age I could have a share in your successes, but evidently like Hercules I
have laboured for the benefit of others. Farewell.   20

Basel, 6 February 1521

* * * * *

3 Wilhelm Nesen (c 1493–1524) was a graduate of the University of Basel, a
  teacher, and a former corrector for the Froben press (1515–16). He was head of
  the new Latin school at Frankfurt-am-Main from 1520 to 1523, when he went to
  Wittenberg and joined the reformers, only to perish in a boating accident the
  following year.
4 Cf Allen Ep 1729:1–3.
5 This passage clearly implies that Nesen was guilty of far more serious offences
  than the sloppy editing of Seneca complained of in the Catalogus lucubrationum
  (Ep 1341A:447–63). Erasmus apparently blamed him for the ill-timed release
  of the Dialogus bilinguium ac trilinguium (CWE 7 330–47), and in a letter of 2
  March 1532 to Martin Bucer (Allen Ep 2615:184–7), Erasmus seems to say that
  Nesen had been responsible for the publication of the Julius exclusus.
6 5 March–19 April 1522
7 The first of the Hapsburg-Valois wars, which had broken out in 1521; see Ep
  1283 n3.
8 Perhaps Antoine de la Marck (Ep 956), abbot of the Cluniac abbey of Beaulieu,
  Verdun, who may have repeated his promise of some preferment for Erasmus;
  see Ep 1065.
9 Erasmus may have contemplated printing the letter after Ep 956 in the edition
  of the paraphrases which Froben published in February 1522. But the abbot's
  reputation for rapacity and licentiousness – he was stabbed to death in 1523 by
  a landowner whose daughter he had wronged – made this inadvisable.
10 Hilarius Bertolph of Ledeberg near Ghent (d 1533) was in Erasmus' service
  1522–4.
11 Ep 184
12 Jan van Campen (1491–1538), professor of Hebrew at the Collegium Trilingue
  in Louvain, 1520–31

1258 / To a Friend

Basel, 9 February 1522

This letter, first published by Allen, survives in a sixteenth-century copy in the Stads- of Athenaeumbibliothek Deventer. The recipient, obviously a close friend, may have been Maarten Davidts (Ep 1254).

In lines 6–13 Erasmus reports what he has heard of the somewhat tumultuous reform movement which took place in Wittenberg in the autumn and winter of 1521–2, during Luther's confinement in the Wartburg (April 1521–March 1522). The principal leaders of the movement were Luther's colleague in the faculty of theology, Andreas Karlstadt (Ep 911:61n), and Luther's fellow Augustinian, Gabriel Zwilling. Their zeal and impatience, expressed in passionate sermons, led to much confusion and disorder, which finally brought Luther back to Wittenberg to impose a more cautious and conservative pace upon the Reformation in that town. Erasmus had evidently not yet heard of the more disorderly aspects of the Wittenberg movement, such as the image smashing which took place in January and early February.

ERASMUS TO A FRIEND, GREETING

The wagons to which Franz[1] was minded to entrust my box[2] are now here. I should have been glad if it had arrived, but am content provided it is in safe keeping; do not send it unless I give the word. I long to know the rest of the story about the prior of the Augustinians.[3] Oecolampadius[4] has thrown off 5
his cowl and left the monastery, because he thought the duke of Bavaria[5] was threatening Altomünster in any case. I hear he has fallen out badly with

* * * * *

1258
1 Birckmann (Ep 1254 n3)
2 Cf Ep 1275:10–12.
3 Proost; see Epp 1254:7–14, 1256:25–7.
4 In 1518 Oecolampadius (Epp 224:30n, 354:6n) took his DD at Basel and accepted a call to be cathedral preacher in Augsburg, where he became deeply perplexed by the phenomenon of Luther and the controversies surrounding him. In April 1520 he sought refuge from the fray by entering the Brigittine monastery of Altomünster near Munich, only to emerge in January 1522 as an active proponent of the Reformation. He became chaplain to Franz von Sickingen at the Ebernberg (Ep 1308 n7), but in November 1522 he returned to Basel to spend the rest of his life as professor, preacher, and leader of the Basel Reformation.
5 There were, in fact, two ruling dukes of Bavaria at the time: Wilhelm IV (1508–50) in Munich and Ludwig X (1514–45) in Landshut. Both were ardent champions of Catholic orthodoxy, which they sought to uphold in their Religionsmandat of 5 March 1522. See also the following note.

Eck.[6] Hence all those tears.[7] Philippus Melanchthon is acting as a public
preacher.[8] Justus Jonas has married,[9] and Karlstadt[10] too, besides many
others. Of the Augustinian monks, some have moved elsewhere and some   10
have changed their dress and are working with their hands. There are
almost no services there now.[11] In the great church there is only one mass
and a sermon. The common people communicate almost daily in both
kinds.[12] Wittenberg has been visited by two fullers, remarkably well
informed but on a few points disagreeing with Luther. They claim to have a   15
spirit of prophecy.[13]

* * * * *

6 Eck (Ep 769) had reacted with threats and fulminations to Oecolampadius'
   Iudicium de doctore Martino Luthero, published in Leipzig c December 1520.
   Even more ominous was the reaction of the nuncio Aleandro (Ep 1256 n11) and
   the emperor's confessor, Glapion (Ep 1275), to the *Paradoxon, quod non sit
   onerosa christianis confessio*, published in Augsburg in April 1521. Aleandro
   denounced Oecolampadius to Rome as 'even worse than Luther,' and Glapion
   urged the dukes of Bavaria to take action against him. These threats caused
   severe tensions in the monastic community at Altomünster, which Oecolampadius decided to resolve by fleeing. See Ernst Staehelin *Das theologische
   Lebenswerk Johannes Oekolampads* Quellen und Forschungen zur Reformationsgeschichte 21 (Leipzig 1939; repr New York and London 1971) 156–7.
7 In the weeks after he fled the monastery, Oecolampadius' letters, one of which
   is known to have been addressed to Erasmus, were rather despondent in tone;
   BAO 1 nos 119, 120.
8 There is no evidence that Melanchthon was functioning as a preacher at this
   time. He was, however, a conspicuous member of the commission that tried to
   bring order to the reform movement in Wittenberg by means of the Wittenberg
   Ordinance of 24 January 1522, which was subsequently disallowed by the
   elector.
9 Justus Jonas (Ep 876), whose wedding Melanchthon reported in a letter of 5
   February to Haugold von Einsiedel; CR 1 546
10 On 19 January 1522 Karlstadt married the fifteen-year-old daughter of an
   impoverished nobleman of Segrehn, near Wittenberg.
11 On 13 October 1521 the Wittenberg Augustinians, under the leadership of
   Gabriel Zwilling, ceased to celebrate mass when their prior refused to permit
   reforms. In November the friars began to leave the cloister and by March,
   when Luther returned, only the prior was left.
12 On Christmas Day 1521, Karlstadt celebrated communion in both kinds at All
   Saints Church, without vestments and speaking the words of institution in
   German. The Wittenberg Ordinance of 24 January 1522, issued jointly by the
   university and the town council (cf n8 above), expressly permitted communion
   in both kinds.
13 Towards the end of December 1521, three men who came to be called the
   'Zwickau prophets' arrived in Wittenberg from Zwickau, a textile and mining
   town in eastern Saxony. Two of them, Nikolaus Storch and Thomas Drescher,
   were weavers. A third, Marcus Thomae (Stübner) had been a student in

They say that in Switzerland a figure of the Crucified painted on canvas has streamed with blood, nor could it be stanched until the Blessed Virgin, who is painted on the same canvas, put her hand to the wound in the Lord's side. The other four wounds had already ceased to bleed in response to the prayers of the common people. Eventually a hard horny substance grew out of the ribs of the Crucified.

It is, however, well established that here in Basel a girl produces coals in plenty from her eyes. She is barely twelve years old, and brings them forth mainly at night. They are perfectly real coals, and come out one after another, being picked off by the bystanders. But this could occur, I am inclined to think, by nature.

I relapsed into an illness worst than the last, and am even now not really recovered.[14] It brings me so low that I do not greatly desire to live much longer; such is the world I see around me. Beware of letters from Germany, and be in no hurry to reply to them. It is dangerous to trust them:[15] this I know only too well. The bishop of Basel,[16] his coadjutor,[17] and many other people are very kind to me. But I must leave Germany because of the stink of the stoves.[18]

Farewell, my dear X, and give my greetings to my friends.   35
Basel, 9 February 1522

1259 / To Willibald Pirckheimer   Basel, 12 February [1522]

On Pirckheimer, see Ep 318. On his recent difficulties with Rome because of charges that he was a Lutheran, see Epp 1182 and 1244. This letter was first published in the *Pirckheimeri Opera*.

Greeting, my honoured friend. I came here in order to be at hand while my

* * * * *

Wittenberg. They called themselves prophets and apostles, claimed direct inspiration by the Holy Spirit, issued apocalyptic warnings, and criticized infant baptism. Their brief stay in Wittenberg added a bit to the confusion and disorder there during Luther's absence, but was of no real consequence.

14 See Ep 1256 n2.
15 Cf Epp 1257:6–9; also 1225:383–7, 1244:41–2, 1278:10–13.
16 Christoph von Utenheim (Ep 1332)
17 Nikolaus von Diesbach (1478–1550) of Bern, canon of the Basel chapter since 1516, and coadjutor to the bishop (see preceding note) since 1519. Erasmus was grateful to Nikolaus for repeated gifts of Burgundy wine, which caused a dramatic improvement in his health; Epp 1342:504–9, 1353:284–99.
18 Erasmus' dislike of stoves (as opposed to fireplaces) is frequently mentioned in the letters of this period; see Epp 1248:13–14, 1249:24–5, 1259:2–3, 1264:10–12, 1302:37–9.

things were printing,[1] and immediately fell seriously ill from the stink of the stoves[2] – the same sort of trouble from which I suffered last time I was here. I had got better, but since then have suffered another attack worse than before.   5

For a long time now I have been waiting to see what will be the upshot of this sorry business over Luther. Unquestionably some spirit is at work in this affair; whether it be of God, I do not know.[3] I, who have never supported Luther, except in so far as one supports a man by urging him towards better things, am a heretic to both sides. Among our own people, a   10 few who have other reasons to dislike me are actually trying to persuade the emperor that I am a leader of the rebels,[4] for no better reason than my failure to publish against Luther. Luther's party in their public utterance tear me to pieces as a Pelagian,[5] because they think I give more weight than they do to free will. Am I not indeed treated very prettily?   15

I have finished a paraphrase on St Matthew, encouraged by the cardinal of Sion.[6] Best wishes, my distinguished friend. Give my greetings to your sisters,[7] and to any who love the teaching of the Gospels.

Your sincere friend Erasmus

Basel, 12 February   20

To the honourable Willibald Pirckheimer, town councillor of Nürnberg

1260 / From Jakob Ziegler   Rome, 16 February 1522

The autograph of this letter is MS Rehd 254.167 in the Rehdiger Collection of the University Library of Wrocław. The letter was first published as Ep 13 in Enthoven.

* * * * *

1259
1 Erasmus' Paraphrase on Matthew (line 16) and a new edition of the *Colloquia* (Ep 1262) were in press at this time.
2 See Ep 1258 n18.
3 See Acts 5:38–9.
4 Cf Epp 1195, 1278; also 1256 n11.
5 This charge (cf Epp 1225:307–8, 1275:31) was originally based on some passages in the *Enchiridion*. News of the Wittenbergers' accusation probably reached Erasmus via Beatus Rhenanus (BRE Ep 206). Luther's first communication to Erasmus had been the suggestion that he should read Augustine's treatises against the Pelagians (Ep 501:49–62). Subsequently, Erasmus' paraphrase of the ninth chapter of Romans became the focus of criticism on this point (Epp 1265:14–19, 1342:1022–78).
6 See Ep 1255 introduction and lines 23–9, 71–6.
7 Pirckheimer's sisters Charitas (d 1532) and Clara (d 1533), both highly learned women, became in turn abbess of the convent of St Clare in Nürnberg.

Jakob Ziegler (c 1470–1549) of Landau in Bavaria studied at Ingolstadt, where he became deeply interested in mathematics and astronomy. In 1500 he left Ingolstadt and nothing is known of him until March 1504, when he was at Cologne. He then spent time in Vienna (1504–8), Moravia (1508–11), and Budapest (1514–20), where he made the connections which secured his invitation to Rome by Leo x (lines 141–4). During his stay in Rome, 1521–5, he was employed at the curia in an unknown capacity and did what he could to defend Erasmus' interests there. After leaving Rome, Ziegler was for a time a partisan of the Reformation, but by 1534 had become an Erasmian Catholic once again.

Cordial greetings. As an old friend of yours, whose affection for you started before you made a name for yourself with works as learned as they are devout,[1] I ought perhaps to begin this belated letter with elaborate compliments, as many people do when they write to you, but my talents are so few and so provincial that I must refrain from that sort of formal opening. 5
Secondly, I ought to apologize for neglecting you these many years; but I do not wish to labour this point either. If I have kept silent, and yet have done all I could to back you up, this silent support ought to please you all the more, for it means that you can take me as evidence to assure yourself that God has left many thousands of men who are devoted to you and have not 10
bowed the knee to Baal.[2]

This letter will, I suppose, find you in Basel, and I very much hope so, for I am sure that there you will be working out something for the public benefit of Christendom. What I want to see is your new edition of Augustine,[3] for the text we have is much disfigured, having been sadly 15
defaced with their barbarous nonsense by unknown Englishmen[4] and men like de Mayronnes[5] who know nothing. On this point I find the judgment of the elder Amerbach[6] sadly at fault. So I long to see that great author cleaned up and restored to his proper grandeur. If I cannot hope at the present time

* * * * *

1260
1 It is not known when Erasmus and Ziegler became acquainted. Perhaps it was in Louvain in 1502–3, before Ziegler's residence in Cologne. That would have been before Erasmus' fame was established.
2 1 Kings 19:18; Rom 11:4
3 See Ep 1309 introduction.
4 Such as those mentioned in Ep 1271 n6
5 François (?) de Mayronnes (d 1327), well-known commentator on Augustine
6 Johann Amerbach (c 1430–1513), famous Basel printer who in 1506 brought out an edition of Augustine in which he relied heavily on medieval commentators

Jakob Ziegler
Portrait by Wolf Huber
Kunsthistorisches Museum, Vienna

for your commentaries on Paul,[7] although they have been promised us so 2
often and dangled before us, the reasons are as clear to me from guesswork
as they are to you from intimate knowledge. We shall welcome them when
they see the light posthumously. In this, in fact, as in many other ways, I feel
somehow what is in your mind.

In your Cyprian you regret the loss of Pontius the deacon.[8] This is at 2
Wrocław, in the possession of either the bishop or the chapter, among
Cyprian's works, a very fine manuscript. You should write to a canon of
Wrocław called Stanislaus Sauer,[9] a good scholar, if he is still alive, or
perhaps better and with more confidence to the chapter, which cannot die. I
saw the book when it was lent for a time to Simon Schönfeld,[10] a doctor of 3
medicine, learned in Hebrew, Greek, and Latin and a long-standing friend
of our dear Reuchlin. This gives you, my dear Erasmus, a way to trace the
volume, and it is worth pursuing with all diligence, for on this subject
Pontius rivalled such eminent authorities as Cornelius, Athanasius, or
Jerome. He equalled in every respect the story of the martyrdom, if you will 3
allow the word, of Pliny in the eruption of Vesuvius.[11] And may some evil
genius repay as he deserves the bungler[12] who defiled and abridged the
work, bringing down the honour of the martyr and his story to the level of
the filth with which he was himself defiled. This scandalous conduct I
attribute to a Frenchman; for it was the French who, in a ridiculous battle of 4
wits against the ancients in every department of learning, banded together

* * * * *

7 See Ep 1341A:1332–5.

8 In his edition of Cyprian (Froben 1520), Erasmus had included a *Passio beati Cypriani episcopi Carthaginensis, per Pontium eius diaconum aedita.* In both the preface to the volume (Ep 1000:43–8) and in an 'annotatiuncula' to the *Passio,* Erasmus voiced doubt that the rather brief *Passio,* which filled slightly more than one folio, was in fact the complete and authentic text of the substantial *Vita Cypriani* which, according to Jerome (*De viris illustribus* 100), Pontius had written. What Erasmus did not know, and never found out, was that the *Passio* that he thought had been derived from Pontius was actually an epitome of the account of Cyprian's martyrdom in the *Acta proconsularia.* The authentic texts of Pontius' *Vita* and of the *Acta proconsularia,* first published in the seventeenth century, are found in PL 3 (Paris 1886) 1541–66 and in CSEL III-3 xc–cxiv.

9 Stanislaus Sauer (c 1469–1535) of Lwówek (Löwenberg) in Silesia, was a doctor of canon law (Padua), a canon at Wrocław, a historian, and an ardent student of Jerome.

10 No such name is known. Schottenloher (*Ziegler* 55 n3) conjectures that the Leipzig physician and Greek scholar, Christoph Sonfelt (Schönfeld) may be intended.

11 Pliny *Epistles* 6.16 and 20

12 Ie, the person responsible for the truncated *Passio* included in Erasmus' edition of Cyprian; see n8 above.

to wipe out the best authors entirely or reduce them to ignorant epitomes, or
made a scandalous use of their names to foist on our own day ignorant
fables, worse than any Iberian trumpery.[13] In the authentic copy I spoke of, a
passage runs: 'He stood on the line (*ad lineam*).' The bungler, as I keep calling   45
him, replaced this with: 'He stood in a linen shift (*in   lineis*).'[14] And his
mistake is more excusable here than elsewhere; for having read that Cyprian
was stripped of his outer garments, he was almost invited by the logic of the
situation to bring the saint on stage in a shift. But this is flimsy, while the
other reading retains its true inherent weight, telling how the martyr was   50
lined up among the guilty, and called forward out of the line to receive his
punishment. I have enjoyed pointing this out to you, so that you can pass
whatever critical judgment on the passage you see fit.

It would be worth while, my dear Erasmus, should you think it right to
devote your efforts and our friend Froben's to the publication of something   55
which you know still needs the finishing touches, to make your desire
known to scholars here a good while before in a published letter. You would
find, I hope, in some unexpected quarter an honest man who would come
forward to lighten your burden.

I made a copy long ago, in Regensburg, in the library at St Emmer-   60
am's,[15] of St Jerome's commentary on the Epistle to the Galatians. I still
remember that much was to be found there in the prolegomena which is
lacking in ordinary copies. Likewise in the commentary on Matthew I feel
something is lacking which I think I read there. It is likely that this contrast of
plenty and poverty in the way of readings is to be discovered in many other   65
passages. I beg you of your kindness to send a suitable person there who can
collate the whole of Jerome with those copies. If you get nothing else out of
it, which I will never believe, at least you will have the very great satisfaction
of having weighed your correction of the text against manuscripts of
venerable antiquity transferred to that place by some emperor from an   70
uncorrupted library somewhere in Italy.

In Rohr, a very well known monastery of canons in Lower Bavaria,[16]
there is a manuscript neither large nor ancient, containing under the name

* * * * *

13 A favourite phrase of Jerome; *Adagia* II iii 9.
14 This passage occurs in the *Acta proconsularia*, not in Pontius' *Vita* (see n8
 above). The Wrocław manuscript was apparently a copy of the former, falsely
 identified as Pontius' *Vita*, as in the case of the truncated version published by
 Erasmus. It appears that Erasmus never saw the Wrocław manuscript. At any
 rate, he made no changes in the *Passio* or the accompanying 'annotatiuncula' in
 subsequent editions of Cyprian.
15 A famous Benedictine monastery founded in the seventh century
16 Twenty-nine kilometres south of Regensburg, founded in 1133

of Jerome three expositions of each of the evangelists, which are short, and
suited not so much to instruct a reader as to refresh an understanding of the   75
text which he has acquired from elsewhere. I can give you no further opinion
on the work, for this is a memory of long ago, but they are sure to be full of
meat and well expressed if the title tells truth about the author. I leave it to
you with your usual energy to arrange for a more up-to-date sampling of this
work, in case by good luck you can make Jerome more complete.   80

There have arrived in Rome two champions of the Holy See, whose
one object this autumn is to maintain it in the status from which certain
persons are working to dethrone it, but they also have hopes of thereby
carrying off rewards and benefices – in fact, of ending up rich by informing
against other men's lives and fortunes. One of them,[17] as you know,   85
established long ago by his confrontations in the schools[18] that he was a
sophist supreme and invincible. Recently too he has often disputed in Rome
at the Sapienza,[19] and has aroused general astonishment by his vehemence,
his way of tossing his head and swaying his body and using expressive
gestures and counting off the points of his case on his fingers and, on top of   90
all this, by his great gaping mouth. And so we expect to secure any and
every result from a man who, under the pretext of a strict theological
definition, seems once and for all and in public to have established a doctrine
entirely contrary to the Christian philosophy – that money-lenders have a
perfect right to exact interest.[20] Some wags say he is the darling of Germany, 95
and have put all the blame on you Germans. For my own part too, except
that 'From one villain learn to know them all'[21] is so misleading, I should
reluctantly accept this slur on a whole nation.

The other man[22] is a different proposition. The way he walks and talks
and his expression and his whole air seem designed to give an impression of   100
modesty. He shows also a skill in impersonation while engaged in putting
his case such as you would scarcely find in great authorities. He is thought to
be quite free from any attempt to ingratiate himself or pursue his own
advantage with men in power, and from feelings of hatred and resentment

* * * * *

17 Johann Eck (Ep 769), who was in Rome October 1521–February 1522
18 As, for example, at the Leipzig Disputation with Luther in 1519
19 Ie, the University of Rome, founded in 1303
20 Eck was a champion of the view that the old ban on interest had to be lifted and
   that five per cent was a reasonable rate.
21 Virgil *Aeneid* 2.65–6
22 Johannes Fabri (Ep 386), vicar-general of the diocese of Constance, who had
   been in Rome since November 1521; see Karl Schottenloher 'Johann Fabri in
   Rom, nach einem Berichte Jakob Zieglers' *Archiv für Reformationsgeschichte* 5
   (1908) 31–47.

towards his opponents such as might make him less trustworthy in practice; 105
and all he thinks or says or writes seems to relate to single-minded defence
of the truth, to an apostolic rule of life, and to the opinions and beliefs of the
ancient commentators. Thus equipped, he has from time to time submitted
books to Rome in support of the standards of conduct and the opinions we
hold,[23] on which in this generation the essence of Christianity hinges, 110
whether we like it or not. By this policy he made people wish to see him long
before his arrival; and this was even more remarkable, inasmuch as he was
in no hurry, though more than once invited by the powers that be, knowing
that his arrival would excite more respect and secure him even greater
situations the more he showed himself a serious character whose company 115
was not to be had for the asking. Nor was it his worldly wisdom that let him
down. Fortune he found on his doorstep and had beguiled almost into his
bosom; but the chance that sways human affairs overthrew all his hopes. At
the moment of his arrival the aged Leo the Tenth breathed his last.[24]

Now pray learn from a single example the wicked opinions which 120
these men cannot tolerate. Somewhere in your part of the world[25] some
hundreds of Christians celebrated the sacrament in both kinds. This the man
reported to us, and made a great thing of it, as though they had committed
sacrilege. We received this as something appalling, we shuddered at it, we
took it to be a crime which every pen and every critic must condemn, 125
presumably because they violated the traditions of our forefathers and the
clear policy of the Scriptures: 'Verily, verily I say unto you, unless you have
eaten the flesh of the Son of man and have drunk his blood, you shall not
have life in you'[26] – and this statement is four times repeated.[27] And in
another passage: 'Jesus took bread, and when he had given thanks, he broke 130
it and gave it to his disciples and said: "Take and eat this: this is my body."
And he took the cup and gave thanks and gave it to them saying: "All of you
drink of this."'[28] And Paul: 'Let a man examine himself, and so let him eat of
the bread and drink of the cup.'[29] And in this passage the same rite is
referred to so often. These are the weapons with which they enter the 135
contest, these champions of public morality and of what have long, and

* * * * *

23 Fabri's *Opus adversus dogmata Martini Lutheri* was published at Rome (M. Silber)
   in 1522.
24 1 December 1521
25 Ie, in Germany; cf Ep 1258 n12.
26 John 6:53
27 In verses 54–8
28 Matt 26:26–7
29 1 Cor 11:28

wrongly, been received opinions. How true it is that your really religious man is not the one who is full of holy reading and immersed in holy things, but he who has his eye single and his spirit lowly and whose mind is taught by God!   140

I arrived in Rome last year precisely on the first of March, having been invited to leave Hungary by Leo the Tenth, whose knowledge of my existence came from Cardinal Ippolito d'Este,[30] who held the richest of all the sees in Hungary,[31] where he had learned to know and like my work. I made my bow to the pope with a book of mine on the heresy of the Picards,[32]   145 among whom I had previously spent three years.[33] I had rushed this out on another occasion, when I was in a hurry to satisfy the bishop of Olomouc,[34] who was asking me for it. Being a hasty piece of work, there was much in it that would not do – more material than was required for a reasonable balance of the whole, arranged in many places very badly, and more warmth   150 in the disputations than the standards of a reasonable Christian or a reasonable man would allow. I made this mistake because I knew from experience how far their *Oratio*[35] differed from their opinions and their way of life. But this is inexcusable in any argument in which you are keen to bring your opponent over to your point of view – to start by embittering a man   155 who might be willing to yield to your case, so that he remembers how you hurt him and keeps off, nor can he have any ground in common with a man who has so bitterly attacked him.

* * * * *

30 C 1478–1530, brother of the duke of Ferrara and cardinal from 1492
31 The archbishopric of Gran (1487–97). The cardinal would have learned to know Ziegler in 1517, during a later visit to Hungary.
32 *Contra heresim Valdensium ... libri quinque* (Leipzig: M. Loter 1512); summary and analysis in Schottenloher *Ziegler* 23–4. The heresy so vehemently attacked in this book was that of the Bohemian Brethren, also known as the Unity of the Brethren (*Unitas fratrum*), a Hussite sect which in 1467 had formally separated itself from the mainline Hussites (known as Utraquists or Calixtines) and spread rapidly in the following decades. The Brethren were not Picards (Piccards, Pickharts, etc), an earlier group of libertine pantheists, long since extinguished, but the name was commonly applied to them by hostile critics. Nor were the Brethren, strictly speaking, Waldensians (Ep 1324A n1), although they had much in common with the Waldensians and had tried unsuccessfully to merge with them in Germany. In the course of the Reformation, the Brethren became Protestants; those in Bohemia merged with the Lutherans in 1542, those in Poland united with the Calvinists in 1555.
33 1508–11, in Moravia
34 Stanislaus Thurzo (Epp 1242, 1267, 1272). Ziegler's book was dedicated to him.
35 *Oratio excusatoria atque satisfactiva*, an official defence of themselves issued by the Bohemian Brethren in 1504; see Allen, Ep 1154:8n.

In Rome, when I was there, your enemy[36] and I were guests at the table
of a man who is very highly thought of, one of the bishops;[37] and there,   160
when we had finished dinner, the conversation turned on Luther, and he
was attacked from various points of view. The prevailing opinion was that
he was a wencher and a drunkard – two vices of the kind men were thought
to suffer from as a rule in Germany. After him, you took the stage, but not
playing your proper part. Your enemy uttered a bitter laugh on hearing that   165
the majority of those who appreciate your religious work in Christ greeted
you as a rising sun.[38] A letter of his own was then read, or perhaps it was
some sort of preface to another work,[39] in which passages were selected for
hostile comment where you attack sham monks, lifeless, repeated prayers,
cowls with scalloped edges, habits with the folds carefully counted, and all   170
the symbols of separate divisions in the church. And that old man, although
no monk but a mere mass-priest, a swarthy, unattractive character, let
himself go completely in an attack on you. His outspokenness found favour
with our common host, maybe because he resented the suggestion that
there was anything distinguished in Germany, and also because he was no   175
great friend of yours personally, and declared loudly that you had hay on
your horns.[40] The fact is that the gospel and the whole canon of Scripture,
the divine scourge of vices, was long ago wiped out by men of corrupted
minds; and in its place they put an unpleasant kind of theology and
traditions which express the wishes of those who invented them, so that   180
with these laws to rely on in future they can let themselves go in all
directions as they please. If anyone brings their behaviour back to the divine
law and weighs it by that standard, they dare not arouse public feeling
against the Scriptures, and in exchange for their resentment they take

* * * * *

36 Diego López Zúñiga (Stunica) (d 1530), theologian of the University of Alcalá
   and one of the contributors to the Complutensian Polyglot. In 1520 he
   published at Alcalá an intemperate attack upon Erasmus' *Novum instrumentum*
   of 1516: *Annotationes contra Erasmum Roterodamum in defensionem tralationis Novi
   Testamenti* (A.R. Brocario). For Erasmus' reply, see Ep 1277 n1. Zúñiga arrived
   in Rome on 9 February 1521 and continued there his attacks on Erasmus' work
   (see n45 below). Erasmus' own account of their bitter controversy is found in
   Ep 1341A:868–927. See also Epp 1277, 1289, 1290. For an extremely useful
   survey of Zúñiga's life and work, see H.J. de Jonge's introduction to ASD IX-2,
   especially 13–34.
37 Possibly Cardinal Carvajal; see Ep 1330:48–51.
38 Allen's note (v 22:148) gives a list of passages in the correspondence where this
   image occurs.
39 Evidently excerpts from the manuscript of the *Erasmi ... blasphemiae et impietates*
   (n45 below).
40 Ie, a chip on your shoulder; *Adagia* I i 81

vengeance on the man who detected their wickedness and wrote an   185
appropriate note on the passage. Thanks to this attitude things had gone
well with him, and he would have avenged himself on your critical nose by
mudslinging of the foulest kind. So I developed a great distaste for this
company, and found myself in an unfair position. We made it up, however,
for I had been very kindly received; and so we parted.   190

Your rival went off to perform his duties, for he held a salaried post in
the Sapienza Romana, and was lecturing on Oppian,[41] whom he regarded as
the most important of all authors. He wanted to show Rome how rich he was
and to pose as an expert in the fish-market – and this was a man who has
spent a number of years on the reading of Holy Scripture, the Old and New   195
Testaments, in Hebrew and Greek and Latin, and has a better right than
most other people to express a judgment on such topics. But I went home
with my head full of threats and already pondering in my mind a suitable
place for challenging this man's insufferable malevolence in the style it
deserved. This I proposed to do in a prologue to the continuous narrative   200
from the four Gospels[42] which Augustine only sketched out in his *De consensu
evangelistarum* and never completed.

While I was still full of this plan, we met again in November, and our
friend Paolo Bombace[43] was in the company. On this occasion that enemy of
yours again brought his old piece[44] onto the stage, but it was no longer a   205
preface, it was a full-sized book,[45] designed to contain all his virulence and
false accusations of heresy, so that you might be thought to be the only

* * * * *

41 Greek texts had been published by the Giunti at Florence in 1515 and by the
   Aldine Press in 1517.
42 Cf lines 303–4, and see Ep 1330 n2.
43 Erasmus and Bombace (Ep 210) had been friends since Erasmus' stay in
   Bologna in 1506–7. Bombace was now secretary to Cardinal Lorenzo Pucci (Ep
   1000).
44 See lines 161–71.
45 During the course of 1521 Zúñiga had completed his *Erasmi Roterodami
   blasphemiae et impietates* in manuscript and had presented a copy to Pope Leo x
   (ASD IX-2 22–3), who had refused him permission to publish it (Ep 1341A:
   914–15). After the death of Leo x, Zúñiga prepared a much abridged version,
   eliminating his own *confutatoria annotamenta* (the bulk of the original work) and
   leaving little more than a series of excerpts from Erasmus' works with
   references to those passages which Zúñiga considered suspect. This abridged
   version was published by A. Bladus at Rome in the spring of 1522 under the
   title *Erasmi Roterodami blasphemiae et impietates per Jacobum Stunicam nunc primum
   propalatae ac proprio volumine alias redargutae.* In June Erasmus replied with the
   *Apologia adversus libellum Stunicae cui titulum fecit, Blasphemiae et impietates
   Erasmi,* published with the *Epistola de esu carnium* (Basel: Froben 6 August
   1522). Text in LB IX 355–75. Cf Ep 1341A:868–88.

begetter of all the perfidy that could ever be invented under heaven or in hell
by desperate minds that have abandoned every scrap of religion. This he
read to the assembled company, and this he had given shortly before to Leo   210
the Tenth; and he had brought men to the point of beginning to have dark
suspicions of you. Paolo Bombace stood up for you in both places, in that
company by his presence with his patron, and before Leo with a prepared
defence; he stood up to their virulence and defended you and your religious
attitude with great spirit. All the same, things were going downhill, and the   215
wrong side might have won, had not Leo died and left their virulence
unsupported.

You know by now what they wanted out of you. This was a test case.
You saw it coming too; and I could see in your letter[46] that you were anxious,
and thought that certain people could not even read you until you were   220
cleared by a pardon from the pope. I saw the three-year space for which you
asked[47] as a kind of truce in the war. I smiled quietly to myself, and more or
less felt like saying 'There's many a slip 'twixt cup and lip.'[48]

Up to now, as long as I thought your enemy was something of a scholar
and a man of high standing as a convinced Christian, all this caused me the   225
greatest concern, and in my impatience I set off at high speed – oars and
sails, as they say[49] – to write a defence[50] of your position. But when we met
several times as the days went on, and every day he showed more in his true
colours, I began to take the man's madness rather less seriously, thinking
that a bad play will soon be shown up by bad acting. And now he is losing   230
his reputation. A fellow-countryman of his,[51] who had spoken with you in
Louvain and knew very well how you order your life, wrote him a letter
about you in the most glowing terms,[52] with the object of making your
enemy realize how good you are and desist from his criminal behaviour.
There are people here who knew him at home, and say that over there he   235
was considered an atheist; at any rate, I have often thought him an

* * * * *

46 Ep 1236:127–31
47 See Ep 1236:135–7.
48 *Adagia* I v 1
49 *Adagia* I iv 18
50 See lines 296ff. The defence, completed by December (Ep 1330 n2), appeared in
     April 1523, not as the introduction to a narrative of the Gospels (cf lines
     200–1) but as a separate work: *Libellus Jacobi Landavi adversus Jacobi Stunicae
     maledicentiam, pro Germania*, published by Froben in combination with the first
     edition of the *Catalogus lucubrationum* (Ep 1341A); summary and analysis in
     Schottenloher *Ziegler* 64–76.
51 Juan de Vergara (Ep 1277)
52 Written from Brussels on 10 October 1521; CWE 8 337–40. See especially lines
     87ff, page 339.

Ebionite.[53] Paolo Bombace with a serious face accused him of being a foul toady, with a criminal system of making money by informing on the innocent. He said he was more horrible than all the heresy they tried to father on Erasmus. The man dodged this attack with a laugh like Domitian's, but he was not the least ashamed of himself.[54] When I and several other people protested at the unlimited bitterness with which he attacked you, he gave us each a different reason. This was not meant for Erasmus, he was attacking the spirit of the age; he only meant to keep Erasmus from going too far; and, what was more outrageous, he hoped to get some reputation out of Erasmus. This mountebank also goes the round of the bookshops, using them to press his slanderous views on everyone whether they will or no; he invites all he can to share his insanity, and has now found a fellow-countryman of the same kidney.[55]

240

245

Copies[56] are now on sale, designed to mobilize an attack on you with all the goblins of Scotism – the things you have always abhorred and kept as far away from as you could – and rout you with hicceities and isthicceities.[57] The author of this sorry business is also preparing in person to refute your later critical text of the New Testament[58] and your annotations on it, hoping to achieve an eruption at a point (if you please!) where he can drag Erasmus down into the crater like a second Empedocles[59] on Etna – and a very frigid one. I could not hope to depict the full frenzy of his feelings for you as they

250

255

* * * * *

53 The Ebionites were an early sect who denied the divinity of Christ; see Ep 1333 n22.
54 The image of the emperor Domitian laughing to cover his shame is Ziegler's invention, albeit one apparently based on specific passages in well-known classical texts. No text mentions Domitian's laugh – he was known, rather, for his frowning severity – but Ziegler probably got the idea from two authors: Tacitus, who in *Agricola* 39 speaks of the happy countenance with which Domitian concealed his displeasure at the news of Agricola's superior accomplishments as a general; and Suetonius, who in *Domitianus* 11 states that Domitian always began pleasantly when he had something cruel to announce. Ziegler seems to have conflated these references with that in *Agricola* 45 to Domitian's crimson face which, because it was always flushed, concealed any shame he might have felt as a result of his cruelties.
55 Sancho Carranza (Ep 1277 n8)
56 Copies, apparently, of the *Annotationes contra Erasmum* (n36 above), which Zúñiga had brought with him from Spain (Ep 1341A:913–14). The *Erasmi blasphemiae* was not yet in print.
57 The 'newly coined expressions and strange-sounding words' of the theologians, which Erasmus parodied in the *Moria*; ASD IV-3 146, 148 / CWE 27 126–7.
58 Ie, the edition of 1519
59 Horace *Ars poetica* 465

deserve. Hatred and spite for you and self-love for himself – these are the mainsprings of his whole mind. But I can give you his character as depicted by another man's pen. You have your enemy to the life – except perhaps that one ought to subtract his pursuit of Thais[60] and her like – apart from that you have at all points the braggart soldier[61] in the play.

I thought you ought to know this, being aware that a speaker cannot put his case precisely as he should until he has fully got to know the temperament, the strategy, and the habits of his adversary. Had this not been my purpose in writing to you, I might perhaps have had some difficulty in defending the levity with which I have thought fit to break the stubborn silence of so many years and write at last, though I should like to depict the passions of mankind.

And so, now that your enemy's behaviour is such as to leave no genuine Christian spirit or conscience in him anywhere and nothing in the way of honourable dealings with his fellow men that is not open to criticism, my own opinion, dear Erasmus, is that in future it will be best for you on no account to bring yourself down to the level of the common herd. When you answer, I mean, keep as far as you can from the line he has marked out for himself to follow, and recall language to its proper level. This is the point at which you should display to all who call themselves Germans, with all the wonderful range and authority of your heroic soul, the criminal activity of foreigners and the way in which they slander the simple integrity and piety and dignity of Germans and put their patience to the test. The outcome of their actions you see for yourself, nor will any other remedy be effective in the long run. What? Are you to wage a long and fruitless struggle, with your weak arms and your feeble body, against a whole river that floods in upon us far and wide from every quarter? Stay at home; erect some dyke on your boundary, however short-lived, against which the weight of waters may subside and its force be broken. Do not misunderstand me, dear Erasmus. I lay down no guidance for that prolific Minerva who inspires you. But let me be allowed to say this much, that, when you understand from the sort of words I use how much I am devoted to you, you may love me in return, and be always assured of the evidence of my sincerity. Many men enjoy your society almost without a second thought, to whom I almost grudge the opportunities that they enjoy; for even among those who take your advice in the serious affairs of life, you would scarcely find one in a thousand who has more need than I have, in this business and in many more, of conversing with you face to face.

* * * * *

60 The courtesan in Terence's *Eunuchus*
61 Thraso in Terence's *Eunuchus*

I am at work on a defence[62] to prove you blameless. It has made good progress from the start; but when it will ultimately finish its appointed course and when it will reach you I do not know. In the process I am led into many fields by that enemy of yours. If I follow these up as the subjects deserve or do not deserve, I should be at some risk when they reach the   300 public; if I were to pass them over and leave them behind, I shall have deserted my post.

Then I plan a narrative of events designed to form a continuous narrative out of the four Gospels.[63] To this I am driven by the same necessity, and it is for these reasons that I regret my separation for so long from you all   305 – from you, I mean, and my friend Froben, and the free part of Germany. But in the name of our friendship as fellow Christians, please let it also be a condition of your receiving this letter that you understand it is intended for your reading and then straight for the fire. On your side, if you mean to send me anything, please have it consigned to Paolo Bombace, my great friend, at   310 least if you think my lodging too much out of the way. It is the Hungarian hospice in the College of San Pietro in Vaticano.

Farewell, dear Erasmus, 16 February 1522

Jakob Ziegler of Landau in Bavaria

To the much respected Master Desiderius Erasmus of Rotterdam, his   315 most honoured teacher and friend, in Basel, at Master Froben's

1261 / From Andrea Alciati   Avignon, 24 February 1522

On Alciati, who was at this time teaching law at Avignon, see Ep 1250.

The passage printed here is all that survives of Alciati's letter to Erasmus in response to Ep 1250. The passage survived because it was quoted by Bonifacius Amerbach in a letter to Alciati (April 1531) about the declamation against monastic life that had been causing Alciati such anxiety ever since 1520 (see Ep 1233A:14–22 and n5). After quoting the letter of 30 March 1531 (Allen Ep 2467) in which Erasmus declares that he had long since complied with Alciati's wishes, Bonifacius continues: 'Your letter from Avignon dated 24 February 1522 runs as follows,' and quotes the passage given below. Erasmus' response to Alciati's letter was Ep 1278.

Allen, using the manuscript in the Öffentliche Bibliothek of the University of Basel (MS C.VIa.54.17v), was the first to print the Alciati excerpt in Bonifacius' letter. The entire letter was subsequently printed as AK Ep 1523.

* * * * *

62 See n50 above.
63 See lines 200–1.

The great pains you have taken to see that my declamation is read by no one fills me with joy, and I am most grateful. You have made me happy by removing this anxiety. But to crown one good deed with another, let me beg you in God's name to put it on the fire. It had been stolen from my desk by Calvo[1] soon after it saw the light ...   5

1262 / To Johannes Erasmius Froben   Basel, 28 February 1522

This is the preface to the new, revised, and enlarged edition of the *Familiarum colloquiorum formulae* (Basel: Froben, March 1522). On the earlier and subsequent editions of the work, see Ep 1341A:285–301. On the 'heresies' discovered in this edition, see Ep 1299:59ff.

Johann Erasmius Froben (d 1549), the younger son of the Basel printer Johann Froben and godson of Erasmus, was about six years old at this time (Ep 635:26n).

ERASMUS OF ROTTERDAM TO JOHANNES ERASMIUS FROBEN, GREETING

I should count you an uncommonly lucky young man, my beloved Erasmius, to be born in such a flourishing home of the best authors as your father's printing-house and brought up among so many men distinguished   5
for their knowledge of the three ancient tongues; but at your age congratulations are not so much to the point as best wishes. And certainly you bear no ordinary load, if you are to satisfy your most affectionate father, to whom you truly are beloved, which your name means in the Greek, and who rests all his hopes on you, as well as Beatus Rhenanus[1] and myself, who took the   10
promise at your christening, and Wolfgang Capito,[2] who stood sponsor at your confirmation. We have seen to it that your first childish prattle should be shaped by Greek and Latin. This book will help you not a little to acquire the rudiments of religion also, and on this score the uncounted host of children of your age will owe you a debt, as being the channel through   15
which they get this great advantage. For I have taken it into my head to become a child again for some days for your benefit, as I schooled my pen

* * * * *

1261
1 Francesco Giulio Calvo of Menaggio, near Como, was a bookseller who had many friends among contemporary men of letters.

1262
1 Ep 327
2 Ep 459

and my matter to suit your tender years. May Jesus keep you always as you
go from strength to strength. Farewell.

Basel, 28 February 1522　　　　　　　　　　　　　　　　　　　　　20

1263 / To [Thomas Wolsey]　　　　　　　　　　　　Basel, 7 March 1522

The manuscript of this letter (British Library Cotton Vitellius B.v.44), first
published by Allen, was damaged by fire in 1731. It is not clear how much of
the letter, which is all on one sheet, is missing: perhaps only a line or two at the
top of the sheet, perhaps one or more sheets preceding. Since the letter was
found among Wolsey's papers, he is presumed to have been the addressee.

... Marino Caracciolo,[1] who was prejudiced against me by Aleandro;[2] and
Aleandro, being a man easily roused, was excited by the most mendacious
detractors,[3] to whom he listened all too readily. In the eyes of God my
innocence might be evidence enough, but among men a good Christian
must protect his own reputation as best he can. Even before Luther had　　5
published his *Assertio*[4] and his *De captivitate babylonica*,[5] there was much in
him I did not like, and I urged both him and his friends to moderate his style
of writing.[6] I tried to prevent the publication of those first books,[7] though in
fact they won almost universal approval. With Luther himself or with any
member of his party I never had any understanding, any more than your　　10
Eminence had. If to instigate a person means to tell him not to, then I did
instigate Luther; if to support a man means telling him to change his tune,
then I was his supporter; if it is defending a man to say that on many points
he is wrong, then I defended him. I always used the same language both to

* * * * *

1263
1 Marino Carracciolo of Naples (1469–1538), since 1518 papal nuncio to
　emperors Maximilian I and Charles V
2 Ep 1256 n11
3 Cf Epp 1268:70–2, 1302:58–9. It is not clear whom Erasmus means here. Allen
　(Ep 1481:61n) thought it was Baechem (Ep 1254 n6). Others have suggested
　Hoogstraten (Ep 1299 n25). But C. Augustijn argues, on the basis of evidence in
　the *Spongia*, that these two must be excluded and suggests that Erasmus may
　have been referring to Aleandro's brother Giambattista, secretary to the bishop
　of Liège. See ASD IX-1 151, footnote to lines 693–5 of the *Spongia*.
4 *Assertio omnium articulorum M. Lutheri per bullam Leonis X novissimam damnatorum*
　(1520); WA 7 94–151.
5 *De captivitate Babylonica ecclesiae praeludium* (1520); WA 6 497–573.
6 Ep 980:45–58
7 See Epp 904:20n, 967:107–9, 1033:52–5, 1143:23–5, 1167:305–7, 1195:143–4,
　1217:107.

men of Luther's party and to his enemies. Evidence for this will be found in 15
the letters I wrote to Luther himself[8] and to his friends, if they are willing to
produce them. Had I had any dealings whatever with Luther's people, they
would produce them, now that they are angry with me. Many letters from
me to my friends are in circulation over here, but one especially which I
wrote from Bruges to the bishop of Rochester, the publication of which I 20
regret.[9] I wrote to him in a hurry and somewhat unguardedly, knowing him
for a wise man and a good friend, and most discreet. This makes it clear that I
do not favour Luther's business. Nor did I say anything different to Duke
Frederick at Cologne[10] or to the king of Denmark.[11] When the captain-
general of Bohemia[12] made me the most lavish offers, I sent him such an 25
answer[13] as makes him now angry with me. In a word, so much am I
Luther's man that in their public utterances his party rend me with abuse
and threaten me with libellous pamphlets.

But, your Eminence will say, whence then this rumour? There are two

* * * * *

8 Of the letters which Erasmus and Luther wrote to one another in the period
between Ep 980 (30 May 1519) and Ep 1443 (15 April 1524) only Ep 1127A
survives.
9 Cf Ep 1265:20–1, where Willibald Pirckheimer also refers to the circulation of a
letter of Erasmus to the bishop of Rochester, John Fisher. No such letter has
survived, which seems odd in the case of a document that was 'published'
either in manuscript copies or in print. This consideration led Allen to
speculate that both Erasmus and Pirckheimer may in fact have been referring
to Ep 1228 (to William Warham, archbishop of Canterbury), which had just
been published in the *Epistolae ad diversos* (August 1521). According to Allen,
such a confusion could have arisen if 1/ the version that circulated had been
based on the original manuscript with its uncertain address (see Allen's
introduction to Ep 1228); 2/ Pirckheimer's identification of the author was a
mistaken guess; 3/ Erasmus saw Pirckheimer's letter, which has no certain
date, before 7 March and repeated his friend's error. All these things are
possible.
10 Elector Frederick 'the Wise' of Saxony, Luther's prince. On 5 November 1520,
when Erasmus and Frederick were both in Cologne in the entourage of Charles
v, the elector sought the great scholar's advice on the Luther affair. Erasmus
criticized Luther's immoderate language (see the *Spongia* ASD IX-1 182:420–4)
but, without endorsing any of Luther's opinions, upheld his right to a fair
hearing; see the *Axiomata pro causa Lutheri*, which Erasmus wrote out for the
elector immediately following their meeting (Ferguson *Opuscula* 336–7). Cf Ep
1155 introduction.
11 Christian II 1481–1559; see Ep 1228:35–9.
12 Probably Arkleb of Boskovice (Ep 1154), who was 'supreme captain' (*supremus
capitaneus*) of Moravia
13 Ep 1183

theologians[14] at Louvain who hate me for the sake of the humanities, of   30
which they are more terrified than of dog or snake.[15] There are a handful of
monks who think my books are responsible for their being undervalued in
certain quarters.[16] They do not care what they do to me, provided they
destroy me; wild beasts they are, not men. This is the truth. At the start I
thought it wrong to brawl in public like madmen, when the evil was not yet   35
past cure. If this had succeeded, Luther would not have gone so far out of his
mind, nor would things have reached this pass. Nor do I yet see any end to
it, unless some fresh approach can be found. We must get to the root of this
evil, so widely has this contagion spread, and it is not sprung from nothing.
One thing I will say, and countless people will back me up: I am so far a   40
follower of Luther that no theologian by his writings or his tirades has been
more of a hindrance to Luther's cause than I have. Had I been willing to
declare myself in two or three words a member of Luther's party, we should
see a very different game being played both here and in Germany from what
we see now. And this is the man on whom they make these murderous   45
attacks – one who under such varied provocation has remained in the
Catholic party, because he would sooner be stoned by both sides than join
any faction.

But, say they, I have published nothing against Luther. I have
published letters, though not books. To write books I had not the leisure,   50
and if I had had, there were strong reasons why it was not wise to write. At
least I frankly made it quite clear, even at some risk to myself, that I was not
doing business with his party. There is no lack of people to write, and there
are other fields in which I can be of more use to Christendom. Posterity will
understand that in all this I have played an honourable part. And in the   55
mean time those who assail me with lies may expect to pay the penalty to
their eternal judge.

I wished your Eminence to know this; and if I can convince you, I know
you will look kindly on your humble servant as you have done hitherto. If
not, I have done my duty, and have not left my innocence entirely   60
defenceless. He must have a cruel heart who cares not what men say of him.

Respectful best wishes to your lordship, to whom I profess my entire
devotion.

Basel, 7 March 1522

* * * * *

14 Baechem (Ep 1254 n6) and Vincentius Theoderici OP (Ep 1196)
15 Horace *Epistles* 1.17.30.
16 Cf Ep 1183:128–41.

1264 / To Nikolaus von Wattenwyl   Basel, 7 March 1522

Nikolaus von Wattenwyl (1492?–1551), who belonged to a distinguished Bernese family, was canon and acting provost of St Vincent's at Bern. In March 1523 he became provost in his own right. In 1525 he resigned all his benefices and joined the reformers.

The letter was first published in the *Opus epistolarum*.

ERASMUS OF ROTTERDAM TO NIKOLAUS VON WATTENWYL,
PROVOST OF BERN, GREETING

Honoured sir, our brief conversation gave me such a taste of your courtesy that after your departure I was seized with a very great desire to see you again, so much so that I have had thoughts of a visit to Bern for longer and 5 more intimate enjoyment of your delightful society. And I had the fortunate offer of a most agreeable guide and companion on my way, who would have been as good as a carriage,[1] in the shape of Henricus Glareanus, who has, I am glad to say, returned to us at last from France.[2] But it was not yet possible for me to leave this treadmill; and had it been possible, it was not safe to risk 10 a journey as long as the stoves are still burning, for at the slightest whiff from them I relapse at once into ill health.[3]

The arrival of my friend Glareanus has brought me such an accession of spirits that I feel a new man. This I think, shows sense on the part of the Swiss, that they value him so highly, for more than anyone he deserves the 15 gratitude of his younger fellow-countrymen, scattering seeds of good judgment and sound learning among his own people which will one day break forth into a bountiful harvest.

I will send you my paraphrase on Matthew,[4] provided it is finished before Glareanus' departure. Once the stoves have cooled down, it will be 20 possible to visit your city, and until then we will converse by exchanging letters. Farewell.

Basel, 7 March 1522

* * * * *

1264
1 An allusion to one of the *Sententiae* (c 17) of Publilius Syrus: 'A witty travelling companion is as good as a carriage.' Erasmus had published the *Sententiae* under the title *Mimi Publiani*; see Ep 298 introduction.
2 Glareanus (Ep 440) settled in Basel in 1514, moved to Paris in 1517, and returned to Basel shortly before this letter was written.
3 See Ep 1256 n2.
4 See Ep 1255.

Autograph rough draft of letter from Willibald Pirckheimer, Ep 1265
Stadtbibliothek Nürnberg

1265 / From Willibald Pirckheimer   [Nürnberg, beginning of March 1522]

This is the autograph rough draft of Pirckheimer's reply to Ep 1259. It survives among Pirckheimer's papers in the Stadtbibliothek Nürnberg (MS PP.323) and was first published by Allen. The text breaks off in the middle of the page. For a possible clue to the date, see Ep 1263 n9. Erasmus' reply is Ep 1268.

Greeting. I was not a little sorry, Erasmus my most valued friend, to learn from your letter that you suffer from ill health; in our eyes it is not only Erasmus who suffers when you are ill, but humane letters are in peril with you. One must put everything in God's hands, and he will dispose of it according to his mercy. I too am sometimes smitten with rheumatism, so 5 that in public I am almost always obliged to go on horseback. Blessed be the Lord, who is the maker of good days and of evil.

That the logic-choppers should wish you ill, as you say they do, is not news; but I am also not unaware of those excellent characters who misrepresent you even to the emperor and the princes as author of the 10 troubles over Luther, though all the time you are deeply suspect in the eyes of Luther's party. I know how much they disapprove of your recognition of free will and, had your friends not prevented it, you would long ago have been reading their attacks upon you. In particular, they criticize your paraphrase on Romans chapter 9,[1] where they protest that you have turned 15 upside-down not only Paul's words and intention but very clear examples too, being taken in no doubt by the commentaries of certain authors. But they are more irritated by the way in which you presume to pick holes in what Luther writes – or so they say.

There is in circulation at the moment a letter in your name to the bishop 20 of Rochester,[2] which touches openly on Luther and his followers; and this, I fear, will rouse them against you like a trumpet. Not that I am afraid you may lack means of defence – who would ever suppose Erasmus to lack shield and sword? – but I am sorry to think, and all your dearest friends regret it with me, that you should incur the hatred of either side. Learning 25 and good literature owe you quite another debt, not unpopularity on their account. Besides which, hardly anyone has such determination, however free of all blame he may be, that he can endure such malicious attacks without some distress of mind, to say nothing meanwhile of the interrup-

* * * * *

1265
1 Cf Ep 1342:1022–78.
2 See Ep 1263 n9.

tion of things more worth doing, and the jeers of the ungodly. God dispose it   30
all according to his goodness! But if fate so dictates ...

1266 / From Udalricus Zasius   Freiburg, 20 March 1522

This letter was first published in Zasius *Opera omnia* ed J.U. Zasius and Joachim
Mysinger (Lyon: S. Gryphius 1550; repr Aalen 1966) v 488.
   On Zasius, see Epp 303 and 1252.

ZASIUS TO THE GREAT ERASMUS OF ROTTERDAM, GREETING
I deeply regret it, great Erasmus, if your opponents are preparing a case
against you, nor do I see what they can object that can count against you, for
if you have aroused some mistaken suspicions, why should you not clear
them up? But I hope things will go better. Your distinguished position, your   5
learning, your character, your high and settled principles – all these men
must take into account before they turn upon you. But if they do show their
claws to any purpose, remember that other men of principle have had to face
similar treatment, and they gain rather than lose in standing from these
venomous attacks. And so, great scholar and great man that you are, pray   10
despise such attacks as may come your way. Think nothing of the brainless
utterances of men born to make trouble, which can do no possible harm to
your reputation nor damage a name already secure in the judgment of all
mankind.
   For my part, I think that to pass judgment on Luther's teaching is   15
beyond me, who know nothing of the subject; but I can say that I approve
some things about it and dislike others. In general, I have always felt that all
teaching which does not come from God soon collapses, but that it endures
if it is directed by the Holy Spirit.[1] As for you, you have your own special
task: press on with the exposition of the Scriptures. You have Dorp,[2] who   20
has outstanding ability, as a colleague in your work; others too, though few
in number, with whom you can work for the benefit of Christendom. Your
teaching is the more authentic, inasmuch as it stays close to the actual text,
and it is all the safer, because it is the real thing.
   Apart from that, we have good reason to be anxious for your help here,   25

* * * * *

1266
1 Acts 5:38–9
2 Maarten van Dorp, the Louvain theologian who in 1515 had criticized
   Erasmus' *Moriae encomium* and his work on the New Testament (Epp 304, 337,
   347). Friendly relations were restored in 1516–17 (Epp 438, 474, 627) and lasted
   until Dorp's death in 1525.

as there is a dangerous dispute between the university and the city,[3] which
has grown so intense that even Velius[4] last night was in some danger, and
other scholars too. Personally, I have decided, unless things improve, to
leave and on Capito's advice to move to Mainz,[5] where a regular chair is now
vacant; for I am not prepared to face these perils any longer. By counsel and 30
advice and in the end by making my voice heard I have urged both parties to
agree, without making one jot of progress. What hope remains in which I
can find comfort? So I would rather leave in good time than postpone my
escape until I have suffered loss, that it may not be said that I was incapable
of looking after myself. Farewell, ornament of our generation. 35

From Freiburg, 20 March 1522

1267 / To Stanislaus Thurzo   Basel, 21 March [1522]

This letter to Thurzo (Epp 1242 and 1260 n34) was first published in the *Opus
epistolarum*, which gives the date 1523. Allen changed this to 1522 on the basis
of internal evidence: Ursinus' departure, Erasmus' attack of the stone, and the
reference to the two books which had, apparently, appeared quite recently.
Moreover, if 1523 were correct, Erasmus would hardly have failed to mention
the paraphrase on St John (Ep 1333).

TO STANISLAUS THURZO, BISHOP OF OLOMOUC,
FROM ERASMUS OF ROTTERDAM, GREETING
My honoured lord, the more pleasure I received from Ursinus' society[1] – he
is at once such a good scholar and such a civilized man that this was very
great – the more I feel his departure.[2] I have nothing of importance to write, 5
but I did not wish him to depart without a letter from me, to assure you that I
am entirely at your service for such duties as a humble but devoted
dependant owes to the best and most generous of patrons.

* * * * *

3 There had been repeated controversies between town and gown since 1516,
  with accompanying tumults since at least 1521. As legal counsel to the
  university, Zasius was deeply involved. See Roderich Stinzing *Ulrich Zasius*
  (Basel 1857; repr Darmstadt 1961) 243–4.
4 See Ep 1252 n1.
5 Capito (Ep 459) was at this time the chief adviser to the archbishop of Mainz.
  The contemplated move never took place.

1267
1 Caspar Ursinus Velius (Ep 1280A)
2 Ursinus had last been at Basel in January (Ep 1252 n1). On 23 March he was still
  in Freiburg (AK Ep 857); but shortly thereafter he departed for Vienna, which he
  reached by May (Ep 1280A introduction).

During the winter months some kind of pestilent rheum[3] troubled me greatly for many days, and then returned after an interval and was worse and more prolonged than ever. Shortly before Lent,[4] when I was more or less recovered, I was suddenly laid low by a stone in the kidneys.[5] The fact is, the crazy habitation of my body, breaking down now in one place and now in another, gives its tenant notice that he must shortly flit, and this I almost think desirable, when I see the tragic mess we are making of this world of ours. All which we owe to certain disputatious persons, of whom one party have some plans – I know not what – to re-establish the liberty of the gospel, while the others consolidate their rule by strengthening their defences even more.

For my own part, I seem to see a way to put the interests of the Christian religion first without commotion.[6] But to play that piece we should need princes devoted wholeheartedly to the public weal, and to the glory of the supreme prince, Jesus Christ, before whose judgment-seat every monarch however powerful must take his stand. I myself have never come to any agreement with any member of Luther's party; I have always tried to recall them to more moderate policies, in fear, of course, that things might end in civil strife. And yet there are people with the effrontery to traduce me even in the emperor's court as a supporter of Luther. Here, Luther's people grind their teeth at me because they say I disagree with him; they tear me in pieces in their public pronouncements and threaten me with venomous pamphlets on top of that. So to both sides I am a heretic.

The New Testament has come out, revised by me for the third time and added to.[7] So has a new paraphrase on St Matthew's Gospel,[8] with the others on all the Epistles of St Paul.[9] Many men, and princes especially, urge me to write against Luther. Personally, if given the choice, I would rather fight against the world for the glory of Christ. Luther will feel no lack of antagonists. My best wishes to your lordship.

Basel, 21 March 152[3]

* * * * *

3 See Ep 1256 n2.
4 5 March–19 April 1522
5 See Epp 1281:17, 1283:10–11, 1285:21, 1294:12, 1302:42, 1311:5–6, 1342:260, 1349:3–4, 1352:18, 1353:23.
6 Probably a reference to the plan outlined in the *Consilium* of November 1520, of which Erasmus and the Dominican Johannes Faber were the co-authors; see Ep 1149 introduction. Erasmus and Faber proposed that the examination of Luther's works be entrusted to a learned commission appointed by Charles v, Henry viii, and Louis of Hungary.
7 Basel: Froben, February 1522
8 See Ep 1255.
9 In the Froben folio of February 1522

1268 / To Willibald Pirckheimer   Basel, 30 March 1522

First published in the *Pirckheimeri opera*, this is Erasmus' reply to Ep 1265. The extant manuscript in the Stadtbibliothek Nürnberg (PP.412) is a contemporary copy.

Greeting. Afflicted as we both are, I only wish it were as easy to restore each other's health as it is to exchange letters of sympathy! Not but what my bodily distempers are the least part of my troubles. As Christ is my witness, my conscience tells me that I desire none of the things of this world, and I shall willingly move from my present lodging as soon as our great   5
commanding officer summons me. Nor should I be reluctant to die in harness, if need be, at my pious task, provided I may be permitted to earn some advantage for Jesus Christ. But I see clearly how weak, or rather how unfortunate, I am, I see how monstrous is this generation, and I do not know to which party to attach myself, except that my conscience does give me   10
some confidence to appear before Jesus my judge. Those who in the pope's name pursue some policy I know not what are so busy tightening every noose of that ancient tyranny that they seem likely to add much to the load rather than take anything away. On the other side, those who under Luther's name proclaim themselves defenders of the liberty of the gospel are   15
animated by a spirit I cannot assess. Certainly many have a finger in that pie whom I should prefer to see at arm's length, if it were my business. All the while, disastrous rifts rend Christian charity everywhere. All the while, men's consciences are left in the air. Those who are naturally prone to licence easily snatch an excuse out of Luther's books; more modest folk are   20
left between the devil and the deep sea. On the one side they see arguments that carry conviction and natural common sense; on the other, the authority of princes and a multitude no man can number.

Where this business will end, I do not know; personally, I do not find a faith extorted under compulsion of much value. Great is the authority of a   25
papal bull,[1] still greater that of an imperial decree;[2] but though such things will perhaps keep men's tongues silent for a time, whether they can convert men's minds I do not know. Would that God might be reconciled with us, and put it into the minds of princes to act together in sincerity, looking

* * * * *

1268
1 The bull of excommunication against Luther, *Decet pontificem romanum*, 3 January 1521
2 The Edict of Worms, May 1521, outlawing Luther, his books, and his followers; cf Ep 1313 n7.

towards nothing save the glory of Christ, while they search out the sources   30
of this evil and find some effective and lasting remedy! – and that too with
the least possible upheaval of the world, which means with the least
possible convulsion of the commonwealth. In a word, things have come to
such a pass that something absolutely must be done to succour the liberty of
all Christian people. So many abuses have crept little by little into the   35
standards of society where, as though established by decree, they have
usurped the force of inescapable law.

On councils I would not dare say anything, unless perhaps this last
Lateran Council[3] was no council at all. There is also much usurpation of
authority by the universities, which has grown imperceptibly until they   40
almost expect their pronouncements to be taken as articles of faith. They are
now carrying on this traffic under the shadow of the Holy See; for one thing
they have made excessive claims in the past, for another they have reached a
pitch of insolence which makes them universally intolerable. Things that
have gradually gathered strength cannot suddenly be torn up by the roots,   45
and open contempt for the authority of the powers that be is neither safe nor
profitable in my opinion. As it is, the affair is carried on, on one side with
bulls and edicts and menaces, on the other with scandalous, not to say
seditious, pamphlets. If the princes are too busy with other things to attend
to this, I am surprised that no men of good will are forthcoming who might   50
devise some prudent policy to withstand such evils.

I myself am not very much concerned. The end of my life cannot be
very far away. But even a dying man must wish for the peace of
Christendom, if we are right in our conviction that Christ is the immortal
head of the whole church. One man has an eye to his private advantage,   55
another is afraid of losing what he already has, another dislikes disorders
and stays quiet; and all the while the perilous conflagration spreads. As for
me, the malevolence of certain people has laid on me such a burden of ill
will that the attempt would be fruitless if I tried to do anything. Certain
theologians I could name, feeling that my efforts to restore the study of the   60
ancients might gradually lead to some loss of their authority, were ready,
even before the world had heard the name of Luther, to set on foot anything
they could against me. To them Luther handed a weapon with which to
destroy me; although I have always kept clear of this Luther business, except
for warning him constantly to change the tone of his writing if he wishes to   65
do any good.

Then Aleandro[4] appeared. Even before there was any mention of

* * * * *

3 The fifth, 1512–17, which produced many fair words but no reforms
4 Ep 1256 n11

Luther, he strove with my poor self as potter with potter[5] – a man high and mighty by nature, bold and irascible, who can never have enough either of profit or of reputation. This man was filled to the brim by certain persons[6] with the most outrageous falsehoods, and roused to such a pitch that he did not care what he said about me, even in the highest quarters, if only he could be my undoing. And yet, when in my company, he used to swear that there was no one living more well disposed to me than he was. When he departed, he left his tools behind him well and truly in position, two Louvain theologians,[7] Master Caracciolo,[8] the bishop of Liège (who changes his tune too often),[9] and a certain Spaniard at the emperor's court, whom I suspect of being Bishop de la Mota.[10] In Rome he has Zúñiga,[11] a man whom everyone knows is crazy[12] and born to make mischief. He had shown Pope Leo a book[13] listing sixty thousand heresies selected from my published works, and I was already in serious danger, had not death carried off Leo, who was in other ways no enemy of my humble self.

Luther's people are now threatening me with scandalous pamphlets, and the emperor was nearly convinced that I was the fountain-head of all the trouble over Luther. And so I am in a splendid position of danger from both sides, though all ought to be grateful to me. I had decided to write something,[14] not against Luther but about steps towards peace; but I see both parties are now so hot that it is better to keep quiet. Not but what I could wish that Luther's people had published an attack on me two years ago: they would have delivered me from a load of ill will. I consulted the most expert theologians whether there was anything in the ninth chapter of Romans,[15] and they said there was nothing wrong in it, unless those men think it wrong that I should attribute anything, however slight, to free will.

70

75

80

85

90

* * * * *

5 Ie, with professional envy; *Adagia* i ii 25
6 See Ep 1263 n3.
7 See Ep 1263 n14.
8 Ep 1263 n1
9 Erard de la Marck (1472–1538), bishop of Liège since 1505, had been a friend and correspondent of Erasmus since 1517 (Ep 738). About 1520 a letter, no longer extant, from Aleandro produced a temporary estrangement of the bishop from Erasmus over the reference to Erard in Ep 980:42–3, but friendly relations were soon restored; see Ep 1127A:83–94 and n23.
10 See Ep 1273.
11 Ep 1260 n36
12 See Ep 1260:229, 248.
13 Ep 1260:210–17
14 See Ep 1275 n7.
15 Ie, if there was any fault in his paraphrase on Romans 9, which had drawn the fire of the Lutherans; Ep 1265:14–17

Farewell, my distinguished friend, and keep your affection warm for me, as
I know you always do.   95
    Basel, 30 March 1522
    Your sincere friend Erasmus, written in the morning in a hurry
    I had no time to reread this letter, so please excuse faults.
    To the honourable Willibald Pirckheimer, town councillor of Nürnberg

1269 / From Joris van Halewijn   Brussels, 31 March 1521/2

The autograph of this letter (=Förstemann/Günther Ep 6) was in the Burscher
Collection at Leipzig (Ep 1254 introduction). The contents leave no doubt that
the letter was written in 1522.
    Joris, lord of Halewijn and Comines (1473–1536), was a humanist scholar
and, at this time, a member of Charles v's court.

JORIS HEER VAN HALEWIJN TO ERASMUS OF ROTTERDAM,
GREETING

Your letter[1] has come, dearest Erasmus, and with it your paraphrases on
Paul's Epistles[2] and on Matthew,[3] and I and my friend Glapion[4] showed
them to the emperor. His Majesty made it clear that the gift was appreciated,   5
as you can see from the letter he is sending you.[5] At this point Glapion made
an open move to support your case and to say something on your behalf; but
he wished you were here, so that he could establish your position more
securely. He wished also that you would write some pieces against Luther as
the enemy of Christian piety; for he said that some things of that kind could   10
snuff out all suspicion and all the malevolence of your detractors. How I
wish you could pay us a flying visit before the emperor leaves,[6] so as to take
thought more securely for your future! I pray that the Almighty may restore
your health[7] and grant that all may be well with you. Farewell.
    The bishop of Palencia, whose name is Mota,[8] a Spaniard, tells me to   15

* * * * *

1269
1 Not extant. Erasmus had written it at the suggestion of Vives; Ep 1256:68–70.
2 Presumably the collected edition of February 1522
3 Ep 1255
4 Ep 1275
5 Ep 1270
6 On 2 May Charles left Brussels, bound for England and Spain; Gachard II 32.
7 See Ep 1256 n2.
8 Ep 1273

send you his warmest greetings. Farewell again, from Brussels, on the last
day of March AD 1521.

To Erasmus of Rotterdam, the man of letters

1270 / From Charles V   Brussels, 1 April 1522

A letter of acknowledgment for the paraphrase on Matthew, which Erasmus
had dedicated to the emperor (Ep 1255). The letter was first published in the
Froben octavo edition of the paraphrase in 1523. According to Allen, the
contemporary manuscript copy of the letter in the Bibliothèque Royale at
Brussels (Sér ii.53 f 16) was apparently made from the printed book rather than
from the original. For Erasmus' references to this letter, see Epp 1299:39–40,
1300:63–4, 1323:20–1, 1331:12–13, 1342:280.

CHARLES, BY DIVINE MERCY ELECTED EVER-AUGUST EMPEROR OF
THE ROMANS, KING OF SPAIN AND THE TWO SICILIES ETC,
ARCHDUKE OF AUSTRIA, DUKE OF BURGUNDY ETC
Right trusty and well-beloved. We derived great pleasure from your
paraphrase on the Gospel of St Matthew which has recently appeared, not   5
so much from its dedication to ourself as from the great applause with which
it has been received by all authoritative and learned critics, but above all for
the great contribution which such an exposition of the pure gospel teaching
will make with its distinguished scholarship to theological studies and to the
Christian religion as a whole. Great as is the reputation you have won by the   10
other products of your labours, which are famous everywhere, by none are
you thought to have earned a richer harvest than by your paraphrases. We
remember for our own part how your many distinguished intellectual gifts
have been exhibited, partly to his Majesty our father of illustrious memory
and partly to us. To him you offered your *Panegyricus*,[1] and to us your   15
Institutio principis christiani,[2] not only for the enhancement of our name but
also to the great profit of posterity. We therefore reckon it part of our royal
duty to show you all our gratitude as occasion may offer, for we are given to
understand that it is no small part of the felicity of men of genius to find in
the prince one who admires their great qualities. In the mean time we will do   20
all we can to promote your religious undertakings and the honourable and
valuable enterprise on which you are at present engaged, and will

* * * * *

1270
1 Ep 179
2 Ep 393

encourage whatever we learn that you have done for the honour of Christ
and the salvation of all Christian people.

Given at Brussels, 1 April 1522

Charles

G. Morillon[3]

1270A / From Battista Casali   Rome, spring (after 1 April) 1522

This letter appears on page 455.

1271 / From Juan Luis Vives   Bruges, 1 April 1522

For the source of this letter, see Ep 1256 introduction.

VIVES TO ERASMUS

Your letter[1] written from Basel on the fourth of February has arrived, and it
arrived with the seal not exactly broken, but so damaged and defaced that it
was easy to detect that it had been opened on the way. That Augustine's *De
civitate Dei*[2] is being published separately[3] is very good news, and I am
immensely grateful to you for arranging this. But I should like to see it also
printed with the rest of Augustine's works, so that the corpus is not a body
lacking this limb; and I think Froben will manage to print some separately
and some as part of the whole. I could have wished that you had read some
pages in the books I sent you, and had told me what you make of them and
written your opinion at some length, so that I could have known what to
avoid and what to follow, and what my policy should be; for in this work I
have tried, so far as I could, to please the public by my brevity.[4] I
encountered some passages in which I could not achieve this, for instance
when there were subjects not very familiar to our divines, such as history
and mythology and philosophy, especially Platonism. Consequently in
books 8 and 10 I have perhaps been longer than I ought to have been, not
only in order to open and display to them these recondite subjects, but also
to leave them not wholly ignorant of Plato and aware that he is by no means
inferior to Aristotle, which may arouse a wish to get to know other
important authors.

* * * * *

3 Guy Morrillon (Ep 1287)

1271
1 Not extant. Doubtless a reply to Ep 1256
2 See Ep 1309.
3 That is, without waiting for the rest of Erasmus' edition of Augustine, which
   was not published until 1529
4 As Erasmus had advised; see Allen Ep 1531:40.

Yet I have not piled up everything that I might have. I have left out far more than I have cited. In other books I easily maintained the brevity I had decided on, for stories taken from Holy Writ are too familiar, even to ordinary people, to need lengthy explanations, and theological questions I 25 have not pursued to any length, being content with a mention of them, or else there would have been no limits. Nor have I been so much a slave to reputation as you perhaps suppose, though I have also given it a thought. But neither the time available nor the nature of the work have left me free to think much about reputation; I should have been glad of more time for work 30 that was to be entirely devoted to giving me publicity and a good name. And then somehow the writing of notes, unless they are notes on Scripture, is not of a nature to get a man a famous name. Work that is to earn an immense reputation will be wholly its author's property, and ought not to be written as a commentary on someone else. But I have brought it to as high a standard 35 of finish as was possible, and do not doubt the reader will recognize that I have tried to do credit both to you, who encouraged me to undertake the work, and to Augustine, and to my own reputation. The jest I made at the expense of a commentator[5] I have not suppressed; and in any case, even had you not told me to, it was my intention to display in my preface what sort of 40 men had written on Augustine; this I propose to do, and shall hold them up for the reader's exquisite amusement.[6] Then in the work itself I intersperse nosegays, as it were, plucked from their commentaries and Passavanti's additions,[7] so that their sweet fragrance may refresh the reader and beguile the tedium of his journey.   45

From the things I now send you, you will see how much I fear any trouble from them. The life of Augustine I should prefer you to add yourself, for I am not confident of putting it together with the good judgment that you

* * * * *

5 Jacopo Passavanti; see following note.

6 In his edition of the *De civitate Dei* Vives included a prefatory essay entitled 'De veteribus interpretibus huius operis' (pages 16–24 in the Leiden edition of 1563). Vives observes that some Dominicans had pronounced his commentary superfluous because members of their own order had already written commentaries 'in such a marvellously learned, skilful, detailed, and successful manner that there was no room for improvement' (page 16). Vives then scornfully catalogues the errors and nonsense to be found in the commentaries of certain Dominicans: the fourteenth-century Englishmen Thomas de Walleys and Nicholas Trivet, and their younger Florentine contemporary Jacopo Passavanti (d 1357). Concerning Passavanti, who had studied in France, Vives asserts that his fellow friars had given him the name 'Passavant' (ie, *pas savant*) as a joke (page 22).

7 Passavanti's notes on *De civitate Dei* were published as additions to the commentaries of Thomas de Walleys (see preceding note); Lyon: J. Sacon 15 October 1520.

show in everything you do; and I shall be thought to have done the saint a
bad turn if what you might otherwise have written about him is written by 50
me, so that my poor efforts make me responsible for depriving posterity of a
brilliant treatment of his life by you. I do beg you and urge you to write it
instead. I send you with this ten books, from 8 to 17, and expect to send the
remaining five just before Easter[8] or soon after. They are mostly finished,
and I am now revising them, and shall proceed at once to have them copied 55
on better paper. The original I shall keep among my most private
possessions, for I can see what an expensive injury I should do to Froben if I
were to give anyone a copy. But I could wish also that he in his turn should
give no one access to what he has printed until he has finished the whole
work; and I say this not without good reason. I perceive that you have 60
always regarded honourable dealing as the safeguard of your whole life; and
this is the one resource relied on by that great orator, even when he has
plunged into the storm and tempest of public life, by which, as he declares,
he easily despises all controversy.[9] And indeed it is impossible that God
should not be well disposed towards you, for you never forget that our life 65
here is too short to deserve that we should stir up troubles and tragedies in
order to preserve it.

    As for Aleandro, I do not doubt that things are as you say, though he
himself, when he returned to Brussels from Liège,[10] swore to me that he
had always spoken up for your reputation in front of the great men. He has 70
now run off to Spain to the new pope,[11] of whom everyone hopes and
expects great things. Christ grant that his election may cure all these great
evils in his church! If friends in your part of the world are afraid that some
people may use their pens as weapons to attack you, this, to use a retort of
Cicero's,[12] is to do service. What grander and more fertile subject could one 75
find than to speak about Erasmus and to defend Erasmus? How easy, how
truthful not only in fact but in appearance, is the task of defending the
innocent! If your way of life wins the approval of your conscience, the most
important witness in everything, can you not be confident that you will have
the approval of others, even if your judge is a personal enemy, as in the story 80
about Scipio?[13]

        * * * * *

8 20 April 1522
9 The reference is perhaps to Cicero's *Pro Milone* 5.
10 There seems to be no other evidence of Aleandro's visit to Liège. It must have
    taken place before 19 February 1522, when Aleandro departed for Spain as a
    member of the emperor's embassy to the new pope (see following note); J.
    Paquier *Jérôme Aléandre et la principauté de Liège* (Paris 1896) 109.
11 Adrian VI (Ep 1304)
12 *Philippics* 2.2
13 Cicero *De oratore* 2.285

As for the black monk,[14] I am sorry it has taken you so long to come round to my opinion; there is much truth in the saying that one should avoid a friend who can do one harm and cannot help one. Zúñiga[15] is preparing a long and savage attack on you; so Vergara[16] told me, and read aloud a letter[17] Zúñiga had sent him from Rome, in which he threatens he will do this. The letter is written in Spanish, answering one from Vergara in Latin; for Vergara is surprised that he should reply to Latin in the vernacular. Such a letter neither Thraso nor Pyrgopolinices[18] would have written. I have never yet spoken of Zúñiga to any Spaniard without his saying how much he dislikes him – arrogant, boastful, slanderous, malicious beyond anything one could explain or believe. He has also written a most virulent book attacking Lefèvre;[19] it has annoyed many people, and lost him most of his friends. They say further that he cannot bear the thought of any people being friends; he is always striving and toiling away, not merely to estrange them from one another but to make them enemies. This I have been told by men who had been most united and had been made bitter enemies by Zúñiga. He sounds like one of the Furies, not a human being. It is greatly to one's credit to be spoken ill of by a man with such a character; no one can enjoy his approval without being suspected of resembling him.

That remarkable verse comes into my head as the best encouragement I can offer you: 'Yield not to evils; march more boldly on.'[20] Maybe I should speak quite differently if I were in your shoes; but in giving advice we say, not what we should do in the same circumstances, but what ought to be done. You have played out the greater portion of your part in the drama of this life; in what remains, devote yourself to earning the approval, not of the audience only, the men you can see, but of Christ, for whom you have endured so many labours, and of your conscience. If you give any weight to the applause of the audience, let it be posterity rather than the present. Posterity, when envy and all the other emotions are done away, will contemplate in you the pure and true Erasmus, and will give you the glory you deserve, all the more generously in so far as the men of your own

* * * * *

14 Perhaps the Dominican, Johannes Faber (Ep 1267 n6), Erasmus' admiration for whom may already have been cooling; cf his comments on Faber in the *Spongia* of August 1523 (ASD IX-1 156:840–9).
15 See Ep 1260 nn36, 45.
16 Ep 1277
17 Dated 9 January 1522, and printed in CWE 8 340–3
18 Thraso is the braggart soldier in Terence's *Eunuchus,* and Pyrgopolinices is the hero of Plautus' *Miles gloriosus.*
19 *Annotationes contra Jacobum Fabrum Stapulensem* (Alcalá: A.G. Brocario 1519)
20 Virgil *Aeneid* 6.95

generation have been unfair to you, and your virtues have been less clearly recognized by the men among whom they were active. We see how this happened to Socrates. I beg you urgently not to distress yourself; remember that, if you consider only yourself and your renown, you have lived long enough and belong now to the ages. You can infer from the judgment of not a few men of good will what will be said of you among peoples yet unborn. If you consider this, you will reckon all the days of your life henceforward as pure gain, and you will live in peace and happiness; this, and this alone, means to live without anxiety and care, and the white hair that protects your old age will make you think nothing of the many barking dogs. You yourself will be as it were above the power of fate, and from a kind of exalted station, which is the approval of all good men, you will see everything beneath your feet.

But I begin to forget to whom I am writing. I think you will get a letter from More[21] by the hands of Clement,[22] who has set off in these last few days for Italy and means to pass through Basel, or so he said. In his last letter to me, More says nothing about his illness. I think he must have recovered, for his earlier letter already indicated that he was improving. At the beginning of Lent[23] I came to Bruges, because Lent in Louvain never suits me; it is so far inland, and we eat no fish except what is already stinking and not cooked so that I can eat it. A few days before my arrival Petrus Laurinus[24] had died, which is no small loss to me. The dean[25] sends you his greetings; he set off last week for Brussels. He told me to send you greetings from the abbot of St Bavo's at Ghent,[26] who this last first of January had a golden new-year's present ready for you against your arrival. I know not what; money, I suppose. About Ferdinand there is still no progress,[27] and I pursue the matter so slowly and languidly that I dare say there never will be any.

The duke of Alba[28] was making me an offer by no means to be despised, had the friars allowed me to hear of it: he was most keen that the grandsons he has in Spain, his eldest son's boys,[29] should be taught by me.

* * * * *

21 The letter to Erasmus is lost, as are the two to Vives (lines 116, 118).
22 See Ep 1256 n40.
23 5 March–19 April 1522
24 Petrus Laurinus (Pieter Lauwerijns), 1489–1522, was the brother of Marcus Laurinus (Ep 1342), dean of St Donatian's at Bruges.
25 Ie, Marcus Laurinus; see the preceding note.
26 Lievin Hugenoys (Ep 1214)
27 See Ep 1256 n24.
28 Ep 1256 n12
29 The duke had two grandsons by his son Garcia, who had been killed in 1512 fighting the Moors. The elder, Fernando Alvarez, 1508–82, later became

When he was making arrangements to send one of his gentlemen of the
bedchamber to me to discuss the proposal and offer me two hundred gold
ducats a year by way of recompense, a certain Dominican friar breaks in and   145
asks the duke whether he has anything to go to Louvain, because he will be
setting off there next day. 'Nothing,' says the duke, 'could be more
opportune. Pray speak with Vives, and find out whether he is willing to be
tutor to my grandsons for this salary.' And at the same time a nobleman
called Bertrand,[30] the man who visited you at Anderlecht,[31] gave him a letter   150
to me containing more details of the whole business. The friar came to
Louvain; he spoke with me ten times and more: not a word about the duke,
nor did he give me Bertrand's letter. The duke, when he saw me hesitate, or
perhaps the friar told him I had said no, handed the boys over from now
onwards to a certain Severus,[32] who is a monk. Knowing nothing of all this, I   155
came to Brussels, and there Bertrand protested that I had never answered
his letter. 'Letter be hanged!' says I, 'what letter?' 'Do you really mean,' he
said, 'What letter?' 'Really,' I said. Then in the presence of many other
people he told me the whole story. Many who were there assured me that
they had been present when the duke gave his commission to the friar. They   160
were very sorry, they said, that I had turned the offer down, for I should
never find a place more to my liking than with them, which meant with men
who liked me very much; but it was not possible now to reopen the question,
because the duke had come to an agreement with Severus. 'What an idea!' I
said; 'Could I possibly reject any offer made to me by the duke, since I have   165
always sought most eagerly for any chance of showing how very desirous I
was of serving the duke?' I was grateful, I told them, for their friendly
feelings, and resented not so much the failure of the offer to reach me as the
criminal behaviour of the friar. And this we suffer from men who call
themselves brethren; how will they treat strangers? Not content with   170
attacking scholarship, they are already encroaching on our worldly positions too. God himself will be our defender. Farewell, my dear teacher.

    Bruges, 1 April 1522

* * * * *

notorious as the Duke of Alba who imposed a reign of terror on the
Netherlands (1567–73). The younger, Bernardino, died in 1535.
30 Unknown
31 Erasmus was in Anderlecht from 31 May to 5 July, and from 31 August to 14
   October; see Epp 1208, 1221, 1232, 1239.
32 Identity unknown. Erasmus mentions someone with the same name in letters
   to Italian correspondents (Epp 1169:31, 1195:171, and 1198:52), but this
   Severus, doubtless a Spaniard, is not likely to have been the same person. For
   another unlikely candidate, see CEBR sv 'Severus.'

1272 / From Stanislaus Thurzo [Kroměříž?], 10 April 1522

This is Bishop Thurzo's reply to Epp 1242–3. The letter was first published
in Erasmus' commentary on Psalm 14, *De puritate tabernaculi* (Basel: Froben
and Episcopius 1536). The probable place of writing is inferred from BRE
Ep 223.

STANISLAUS THURZO, BISHOP OF OLOMOUC, TO DESIDERIUS
ERASMUS OF ROTTERDAM, GREETINGS

I cannot fail to admit, dear Erasmus, most learned of men, that I am filled
with incredible happiness and joy whenever I remember (as I constantly do)
the benefit that I owe to your exceptional generosity, in which you show   5
yourself so kind as to admit me to the same place in your affection in which
in a saintly and loving spirit you once held my brother the bishop of Wrocław,[1]
now torn from me by an early death; for this there is abundant evidence in
the most open-hearted letters which you wrote me recently. These letters I
treasure as highly as the most valuable gift I ever received. Could anything   1
more precious come my way than for Erasmus, the great man of our time,
Erasmus the unchallenged leader without exception in every branch of
learning in both tongues, to admit me readily and gladly to be his friend? –
and this when he has not yet met me, and I have done him no service worth
the doing, but moved solely by the persuasion, such as it is, of Caspar   1
Ursinus[2] or, to speak more truly, by his own inborn kindness, which he
shows in equal measure to almost everyone devoted to the humanities. Why
then should I not rejoice, why not think myself remarkably fortunate, that
such a blessing as I could never deserve has come my way unasked?

It is at any rate a long time since I first felt awe, respect, and admiration   2
for Erasmus, as a kind of divine being sent down to us from heaven. In all my
travels I have you always as a companion at my elbow, for your most
scholarly and pious writings make me not only a better scholar but a better
man. But now that mutual affection has been added to all these, as I hope for
salvation by the pleasure of our great Saviour, I know no words in which to   2
express how much I rejoice and how much I love to see you famous. But this
I must not fail to ask (for Love's an anxious being,[3] as you are aware), do not
forget me and let me slip from your heart; and if you love me, I in return will
enfold you in immortal affection and will perform most readily for your sake

* * * * *

1272
1 Johannes Thurzo, 1464/5–1520 (Ep 850)
2 Caspar Ursinus Velius (Ep 1280A)
3 Cf Ovid *Heroides* 1.12.

whatever gratitude and constant affection could do and ought to do. Caspar   30
Ursinus was warmly commended to me long ago by his gifts, his literary
attainments, and his many services as well; but now that you too give him
such a warm recommendation, I will gladly add something further to what I
have done for him before, so that he may see how far from fruitless is the
support of a great man and a very wise one.   35

I send you for the time being a small token of my respect for the great
man that you are, to which with your usual courtesy I know you will give a
kind reception, four gold coins of virtuous emperors. For I have heard that
you take great delight in such relics of the past. If there is any other way in
which I can gratify you as a dear friend, ask me, or somehow let me know,   40
and it is as good as done. Farewell, and best wishes.

10 April 1522

1273 / To Pedro Ruiz de la Mota   Basel, 21 April 1522

This letter, first published in the *Opus epistolarum*, is probably a response to the
compliment relayed in Ep 1269:15–16. The bishop's reply was likely the letter
mentioned in Epp 1299:43, 1300:65, 1331:16–17, 1342:283.

Pedro Ruiz de la Mota of Burgos (d 19 September 1522), had already been in
Hapsburg service for several years when in 1511 he was appointed chaplain
and almoner to the future Charles v. In 1517 he became a member of the
Council of Flanders and in 1520 bishop of Palencia. At the time this letter was
written, Mota was one of the most powerful men at the imperial court. Despite
his show of good will towards Erasmus, the latter's suspicions of him (Epp
1268:77–8, 1302:59–62) may have been well founded. Mota, who was reputed
to be 'more ambitious than honest,' may have said what was necessary to
please Erasmus' friends at court, such as chancellor Gattinara (Ep 1150), while
at the same time currying favour with Aleandro (Ep 1256 n11) in the hope of
further ecclesiastical advancement (a cardinal's hat, the archbishopric of
Toledo).

It was apparently in the interval between Ep 1268 and the present letter that
Erasmus made the unhappy Rhine journey described in Epp 1302 and 1342:
333ff. His aim was to go on to Brabant to pay his court before the emperor's
departure for Spain (Ep 1269 n6), and to arrange in person for the payment of
his two pensions (see Ep 1245 and n4 to this letter). But on the journey his
health quickly broke down. He rested for two days with Johannes Gallinarius
(Ep 1307), parish priest in Breisach, then struggled on to Sélestat, where he
spent four days with Beatus Rhenanus (Ep 327). Too ill to go on, he turned back
to Basel, which he reached only after stopping to rest once more with
Gallinarius. Back in Basel, he dispatched Hilarius Bertolph (Ep 1257 n10) with a

packet of letters (Epp 1273–6, and doubtless others: see Ep 1281:23–5, 82–3), hoping to accomplish by mail what he could not perform in person.

ERASMUS OF ROTTERDAM TO THE BISHOP OF PALENCIA, GREETINGS

Right reverend prelate, the news that you so generously both took my part and spoke well of me before the emperor, and your kind words, gave me the greater pleasure because I neither expected this[1] nor deserved it. But meanwhile the life of those who like myself write books is no better than that of the actors of antiquity who presented a play on the stage before the public. They had to learn their parts, to rehearse their production, to do all that was humanly possible to satisfy their audience – that motley throng, truly a beast of many heads, few of whose members have the same tastes, nor are they always consistent, and, what is worse, the greater part of them are led by prejudice rather than judgment. On their thumbs the poor mountebank is wholly dependent; he must worship the lowest of the mob, and after superhuman exertions thinks himself happy if he has secured a hearing for his play. If he is hissed off the stage, he must find a tree and hang himself. Surely books have to face critics who are no less various, no less difficult to please, no less distorted by prejudice. In one way our fate is the more unfair, in that we put on our show at our own expense, while the actors get their fee. And they, if the dance is a failure, merely look foolish; we, if we fail to please, are heretics.

My own wish has always been not so much to please as to be of use to all men. And all was going well, had not this tragedy of the new gospel interfered with everything; which, when it opened, somehow won enthusiastic plaudits from almost the whole world, but each act proved worse than the last, and it has ended in uproar and madness as a finale. I disliked it when it first came on, for this reason among others that I could see it must end in subversion. I for my part have never approved of truth in a subversive form, and heresy still less. Even so, there are men where you are now who make me out to be one of Luther's party, although their consciences tell them they lie – their object being no doubt to drive me willy-nilly by their spiteful attacks into Luther's camp. For my own part, neither death nor life shall tear me from the society of the Catholic church. How close I am to Luther is shown by Luther's own people, who attack me ferociously with public calumny and vicious pamphlets. I have no wish, however, to claim credit for deserting Luther. Let me be called Luther's man still, if I have ever

* * * * *

1273
1 Cf the suspicions about de la Mota expressed in Ep 1268:77–8.

been one. Not but what in the beginning I did disapprove of the subversive   35
clamour of certain monks, who not merely ranted against Luther with
spiteful falsehoods worthy of any fishwife, but likewise attacked the ancient
tongues and the humanities one and all, while I was shamelessly torn to
pieces by name in their public sermons.

Our new pope,[2] with his scholarly wisdom and wise integrity, and at   40
the same time a spirit in our emperor that seems more than human,
encourage me to high hopes that this plague may be rooted out in such a way
that it may never grow again. This can be done if the roots are cut away from
which this plague so often sprouts afresh, one of which is hatred of the
Roman curia (whose greed and tyranny were already past bearing), and   45
along with that, much legislation of purely human origin, which was
thought to lay a burden on the liberty of Christian people. All these can
easily be cured, without setting the world by the ears, by the emperor's
authority and the integrity of the new pope. I myself am nobody, but to the
best of my ability I do not, and I will not, fail to do my duty. Only let the   50
emperor in his mercy[3] provide that my salary[4] shall be permanent, and
ensure that my reputation is kept in good and sound repair against the spite
of certain enemies;[5] I shall see to it that he will not regret making me a
councillor.[6] My best wishes to your noble self, whose servant, such as I am, I
subscribe myself.   55

Basel, Easter Monday 1522

1274 / To Luis Núñez Coronel   Basel, 21 April 1522

Luis Núñez Coronel of Segovia (d 1535), studied at Salamanca and then at
Paris, taking his DD in 1514. From 1519 he was councillor, preacher, and
confessor at the court of Charles v. In 1521 and 1522 he assisted in the work of
the Inquisition at Brussels, Ghent, Bruges, and Antwerp. His opinion of
Erasmus was extremely favourable. To Vives he described the Dutch scholar as
another Jerome or Augustine (Ep 1281:48–9). After his return to Spain with
Charles v in 1522, Coronel became secretary to Alonso Manrique, archbishop
of Seville and grand inquisitor of Spain. In this position Coronel was able to
assist Erasmus against his Spanish critics, especially during the theological

* * * * *

2 Adrian vi (Ep 1304)
3 The emperor's good will had recently been expressed in Ep 1270.
4 Ie, his annuity as an imperial councillor. See Epp 370:18n, 1275:58–9, 1276:9,
   1287:27–34, 1303:62, 1306:50–1, 1319:21–2, 1341A:1797–8, 1342:101, 286–7.
5 See Ep 1263 n14.
6 See Ep 370:18n.

examination of Erasmus' works at Valladolid in 1527 (cf Ep 1334 introduction).
This letter was first published in the *Opus epistolarum*.

ERASMUS OF ROTTERDAM TO LUIS CORONEL, GREETINGS

Honoured sir, Luis Vives, who gave me in passing a sketch of your
admirable qualities,[1] had kindled in my mind the desire to win your
friendship, and this spark was strongly fanned by Ludwig Baer,[2] who
described fortissimo, as they say, and with great warmth your lively 5
intelligence, which to a mastery of theological literature adds an elegant
familiarity with mathematics. And now a rare kind of freshness in your
attitude and a truly Christian good will towards myself, although a man of
no account, have been made fully known to me in a letter from Guy
Morillon,[3] so that I regret quite particularly my failure to have secured such a 10
friend, to some extent at least, before I left.[4] I was filled with a desire to pay a
flying visit to your part of the world before the emperor's departure.[5] I
would have made nothing of my state of health, which has lately been so
much weakened by constant illness[6] that I find life a burden; nothing of the
length of the journey; nothing of the learned labours[7] which I have now in 15
hand and which are now printing on Froben's presses; nothing of certain
other obstacles not lightly to be overlooked. But chiefly I was afraid of the
journey, which is more than usually notorious now for robberies.[8] I have
often travelled that way successfully in the past; but if anything should
happen, it would be the end of me. 20

* * * * *

1274
1 At just about this time Erasmus would have received Vives' notes to
  Augustine's *De civitate Dei* (Ep 1271:53–4) where, in the note to 13.24 (page 411
  of the edition of September 1522), Vives thanks Coronel for the loan of the first
  volume of the Complutensian Polyglot, calling him a distinguished theologian
  and commending his zeal for the common good.
2 Ludwig Baer (Ep 305:201n), who must have known Coronel during his student
  days at the University of Paris
3 Not extant; presumably contemporary with Ep 1270
4 Ie, before Erasmus' departure from Louvain for Basel in the autumn of 1521;
  see Ep 1242 introduction.
5 For Spain in May 1522; Ep 1269 n6
6 See Ep 1256 n2.
7 See Ep 1294 n9. In addition to the works mentioned there, Erasmus wrote just
  at this time the *Epistola de esu carnium*, addressed to the bishop of Basel on 21
  April and printed by Froben in August; see Epp 1341A:1306–13, 1353 n13, 1293
  n8.
8 On his journey from Louvain to Basel in the autumn of 1521 (n4 above)
  Erasmus had taken advantage of the protection offered by a troop of disbanded
  soldiers who were travelling up the Rhine; Epp 1302:17–20, 1342:168–71.

As regards my preface and the paraphrase,[9] I am most grateful for the points you so kindly make. The preface[10] was added without much care, to please the printer, who complained that a few pages would be empty unless I added some trifle or other. Such as it is, however, it is my own child – my miscarriage, if you prefer. One ought not to detest any heresy to such a degree that hatred of it leaves one no courage to point out what is right. Jerome is not afraid to praise virginity because the Marcionites condemned marriage; he is not deterred from recommending marriage to one wife only by Tertullian's condemnation of second marriages. If there is any danger in the widespread reading of the Gospels, why did the apostles put them out in the most widespread language of the day? I do not believe there is any danger, provided the laity read the Scriptures in the manner I there lay down. What Luther's teaching is, I do not know; my paraphrase on Matthew I was moved to undertake more by the authority of Matthäus, cardinal of Sion, than by my own judgment, a fact I do not conceal in the preface.[11] In the apostolic Epistles, if your judgment finds my work more satisfactory, this is due to the subject-matter, and none of my doing. In a version, the sense is rendered literally; in a paraphrase, it is legitimate to add something of your own as well that may make the author's meaning clearer. The scope allowed to the writer of a paraphrase can easily be seen by anyone who compares Themistius[12] with Aristotle. For a paraphrase is not a translation but something looser, a kind of continuous commentary in which the writer and his author retain separate roles.

But how I wish it might be possible for me to have the benefit of your most friendly advice face to face, and correct my manner of writing by the criteria of your most polished judgment! I wonder there can be people in your part of the world so stupid or such shameless liars that they can call me a supporter of Luther. The beginning of this tragedy always distressed me, for I saw that it must end in subversion, although there was some hope that the man would turn over to a more sensible policy. Nor did I like the subversive clamour raised by some noisy rascals before popular audiences. As things are now, Luther's party behave everywhere as though they had

* * * * *

9 On Matthew; Ep 1255
10 Not Ep 1255, but a letter to the reader, dated 14 January 1522, added in order to fill the blank opening sheet. In the letter Erasmus maintained, as he had in the *Paraclesis*, that the Bible should be read not merely by scholars but by all classes, to whom it should be made available in translation. See Allen's introduction to Ep 1255.
11 That is, in Ep 1255:26–31
12 A fourth-century philosopher and rhetorician, author of paraphrases of several works of Aristotle

no interest in their own safety. Here, I am so far from being regarded as Luther's man that some of his supporters write and ask me not to use my pen against him, while others threaten me with vicious pamphlets. How I wish they had attacked me with them two years ago! – they would have freed me from a great burden of unpopularity. In Louvain there are two or three people[13] instigated to attack me by private spite, because long ago I gave devoted support to the humanities, which they judge to be unsuited to their own way of life. But it is not like our merciful emperor to hand over a man who labours for the glory of Christ and the honour of the empire to the resentment of such as they. Had I supported Luther even a little, I do not wish to boast what effect I might have had in Germany. But I would sooner meet death ten times over than start or encourage a perilous schism. This is already understood in Germany,[14] and I will see to it that all men soon understand the unflinching course I have taken in this affair. I am confident therefore that a man with your sense of justice will defend me against such shameless falsehoods.

Farewell. From Basel, Easter Monday 1522

1275 / To Jean Glapion   Basel, [c 21 April] 1522

First printed in the *Opus epistolarum*, this letter is clearly contemporary with Epp 1273–4 and 1276. Glapion's reply is mentioned in Epp 1299:42. 1300:64, 1331:15, and 1342:282.

Jean Glapion (d 14 September 1522), who was from northern France (probably Maine), studied at the University of Paris and became a Franciscan Observant. In 1520 he became personal confessor to Charles v, over whom he exercised great influence. Erasmus and Glapion met only once, in Brussels in the summer of 1521, but they exchanged letters afterwards (ASD IX-1 154:810–12). This letter is all that survives of that correspondence.

ERASMUS OF ROTTERDAM TO JEAN GLAPION, GREETINGS
For my part, dear Glapion, I think our most intelligent emperor is to be congratulated on this perhaps above all, that he has to advise him a man like you. I entertain a most certain hope that you, singularly uncorrupted as you are by worldly desires, will give that most powerful monarch advice which will tend to the general advantage of the world and to Christ's glory, as I

* * * * *

13 See Ep 1263 n14. A third might have been Laurens Laurensen OP (Ep 1166 n6).
14 Cf Ep 1275:29ff.

think you have done hitherto. Apart from that, your kindness towards me[1] I must acknowledge so often that it makes me blush. I would have made nothing of all else – my state of health,[2] the length of the journey, the risk of being robbed,[3] the work that I have in hand and that is now printing,[4] and a great box of my belongings which has now at last been brought as far as Frankfurt but has not reached me yet – and would eagerly have paid you a flying visit, as surely as I treasure the love of the Lord Jesus, but I was afraid that when I had done everything possible, I might not have found his Majesty the emperor where you are now, for he was said to have been held up for some time already on the coast, waiting for nothing but favourable winds – and winds are the only creatures that do not know an emperor when they see one. I wanted also to visit Calais to greet some of my patrons,[5] who would be there, I thought, with the emperor.

If there is any way in which I can oblige the prince my master, or serve the cause of his honour or the Christian religion, send me a brief note by this young man,[6] who is thoroughly to be trusted. I am to be sure a man who knows how to keep silence. I had already made a fair start with a short treatise on how to end this business of Luther;[7] but ill health has interrupted all my work. In the mean while, I have restrained by both speech and writing[8] many people who were greatly attracted by Luther. I have also made it clear in my published letters[9] that I have never come to an agreement with any of Luther's party, but that business which must end in sedition is a thing I have always disliked. This is by now so well known all over Germany that no true Lutheran wishes me well;[10] some threaten me with vicious pamphlets; others attack me with clamorous abuse, calling me a Pelagian[11] and a time-server instead of a herald of the gospel teaching. I at least shall

* * * * *

1275
1 See Ep 1269:6–7.
2 See Ep 1256 n2.
3 See Ep 1274 n8.
4 See Ep 1274 n7.
5 Erasmus apparently expected some of his English patrons to be among those who crossed to Calais to meet Charles on his way to England.
6 Hilarius Bertolph; see Epp 1257 n10, and 1281:23.
7 Erasmus gives a full account of this project in Ep 1341A:1338–1416. The *libellus* would doubtless have amplified the proposals put forward in the *Consilium* of 1520 (Ep 1267 n6), but it was never completed. Cf Ep 1268:86–8.
8 As, for example, in Ep 1202. Also in Epp 947:40–3, 983:11–18. Cf Ep 1225:298–9.
9 Such as Epp 961, 967, 1033, 1041. Cf Ep 1225:168–70.
10 Cf Ep 1274:64–5.
11 See Ep 1259 n5.

never be torn by either life or death from obedience to the church and from the integrity of the Christian faith.

Yet this is a point, my excellent friend, which I should like you to 35 consider – how unfairly I am treated. I have devoted all this labour to advancing the general standard of knowledge and the Christian religion; I have always urged Luther's party not to pursue this subversive course; I have never let myself be influenced either by reasoning or by spiteful attacks and threats to yield even a scrap of ground to their faction, though I could 40 have aroused great tumults here had I been the man they say I am; and now I am handed over to the private resentment of certain people to be torn to shreds and am forced into a position where it is not safe for me to live either in your part of the world or in Germany – here on account of Luther's party, who are said to be planning some great political disturbance I know not 45 what, and there because of two or three men[12] who are my enemies on personal grounds. My genius, which you call divine, is small enough, to be sure; but such as it is, it shall always be devoted to Christ's glory and, next after him, to the honour of the prince my master.

And I might still be able to support these labours for some years to 50 come, if I were allowed peaceful and uninterrupted leisure. But I cannot fail to be aware of the spite with which some men attack me and the things they are preparing to do, their object no doubt being to drive me willy-nilly into the Lutheran camp. But this they shall never do. They shall kill me before they corrupt me, and I will revenge myself on them in a way that shall best 55 prove my integrity in the sight of all men. Such revenge will suffice for a Christian spirit. I like Brabant greatly, and especially that rural retreat at Anderlecht[13] –if only the prince in his mercy would give the word for my annuity[14] to be permanent and would defend me against certain men who seek to gratify their private spite under the guise of religion. 60

How bitter that spite is, you may guess from this instance among many. A decree was passed in Cologne by the Dominicans that all books written by Erasmus should be thrown out of the libraries of the entire order.[15] Among these are the New Testament and Jerome! And there are

* * * * *

12 See Ep 1263:1–3.
13 See Ep 1271 n31.
14 See Ep 1273 n4.
15 It has proved impossible to verify this report. On 19 September Michael Hummelberg (Ep 1253 n6) reported having heard that certain of Erasmus' opinions had been condemned by the theologians of Cologne; BRE Ep 226.

men in Louvain who still openly display the old hatred of the humanities.[16]   65
Their rash behaviour is likely to end in open subversion, and it ought to be
restrained by the authority of the prince and the prelates. If any point
emerges on which Luther's opinion ought to be refuted, let them do this
with appropriate arguments and clear evidences from the Scriptures. On
other men, who have not been condemned by the authority of universities   70
or popes or the prince, let them keep silence and not defile the place where
they should preach the gospel with their foolish and poisonous scurrilities.
My own heart is set on defending the Christian faith and advancing the
honour of the emperor; but that I may be enabled to fulfil my desire lies
largely in the emperor's own hand, who has in his hand the sum of things. I   75
do not ask him for great positions. Let him but give me leisure and
tranquillity, and I will see to it by every means in my power that his Majesty
shall never regret his humble councillor.[17] You wish me to put my trust in
deeds not words; so you say in your letter. Unless at no distant date I keep
my promise[18] you shall list the name Erasmus among men of straw.   80

When I was writing this, I had not yet made up my own mind
definitely about my journey; my mind is so much disposed to your part of
the world that, with even a very little weight in the scale, I should follow this
Dromo[19] of mine. Meanwhile let your deeds show that you are a true friend,
and may the Lord Jesus bless your pious intentions. The primacy of the pope   85
has now been so clearly asserted by Cajetanus,[20] Silvester,[21] and Eck,[22] that
there is no need of help from me; for Catharinus'[23] handling of the question
is not so skilful. My views on the sacraments I have now made clear in some

* * * * *

16 See Epp 1299:10–14, and 1330:53–6. On 3 September Paul Volz had heard that
   Erasmus' paraphrases had been burned at Louvain University; BRE Ep 225
   (page 310). See also Ep 1342:644–7.
17 See Ep 370:18n.
18 As Allen suggests, this promise seems to refer not to the completion of the
   libellus against Luther (lines 23–4 and n7 of this letter) but rather to the
   completion of such projects as the edition of Augustine (Ep 1309) despite the
   bitter opposition of conservative theologians.
19 Ie, Bertolph (n6 above). Dromo is the name of a slave in two of Terence's plays,
   Heautontimorumenos and *Adelphi*.
20 Ep 256:49n
21 Silvester Prierias; Ep 872:19n
22 Eck (Ep 769) had published his *De primatu Petri adversus Ludderum* at Ingolstadt
   in 1520.
23 Lancellotto de' Politi of Siena (c 1484–1553), who took the name Ambrosius
   Catharinus Politus when he joined the Dominican order, denounced Luther in
   two works: *Apologia pro veritate catholice fidei* (Florence: G. Giunta 1520), and
   Excusatio disputationis (ibidem 1521).

verses added to the small book known as the Cato.[24] On the same subject
there is a treatise by the king of England,[25] which some people in Rome and   90
here wrongly suppose to be by me.[26] How fortunate these suspicions would
be for me if only they could change their country – if the English would
suspect what they suspect in Germany! I suppose this guess was suggested
by the style. For the king when he was a boy read nothing more diligently
than my writings, and from them he may perhaps have picked up   95
something of my style, if indeed there is anything of mine in his book.

But really I am too discourteous, taking the time of a man of your
eminence, so burdened with business, with such a talkative letter; and
indeed I am very busy myself. Farewell, and show yourself a true friend.

Basel, 1522   100

1276 / To Jean de Carondelet   Basel, 23 April 1522

Jean de Carondelet (1469–1544?), whose father (also Jean, d 1501) had been
Burgundian chancellor, rose to power and prominence in Hapsburg service in
the Netherlands. In 1497 he joined the household of Archduke Philip and in
1504 became a member of his council. In 1515 he was appointed to Charles'
council and accompanied him to Spain in 1517. On the death of Le Sauvage (Ep
301:38n), Carondelet was briefly acting chancellor of Castile. Returning to the
Netherlands, he quickly became the chief counselor to Margaret of Austria,
Charles' aunt and regent. Dean of Besançon since 1493, he was appointed
archbishop of Palermo in 1519 and provost of St Donatian's at Bruges in 1520.
From 1531 to 1540 he was president of the Privy Council of the Netherlands.

Erasmus found in Carondelet a reliable patron (cf Ep 1320:14–18) to whom
he could write about such delicate matters as his annuity from the emperor and
to whom he dedicated his edition of Hilary (Ep 1334).

This letter first appeared in the *Opus epistolarum*. Carondelet's reply is
mentioned in Epp 1299:42 and 1331:18.

ERASMUS OF ROTTERDAM TO JEAN DE CARONDELET, ARCHBISHOP OF
PALERMO, GREETINGS

I am told, my Lord Archbishop, in letters from my friends[1] to present myself

* * * * *

24 Ie, in the *Institutum christiani hominis carmine pro pueris*; Epp 298, 679
25 Henry VIII's *Assertio septem sacramentorum adversus Martin. Lutherum* (London:
Pynson 1521)
26 Cf Epp 1298:16–19, 1313:74–92.

1276
1 Cf Ep 1269:11–13.

in your part of the world before the emperor's departure; but the bearer[2]
informed me that his setting out for England was being advanced, so that I   5
fear even my letter may prove fruitless. I will follow,[3] however, if I find that
the emperor will remain longer. But meanwhile may I ask you, if I seem to
have done anything of value for the humanities by my labours, to
strengthen my case with your support, that my annuity[4] may remain intact
and that the emperor's favour may defend me against the baseless attacks of   10
certain shameless individuals. My conduct here is such that all Luther's
party hate me passionately and pile slanders on me; some of them even tear
me to pieces in pamphlets. For my part, I shall never prove false either to the
faith of Christ or to the glory of the emperor. Need I say more? I shall see to it
that he never regrets making me a member of his council.[5] In olden days   15
four-footed beasts that had caused damage were delivered over to punishment; how cruelly unfair that I for doing service to the public should be
delivered over to certain noxious beasts, or rather to jealousy, which is a pest
more virulent than any viper! May Almighty Jesus have your Highness
always in his keeping.   20

Basel, Wednesday after Easter 1522

1277 / From Juan de Vergara   Brussels, 24 April 1522

Juan de Vergara of Toledo (1492–1557) studied at the University of Alcalá (MA
1514, DD 1517) and contributed translations of Greek versions of several Old
Testament books to the Complutensian Polyglot. In 1516–17 he became
secretary to Cardinal Jiménez, the archbishop of Toledo. In the spring of 1520
Vergara sailed to Flanders to join Jiménez' successor as archbishop, Guillaume
de Croy (d 1521), the son of the chancellor, Chièvres (Ep 532:30n). That
summer Vergara met Erasmus at Bruges and Louvain and quickly undertook
the thankless task of trying to mediate peace between Erasmus and Zúñiga (Ep
1260 n36). When Vergara wrote this letter, he was still in the Netherlands,
attached as a chaplain to the imperial court, but he returned to Spain later the
same year. There he was a constant supporter of humanist scholars and
remained sincerely devoted to Erasmus. In the 1530s this devotion earned him
repeated trouble with the Inquisition.

This letter was first published by Allen from a manuscript (an eighteenth-
century copy) that was in the so-called 'Heine Collection' at Munich. For

* * * * *

2 Hilarius Bertolph; see Epp 1257 n10 and 1281:23.
3 Cf Ep 1275:82–4.
4 Cf Ep 1273 n4.
5 See Ep 370:18n.

details on this collection, the subsequent fate of which is unknown, see Allen
IV 620–2 and CWE 8 336. Erasmus' reply is Ep 1312.

JUAN DE VERGARA TO ERASMUS OF ROTTERDAM, GREETING

The *Apologia*[1] in which you answered Zúñiga's *Annotationes*[2] I sent[3] to
Zúñiga himself in Rome, as I told you I would in St Peter's at Louvain;[4] and
in doing so, I urged him in my letter (for he is a friendly person) to bring the
dispute to a final end at that point, and to overlook all minor causes of   5
offence and make friends with you, a thing which all scholars alike must
wish to see. I also said that if I could be of any service in making peace, I
would help him all I could. I reminded him of Lee's efforts[5] – how unpopular
they had proved with all scholars[6] and how little glory they had brought to
him personally. I added a good deal in praise of you, though compared with   10
what I feel it was very little. None of this moved him much; he seems so
determined not to alter course that he threatens all over again an even more
savage war, according to a letter he sent me[7] – a ferocious letter, all outrages
and thunderbolts – it is no longer a matter of javelin and dart, he threatens a
whole artillery of missiles, mangonels, and catapults, with which hencefor-   15
ward he mows down his adversaries in swathes, routs them, pursues them,
and lays them flat. Not only will he answer your defence; he will show quite
clearly that the second edition of the New Testament and the notes on
Jerome and many of your other works are stuffed with ten thousand errors
and flavoured with Lutheran impiety. Nor is this activity his own special   20
preserve: he says a large and picked force of learned Italians is now
mobilizing, who will make a sortie and bear down headlong on your
writings.

Meantime, while he is getting together all the tackle needed for a
pitched battle, a book has been sent out like a reconnaissance-party, not by   25

* * * * *

1277
1 *Apologia respondens ad ea quae Jacobus Lopis Stunica taxaverat in prima duntaxat
   Novi Testamenti aeditione* (Louvain: Dirk Martens, September 1521). An
   enlarged version was printed in the *Apologiae omnes* (Basel: Froben, October
   1521– February 1522); critical edition by H.J. de Jonge in ASD IX-2.
2 See Ep 1260 n36.
3 On 10 October 1521; see Vergara's letter to Zúñiga in CWE 8 337.
4 Erasmus may have been in Louvain in mid-September 1521 in connection with
   the printing of the *Apologia* in reply to Zúñiga; see Ep 1235:36.
5 Edward Lee (1482–1544), the English theologian with whom Erasmus had a
   long controversy over Lee's critical notes on the *Novum Testamentum*; see Epp
   765 introduction, 1037 introduction, and 1341A:823–30.
6 See Ep 1083 introduction.
7 Dated 9 January 1522; printed in CWE 8 340–3

any means with Zúñiga himself as its author (he of course captains heavier
troops), but one Sancho Carranza of Miranda,[8] a Spaniard, a man of high
position and reputation among the theologians of Alcalá, who handles the
business of the Spanish church in Rome. Gathering from my letter to Zúñiga
how high an opinion I have of you and how much I admire you as a scholar   30
of great distinction, he naturally supposed this judgment to arise from close
familiarity and friendship with you. He therefore sent the book to me as a
friend of yours, and asks me in the prefatory letter[9] to assure you that his
feelings towards you are not at all hostile, but entirely open-minded and
respectful. Indeed you will see this for yourself much more clearly from the   35
letter. I would like to add that the man is a real expert in philosophy and
theology of the subtle sort, with a critical mind, a balanced judgment, and
wide reading in that field. In short, in the study of philosophical trivialities
he has few rivals; besides which his character is upright, modest, and far
from difficult to get on with. This leads me to believe that he did not think of   40
writing this out of jealousy or spite, but was swept away by a strong and by
no means improper spirit of contention, such as often exists on literary
subjects between learned men, with no loss of personal good will. But all
this you will discover with far greater insight than mine as you read the
book; so let me in the mean while refrain from any premature verdict.   45
    As for myself, pray think of me as a passionate devotee of the
humanities, for thus you will recognize at the same time that I must be
devoted to Erasmus, whose cause I have always regarded as closely linked
with the cause of liberal studies. For there is one blessing I clearly owe to my
destiny, which in other respects has been far from generous: having been   50
consigned in early boyhood to harsher studies (but the decision was taken
by others), I preferred the gentler Muses all the time and more civilized
learning to all trifling, however ingenious, but decided that humane
learning must be reconciled and allied with the more severe speculations of
philosophy, divine and human. This is just what you have set yourself to do   55
in our time, with immense efforts but with great success, and all men of

* * * * *

8 Sancho Carranza of Miranda in Navarre (d 1531), theologian at Alcalá. In
  March 1522 he published at Rome, where he lived 1520–3, *Carranzae opusculum
  in quasdam Erasmi annotationes* (A. de Trino), in which his criticisms were
  moderate and respectful in tone. Erasmus reprinted the work, together with
  his *Apologia de tribus locis quos ut recte taxatos a Stunica defenderat S. Caranza
  theologus*, with the *Epistola de esu carnium* (Basel: Froben 6 August 1522). The
  text is in LB IX 401–32.
9 Ie, the prefatory epistle to Vergara, 27 December 1521, in Carranza's
  Opusculum (n8 above). The passage Vergara refers to is quoted in Bataillon 132
  n1.

good will owe you not only hearty support and best wishes but all the help and assistance in their power. And though to help you is not possible for a modest creature like myself, I can at least promise my support without fear of perjury; and so I do, as best I can, and long have done so too.　　60

And so, dear Erasmus my most learned friend, although I feel it to be unnecessary, I do urge you and exhort you and adjure you, by the most fruitful outcome of your labours, not to relax your efforts in the cause of good literature, which is raising its head but still faces toil and trouble, and not to let the crazy prejudice of certain wretches deter you from so lofty and　　65 so honourable an enterprise. This is a plague of long standing. There have long been, and there always will be, certain bitter and malignant characters who love a fight, foolish, ignorant, and voluble, who, when their purblind eyes have once perceived the splendour of a learning they do not possess, move without hesitation against everything good and profitable that　　70 appears in print. Insidiously at first and privily they carp at it; then cast off all shame and attack it openly, tracking down mistakes in it with the greatest subtlety in all directions, concentrating on other men's errors without concern for their own, for they never publish anything. And you ought to stand firm and unmoved against the lot of them, rather than engage them　　75 individually.

By this I do not mean to convey that I put Zúñiga or Sancho in that class, and mean to attack them as malignant critics. They are my friends, and in themselves they are good men and good scholars, very far removed from any fault of the kind. But when I see everywhere so many men like that　　80 (monstrosities rather than men I would call them, were they not so common), it really makes me fear that the resolution of good men, men like yourself, may one day be unable to withstand such frenzy. But why run on about this at such length? I am more than satisfied, provided it is clear to you that I am a man sincerely devoted to liberal studies, and one who for their　　85 sake will never fail to stand by you with all the devotion and all the assistance that may lie within my modest powers.

The book itself, together with this letter, I was minded to give to Herman (surname?),[10] a man who is (as I can clearly see) a great admirer of yours; he is a new acquaintance, whom I took to immediately, able and　　90 agreeable and an unusually good scholar. He is the only person I have allowed to see the book, he having offered to transmit it to you, for I did not like the idea of its passing from hand to hand until you had seen it. If you do sometime decide to write an answer, mind you do not forget your usual moderation – for your own sake first of all, and then for the sake of the　　95

* * * * *

10 Perhaps Herman Lethmaet (Ep 1320)

author himself, who speaks of you throughout the work with the greatest respect, and partly, please, for my sake too. If anything further appears from Zúñiga while the emperor has not yet set off for Spain, I will arrange to send it to you, provided there is someone to whom I can safely give it. Farewell, and think of me among your friends.   100

Brussels, 24 April 1522

Herman having returned the book to me some days later, saying he has no opportunity of a courier going in your direction, I have entrusted to Luis Vives the task of conveying it to you,[11] being myself about to sail for Spain any day now. If you think of sending any answer (which would be highly   105 welcome), a letter can conveniently reach me through that same Luis. Farewell.

To Master Erasmus of Rotterdam, the distinguished theologian

1278 / To Andrea Alciati   Basel, 25 April 1522

This letter was first published by Allen. The manuscript, in a secretary's hand with corrections by Erasmus, was in the Burscher Collection at Leipzig (Ep 1254 introduction). The Öffentliche Bibliothek of the University of Basel has a copy made by Bonifacius Amerbach (MS G.II.13.131).

For Alciati, see Epp 1250, 1261.

ERASMUS OF ROTTERDAM TO ANDREA ALCIATI

Greeting. Other people, when they find a reliable courier, usually write at length about everything. I on the other hand think that I can write very briefly for the same reason, having got Bonifacius Amerbach[1] to carry my letter, for I could be blessed with no one more completely reliable or more   5 devoted to us both. Why need I write at all, when there is nothing about me that he does not know? About that pamphlet[2] I beg you most seriously not to worry. Pyrrhus'[3] death distresses me, and I welcome all the more your true friendship, which has not allowed your friend's memory to perish.[4]

* * * * *

11 From Ep 1281:39–40 it appears that Vergara did not in fact give the book to Vives.

1278
1 Ep 408. On Amerbach's journey to Avignon, see Ep 1288 introduction.
2 See Ep 1261 introduction.
3 Jean Pyrrhus d'Angleberme (d 1521), lecturer in law in Orléans, had studied Greek with Erasmus in Paris and corresponded with him at intervals thereafter.
4 Alciati had composed an epitaph for d'Angleberme's tomb; see *Nouvelle Biographie Générale* (Paris 1855–66) II 659–60.

A year ago some Germans I could name[5] who are too much devoted to 10
me reprinted an immense volume of my letters, among them some which I
fear may get me into serious trouble, especially in these days when
everything is instantly seized upon as material for suspicion or calumny. At
the imperial court I can scarcely hold my ground, thanks to certain persons[6]
who will have it that I am responsible for Luther's faction, not because they 15
really suspect this, which they themselves know to be absolutely false, but
partly for the pleasure of doing me harm whatever the excuse and partly in
order to push me willy-nilly into Luther's camp – which, however, they will
never succeed in doing. On the other side, here among the Germans those
same logic-choppers who wish for my ruin are spreading a monstrous 20
rumour among Luther's partisans that I am preparing large, ferocious
volumes[7] to attack, and indeed utterly to overthrow, all the citadels of
Luther's supporters. So they too rage against me, and already have books
with long teeth at hand with which to rend me limb from limb. So things are
quite topsy-turvy: men denounced as heretics by pope and emperor regard 25
me as a heretic, unless I am willing to turn heretic. There is in Rome one
Zúñiga, a Spaniard, who has now spewed up a second volume[8] loaded with
violent abuse directed at me. How I wish Luther's party had attacked me in
print two years ago! They would at least have taken a load of ill will off my
back. But no tempest shall divert me from the course I have set. 30
Unless I were sincerely and singularly devoted to you both, Alciati and
Bonifacius, I should envy each of you the other's society. My life upon it, I
have never seen anything more sincere and genuine than that young man,
or a truer friend. He never tires of singing the praises of his friend Alciati. I
only hope that envious Fate will keep her hands off him, for his gifts are 35
outstanding; one day he will be the pride of his native Germany. I know that
you with your generous heart will do all you can for a man whom you have
known and loved for so long. Otherwise I would ask you urgently to add to
your kindness towards him on the grounds of a recommendation from me.
Farewell, my most excellent friend, and let the name of Erasmus stand 40
written among those who cordially wish you well.
Basel, the Friday in Easter week 1522

* * * * *

5 Ie, the Froben editors responsible for the *Epistolae ad diversos*, the printing of
  which had begun a year ago; see Epp 1206 and 1258 n15.
6 See Ep 1263:1–3. For Erasmus' efforts to secure his reputation at the imperial
  court, see Epp 1269, 1273–6, 1300.
7 Cf Ep 1275 n7.
8 See Ep 1260 n45.

1279 / From Leonhard Müller   St Georgenberg, 7 May 1522

This letter was first published in LB. The original manuscript is in the Rehdiger Collection in the University Library at Wrocław (MS Rehd 254.95).

Leonhard Müller (d 1525) was during the last ten years of his life abbot of the Benedictine house at St Georgenberg in the Inn valley, about twenty-six kilometers south of Innsbruck. According to the records of the community, he was a learned man and a wise ruler who undertook the rebuilding of the monastery, which had burned down in 1448.

LEONHARD, BY THE GRACE OF GOD ABBOT OF THE MONASTERY OF
ST GEORGENBERG IN THE INN VALLEY ETC, SENDS GREETING
You must not be surprised, Erasmus most learned of men, to receive this letter from a stranger. A stranger I may be to you, but you have been for a long time very familiar to me, and I converse daily with the more exalted half   5
of you,[1] for among abbots there are several, and among monks a great many, who are your zealous followers. I however am specially devoted to you, for I have a special aversion to the superstition of many abbots and monks, combined as it is with a hatred of honourable studies, and a great devotion to you and others like you. For I see no purpose in the monastic habit except   10
that we should be good Christians and not consider ourselves cut off from men of any honourable calling.

And why then do I write to you? I am sending the bearer of this, our Brother Kilian,[2] a long-standing disciple of yours, who much desires to see you, to pursue the study of the humanities in Basel. May I beg you, my dear   15
sir, with your unfailing kindness towards all men of good understanding, to help him with your support and recommendation. Pray believe that I make this request in few words but with all the emphasis of which I am capable. I have an impoverished monastery which, when almost ruined by the negligence of my predecessors, was entrusted to me for restoration, and   20

* * * * *

1279
1 Ie, his books
2 Not much is known about Kilian Praus, who sometimes signed himself Kilian Clemens (BRE Ep 239). In May 1522, on his way to Basel to pursue the studies mentioned here, he visited Johann Botzheim in Constance (Ep 1285:55–7). In Basel, Beatus Rhenanus (Ep 327) took an interest in him, helping him to obtain a BA and make plans for further study. In 1523 Praus moved to Sélestat, where he may have worked for a printer. Because of his associations with Eppendorf and Hutten (Epp 1283 n4, 1331 n24), he later had to defend himself against Erasmus' suspicions that he was siding with those two former friends turned enemies (Ep 1449).

hence I have had severe difficulty in providing this brother of ours with
money for his essential expenses. One word from you will be able to help
him in all directions, both in living in your town at less expense and in
qualifying (as they call it) for some degree in less than the traditional period
of time. For I hear that the practice is still maintained in certain universities   25
of allowing no one the title to a degree until he has fulfilled the stated time.

If this letter is written by my secretary in German script, please take
this in good part. Farewell.

From our monastery, 7 May 1522

To Master Erasmus of Rotterdam, most learned and eloquent teacher   30
and expositor of theology

1280

This letter to Maartin Davidts has been redated to 1528 and will be published in
volume 14 of this edition.

1280A / From Caspar Ursinus Velius   Vienna, c May 1522

This letter was first published in Ursinus' *In hoc libello habentur Oratio dominica
… Epistola ad D. Erasmum Rhoterodamum* (Vienna: J. Singriener 1524). Although
Allen knew of the existence of the letter (see his note to Ep 1267:3), he did not
include it in his edition. At the suggestion of Professor Peter G. Bietenholz,
who had used the letter in his own research ('Erasmus und die letzten
Lebensjahre Reuchlins' *Historische Zeitschrift* 240 [1985] 63), the Editorial Board
decided to include the letter in the CWE edition.

Caspar Ursinus Velius (Kaspar Bernhard), c 1493–1539, of Świdnica in
Silesia was a canon at Wrocław, a gifted poet, and a successful teacher of
Greek at the University of Vienna. He left Vienna in July 1521, evidently to
escape the plague. Wishing to meet Erasmus, he went to Basel, where the
university records indicate that he matriculated on 1 August, although other
evidence suggests that he may not have arrived in town until a few days later
(AK Ep 817 introduction). Sometime in October he moved on to Freiburg im
Breisgau (ibidem n1, Ep 1242), where he registered at the university on 1
February 1522 and attended the lectures of Zasius (Epp 1252, 1266). Soon after
23 March (Ep 1267 n2) he embarked upon his return journey to Vienna. This
letter is Ursinus' account of that journey.

An approximate month-date can be assigned. Ursinus arrived in Passau on
or about Easter, 20 April (lines 131–4). Proceeding to Vienna, he arrived after
having been away for 'ten months' (line 183). On 26 May he addressed a letter to
Beatus Rhenanus from Vienna (BRE Ep 223). Assuming that Ursinus wrote this
letter soon after his return, the date 'c May 1522' is a reasonable estimate.

The letter is written in verse. Versified accounts of journeys have a long history in Latin poetry, going back to Lucilius and Horace. Ursinus' poem owes much, including the use of dactylic hexameters, to Horace's 'Journey to Brundisium' (*Satires* 1.5). Other borrowings from Horace are mentioned in the notes. This translation into English pentameters is the work of Ann and Alexander Dalzell.

Leaving the borders of th' Helvetian land,
Where sturdy farmers plough the Rauric fields,[1]
I said farewell to lovely Basel's walls –
The town is German though its name is Greek[2] –
And reached a region, rich despite its size,   5
A region chiefly known for grain and vines,
Whose people rose in arms to oust their duke.[3]
There noble Reuchlin warmly welcomed me
To his small city, washed by Neckar's stream,[4]
And when he read the graceful note you sent,   10
Received me, though a stranger, to his home.
We lingered over dinner, as we talked
About Erasmus the magnificent.

From here I made my way through Swabian towns
To Danube and the walls of smiling Ulm.   15
My thought was here to buy a little boat
And drift downstream, borne on the river's flood.
But some rapacious merchant wrecked that plan
By leasing all the boats at bargain rates.
We boarded cheerfully – the wind was right –   20
And set our course for ancient Lauingen.

* * * * *

1280A
1 The Raurici or Rauraci, mentioned in Caesar's *Bellum gallicum*, were a Gallic tribe who lived in Switzerland in the region of Basel.
2 Ursinus incorrectly derives the name of the city from the Greek βασιλεύς (king).
3 Duke Ulrich of Württemberg (ruled 1498–1519, 1534–50), whose mistreatment of both subjects and neighbours caused the Swabian League, an alliance of South-German princes and cities, to invade Württemberg in 1519 and force him into exile. After being restored to his duchy in 1534, Ulrich introduced the Reformation there.
4 Stuttgart, where Reuchlin (Ep 290) spent his last years

But here our crafty host showed us to bed
Before we'd had our fill. When morning came,
He packed us off with nothing for our lunch.

Then dawned for us a most ill-omened day.   25
As Phoebus'[5] car forsook the crest of heaven,
A sudden tempest whirled across our course,
Boatman and barge were dashed against a bridge.
Then panic filled my heart: I seized the pole,
And begging heaven for help, made one great leap,   30
And nimbly reached the bank and marshy shore.
The boatman used the paddle[6] for support,
And safely swam to shore. With help from me,
He fixed a stake and tied the hawsers fast.
Soaked by the waves and trembling, all the rest   35
Leaped overboard and, linking arm in arm,
Managed to struggle safely to the bank.

We walked to Verda[7] under thundering skies.
Rain pelted down in torrents from the heavens.
A kindlier host received us than before,   40
An older man, who with his pretty wife
Set off for bed as soon as it was dark:
His portly steward attended all our cares.

During the morning hours the boatman knocked,
Calling us forth – the barge had been repaired.   45
He put us all on board, and sturdy youths
Bent to the oars in turn. When we had passed
The Histrian bridge, where Lech with waters wild
Enters the Danube,[8] Phoebus stood beyond
The mid-point of the sky. Fierce hunger growled   50
Within our famished bellies. All our minds
Were dominated by the thought of food.

* * * * *

5 Phoebus Apollo, the sun-god in whose chariot the sun moves across the sky
6 Probably a long oar used to steer the boat, though the Latin is not clear
7 *Verda* (or *Werda*) *danubiana,* ie, Donauwörth
8 This is a puzzle. There was a bridge on the river Lech near the point where it
  meets the Danube. But it seems unlikely that Ursinus would have 'passed' a
  bridge some distance up the Lech or that he would have called it 'Histrian,' ie,
  Danubian.

We left the boat and found a wretched hut,
Smoke-filled and poor, whose owner took us in.
It was his rule never to eat cooked food   55
And to abstain on certain days from wine.
Wishing to bind me by his strange belief,
He set before me water and coarse bread.
A boy then followed with a dish of salt.[9]

We had to leave with bellies angry still[10]   60
And sweep the sluggish stream with stronger oars,
Till late at night we came to Ingolstadt,
And soothed our barking stomachs[11] there with food.
But brief the rest our weary limbs received,
For soon before the rosy-fingered bride   65
Of old Tithonus[12] with her saffron robe
Had spread her kindly light upon the earth,
The boatman's voice rang in our sleepy ears
And ordered us to board our floating bark.

Then did our little boat, impelled by oars,   70
Race down the headlong current till it reached
That city ringed with hills where grapes are picked
To make a wine more sharp than vinegar.[13]
All of us rushed ashore with thoughts of food.

Now at the inn there lived a crafty cat.   75
It happened that the simple serving maid
Failed to observe the creature's crafty wiles
As from the plate it dragged our tasty fish.
The angry mistress chased the fleeing maid,
And round her head flew blackened pots and pans   80
And greasy plates. Meanwhile we gathered up
From rapier talons, jaws, and stubborn teeth
The stolen fish, our spoiled, half-eaten meal.

* * * * *

9 Cf Horace *Satires* 2.2.18: 'Bread and salt will appease your barking stomach
  well enough.'
10 Horace *Satires* 2.8.4
11 See n9 above.
12 Aurora, goddess of the dawn; cf Virgil *Aeneid* 7.26.
13 Perhaps Kelheim

Thence did we make our way to Regensburg
(Named from the river Regen), once a rich,   85
But now a humble city; for its wealth
Has shamefully declined since it became
More than a hundred years ago the prey
Of filthy Jews. At dawn we all set out,
Changing our barge for a much larger craft.   90

The number of our company increased,
Because the boatman, grasping after gain,
Packed more on board. A mighty cry arose
As we besought the gods for gentle winds
And raised to heaven's host our artless hymns.   95

There was a soldier in our company,
Charming and handsome, elegantly dressed,
Who, with his gentle talk, tried to console
A girl who cried and sobbed incessantly.
His words had no effect, and when he asked   10
The reason for her sorrow, she replied,
'My tears are for a lover left behind
Whose bed and board for many years I've shared,
And always in his manner he's been kind.'
This marvellously witty, genial knight   10
Began to say such cheerful, funny things,
So interspersed with lively wit and jest,
That even children, cruelly bereft
Of both their parents, would have laughed aloud
While leading the procession to the grave.   110
She like Niobe sat,[14] by nothing moved,
Till, pitying her tears, the knight spoke thus:
'O might you sooner perish, gleaming stars
That light the universe, than she destroy
Such starry eyes with tears! Th' Oebalian twins[15]   11
Guide sailors through strange waters, but her eyes

* * * * *

14 Niobe, wife of Amphion, king of Thebes, whom Zeus turned into a stone that
   shed tears in memory of her children, who had been killed by Apollo and
   Diana
15 'Oebalian' (from Oebalus, king of Sparta) is used in classical poetry as an
   ornamental epithet meaning 'Spartan.' The Spartan twins are Castor and
   Pollux, the traditional helpers of sailors in peril on the sea.

Propel her amorous lovers where she wills.'
At that fine speech all smiled a happy smile;
She dried her eyes and laughed enchantingly.

And now the sight of Passau on its wedge[16]   120
Puts thoughts of profit in the boatman's mind.
He tells the boy to extricate the fare
From every passenger. Our soldier friend
Conceals three comrades underneath a pile
Of sacks and matting, setting us on top.   125
The simple child is cheated of the fare.
When his ill-humoured master learns the trick
And we have left and gone our separate ways,
He chides the boy for sloth and sends him off –
No dinner and a cold night out of doors!   130

The forty days were past, the festal day
Had dawned, that welcome time, when for mankind
The long-awaited freedom comes again
Of eating what one wills.[17] The world rejoiced.
I went to church, then visited my friends,   135
Who joyed to see the long-lost traveller.
Thus passed two days: the third saw me again
Back on the river, parted from my friends,
Though hard it was to leave such company.

Passing the walls of Linz, we sailed downstream   140
Until we saw the town of Mauthausen,
Tamed by th' imperious power of Vulcan's fire;[18]
The north wind's blast had fanned the deadly flames.
Here the whole night I hardly slept a wink,
My left side punctured by th' unyielding bed.   145
A year-old infant wailed with goatlike sound,
But nothing could arouse his sleeping nurse.
Everyone heard his bitter, tearful cries,
As endlessly he pleaded for the breast.

* * * * *

16 The old city of Passau lies on a wedge of land between the Inn and the Danube.
17 Easter: 20 April 1522
18 Vulcan was the Roman god of fire. No information is available about a fire in
   Mauthausen at this time.

The day that dawned was radiantly bright.   15
The cargo was in place; the boatman blew
The signal on his raucous horn. At once
A motley troop of travellers rushed the ship.
Look at that man, dragging his wife along!
He leaps on board, extends his hand to hers   15
Across the stern. Thoughtless, she sets her foot
Upon some fish-tanks moored along the bank
Like little boats, not thinking she would sink.
But down she sinks, into the icy stream
Beyond her waist. Seizing her by the head,   16
Tugging her arms, we fish her up half-faint –
A young and pretty wench. Her husband's face,
From fear and anger mixed, turned white as death.

I tried then to console her if I could
With pleasant trifles; talked of Pyrrha's flood[19]   16
And how the same will one day come to us
When once Aquarius inverts the urns;[20]
Then all together mountains, fields, and towns
(Dreadful to think upon!) will be submerged
By ocean, and the land will disappear.   17
Such was the portent of some cruel star,
The fearful prophecy of men who know
The will of heaven and can unlock the minds
Of all the gods,[21] as if from Jove's own lips

* * * * *

19 Deucalion and his wife Pyrrha were the only survivors in the classical myth of
   the flood; cf Ovid *Metamorphoses* 1.313–415.
20 Aquarius, the water-carrier, one of the signs of the zodiac. He is represented in
   ancient art with one, or sometimes two, urns.
21 The reference is to the astrological prediction that a second universal deluge
   would engulf the world on 25 February 1524. This prediction had its origin in
   an almanac by Johann Stöffler von Justingen (1451–1531) that was printed at
   Ulm in 1499 and reissued at Venice seven times in the period 1504–22. Stöffler
   did not actually predict a flood, but his observation that profound consequences would ensue from an extraordinary number of planetary conjunctions
   'in a watery sign' in February 1524 caused vulgar astrologers to jump to the
   conclusion that there would be another universal deluge. These predictions
   apparently caused widespread apprehension. See Lynn Thorndike *A History of
   Magic and Experimental Science* IV (New York 1934) 483 and V (New York 1941)
   181. Ursinus is clearly mocking the prophecy.

They knew the future and were given a place   175
At all the feasts and councils of the Twelve.[22]

And now our ship was driven by favouring winds
All day along the pleasant river's flow
Until it brushed the sprawling docks that form
Pannonian Vienna's[23] anchorage.   180
All disembarked with pleasure and approached
The famous city walls, which I last saw
Ten months ago. Dear Collimitius[24]
And all my friends were there, safely returned
As if from exile; for the dreadful plague   185
Had forced them to escape to diverse lands.
I greeted all. Gundelius had been last
To make the journey back from chilly lands[25]
– I noticed that his hair was turning grey.
No man now lives more charming, none more dear   190
To Decius,[26] the patron of our group,
Who loves those studies which the gods protect,
Augur Apollo[27] and the Muses chaste.
It was his passion for his new-found wife,

* * * * *

22 Ie, the Olympian deities
23 Ie, Vienna in the Roman province of Pannonia as opposed to Vienna (Vienne)
   in Gallia Narbonensis
24 Collimitius was the name taken by Georg Tannstetter of Rain in Bavaria
   (1482–1535). He became professor of medicine and mathematics at the
   University of Vienna and personal physician to Emperor Maximilian and
   Archduke Ferdinand. On 20 March 1523 Tannstetter, himself a well-known
   astrologer, addressed to Archduke Ferdinand a *Libellus consolatorius* debunk-
   ing the idea of a deluge in 1524. See Thorndike (n21 above) v 221–5; *Neue
   Deutsche Biographie* III (Berlin 1957) 322–3.
25 Philipp Gundelius of Passau (1493–1567), a doctor of law who in 1518 became
   the successor of Vadianus (Ep 1314 n5) as professor of rhetoric at Vienna.
   Fleeing Vienna in 1521 to escape the plague, he went to Cracow, the home of
   his patron Decius (see following note), where he taught law. After his return to
   Vienna, he devoted the rest of his academic career to law, becoming dean of the
   faculty in 1530 and rector of the university in 1540. His publications, none of
   them in the field of law, include poems, speeches, and editions of classical and
   humanist authors. See the *Allgemeine Deutsche Biographie* x (Leipzig 1879)
   124–5.
26 The German-Polish businessman and statesman Justus Decius (Ep 1341A
   n210), who lived in Cracow
27 Cf Virgil *Aeneid* 4.376.

I'm sure, which kept him later than the rest.   1

His marriage was a secret, no one guessed,

Till with a stepson he returned at last.

Thus to this city came I wearily;

Here ends my letter, here my odyssey.

1281 / From Juan Luis Vives   Bruges, 20 May 1522

> For the source of this letter, see Ep 1256 introduction. The letter was obviously
> written in several stages (see lines 70–1). The first stage ends at line 40. Then
> Vives had his interview with Coronel and added lines 41–57. The paragraph
> beginning at line 58 is probably also a subsequent addition. From the
> movements of the court (see n16), it appears that the first part of the letter
> cannot be dated before 15 May. If the date of the bishop of Liège's arrival in
> Bruges were known, a more precise dating would be possible.

VIVES TO ERASMUS

The letter[1] you wrote me on 20 March arrived on 7 May; how it took so long
to come I do not know. I gave[2] the chancellor[3] the letter you wrote to him;
when he had read the address, he smiled as he broke the seal and turning to
me – Narcisus[4] his physician was there too – he said, 'Erasmus has made a   5
mistake in the name.' For you had first written Guglielmo, and then struck
that through and written Mercurino above it. But I have no doubt that what
made him smile was not so much the reason he put forward as pleasure at
receiving a letter from you. Then he read what looked to me like two letters,
one of them not written in your hand or in an Italian script, and he read that   1
one first;[5] then one written by you or one of your household, and he read it
with attention and not superficially. Then he asked me whether you had
written him anything else; I said I had nothing else meant for him. 'And yet,'
he said, 'this letter seems to hint at something else.' I replied that I knew
nothing about that. 'He speaks here,' he said, 'of some approach,[6] but does   1
not explain what he means.' Narcisus asked how you were, and he

* * * * *

1281
1 Not extant; contemporary with the letter to Gattinara (line 2), which, to judge
  from its contents (lines 14–16), was contemporary with Ep 1267
2 Not before 13 May; see n16.
3 Gattinara (Ep 1150)
4 The name appears in the list of Charles' retinue at this time; LP III 2288.
5 The nature of this enclosure is a mystery.
6 See Ep 1267 n6.

answered that you were suffering from the stone[7] when you wrote. After that, he was silent, and so I took my leave and departed.

The cardinal of Liège[8] had not yet come; he arrived after dark. Next day[9] when I went to see him, I found him in the entrance hall getting ready to go to the emperor, and gave him your letter.[10] He seemed glad to have it, and said he would read it; then he mounted his mule, broke the seal, and began to read. On my return I found our friend Hilarius[11] knocking at my door, and he brought the news that you were well, which rejoiced me not a little. About your coming here he said he knew nothing definite, except that he had no doubt that you would not be away for long. Many want to have you here, even those who have most influence in this court and are thought to be the great judges of ability and research, unless they are taking everyone in and are parading marvellously well counterfeited opinions – which is nothing new in any court and not rare in this one.

Today[12] I shall speak with Coronel,[13] whom I have not yet met since he got here. If I discover anything from him that I think it important for you to be aware of, I will add it to this letter, provided I have not sent it; and if I have, I will write by other hands. Vergara[14] sends you his greetings; he told me that a certain Spaniard now living in Rome, Miranda[15] by name, has written on three or four passages in your annotations on the New Testament. But he does this like one giving counsel with great modesty and respect rather than like a man full of criticisms and objections. Vergara told me the work was dedicated to himself. They said some people here at court had a copy; if I can get one, I will give it to Hilarius here to take to you.

I have spoken with Coronel and, moreover, at length, so you can marvel at my good fortune. First he described to me all the business he is engaged in against Luther's party; he said that was why he could not answer your letter, which he showed me, but he would answer before leaving Bruges.[16] He said he was afraid of your critical eye, and therefore could not work out any means of replying; he is always most ill equipped in both

* * * * *

7 See Ep 1267 n5.
8 See Ep 1268 n9.
9 Not earlier than 14 May; see n2 above.
10 Apparently of the same date as those to Vives and Gattinara; see n1 above.
11 Bertolph (Ep 1257 n10). He was doubtless bringing Epp 1273–6.
12 15 May at the earliest; see n9.
13 Ep 1274
14 Ep 1277
15 Carranza (Ep 1277 n8).
16 The imperial court, of which Coronel was a member, spent 13–22 May at Bruges before proceeding on its way to England via Calais; Gachard II 32.

matter and language, but in language especially. He regards you, if he really
thinks as he spoke to me, and he swore he was speaking his mind, as a
second Jerome or Augustine, and he says he is devoted to advancing your
reputation; he admires what you write, which he declares is absolutely   5
untainted and perfectly Christian, and will defend it just as he would defend
Christ's gospel. 'How is it then,' I said, 'that there are men who attack him as
though he were a member of Luther's party?' 'There are not,' he said; 'they
no longer speak like that, and only stupid people think so.' That was the
chief matter of our discourse, and we were parted by supper-time. They do   5
not have Miranda's pamphlet; but they say it is in Brussels. If I can, I will
unearth a copy for you from somewhere else.

There came to me today a servant of my lord of Liège, a Spaniard[17]
who once worked for me, and he told me that his lordship had handed your
letter[18] to a certain Domenico,[19] an Italian whom Aleandro[20] had left here   6
with him, and whom I suspect is a kinsman of Aleandro's. This Domenico
after reading the letter said to those who were present: 'Erasmus defends
himself though no one accuses him, and complains of Aleandro, though
Aleandro has always spoken of him with great respect and has written the
pope a letter brim-full of good will towards him.'[21] Mijnheer van Praet[22] is to   6
leave for England today or tomorrow as permanent envoy; and he told me
that the bishop of Liège had shown him your letter, and was anxious
because you were ill[23] when you wrote. That the chancellor[24] is your keen
supporter I have heard even from quite ordinary people about the court.

This letter is put together, as you see, from odd pieces; but as I got to   7
know of everything, I wrote it straight down. But you would rather have a
letter like this to tell you about everything than a highly polished one in
which there are nothing but elegant commonplaces.

While Hilarius was with me yesterday,[25] that Spaniard who is in the
household of my lord of Liège came;[26] and he said in Hilarius' hearing that   7

* * * * *

17 Mentioned also in line 74; identity unknown
18 See n10 above.
19 Identity unknown
20 On Aleandro's whereabouts at this time, see Ep 1271:67–71.
21 No such letter to Pope Adrian is extant.
22 Louis of Flanders, heer van Praet (d 1555), leading Netherlandish soldier,
   administrator, and diplomat during the reign of Charles v (Ep 1191). His
   credentials were dated 14 May at Bruges; LP III 2255. Cf Ep 1286:42–90.
23 See n7 above.
24 See n3 above.
25 19 May
26 See nn8, 17 above.

there is no man under the sun to whom his lordship is more attached than you, and that he always has your works in his hand, reads them constantly and with admiration, and defends you, if anyone attacks you, as he would hearth and altar. He said he had often been present at supper or at dinner when you were mentioned, and my lord had defended you and your 80 reputation and your scholarship against certain Italians in such a way that it was clear that he was very fond of you. Your man Hilarius was most diligent in demanding answers from the people you had written to,[27] but this court has a genius for putting things off and procrastinating.

My Augustine,[28] on the arrival of some friends from court, has been 85 laid aside for the moment; but as soon as ever they leave here, I shall run over to Louvain. There I shall very quickly add the finishing touches; for only five books are lacking. Froben has seventeen. I recommend Hilarius[29] to you, the bearer of this; he and I were fellow pupils once in Paris, and I think in any case he is very well recommended to you. 90

Farewell, from Bruges, 20 May 1522

1282 / To Ennio Filonardi   Basel, 21 May 1522

Filonardi (c 1466–1549), bishop of Veroli since 1503, was at this time doing a second tour of duty (1521–6) as papal nuncio in Switzerland. In April 1522 he had moved his headquarters from Zürich, now in the early stages of its Protestant Reformation, over the border to Constance, where he gave Erasmus a cordial reception in September of the same year: Epp 1316:16–17, 1342:474–88.

The letter was first printed in the *Opus epistolarum*.

ERASMUS OF ROTTERDAM TO ENNIO, BISHOP OF VEROLI, GREETING
My Lord Bishop, that bundle of papers, together with your lordship's letter,[1] was faithfully delivered to me, and gave me pleasure on many grounds. In the first place, I learned certain things from them which it was important for me to know. And then this made me see clearly the sincere 5 good will of Matthäus,[2] cardinal of Sion, though from this evidence I do not now learn for the first time of his kindness to me. Above all, I made as it were a new acquisition on the side – your own feelings towards me, who are so

* * * * *

27 Epp 1273–6
28 Vives' edition of the *De civitate Dei*; see Ep 1256:108–17, 148–62.
29 Bertolph left Louvain on 31 May to return to Basel; Ep 1296:14–15.

1282
1 Not extant
2 Schiner (Ep 1295)

Letter from Erasmus to Duke George of Saxony, Ep 1283
Staatsarchiv Dresden
Only the signature is in Erasmus' own hand.

ready to earn my gratitude, although up to now I have known you only by
name. I welcome your offer with both hands, and am sincerely grateful. On   10
my side, to be sure – for it is all I can do – I can promise one thing, a grateful
heart that does not forget, such as befits the faithful dependant of a generous
patron and benefactor. Farewell.

Basel, 21 May 1522

1283 / To Duke George of Saxony   Basel, 25 May 1522

The manuscript of this letter is found in a volume in the Staatsarchiv Dresden
entitled 'Dr. Martin Luthers Lehre und andere Sachen, 1522–49' (Loc 10300).
The letter was first published by Christian Saxius in *De Henrico Eppendorpio
commentarius* (Leipzig 1745). Duke George's reply is Ep 1298.

Duke George of (Albertine) Saxony (1471–1539) was an ardent champion of
ecclesiastical reform and an inveterate cataloguer of the *gravamina* of the
German nation against Rome. At the same time, however, he was (in contrast
to his relatives, the princes of Electoral Saxony) a bitter opponent of Luther and
his followers.

Greeting, most excellent Prince. I have no particular reason to write to your
Highness except that, having unexpectedly found a reliable person to carry a
letter, I wished to assure you in a few words that I do not forget you and
never shall. I only wish I may have an opportunity to show in something
more than words that the man to whom you so generously offered your   5
friendship is anything but ungrateful. The task of seeing some works of
mine through the press has recalled me to Basel, with what profit to learning
I know not, but undoubtedly at great peril of my life. I have suffered
repeated attacks of an illness[1] which has now become so habitual that I fear it
may never leave me; and it is the most serious thing one can have – stone in   10
the kidneys.[2] My personal sufferings are increased by the disastrous times
we live in, as I contemplate the whole world plunged by disputes between
two rulers into savage wars.[3] Nor is there any less turmoil in the world of
learning than between one country and another. May God Almighty turn
the hearts of princes towards policies that will bring peace!   15

* * * * *

1283
1 See Ep 1256 n2.
2 See Ep 1267 n5.
3 Ie, the Hapsburg-Valois wars between Charles v and Francis i, which broke out
  in 1521 and lasted, off and on, until 1544, only to be revived in the 1550s under
  Francis' successor, Henry ii.

My one comfort in these great troubles is Heinrich Eppendorf,[4] a young man both scholarly and civilized, whose character attests his noble birth.[5] He has been in Basel now for some months, where he is popular with every man of any judgment. If there is anything in which your Highness can use the services of your dependant, please be assured that everything is at your disposal which zeal and pains on my part can achieve. May Christ Jesus long preserve your illustrious Highness in health and wealth.

Basel, 25 May 1522

Your Highness' humble servant, Erasmus of Rotterdam

To the most illustrious Prince George, duke of Saxony, landgrave of Thuringia, margrave of Meissen, most clement lord

1284 / To Nicolas Bérault   Basel, 25 May 1522

This is the preface to the edition of *De conscribendis epistolis* which Froben published in August 1522. Erasmus wrote the earliest version of the work in Paris before the turn of the century. He revised it several times with the intent of publication but then abandoned the project in 1511. In 1521 an unauthorized version of one of Erasmus' drafts was published by John Siberch at Cambridge. Incited by this bit of piracy, Erasmus produced a new version, so much revised and expanded that it was virtually a new work. For more details see Ep 71 introduction and CWE 25 2–9. There is a critical edition by Jean-Claude Margolin in ASD I-2 157–579 and a translation in CWE 25 12–254.

* * * * *

4 Heinrich Eppendorf (d post 1551), a Saxon who studied at Leipzig (BA 1508). Little else is known of him until his visit to Erasmus at Louvain in 1520 (Epp 1122, 1125). Early in 1522, after a period of study at Freiburg paid for by Duke George (Ep 1437), Eppendorf appeared in Basel and attached himself to Erasmus, whom he accompanied on his visit to Botzheim at Constance in September 1522 (Ep 1316 introduction). In December 1522 Erasmus still spoke well of Eppendorf to Duke George (Ep 1325). But when the quarrel between Erasmus and Hutten broke out early in the next year (Epp 1331 n24, 1341A:1020ff), Eppendorf sided with Hutten. Indeed, Erasmus became convinced that Eppendorf had deliberately engineered the breach between him and Hutten and, as a consequence, became involved in a rancorous feud with Eppendorf which lasted until 1531. Erasmus' account of the origins and early stages of the dispute is found in Ep 1437. From 1523 Eppendorf lived at Strasbourg, devoting himself largely to scholarship and winning deserved fame as a translator of the classics into vigorous German prose.

5 Saxon correspondents eventually informed Erasmus that Eppendorf was, in fact, of humble birth (Allen Epp 1437:83–4, 1551:10–11). Erasmus subsequently lampooned Eppendorf in the colloquy Ἱππεὺς ἄνιππος, *sive Ementita nobilitas*, first printed in the edition of March 1529 (ASD I-3 612–19 / Thompson 424–32).

Nicolas Bérault of Orléans (c 1470–after 1545), whom Erasmus first met in 1506 (Ep 535:42–54), had a distinguished career as teacher and editor. Among his works was an edition of Valla's *Elegantiae* (Paris 1508), and among his pupils was Gaspard de Coligny, the future Huguenot leader and statesman.

ERASMUS OF ROTTERDAM TO NICOLAS BÉRAULT, GREETING

Once that man Hollonius[1] was no more in the land of the living, dear Bérault, my most learned friend, I supposed I had no one else to fear who might publish to the world the trifles I had written as a young man either to practise my pen or to comply with my friends' wishes, with publication as   5 the last thing I intended. Lo and behold, a second Hollonius has suddenly appeared in England, who has printed a book on the art of letter-writing which I began to write in Paris about thirty years ago[2] for the benefit of a friend of dubious loyalty,[3] whom I wished to please with a present on his own level – like lips, like lettuce, as the proverb has it.[4] The necessary   10 reading and the writing of it together cost me less than three weeks, and so far was I at that time from any intention to make a finished work of it that I gave the original to the man to carry away (for he was making preparations to set out on a long journey) and kept no copy by me. Some time after that, certain friends,[5] who by some chance had lighted on this trifling piece and   15 copied it, obliged me by their importunity to finish the work I had roughed out; for it was not only rough but incomplete and mutilated. So I sat down to it; but as I revised I still did not care for it and rejected it entirely, never suspecting that anyone would be shameless enough to publish my draft notes while I was still alive to protest. But printers, I perceive, have lost all   20 sense of shame. Now that they have discovered that nothing is more eagerly bought than the most trifling rubbish, they leave the classics and authors of repute on one side till further notice, put a bold face on it, and follow the satirist's advice: 'Profit smells sweet, whate'er the source of it.'[6]

And so, though I was so much put out that I now realized for the first   25

* * * * *

1284
1 It was Lambertus Hollonius of Liège (Ep 904) who in 1518 showed Erasmus' manuscript of the *Colloquia* to Beatus Rhenanus, who immediately published it, much to Erasmus' annoyance (see Ep 909 introduction).
2 Erasmus had arrived in Paris twenty-seven years earlier, in 1495.
3 Robert Fisher (Epp 62 and 71)
4 *Adagia* I x 71
5 Perhaps Adolph of Burgundy, heer van Veere (Ep 93) or Lord Mountjoy (Ep 117), or both
6 Juvenal *Satires* 14.204–5

time the full force of the feelings that made Horace write 'Long as the night
...' (you remember how it goes on),[7] I laid aside my labours of a more or less
religious kind, which are now more suitable to a man of my years and much
more agreeable to my present state of mind, and wasted some days on the
revision of what had already appeared. How great the loss to scholarship, I
do not know; to me at least the tedium was very great. To prevent too many
repetitions of this, I urge you most seriously, my dear Bérault, to contrive
somehow that this young man,[8] who has it seems an excessive devotion to
me, should take this book, which you say he has bought at a high price from
some knowledgeable dealer, and either destroy it or at the least hand it over
to you to be sent on to me, so that I can pronounce on it in complete freedom.
As for the printers, what fate can I invoke for them except that they may be
given better judgment? In any case, I would gladly warn the young who
wish to advance their education to waste as little time as possible on this sort
of rubbish.

I perceive, and the sight is torment to me, that this war between the
Germans and the French gets more and more bitter every day.[9] What a
calamity for the whole of Christendom that the two most powerful
monarchs in the world should contend like this in such disastrous conflict! It
would be a lesser evil if the question could be decided by single combat
between those whose interests are at stake. But what have citizens and
country folk done to deserve this, who are robbed of their livelihoods,
driven from their homes, dragged off into captivity, slaughtered and torn in
pieces? The spirit of princes must be hard as iron if they consider this and let
it be, stupid if they do not understand it, idle indeed if they do not think it
worth a thought. I had some hopes of our new pontiff,[10] in the first place
because he is a theologian, and then because his high character has been
obvious all his life; but somehow or other papal authority carries more
weight in stirring up war between princes than in bringing it to an end.

But these upheavals do not breach alliances knit together by the
Muses, nor can this intercourse between us be broken off by the laws of war.
There is no agreement between the emperor's supporters and the French,
but comrades in honourable studies agree together very well. Farewell
therefore, most civilized of men, and at the same time, given the oppor-

* * * * *

7 *Epistles* 1.1.20
8 Probably one of Bérault's students who had bought a copy of the unauthorized
   version
9 The first Hapsburg-Valois war; cf Ep 1283 n3.
10 Adrian VI (Ep 1304)

tunity, please convey my warmest greetings to Budé,[11] Deloynes,[12] Brie,[13]   60
and all my other friends.

Basel, 25 May 1522

1285 / From Johann von Botzheim   Constance, [26 May?] 1522

The manuscript of this letter is in the Rehdiger Collection in the University
Library at Wrocław (MS Rehd 254.38). The letter was first published by Karl
Hartfelder in the *Zeitschrift für Geschichte des Oberrheins* 8 (1893) 29.

Johann von Botzheim (c 1480–1535), often called Abstemius (see Ep 1341A
n1), was a member of a noble Alsatian family, a doctor of canon law, and since
1512 canon at Constance, where his home was a centre of hospitality for artists
and scholars. Erasmus first corresponded with him in 1520 (Ep 1103), visited
him at Constance in September 1522 (Ep 1316:12–14), and remained his friend
for life. Botzheim elicited from Erasmus the *Catalogus lucubrationum* of January
1523 (Ep 1341A). At first favourably disposed toward the Reformation,
Botzheim eventually was repelled by its excesses and, like Erasmus, found
both sides hostile to him. In 1527, when the Reformation triumphed in
Constance, Botzheim accompanied the cathedral chapter to Überlingen,
where he spent the rest of his life.

The month-date in the manuscript (line 71) is impossible: *26 Cal. Junias* (ie,
'26 the first of June'). Allen thought that Botzheim might have begun by dating
on 26 May and then, because Praus' departure was delayed, have changed to
1 June without erasing the 26.

When you give the length of the journey, my dear Erasmus, most beloved
and most learned of teachers, as an excuse for not coming to see us in
Constance, I take this in good part, in so far as I recognize on many grounds
that Sélestat has snatched you from us not unjustly,[1] although we suffer for
it; for apart from other drawbacks we have lost the glory of entertaining   5
Erasmus as our guest. But, given the option, who would not choose the
better course? – though all the same I think I have some reason for lodging a
protest with you. I came close to transferring myself likewise to Sélestat
when I heard your news, so envious was I at the time to see this glory fall to

* * * * *

11 Guillaume Budé (Ep 1328)
12 Ep 494
13 Germain de Brie (Ep 212:2n) was now canon of Notre Dame de Paris and
    almoner to Francis I.

1285
1 See the introduction to Ep 1273.

my very dear friends there who are such immoderate gluttons for good   10
literature. I seemed to hear and see my friends with my own eyes all
laughing and gesticulating and mutually congratulating themselves with
beaming faces on their having snatched from us the triumph of entertaining
you. I do indeed owe a great debt to Wimpfeling,[2] my respected teacher; to
the two Pauls, Volz[3] and the parish priest;[4] to Beatus Rhenanus,[5] who is   15
triply your friend; to Sapidus,[6] and others of the same kidney – all admirable
men that is – I owe them a debt which, given the opportunity, I will repay in
such a fashion as to make them all feel, though reluctantly, that I am
perpetually devoted to them and their sincere well-wisher.

As for that tyrant who is such a deadly foe to the welfare of   20
Christendom, that stone[7] in the kidneys which is so cruel to you, would that
I could drive it far hence to the Caudine Forks[8] at my own risk! As regards
that, you would not be far off the mark if you were to parody Hutten's
famous fever,[9] just changing the name, and consign it to one of the Fuggers
or to some ignorant cardinals or portly abbots. I hate the thought of that   25
sickness that reawakes in you from time to time, until I am beside myself
with impatience, so that there is no evil anywhere in the world that I do not
wish it from the bottom of my heart for causing such a loss to Christendom
by its attacks on you! But Christ with his wonted mercy will see that his
purpose in you does not fail.   30

In any case, if you will not be able to leave the things that are printing
for the next fair, this is a reason I highly approve; so far am I from offering
you an excuse to abandon them; for I look forward to sharing the results of

* * * * *

2 Jakob Wimpfeling (1450–1528) of Sélestat, the distinguished Alsatian humanist (Ep 224), was spending his last years in the city of his birth. In 1517 he
  founded there the humanist literary society, of which the others mentioned
  (nn3–6) were members.
3 Paul Volz (Ep 368), to whom the preface to the 1518 edition of the *Enchiridion*
  (Ep 858) was addressed
4 Paul Seidensticker, known as Paulus Constantinus Phyrgio (c 1483–1543) of
  Sélestat, where he became parish priest and welcome member of the literary
  society in 1519. Later he went over to the Reformation and in 1535 became
  professor of the New Testament at Tübingen.
5 Ep 327
6 Johannes Sapidus (Ep 323)
7 See Ep 1267 n5.
8 Narrow passes near the town of Caudium in Santium (central Italy), famous as
  the site where the Roman army surrendered to the Samnites in 321 BC
9 A reference to the dialogue *Febris [Prima]*, 1518 (Böcking IV 29–41), of Ulrich
  von Hutten (Ep 1331 n24). In the dialogue, Fever is banished to dwell among
  the representatives of wealth and power: the Fuggers, cardinals, and abbots.

that labour with many others and deriving great profit from it, if I maintain
my resolution. I had got a place ready where you could live as you like 35
without a care, nothing splendid, but such that you could easily judge from
it how devoted to you I am. I occupy it with greater pleasure and all the more
often because it was got ready for my friend Erasmus.

As regards my version of that preface[10] of yours, your warning comes
too late, for I have sent it to be printed, not suspecting that any man would 40
have sufficient effrontery and be so unchristian at heart as, out of hatred of
Luther, whoever he may be, to persecute the very truth of Christ and the
gospel where it is clearer than daylight, simply because Luther had touched
on this as well. I do not believe it will pay to sink to such a level of cowardice
that, if we have some service we can render to Christians for their salvation 45
(and you are always doing this), we should hold back for fear of any good
master doctors you can name, be they Spaniards, Jews, or Coronels.[11] Surely
everyone is under a heavier obligation to Christ than to any good master
doctor, however enlightened. You detected, rightly enough, that the laconic
brevity of your epistle[12] might arouse suspicions that your feelings towards 50
me are somehow growing cool, unless you had indicated what a mountain
of work (of which I am well aware) hangs over you. For it is not right to
spend on the Botzheims of this world the time that is much more properly
reserved for the general good.

I send you, dear Erasmus, better half of my soul, two enthusiasts for 55
liberal studies, as their conversation shows: one Kilian Praus,[13] a Benedictine monk from St Georgenberg[14] in the Inn valley, and the other Simon
Minervius,[15] who was previously (I understand) not altogether unknown to
you. I myself had never seen them before; but when they reached
Constance, they made diligent inquiries in their inn whether there was 60
anyone in the town devoted to Erasmus. They were given my name, and
when I heard the story I sent for them. Their courtesy extracted from me
something I myself already had in mind, that I would give them a letter to

* * * * *

10 Perhaps the letter to the reader, 14 January 1522, printed with the Paraphrase
on Matthew (see Ep 1274 n10). A German version of it, *Ein schon Epistel das die
Euangelisch ler von jederman sol gelesen vnd verstanden werden*, was printed twice
in 1522, but with no indication of the translator's name. Holeczek 121 identifies
Botzheim as the most likely translator.
11 Ep 1274
12 Not extant
13 See Ep 1279 n2.
14 See Ep 1279 introduction.
15 Simon Schaidenreisser, a kinsman of Praus (see Allen Ep 1449:41).

take to you which they hoped would secure them a welcome; for to see you
was, they said, their object in visiting Basel.   65

Last but not least, I long to hear from you what your next publication
will be from Froben's presses. Whatever you have in hand, try hard to take
your state of health into account. Farewell; and spare sometimes even a brief
word for your devoted Botzheim, who sends you his most affectionate
greetings.   70
From Constance, [26 May?] 1522
Your sincere friend Johann von Botzheim

1286 / From Gerard Bachuus   Bruges, 27 May 1522

This letter was first published as Ep 18 in Enthoven from a manuscript in the
Rehdiger Collection in the University Library at Wrocław (MS Rehd 254.14).
The manuscript belonged to that portion of the Rehdiger Collection lost in
World War II.

Gerard Bachuus (d 1569) was a priest, canon of St Donatian's at Bruges, and
'submonitor' at the chapter school until he became rector in 1523. He had been
tutor to Louis of Flanders (lines 42–90) for two years.

I was wondering the other day, O prince of scholars, where our great man
Erasmus was, what he was up to, and whether he was well or ill, when I ran
into one of my old friends in Bruges, who gave me, I must say, the most
splendid news. He told me that a member of the household of my old master
Erasmus had arrived from Germany and was in Bruges.[1] I could hardly   5
restrain myself from trotting off there and then and ranging up and down to
find the man, longing to ask him whether he had any news and had he not
something stupendous to communicate? I tracked him down, and asked
him how he left Erasmus. 'Very well indeed,' says he. I rejoice to hear that
you are well, and I do not believe (never trust me if I don't speak the truth)   10
that you could have found anyone among your friends at that moment more
steeped in delight. What news could give me greater relief and pleasure than
to know that all is well with Erasmus? It is a law of friendship that we rejoice
in our friends' good fortune and grieve with them when things go wrong.
We had a most friendly conversation, as two devotees of the Muses should,   15
and he told me he had brought some things that had not yet reached us, in
the way of works not devoid of learning – as one could easily suspect, when

* * * * *

1286
1 Hilarius Bertolph (Ep 1257 n10), who arrived in Bruges on about 14 May; see Ep
  1281:19–24 and nn9 and 11 in that letter.

I heard they came from your own literary workshop. Everything is beautifully finished, and everything is sound all through, that bears Erasmus' name. Your book of colloquies,[2] he told us, has been printed in an enlarged form with new material. 'What you say gives me great joy,' said I. 'How so?' he asked. 'Nothing,' I replied, 'could give me greater pleasure, for I know what I am talking about, and I hope we shall see old men and young men alike eagerly poring over this book with the same enthusiasm and thumbing it and learning it by heart, for they will get no small profit out of it.' Is there anyone too stupid to see how readable they are, how witty and, on top of that, how instructive? Nor is anyone, I believe, so idle that he would not rather have in its most lucid and most perfect form a thing which touches him so closely and which we use almost every hour. As far as I am concerned, I am confident that the youth of Bruges will emerge from reading your *Colloquia* far better educated than any others, having learned something which will make them a pleasure to every educated man and kindle a zeal for education in their parents. For parents love to hear their children speaking like well-taught, educated people, and they give others the same ambition. Then there is the publication of your paraphrase on Matthew,[3] your useful book on letter-writing,[4] and last but not least some pieces written by you against Luther,[5] but what they are like I have not yet been able to see. I reckon our generation is truly fortunate, in which I see the rebirth and restoration of learning, all through the efforts of this one man of Rotterdam. If only fate would allow us more of the same kind! And so we parted: he went one way to get on with his business, and I another.

So much to give you an idea of our conversation. Now let me give you news of heer van Praet.[6] He is in extremely good health. He is devoted to the Muses, as usual, and pursues them with all his might. Among all the members of the court there is no one who reads as much as he does or shows a more sincere affection and respect for literature and literary men. He enjoys their society, he shows no reluctance to entertain them, he helps them to appointments in the most generous way – all evidence of a really humane person. I would dare swear, believe me, that in the continuous two years that I have been his unworthy tutor, not a day has been so idly spent that there was nothing to show for it in the way of reading or writing, no day so busy that he would not steal an hour or even part of an hour from public

20

25

30

35

40

45

50

* * * * *

2 See Ep 1262.
3 See Ep 1255.
4 See Ep 1284.
5 See Ep 1275 n7.
6 Louis of Flanders, heer van Praet (Ep 1281 n22).

business. In brief, he is a very keen reader, he admires you beyond anyone,
calls you a light of the world, the eye of Germany, the prince of Italians, the
glory of Holland and Flanders and other seafaring people, the most learned   55
of theologians, most stylish of orators, and among poets both inspired and
expert beyond all others. 'To paint the man in his true colours,' he says, 'he
is a man for all seasons, and perfect at all points.' He is entirely devoted to
you.

    Now let me speak of letters. When he saw the letter you wrote him last   60
year now in print[7] – he had it from Vives before I did – he sent for me to share
his delight. I wish you could have seen him beaming from ear to ear, so
pleased with himself! You would hardly have recognized the old heer van
Praet, he was so beside himself with joy. 'Happy?' he said; 'of course I'm
happy, if Erasmus thinks I deserve to be added to the list of his friends. He   65
couldn't give me any present more acceptable. What is worth more than
immortality? – which cannot be gotten for gold or jacinth. Erasmus has
given me something with this bit of paper which no wealth could buy. How I
wish,' he said, 'that he would write to me oftener and more freely! There is
nothing I should more appreciate. Nothing would set me up more when I   70
am weary with public business. Unfortunately my position in the world is
not grand enough to repay someone like Erasmus adequately. But I am
confident of being able to oblige him, and at least I shall do it with a will. I
would have recommended him to the emperor, but least of all men does he
need recommendation there.' He used to add much else of the same sort; but   75
if I went on to recount that, I fear that the brief letter I intended would turn
into an Iliad. And so I do beg you and urge you, dear Erasmus, to be fond of
van Praet and to write to him. He is a real friend; he is a man both willing and
able to do something for you. He could do something particularly at this
moment, for he is being sent to England as envoy, and in sole charge, what's   80
more. There are some people at court who, when he was chosen, were
against it, and some who were for giving him a colleague; but Charles will
have no one else with him, saying that he is too well equipped for such a post
to need a second man. Van Praet was too much for their jealousy and for
their intrigues. Nobody has any doubt that he is capable of carrying out and   85
completing everything with great distinction and much to the glory of the
emperor; and may God bless the outcome! Let me tell you how the emperor
values him; he has imparted to him such secrets, so abstruse, as no member
of the court has ever heard; there was no one whom the emperor could trust
with such things except him.   90

      * * * * *

7 Ep 1191, which had just been published in the *Epiostolae ad diversos*.

My wife is expecting, and may be brought to bed any day now. I hope
Lucina[8] will be kind, and she will have a child worthy of both parents.

And so, most generous of friends, you have all our news. One thing
please let me get out of you: do not attribute my slowness in writing to
laziness, but put it down to my modesty, which is obstinate enough. I was   95
afraid to send you my foul papers, rough and rude as they are, with not a
breath about them of Aristophanes' learned lamp.[9] Your kindness was at
length too much for me, for you readily give a kindly reception to anything
that comes from a friend; your Hilarius was too much for me too, for he
persuaded me to take the risk, saying that you were far too kind-hearted to   100
despise anybody. Heer van Praet has told me to send you his greetings.
Farewell, best of teachers, and keep your young friend Bachuus at least in
the bottom row.

From Bruges, 27 May 1522

Your entirely devoted (for what he is worth) Bachuus   105

To Master Erasmus of Rotterdam, most learned of theologians, his
much esteemed teacher

1287 / From Guy Morillon   Bruges, [c 27 May 1522]

The manuscript of this letter, first published in Enthoven (Ep 15), is in the
Rehdiger Collection of the University Library at Wrocław (MS Rehd 254.110).
The approximate date is based on the references to the movements of the
imperial court (see n1) and to Epp 1273–6, which Bertolph had delivered (Ep
1286 n1).

Guy Morillon of Burgundy (d 1548) first appears as a teacher in Paris, where
in 1507–8 he prepared editions of several classical authors for the use of his
pupils. By 1515 he was living in Brussels, where he entered Hapsburg service
as a client of the chancellor, Jean Le Sauvage (Ep 301:38n). Upon the latter's
death (1518), Morillon became imperial secretary. He accompanied Charles to
Spain in 1522 and remained there until 1531.

Most honoured lord, your esteemed letter found me on the road, for I am
following the court, which I hear has already reached Calais,[1] as fast as I can.
I stopped some days in Brussels, getting together what I need for this

* * * * *

8 The goddess who brings to light and thus presides over the birth of children
9 *Adagia* I vii 72

1287
1 Charles arrived at Calais on 25 May and crossed to Dover the following day; see
   Ep 1281 n16.

journey to Spain, and could be of no use to Hilarius[2] because of my absence. Though I do not see what I could have done for him, he has arranged 5 everything with such care, and he is already too well known in the court here to need help from me or anyone else. In fact he can make himself useful to other people (myself included), as can be seen in the dispatch of letters.

The power of attorney[3] which you suppose to have been sent by our friend Barbier[4] I have been unable to see anywhere; but there is no call for 10 you to be afraid of losing money even if it falls into unauthorized hands, as I do not think it has. For Barbier wrote the other day to his brother[5] and to me how he wished to resign his benefices in favour of that same brother. So far is this from meaning any loss to you, if it comes off, that it will much improve the security for your annuity.[6] In a resignation in this form, Barbier reserves 15 to himself the profits of the benefice and the right of re-entry, so that, should his brother predecease him, it would revert to him again; and if his brother survives him, he is under the obligation of paying the annuity, and would pay it in any case, even were he not so bound. Thus, whether the benefice is resigned or no, the annuity always remains in Barbier's hands. And in fact, if 20 Barbier were to die after his resignation, the annuity survives intact in the person of his brother.

Those letters[7] in which you make it clear that you are not and never have been a supporter of Luther – I long to see them, and will get them from Glapion[8] when I reach the court. All the great men here seem to be your keen 25 supporters. Your writing to them all did a lot of good.

Your annuity will not merely be kept intact in the emperor's hands;[9] it will be paid immediately, if you will first authorize some agent to receive it or will simply write to master Jean Ruffault,[10] the treasurer, who is well disposed to you, as he told me last night. He will remain here with the most 30 illustrious Lady Margaret.[11] It will be possible for you to write to Pieter Gillis[12] or some other person who can collect the annuity for the past year,

* * * * *

2 Bertolph had visited the court at Bruges in mid-May and was already on his way back to Basel; see Ep 1281:23–6 and n29 in that letter.
3 See Epp 1245:33–4, 1254:17–19.
4 Pierre Barbier (Ep 1294)
5 Nicolas Barbier, known only from his correspondence with Erasmus (Ep 613)
6 Ie, Erasmus' pension from the living at Courtrai; see Epp 436, 1094, 1235, 1245.
7 Epp 1273–6
8 Ep 1275
9 See Ep 1273 n3.
10 Jean Ruffault, seigneur de Neuville, treasurer-general to Charles v and good friend to Erasmus; see Ep 1342:100–2, and Allen Ep 1461:9–10.
11 Margaret of Austria, aunt of Charles v, regent in the Netherlands
12 Ep 184

and in the letter you write to the treasurer himself to nominate the man to
whom the annuity is to be paid. If I were to stay here I could arrange this
admirably. But who can say whether I shall be here or in Spain? – especially   35
as for two months there have been only light winds.

Your request[13] that the Carmelites and the Dominicans may be
prohibited from vulgar abuse of you in their sermons may easily be met
without an imperial edict, if the cardinal of Liège[14] and the bishop of
Cambrai[15] order them to be silent; for this is entirely their responsibility and   40
not the emperor's. You should write about this to his Grace of Liège and the
other bishops concerned. I do not doubt that this will be easy to arrange,
especially with my lord of Liège, who habitually speaks of you in such
glowing terms. Nor do I think he has been aroused by Aleandro,[16] for whom
he has a great dislike, as I learn from those in a position to know.   45

Your letter to Barbier[17] shall be entrusted only to safe hands. I shall
speak with More in England. How I wish I had a letter for him from you, and
one for the cardinal of York[18] as well! I should much have liked to see you
before I leave for Spain. Write often, I beg, to all the great men at court, and
tell me if there is anything I can do for you. Farewell.   50

From the dean's[19] lodging at St Donatian's in Bruges, your lordship's
most devoted servant, G. Morillon

To my most honoured lord, Master Erasmus of Rotterdam. In Basel

1288 / From Andrea Alciati   [Noves, c 29 May 1522]

On Alciati, see Ep 1250. This is Alciati's reply to Ep 1278. First printed by Allen,
the letter survives in the Öffentliche Bibliothek of the University of Basel (MS
G.II.13a.48) in a copy made by Bonifacius Amerbach (Ep 1293). On about 1
May, Amerbach left Basel bound for Avignon to resume his studies under
Alciati (AK Ep 899:9ff), carrying Ep 1278 with him (Ep 1278:4–5). Reaching Lyon
by 20 May, he learned that Avignon was still not free of the plague that had
driven him home the previous year and that, as a consequence, Alciati had
retired to Noves, eleven kilometers southeast of Avignon (AK Ep 868). (In his
editions of Epp 1278 and 1288 Allen incorrectly identifies Alciati's place of
retreat as Châteauneuf de Gadagne; cf AK Ep 780 n2.) Amerbach arrived at

* * * * *

13 In Epp 1275:58–60, 1276:8–11
14 See Ep 1268 n9.
15 Robert de Croy (Ep 1256 n28)
16 Ep 1256 n11
17 See Ep 1302 n1.
18 Wolsey
19 Marcus Laurinus (Ep 1342)

Noves by 28 May (AK Ep 869), so the date of this letter can be placed at the end of May.

Our friend Amerbach has at last arrived, and brought me your letter. So he made me quite uncertain which gave me greater pleasure: his arrival is a very great joy to me, and anything that comes from you is regarded by me with great veneration, as though it were holy. And so that young man brought me near beatitude on both counts; and yet you recommend him to me, as if he did not already deserve, without any recommendation from anybody, whatever one man can do for another. Perhaps it was your exceptional kindness and sincere and loving nature that made you write as you did; for a friend's sake you do not hesitate to be over-anxious, and never feel you have done enough for the claims of mutual affection. A generous mind indeed and the heart of a true Christian! which all men ought to love and reverence and do all they can to serve, drawing upon it for examples of the true way of life, just as the painters of antiquity used to draw on what they called the canon.[1] Those who do not know how to do this, but instead go out of their way to attack you, do not understand the blessings of our age into which you were born, and suffer from an incurable disease of the judgment.

Suppose Luther's party do threaten books with long teeth to tear you in pieces; it is no cause for distress if you incur the disapproval of those whom all men of sound mind disapprove of. This is still further to your credit. They might perhaps have been able by that first publication[2] of theirs to convince many people (as they convinced me) that they are moved by zeal for Christian piety; but what they have published since, and what they set on foot under this head every day, is against that. I have heard that they have overstepped the limits of decency and Christian moderation and break out into strife and contumely and deadly hatred, sometimes even come to blows, and that contrary to the traditions of the gospel everything is done in the most scandalous fashion. In the same way you ought to stand firm against those who with greater cunning, as it seems to me, accuse you of belonging to the Lutheran faction in order to push you into that camp willy-nilly, which is the most impious plan, I think, that can be conceived. But you will defend yourself with the shield of St Jerome, and will not allow

* * * * *

1288
1 Ie, the work of Polycletus; see Pliny *Naturalis historia* 34.8.55.
2 Perhaps the composite volume of Luther's works published by Froben, without name or place, in October 1518

to be said of you what he said of Tertullian[3] – being so much fired by some
people's ill will or abuse that you deviate into a doctrine different from that
in which you have lived hitherto in perfect orthodoxy and with the greatest   35
credit.

One thing ought to be a great consolation to you, that, as you well
know, none of the ancient Fathers, even the most saintly of them, found his
efforts so successful that he had no experience of these quarrelsome gentry;
and your situation is in a way better than that in which the ancients found   40
themselves, because in those days there were so many more men of great
learning that they could not achieve such an outstanding reputation, and so
were an easier target for their enemies and those who lay in wait for them.
But you, as the leading light of our generation, stand above all the hazards of
ill will, so that, let them bark as loud as they please, they cannot weaken   45
your authority, for such accusations find credence nowhere. Go valiantly on
your way then, and continue to support the republic of letters as you always
have.

1289 / From Maternus Hatten   Speyer, 4 June 1522

The autograph of this letter (=Ep 8 in Förstemann/Günther) was in the
Burscher Collection at Leipzig (Ep 1254 introduction).

Maternus Hatten (d 1546), vicar and precentor of the cathedral at Speyer,
had once extended hospitality to Erasmus as he travelled to or from Basel (Epp
355, 361). In 1527 Hatten was denounced as a Lutheran and deprived of his
post in Speyer, whereupon he moved to Strasbourg and became a canon of St
Thomas' church.

Greeting. The lord bishop of Basel,[1] most learned Erasmus, has now sent us
a special courier, and wishes my masters to let him have a copy of the decree
lately published in our synod at Speyer by our own bishop.[2] The presence of
this courier I discovered at the last minute, so I must be brief if I am to tell
you what I thought you ought to know.   5
On the eve of the Ascension[3] there arrived from Rome for one of our

* * * * *

3 *De viris illustribus* 53

1289
1 Christoph von Utenheim (Ep 1332)
2 Georg Palatinus, bishop from 1513 to 1529
3 28 May

Romanists an attack[4] on you published by Diego López Zúñiga,[5] consisting
of seven duternions, as they call them.[6] I would have had it copied out and
sent it to you, had not I, as a friend of yours, been so far refused access to it.
But our dean,[7] who is also your friend, got me the book yesterday evening,   10
and last night with the help of friends who are well disposed to you I had a
copy made of the title and prefatory letter and at the same time of the list of
chapters and the beginning and end of each. The object of this impostor is to
show that you are not only, as he maintains, Luther's supporter but the
standard-bearer of Luther's whole party. All this I enclose, and beg you to   15
believe that I have the most friendly feelings in sending it you.

Apart from that, I should be glad to know whether Froben safely
received the Hilary[8] and the other things that I sent him by Marcus the
Sélestat carrier on 22 May and what is happening about Arnobius.[9] And if it
is convenient for him, will he please send me some New Testaments in large   20
and small format. Many people here have read the English king's book[10]
with great pleasure; and now Zúñiga's attack on you is being circulated by
some men I know (but not many) with equal zeal. May God Almighty long
and ever preserve you in good health for the benefit of liberal studies and of
us your friends. The dean greets you most warmly. Farewell, most learned   25
Erasmus. I very much hope that Beatus,[11] Froben and his delightful
spouse,[12] Hieronymus,[13] and my other friends are flourishing.

Speyer, 4 June 1522

Your most sincere friend Maternus Hatten

* * * * *

4 *Erasmi Roterodami blasphemiae et impietates*; see Ep 1260 n45.
5 Ep 1260 n36
6 Latin *duternos*, an otherwise unknown word. According to Dr. H.J. de Jonge of
   the University of Leiden, who has examined the copy in the Rotterdam
   Municipal Library, Zúñiga's book comprises seven quires of four leaves (or
   eight pages) each, which makes a total of twenty-eight folios or fifty-six pages.
   Each quire, moreover, is formed of one sheet folded twice to quarto format.
   Had the quires consisted of two sheets folded once to folio format, they would
   have been called 'quaternions,' a familiar term. Thus *duternus* must have been a
   neologism coined to describe something conceived of as half a quaternion, ie, a
   quire containing half as many sheets folded into pages half the size.
7 Thomas Truchsess, d 1523 (Ep 355:50n)
8 Apparently a manuscript for use in Erasmus' edition (Ep 1334)
9 See Ep 1304.
10 See Ep 1275 n25.
11 Ep 327
12 Gertrud Lachner, Johann Froben's second wife, whom he married in November 1510
13 Froben's son by his first wife (1501–63), since 1518 working in his father's firm

To the great scholar in Greek and Latin Master Erasmus of Rotterdam,   30
the vigilant champion of the humanities, his dear friend and teacher. In
Basel, Zum Sessel[14]

1290 / From Wolfgang Faber Capito   Nürnberg, 5 June 1522

The manuscript of this letter, which was first published in LB, is in the Rehdiger
Collection of the University Library at Wrocław (MS Rehd 254.45). On Capito,
who was at this time cathedral preacher in Mainz and chief adviser to
Cardinal-Archbishop Albert of Brandenburg (Ep 661), see Ep 459.

Some passages of this letter, especially in the second paragraph, were
written in Latin that is opaque – full of undefined antecedents and obscure
references. The translation faithfully reproduces the bewildering vagueness of
the original.

Greetings. Zúñiga's book is likely to please Luther's party. The title-page
reads 'The Blasphemies and Impieties of Erasmus of Rotterdam, collected
etc by Diego etc.'[1] Over the page is a pompous letter by Zúñiga, in which he
assures us that he will prove Erasmus to be the standard-bearer and prime
mover of Luther's party. After that, pieces from your *Annotationes* on the   5
New Testament, your notes on Jerome, and your other books, most of them
things that suit the public taste and that of anyone who wishes to see a
change for the better. Each subject has its own heading, like this: 'The
Canonical Hours,' 'The Primacy of St Peter over the other Apostles,' 'Of
Ordinances Made by Man,' 'Of the Paris Articles,' and so forth. Then he   10
adds what you wrote, none of which can be taken amiss by any of your
opponents with the slightest intelligence, such is the charm of style, the
virtuosity of judgment, and the prudence you display in everything.

I congratulate you on the acquisition of such a helpful opponent,
whose efforts, intended as they are to damage you, can only recommend   15
you to every man of good will; by which I mean that he almost paints a
picture of the sort of man you are, so far as indifferent sight can form an idea
of this. You would have felt Luther's opponents by no means to be despised
just lately, on account of the letters and the book published by the king of

* * * * *

14 Froben's house and printing press, where Erasmus lived until the autumn of
   1522; see Ep 1341A:1790 and Allen Ep 1528:54–5.

1290
1 See Ep 1260 n45. Cf Epp 1289:6–15, 1291:24–35.

England;[2] it is not so very different, they assure me, from your own style and   20
language.[3] Zúñiga has unintentionally calmed them down by producing a
unique book, of the sort some friend of yours would have been obliged to
put together one day out of what you have written. I am delighted. Nothing
pains me more than to see my Erasmus torn to pieces by ill-natured
pamphlets which are likely to survive. For your writings are full of happy   25
strokes of genius which just catch the spirit of posterity, and of matter that
suits you; if they choose to engage you in this field, they will prove this, not
to mention that there will be so many more of them. An age is coming to
birth much more blessed than this, which will set equal value on a spirit
consistent with itself and a mind trained in the humanities, and will expend   30
its energies not so much in the cult of the Muses as in devotion to Christ.
Such is the progress now to be seen everywhere, so far as I can gauge from
the present case. And so all of us who value you highly beseech you to
consider your peace and quiet by holding aloof from this sorry business, not
by tacitly agreeing with the powers that be against your convictions, nor yet   35
by resisting those who spring up after you and in fact grow from the
seed-corn that you have harvested. Maybe you could not write otherwise
than you did; the manner suggested by your mild character and your mild
pen is very different. How therefore will you use the same arguments to
reprove the same policy in another man, just because he has acted more   40
unwisely and has run greater risks, paying no attention to his own safety?

They make a great deal here of a pamphlet by Erasmus attacking
Luther.[4] I have not seen it yet, nor do I suppose you have boldly done
something you would rebuke me for doing. My prince's[5] advice is that you
should not reply to Zúñiga, and I urge the same thing. Whichever side you   45
steer towards, you will have to endure hatred from the other one. Some
would prefer to see you move towards the better rather than the more
successful party; for this, they think, is in a state of flux and uncertain of
itself, while the other, growing as it does on its own roots, and founded
upon the Rock that is Christ, gains in strength day by day; though the safer   50
course is to remain free and uncommitted and out of bowshot, if we think of
ourselves and not of the public weal.

You must take this in good part, for it comes from a straightforward
soul who has a great respect for you, and it has been wrung from him by very

* * * * *

2 The book is Henry VIII's *Assertio septem sacramentorum* (Ep 1275 n25). The
  letters referred to may be Henry's two prefaces, without dates, addressed to
  Leo x and the reader, in the *Assertio*.
3 See Ep 1275:89–91.
4 See Ep 1275 n7.
5 Ie, Archbishop Albert

severe criticisms of you from men of high character, and also by the   55
revolution in progress at this very moment. As far as religion is concerned,
either this world of ours will turn Christian, or it will drive the whole idea of
Christ off the stage; there is no third course. Farewell in the Lord, and keep
up your love for Christ and the public peace, as I know you do, my dear
Erasmus.   60

    Nürnburg, 5 June 1522. Your sincere friend Fabricius Capito

    To the incomparable Erasmus of Rotterdam, with all the esteem of a
son for his father

1291 / From Johannes Caesarius   Cologne, 14 July [1522]

> This letter was first published by Allen on the basis of the autograph in the
> Öffentliche Bibliothek of the University of Basel (MS G.I.25.15). The year-date is
> inferred from the mention of Zúñiga's book and of Buschius' presence in Basel.
>   On Caesarius, see Ep 374.

Greeting. The man who brings you this letter from me, Erasmus dearest of
all my friends, has lain low in my house for several days, for a reason which
he himself will be able to make luminously clear,[1] and therefore I need not
tell you the whole story at some length, as I had otherwise intended to do.
But he will not be able to put as much resentment into his narrative as will, I   5
am quite certain, overwhelm you when he sets out everything as it occurred.
Christendom seems to me to have reached such a state that there is simply
nothing for it but despair, unless Christ, our only and our final hope, is
willing to take pity on us. Everywhere evil confronts us; all the world over,
the prospect is darkened by war. Heaven itself has turned against us. And   10
all the time our self-satisfaction, our readiness to live as we always have,
continues unimpaired, and we see no need to diverge a hair's breadth from
our former habits. Today, it is not merely nation rising against nation; in our
very cities citizen and citizen do not agree. New factions constantly arise,
not to say persecutions. The laity are hostile to the clergy, and the clergy   15
regard the laity almost with abomination. It is not so much sickening as
dangerous to describe the outrages recently inflicted by the citizens here on

* * * * *

1291
1 Allen speculates that the bearer may have been Antoine Brugnard (Ep 1318),
  who left Antwerp c 5 June after two of his friends (Ep 1299 nn23 and 24) had
  been condemned as heretics in Brussels. Brugnard, however, did not enter
  Basel but turned off to Montbéliard, arriving there c 22 June. Therefore, if he
  was the carrier, Erasmus cannot have received the letter promptly.

some of the clergy.[2] It is at present impossible to discern the cause and origin of this evil. And yet, great as is the discord between them, I believe something even worse to be impending in literary circles – not merely between those who pursue such studies on quite different principles, but those too who can be shown to have been equally devoted to the humanities.

I saw a book[3] lately in which a certain Zúñiga, a scholar above the average who is, they tell me, a regular professor in Rome and a Spaniard by birth, has collected a number of passages scattered through your works under some sort of headings, of which the worthless fellow is very proud; he promises that he will shortly publish another book to prove you not merely blasphemous but impious too. When I read the book, in common with everyone else here of any decent education, we guessed at once easily enough what had roused him to the effort of attacking you like this: it was to make you detested by the hierarchy of the church (to which he was moved not so much by personal ill will as, I have little doubt, by the influence of some people in the city of Rome), and meanwhile to ingratiate himself with that hierarchy in hopes of somehow or other securing benefices. But I have no doubts about your courage, or that you are afraid of anything he can do to you; only let the question at issue between you be assessed by reason and not private spite, with judgment and not jealousy. Are these the rewards which such great gifts must earn at last? Perhaps it will prove more profitable to do harm than to care for the public weal, if this is the treatment in store for those who try to do good unto all men, to recall the fallen from their errors, to rebuild that which has fallen, and to restore what is now corrupt.

But I hold forth to you on this more fully maybe than I should. I had my reasons for so doing, though as I write it is already the eleventh hour of the night. Every good wish, and pray convince yourself that I am wholly devoted to you. Farewell again and again.

Cologne, the Saturday after Pentecost

Johannes Caesarius

*****

2 The specific 'outrages' referred to here cannot be identified, but the period 1519–25 saw frequent conflicts between citizenry and clergy in Cologne as in many other towns. Contemporary documents (excerpts from which were generously supplied by R.W. Scribner of Clare College, Cambridge) indicate that in Cologne as elsewhere these conflicts were frequently accompanied by violence against the persons and property of the clergy.

3 Ep 1260 n45. Cf Epp 1289:6–15, 1290:1–13.

Pray give my greetings to Hermannus Buschius[4] and everyone else   50
whom you know to be my acquaintance.

To the excellent Master Erasmus of Rotterdam, his dear and much
respected friend

1292 / To Conradus Goclenius   Basel, 16 June 1522

Another letter first published in the *Vita Erasmi* (Ep 1257 introduction). On
Goclenius, see Ep 1209.

ERASMUS OF ROTTERDAM TO THE DISTINGUISHED GREEK AND
LATIN SCHOLAR CONRADUS GOCLENIUS

Thank you for your letter.[1] You have seen Georg[2] by now, I suppose, and
have learned the story[3] from him. Tell that non-priest[4] that, if he has decided
to leave (which however I do not think right), he must take courage. The first   5
encounter, you know.[5] The man is a great scoundrel. Let him come here next
fair-time, and good luck to it. He will not fail to receive a good offer. Yet I
would rather the circle[6] did not break up, for many reasons. The end will be
different from what they think. About the humanities, I mean. I had written

* * * * *

4 Hermannus Buschius (1468–1534), a knight of Westphalia whose real name
  was Hermann von dem Busche, was a humanist, a poet, and since 1515 a friend
  of Erasmus, who may have tried to secure him for the Collegium Trilingue at
  Louvain (Epp 884 introduction). At this time Buschius was in Basel, where he
  joined the reformers and forsook poetry for theology. In 1523–4 he sided with
  Hutten against Erasmus (cf Ep 1341A n285), and later (1526–33) taught at the
  new Protestant University of Marburg.

  1292
1 Not extant; probably dated c 31 May and carried by Hilarius Bertolph (see Ep
  1296:12–15)
2 A messenger who left Basel about 8 June (Ep 1296:14–15) and returned bearing
  a letter from Vives (Ep 1303:20)
3 Perhaps some communication about the property that Erasmus had left in
  Louvain in the care of Neve and Goclenius at the College of the Lily; Epp
  1296:16–18, 1355:20–43
4 Unidentified. Allen's suggestion of Melchior Vianden seems most improbable
  in the light of Ep 1257:1–5 (unless one or the other of these utterances is not to
  be taken seriously). Cf Ep 1237:44–7.
5 Cf Terence *Phormio* 346.
6 The circle of Louvain scholars described in Ep 1237

about Hoorn.[7] At any rate let him come. Be silent and sensible, sober and   10
sceptical, keep your courage up, and so farewell.[8]

Basel, Trinity Monday 1522

1293 / To Bonifacius Amerbach   Basel, 24 June 1522

> This letter, which was first published in the *Epistolae familiares* (Basel: C.A.
> Serin 1779), has also been published as AK Ep 873. The manuscript is
> AN.III.15.1b in the Öffentliche Bibliothek of the University of Basel.
>
> On Bonifacius Amerbach, who was at this time (1520–4) studying law with
> Alciati (Ep 1250) at Avignon, see Ep 408.

Wishing as I do, dear Bonifacius, that all may go well with you, my mind
somehow misgave me as you set off for where you are now.[1] But I dared not
fight against God,[2] which means against your wishes and your love for
Alciati. Life must come first; better face the risks of a return than stay where
you are and perish. The whole world seems poised for some great change;   5
and if this comes about, law will perhaps turn into lawlessness. Above all,
dear Bonifacius, have a care of your life and health. Achilles himself found
no joy among the shades.[3]

As for me, I begin to recover physically,[4] but have much to distress my
mind, and specially a rumour that reached us through the Carthusians that   10
Pieter Gillis had been arrested as a follower of Luther.[5] And lo, here comes
my servant[6] with a letter, and nothing sinister has been said. Meanwhile I
had dispatched another servant.[7] Oh, this monkish tyranny! How I envy
you! Here there is astonishing uproar over the gospel.[8] But of this when we

* * * * *

7 Jacobus Ceratinus (Jacob Teyng) of Hoorn; Epp 622:34n, 1237:25–9
8 This last sentence is in Greek. The admonition to be 'sober and sceptical' is
  adapted from a fragment of the comic poet Epicharmus much cited by Greek
  and Roman writers, eg, Polybius (18.40.4) and Cicero (*Ad Atticum* 1.19.8).

1293
1 Amerbach had just returned to Avignon, whence the plague had driven him
  the year before; see Ep 1288 introduction.
2 Acts 5:39
3 Homer *Odyssey* 2.475–6, 489–91
4 Cf Epp 1256 n2, 1294:12–13.
5 The rumour was false, but Gillis (Ep 184) feared the possibility of such action
  against him; see Epp 1296:4–6, 1318:3–7.
6 Hilarius Bertolph; see Ep 1292 n1.
7 Perhaps Georg; see Ep 1292 n2.
8 On Palm Sunday (13 April) a number of citizens had defiantly eaten pork, thus

meet. Only please arrange that I may see you. You see how the world is in 15
tumult. Please play the part of a letter from me to Alciati,[9] a man whom I
value more than I do anyone.

I have written this after supper, rather than not write at all, dear
Bonifacius. Give my greetings to Basilius,[10] who since you left has never
come to see me.   20

Basel, St John Baptist's Day 1522
Your truly devoted friend Erasmus
To the worthy Bonifacius Amerbach of Basel. In Avignon

1294 / To Pierre Barbier   Basel, 25 June 1522

As early as 1501 Pierre Barbier of Arras (d 1551) was a chaplain at the Hapsburg
court in the Netherlands. By 1516 he was chaplain and secretary to the
chancellor, Jean Le Sauvage (Ep 301:38n), whom he accompanied to Spain in
1517. After the death of the chancellor (1518), Barbier remained in Spain and
joined the household of Adrian of Utrecht. When Adrian was elevated to the
papacy, Barbier went with him to Italy. The new pope left Saragossa on 11 June
1522 and arrived in Rome on 29 August (Pastor IX 59–66). In his letters (see line
1) Barbier must have announced his imminent departure for Rome, since
Erasmus sent the letter to him there (Ep 1302:5–6). All the persons to whom
Erasmus sent greetings were in Rome at the time.

The letter was first published in the *Opus epistolarum*.

ERASMUS OF ROTTERDAM TO PIERRE BARBIER, GREETING
The parcels which you sent from Spain, both the books and the letters,[1] have

* * * * *

provoking an uproar which lasted throughout the summer; see Zw-Br Epp 204
and 206, with Egli's informative notes. Erasmus' *Epistola de esu carnium*,
published in August, was a by-product of the controversy; cf Ep 1353. There
had also been considerable controversy over Wilhelm Reublin, priest at St
Alban's and future Anabaptist leader, whose sermons attacking vigils, masses
for the dead, and other Catholic ceremonies, as well as the bishop himself, had
drawn audiences of up to four thousand. On 13 June he substituted a Bible for
the reliquary in the Corpus Christi procession, for which he was banished on
27 June, 'non sine magno tumultu parochianorum' (AK Ep 877). See also G.H.
Williams *The Radical Reformation* (Philadelphia 1962) 88.

9 To answer Ep 1288
10 The brother of Bonifacius (d 1535). In a letter dated 14 August, Bonifacius
urged Basilius to cultivate Erasmus' friendship more assiduously; AK Ep
882:84–90.

1294
1 Not extant

arrived safely. As for Matthäus, cardinal of Sion,[2] you must take the place of
a letter from me to him. His kindness to me is exceptional, and I feel how
much I owe him. If he were my brother, he could hardly be more devoted. I   5
am sorry that I ever thought Zúñiga worth an answer.[3] Now Carranza[4]
follows him, no toothless babe in arms. Everyone thinks the *Blasphemiae*[5]
ridiculous, and they are all indignant with Zúñiga for publishing things in
his anthology which support Luther's case, or so Luther's own people think.

Some time back, they said that the journey to your part of the world   10
was risky, and I was in no state to be fit to travel.[6] In fact, as I write this, I
have a serious attack of the stone,[7] although for some days now I have been
in fair shape.[8] And I am tied down to the printing of my books[9] and cannot
get away before the end of August. Then, if I am even tolerably well, I shall
hasten to visit you. Give a thousand greetings to all my friends, to Pace[10] and   15
Fabri[11] and the provost of Wrocław[12] and Herman of Friesland,[13] for whose
gifts I have a particularly warm feeling, and Landau the Bavarian.[14] I will
write soon[15] to all of them, when I have a more reliable courier and am in
better health.

Basel, morrow of St John the Baptist 1522   20

1295 / To Matthäus Schiner   [Basel, c 25 June 1522]

This is a fragment of a letter which, according to Allen, the editors of the *Opus
epistolarum* mistook for a postcript to Ep 1410; see his introduction to that letter.
Though the letter to Schiner was probably not completed at this time (see Ep
1294:2–3), the fragment may be conjecturally dated as shown, when Schiner's

* * * * *

2 See Ep 1295.
3 The first *Apologia*; Epp 1260 n36 and 1277 n1
4 Ep 1277 n8
5 Ep 1260 n45
6 For a recent, unsuccessful attempt to travel, see Ep 1273 introduction.
7 See Ep 1267 n5.
8 Cf Ep 1293:9.
9 *De conscribendis epistolis* (Ep 1284) and new editions of the *Colloquiorum formulae*
  (Ep 1262) and the *Parabolae* (Ep 312) were printed by Froben in August 1522.
  Erasmus' edition of Arnobius' commentary on the Psalms (Ep 1304), to which
  Erasmus' own commentary on Psalm 2 was appended, followed in September.
10 See Ep 1342 n85.
11 See Ep 1260 n22.
12 Georg Sauermann (Ep 1342 n88)
13 Haio Herman of Emden in Friesland (Ep 903:14n)
14 Jakob Ziegler (Ep 1260)
15 See Ep 1302.

offer of financial support had recently been renewed (Epp 1282:5–7, 1299:49–50).

Matthäus Schiner of Mühlebach (c 1470–September 1522), the son of a Valais peasant, had become bishop of Sion (Sitten) in 1499 and cardinal in 1511. A noted diplomat and champion of Swiss alliance with the papacy against the French, he settled in Rome in 1522 a short time before his death. During his diplomatic journeys he had several meetings with Erasmus, who wrote the paraphrase on St Matthew at his suggestion (Ep 1255:30–1). The paraphrases on the Epistles of St James and St John (Epp 1171 and 1179) were also dedicated to Schiner.

ERASMUS OF ROTTERDAM TO MATTHÄUS, CARDINAL OF
SION, GREETING
The five hundred ducats[1] a year which you so generously offer me I feel as though I had already received, and am no less grateful than I should be if they were already mine.   5

1296 / From Conradus Goclenius   Louvain, 26 June [1522]

On the writer, see Ep 1257.

This letter was first published by Allen from MS G2.II.66 fin in the Öffentliche Bibliothek of the University of Basel. Besides the mention of the *Colloquia* and the apology against Lee, the connection with Epp 1292, 1293, and 1303 shows beyond doubt that Erasmus is the addressee. The relationship to those letters also establishes the year-date. The fictitious name in line 36 was probably used as security against hostile interception. The direction to Constance may have served the same purpose, unless Goclenius believed Erasmus to be on a visit to Botzheim at the time (see Ep 1285:1–3).

* * * * *

1295
1 The current exchange rates for the Venetian ducat (3.56 grams fine gold) and the Florentine florin (3.54 grams fine gold) were: 6s 8d (80d) gros Flemish in the Low Countries; 41s 6d tournois in France; and 4s 6d (54d) sterling in England. Thus an annuity of 500 ducats was then officially worth about £166 14s gros Flemish, £112 10s sterling, or £1,037 10s tournois. This sum is clearly expressed in terms of the current Venetian gold coin, even though in Venice itself the coin was then called the *zecchino*; the term ducat had come to be reserved for the silver-based money-of-account fixed in value from 1517 at 6 lire 4 soldi Venetian. See Denis Richet 'Le Cours officiel des monnaies étrangères circulant en France au XVIe siècle' *Revue historique* 225 (1961) 377–96; Jean Lafaurie and Pierre Prieur *Les monnaies des rois de France* II, *François Ier à Henri IV* (Paris 1956); Robert Steele ed *Bibliography of Royal Proclamations of the Tudor and Stuart Sovereigns, 1485–1714* (London 1910) I 9; CWE 1 314; and CWE 8 349–50, Tables A, B.

Heaven reward as they deserve those scoundrels who enjoy spreading unpleasant news![1] But may the severest penalties be reserved for those who deliberately invent such things in order to bring torments of grief on all men of good will! It is such men's irresponsible malignity, feeding as it does on the sorrow of others, that has plunged you in this baseless fear for Pieter 5 Gillis.[2] We ought to be quite content, and even regard it as a great triumph, if their rumours are proved false; but none the less it pains me greatly to think how the wickedness of these rascals has plunged you in such consternation as I could discern in your letter.[3] I hope we shall soon see that breed of utter liars have their hands full, with real and not invented misfortunes of their 10 own to report. But this we must leave to fortune. No doubt you have already been relieved to a great extent by Hilarius[4] of the anxiety arising from this false rumour; for as I reckon the days I suppose he must have returned to Basel the day after Georg left you[5] or not much later, since he left Louvain on 31 May. Meanwhile however I have sent you another letter by Pieter, the son 15 of Dirk of Aalst,[6] who left here on 15 June. As to your things,[7] I expected to get my instructions from Georg, but he said you were not minded to make any changes or move to any other quarters[8] unless the outlook is doubtful. And so no efforts have yet been made. Should there be any sudden alarms, or signs of some impending storm or even calamity, I will without fail take 20 steps to see that your position is watertight.

In Louvain all is peace, for those who stir things up[9] have been away for some time; except that some people object very strongly to certain

* * * * *

1296
1 See Ep 1293:10–11.
2 See Ep 1293 n5.
3 Not extant: probably dated c 8 June and carried by Georg (Ep 1292 n2)
4 Bertolph (Ep 1257 n10), who doubtless carried Epp 1281, 1286, 1287, and the lost letter from Goclenius mentioned in Ep 1292:1
5 See n3 above.
6 Dirk Martens of Aalst (c 1450–1534) spent a long and distinguished career as a printer in Antwerp and Louvain. A devoted friend of Erasmus, he published, among other things, the first edition of the *Enchiridion* (Ep 1341A n174). Of his son Pieter little is known but the name, which appears in the colophons of three books published at his father's press in 1524.
7 See Ep 1292 n3.
8 Ie, to quarters other than those in the College of the Lily, where Erasmus' property, including his library (Ep 1355) was stored. Ep 1322:14–15 indicates that a room had been set aside for him at the Collegium Trilingue.
9 Erasmus' enemies among the friars; Ep 1263 n14

passages in the *Colloquia*,[10] on which I have lately made notes. But I know
that you will have no lack of material with which to defend them, and in fact   25
have done so to a great extent in your defence against Lee[11] and his ravings.
But men of that sort do not read your answers; they read only what might
seem to tell against you, for they hate you worse than they hate dog or
snake.[12] But only a few, and those bad hats. 'Yield not to evils; march more
boldly on,'[13] as you do already. And so farewell, and all good wishes to the   30
great glory of our age.

Louvain, 26 June
C.G.

My friend Karl[14] tells me to send you his greetings, which he will
shortly tender in person.   35

To master John the tithe-collector, his most respected friend. In
Constance

1297 / From Jacobus Piso   [Prague, c June 1522?]

The autograph of this letter (=Ep 7 in Förstemann/Günther) was in the
Burscher Collection at Leipzig (Ep 1254 introduction). The manuscript ended
abruptly at the bottom of a page. The letter answers one, now lost, which
reached Piso via Stanislaus Thurzo (Allen Ep 1662:27–30). This suggests that
Erasmus' letter may have been written c 22 November 1521 and enclosed with
Epp 1242–3, which were addressed to Thurzo. Piso's reply, the present letter,
was lost among his papers for four years (Allen Ep 1662:30ff) and was finally
sent, undated, along with Ep 1662 (1 February 1526). The approximate date
derives from the account of the dinner at Prague (lines 58–82), which took
place shortly before 1 June 1522 (LP III 2299); see also n10.

Jacobus Piso or Borsody (d 1527) was a native of Medgyes in Transylvania.
He was the Hungarian ambassador in Rome when he met Erasmus there in
1509. Returning to Hungary in 1516, Piso became tutor to King Louis II of

* * * * *

10 Baechem (Ep 1256 n6) had found in the new edition of the *Colloquiorum formulae*
   (Ep 1262) four passages (on vows, indulgencies, confession, and fasting) that
   he labelled heretical; see Epp 1299:59–79, 1300:1–47, 1301. In the new edition,
   c August 1522, Erasmus introduced changes in response to Baechem's denunciation.
11 The *Apologia qua respondet* (Ep 1341A n225), in which Erasmus responded to
   Lee's charge (Ep 1061:374–440) that two passages in the *Colloquia* were
   indecent; see Ferguson *Opuscula* 289–93.
12 Horace *Epistles* 1.17.30
13 Virgil *Aeneid* 6.95
14 Probably Karl Harst (Ep 1215)

Hungary (see n7), for whom he later discharged various diplomatic missions, some of which are referred to in Allen Ep 1662.

It was easy enough, dear Erasmus most learned of men, to discover how to thank my friend Velius[1] forthwith for being the cause of your writing to me; but I can neither find nor invent any words to thank you even now for actually writing with your own hand, especially to the extent that your kindness deserves. Velius perhaps owes some requital to my humble self, mutual affection at least and an equal return of friendship, if nothing else. But my debt to you is too long-standing and too great to be redeemed by any service, to say nothing of requital. As far as I am concerned, however, I shall think myself lucky enough in this respect, and truly happy, if you do not displace me from my old position among your friends; for honestly I have always treasured your friendship so highly, and always shall, that, when I must abandon life itself, I do not feel as though I should ever abandon that place, especially if there is any trusting to the written word one day, when we are all dust and ashes. I am not thinking of my own writings, which are in any case too ill written for me to wish them to survive me, but of the men who of their own accord have testified to you of my unshakeable devotion – and in this class there were not a few who found my opinion of Erasmus not uncongenial. And now my friend Velius is added to their number, from whose conversation you learned, as you say in your letter, that I never vary, and am your most keen and active supporter. In this regard, what I can do for you I do not see, for you enjoy already such a reputation among men of good repute themselves that you need no *curio*[2] to sing your praises, much less a *Piso*.[3] Furthermore, having once known Erasmus in private life 'inwardly and under the skin,'[4] how can I fail to praise him continually and consistently in public, and pay him honour and respect? Let each man make up his own mind on this, all's one to me: for my part I pay him, and him alone, a tribute I would not pay to any other author I have read. I speak of those among the moderns who wish for the true welfare of Christian theology; for those quarrelsome wits who are only at home in the lecture-room have always been my aversion. And how I wish that from my boyhood until now I had never opened a book by anyone except Erasmus! Yet at this point someone will be found to say that I have read nothing

* * * * *

1297
1 See Ep 1280A.
2 Ie, a herald; see Martial 2 praef.
3 That is, someone without eloquence; see Cicero *In Pisonem* 1.1.
4 Persius 3.30

else. I have read very little, I agree, if I reckon the good it has done me; if I count the loss of toil and time, I have read too much. My natural cast of mind always suggested that more self-advertisement has been introduced into the   35
gospel of Christ by some commentators (let me not call them hare-brained purveyors of conjecture) than the pure and simple truth itself would have demanded. What profit I have found in them, I know not; but this one thing I know full well, that I have derived more sauce to the dish from two or three pages of Erasmus than from whole volumes by all those learned doctors in   40
between. I speak of my own taste, and how from time to time it seems diametrically opposed to others, like the one guest in any group of three.[5] In this matter I have always been consistent, I have never blown hot and cold at the same time, though it might have been to my advantage, public and private. And this is now well known everywhere to those with whom I have   45
had to do business; so that if I wish to change, even for some good reason, I could not do it, unless perhaps I wished to be untrue to myself, and nothing could ever be further from me than that. Kings have heard me on this topic, bishops have heard me and princes, and friends above all of my own standing, to whom I have sung the praises of Erasmus the scholar and   50
teacher and no less of Erasmus the man. They plighted their agreement in friendly fashion, not so much with what I said as with the facts, even if men were not wanting here and there who, while agreeing cordially with all the rest, seemed to resent that you were thought to have encouraged Luther (if I may say so) to cause the world so much trouble. That many people bring this   55
up against you, you cannot deny.

But I must not repeat old tales which have long since been told more than once, so I will add one thing at least for its novelty.[6] At dinner lately in Prague the king[7] and queen[8] entertained, as it happened, Andrea da Borgo,[9] the emperor's envoy and a most gifted man, the most illustrious margraves   60
of Brandenburg, Albert, grand master in Prussia, and his brother George,[10]

* * * * *

5 Horace *Epistles* 2.2.61–2
6 Horace *Ars poetica* 16
7 Louis II of Hungary and Bohemia (b 1506), who had succeeded his father, King Vladislav II, in 1516 and was killed at the battle of Mohács in 1526
8 Mary of Austria (1505–58), sister of Charles v. After the death of her husband (see preceding note), she became regent of the Netherlands (1530–55).
9 An Italian in Hapsburg service since 1505. In 1519 he was sent as ambassador to Hungary.
10 Two sons of Frederick, Margrave of Brandenburg-Ansbach: Albert (1490–1568), last grand master of the Teutonic Order in Prussia, 1512–25; and George (1484–1543), who in 1527 succeeded his brother Casimir in the margraviate. Albert and George were nephews of King Vladislav of Hungary and Bohemia

and two magnates from Bohemia. By some chance the conversation turned to Luther, which did not much please my own princes. When one of the margraves saw this, in hopes of pacifying the princes, who support you as a monarch should, he added that to start with Luther had got everything from Erasmus, and that there was a good understanding between them. I was frank, and did not deny that I had indeed heard this, from many people too, but I showed them that the facts were quite different, with plenty of proofs, of which the strongest was what I produced from your letter,[11] which had lately arrived. Some of them none the less maintained their former opinion. Meanwhile I ordered that your letter should be sent for. When it arrived, first of all the queen seized it, eager to recognize your hand, and then the king; but he had got to know it already from the letter you sent me from Siena[12] while I was still in Rome. The letter then flitted everywhere from hand to hand; silence fell while they read it, and the received opinion melted away. On the spot, those who were standing (and there was a circle of courtiers standing round) voted with their feet for my proposal, and those who sat, with their hands. I thought that by this I had richly deserved a victor's crown, or at least a civic one, for at the same moment I had saved a most distinguished citizen who had deserved so well of the republic and throttled more than one obstinate foe, and all that without moving from my position in that engagement.

Perhaps I ramble on too much, especially on so desperately serious a business; for I do not fail to see that there is absolutely no place here for humour, on a topic that threatens a very grave outcome in the near future. Indeed I very greatly fear that any consultations will be far too late, even did Luther himself start now to sing a palinode. They are very, very far astray, in my opinion, all those who limit the outcome of this dreadful business by supposing that, once popular resentment has been vented against religion and the clergy, they will at once refrain from touching the things of this

* * * * *

(see n7). George had been at the Hungarian court since 1506 and had since 1516 supervised the education of young King Louis. Albert, recently at war with another uncle, Sigismund I of Poland, was in Prague from early May until the end of July 1522 (see the information on his itinerary in Förstemann/Günther 405). Both brothers eventually became important supporters of the Lutheran cause. In 1525 Albert turned Prussia into a secularized, Lutheran territory with himself as the first duke. Starting in 1528, Margrave George and the city council of Nürnberg co-operated in the ecclesiastical visitation of their contiguous territories and in the preparation of a common church order, which went into effect in 1533.

11 Not extant; see introduction.
12 Erasmus was apparently in Siena in the spring of 1509; see Epp 216 introduction, and 1206:27–9.

world. In this business the fall of the dice will be quite different: once they
have seized this pretext to get arms at last in their hands, we shall hear how
they turn against all social order and all government and even (God save the
mark) against princes and kings, and plunge the drawn sword into their
throats – yes, we shall see this with our own eyes. What can be sacred and   95
abiding, what in the last resort can be even safe, if the people are once
released from religion and law? ...

1298 / From Duke George of Saxony   Dresden, 9 July 1522

This letter, which is Duke George's reply to Ep 1283, was first published by
Allen from a sixteenth-century transcript which Professor Henry de Vocht of
Louvain discovered among the papers of Frans van Cranevelt (Ep 1317). De
Vocht himself later published the letter as Ep 9 in his Literae ad Craneveldium.

GEORGE, BY THE GRACE OF GOD DUKE OF SAXONY,
LANDGRAVE OF THURINGIA, AND MARGRAVE OF MEISSEN, TO THE
MOST LEARNED ERASMUS OF ROTTERDAM, GRACE AND FAVOUR
We have received your letter, most learned of men, and it gave us all the
more pleasure as we fully learned from it the warmth of your feelings   5
towards us. It also suggested to us that, though at the moment almost no
reason occurred to us for writing, yet as we had the opportunity, we should
not allow your courier to return without a letter; and there is one subject in
particular on which we thought it well to write. There is in general
circulation among us here a small book,[1] which in our opinion is note-   10
worthy, attacking the works of Luther and his propositions,[2] under the style
and title of his serene Majesty the king of England, our much respected lord
and friend, which is a most scholarly and elegant performance and appeals
to us almost more than we can put into words. Now, though in view of his
royal Highness' outstanding intellect and erudition, which are common   15
knowledge, I have no doubt that it comes from his own workshop, yet many
men suggest, and indeed assert, that he had some further help from you.[3]
Indeed, if the king's book is compared with your own writing, this can easily
be detected from the style. However this may be, we most certainly hope
that this book, published as it is under the name of that eminent and learned   20

* * * * *

1298
1 See Ep 1275 n25.
2 King Henry's book was a reply to Luther's De captivitate babylonica of October
1520.
3 See Ep 1275:89–91.

king, will carry no little weight in opposition to Martin's frivolous propositions, which he has circulated for some years now among the common people.

We also believe sincerely that it would do much good in this regard if you, who brilliantly surpass all other men as a scholar and a fluent speaker and writer, were to descend into this arena. In these last few days two pamphlets by Martin Luther have again appeared in our German vernacular,[4] on the title-page of one of which he has described himself as a preacher, *ecclesiastes*. Both these I send you; in both Martin has, in our opinion, written on the sacraments of our religion and on the leading figures in the church such filth and obscenity and such conceited and unbridled nonsense, that anything more filthy, more obscene, more conceited and unbridled can hardly be imagined.

Arise, most learned Erasmus, and for the love of Christ Jesus turn all the force of your great natural gifts to meet this challenge. Let this be the target for all your energies in speaking and in writing, that at length you may so effectively silence this man with his unbridled conceit that henceforward he may cease to deploy his headstrong and profane presumption with uncontrolled impunity against holy things. In this you will undoubtedly do what is pleasing to Almighty God, far from unprofitable – in fact, a blessing – to Christendom, honourable to yourself, and most welcome of all things to us; and in particular you will win the good will of all those especially who have hopes for the future of Christendom, and will make your name immortal among posterity. Farewell, and give a favourable hearing to this request, and also wish us well, as I know you do.

From our castle in Dresden, on Wednesday the ninth of July in this current year fifteen hundred and twenty-two

George, duke of Saxony etc, with my own hand

1299 / To Joost Lauwereyns   Basel, 14 July 1522

Joost Lauwereyns of Bruges (d 1527) was an able jurist who in 1515 entered the service of Charles of Hapsburg as a member of the Grand Council of Mechelen. In March 1522 he became president of the council. In May, the decisions of the Netherlands Inquisition were made subject to his review as superintendent. It was in that connection that Erasmus wrote the present letter to him, appealing for protection against the attacks of the conservative theologians Nicolaas

* * * * *

4 *Von beyder Gestallt des Sacraments zu nehmen vnd ander Newerung* (April 1522), WA x-2 11–41; and *Wider den falsch genannten geystlichen Stand des Babst vnd der Bischoffen* (July 1522), ibidem 105–58.

Baechem and Jacob of Hoogstraten. Lauwereyns seems to have responded
coldly to this overture and subsequently sided with anti-Erasmian theologians
such as Jacobus Latomus. This caused Erasmus to characterize him as a mortal
enemy of good letters (Allen Epp 1717:16–18, 1747:28–30), a harsh judgment
not shared by Vives and others who knew him.

The letter was first printed in the *Opus epistolarum*.

ERASMUS OF ROTTERDAM TO JOOST,
PRESIDENT OF THE GRAND COUNCIL OF MECHELEN, GREETING

I am told, honoured sir, and sincerely rejoice to hear, that supreme authority
in the Luther affair has been entrusted to your Excellency, whom I know to
be not only a perfect master of the law but a man of spotless character and   5
complete impartiality. For while our efforts must be devoted to laying
Luther's faction to rest, we must be careful at the same time not to abandon
men of high character, whose labours have done good service to the public
cause of learning, to the private spite of certain individuals.

Nicolaas Baechem[1] is universally known in Louvain for his obstinate   10
and vindictive spirit, if he has taken a dislike to someone. Between him and
myself a long-standing and bitter hatred arose, even before the world heard
of Luther's existence, on account of the learned tongues and the humanities,
which he hates even more bitterly. Although he has gone to the length of
attacking me so frequently in his sermons and lectures with transparent   15
falsehoods, not refraining even from trumping up accusations of heresy, he
yet finds it intolerable that in a piece in my own defence,[2] in which I do not
even mention his name,[3] I reject his outrageous charges. And now I hear
that at every drinking-party, and at Mechelen in a public sermon, he has
branded me as a heretic in common with Luther. This at least is no part of his   20
instructions,[4] either from the emperor or the pope, this way of satisfying the
hatred in his heart. Personally, I have never had anything to do with Luther,
except that I have always urged him not to go on setting the world by the
ears with this sort of pamphlets, for I already prophesied even then what we
now see has happened. Both in this country and in yours, both in   25
conversation and by correspondence, I have detached many men from
Luther's faction; nor has any single thing more depressed the spirit of

* * * * *

1299
1 Ep 1254 n6
2 The *Apologia de loco 'Omnes quidem,'* February 1522; see Ep 1341A n269, and cf Ep
1235.
3 Cf Ep 1341A:940–2. Baechem was, however, sufficiently well described to
make his identity perfectly clear; LB IX 434B–C.
4 As assistant inquisitor

Luther's party than my open declaration in my published works that I support the Roman pontiff and disapprove of Luther's business. Had I supported Luther, as these men affirm, I should not have lacked princes to back me up. Nor is that way of thinking yet so extinct in men's bosoms as they suppose and as I myself would wish. In this country there are more than a hundred thousand[5] men who hate the Roman see, and to a great extent approve of Luther.

Observe now how unfairly I should be treated if, when I have lost the friendship of so many scholars in Germany and aroused against myself all Luther's party, who now attack me in their virulent pamphlets, these men were to abuse their victory, which they owe in great part to me, by making a major assault upon me, and were to denigrate me as a heretic for no better reason than that I like the humanities and do not like the character of Baechem, which almost every honest man dislikes. I have had letters from his Imperial Majesty,[6] from Jean Glapion, from the archbishop of Palermo, the bishop of Palencia,[7] Mercurino[8] the chancellor – letters full of sympathy, urging me to continue in my labours for the cause of learning. I have had letters from other learned men and especially Matthäus, cardinal of Sion,[9] and the cardinal of Mainz,[10] and a great many others, expressing their appreciation and promising me every kind of support and generosity, because in the business of the church I display the spirit which they wished to see. My lord of Sion even offers me five hundred ducats a year and lavish provision for my journey, if I am willing to move to Rome.[11] What could be more monstrous, than that when I have made myself an enemy of Luther's party and am at peace with the world's chief princes, I should be torn in pieces by an individual Carmelite? I lived all those years in Louvain; why did he not charge me with my errors then? In fact Atensis[12] approved all I wrote

* * * * *

5 In Epp 1300:90–1 and 1302:113, Erasmus gives a much higher figure.
6 Ep 1270
7 The letters of Glapion, Carondelet (Palermo), and Mota (Palencia) were evidently answers to Epp 1275, 1276, and 1273, which must have been delivered early in May (Ep 1281 n11).
8 Answering the letter mentioned in Ep 1281:2–3
9 His letter was perhaps an answer to Epp 1248–9.
10 Ep 1302:74–5 mentions more than one letter, but none from this period survives. For some of the matters raised in those letters, see Epp 1305:12–13, and 1323:22–4. See also Ep 1308:19–24.
11 See Epp 1295, 1300, 1302, 1305, 1311, 1342:346–52.
12 Jan Briart (Ep 670), professor of theology at Louvain from 1506 and the university's leading administrator. Despite his conservatism and his discomfort with Erasmus' views, the two had generally cordial relations (but see Ep 1341A:839–57). On his approval of Erasmus' works, see Ep 1225:130.

without exception; then, when at my request he had criticized two or three   55
passages, I replied and gave him satisfaction on them all. And now, in the
emperor's absence,[13] they are preparing to misuse his authority to attack
me, and thus to satisfy their ancient hatred.

I have lately published a small book of colloquies.[14] Several things in
this Baechem loudly proclaims to be heretical.[15] Now in the first place, in   60
these imaginary conversations I impart, not the principles of the faith but the
art of self-expression. Nor do they contain anything of the sort, but his
hatred makes him think so. I do not condemn indulgences,[16] there or
anywhere else; but I have a character who laughs at his friend because,
though a worthless fellow, he thought he could get to heaven under the   65
protection of a papal bull.[17] Confession I actually approve; only there is a boy
who says he would be satisfied to make his confession to God, if that were
acceptable to the leaders of the church; and yet he admits that he confesses
to priests as well.[18] As though it were not sufficient for a child to obey the
leaders of the church in the confession of his sins, or as though Christ were   70
not one of the leaders of the church; or as though I were certain that it is an
article of faith that this form of confession was instituted by Christ! And yet
on this subject I have always submitted the verdict of my own mind to the
judgment of the church. Someone in the book says he hates fish,[19] and is
surprised that prelates have been ready to bind us to eat fish on pain of   75
hell-fire. And yet the man who says this admits that he is an Epicurean.[20]
Although this is not clear to me either, whether the pope's state of mind was

* * * * *

13 See Ep 1274:12.
14 See Ep 1262.
15 See Epp 1296 n10, 1300:1–47, 1301. See also Franz Bierlaire 'Le *Libellus
    Colloquiorum* de Mars 1522 et Nicolas Baechem, dit *Egmondanus'* in *Scrinium
    Erasmianum* ed J. Coppens (Leiden: Brill 1969) 2 vols, I 55–81 and, by the same
    author, *Les Colloques d'Erasme: Réforme des études, réforme des moeurs et réforme de
    l'église au XVIe siècle* (Paris 1978) 203–12.
16 Cf Ep 858:430–33. But in private statements, Erasmus was less circumspect; Ep
    786:25–6.
17 In the *De votis temere susceptis*, first published in March 1522; (ASD I-3 149–50 /
    Thompson 7)
18 In the *Confabulatio pia*, also new; (ASD I-3 177–8 / Thompson 38–9). But
    Erasmus' views on this question had already got him into trouble; Epp 1153
    n10, 1225 n29.
19 In a passage newly inserted into the dialogue *Convivium profanum*; ASD I-3
    207–8 (March 1522), 227–30 (augmented version in edition of July-August
    1522) / Thompson 602–5 (augmented version)
20 This was in the earlier editions; ASD I-3 198, 202 / Thompson 594, 598.

such that, except in cases of scandal and contempt, he wished to make the eating of fish obligatory upon us on pain of eternal damnation.

I can hardly think that their action against me is in accord with the imperial edict.[21] At any rate, the most recent edict[22] has not reached us here, nor has it ever been exhibited either publicly or in private. I therefore beg you, my distinguished friend, to moderate their hatred and their bitterness with your usual sense of justice. As far as I am concerned, I know what they have in mind: they would like to force me even against my will into Luther's faction, and that is something they will never do. But the point is worth taking whether it would be expedient to drive me to such lengths. It will give the greatest pleasure to Luther's supporters if they commit any outrage against me. If they have any fault to find with me, let them put me on notice first; it may be that I shall reply in a way that more than satisfies them. This is no place for making idle sport of the books of other men. There are countless thousands of men who do not hate their Erasmus, because of the benefit they have derived from my books. And I could set the world by the ears, were I so minded; but I would rather die than be responsible in the future for some new upheaval. Such being my resolve, it will be all the more unfair to act in such a way that I am abandoned with impunity to the implacable hatred of two or three individuals. If courteously treated, I will ensure that no one finds me wanting in a Christian's duty. It has always been my aim to be of use to all men, nor does anyone abhor dissension more than I do.

I am not pleading now for N.B.,[23] for I do not know what he has admitted to. But this I know, that there was no man in Antwerp of more unblemished character, more popular with his fellow-citizens, or of more value to the community in the education of the young. Nor do I express any opinion about his colleague;[24] for of his case, where it concerns Luther, I am

* * * * *

21 Ie, the Edict of Worms, May 1520, condemning Luther; see Ep 1313 n7.
22 Ie, the decree of 29 April 1522 conferring on Frans van der Hulst (Ep 1345 n8) full powers to extirpate heresy in Brabant. In May, these activities were made subject to review by Lauwereyns (see introduction to this letter).
23 Nicolaas van Broeckhoven of 's Hertogenbosch (Buscoducensis), c 1478–after 1550. A friend to all the humanists active in the Netherlands, Broeckhoven became master of the Latin school in Antwerp c 1520 but got into trouble on account of his religious opinions. In 1521–2 he was imprisoned and forced to abjure his errors; Epp 1302:97–102, 1318:12–16, and Allen Ep 1358:32–3. In 1528 he joined the reformers, settling first in Bremen, then at Wesel, where he became rector of the Latin school. He died as pastor at Blankenburg in the Harz.
24 Cornelis Schrijver (Cornelius Grapheus) of Aalst, 1482–1558, was a humanist and poet, befriended by most of the great humanists of his time, including

ignorant. But this I know, that he is a good scholar, versed in many 105
languages, and his character is spotless, except that he is a rather unguarded
talker. Baechem no doubt treated him with greater severity, having suffered
from his attacks in private. It is common knowledge that Hoogstraten[25] and
Baechem aim at the extinction of the ancient tongues and the humanities,
and seek above all a handle to attack those who teach them. In my opinion 110
they would do better if they were content with their victory and did not
arouse further tragic disturbances in this world of ours. The world will bear
it somehow, if deprived of Luther; to be deprived of the tongues and the
humanities, it will never bear.

But I take up your Excellency's time by my great length; so let me most 115
strongly urge you to use all your wisdom and your sense of justice to control
the outbursts of others and, if there is any truth in the rumours that have
reached us, not to allow a servant of the public like myself to be abandoned
to the hatred of two individuals. Beyond question, this is the wish of our
merciful emperor and of our saintly pope, and the general desire of all good 120
men. My best wishes, honoured sir, to your Excellency, and pray add my
name to the roll of your dependants.

Basel, 14 July 1522

* * * * *

Erasmus. By 1520 he had become one of the secretaries of the town of Antwerp.
His lively interest in schemes of moderate ecclesiastical reform led, in February
1522, to his arrest on charges of propagating Lutheranism. The price of his
release was an abject recantation (Epp 1302:97–102, 1318:8–12, and Allen Ep
1358:31–2). Thereafter carefully avoiding theological questions, he slowly
re-established his reputation through literary work and, by 1540, was restored
to his town secretaryship.

25 Jacob of Hoogstraten op (d 1527) was a Dutchman by birth but, after taking his
DD at Cologne in 1504, resided mostly in Germany. From 1510 he was prior of
the Dominican convent at Cologne and inquisitor for the archdioceses of
Cologne, Mainz, and Trier. His earliest university training had been at Louvain
(MA 1485), where he subsequently retained friendly contacts, especially with
Baechem. Although a capable theologian, Hoogstraten was a fanatical and
intemperate inquisitor. In the Reuchlin affair and other controversies he
manifested bitter opposition to humanist scholarship and was indiscriminate
in his charges of heresy. Erasmus, whose initial contacts with Hoogstraten had
apparently been agreeable (Ep 856:28–34), had no serious quarrel with him
until the autumn of 1519, when Hoogstraten denounced Erasmus at Louvain
and at the imperial court in Brussels as an accomplice of Luther, using Ep 980 as
his evidence. Early in 1520 Erasmus and Hoogstraten met, settled their
differences (Ep 1064), and restored tolerably agreeable relations (Ep 1342:670–1).
However, Erasmus continued to link Hoogstraten and Baechem as enemies of
the humanities (Ep 1330:53ff).

1300 / To Jeroen van der Noot   Basel, 14 July 1522

> The manuscript of this letter (British Library Add MS 38512 f 2) is in a secretary's
> hand, with corrections and signature by Erasmus. It was first published by
> Allen.
>
> Jeroen van der Noot (d 1541), who had studied law at Orléans, was
> chancellor of Brabant (1515–31) and thus one of Charles v's chief ministers. It is
> not clear whether Erasmus knew him personally.

Greeting, most honoured sir. I learn from many correspondents that in your
part of the world Dr Nicolaas Baechem[1] is attacking me everywhere at social
gatherings and in public sermons, and frequently calls me a heretic, and that
he is taking steps to secure authority from the emperor's court to burn my
book entitled *Colloquia*,[2] on the ground that in it on the subjects of   5
confession, of fasting, and of man-made legislation I think as Luther thinks.
Anyone who reads the book will find this very far from the truth; but he so
interprets it because he suffers from long-standing hatred of me and of the
ancient tongues and the humanities. I have therefore thought it well to
forewarn your Highness not to be misled by his calumnies into taking some   10
decision against me which I do not deserve. If you are prepared to comply
with his hatred, there will be no end of harsh measures against those who
love the humanities. I found it easy to suspect that in the emperor's absence[3]
he would start some new campaign.

In the first place, in that book I teach Latin conversation, I do not   15
impart the articles of the faith. Yet not a word in it is contrary to the faith.
There is a boy in it who says that he makes his confession every day to God.
When asked whether he thinks this sufficient, he replies that he himself
would be satisfied, if that were acceptable to the leaders of the church.[4] This
Baechem interprets as asserting that confession is a matter of man-made   20
law. It is an established fact that the confession we use is largely a matter of
man-made law; it is a fact that our making our confession once a year, and
making it to this or that person, stems from the chapter *Omnis utriusque
sexus*.[5] Thus we are encouraged to make our confession once a year by the
authority of the bishops. The boy therefore does nothing wrong if on the   25

* * * * *

1300
1 See Ep 1254 n6.
2 See Epp 1262, 1296 n10, and 1299.
3 See Ep 1274:11.
4 See Ep 1299 n18.
5 *Decretales* v.38.12

subject of confession he follows the authority of the episcopate, even if he
doubts whether it is part of divine law or no – a point on which, to speak the
truth, my own mind is not yet quite clear. Not but what among the leaders of
the church Christ has first place, I should suppose. The boy also says that he
confesses only those sins that are certainly mortal or very strongly suspected   30
of being so. This, I suppose, no one says is unorthodox.

Fasting is not mentioned in the book;[6] one character merely discusses
the eating of fish.[7] Fasting is enjoined upon us by Christ and the apostles.
The scrupulous choice of food is condemned in many passages of the gospel
text. Yet there is no condemnation in the book of the practice of the church: 35
merely a discussion at table whether it was the intention of the bishops to
compel all men without distinction to eat fish under pain of hell-fire, even
supposing they had power to do this – I always make an exception of
scandal and contempt. As a sensible man, you can see that in this there is
nothing that disagrees with the rule of faith. It is not Baechem's business, it   40
is for the pope himself, to explain what he means.

Indulgences are condemned by no one in the book, but one of the
characters laughs at his boon companion[8] because, though a man of evil life,
he had none the less thought himself secure of heaven under the protection
of a papal bull. What is there heretical in this? Is there any divergence from   45
the teaching of the papal bulls, which demand a contrite heart from the man
who seeks indulgences?

How much I have done for the general cause of learning, the facts
themselves declare. As for Luther's party, I was the very first man to deter
them from their presumptuous programme. Had I been willing to support   50
him, that Carmelite[9] of yours would not rule the roost as he now does. I have
lost the friendship of innumerable scholars in Germany because I made it
clear that I do not think as Luther does. And now Luther's party are
resentful, and rave against me in abusive pamphlets. I have estranged more
men from Luther than ever Baechem will, whose opinion carries no weight   55
here. And for these services shall I be abandoned to the spite of one
individual, who is so beside himself that he cannot attempt to conceal his
loss of self-control? The emperor's intentions were good, and I approve
them; but I wish his Majesty had committed so perilous a task to someone
else. The emperor's proclamation[10] armed them, not against those who are   60

* * * * *

6 Erasmus must have forgotten that fasting is discussed briefly in the *Confabulatio pia*; (ASD I-3 177 / Thompson 38).

7 See Ep 1299 n19.

8 See Ep 1299 n17.

9 Ie, Baechem

10 See Ep 1299 n22.

devoted to the humanities and the ancient tongues, but against heresies. And yet this is the target against which they will misuse their authority, unless you in your wisdom restrain them. His Imperial Majesty himself wrote to me most kindly.[11] I had a most friendly letter from Dr Jean Glapion, more than once. A letter from the bishop of Palencia. A letter from the lord 6 high chancellor Mercurino. Letters from Rome from, among others, his Eminence the cardinal of Sion, offering me in addition a most generous stipend if I were prepared to betake myself to Rome. A letter in a most friendly spirit from the cardinal of Mainz. They think nothing more damaging to the papal cause than that I should be forced by the private 7 animosity of certain individuals into Luther's faction. These men may try hard to do so, but they will never succeed. My conduct in this business has been such as to give me no fear of Christ's judgment-seat; nor shall I prove untrue to myself. If they have anything against me, let them at least put me on notice. I did on one occasion reply to Atensis[12] on points that had been 7 criticized, and I satisfied him and all the others. They make much of mistakes, I know not what; personally, I have failed so far to find a single one in my books without the assistance of perverse interpretation, which can make the most admirable statements sound very dangerous.

As for this business of Luther, though it is nothing to do with me, you 8 in your wisdom must take precautions to prevent severe steps being taken, and beyond all reason, against men who have done no harm. In the first place, it is not the articles of the faith that are in question but the authority of the Roman pontiff, who has hitherto been given too much power; indulgences, which have hitherto been allowed too much indulgence; and 8 man-made legislation, which has hitherto been given more weight than the gospel. Luther has gone too far, but the passion which roused him to take up this business was not wholly without cause. Furthermore, were this way of thinking confined to the few, it could be restrained by savage measures. As it is, there being more than twenty million[13] people who support Luther in 9 part and hate the pope, savagery against such numbers would be fruitless, especially since no one openly confesses himself a champion of Luther's faction. It is also expedient for the cause itself not to exacerbate too many people. Support for Luther is better left to evaporate than crushed.

But you in your wisdom will see these things more clearly than I. In my 9 own case I ask only that no concessions should be made to Baechem's spite,

* * * * *

11 For this and all the other letters listed, see Ep 1299, nn6–10.
12 See Ep 1299 n12.
13 Cf Epp 1299:33, 1302:113.

unless I am given notice and can reply. All good wishes to your Excellency, to whom I profess myself entirely devoted.

Basel, 14 July 1522

Erasmus of Rotterdam, your Excellency's most humble servant   100

To the right honourable Sir Jeroen van der Noot, knight, chancellor of Brabant, my most respected lord. In Brussels

1301 / To the Theologians of Louvain   [Basel, c 14 July 1522]

This letter exists in two versions: a shorter one, first published in the *Vita Erasmi* (Ep 1257 introduction); and a much longer one, printed with the first edition (April 1523) of the *Catalogus lucubrationum* (Ep 1341A). The shorter version, written in haste on receipt of the news of action impending against him in Louvain, is clearly the earlier one, and probably the one actually sent. It closely resembles Epp 1299 and 1300 and was probably written and dispatched at the same time. The longer version, written after the arrival of more information, may never have been sent to Louvain, Erasmus being content to publish it as his considered defence of the points attacked. Allen published the shorter version, giving the variants from the longer version in notes. Reversing Allen's procedure, we present here the longer text, which is by far the more interesting historically, with the most important variants in the notes. Variants which do not affect the substance of the letter are not noted.

ERASMUS OF ROTTERDAM TO THE THEOLOGIANS OF LOUVAIN,
HIS DEARLY BELOVED BRETHREN IN THE LORD, GREETING
A matter has reached me not only by hearsay but in letters from friends of standing, who tell me precisely the language, the place, and the audience chosen for a slanderous attack on me. The person responsible[1] always runs   5
true to form, and his character and record make it easy to accept as fact what would otherwise have been merely probable. I do not think therefore that I should overlook it, especially in front of you, whose business it was to restrain his unbridled impertinence, if not to please me, at least for the credit of your own faculty.   10

He puts it about with full use of his lungs that in my book of *Colloquia*[2] there are four passages which are worse than heretical: on the eating of meat and on fasting, on indulgences, and on vows. Although he asserts this emphatically and without restraint, anyone who reads the book with an

* * * * *

1301
1 Baechem (Ep 1254 n6)
2 See Epp 1262, 1296 n10.

open mind will understand that it is not so. For those who have no time to   15
read such trifles, I will expound the point in brief.[3]

But before I begin, there are three points which I would like to make by
way of preface. First, there are no grounds in this case for accusing me of
contempt of the imperial edict;[4] for I am told that this was published on 6
May 1522, while my book was printed long before that – and in Basel, where   20
even to this day no edict of the emperor has been displayed either in public
or in private. Then it must be remembered that in the book I impart, not the
doctrines of the faith, but phrases for those who wish to speak Latin,
although I bring in some things in passing which contribute to the building
of character. Suppose the grammar-master, after setting his boys a theme in   25
French or German, were to teach them to turn into Latin an expression like
this: 'May those who imposed these fish-days upon us eat nothing but
garlic!' Or this: 'I wish those who compelled free men to accept the necessity
of fasting would starve to death!' Or this: 'Men who deal for a high price in
the smoky trade of dispensations and indulgences deserve to perish in the   30
smoky flames of the fire!' Or this: 'Those who keep people against their will
from marrying really ought to be castrated themselves!' Surely no one would
be compelled to defend himself on a charge of heresy if he taught his
students to translate such sentiments, wicked though they may be, into
good Latin. No one surely would be so unfair as to think this a fair   35
proceeding. Third, I would say one ought to consider particularly what sort
of character it is to whom I attribute a particular remark in the dialogue. In
that passage I am not portraying a doctor of divinity in the pulpit, but
presenting a trivial conversation among elegant young gentlemen. Anyone
who would be so unjust as to refuse to let the difference of character tell in   40
my favour would have to hold me responsible in the same work when a
certain Augustine,[5] I think his name is, despises the morality of the Stoics
and prefers the Epicureans, who chose pleasure as the highest good. The

* * * * *

3 These two opening paragraphs correspond to the first paragraph of the shorter
   version (Allen Ep 1301:1–5): 'A matter has reached me by hearsay only, though
   it is likely enough, and so I will reply with the sole object for the moment of
   preventing hasty action based on calumny before my case has been heard. A
   certain person is putting it about in public that in my new *Colloquia* there are
   three or four places in which I side with Luther – on confession, that is, and on
   fasting. That this is not so will be clear to anyone who reads the book with an
   open mind.'
4 See Ep 1299 n22. It was published in Antwerp on 6 May.
5 Augustinus Vincentius Caminadus (Ep 131), who appears as a character in the
   Colloquiorum familiarum formulae. He is the Epicurean hater of fish referred to in
   Ep 1299:74 and 76.

same man should hold me responsible when a soldier in the book, among
many other remarks which are highly appropriate for a man of war, says he   45
is minded to look for a priest with as little sound sense as possible, to whom
he may make his confession.[6] I suppose he would also ascribe it to me if, in
the dialogue, I had put into the mouth of Arius some words which
conflicted with the teachings of the church. If it would be absurd to ascribe
these remarks to me, why not consider in other places what kind of character   50
is speaking? Unless perhaps, if I were to introduce a Turk as one of my
speakers, they should think fit to attribute to me whatever he might say.

With this by way of preface, I shall now make a few general remarks
about the passages with which he found fault. In the first of them a boy of
sixteen says that he goes to confession, but only confesses those sins which   55
are certainly capital or are strongly suspected of being so,[7] although the
followers of Luther, I am told, teach that it is unnecessary to confess all one's
capital sins.[8] So it is clear that what the boy says differs greatly from the
point of view which you condemn. A little later, when the same boy is asked
whether he is satisfied to make his confession to Christ, he replies that he   60
would be happy in his own mind, if the leaders of the church had been of
that same opinion. From this my critic deduces, not by any logical argument,
but out of a spiteful desire to stir up trouble, that I am responsible for the
view that the practice of confession which we now follow was not instituted
by Christ, but by the bishops of the church. This inference might have an air   65
of plausibility, if Christ were not one of the leaders of the church, since,
according to the words of Peter,[9] he is the chief of shepherds, and he is
described in the Gospels as 'the good shepherd.'[10] So whoever speaks of the
leaders of the church does not exclude Christ, but includes him as well as the
apostles and the successors of the apostles, just as those who mention the   70
principal parts of the body do not exclude the head. But if this reply seems to
some to be somewhat disingenuous, let me concede that the boy was
thinking of those who are merely human beings, the princes of the church.

* * * * *

6 *Militaria* (1522) ASD I-3 157 / Thompson 15
7 See Ep 1299 n18.
8 The shorter version (Allen Ep 1301:30–1) says: '... it is unnecessary to confess
   all one's mortal sins, but only those which are manifest.' It is not clear why
   Erasmus here changes the 'mortal sins' (*peccata mortalia*) of the shorter version
   into 'capital sins' (*crimina capitalia*). At any rate, Luther's point was that we
   need confess only those sins of which we are aware; see his *Sermo de poenitentia*
   of 1518 (WA I 322:22–5). Erasmus summarizes Luther's view rather more clearly
   in Ep 1153:49–52).
9 1 Pet 5:4
10 John 10:14

Is it not sufficient, then, that in making his confession he follows their authority, although he does not know whether bishops were able to institute this on their own authority or whether it was Christ's institution and they handed it on to us? For it is his intention to obey, whatever the channel of transmission. I myself am not entirely clear that the church has laid it down that the present practice of confession is of Christ's instituting. For there are very many arguments suggesting the opposite which I at least cannot resolve. And yet I submit this feeling of mine at every point to the judgment of the church; my ears are open and I will readily follow as soon as I hear her voice loud and clear. Suppose by all means that this had been expressly laid down in the bull of Pope Leo,[11] and that someone either did not know this or did not remember it, it would suffice for the moment, I think, to bow in this matter to the authority of the church with the intention to obey, if that too could be established. Nor is it logical to argue, 'This confession is of human institution; therefore it does not carry the authority of Christ.' The apostles instituted the practices of the church, doubtless in accordance with Christ's teaching. They instituted baptism, they instituted the episcopacy, but in accordance with the authority of Christ. And yet it cannot be denied that much in the practice of confession depends on the legislation of the bishops, namely, that we make our confession once a year, that we do so at Easter, that we make it to a particular priest because not every priest can absolve us from every kind of sin. These examples, I think, make it evident what a blatantly scurrilous attack this is, so far as my views on confession are concerned.

Moreover I say nothing in the work about fasting,[12] though fasting is something which we are encouraged to observe by the Gospels and the apostolic Epistles; rather I am concerned with the scrupulous choice of food, which is specifically rejected by Christ in the gospel and not infrequently condemned in the Pauline Epistles, especially where some Jewish superstition is concerned. Someone will say that this is to accuse the Roman pontiff of enjoining what the Apostle condemns. What the gospel teaches is abundantly clear. It is up to the pope to explain what he has in mind when he demands something which the gospel does not require. Yet no one says in my work – what may possibly be Luther's position – that episcopal constitutions do not render us liable to the charge of sin unless there is an

* * * * *

11 The shorter version (Allen Ep 1301:50) says simply 'in a bull.' Presumably the reference here is to the bull *Exsurge domine* against Luther (Ep 1313 n6).
12 See Ep 1300 n6.

element of contumacy as well.[13] Indeed the speaker in my work concedes
that a bishop is able to institute this requirement,[14] only he raises the   110
question whether it was the bishop's intention to lay all men equally under
an obligation to abstain from meat, meaning that anyone who did take it
would be liable to hell-fire, even if there is no wrong-headed contumacy as
well. And the character who says this in the *Colloquia* adds that he has no
more liking for fish than for a snake.[15] Moreover there are people who are so   115
constituted that fish is poison to them, just as you will find people who react
similarly to wine. If someone who is affected by fish in this way is prevented
from having meat or dairy foods, will this not be harsh treatment? Will
anyone want to make such a person liable to the punishment of hell if he eats
meat in response to the needs of his body?   120

If any pontifical or episcopal constitution whatever exposes us to the
penalty of hell-fire, the position of Christians is hard indeed. If some
constitutions bind us and some do not, no one is in a better position to make
his purpose clear than the pontiff himself. Such a clarification would be
helpful in bringing peace of conscience. But suppose the pope were to lay it   125
down that priests must wear a belt when they appear in public, do you think
it likely that he would have intended that anyone who left off his belt
because of pain in the kidneys should render himself liable to hell-fire? I do
not think so. St Gregory once laid it down that anyone who had had carnal
knowledge of his wife during the night should not enter church the   130
following day.[16] If someone had kept quiet about having intercourse and
entered the church simply to listen to the preaching of the gospel, do you
think he would have risked hell-fire? I cannot imagine that that saintly man
was so hard-hearted. If a husband were to eat meat with his ailing wife, who
could not otherwise be persuaded to eat and her health made it essential that   135
she take nourishment, surely the pontiff would not intend him for that
reason to be at risk of hell-fire? This question is merely raised in the book and
no positive statements are made. And certainly before the imperial edict it
was permissible to raise questions about these matters.

Furthermore neither in this work nor elsewhere do I simply condemn   140
episcopal indulgences,[17] although too much indulgence has been allowed

* * * * *

13 The opinion here attributed to Luther is not found in his writings. In the earlier
   version (Allen Ep 1301:60–1) Erasmus had asserted more confidently that this
   is 'what Luther teaches.'·
14 ASD I-3 228 / Thompson 603
15 ASD I-3 207 / Thompson 602
16 PL 77 1196 (*Register epistolarum* XI, Ep 64)
17 See Ep 1299 n16.

them hitherto. All that happens is that someone makes fun of a boon
companion because, though in all other respects a worthless fellow (for that
is how he is portrayed), he thought all the same that under the protection of
a papal bull he would get to heaven.[18] So far am I from thinking this heretical   145
that I believe nothing could serve religion better than to tell the public not to
put their trust in papal bulls, unless they take serious steps to change their
way of life and amend their corrupt affections.[19]

But, say they, the book makes a mock of vows of pilgrimage. Not at all:
the objects of mockery and protest are the men – and there is a large crowd of   150
them – who leave their wives and children at home because they have taken
some rash vow in their cups with a few boon companions, and go ranging
off to Rome or Compostela or Jerusalem,[20] though in the present state of
society I think it more religious to urge men to abstain from such vows
entirely rather than encourage them. And these, if you please, are the   155
outrageous heresies which this keen-eyed Lynceus[21] has detected in a
child's school-book! I wonder he does not go carefully through my poor little
Cato and my *Mimi Publiani!*[22] Can anyone fail to see that the origin of all this
is some personal vendetta? Though I personally have never done him any
harm, except that I have supported the humanities, which he hates worse   160
than death without knowing why. And all the while he prides himself that
he too has a weapon with which he can retaliate. If anyone across the
dinner-table calls him a fathead or a drunkard, he in his turn will proclaim in
his next sermon that the man is a heretic or a forger or a schismatic. I believe,
if his cook served up his meat overdone, he would proclaim in his sermon   165
next day that she was suspected of heresy. He knows no shame and no
repentance, though the facts have so often shown him up as a flagrant liar.

To begin with, look at the idiotic and crazy nonsense with which he
greeted my revision of the New Testament.[23] Then what could be crazier

* * * * *

18 See Ep 1299 n17.
19 At this point the shorter version (Allen Ep 1301:81–4) concludes with the
following paragraph: 'So much with reference to the rumour that has reached
me; when I have more certain knowledge, I will send a more detailed answer.
Now pray consider whether you can tolerate a man who is so distraught with
hatred for a fellow Christian that at the dinner-table and in the pulpit he calls
Erasmus a heretic on no better grounds than these.'
20 ASD I-3 147–50 / Thompson 4–7 (*De votis temere susceptis*)
21 The most keen-sighted of the Argonauts
22 See Ep 298 introduction.
23 Among other things, Baechem had proclaimed that the publication of
Erasmus' New Testament would inaugurate the reign of Antichrist; Epp
948:141–9, 1196:128–35, 598–613.

than the charges he hurled at Jacques Lefèvre and myself,[24] when it was   170
clear from the facts that he had no idea what I had in common with Lefèvre
and what our points of difference were?[25] What could be more brazen than
to accuse me in a public lecture of forgery and heresy because I had followed
the Greek texts in my translation and written 'We shall not all rise, but we
shall be changed?'[26] What could be more insane than the warning he gave in   175
a public sermon in Mechelen that ordinary people should 'beware of the
heresy of Luther and Erasmus?'[27] Need I now recall the words he hiccups,
rather than utters, after some gross meal, and all the occasions on which his
zeal for the Lord's house has had its source in liquor? In Holland the other
day he said that in the theology faculty at Louvain I was known as a forger;   180
so I was told by someone who was there and heard him. And when asked
why, he replied, 'Because he is constantly revising the New Testament.'
What a stupid thing to say! How often did Jerome revise the Psalter – and
does that make him a forger? And finally, if the man who through
inadvertence or ignorance makes a mistake in translating is a forger, that   185
man was a forger whose translation the church uses at the present day.

And what good does it do him to behave like this? All men laugh at him
as a blockhead, shun him as a madman, and shrink from him as a savage
whom they cannot deal with. They must inevitably sympathize with a man
he attacks so unpleasantly. Yet though no one can stand him, the one man   190
whose good opinion he cannot lose is himself. He seems to think there is an
imperial edict to the effect that he can use this virulent and insane language
to attack anyone he chooses. That is how this sapient and serious character
supports the cause of the orthodox faith. There is no zeal for God in this
hurting of the innocent; it is a madness from the devil. On one occasion there   195
was Jewish zeal in Phineas[28] which received high praise; but not so as to set
any precedent for Christians. And yet he killed those who were openly
heathens; in this man's eyes whatever he hates is Lutheran and heretical.
On this footing thin beer, watery wine, and a tasteless stew would be called
Lutheran, I suppose; and Greek, a language for which he has a special   200
dislike, no doubt because it was so greatly honoured by the apostles that
they wrote in no other, will be called Lutheran; and study of the poets,

* * * * *

24 See Ep 1192:56–9, 1196:614–23.
25 The controversy was over Erasmus' annotation on Hebrews 2:7; see Ep
   597:37n.
26 This accusation elicited from Erasmus the *Apologia de loco 'Omnes quidem'*; see
   Ep 1299 n2.
27 Cf Ep 1302:68–9.
28 Num 25:7–8

which he hates too, much preferring potations, will be Lutheran. He proclaims loudly that I undermine his authority, and that in what I write he is made a laughing-stock; but it is he who offers himself as a butt to all 205 educated and intelligent men, and that without ceasing. I reject his calumnies. And if educated men and good men have a low opinion of those who cast calumnies at one who does not deserve them, whose fault shall we say it is, the man who rejects what he ought not to accept or he who casts aspersions out of malice? If anyone were laughed at for asserting that 210 donkeys in Brabant have wings, it would be because he made himself ridiculous. He declares that the whole of Luther is to be found in my books and that they are full of heretical errors everywhere. But when those who read my books find nothing of the sort, they may know no logic but they can easily draw the obvious conclusion. He is authorized by the emperor.[29] Let 215 him therefore do his business in the spirit of the emperor, who would have those who do wrong corrected rather than punished, and at any rate has no wish to see the innocent suffer harm. He entrusted this office to a man he did not know; and when he learns what the man is like, he will without doubt recall the power entrusted to him. Neither the mildest of emperors nor the 220 most upright of popes is minded to see those who by their nightly vigils strive to adorn and improve the body politic abandoned to the resentment of such men as he, even if there has been some human error; much less do they wish to see good men and honourable men treated as strangers and driven into the opposite camp. 225

This is more your affair than mine. This man's character casts great discredit on your faculty, for the common folk judge you all by his example; wrongly, I agree, but men are like that. And not a few people are turned away from the study of theology by his brutality. I know that you dislike everything about the man, except for two or three boon companions[30] and 230 one sly fox[31] who uses this man's folly to further his own ambition. But your disapproval will not be generally understood until, since there is no controlling him, you throw him out of your society. This will be most difficult, I well know. Such people are not easily torn away from the delicious smell of meals rich, regular, and free. All the same it bears 235 directly on the honour of your order, which I quite rightly have at heart. Farewell.

* * * * *

29 Ie, as assistant inquisitor
30 According to Ep 1330:53–5, these would be Jacob of Hoogstraten (Ep 1299 n25) and Vincentius Theoderici (Ep 1196).
31 Probably Jacobus Latomus; see Ep 1330 n17.

1302 / To Pierre Barbier   Basel, c 14 July 1522

This letter, first published in the *Opus epistolarum*, is apparently incomplete. It is contemporary with Epp 1299 and 1300, which deal with many of the same topics.

On Barbier, see Ep 1294.

ERASMUS OF ROTTERDAM TO PIERRE BARBIER, GREETING
I wrote you a letter,[1] my incomparable friend, by Morillon, a truly open-hearted friend of mine, which will bring you up to date on the condition in which your poor friend Erasmus finds himself, for I am just about finished, if to be finished means to be face to face with death. I wrote to   5
you the other day[2] (but it was only a short letter) and addressed it to Rome, as it was not certain whether you were likely to be there. I always had a suspicion that Pope Adrian would not go to Rome either before the autumn or without the emperor.

As it is, you ought not to be left unaware of the fate that has finished off   10
a dependant of yours who has hitherto enjoyed your support. There was in the press here, apart from certain other things, my New Testament, revised and enlarged for the third time;[3] and although I had more than once had a cruel reception[4] in Germany, I was like a donkey, which is said to brave the heart of a fire to bring help to its offspring, and was no less anxious to come   15
to the help of my own work, even at the risk of my life; for it would undoubtedly have been ill-treated, had I not been on the spot. When therefore I was offered the company of a large party of soldiers who were returning home at that moment after being discharged by the emperor, I summoned up courage to risk the journey.[5] For in my country retreat at   20
Anderlecht I had recovered my health,[6] or rather, had somehow become young again, to such a degree that I could face anything with a certain

* * * * *

1302
1 The letter, mentioned in Ep 1287:46, was evidently sent with Epp 1273–6 to Morillon for delivery to Spain.
2 Ep 1294
3 See Ep 1174 n6.
4 Epp 412:1–10, 867:29–30; cf Ep 1274 n8.
5 For a discussion of Erasmus' reasons for leaving Louvain to return to Basel, see Ep 1242 introduction. For an attempt at a detailed reconstruction of the journey, based largely on this letter and on Ep 1342, see Allen's introduction to Ep 1242.
6 Cf Epp 1208:1–2, 1223, 1238:12–15, 1342:25–6.

amount of courage. Thus, as the wisest of men puts it, does a haughty spirit go before a fall.[7]

In this regard it was already most unfortunate that, when a sudden chance presented itself, I had departed without having had a talk with Jean Glapion,[8] whom I have found to be a true and sincere friend. He had wanted to see me, and I was extremely anxious to meet him; but when he called at my house I happened to be away in Antwerp, harvesting my annuity,[9] and in the mean time he followed the emperor, when he abandoned Valenciennes for the Tournai campaign.[10] And so, despairing of an opportunity for an interview, I set out for this place, consoling myself with the hope that once I had finished what I had in hand I might return to my native country before the emperor left it.

Whereupon, in Worms, I fell ill at once from the stink of the stoves.[11] That trouble was relieved by riding, and at Speyer I spent some days recovering as a guest of the dean of the cathedral.[12] Again in Basel, as a result of the smell of a stove, I was seized, not by the phlegm but by the plague pure and simple.[13] This trouble too was overcome by the force of nature. I smelled them a third time, and succumbed to a permanent headache, which was with me for several months. On top of this and even taking its place had come an attack of the stone,[14] which is so far from leaving me that it shows me less mercy every day. There is no end to it, and no time off; one birth follows close on another, and several are in gestation all the time. The process of giving birth often puts me in grave peril of my life, and the torment is such as to give me good reason not to fear death and often to envy sufferers from the plague or shaking fevers. A fortnight ago I almost died in bringing forth. It was an enormous stone; my appetite completely deserted me, and even now cannot be entirely restored. Altogether your friend Erasmus is nothing but skin and bone.

The result of all this was that, though I perceived it to be of the greatest importance for me to be present in Brabant before the emperor's departure, my health none the less made this impossible. I had got as far as Sélestat,[15]

* * * * *

7 Prov 16:18
8 Ep 1275
9 Ep 1273 n4
10 Charles' siege of Tournai began in September 1521. The city surrendered in November; LP III 1819.
11 See Ep 1258 n18.
12 Thomas Truchsess (d 1523); see Ep 355:50n.
13 See Ep 1256 n2.
14 See Ep 1267 n5.
15 See Ep 1273 introduction.

which is two days' journey; but a fever contracted from the hot weather forced me to return home; and even that I accomplished with difficulty after 55 staying four days with Beatus Rhenanus to recuperate. I did my business, however, as best I could by letter.[16] I easily guessed that Caracciolo and Aleandro,[17] who had been set against me by false accusations and wicked lies,[18] were campaigning against me in the emperor's court. And there was someone at court who was my bitter enemy; who it is, I have not yet been 60 able to detect, but I suspect he is a Spaniard,[19] and they say he has great influence over the emperor. But the paraphrase on Matthew[20] won me fresh support from the emperor,[21] with the timely help of Glapion, the bishop of Palencia,[22] and other well-wishers. For when the emperor was in England,[23] he was dining with the king, and, my name happening to come up, he spoke 65 of me in most honourable terms[24] and gave my labours high praise. And I know from definite evidence that the king of England is sincerely on my side.[25] Moreover the college of cardinals made it pretty clear that they support me when they published an order[26] forbidding the printing of a pamphlet by Zúñiga of which the title, accurately enough, was *Blasphem-* 70 *ies*,[27] and when it was printed secretly they forbade the sale.[28] The cardinal of Sion over and over again[29] offers me five hundred ducats a year from his private means, besides a sum for travelling expenses which is a compliment in itself. The cardinal of Mainz often writes to me in the warmest and at the

* * * * *

16 Epp 1273–6, and doubtless others as well
17 See Epp 1263:1–2, 1268:74–6, 1305:20–1.
18 See Ep 1263 n3.
19 See Ep 1268:77–8.
20 See Ep 1255.
21 See Ep 1270; also Epp 1305:21–2, 1314:5–6.
22 Mota (Ep 1273)
23 26 May–6 July 1522; Gachard II 32
24 Cf Ep 1342:289–92.
25 Cf Ep 1313:74–92.
26 Cf Epp 1305:8–9, 1306:27–9, 1312:10–14, 1314:6–7, 1341A:877–80, and LB IX 357A–C (*Apologia ad blasphemias Stunicae*).
27 Ie, Zúñiga's *Erasmi Roterodami blasphemiae et impietates* in the abridged form in which it was published; Ep 1260 n45
28 Leo X had forbidden the publication of the original, unabridged version (Ep 1260 n45). The Vatican Archives have yielded no documentary confirmation of Erasmus' repeated assertions (see n26) that the cardinals had placed a special ban first on the publication and then on the sale of the abridged form of Zúñiga's work; ASD IX-2 23 n95. However, it is clear from Zúñiga's own report that the cardinals had prohibited the sale of any of his books in Rome; CWE 8 346:9–13.
29 See Epp 1282:5–7, 1295, 1299:48–50.

same time most complimentary terms.[30] Nor do I see any danger at all   75
awaiting me, unless it be from a certain number of pseudo-monks.

As for Baechem,[31] I foresaw without difficulty what actually happened, that on the emperor's departure he would begin to play the bully as
usual. He began at once to declaim against me, and at Mechelen in a public
sermon he warned a large audience to be on their guard against the heresy of   80
Luther and Erasmus. In drinking-parties all over the place he maintained
that Erasmus is a worse heretic than Luther, and uttered dire threats of what
he would do if I were present. There is another man who attacks me more in
secret, but does more harm.[32] You, my dear Barbier, judge him by his
original character, which I also found agreeable, when he was still in a junior   85
position; but since he has felt the breeze of fortune in his sails he has become
so ambitious that even certain of the theologians cannot stand him, to say
nothing of all men of good will. For the religious spirit of the prince I have
nothing but the highest praise; but had he been sufficiently well informed
about the whole business he would not have entrusted a question of such   90
importance to a fool and a madman like Baechem and to a second colleague
very like him,[33] both of whom hate the classical languages and the
humanities worse than they would a snake.[34] The Carmelite[35] rages against
none so much as my supporters, and those who love good literature, or
those by whom he has been injured. He boasts that he is dead to the world;   95
but no one has a keener appetite for revenge.

X,[36] an excellent young man and a good scholar, was treated by him
with a tyranny worthy of Phalaris[37] because he once called Baechem a fool.
Raving mad as he was, he could not forget this, although in public they went
through the farce of a withdrawal. Another man[38] whom he had once let out   100
of his clutches he dragged back again and put in prison – and he one of the
best men in Antwerp; I think you know him. What their opinions on Luther
may be, I do not know; in my hearing, at least, they have never maintained
anything of the sort, but they have a lively dislike for certain Dominicans
and Carmelites, who do undoubtedly behave in such a way that every   105

* * * * *

30 No such letters from this period survive. Cf Ep 1299 n10.
31 Baechem (Ep 1254 n6); see Epp 1299–1301.
32 Probably Jacobus Latomus; see Ep 1330 n17.
33 Vincentius Theoderici (Ep 1196)
34 Horace *Epistles* 1.17.30
35 Baechem
36 Cornelis Schrijver (Ep 1299 n24)
37 Phalaris, ruler of Agrigentum in Sicily (570–554 BC), achieved proverbial fame
    for cruel tyranny.
38 Nicolaas van Broeckhoven (Ep 1299 n23)

right-thinking person must detest them. You would agree to the truth of
what I say if you were here in person. The Carmelite's fixed opinion is that
the movement must be stopped by severity. But while severity may perhaps
be used against those who defend Luther openly, we have no one like that
here. Dislike of the monks and of the see of Rome has won him some   110
support here among the common people universally and most of the leading
men. If this feeling is to be so severely punished, there are here and in my
own country twenty million people[39] who share these feelings, and all they
need is a leader. Behind an honourable façade this business is all mixed up
with a passionate desire to seize what belongs to others and an itch to settle   115
private scores.

1303 / From Juan Luis Vives   Louvain, 14 July 1522

> For the source of this letter, which answers one from Erasmus written on 16
> June (lines 38–9), see Ep 1256 introduction. Further clues to the contents of
> Erasmus' letter are found in Ep 1306.

VIVES TO ERASMUS
I have finished at last, thanks be to Christ, the twenty-two books of *De
civitate Dei*,[1] and the last five of them, which were still left, I send herewith by
the hand of this young man from Cologne,[2] together with a letter of
dedication[3] to the king of England, a preface, a note on the ancient   5
commentators, and finally another note on the Gothic ones. These four
pieces are to be placed at the beginning of the work, for they form a kind of
introduction. As for the preface itself, I have touched on a few points out of
the immense field of what we all owe to you;[4] and I only wish I could do this
with as much style and scholarship as I can with truth, and with the full force   10
of my own feelings. Please read all this before it is printed, and adjust
everything as you think best; please make additions and alterations at your
discretion, provided you do not reduce the scope of what I have said, or
there will be nothing left. And then, if there are any mistakes, not only in the

* * * * *

39 Cf Epp 1299:33 and 1300:90–1.

1303
1 See Epp 1256:108–17, 1271:3–67, and 1309.
2 Cf Ep 1306:2.
3 Dated 7 July 1522, Louvain
4 Vives praises Erasmus for his work on Jerome, Cyprian, and Augustine and
testifies to the great usefulness to him of Erasmus' library. This praise was
subsequently withdrawn; see Ep 1309 introduction.

Greek and the orthography but in history or mythology as well, or 15
philosophy or theology, or in the language, I entrust it all to you for
correction, being ready to approve any changes you may have made in the
work no less than if I had made them myself, and to think you have done me
a very great service, for you will have taught me something as well as
making my work better. The notes, such as they are, they will no doubt have 20
added in the margins, following the precedent I set in the first two or three
books,[5] or their own, for that matter, for they have more experience in these
things. It will then not be difficult to put together an index,[6] about which I
have already sent you another letter carried by Georg.[7] You must tell me
what you wish me to do about the book from Cologne,[8] since it will not be 25
much use to me in future, unless perhaps on a later occasion for a new and
revised edition of the same work. I should like to collate it afresh with
ancient copies of Augustine; please see that I am sent a full account of your
wishes in this regard. The whole question of finance I leave to your
judgment and Froben's. You know yourself that I am not greedy for money; 30
and yet one has to live in these very difficult days, and in a region where
costs are high and earnings non-existent[9] – such, at least, as are acceptable to
a civilized mind. If he sends me anything, let him take care to get it to me by
some reliable hand and without delay. I will say no more on this point for
fear you may suspect that I have changed my ways, to which you have 35
actually borne witness in print.[10] But mind you think of yourself as well: you
know what you lent[11] me when we were here together.

I now come to your letter, which I got I suppose three or four days ago
– the one you wrote on Trinity Monday[12] and sent me via Antwerp. For that
man of yours,[13] by whom you tell me to send my work, I have not seen, nor 40
has he reached here. Pieter Gillis[14] wrote to Conradus[15] that he would be
returning to you by a roundabout route and take longer than I thought in
present circumstances it was right to hold things up; nor is Karl,[16] who had

* * * * *

5 This was done.
6 No index was provided.
7 See Ep 1292 n2.
8 A manuscript of *De civitate Dei* procured by Erasmus at Cologne and said to be
    written in the hand of St Ludger (d 809); see Allen v 117.
9 Vives was apparently teaching at a school in Bruges; see Ep 1306:47–9.
10 See Ep 1082:28–61. Ep 917 was not published until 1529.
11 Eight gold florins (presumably Rhenish florins). See Allen Ep 1362:3–4.
12 16 June
13 Hilarius Bertolph; see Epp 1281 n29, 1306:5–7.
14 Ep 184
15 Probably Conradus Goclenius (Ep 1209)
16 Probably Karl Harst (Ep 1215)

said he was going to set out when Georg was here, clear enough when he
will go. So Conradus has engaged this man, Johann Andernach,[17] and come   45
to terms with him in the way I expect you will learn from his letter.
Personally I had no leisure to look for someone or to make any such
arrangements, being extremely busy revising and making a fair copy of the
end of my work and the introductions, and in poorish health[18] as well.

Of Zúñiga[19] I have heard nothing for some time; I hope you will have   50
plenty of support of the kind your hard work, your ability, your learning,
and your integrity deserve. I sent you Carranza's book[20] by Georg; but I see it
has reached you already. I will show part of your letter to Dr Joost[21] when I
have a chance, as I would have done even if you had not told me to. You tell
me to pass on a letter, I do not know which, to Mauritius;[22] but not having   55
seen your man,[23] I have equally seen no letter of yours except the one you
wrote me. I have no doubt that Pieter Gillis will have done what you told me
to do. Mauritius is away, in England. I send herewith two letters from W.
Thale,[24] who is very anxious to know whether you ever got the letter he sent
you in Lent.[25] My friends – and yours too – Cranevelt[26] and Laurinus[27] and   60
Fevijn[28] send you their greetings; so do Wouters[29] of the Council of Flanders
and my friend Ruffault,[30] who has not lost sight of your business[31] and
actually wrote to his father today on the subject. You can give the bearer of
this when he returns some volumes of the printed edition, if you think this a
good plan, for him to bring them to me. Please give my greetings to all your   65
friends in your part of the world, who by the same token are my friends too,

* * * * *

17 Presumably a professional messenger
18 Cf Ep 1306:9–13.
19 Ep 1260 n36
20 See Ep 1277 n8.
21 Perhaps Joost Vroye of Gavere (Ep 1347); or Joost Lauwereyns (Ep 1299)
22 Ep 1256 n32
23 See n13 above.
24 Ep 1224
25 5 March–19 April The letter is not extant.
26 Ep 1317
27 Marcus Laurinus (Ep 1342)
28 Ep 1317 n7
29 Jan Wouters, or Vaulterus (1484–1560), lord of Vinderhoute, near Ghent, and
   member of the Council of Flanders from 1509 until his death
30 Jérôme Ruffault, son of the treasurer-general (Ep 1287 n10) and a favourite
   pupil of Vives
31 The payment of Erasmus' pension from the emperor; see Ep 1273 n4, and Ep
   1306:49–51.

and above all to Froben and his household. Farewell, from Louvain, 14 July 1522.

I had two letters[32] from More a few days ago, in which he said he was in excellent health, heaven be thanked.

70

1304 / To Adrian VI   Basel, 1 August 1522

This is the preface to the *Commentarii in Psalmos* by Arnobius the Younger, which Erasmus was the first to publish (Basel: Froben, September 1522).

Unaware that there had been two Latin Fathers with the name Arnobius, Erasmus assumed that the author of the manuscript found at Frankenthal (lines 36–41) was Arnobius Afer (died c 330) who, as Jerome reports (lines 121–8), was a rhetorician at Sicca in proconsular Africa. Lactantius was his pupil. The real author, however, was Arnobius Junior, another African who c 450 was a monk in Rome, where he attacked Augustine's doctrine of predestination as heretical.

The new pope was an old friend and fellow-countryman of Erasmus (see lines 12–13 and n2). Born Adriaan Floriszoon of Utrecht in 1459, he became in 1493 professor of theology at Louvain, and in 1507 tutor to the young Prince Charles of Hapsburg. In 1516 he accompanied Charles to Spain, becoming bishop of Tortosa in 1516 and cardinal in 1517. Until his election to the papacy in January 1522, he remained in Spain as Charles' personal representative. Although Adrian was an academic theologian, 'not wholly well disposed to the humanities' (Ep 1311:18–19), he had always been personally well disposed towards Erasmus and his work. As bishop of Tortosa, he supported Erasmus against the Louvain theologians (Allen Ep 1581:484–90) and welcomed his New Testament, urging him to translate the Old Testament as well (Allen Epp 1571:46–8; 1581:291–4, 670–3). On the other hand, Adrian was also an implacable foe of Luther and had in 1519 applauded the Louvain theologians for condemning the Wittenberg reformer (Pastor IX 43). Consequently, Erasmus feared that Zúñiga and others in Rome and elsewhere who regarded him as an accomplice of Luther (see Ep 1260) might succeed in turning Adrian against him (Epp 1310:27–38, 1311:11–19). This fear was finally allayed by the receipt of Ep 1324.

TO OUR HOLY FATHER ADRIAN, SIXTH OF THAT NAME,
ROMAN PONTIFF NEWLY ELECTED, FROM ERASMUS OF ROTTERDAM,
GREETING
It was not difficult to foresee, most holy Father, with what an ostentatious

* * * * *

32 Not extant

outburst of delight Rome was likely to welcome the arrival[1] of one who is by   5
far the most popular of popes, and especially as she has now longed for so
many months for his arrival. And so I sought for some way in which, amidst
the rejoicing of so many thousands, amidst all those cheering and
applauding crowds, amidst the blare of trumpets and the thunder of
cannon, you might hear the small voice of a man of lowly estate and one   10
moreover who lives far off, and thus might recognize that your Erasmus was
not wholly silent; for just as he listened long ago to your teaching as a
theologian and admired you for your nobility of character,[2] so now he is a
humble sheep in the flock of which you are the apostolic shepherd. Thus did
Zacchaeus,[3] as a man of small stature, seek the support of the sycamore-tree,   15
that he might see Jesus and be seen by him. It would be truer to say, not that I
sought a way to do this but that it offered itself unsought. For the goodness
of the Lord Jesus (by whose special will it was, as all men are convinced, that
you were summoned to your present office) having promised that those
who have sought shall find,[4] offered me without my seeking an instrument   20
highly adapted, if I am not mistaken, for the performance of my duty of
congratulating you, and that too in no ordinary fashion. For he offered me
David's psaltery, making what is, I think, its sweetest music under the
fingers of a most skilled performer on that instrument, Arnobius. And if
blazing cressets and flaming torches contribute to the splendour of an   25
occasion, this instrument produces not merely animating notes that are
sweet in the ears of pious folk; it has its fire as well, it has its sparks of flame,
shining with Christ's own fire, which he came to spread over the earth. Such
a tribute is far more seemly for one who is truly a theologian and a most
upright pope; and so I doubt not that it will be far more welcome to a spirit   30
like yours than the sounding of trumpets, the crack of bronze artillery, or the
tumultuous plaudits of popular enthusiasm.

But enough of these tedious riddles; let me give you a plain statement
of the facts. About the time when the news that was so welcome to all ears
first reached us, that the overwhelming majority of the cardinals had   35
summoned you to that exalted position, the Roman see, I received from an
ancient community with an outstanding reputation for religious obser-

* * * * *

1304
1 See Ep 1294 introduction.
2 In 1502–3, when Adrian was professor of theology at the University of
Louvain; see Ep 171:15–16, and cf Epp 1311:16–17, 1324:113–15, 1332:70–1,
1338:20–1.
3 Luke 19:2–4
4 Matt 7:7; Luke 11:9

vance, which lies between Worms, capital city of the Vangiones, and
Speyer, capital of the Nemetae, and is commonly called Frankenthal,[5] a
commentary on the Psalms of David bearing at its head the name of
Arnobius.[6] The senders had no confidence that it would be welcome, either
because they found it thin in texture or because the style was unpolished
and the work seemed full of obvious grammatical mistakes. As soon
however as I had read two or three pages to get a sample of the work, I found
at once that this was not the unskilled utterance of some common scribbler
but a most artful artlessness and copious brevity; in the language indeed I
found an element that was mean and slovenly, but in the subject-matter all
was grand and brilliant. And as I got further into it, my admiration for the
work increased, so that I clearly realized what a distinguished treasure had
been offered me, only (to use Paul's phrase) in an earthen vessel.[7] I have
always been attracted, I confess, by purity of style, even in sacred authors,
and repelled by bad Latin; but I only wish we might be blessed with more
people who can write bad Latin about the mysteries of Scripture to the same
good purpose as this Arnobius can, with so much brilliance, so much
learning, such pregnant brevity and (last but not least) such true religious
feeling!

But I should be sorry if prejudice arising from the unskilful and in
many ways ungrammatical style of the book were to reduce its authority,
especially in the eyes of those who habitually measure the wisdom or
learning of a writer by his faults of style; and so, before I attempt to speak of
the merits of our author and his work, I should like to warn the reader in
advance that whatever grammatical errors he may find here arise not from
ignorance but intentionally, and should be ascribed not to the man but to the
age in which he lived. It is known that Arnobius was a celebrated teacher of
rhetoric even before he was initiated into the mysteries of our faith; the fact
that Lactantius was his pupil is enough to show how far from inarticulate
that man must have been as a teacher; and while still a catechumen he
published those notably well written books *Adversus gentes*,[8] following
Tertullian's example,[9] as Lactantius in turn followed his.[10] All this shows

* * * * *

5 A house of Augustinian canons eleven kilometres south of Worms, founded in
   1135
6 The manuscript Erasmus used is now part of the Palatine collection in the
   Vatican Library (Pal Lat 160:xc).
7 2 Cor 4:7
8 Seven books, known both as *Adversus gentes* and *Adversus nationes* PL 5
   713–1288 / CSEL 4
9 *Apologeticus adversus gentes pro christianis* PL 1 (Paris 1878) 305–604
10 *Divinarum institutionum libri septem* PL 6 111–822 / CSEL 19

that it cannot be ascribed to lack of skill that so many mistakes should be 70
found in this present work, especially as they are so obvious that scarcely a
Holcot[11] or a Bricot[12] could have made grosser blunders.

Yet this is no reason to suspect that our Arnobius is different from the
man whose *Adversus gentes* has such a reputation, not least for the elegance
of its style. The same man wrote our book, but he did not write it for the 75
same readers. The other work was meant for the educated public and this
one for the common people. It is known that in Spain, in Africa, in Gaul, and
in the other Roman provinces the general use of Latin was so widespread
that a man who preached in Latin would be understood even by cobblers,
provided the speaker adapted his language in some small degree to that of 80
the common people. This is made clear by certain sermons of Augustine and
by several disputations conducted by him before a public audience, which,
as that very fact proves, were not written out by Augustine but taken down
by shorthand writers, who included in their written report not only what
was said but what was done. If anyone wishes to have these pointed out 85
precisely so that he may test this for himself, let him read Augustine's debate
with Maximinus, and compare the opening of the discussion, which was
taken down by reporters,[13] with the end of the same work,[14] which he wrote
himself after Maximinus had withdrawn from the confrontation. Let him
read the two sermons[15] in which he clears up the scandals that were being 90
spread publicly about his clerks; let him read the speech[16] in which
Augustine designates the man who is to be his successor in accordance with
the popular vote and is to be his representative in less important business;
let him read the rhythmical composition against the Donatists,[17] which he

* * * * *

11 Robert Holcot OP (d 1349), nominalist theologian who taught at Oxford and
Cambridge. He had great interest in classical studies but no classical style. His
Super libros sapientiae (Haguenau 1494) was extremely popular all over Europe.
See Heiko Augustinus Oberman *The Harvest of Medieval Theology* (Cambridge,
Mass 1963) passim.

12 Thomas Bricot, a nominalist theologian trained at the University of Paris (DD
1490), where he taught until his death in 1516. He played a conspicuous role in
the proceedings of the faculty of theology, over which he often presided as
acting dean in the period 1506–16. He was the author or editor of many works
on logic and philosophy, several of which were designed to help students in
the faculty of arts master their Aristotle. See A. Renaudet *Préréforme et
humanisme à Paris, 1494–1517* (Paris 1916) passim.

13 *Collatio cum Maximino arianorum episcopo* PL 42 709–42

14 *Contra Maximinum haereticum arianorum episcopum libri duo* ibidem 743–814

15 PL 39 1568–81 (sermons 355 and 356)

16 Letter 213 PL 33 966–8 / CSEL 57 372–9

17 *Psalmus contra partem Donati* PL 43 23–32 / CSEL 51 3–15

wrote to be sung in public in the language that the public used. Anyone who   9
compares these with what he wrote for educated readers, the *De Trinitate* for
example or the *De civitate Dei*, will perceive without difficulty what a
difference there was between the language of the educated and that of the
unlettered multitude. Even in Rome itself, in the heyday of the language,
everyone did not speak as Cicero spoke. Even in those early days the   1
common people took certain liberties as of right, which were condemned by
the learned.

It may be asked how Arnobius, a man noted for his eloquence, took it
into his head to entrust this commentary to the language of the common
people. The first answer is that in the olden time nothing was nearer to the   10
hearts of the people than the Psalms of David: they gave the ploughman
something to sing at the plough-tail, the helmsman at his tiller, the sailor at
the oar, the digger at his trench, the weaver at his loom, and his wife at her
distaff; even children in arms longed to sing some scrap of the Psalms to
their nurses before they knew how to talk – so great was the love for this   11
divine music in the old days in every heart – and now the majority even of
priests are tired of it. And so Arnobius wished everyone to understand what
he perceived that everyone sang. He was moved to do this by Christian
charity, which tries to do good to as many people as it can. He thought that
to write bad Latin and be useful to the many was better than to win a   11
reputation as a writer from the chosen few. And this popular language was
no less intelligible to the educated, so that they too for their part did not lose
the benefit of an understanding of the hidden meaning; and he who has his
share of that ought not to clamour for the trappings of rhetoric.

I will add a second reason whose existence I suspect, which is in my   12
opinion plausible enough. St Jerome, in a sort of appendix which he added
to the chronicle of Eusebius of Caesarea, records that this Arnobius, while
still a pagan and teaching rhetoric to the young in the city of Sicca, was
driven by a dream to ask for baptism, and when he could not secure what he
wanted from the bishops (for they could not be brought to believe that he   12
genuinely wished to adopt a religion which he had attacked hitherto), he
wrote elaborate and fully argued books against his original religion, and by
giving these as hostages, as it were, made his peace with the true faith.[18]
Furthermore, in order to leave no suspicion in the minds of simple
Christians, who either hated or suspected the proud, ornate, and artificial   1
style of his earlier life, he divested himself in this commentary of all his noisy
rhetoric and brought himself down to the language of the lowest of the

* * * * *

18 PL 27 (Paris 1866) 497–8

people, in order to show that he was now wholeheartedly a Christian. For he undertook this task on the instructions of two bishops, Rusticus and Laurentius, as he tells us himself in his preface; and this he describes as an act of obedience, so that we may infer that he speaks as a catechumen or, at most, as a Christian of no long standing. And so anyone who considers for whom Arnobius writes this ought not to regard it as a blunder if he happens on something alien to the habits of more correct writers; it would in fact have been a blunder had he not so written. Suppose a man were to address the common people of Rome in our own day as St Gregory used to address them in the old days, when the popular language was still comparatively unspoiled; or suppose a man to address an audience of Spaniards in language not accepted by the common custom of that country; he would be rewarded with a twofold setback for his pains: first, his audience would not understand him, and secondly, he would give offence and be laughed at as a barbarian.

Thus the example of this author gives no support to those who, though they write for educated readers and in a language which in these days has nothing in common with ordinary people, yet expect actually to earn credit for the way in which the ineptitude of their style is surpassed by the ineptitude of their clever ideas. For the power of eloquence chiefly resides in the choice of subject-matter. Though even now a neat and simple style is not to be despised in a Christian author, provided the absence of rhetoric and claptrap is matched by an absence, on the other side, of meanness. For Arnobius would not commit the same blunders if he were writing today; he would either write in straightforward French, if he were writing for a French public, or in good Latin, if he were writing for educated readers. The language of the apostles, we may be sure, was the kind of thing in which they have given us the New Testament in writing. That was how wagoners and sailors talked then. Such was the language in which the books of the New Testament were first translated into Latin; and if there are blunders in them which nowadays offend an educated ear, they should be ascribed to the customary practice of those distant days rather than to the translators' lack of skill. In those days it was advisable to write like that, because one was writing for the common people; and in the same way it is folly now to parade one's blunders, which are no help to those who are not educated and a stumbling-block to those who are, and which obscure the meaning and reduce the influence the writer can exert.

In any case, since it is well known that popular usage corrupted the purity of the old Roman tongue, it is likely that different nations and different periods of time will have corrupted it in different ways. We find at least two things in this commentary which on the evidence of St Augustine

were as a rule wrongly pronounced in the popular speech of his own day. In his commentary on Psalm 138 Arnobius more than once writes *ossum* for *os*   1·
(the word which makes *ossis* in the genitive and *ossa* in the plural) and *floriet* for *florebit*, and does this in such a way that it is pretty clearly not an accident; and when he used the word *os*, he added '*ossum*, that is' as though explaining to the people what he meant. St Augustine mentions both words in the book he called *De doctrina christiana*. In chapter 3 of the third book,   18
where he is discussing words whose meaning is ambiguous, he says: 'Where the text reads *Non est absconditum a te os meum, quod fecisti in abscondito*,[19] it is not clear as one reads whether *os* should be pronounced with a short vowel or a long one. If one shortens it, it comes from the word of which the plural is *ossa*; if one lengthens it, one understands it as the singular   18
of the word the plural of which is *ora*. But such questions are settled by inspection of the text in the underlying language; for in the Greek the word is not *stoma* but *osteon*. In such cases the habits of popular speech are often a better guide to the meaning than the accurate language of the educated. I would rather they said *Non est absconditum abs te ossum meum*, though it   19
involves a blunder, than that the words should be less well understood because they are more like Latin.' Again, in chapter 13 of the second book, when discussing faults of language he says: 'Then there is that phrase which you hear from congregations when they chant the Psalms and which it is no longer possible to suppress: *Super ipsum floriet sanctificatio mea*.[20] It means   19
not one scrap less; and yet a more educated person who hears it would gladly have it corrected to make them say *florebit* and not *floriet*, nor is there any obstacle to the correction except the habits of people when they chant.' From these remarks we can infer that this commentary was written for Africans, and that it was written in those very early times.   20

It may perhaps be a good plan to point out a few other barbarisms, so that the reader, being forewarned, may take less offence when he comes across them, and may not alter them on the spot under the impression that the text has been corrupted by scribes. It is not rare for Arnobius to use *poenitemini* as a deponent. Often too he puts *tribulantes* for those who suffer   20
tribulation, not for those who inflict it; and in the same way *confundentes* for those who are confounded with shame, as though *tribulari* and *confundi* were deponent verbs and not passives. He constantly writes *hoc flos* and *hoc ros* as neuters on the analogy of *os, oris*. He constructs the verbs *careo* and *utor* with the accusative. He inflects *manna* with *mannae* genitive, as we do *Anna*,   21

* * * * *

19 Ps 139 (Vulg 138):15
20 Ps 132 (Vulg 131):18

Annae. Following the precedent of Greek he often uses a nominative absolute instead of an ablative, for instance in the commentaries on Psalms 114 and 84. Sometimes he adds a case appropriate not to the words he uses but to the verb which his phrase replaces, for example *memor esto apostolos* for *memento apostolos* in Psalm 88. In one passage he wrote *adtropare* for *per*   215 *tropologiam applicare,* the former being at that date, I suppose, the current rather than the correct usage. The word *paratura,* which is a speciality of Tertullian, you will sometimes find in him too; for though Tertullian was earlier than Arnobius, they were of the same race. Some things not unlike these are to be found in Augustine's books, especially in those which were   220 addressed to the public: *subdiacones* and *diacones,* for instance, and *baptismum* as a neuter.

I thought these points worth mention, to discourage anyone from underrating a work of scholarly as well as religious value on account of these faults of language and others like them, though they were so far from   225 seeming faults to the contemporaries for whom he wrote that he himself would have been thought illiterate had he written otherwise. By changes of phrasing and a few additions I could without much effort have transferred the credit for the whole work to myself. But, for one thing, to steal someone else's reputation has always been utterly foreign to my character; besides   230 which, Arnobius strikes me as a man who ought not to be deprived of his meed of praise among posterity.

We have lost the polemical work *Adversus gentes,*[21] which is well spoken of. Let this at least be the surviving memorial to a gifted man, of whom Jerome so often speaks highly. Yet this particular work is not   235 mentioned by Jerome in his catalogue of illustrious authors, the reason perhaps being that, as the book was designed for a popular audience, its circulation was confined to Africa, or it was too well known and too universally read to be thought by Jerome to need mentioning. Thus it is that excessive popularity has caused some things to be forgotten. This is no   240 doubt the reason why we are now deprived of the titles of the works of Origen; and a similar mischance would have left us in ignorance of the books of Tertullian, had not providence relented towards the cause of learning and lately brought to light some part of them.[22]

I will put forward a further indication from which, over and above   245 inferences from the style, one can gather that the writer is early. He refers, as occasion offers, to several heretics, Manichaeus, Novatian, and Arius, but to

* * * * *

21 Arnobius Afer's *Adversus gentes* (see n8 above) was first published in Rome in 1542–3 by the Vatican librarian, Faustus Sabaeus of Brescia.
22 In Beatus Rhenanus' edition of 1521, published by Froben at Basel

none later than the age of Arnobius.[23] For the rise of the Arian heresy clearly
belongs to that period, since he flourished under the emperor Diocletian
about the year 329 of the Christian era. Apart from that, he mentions neither   250
Donatists nor Pelagians, though both those pestilential sects arose in Africa;
the first of the two clearly took its rise after our author's death or in his
extreme old age, and the other is known to have come into existence in the
age of Augustine.[24] And yet our Arnobius in two or three places discusses
the freedom of the will, and he could not have failed to mention Pelagius had   255
Pelagius preceded him.[25]

    It has been shown then that the only features which might give offence
contain no element that should offend anyone; the author is warmly
recommended to us by no less an authority than Jerome, and the work itself
by its very early date; now for a few words of explanation of the qualities in   260
this volume which have so much filled me with admiration. In the first place,
it is generally agreed that among all the books of Holy Scripture none is full
of such recondite mysteries as the book of Psalms, and no other book is
wrapped in such obscurity of words and meaning. On such a subject to be at
once both brief and clear – and our author is both to a surprising degree –   265
seems to me the mark of a man with peculiar powers of expression, and
equally with a thorough understanding of the subject-matter. No one can
explain briefly what he does not understand; no one could expound such
obscure material so lucidly except a man very well versed in all the arts of
communication. Nowhere does he distract his reader with roundabout   270
prefatory matter and digressions, but all the time as a master of his craft he
'keeps up his speed, and in the heart of things / Plunges his reader as
though he knew it all,' as Horace says[26] in admiration of Homer. At no point
does he cite the testimony of Holy Writ for mere display; but his whole style
is skilfully put together like inlay or mosaic from scriptural elements, and   27.
often he weaves together several verses of the psalm he is expounding with
such skill that the addition of a few words enables him to throw light even on
what he does not expound, and sets them out in such a way as to produce a
continuous and coherent sense with its own power to please.

                    * * * * *

23 The putative author, Arnobius Afer (died c 330), was a contemporary of Arius
   (died c 336). Manichaeus (Mani) lived c 216–76, and the Roman presbyter
   Novatian (whom Erasmus calls 'Novatus') started a schism in 251.
24 Donatus started his schism in North Africa in 311. Pelagius first published his
   views in Rome before its conquest by Alaric in 410. Fleeing to North Africa to
   avoid Alaric, Pelagius there encountered the formidable bishop of Hippo.
25 A splendid example of the danger of the *argumentum ex silentio*; the real author,
   Arnobius Junior, was active in Rome more than a generation after Pelagius.
26 *Ars poetica* 148–9

He does something, again, which is a great achievement even when   280
the subject-matter is crystal-clear: he imparts instruction quite openly, while
at the same time fully retaining his hold over our feelings. His language
suggests more than it expresses, and as he speeds on his way he leaves in the
reader's mind plenty to think about and plenty to spur it into activity, so that
you cannot say which is the first effect he produces in you, understanding or   285
enthusiasm. This again is the hallmark not merely of a good scholar but of a
teacher who loves his subject. Should anything present itself that needed a
reference to some obscure passage in ancient history or to the work of
writers on natural history or other subjects, nothing is so abstruse in secular
or sacred literature that he cannot suggest it in a few words without any   290
ostentation or desire to show off the extent of his learning, a fault that I often
find tedious even in some writers of the highest reputation. His essentially
religious subject he treats with an almost apostolic plainness and singleness
of mind. He neither collects irrelevant matter nor ever forces the sense of
Holy Scripture; whatever he cites seems meant by nature for that context, for   295
in his quotations he has gone for quality, not quantity. Furthermore, though
he refrains from humour, which was excluded by the serious nature of his
subject-matter, you feel all the same that his style is suffused throughout
with some sort of continuous cheerfulness and charm. He himself is
nowhere dull or drowsy, and the liveliness of the writing cheers and   300
refreshes the reader. He opens in a way that gives one at once a fresh start;
he makes such good speed that sleep cannot overtake us; he ends by
sending us away still hungry and anxious to hear more.

Again, while in the works of Tertullian and Origen and almost all the
early Fathers there are elements either of manifest error or of dubious   305
doctrine, Arnobius as an author is so well balanced that I have never
observed anywhere what could be close to any heresy. For when he writes in
his commentary on Psalm 14, 'Jesus however, himself alone without taint,
entered the Virgin's chamber, and so freed the tabernacle itself from all taint
of the flesh,' he was not thinking of taint which might have been in Mary   310
before Christ's entry, but of that which was normally to be found in other
women, from which Christ preserved his mother unspotted; he did not
defile her chastity but reinforced it. He seems too to pay the church in Rome
the honour of supposing that anyone is outside the Catholic church who is
alienated from Rome, since Rome enjoys the headship of the whole church   315
and was found worthy to have Peter, prince of the apostles, as its shepherd.
That passage is in chapter 106 of the commentary and in the commentary on
Psalm 138. He teaches that some very special power was given to Peter by
Christ, whom he had thrice denied, meaning undoubtedly the power of
feeding his sheep. Vows are sometimes mentioned, but only those by   320

which, when we professed Christ in our baptism, we renounced the world
and Satan, not that I think he despised all other vows, but because he took
these to be the most important, as indeed they are. Nor do I doubt that in
these notes he derived some assistance from the labours of Origen, who
published more dense annotation on the Psalter than on any other book of   3
Scripture. For in several places he makes it clear that he knew Greek well.

All this time someone is waiting to ask me, 'What thanks do you expect
for yourself out of this, if you make no generous contribution of your own?' I
do not object if Arnobius gets all the credit, provided as much profit as
possible flows from this source to those in search of true religion. And yet it   3
is something to have made publicly accessible a book which was hitherto
obscure and which was even despised for its faults of style. It is something to
have got Johann Froben to the point of printing an unknown work at his
own expense and his own risk, for in the hazardous business of publishing
his types are not always equally fortunate. Lastly, hardly anyone would   3
credit how much toil it has cost me to correct the errors of the scribe, for
which purpose I often had to reread the whole psalm in hopes of scenting
out the reasons for the slip. I had to keep careful watch on the solecisms and
barbarisms characteristic of this work. In some places the problem fairly
called for some Delian swimmer[27] or, better still, a sibyl.[28] I will give one   34
example of this kind of thing. In his comment on Psalm 77 the scribe, losing
the thread, had copied down *quod aures in faciens*. These words being quite
meaningless, I tormented myself for some time, and then guessed the right
answer, that what had been written was *quod auxesin faciens*; for in many
scripts the letter *x* is in shape very like an *r*. And so a scribe completely   34
ignorant of Greek and knowing very little Latin had turned *auxesin* into *aures
in*. And on Psalm 105 the written text ran *Suscipiat regulam poenitentiae,
excluso nova ita ut centesimum quintum psalmum* etc, and I have restored by
conjecture *excluso Novato* or *Novatiano*; for both followed the same heresy
and would not admit penitents.   35

So this is a new work, and I dedicate it to a new pope, a work of religion
and theology to a pope who is himself a theologian of outstanding personal
religion. Your Holiness will, I hope, accept it the more readily inasmuch as I
have no ulterior motive in making this modest offering, for I am content with
my humble position in the world, slight though it is. All I want is to secure   35
your patronage for this work as it issues forth into men's hands; for of course
it will win a heavier harvest of piety if commended by the approval of one

* * * * *

27 Ie, a powerful swimmer, someone who would not be daunted by the book's
   difficulty; see *Adagia* I vi 29.
28 Ie, someone who can divine mysteries

who, like yourself, has been raised to that exalted station not by ambition or by any help from men but, as we all believe, by the will of a beneficent deity, to provide someone combining the greatest nobility of character with 360 supreme authority, who may eventually lay to rest these godless disorders in the Christian world that have been with us, alas, far too long and grow continually worse. We behold two of the world's leading princes at loggerheads[29] with enmity in their hearts, and scarcely any part of our world free from war, from bloodshed, and from pillage. And although the 365 Christian religion, which once had spread over all the regions of the world, is now less extensive than the narrow bounds of Europe, yet Europe too is pitifully torn asunder by perilous differences between sects and schisms. And all the time over our wrangling hangs the menace of the Turks.

With things in such a sorry state, the hearts of all men of good will are 370 filled by something like a mighty hope that even now the storm-clouds may be dissipated and clear shining and tranquillity return to us through you.[30] There is much else that promises us this, but above all your distinction as a man of learning and that nobility of character which all men have remarked on from your earliest years down to this present day; then there are your 375 advancing years, which will permit you to pursue no other goal except Christ's glory and the advancement of his true religion; last but not least the union of minds between you and the emperor Charles, whose power and authority will secure for you the ability to achieve what you judge will be for the best.   380

At any rate, to expel this vast contagion of moral corruption we need powerful spells, and some sort of enchanter, a master of his art, who can charm wisely. For this purpose I have provided almost a new weapon, not that the Psalms of David did not exist, but for most people they lay silent. It is a property, they say, of man-made music that it can either rouse the 385 emotions or control them if a skilled performer makes an appropriate use of specific harmonies. It is said that Timotheus could kindle the heart of Alexander of Macedon with warlike fire by playing in certain particular modes.[31] Pythagoras, by playing spondees in the Phrygian mode, trans-

* * * * *

29 See Ep 1283 n3.
30 Adrian failed in his efforts to restore peace between Charles v and Francis I; see Pastor IX, ch 5. Cf Ep 1353 n30.
31 The legend of Timotheus and Alexander was popular in the Renaissance (see, for example, Castiglione's *Courtier* 1.4) and eventually became the basis for Dryden's *Alexander's Feast*. Erasmus probably knew the story from at least three sources: Dio Chrysostom *Discourses* 1.1–3; Basil the Great *To Young Men, On How They Might Derive Profit from Pagan Literature* 8.7–8; and *The Suda* sv Τιμόθεος (T 620).

formed a young man mad with love and restored his sanity. A similar story   3
is told of Empedocles, who is said by the use of some particular musical
modes to have recalled to his proper wits a young man already beside
himself with rage and hell-bent on murder. The tales told in antiquity of
Mercury and Orpheus playing on the lyre look like fables; and yet these
fictions were inspired by the wonders music can perform. Certainly   3
Terpander and Arion in Lesbos and in Ionia are said by the historians to have
cured many serious diseases as a regular thing by the use of musical
harmonies. Ismenias of Thebes in Boeotia is recorded as relieving the
torments of many sufferers from gout in the hip with appropriate melod-
ies.[32] When Virgil says that 'the clammy snake in the meadows is burst by   4
the singing of spells,'[33] this might be ignored as merely the utterance of a
poet, had not our own Scriptures mentioned the charmer who charms so
wisely and the adder that will not listen.[34] David used his harp to come to the
aid of Saul,[35] whenever he was vexed by an evil spirit from the Lord.

If then man-made music has such power to change the affections of   4
both body and soul, how much more effective we must suppose this
heavenly and divine music to be in purging our hearts of spiritual diseases
and the evil spirits of this present world! Ambition is an overmastering
disease, ill will and jealousy are a most evil spirit; and the majority of
Christians are victims of this kind of plague, even those being often not   4
exempt whose duty it was to cure their fellow men. The pagans of old
possessed 'both words and spells,' with which they could 'of their
distemper lose the greater part, / And soothe the gnawing canker of the
heart.'[36] And surely Christ's music has words and spells with which we can
charm out of our hearts the love of things transient and charm into its place   4
the love of heavenly things. Pythagoras commanded musical modes
whereby he could recall to sanity a young man beside himself with
infatuation; and does not the Christian psalmist command modes whereby
he can recall to the love of peace the princes who are endlessly at
loggerheads in these most crazy wars? But we must first use this music to   4
cure ourselves before we attempt to cure other men's diseases. There is no
part of Holy Scripture that does not have these powerful modes at its

* * * * *

32 The stories of Pythagoras, Empedocles, Terpander and Arion, and Ismenias
   are all found in Boethius' *De institutione musica* 1.1. Basil the Great *To Young
   Men* (see preceding note) 9. 9–10 and Quintilian 1.10.32 also tell the Pythagoras
   story.
33 *Eclogues* 8.71
34 Ps 58:4–5 (Vulg 57:5–6)
35 1 Sam 16:23
36 Horace *Epistles* 1.1.34–5

command, provided that we do not stop up our ears like deaf adders for fear
that the strong magic of the divine enchanter may penetrate into our hearts.
But in my view no modes are more powerful than the music of the Psalms;   425
for in this book it was the will of that divine spirit to lay up a store for us of his
most secret and delightful mysteries, and in it he enshrined certain musical
modes of greatest power, by which we might be changed into a frame of
mind worthy of Christ, provided only that there is someone at hand who can
wake the strings of this psaltery with proper skill.   430

This is the special duty of bishops and priests; and yet every individual
might learn to play for himself. The spirit will help him as he plucks the
strings and will breathe secret power into his inmost parts, if only he
provides a pure and fervent heart – the ears, that is, with which a mind that
has been purified can listen. Oh that your Holiness might be our new David   435
– that consummate master of this kind of music! – who not only played
himself but taught many other singers to do the same. And David was a
prototype of Jesus Christ, our psalmist, who, when his body was strung like
a harp upon the cross, played nothing common, nothing earthly, but such
melodious music as the Father loves, the moving force of which we feel.   440
What harmony of the divine love sounded in that chord: 'Father, forgive
them, for they know not what they do'!37

The world too has its instruments, but their infernal notes return an
unlovely sound. How speak the strings of anger? 'Revenge and rapine, Cast
them out, Cut them down!' What tune does ambition play? 'On, on! extend   445
your realm, think not of oaths nor of religion when dominion is the prize.'
What twangling notes we hear from avarice! 'You see no man is happy save
him who has great possessions; by fair means or by foul get, get and pile and
keep!' How sound the chords of luxury and lust? 'Live now to please
yourself, for you know not what your portion will be after this life.' No less 450
discordant are the chords played by jealousy and spite. This is of course the
music of the world, which by such dreadful strains calls up pestilential
appetites within us, and like the Sirens lures us to destruction with notes as
sweet as they are fatal. This is the music that intoxicates and maddens us,
and so we fight wars, we raise rebellion, we are ambitious, greedy, wrathful, 455
and vindictive; we bite each other and are bitten in turn.

But it was heavenly music that inspired the man who wrote, 'How
amiable are thy tabernacles, O Lord of hosts! My soul longeth, yea even
fainteth for the courts of the Lord.'38 And again, 'My heart is like wax; it is

* * * * *

37 Luke 23:34
38 Ps 84:1–2 (Vulg 83:2–3)

melted in the midst of my bowels.'[39] Such were the harmonies whose power   460
had breathed upon the apostles when they said, 'Lord, whither shall we go?
Thou hast the words of life.'[40] Sweet and tuneful indeed is the concerted
sound when love, chastity, sobriety, modesty, and the other virtues sing
together in harmonious variety. And this music has different styles to suit
different themes. In some which, mournful though they are, are pleasing in   465
the ear of God, we lament our sins. Some give us strength and courage
boldly to resist the devil. Some are cheerful and full of joy, to use when we
give thanks to God for his goodness to us. Some are used to console and
comfort the afflicted. In a word, this life offers no kind of trouble that we
cannot easily endure, if, as St Paul puts it in his letter to the Colossians, we   470
instruct and admonish each other, with psalms and hymns of praise and
spiritual songs singing gratefully in our hearts to the Lord, and if, whatever
we do in word or deed, we do all in the name of the Lord Jesus, giving thanks
to God and the Father through the Son.[41] And this music will be the more
pleasing to God if performed by a numerous choir in harmony of hearts and   475
voices.

But to return to the Psalms of David, no man can appreciate how sweet
this music making is unless he has perceived its mystic meaning. What is the
reason, otherwise, why so many monks and priests find it so tedious to
intone these famous psalms? Surely because they sing them with their   480
mouths, not with their minds. And if any of them have no time to turn the
pages of long commentaries by other authors, such men, though hard to
please, will find Arnobius a help, for his note is often shorter than the psalm
itself, and if they read his brief disquisition they will have sung the psalm
and learned its meaning at one stroke. All priests should therefore take   485
special care to master once and for all what they sing every day. As a result
they will find more comfort in one psalm which they have learned to
understand and have sung with the mind, than in forty sung merely with
the mouth. Of one thing above all others our would-be psalm singer must be
perfectly convinced, that it was the purpose of the Holy Spirit, and a very   490
wise purpose too, to wrap up the mysteries of heavenly wisdom under these
layers of metaphor. The way to unwrap the mystery has been marked out for
us by Christ himself in the gospel and by the writings of the apostles.
Following in their footsteps, the orthodox Fathers have shown us the rest;
but none, in my judgment, in a more religious spirit than Arnobius. He is   495

* * * * *

39 Ps 22:14 (Vulg 21:15)
40 John 6:68
41 Col 3:16–17

specially concerned, it is true, to expound any sense which has a bearing on the gospel history, so that, in the words of the Apostle Paul, the knowledge of Christ may be confirmed in us all the more from faith to faith,[42] when we clearly see that whatever we read of as happening in the Gospels was foretold in the Psalms. This is indeed the most difficult aspect in the treatment of the Psalms, and those who have rightly understood it easily conjecture the other meanings even without outside help, once they have had some practice in the detection of mystic meanings. On this topic I have made some observations in the essay I have lately devoted to the interpretation of the psalm 'Why do the heathen.'[43]

But I must draw to a close. Most holy Father, there is this one thing which Christian people hope and expect of you more than all else. Take up Christ's psaltery and play on it some truly apostolic melody which can unite the hearts of princes and peoples in Christian concord, break up these dangerous conflicts of opinion, and fire with love of the heavenly promises those who are destined for the kingdom of heaven. I do not congratulate you on your exalted rank, I do not congratulate the country, and indeed the diocese,[44] which I share with you, which now for the first time has the privilege of providing a Roman pontiff. I have no ambition to advance my standing with you either by our common origin or by our long-standing friendship. But I certainly shall congratulate the Christian world if you fulfil your apostolic office (as I am confident you will) in such a way as to make the world understand that it has at last a Roman pontiff who puts Christ's glory first, who recalls the spirit of Peter and Paul rather than their titles, who does his duty as Christ's vicegerent in such a way that the world feels the spirit of Christ in him alive and active. The people will listen, I do assure you, to the voice of a true shepherd, and he who goes before them in Christ's footsteps will readily be followed by his flock; they will not hesitate to recognize the power of the apostolic see, when they know it stands for apostolic piety. As you attempt this task, may the Lord Jesus, chief shepherd of them all, grant you a favouring wind. Amen.

From Basel, 1 August 1522

* * * * *

42 Rom 1:17
43 Ps 2. Erasmus' commentary on this psalm was appended to the edition of Arnobius.
44 Utrecht

1305 / To Petrus Mosellanus Basel, 8 August 1522

Petrus Mosellanus was the name used by Peter Schade (c 1493–1524) of Bruttig on the Mosel above Koblenz. From 1517 until his death he taught Greek at Leipzig University.

The letter was first printed by J.G. Weller in *Altes aus allen Theilen der Geschichte* (Chemnitz 1760), one of the miscellanies that were so popular in eighteenth-century Germany. Weller did not say where he obtained the letter, and no manuscript survives.

TO THE HONOURABLE PETRUS MOSELLANUS OF BRUTTIG,
HIS INCOMPARABLE FRIEND, FROM ERASMUS, GREETING
I rejoice to hear of your new position, and the chance of seeing you will be a very great pleasure. You will perhaps have me as a companion on your journey,[1] for I am invited to Rome by lavish promises from the cardinals, 5 especially my lord of Sion;[2] yet I have friends who advise against it. Zúñiga is in Rome,[3] raving mad as any Orestes;[4] every month he spews forth a fresh pamphlet full of blasphemies.[5] He has been forbidden by a veto from the cardinals[6] to rant against your friend Erasmus. He has a boon companion, a theologian by the name of Carranza, to whom I am replying in such terms 10 that, if he has any sense of shame at all, he will not attack me a second time.[7] To Zúñiga's crazy pamphlet I reply in a tone of disdain: for the cardinal of Mainz wrote to tell me to answer the Spaniard.[8] He is a shameless buffoon and an ignorant blockhead. This monk is in Rome what Pfefferkorn[9] was in Cologne. I am not surprised to find someone as mad as that in Rome, but it 15 does surprise me that there should be people who think they need be afraid of a brawling rascal like this. Here my German fellow-countrymen are

* * * * *

1305
1 Mosellanus' proposed trip to Italy via Basel, mentioned again in Ep 1326:5–7, evidently never took place.
2 See Ep 1299 n11.
3 Ep 1260 n36
4 Orestes was driven mad by the Furies after he murdered his mother Clytemnestra.
5 Ep 1260 n45
6 See Ep 1302 n26.
7 See Ep 1277 n8.
8 The cardinal's letter is not extant; see Ep 1299 n10. He had evidently changed his mind on the subject of Erasmus' responding to Zúñiga; see Ep 1290:44–5.
9 Johann Pfefferkorn (Ep 487:22n)

wonderfully bold where moderation was called for, and wonderfully timid when the business needed determination.[10]

The Louvain people and certain monks, Aleandro and Marino,[11] have 20 made desperate moves against me, but so far in vain. I have the emperor on my side, as I know quite for certain, and the king of England, and in Rome nearly all the cardinals.[12] But they would all like me to attack Luther; and I, though I do not approve this Luther business, have many reasons all the same why I would rather do anything than make this my concern. Yet there 25 are members of Luther's party who make far worse mistakes than Luther himself. I can see that there is no doing business with either side. I should be sorry, if it could be avoided, to see the good things in Luther destroyed on account of some bad things; and those on the other side cannot fairly be compared with him. 30

Of your translation[13] I could form no opinion without comparing the texts, and for this I simply had no leisure; even now I have no time to spare. When I am allowed any leisure, I will not fail to do my duty. The rest we will speak of when we meet. Farewell.

Basel, 8 August 1522 35

1306 / From Juan Luis Vives   Louvain, 15 August 1522

For the source of this letter, see Ep 1256 introduction. The content is closely related to that of Ep 1303, which was written a month earlier.

FROM VIVES TO ERASMUS

I am in great anxiety, and shall remain so until I learn whether the rest of the book reached you safely. I sent it by a young man from Cologne,[1] as Conradus[2] advised, on 15 July, because Karl[3] had decided differently about his leaving from what he had said when Georg[4] was here. Nothing is left to 5

* * * * *

10 See CWE 3 xii and the index to that volume under 'Germany, Germans.'
11 Aleandro (Ep 1256 n11) and Marino Caracciola (Ep 1263 n1)
12 See Ep 1302:62–71.
13 The reference is probably to Mosellanus' translation of Gregory Nazianzen's *De theologia libri quinque* (Basel: Froben 1523), the preface to which is dated 13 June 1522.

1306
1 See Ep 1303:2–4.
2 Probably Goclenius, as in Ep 1303:41 and 45. Cf line 30 of this letter.
3 See Ep 1303:43–5.
4 See Epp 1292 n2 and 1303:23.

be sent with Hilarius,[5] whom I have not seen yet; they say he has gone to
Antwerp, and will be back shortly. I plan to send this letter by him; as I write,
I am not wholly recovered or well again, but rather more free from pain than
I was a few days ago. Ever since I finished Augustine, I have never been as
well as I could wish;[6] last week and this week, my whole body has been   10
much afflicted and my energy borne down by a kind of weariness and
weakness – it feels as though ten steeples were resting on my head with
unspeakable weight and pressure more than I can bear. This is the reward of
all my labours, the recompense for the splendid work I have done; of what
avail now the service and the toil? What you say about the mother of a   15
new-born child fits me so neatly, that now that Augustine has been out of
my hands for three days, I have begun another book.[7] 'So true is it,' you will
say, 'that work is what feeds the mind';[8] but believe me, I need to spend two
or three whole months regaining my mental vigour, so that I can recover it
by rest and idleness like a fallow field.   20

I long to see how you have answered Carranza,[9] and the other things
you are said to have written where you are now, which are so particularly
numerous and important. About Carranza I was clearly wrong; I had been
imposed upon by the pretence in his letter,[10] which was the only part of his
whole work that I had read. Your letters to More and to the archbishop of   25
Canterbury I sent off to England today;[11] they will get them soon, for many
people now return to England every day from the Antwerp fair. I rejoice to
hear that you have the support of their Eminences,[12] and that they are so
much in favour of your genius and your learning – if it is true, as I was told
by someone here who had it from Conradus, about this offer of an annuity,[13]   30
which is a great honour. I wonder you grudge a keen admirer like myself the
pleasure of knowing this, for I am the one person you never write to with
news of this kind – as though I should enjoy it less than other people or, if it
had to be concealed, I could not keep a secret. However that may be, I shall

* * * * *

5 Bertolph; see Ep 1303:39–41.
6 Cf Ep 1303:49.
7 Perhaps the *De institutione foeminae christianae*, which was completed in April
   1523 but not published until 1524 (Antwerp: M. Hillen)
8 Ovid *Ex Ponto* 1.4.21–2
9 See Ep 1277 n8.
10 Ie, in the letter to Juan de Vergara, 27 December 1521/2, which served as the
   preface to Carranza's book against Erasmus (see the preceding note)
11 Neither letter is extant.
12 Ie, the college of cardinals, who had banned the publication of Zúñiga's book
   against Erasmus; see Ep 1302:68–71.
13 Cardinal Schiner's offer; see Ep 1299 n11.

rejoice at all your promotions and at every success worthy of what you   35
deserve, however I come to hear of it; I would rather hear from you, for the
more certain the news, the more certain my joy.

I do in fact need money, but I shall approve whatever you and Froben
decide;[14] if you send me something, the two of you, give instructions for it to
be remitted as soon as possible. If you wish to write to Vergara,[15] send it to   40
me here. Next month I think of crossing to England. If you have any
commissions for me, write to me by way of X[16] when he returns from the
Frankfurt fair. At the same time I beg you to send me by the same hand some
letters of introduction[17] to your friends there, so that at least they may know
that I am a friend of yours and make more of me accordingly; though I do not   45
plan to stay there more than three months or four at most – about which I
think I spoke to you at Bruges[18] – I am so tired of teaching that I would do
anything rather than return to this dreary life and have schoolboys for
company. Ruffault sends you his warmest greetings; he says he will soon be
seeing his father, and will make sure when he meets him that this payment   50
to you is not delayed any longer.[19]

Here all is peace. There is a surprising silence on all subjects; all men of
good will support you more warmly than ever. Many of the old croakers
have fallen silent, and those who croak still will be silenced by death. I hope
you will live to see men's feelings towards you become such as what you   55
have done for them deserves, and to behold your own spiritual heirs; those
are the days for which you ought to preserve yourself. For he[20] told me that
you are damaging your health by excessive study. Here all your friends are
longing for you with impatience, and we pray God that he will restore you to
us safe and sound.[21] We make ready for battle here with more spirit than we   60
show in actual fighting;[22] and would that we showed less on both sides!
Some thousands of Spanish troops are said to have landed in England to be
absorbed into the English ranks.[23] Great things are expected of the new

* * * * *

14 As payment for Vives' work editing the *De civitate Dei*; cf Ep 1303:29–30.
15 See Ep 1312.
16 Probably Franz Birckmann; see Epp 1254 n3 and 1256:145–6.
17 One of these, Ep 1311, survives.
18 Presumably during Erasmus' visit there in August 1521
19 See Ep 1303:62–3.
20 Presumably the informant mentioned in lines 29–30
21 On Erasmus' intention to return to Louvain, see Ep 1257:12.
22 In June 1522 Charles v and Henry viii had, at Windsor and Waltham Cross,
   signed treaties committing them to a joint assault upon France; LP III 2333,
   2360.
23 There was no truth in this rumour.

pope. So far he has been a disappointment; but people think he will warm up at this meeting with the emperor, who landed on the coast of Cantabria on 16 July.[24] I fear he will remember, not so much that he is now pope as that he was once the emperor's subject,[25] so that the weight of the authority he used to recognize may drag him to side with the emperor. If only he will bear in mind what he is now and not what he was, there is good hope of peace.

But this we must leave to fate. As to Schrijver[26] and other things, I suppose that you hear from Pieter Gillis[27] and others who know about them. For I am always buried at home and hear nothing; or I hear so late that the news reaches you faster than it does me. In these last few days of the vacation Clava[28] has paid us a visit from Ghent, simply to attend lectures from some Greek or other. What an industrious old man he is! – and we younger men sleep and are not ashamed. Farewell many times over, my beloved teacher.

Louvain, feast of the Assumption 1522

1307 / From Johannes Gallinarius   Breisach, 15 August [1522]

The autograph of this letter, with the address-sheet missing, is in the Rehdiger Collection of the University Library at Wrocław (MS Rehd 254.42). The letter was first published as Ep 158 in Enthoven.

Johannes Gallinarius was the name taken by Johannes Henner or Henlin of Heidelberg, a kinsman of Wimpfeling. Educated at Heidelberg (matriculation in 1495), he later moved to Strasbourg, where he became involved in publishing. Still later he became a priest. At the time he wrote this letter, which is all that survives of his correspondence with Erasmus, Gallinarius was parish priest in Breisach, a post he had assumed in 1516. The last historical trace of him is a letter to Beatus Rhenanus of March 1525 (BRE Ep 446).

Greetings and best wishes. If your health,[1] dear Erasmus, father of learning,

* * * * *

24 At Santander; Gachard II 66
25 As a Dutchman, Adrian had been the subject of Charles of Hapsburg, the future emperor.
26 See Epp 1299 n24 and 1302:97ff.
27 Ep 184
28 See Epp 175:13n, and 301:39n.

1307
1 Gallinarius had witnessed the breakdown of Erasmus' health during the latter's aborted journey to Brabant in the previous spring. See Ep 1273 introduction.

is on the mend, as I learned from your letter, I am delighted – so much delighted that it makes me reckon myself too in good health. And so, to give me my due, please share my delight with me. Only the day before yesterday I got a work in several books[2] by his most serene and at the same time most   5 intelligent Majesty your friend the king of England, attacking Martin Luther, which maybe you have seen already. The great joy it gave me I can hardly describe, especially as issuing from such a most noble prince against a man at whom not one of our better scholars either could or would let himself go. I believe this was the will of heaven. It is as if that lofty debate   10 which has for so long disrupted the peace of Christendom demanded none but the highest protagonists, the subject of his book required the greatest theologians, and the writing of it were a proper task for a noble and lively mind: all these qualities, united and in good measure, have now, as it seems to me (for I have read the book right through), found a worthy representa-   15 tive in this one most illustrious king. If only our German satraps would regard this prince as the pattern they should follow – and our bishops too, and theologians and monks of this description, our grand doctors of divinity and ordinary mass-priests – it would be greatly to the benefit of Christen- dom. By his brave onslaught on Luther's basic position, his untiring   20 demolitions, his well-thought-out refutations, this most intelligent monarch has earned all the more credit from Christendom, if we think how few theologians have appeared, though they have most to gain from cutting this hydra in pieces, who have the learning and wisdom to attack the man. In short, in this secular prince I see a combination of theology and eloquence   25 which in our countries is a rare bird[3] indeed. But a prince of such gifts has no need of me to spread his name. You, dear Erasmus, greatest of men, you are very near to him, you are his friend, you know his genius well; and so it has been a pleasure to speak of him to you at undue length, for I am a passionate admirer of you both.   30

The printer has struck him off in very poor type unworthy of the distinguished subject-matter. They have added, I see, two of your letters;[4] and all this will give you, I suspect, no great satisfaction. There is one request I would like to make, my most learned friend: that in view of my most sincere and genuine devotion and affection for you you would some   35 day write and tell me your opinion of that prince. So I send you a copy of the

* * * * *

2 See Ep 1275 n25.
3 Juvenal 6.165
4 Epp 1219, 1228. These were included in the edition published by Johann Grüninger at Strasbourg on 9 August 1522 and in another edition from the same press the following month.

book, using a prince for whom I know you have a great regard as a courier to convey my greetings.

I gave our friend Rhenanus[5] a stinging rebuke yesterday for writing so seldom to Erasmus, and hope he will soon reply. And now I have no prayers 40 and wishes, except that I may keep my own health long enough to see Erasmus our glory achieve in health and wealth the age of Nestor;[6] and I assure him that I am most sincerely his. Farewell, from Breisach, on the feast of the Assumption of the blessed Virgin.

Your disciple and faithful servant, Johannes Gallinarius, pastor of the 45 church of Breisach

1308 / From Wolfgang Faber Capito   Mainz, 17 August 1522

The autograph of this letter (=Förstemann/Günther Ep 9) was in the Burscher Collection at Leipzig (Ep 1254 introduction).

On Capito, see Ep 1290.

Greeting! All sorts of stories are spreading about you. Be careful, while you try to keep on good terms with both factions, not to get yourself disliked by both; for I scent something of the kind. The more sagacious members of the papal party detest you as the source and origin of the trouble; to Luther's men on the other hand you are anathema as a deserter from the right side. 5 Hoogstraten[1] in Cologne condemned your writings long ago, I know not which. At Wittenberg to show their contempt they do not yet mention you in what they write; but I fear that your too outspoken letter[2] to Duke George of Saxony will make you the target of many pens. Luther has written a bitter and most abusive answer to the king of England.[3] If we of the papal party 10 were not pretty foolish and at such odds with the truth, the world would never stomach such virulence in attack. Up to now they have tried the pen; we are already nearing the use of force. Feelings are getting up, in the

* * * * *

5 Beatus (Ep 327) was apparently summering in Sélestat; see the address on BRE Ep 224 (=Zw-Br Ep 222) of 30 July.

6 Ie, great old age. Nestor, king of Pylos, ruled over three generations of men; see *Adagia* I vi 66.

1308
1 Ep 1299 n25
2 Ep 1125, which had just been published in the *Epistolae ad diversos*
3 In the summer of 1522 Luther replied to King Henry's *Assertio* (Ep 1275 n25), first in German (*Antwort deutsch auf König Heinrichs von England Buch* WA x-2 227–62) and then in Latin (*Contra Henricum regem Angliae* ibidem 180–222).

direction of battle and bloodshed; there is such a fever of plotting, so much
forming of alliances; and everywhere Christ the author of peace is the   15
pretext. I long for the old security. I am no longer out of bowshot,[4] being
caught in the service of a prince who thinks more highly of me than I could
wish. So much has the court, that necessary evil, tied my hands. In any case,
the prince cannot stand that blockhead Hoogstraten. He commissioned me
to encourage you to despise a grubby, grovelling opponent, who can bark at   20
your heels, but cannot get his teeth into your reputation. He read your
paraphrases on Matthew[5] most attentively, and says he never read anything
that had more kindled his love towards Christ. He wished me to ask you on
his behalf to devote the same care to explaining John.[6] I have no time now to
write more on this. Please let me have an answer.   25

Farewell, from Mainz, 17 August 1522. Capito

Johannes Oecolampadius sends his greetings;[7] so does my friend
Hedio,[8] who is a powerful screecher – preacher, I should have said. You will

* * * * *

4 During his tenure at the archiepiscopal court of Albert of Brandenburg in
  Mainz, Capito tried to play a mediating role between Luther and his enemies in
  order to prevent religious conflict and thus preserve an atmosphere congenial
  to the humanist programme of enlightened piety. Capito did much, for
  example, to frustrate Aleandro's attempts to secure the enforcement of the
  Edict of Worms against Luther. But when, in the winter of 1521/2, Capito tried
  to restrain Luther's opposition to Archbishop Albert's resumption of the sale of
  indulgences, Luther denounced him for indifference on vital questions of right
  and wrong. In March 1522 Capito made his way to Wittenberg to receive
  pardon. The process of his conversion from humanist into Protestant, which
  took about a year, had commenced, making his position in Mainz increasingly
  uncomfortable. See James M. Kittelson *Wolfgang Capito: From Humanist to
  Reformer* (Leiden 1975) 50–111.
5 See Ep 1255.
6 See Ep 1333.
7 Since leaving Altomünster (see Ep 1258 n4), Oecolampadius had been living at
  the castle of the Ebernburg (southeast of Mainz), serving as chaplain to Franz
  von Sickingen (Ep 1342 nn33–4), an early and enthusiastic supporter of the
  Reformation. At the Ebernburg, Oecolampadius had joined with Martin
  Bucer, the future reformer of Strasbourg, in the introduction of vernacular
  readings from Scripture into the traditional Latin service. In August, Sicking-
  en's invasion of the archbishopric of Trier touched off the Knights' Rebellion,
  which ended disastrously in the spring of 1523. Meanwhile, in the autumn of
  1522, Oecolampadius moved to Basel, where the atmosphere was more
  congenial to one of his pacific and scholarly temperament.
8 Caspar Hedio was the name taken by Kaspar Heyd (1494–1552) of Ettlingen
  near Karlsruhe. He matriculated at Freiburg in January 1513, took the MA in
  1516, and in April 1519 commenced theological studies at Basel, where he
  became closely attached to Capito and was on intimate terms with Erasmus'

see everything now poised on the edge of a precipice. It must soon tilt
without a doubt, one way or the other, the whole thing.   30

To Erasmus of Rotterdam, first of theologians, glory of the world, his
beloved teacher. In Basel

1309 / To the Reader   [Basel, c August 1522]

This is a letter that Erasmus contributed to Vives' edition of Augustine's *De
civitate Dei*, published in Basel by Froben in September 1522. Written after all of
Vives' introductory material had been received (see Ep 1303), the letter was
printed on the verso of the title-page. Only an approximate date can be
assigned.

Vives' edition of the *De civitate Dei* was intended to form part of a new edition
of Augustine more complete and correct than that published by Johann
Amerbach in 1506. Froben had proposed the undertaking to Erasmus in 1517
(Ep 581:22), and by the following year Erasmus was at work on it (Ep
844:275–6). But in 1519 Augustine was laid aside in favour of Cyprian (Epp 975,
984, 1000). By September 1520 Erasmus was again at work on Augustine (Ep
1144) and made steady progress for about a year (Epp 1174, 1189, 1204, 1212,
1218) until the move from Louvain to Basel in November 1521 and the
completion of the third edition of the New Testament (Ep 1174 n6) caused
further delays.

Meanwhile, the immensity of the task of editing the whole of Augustine
anew made Erasmus decide to divide it among a number of scholars (Ep
1341A:1417–40). In the autumn of 1520 Vives agreed to undertake *De civitate
Dei* and by the following summer could report considerable progress (see
Ep 1222:28–30; see also Epp 1256, 1271, 1281, 1303, 1306). The immense
popularity of Augustine's great apologetic treatise in the early days of printing
– two dozen editions before 1496, not counting translations – doubtless played
a role in the decision to publish it in advance of the rest of the edition.

When the complete Augustine in ten volumes was finally published in
1528/29, *De civitate Dei* appeared as volume 5. The last of the volumes actually
to go to press, it was printed as plain text, without Vives' prefaces or notes.
This was probably the result of the printers' original desire to omit *De civitate
Dei* from the edition on the ground that it had not sold well (Allen Epp

* * * * *

circle. In October 1520 he followed Capito to Mainz, where he was appointed
cathedral preacher. In 1523 he followed Capito to Strasbourg, where he
became preacher at the cathedral and a member of the circle of Strasbourg
reformers. Despite his adherence to the Reformation, his relations with
Erasmus always remained amicable.

1531:36–7, 1889:15–16). When it dawned on them that this was hardly possible in a collected edition, they evidently decided to repair the omission by printing the bare text in 492 pages instead of the 810 annotated pages of 1522. When a revised edition of Augustine (based on the Froben edition) was published by Chevallon at Paris in 1531, *De civitate Dei* was published with all Vives' notes and with a new preface in which Vives' eulogy of Erasmus (Ep 1303 n4) was cut down to a brief formal acknowledgment. Thus the mistreatment of Vives in this matter may have caused some temporary bad feelings between him and Erasmus, although there is no evidence of it in their surviving correspondence.

ERASMUS OF ROTTERDAM TO THE READER, GREETING

Importunate requests[1] from the learned have assailed me for some time with the demand that I should do for the entire works of St Augustine what I had done for Jerome's letters.[2] I knew already by experience that no labour is more wearisome or brings less credit and popularity to the man who   5
undertakes it, and I was further deterred by the immense size of the undertaking; but none the less I had begun to turn my unwilling and reluctant mind in that direction. The plan of the whole work which I had formed ran as follows.[3] I had allocated first place to his practice-pieces, those, that is, which he wrote as a catechumen; the second place to the   10
letters, many of which he wrote while still a young man, and which therefore are even more redolent of the study of rhetoric. Third place was reserved for the theoretical or contemplative works, which contribute to the kindling of our minds with love for the things that are eternal, in which class fall his *Confessions* and the *Soliloquia*. To these I should have added the books   15
which relate to the right ordering of life. The fourth was destined for the didactic works, those, that is, in which he teaches the science of theology, in which class fall the books *De doctrina christiana* and *De Trinitate*. The fifth would have contained the controversial pieces, in which he combats various plagues in the way of heresiarchs; and their arrangement would have been   20
dictated by the dates at which the heresies arose and kinship between their errors. For in this department he wrote a great deal, including his *De civitate Dei*. The sixth would have displayed the exegetical works, in which he expounds the books of Holy Scripture, which I was intending to arrange

* * * * *

1309
1 See, for example, Ep 922:39–50.
2 See Epp 326, 396.
3 This scheme is reproduced in the *Catalogus lucubrationum* of January 1523 (Ep 1341A:1419–37), but was not followed in the actual edition of 1528/9, which was expanded to ten volumes.

according to the order of the books of the Bible upon which he comments.   25
For instance, the commentaries on the Psalter would have preceded the
commentary on St John's Gospel, and the gospel commentary would have
come before that on the Epistle of the same apostle, and so with the
remainder. The seventh would have pointed out the doubtful and spurious
pieces – those, that is, concerning which one might well doubt whether they   30
are Augustine's, and then those which are falsely ascribed to him. I also
intended to point out those books which have succumbed to the assaults of
time. The Greek I should have restored. Errors, introduced by the fault
either of scribes or of men with little learning trying to correct what they did
not understand, I should have removed, with a full sense of responsibility,   35
and not without the help of ancient and correct copies,[4] of which I had
already got together for the purpose several which would seem to have been
written in Augustine's own day.[5] The entire work, in view of its immense
size, I had decided to divide among a number of scholars, men who would
be equal to the task, but so as to provide that each of them would be sure of 40
receiving his own share of the credit without deduction. For this generation
of ours includes a great number of men born under happier auspices than I,
who can achieve in this department more than I can.

By these means I was hoping to secure that Augustine, the saintly and
scholarly Augustine, should henceforward reach a larger public, who would   45
also read him with more profit, as has clearly happened with the works of
Jerome – so clearly that even my enemies cannot deny it. Yet when certain
brethren of the Dominican fraternity got wind of this audacious enterprise,[6]
it was not only at drinking-parties, but even in public sermons that clamour
broke out: it was insupportable, and a thing that public opinion could no   50
longer stand, that Erasmus should now proceed to correct the text of
Augustine as well, of whose works he did not understand one jot. They
even called it heresy to assert that there could be anything in the great man's
books that was erroneous or spurious or misunderstood by theologians. For
my own part, I have never claimed to be an expert in the rare science of   55

* * * * *

4 Vives' was the first of the early printed versions of *De civitate Dei* to indicate the
  manuscripts used. He had used three: one procured by Erasmus from
  Cologne, said to date from the eighth century; one lent by Marcus Laurinus (Ep
  1342) from St Donatian's at Bruges; and one shown Vives by the Carmelites at
  Bruges. See Allen's introduction to this letter.
5 This estimate is probably no more accurate than Erasmus' later statement that
  the twelfth-century Codex Reuchlini (used in his edition of the Apocalypse)
  appeared to have been written in the apostolic period; see his annotation to
  Rev 3:7 (*Qui aperit, et nemo claudit*) LB VI 1097–8 (added in 1527).
6 Cf Ep 1271 n6.

theology, and yet I do not have so low an opinion of such brains or learning as I may possess as to think that I understand nothing that Augustine wrote, when these potbellies, born for the plough-tail rather than the study, understand it all. The truth of this, dear reader, you would readily accept, if I gave you the names of three or four who are continually pouring out this kind of rubbish, in Louvain and Cologne especially.[7] I have no quarrel with the order;[8] it is those noisy rascals I detest, who boast themselves champions of the gospel and behave like lickspittles – men whom the order would discipline or dismiss, had they any wish to take thought for their own reputation.

And yet in this affair my business is not with theological subtleties but with the correction of the text. I take upon myself a schoolmaster's part; questions of truth and falsehood I leave to those master-minds. If they have found my labours of great value to all who wish to learn in the restoration of Jerome, why have they chosen to protest at this stage, rather than form a provisional view of what I was undertaking on the basis of my earlier success? For instance, the question whether anything is falsely ascribed to Augustine will cease to puzzle anyone who has read *De vera et falsa poenitentia*, in the seventeenth chapter of which Augustine himself is quoted, and quoted in a way that shows that the author of that work disagrees with him.[9] The same thing has happened in a preface prefixed under the name of St Aurelius Augustinus to the commentary on the Psalms, though Augustine himself receives honourable mention in that preface.[10] There is another book put together by some industrious person like a kind of patchwork from the writings of Augustine and others, and ascribed to Augustine.[11] These gross facts are not perceived by our friends, who think themselves more clear-sighted than any roe-deer, any eagle. Last but not least, I too was convinced that there were fewer mistakes in Augustine's works than in Jerome's. But when I corrected a few books by way of experiment, the facts soon taught me that monstrous corruptions were commoner in this author than I had found them to be in Jerome or

* * * * *

7 See Epp 1263 n14, 1274 n13, 1299 n25, and 1330:53–8.
8 Though Erasmus frequently wrote of Dominicans, individually and collectively, with great bitterness, on occasion he also expressed genuine respect for the order because it was relatively unburdened with ceremonies. See, for example, Ep 1196:293–5. For further references, see Ep 1006 n1.
9 See PL 40 1111–12.
10 In PL 36 61–4, this appears as 'Praefatio cujusdam recentioris in commentarios Augustini, quos scripsit in Psalmos.'
11 *Quaestiones Veteris et Novi Testamenti* PL 35 2207–2422

Cyprian.[12] For this, Augustine no doubt has to thank these exceptional admirers of his who alone understand him.

That I am not making all this up will be abundantly proved by the result, if these men once allow me to finish what I have begun. In the mean time I will produce two or three passages from which an intelligent reader can estimate conditions elsewhere. In book 16, chapter 24 of the *Adversus Faustum Manichaeum*, in books of which more than one edition has appeared in print,[13] the text ran as follows: *quem dominus Jesus Christus eadem commendatione commemorat, eiusque autoritatis adductae, eorum refellit errorem resurrectionem negantium*, although in a very ancient codex the uncorrupted reading was preserved: *eiusdemque autoritate Sadduccaeorum refellit errorem*. For Augustine has in mind the passage reported in Matthew chapter 22. Again, in book 16, chapter 33 the text had been doubly corrupted: *vides nequaquam* or *vides ne quamquam*, when one ought to write *videsne quam tibi non dicam* etc. For Augustine refers to Faustus' words which had preceded in chapter 8 of the same book: 'Elsewhere he said, "If you are a Christian, you must believe Christ when he says that Moses wrote of him; if you do not believe that, you are not a Christian." This is always a weak and silly argument, which shows that those who use it have no evidence to which they may point.' So Faustus had represented Augustine as saying, 'If you are a Christian, you must believe Christ when he says, etc,' and Augustine denies that he had ever dealt with Faustus like that.[14] A little further on, in chapter 33 of the same book, *nec illud sibi patere praecipitium* had been written by mistake for the true text, *nec illud sivi patere*. In chapter 6 of the same book, in words spoken by Faustus, who had used an idiomatic expression from the old translation and put *virorum virorum quisquis hoc non gestaverit, exterminabitur*, they had corrupted it to *utrorum virorum*. For Hebrew uses *viri viri* for *quicunque viri*, 'whatsoever man.'

There are countless things of this kind, but this is no place at the moment to recount them, and they can scarcely be recounted without weariness even in their proper places. This is my programme: at my own

* * * * *

12 See Ep 1000.

13 Allen could find no edition other than Amerbach's of 1506. None earlier is listed in CSEL.

14 In the dispute between Faustus and Augustine over the importance for Christians of the teaching of Moses, Augustine relied on John 5:46: 'For had ye believed Moses, ye would have believed me: for he wrote of me.' Faustus argued that the text was spurious because there is nothing in the Mosaic books that points to Christ. Augustine defended the text and used it to demonstrate that all that Moses wrote was of Christ. In the passage referred to, however, he denied ever having said that those who disagreed were not Christian.

expense and with incredible efforts, I offer them the standard authorities of
our religion in a more accurate and more intelligible shape; and this these
pillars of religion, themselves devoted to nothing but their bellies and their   120
appetites, have thought proper to attack in harangues that might cause a
breach of the peace. How I wish for one of two things! Either let them devote
themselves to studies worthy of men who profess themselves dead to the
world or, if they will not mend their ways, let the world mend its own ways
and get rid of these styes in its eyes, these drones in its beehives, so that, if   125
they are unwilling to be of any service themselves, at least they may no
longer get in the way of others who wish to serve the interests of all men of
good will. The support of good men will stimulate my labours far more than
the snarling of bad men will discourage them.

   And now, in the mean while, here is that admirable book, *De civitate*   130
Dei, more correct than it was before and with more learned explanatory
notes – how much more, I would rather the reader discovered from the work
itself than took on trust from me. For Luis Vives has extolled my merits far
beyond what they deserve,[15] with the result that it would be legitimate to
praise him in my turn even did he not deserve it. Farewell, and pray ensure   135
that Johann Froben need not regret his outlay and his toil, for he refuses
nothing that can adorn and further and assist the cause of learning.

1310 / To Adrian VI   Basel, [c September] 1522

   This is the covering letter for the presentation copy of Arnobius (Ep 1304).
   Thus an approximate month-date can be assigned. The letter was first printed
   with the 1524 edition (Basel: Froben) of the *Exomologesis*, along with Epp 1329,
   1324, and 1338. Subsequently it appeared in all the collections of the *Epistolae*.
      Pope Adrian's reply is Ep 1324.

TO HIS HOLINESS ADRIAN VI, PONTIFF-DESIGNATE,
FROM ERASMUS OF ROTTERDAM
Another man, most holy Father, might at this juncture deploy the whole
arsenal of rhetoric in the task of congratulating you on your elevation to the
greatest eminence that can fall to a man's lot upon this earth. For my part, I   5
will expend no effort in so doing, for I know well enough how reluctantly
you have assumed this office, so unexpectedly conferred upon you. I should
perhaps look foolish, were I to express rejoicing at what is for you a source of
sighing and groaning, for I am not unaware how hard it is to perform your

          * * * * *

   15 See Ep 1303 n4.

new duties in such a way as to make your performance acceptable to Christ   10
your master, to whom sooner or later you must give an account of all that
you have done – especially in times like these, when the whole body of
Christendom in both its parts[1] is beset by such great evils, even were they
not aggravated by the savage threats of the Turks, and lately indeed not
threats alone. But the less reason we have to rejoice with you as an   15
individual, the more emphatically we can congratulate the whole Christian
world. This tempest in human affairs absolutely demanded a man like you at
the helm. For many indications invite us to expect that you will administer
the duties divinely entrusted to you to the advantage of no one save only
Jesus Christ and his flock; and may he of his goodness deign to bring your   20
most saintly efforts to good effect, without whose favour every mortal effort
is in vain.

   As a sort of earnest of my feelings towards you, I now send you
Arnobius, whom I happened to have in hand when the best of good news
reached us here – that Adrian vi had been set at the helm of affairs; and I will   25
establish those feelings to better purpose and more fully when the
opportunity presents itself. Well acquainted as I am with my own
unblemished conscience and your native wisdom and sense of justice, I see
none the less how great is the influence in this generation of malicious
tongues; and I therefore thought it advisable to protect your Holiness   30
against their virulence by a kind of antidote, so that, should any hostile
report of me come to your ears, you may either reject it entirely or, if you
have any hesitation, may keep an open mind until you have heard my
defence. For I have no doubt that before you, the most upright of judges, I
shall give a full and sufficient reply to their malignity. Though I know that 35
you would do this of your own accord, I have yet been moved by the
wickedness of certain persons who know no rest anywhere, not so much to
make a request of you as at least to put you on notice. Hitherto in religious
matters I have shown the spirit proper to an orthodox Christian, and so I
shall do to the day of my death. If I can persuade neither side[2] to approve my   40
position, I am confident at least of securing Christ's assent that my
conscience is clear. Let this be taken as the solemn utterance, not of the
proverbial priestess on her tripod,[3] but of an honest heart.

   The brevity of this letter will be made up for by a longer preface to the

       * * * * *

1310
1 Ie, European society (Christendom) in both its temporal and ecclesiastical
  aspects
2 Ie, neither his Lutheran nor his Catholic critics
3 Pythia, the priestess of Apollo who uttered oracles at Delphi

Arnobius. May the Lord Jesus, saviour of all men, long preserve your   45
Holiness to our advantage, and ever deign to be with you as his vicegerent
on earth.

Basel, 1522

1311 / To John Fisher   Basel, 1 September 1522

> This is evidently one of the letters of introduction written at the request of
> Vives (Ep 1306:43–5). It was first published in volume 2 of J. Jortin's *Life of*
> *Erasmus* (London 1758/60), where the text is inaccurate. Allen used the
> autograph in the British Library (MS Harl 6989.9) as the basis of his version.
> Since the manuscript is badly worn away in many places on both edges, Allen
> had to employ a good deal of conjecture in order to produce a complete text.
>
> John Fisher (1469–1535), since 1504 chancellor of Cambridge University and
> bishop of Rochester, had been a friend and patron of Erasmus since the latter's
> second sojourn in England, 1505–6.

TO JOHN FISHER

Most peerless of prelates, your letter[1] was a great solace to me in all my
troubles. For I am brought low, not so much by the burden of my
researches,[2] without which I could not go on living, as by the frequent
attacks of illness, first a pestilent rheum[3] accompanied by fever and then the   5
stone,[4] every attack of which – and it attacks me roughly every four days –
brings me to death's door. The last onset, which was the most serious of all,
caused such inward upheaval that nature cannot reassert herself. The
weakness continues, and has been made worse[5] by fever, while my poor
body is daily more and more reduced by looseness of the bowels. It seems   10
like some sort of consumption due to old age. My discomforts are somewhat
increased by certain blockheads who persistently conspire against me. The
last part of the story is now being played out in Rome. The Dominicans are
stirring up one Zúñiga,[6] a Spaniard, who is beside himself with ambition
and effrontery. All depends on the disposition of the new pope. What he   15

* * * * *

1311
1 Not extant
2 See Ep 1330 n6.
3 See Ep 1256 n2.
4 See Ep 1267 n5.
5 Reading *accessit*; Allen's *successit*, 'fever has taken its place,' can hardly be
  right.
6 See Ep 1260 n36.

was like some time ago, I well know;[7] what he will be like in such exalted office, I know not. One thing I do know: he is entirely a scholastic,[8] and not wholly well disposed to the humanities. His friendliness and loyal spirit I know and have not forgotten.

The subject[9] I should treat of had already occupied my thoughts for 20 several days when your letter arrived, and I will work hard at it, once I have settled somewhere, for ill health compels me to move. I get many letters inviting me to Rome. My lord of Sion renews his offer – five hundred ducats a year, besides the expenses of the journey.[10] But I am terrified by the Alps and the Appennines, to which I doubt whether it would be safe to entrust a 25 frail body like mine. I am expected in France too. The king sent me a safe-conduct with pleasure.[11] But I would rather the monarchs made peace first.[12] In Brabant there is great uproar over Luther.[13] The business has been entrusted to men who hate me, not on account of Luther – they hate me more bitterly than they do Luther himself. My spirit abhors contention. And 30 yet, whatever I intend to do, I must do soon. Whatever it is, I will let you know. I could have spent the winter nowhere more conveniently than here, for things are still plentiful: but the wines of this region do not agree with me.

The bearer of this letter is Luis Vives. I expect you already know his 35 quality by what he has written, and you will learn the rest from talking with him. He is among the number of my friends. Your Robert[14] is at Tübingen as professor of Greek and Hebrew, with a fairly generous stipend. Reuchlin has preceded me to the next world. I have promoted him to the ranks of the gods in a new edition of my *Colloquia* printed this summer.[15] And so farewell 40 to your lordship, and may he who is the source of all our blessings long bless

* * * * *

7 See Ep 1304 introduction and n2.
8 See Epp 969:21–4 and 1304 introduction.
9 Either the Paraphrase on John (Epp 1323:22–5, 1333) or the *Ecclesiastes* (Ep 1332:41–3)
10 See Ep 1299:49–50 and n11, Ep 1342:348–52.
11 See Ep 1319:5–8.
12 See Ep 1306 n22.
13 Probably a reference to the persecution of Nicolaas van Broeckhoven and Cornelis Schrijver; Epp 1299:100–7, 1302:97–102.
14 Robert Wakefield (d 1537), English Hebraist, educated at Cambridge and Louvain. In the summer of 1522 he accepted an invitation to Tübingen to replace Reuchlin (Ep 290), who had died on 30 June. By March 1524 Wakefield was back in England where, under royal patronage, he had a successful career first at Cambridge and then at Oxford.
15 Reuchlin is celebrated in the *Apotheosis Capnionis*, first printed in the Froben edition of August 1522.

and preserve you. To him you will sometimes be so good as to commend my poor self in your prayers.

Basel, 1 September 1522

Erasmus, your lordship's most devoted servant   45

To the right reverend father in Christ John, bishop of Rochester. In England

1312 / To Juan de Vergara   Basel, 2 September 1522

This is a reply to Ep 1277 and was evidently written in response to Vives' offer to carry a letter to Vergara (Ep 1306:40–1). It was first published by Allen from the manuscript, which was an eighteenth-century copy in the Heine Collection at Munich (see Ep 1277 introduction).

I was extremely grateful for your letter, scholarly and elegant as it was, and exhaling a sort of affection for me of no common kind. I am resolved to follow your advice. I have no spirit to take on individuals, especially if they are like Zúñiga[1] and Carranza,[2] both of whom you present to me at length as men of integrity and learning. Perhaps they have these qualities at heart; in   5 what they write, at any rate, there is no sign of them. All the same, I was pleased here too with your native courtesy. I have answered those two most abusive and ignorant pamphlets by Carranza and Zúñiga.[3] The three promised by Zúñiga are still to come;[4] but I undertook not to reply.[5] The college of cardinals had forbidden the printing of his book, so appropriately   10 named *Blasphemies*; it was printed secretly by certain monks for whose

* * * * *

1312

1 See Ep 1260 n36.

2 See Ep 1277 n8.

3 Zúñiga's *Erasmi blasphemiae et impietates* (Ep 1260 n45) was certainly abusive, but Carranza's *Annotationes* (Ep 1277 n8) were not. For Erasmus' replies see the notes cited.

4 The title of Zúñiga's latest pamphlet attacking Erasmus was *Libellus triorum illorum voluminum praecursor, quibus Erasmicas impietates ac blasphemias redarguit* (Rome: A. Bladus 1522). The three *volumina* in question were evidently the three 'books' of the *Blasphemiae et impietates* in its original, unabridged form, the publication of which had been banned by Leo x (Ep 1260 n45) and by the college of cardinals (see n6 below); ASD IX-2 26. Zúñiga's attempt to secure the permission of Adrian VI for publication also failed; Ep 1341A:919–20 with n261.

5 Erasmus promised this in the *Apologia ad prodromon Stunicae*, published as an appendix to the *Apologia* of June 1522 (Ep 1260 n45). But he was provoked to further apologies in March 1524 (Ep 1428) and in June 1529 (Ep 2172).

benefit he is acting this part. Then the sale of it was banned; such is its reception by the leaders of the church.[6] I intend in future not to scratch a scab like this.

Of you, my dear Vergara, I form the highest hopes, I do assure you, on   15
the basis of that letter of yours, which promises nothing common or ordinary. You had deceived me up to now – I had no idea you were such a favourite of the Muses in both tongues. Farewell.

Basel, 2 September 1522

Your sincere friend Erasmus   20

In haste, with my own hand

To the most polished theologian and practised scholar in both the tongues, Juan de Vergara. At the emperor's court

1313 / To Duke George of Saxony   Basel, 3 September 1522

On Duke George, see Ep 1283.

This letter, which is Erasmus' reply to Ep 1298, was written at the beginning of a period of nearly two years during which the correspondence between Erasmus and Duke George was frequently intercepted, perhaps by brigands (Ep 1325:6–7), perhaps by hostile Lutherans (Allen Ep 1499:5–6), perhaps by Heinrich Eppendorf (Allen Ep 1437:90–5) showing his true colours (see Ep 1283 n4). The letter failed to reach Duke George, so three months later Erasmus dispatched a duplicate along with Ep 1325. The duke responded with Ep 1340, but that was intercepted. In the spring of 1524 Erasmus wrote the duke a letter that is now lost. The duke replied with Ep 1448 and sent a copy of Ep 1340. These were delivered in September 1524 (Ep 1499), and communication was thus re-established.

Two contemporary copies of the letter survive. One is in the papers of Frans van Cranevelt at Louvain (see Ep 1298 introduction). The other, the duplicate sent to Duke George, is in the Staatsarchiv Dresden (Loc 10300). For the version published in the *Opus epistolarum*, Erasmus made numerous revisions. Allen's version is based on the Louvain manuscript. The letter has also been published as Ep 14 in de Vocht *Literae ad Craneveldium*.

The attitude toward Luther expressed here forms an interesting contrast to that in Ep 1275.

Greeting, most illustrious Prince. It came as a great joy to me that you should have honoured me with your most gracious letter, when I had been so

* * * * *

6 See Ep 1302:68–71 and the notes indicated there.

neglectful in writing to your Highness, being in fact extremely busy and also
in indifferent health. That this most perilous division in the world around us
should displease you is not surprising; what man could take pleasure in it   5
who has the spirit of a Christian? I only wish that princes would use all their
vigilance and unfeigned zeal to lay this great evil to rest, to such good
purpose that it never grows again. Which side is at fault is a question it is
now perhaps too late to ask. Luther – and this cannot be denied – had
chosen an admirable programme, and had begun to perform Christ's work   10
before an approving world when Christ had almost disappeared. If only, in
carrying on this great campaign, he had followed more responsible and
steadier counsels, and shown more moderation both in his spirit and in
what he writes! How I wish that his writings did not contain so many good
things, or that he had not ruined his good things by insufferable faults! And   15
yet in this regard certain of Luther's supporters are more seriously in the
wrong than he is himself. As it is, since there is now an atmosphere of bitter
hatred on both sides, there is some risk that all these good things (which I
should be sorry to see destroyed,) will perish together in Luther's
overthrow, and then that the victorious party will inflict certain things upon   20
us which no lover of Christ will be able to bear and which seem likely to lead
to serious damage to the glory of Christianity and the purity of the gospel.

For if I may be allowed to speak freely before a prince who is as wise as
he is kind, the world was sound asleep, pillowed on the opinions of the
schoolmen and the petty codes of human legislators, and all it heard of was   25
indulgences and satisfactions and the power of the pope of Rome. Even
were these things beyond question true in themselves, they contribute little
to the vigour of the gospel, they do not inspire us to despise the world, they
do not kindle us to love of heavenly things. Yet these above all else are what
should be brought home to us. The pope's authority should not be made   30
light of, but all the glory should be transferred to Christ alone. And with this
support[1] some sat upon the papal throne who seek not the things that are
Jesus Christ's but, like that Demas condemned by the apostle Paul,[2] are
lovers of this world. From this slumber it was essential to arouse the world,
and blow the spark of gospel vigour into flame. If only this could have been   35
done with the mildness and the care appropriate to a cause so near the heart
of our religion! It was certain monks and theologians who think like monks
who took a hand in this business, who aggravated the evil by their foolish,

* * * * *

1313
1 Supported, that is, by 'the opinions of schoolmen' and 'the petty codes of
human legislators'
2 2 Tim 4:10

ignorant, and subversive clamour; what was bad enough they made very
bad, and what was small they made great. For at the start there was nothing   4
at risk except the profits of those who sold indulgences. And just as much of
what Luther writes is more than most men's ears can bear, so do these
people drag in many things which good men and educated men can see will
do nothing but harm to the religion that is truly of the gospel. And yet those
who write these things are not forwarding Christ's business or the pope's,   4
but their own. It is in their eagerness for personal gain that they undermine
the papal cause and cast a shadow on Christ's glory. They neither allow us to
approve the elements in Luther that are really Christian, nor do they relax
any of their own tenets, but add things still harder to bear to what was there
before.   5

   And so, since I saw plainly that both sides were being swept off course
by some violence they could not resist, I did not get myself mixed up very far
in this confusion, only making it quite clear that I had come to no
understanding with Luther's supporters, and that I hate nothing so much as
subversion. Though in other ways too I saw that I was no match for so   5
perilous a business, even had I had the leisure to read what they write on
both sides; for it all had to be read. Besides which, my age and state of health
are already demanding my release from more serious studies. I could never
write against Luther bitterly enough to avoid seeming lukewarm to the other
party. And furthermore, seeing how terribly Luther's men threaten me   6
already,[3] they would tear no one in pieces so readily as myself if I took the
field against them. Enough pamphlets attacking Luther exist already,[4] if that
was the way to overwhelm him, and there are men far more effective in this
cockpit than myself. Last but not least, it was always my opinion that
nothing would lull this sad business to rest so effectively as silence.[5] This is   6
the view of those cardinals and great laymen who are the most intelligent.

* * * * *

3 According to a contemporary account, which Allen quotes at length, Erasmus
   had recently been much exercised by a rumour that Melanchthon was writing a
   book against him. Earlier in the year, Erasmus had believed that Melanchthon
   was going to challenge him by publishing his own paraphrases on St Paul;
   Zw-Br I 502 (Ep 201).
4 See the long list in Friedrich Lauchert, *Die italienischen literarischen Gegner
   Luthers* (Freiburg im Breisgau 1912; repr Nieuwkoop 1972) 688–9. For a list of
   works by Luther's northern opponents, see Karl Schottenloher *Bibliographie
   zur deutschen Geschichte im Zeitalter der Glaubensspaltung 1517–1585* I (Stuttgart
   1956) 458–60.
5 Ie, a silence imposed on all parties; see Ep 1007:118–27.

The pope has published a most savage bull,[6] and its only effect has been to embitter the conflagration. It was followed by an even more savage edict from the emperor,[7] who is entirely devoted to this question. This is restraining some people's tongues and pens, but it cannot change their minds. The emperor's pious intentions do him credit; but his judgment in this matter is commonly attributed to men to whom the learned give little weight.

For the rest, I have never had any doubts that the book by his Majesty the king of England,[8] which you have good reason to speak well of, was fashioned by the intelligence of the same man whose name it bears, by his own bow and spear as the saying goes.[9] That prince has a wonderfully fertile and subtle intelligence, which is extraordinarily effective in any field upon which he turns it. And as a boy he practised his pen with some diligence, even writing letters to me personally.[10] It is not many years since he composed a theological disputation on the theme whether a layman has an obligation to pray out loud.[11] It is his wont to have some acquaintance with books of scholastic theology, and he enjoys the discussion of some theological point even over his wine. Sometimes the discussion on some

* * * * *

6 The bull *Exsurge domine*, published at Rome on 15 June 1520, threatened Luther with excommunication if he did not recant forty-one enumerated errors within sixty days of the bull's official publication in Germany, which took place at the end of September. Luther's books were to be burned. The bull was immensely unpopular in Germany, where it was felt that Luther had been condemned without a fair hearing, and most magistrates refused their co-operation in the execution of the bull. Luther not only wrote in defence of the condemned articles (WA VII 308–457) but also symbolically burned the bull, along with a copy of the canon law, at a public bonfire outside the Magpie Gate at Wittenberg (10 December 1520). The bull formally excommunicating Luther, *Decet pontificem romanum*, was published at Rome on 3 January 1521.
7 The Edict of Worms, based on a draft by Aleandro (Ep 1256 n11), signed on May 1521, outlawed Luther and forbade the reading or the dissemination of his writings. It also subjected the publication and sale of all books to episcopal censorship and placed religious works under the supervision of the theological faculties. But effective enforcement of the edict was impossible because of widespread popular support for Luther, patriotic resentment of Rome, and the feeling that only a general council could render authoritative judgment on the issues raised by Luther.
8 See Ep 1275 n25.
9 *Adagia* I vi 19
10 See Ep 206.
11 See Ep 964:132n.

literary topic is prolonged until late at night. His queen[12] has had an elegant   8
education. If however he had had any help in the writing of that book, he
had no need of any assistance from me, for his court is stuffed full of men
who are excellent scholars and write with great style.[13] If his way of writing
has something about it not unlike my own, there will be nothing new or
strange in that, since as a boy he applied himself studiously to my works at   9
the suggestion of my honoured lord William Mountjoy,[14] whom he had then
as the companion of his studies.

Two pamphlets by Luther[15] were sent me by your Highness to no
purpose, since I cannot read the language in which they are written.[16] –
though I am told that they were in circulation here a long time before you   9
sent them. It seems to me the height of folly to challenge those whom you
cannot beat. All the same, to remind princes and bishops of their duties, as
often as the actual facts give you an opportunity, has its value, and is
covered by the example of the most acceptable authors. Jerome does it
sometimes, and so do Chrysostom and Bernard. There always have been   1
bishops and there always will be, and perhaps there are some today, who
are intoxicated by the sweets of fortune and forget what it means to behave
as a bishop should. And what is said of a class ought not to be twisted into
criticism of any individual; provided only that it is said with no subversive or
offensive intentions, and that the bitterness of the strictures is tempered   1
always with the sweetness of Christian charity. The authority of bishops
ought not to be diminished, but the best way to obtain it and preserve it is to
be a good bishop. The whole of this evil, or at least a great part of it, arises
from ourselves: we devote ourselves wholeheartedly to the world, and yet
we shelter under titles that are Christ's. If we could cut off this evil at the   1
root, the world would accept us with enthusiasm as fathers; as it is, it hates
us as tyrants, and it rebels.

I wait to see which way the new pope will invite us to follow.[17] Perhaps

* * * * *

12 Catherine of Aragon, whom Erasmus greatly admired; see Epp 296:124,
  855:34–6, 948:226–7, 964:80, 968:14–17, 976:44–5, and Allen Epp 1381:38–40,
  1404:24–5.
13 Cf Epp 821:1–2, 832:38–41, 855:32–51, 917:14–21, 966, 968–70, 976, 1004,
  1005:35–7, 1028:1–2, 1031:21–5, 1032:24–6.
14 Ep 79
15 See Ep 1298:26–33 and n4 to that letter.
16 Cf Ep 1342:830–1. Duke George refused to take this spurious claim seriously;
  Ep 1340:15–18. In Allen Ep 1499:10–12, Erasmus repeated it even more
  strongly. Erasmus in fact knew German well enough to review translations of
  his own works and to demand extensive revisions; see Holeczek 228–9.
17 See Ep 1304 introduction.

he will show us some way of putting an end to this evil, which has spread
widely over so many parts of the world, and has taken deep root in many   115
hearts. For myself, as far as age and brains and strength and time permit, I
shall not be found wanting in the cause of Christian faith and Christian
concord, as indeed I have done hitherto to the best of my ability. You in your
wisdom, most illustrious Prince, must see to it that what I now write to you
with some freedom is not allowed to damage me in the eyes of other men,   120
who can twist anything into a cause of scandal. May your illustrious
Highness long be preserved in health and wealth by Jesus the Almighty
Lord.

From Basel, 3 September 1522
Erasmus of Rotterdam   125

1314 / To Huldrych Zwingli   Basel, [3?] September 1522

This letter (=Zw-Br Ep 235) was first published in Johann Kaspar Hess
Lebensbeschreibung M. Ulrich Zwinglis (Zürich 1811), II (=the 'litterarisch-
historischer Anhang' by Leonard Usteri) 563. The autograph is in the Rehdiger
Collection (MS Rehd 243.135) of the University Library at Wrocław. The
month-date in the manuscript, '5. *Nonas Septembr.*,' obviously needs correction since there is no such date in September. Allen accepted the suggestion of
the editors of the Zwingli correspondence that the invitation to Erasmus to
come to Zürich (see below) was the result of Michael Hummelberg's letter of 26
August (Zw-Br Ep 232) but that this friendly letter probably preceded the
sharply critical Ep 1315. It thus seems likely either that 5, which is unmistakable in the manuscript, was a miswriting for 3, or that Erasmus calculated in
September as for October.

Zwingli and Erasmus had exchanged letters in 1516 (Epp 401, 404), when
Zwingli was still parish priest in Glarus and an ardent Erasmian humanist. In
January 1519, after two years as chaplain to the abbot of Einsiedeln (November
1516–December 1518), Zwingli became parish priest at the Grossmünster in
Zürich, where he soon crossed the threshold from Erasmian reform to
Protestant Reformation. By the time Erasmus wrote this letter to him, Zwingli
had long since become the acknowledged leader of a reformation being carried
out under the authority of the city magistrates in defiance of the bishop of
Constance. In March 1522 a number of Zwingli's supporters violated the
Lenten fast, an action which he defended from the pulpit and in print. When
the bishop complained of this and other violations of church law, Zwingli
responded in August with the *Apologeticus Archeteles*, his first extensive
defence of the Reformation at Zürich against the charges of heresy and
innovation. Learned in content but often indignant and ironic in tone, the

Huldrych Zwingli
Portrait by Hans Asper, 1531
Kunstmuseum Winterthur

Apologeticus attacked Catholic institutions and traditions from the basis of *sola scriptura*. In the interest of civic peace, however, the pace of reformation in Zürich was deliberately slow: not until April 1525 was mass formally abolished.

In 1522 Zwingli still retained his high regard for Erasmus, who he hoped would be won for the Reformation. He reportedly visited Erasmus in Basel in January 1522; *Die Vadianische Briefsammlung der Stadtbibliothek St. Gallen* ed Emil Arbenz II (St Gallen 1894) Ep 301; Zw-Br Ep 200. Moreover, in letters no longer extant Zwingli proposed that Erasmus accept citizenship in Zürich (Ep 1342:585–9), which presumably would have involved taking up residence there. This letter is Erasmus' response to that proposal.

I am most grateful to you and your city for your kindly thought. My own wish is to be a citizen of the world, to be a fellow-citizen to all men – a pilgrim better still. If only I might have the happiness of being enrolled in the city of heaven! For it is thither I make my way, under the constant attacks of all this illness.[1] Nor do I see why I should want what you offer me. I know for 5 certain that the emperor's feelings towards me are friendly.[2] The order of cardinals as a whole supports me.[3] Nor is there any danger except from some raving Jacobins[4] whom I could name. Even that city of yours could not restrain them from ranting against me and my books to their hearts content.

I like Vadianus[5] no less now that I have seen him[6] than I did on reading 10

* * * * *

1314
1 See Epp 1302:35–50, 1311:3–11.
2 See Ep 1302 n21.
3 See Ep 1302 n26.
4 The Parisian name for the Dominicans, whose convent was in the Rue St Jacques, near the church of the same name
5 Joachim Vadianus, the name taken by Joachim von Watt (1484–1551) of St Gallen. Educated at the University of Vienna (MA 1508, MD 1517), he taught there in the arts faculty from 1514, becoming professor of rhetoric in 1516 and serving as rector in 1516–17. Among the works written in this period was a volume of scholia on the *De orbis situ* of Pomponius Mela, published at Vienna in 1518.
In 1518 Vadianus returned to St Gallen, where he was appointed town physician. In 1521 he succeeded his father as a member of the city council, and at the end of 1525 he became burgomaster. Meanwhile, he had adopted the reformed faith and in the years 1524–7 directed the introduction of the Reformation into the city. Thereafter he devoted his energies to his medical and municipal duties and to the composition of geographical and historical works, including a voluminous chronicle of the abbots of the famous monastery at St Gallen.
On two occasions that we know of, Vadianus attempted to initiate a friendly

what he writes.[7] He is the most open-hearted of men. I gave him a lukewarm welcome – conversation only. My health insisted on that, for it cannot face dinners. We shall soon see which way Christendom is turning. Our new pope is a theologian.[8] For my part, so far as the world we live in allows, I shall not be wanting in Christ's service as long as I live. Fight on, dear Zwingli, not only with courage but with prudence too. Christ will grant that you fight also with success. Farewell.

From Basel, [3?] September 1522

Your sincere friend Erasmus

To that most unsleeping of pastors Huldrych Zwingli. In Zürich

1315 / To Huldrych Zwingli   Basel, 8 September 1522

The autograph of this letter (=Zw-Br Ep 236) is in the Staatsarchiv Zürich (E.II.339:87). It was first published in J.H. Hottinger *Historia ecclesiastica novi testamenti* VI (Hannover 1665).

Greetings, dear Zwingli, my most learned friend. I have read some pages of your *Apologeticus*.[1] I beseech you by the glory of the gospel – which I know you have at heart above all else, as all of us are bound to do who are enlisted under Christ's name – if you publish anything in future, it is a serious task, and you must take it seriously. Do not forget the modesty and the prudence demanded by the gospel. Consult scholarly friends before you issue anything to the public. I fear that defence of yours may land you in great peril, and even do harm to the church. In the little I have read there was

* * * * *

relationship with Erasmus, whom he greatly admired: by letter (now lost) in 1518, and by means of a personal visit in 1522 (see the following note). But Erasmus reacted coldly and no correspondence between the two men developed. Vadianus nevertheless retained his high opinion of Erasmus, whom he later eulogized, along with Luther and Zwingli, as one of the fathers of the Reformation; *Deutsche historische Schriften* ed Ernst Götzinger I (St Gallen 1875) 6–7, 469.

6 Vadianus apparently visited Erasmus in Basel in the summer of 1522. Erasmus' brief, rather frosty comments in this letter are the only historical record of that visit.

7 Perhaps a reference to the second edition of Vadianus' scholia on Pomponius Mela (see n5), published by Cratander at Basel in January 1522, in which (page 160) Vadianus praised Erasmus as a 'true Camillus of sacred letters and true theology.'

8 Cf Epp 1311:17–18, 1304 introduction.

1315
1 See Ep 1314 introduction.

much on which I wanted to see you put right. I do not doubt that with your
sound sense you will take this in good part; for I write with the warmest 10
affection for you, and late at night. Farewell.

Nativity of the BVM 1522

Your friend Erasmus

To the most worthy Master Huldrych Zwingli, pastor in Zürich

1316 / To Konrad Heresbach   Basel, 18 October 1522

This letter first appeared in the *Opus epistolarum*.

Soon after writing Ep 1315, Erasmus, accompanied by Beatus Rhenanus (Ep
327) and Heinrich Eppendorf (Ep 1283 n4), paid a visit to Johann von Botzheim
(Ep 1285) in Constance. The visit lasted about three weeks (Ep 1342:500). One
of Erasmus' reasons for making the trip was concern for his health, which was
adversely affected by the local wines in Basel (Ep 1311:22, 33–4). His intention was to go on to Rome in response to the numerous invitations he had
received. But a bad attack of the stone at Constance and reports of the dangers
facing a traveller to Rome compelled him to abandon the thought of so long
and arduous a journey (Ep 1319:11–16). With the aid of some agreeable wine
from Burgundy (lines 26–8) his health improved, and by the end of September
he was back in Basel, though still determined to move elsewhere as soon as
possible (see Ep 1319 introduction). Either on the way to Constance or on the
way back, Erasmus received a most flattering welcome in Schaffhausen (BRE
Ep 228). An expected visit to Zürich (Zw-Br Ep 237) did not take place. At
Constance, Botzheim was a splendid host, and men of every station treated
Erasmus royally. Ep 1342:369–503 provides an unusually detailed account of
the visit, and there is a brief account of it in the colloquy Ἰχθυοφαγία, 'A Fish
Diet' (ASD I-3 530–1; Thompson 350–1).

Konrad Heresbach (1496–1576) was a young humanist of whom Erasmus
had a high opinion (Ep 1364) and whose successful career Erasmus helped to
launch. After graduating MA at Cologne in 1515, Heresbach studied law in
France for two years (1517–19) before returning to Cologne. Following
Erasmus' visit to Cologne in November 1520, and conceivably as a result of it,
Heresbach was by December of the same year working as a corrector for
Froben in Basel. In 1521, again possibly on Erasmus' recommendation,
Heresbach became professor of Greek at Freiburg. The following year he
visited Italy briefly in order to become a doctor of civil law at Ferrara. Erasmus
and Heresbach no doubt discussed the latter's future during Erasmus' visit to
Freiburg in March 1523 (see n1). With the help of Erasmus and Johann von
Vlatten (Ep 1390), Heresbach became in September 1523 tutor to young Duke
William V of Cleves, a post he held until 1535, when he became privy

councillor. He exercised a decisive influence on the Cleves ecclesiastical ordinances of 1525, 1532, and 1562. He also played an important role in the legal and educational reforms of the period 1550–61. To the end, Heresbach was an Erasmian moderate, aiming at the reconciliation of the confessions and refusing to break with the old church.

ERASMUS OF ROTTERDAM TO KONRAD HERESBACH

I must say, my most learned friend Konrad, you have not far to go to find happiness, if such a little thing will make you happy. You say in your letter that you would be happy, the moment it is your good fortune to have me as your guest.[1] Great indeed is the felicity for which you envy Constance, and such other poor towns as I have honoured (so you put it) with my presence! I on the other hand lament my own infelicity, for I am weighed down with so many troubles that wherever I take refuge I am not merely a burden to myself (my complaint being so unmerciful and my health such a handicap[2]), but I am obliged to be burdensome even to those to whom I should most wish to give pleasure.

In Constance I was ill all the time, staying with Johann von Botzheim, who, besides being a good scholar and a man of the highest character, is such good company that he could cheer up a corpse. The bishop of Constance himself,[3] the mildest and worthiest and most honourable of men, did all he could to show me kindness. I had no less courteous welcome from Ennio, bishop of Veroli,[4] the apostolic nuncio. Hummelberg too[5] – a really charming person – paid me a visit immediately, and so did many others. Had none of these been available, I had the company of the most agreeable man I know and my dearest friend, Beatus Rhenanus. Is Beatus ever without a smile? My life upon it, he is the most civilized and intelligent man I ever met. To all of them I brought nothing but trouble; and on this account, as you may suppose, found my complaint even more troublesome, though it caused me infinite trouble taken by itself. If only I could find their stove-heated rooms[6] and their wine as agreeable as I do their climate and the kind of men they are! At last, when I had given up hope, I secured some

* * * * *

1316
1 Heresbach's letter is not extant. Erasmus subsequently accepted the invitation, visiting Freiburg early in March 1523; Ep 1353 introduction.
2 See Ep 1256 n2.
3 Hugo von Hohenlandenberg (d 1532)
4 Ennio Filonardi (Ep 1282)
5 Ep 1253 n6
6 See Ep 1258 n18.

Burgundy,[7] and learned from the results that all my sufferings hitherto had come from the thin fluids of this part of the world. So, unless Burgundy sends wine here, I have made up my mind to go to Burgundy. Count Arnold,[8] who is indeed just the man you described, once did me the honour   30 of coming to supper.

I will not ask you to give our little Erasmius[9] the education that will make him worthy of his excellent parents and of you as his tutor, nor will I lay down how that should be done, for fear I seem to have too low an opinion of your sense of duty or your common sense. I will say only this,   35 that by doing us that service you will earn no less gratitude from me than from his parents, although quite rightly they are specially devoted to the child; and apart from the affection they both feel for you, you know that neither of them is mean or ungenerous.

I have no feelings against a visit to Freiburg before midwinter, but I am   40 frightened of the stoves and the wine. I have now moved into another house[10] and set up as an apprentice householder. Henricus Glareanus[11] – and may there be a blessing on it! – has a wife after his own heart. The wedding ceremonies will shortly take place with dance and song;[12] so you have good reason to wish him well. He is, to be sure, one of the most   45 straightforward of men, in my opinion, and deserves that not only this marriage but everything should go well.

Farewell, best of teachers in the best of subjects, and give my greetings to all those in your part of the world who wish me well.

Basel, St Luke's day, 1522   50

* * * * *

7 A gift from Nikolaus von Diesbach (Ep 1258 n17). From this point on, Erasmus preferred Burgundian wine to any other (see Epp 1319:17, 1341A:1494–5, 1838–9, 1342:504–41).
8 Unidentified
9 Froben's youngest son (Ep 1262), who was in Freiburg being tutored by Heresbach (AK Epp 874:15–16, 879:28)
10 The house 'zur alten Treu' on the Nadelberg, which Erasmus had occupied on an earlier visit. Froben had purchased it on 18 December 1521, perhaps with the intention of making it available to Erasmus; see AK Epp 902:23 with n3 to that letter, and 915:19–20. The attraction of the house was that in one of the rooms there was an open fireplace rather than a stove (Allen Ep 1422:28–9). Froben offered it to Erasmus rent-free, but he insisted on paying; Ep 1342:582–4.
11 Ep 1264 n2
12 By 28 November the ceremonies had taken place. Erasmus, who could not attend because of the stoves, sent two coins, one of Trajan and one of Alexander the Great, as a present; Zw-Br Ep 252.

1317 / From Frans van Cranevelt   Mechelen, 24 [October 1522]

As in the case of Epp 1298 and 1313, the manuscript of this letter is part of the Cranevelt collection discovered by Professor de Vocht at Louvain. Allen's edition appeared first; de Vocht's is Ep 20 in his *Literae ad Craneveldium*. The manuscript is apparently Cranevelt's rough draft rather than the letter actually sent. The beginning of the manuscript and the right-hand edge have been destroyed, leaving small gaps that had to be filled by editorial conjecture. The month and year were easily deduced from internal evidence (lines 9–12).

Frans van Cranevelt (Ep 1145) had been town pensionary of Bruges, ie, chief legal adviser to the town magistrates, since 1515. In Bruges he formed close ties of friendship with Vives, among others. He probably first met Erasmus in Louvain, which he often visited, in the summer of 1517, though an earlier meeting in 1514 is possible. At any rate, they became and remained steadfast friends. In 1522 Cranevelt became unhappy with his circumstances in Bruges because the magistrates, despite their high opinion of him, would not give him the salary he thought necessary to support his large family. In September of that year he was appointed to the Grand Council of Mechelen, the highest court of justice in the country, a post which he held for the rest of his life. His duties left him ample leisure to write poetry, to study Greek, and to follow other humanist pursuits.

I wrote to you the other day, only a brief letter, but with a very definite purpose, for being uncertain of my future and whether I was in or out of luck, I wanted even so, and with apologies, to extract something from you in the way of a letter. You know the position I have held for some years in Bruges. The disasters of this war[1] have brought Flanders so low that she   5
could no longer maintain a man who cost her so much, and with a hen and numerous chickens too. They wanted to give me less pay than had been the practice, while I on the other hand was asking for a little more. So there was a split. I was invited to Mechelen at a higher salary and to a more distinguished post with the council of his Imperial Majesty.[2] In which   10
nothing was more troublesome than the move. The day before yesterday my wife and children arrived,[3] and we are busy finding a place for our

* * * * *

1317
1 See Epp 1283:11–13, 1284:41–2, 1306:60–1.
2 Cranevelt's letter of appointment was dated 27 September 1522; de Vocht *Literae ad Craneveldium* liii.
3 Cranevelt's wife and family arrived in Mechelen on 22 October 1522; ibidem.

belongings. We are still the guests of Dr Jan Robbyns,[4] the dean of Mechelen, where your man Hilarius[5] found me, bringing a letter from you[6] and one from my friend Fevijn,[7] whom I should much like to have, need I   15 say, as my Hercules in the rescue of Theseus,[8] if I may compare small things with great.[9] Farewell, my distinguished friend.

From Mechelen, 24 [October]

Such as he is, your most devoted Cranevelt

1318 / From Antoine Brugnard   Montbéliard, 4 November 1522

Antoine Brugnard (fl 1522–47) came from the little village of Brugnard near Montbéliard. Some time after writing this letter he received a canonry in his native town. In March 1532 he became principal of the College of Grammar at Dôle. In 1539 he left Dôle to teach in Orléans, but in 1542 he returned to Dôle and resumed his principalship until 1547. After that, nothing is known of him.

The autograph of this letter (=Förstemann/Günther Ep 10) was in the Burscher Collection at Leipzig (Ep 1254 introduction).

TO ERASMUS OF ROTTERDAM, THE EMINENT TEACHER OF
REAL LEARNING, GREETING

Expecting to leave Antwerp on 5 June, I asked Pieter Gillis[1] whether, as I was setting off in your direction, he proposed to give me a letter for you. He at once said he would, but he did not do so, being afraid perhaps that it might   5 be intercepted; for he was so anxious to avoid any suspicion of the Lutheran heresy that he did not even dare exchange a word with me. He had heard in Brussels and seen for himself in Antwerp how his colleague Cornelis

* * * * *

4 Jan Robbyns (d 1532) was elected dean of St Rombout's in Mechelen in 1502. He was a frequent visitor in Louvain, where he and young Dr Cranevelt became close friends.

5 Bertolph (Ep 1257 n10). For his journey at this time, see Ep 1322:1.

6 Not extant

7 Jan van Fevijn (1490–1555), who had studied law at Louvain and in Italy, was canon of St Donatian's at Bruges, where he was an intimate friend of Marcus Laurinus (Ep 1342) and Cranevelt. Over ninety letters from Fevijn to Cranevelt are found in de Vocht *Literae ad Craneveldium*.

8 Perhaps a reference to Nicolaas van Broeckhoven or Cornelis Schrijver, both of whom Erasmus was attempting to get released from imprisonment; Epp 1299:100–7, 1302:97–104, 1318

9 Virgil *Georgics* 4.176

1318

1 See Ep 1293 n5.

Schrijver had been made a public butt and compelled to recant,[2] dressed in a
yellow sheet, and how, all his property having been confiscated, he would   10
have to remain there in some form of confinement until the emperor should
decide otherwise. There was also a rumour that Nicolaas,[3] the headmaster of
the Antwerp high school, and a certain number of priests had been
condemned to life imprisonment on a diet of bread and water, and that some
laymen too had had their property sequestered and had themselves been   15
mutilated. Such terror had seized everyone there who had ever spared
Luther a thought that scarcely anyone thought himself safe, and they all
looked as though some baleful star had struck them.

Finding myself in the same boat, I thought it wiser to retire to a safe
place than to remain in jeopardy, especially as, not long before, my pupil's   20
guardians had dismissed me. So I came here, a sixteen-day journey; but I did
not get to Basel to see you and pay my respects, for my travelling
companions had no business to do there and did not want to make the
detour. I myself, knowing no German, was very much afraid that if I went
off on my own I might fall among rascals; nor have I yet had the chance to do   25
so, or even to write. I have also been prevented by fate, which has thrown all
my affairs here into confusion, coupled with travel and ill health. But now
that I can, I do what I ought. So here I am writing, more unskilful stuff than
you can be expected to read or listen to, but I write all the same, for fear of not
paying my debt, by which I mean not sending you greetings and assuring   30
you how devoutly I hope you are well, and at the same time to let you know
how I am situated, for you are the most reliable of benefactors whether in
deed or word to all that flee to you for help. This is no place for me. Here
anyone who loves letters is deemed a nobody; indeed, anyone who has had
even a sniff of them is laughed at or disliked. What I want, you can guess   35
from this: I want to go somewhere else, and not wither away here doing
nothing. Teaching or, better still, learning – there is nothing I would rather
have than that. And so this is the one thing I do earnestly beg of you, that if
you know of anyone who can use me, be so kind as to write to him or have a
word with him.   40

Farewell, from Montbéliard, 4 November 1522

Antoine Brugnard, lately tutor to François Gualthierot[4]

To Master Erasmus of Rotterdam, most scholarly teacher of sound
learning. In Master Froben's house, in Basel

* * * * *

2 See Ep 1299 n24.
3 Nicolaas van Broeckhoven (Ep 1299 n23)
4 Unidentified

1319 / To François de Tournon   Basel, 10 November 1522

This letter was first published in the *Opus epistolarum*. It is the first surviving
letter in which Erasmus discusses his plans to leave Basel, where not only the
local wines (Ep 1316 introduction) but also the growing 'uproar over the
gospel' (Epp 1293 n8, 1327:11–13) were a source of increasing distress to him. A
projected trip to Rome was abandoned for the reasons stated here (lines 10–16).
But the idea of migrating to France (lines 19–21), a move from which Erasmus
expected great benefits (Ep 1342:616–26) and for which he had already been
laying the groundwork (lines 4–7, Ep 1342:599–608), was still alive. That the
move did not take place may be attributed to the discovery that Burgundian
wines could easily be sent to Basel and, more important, to the disappointment
of Erasmus' hopes for the restoration of peace between Francis I and Charles V
(Epp 1342:590–637, 1345:2–6).

François de Tournon (c 1489–1562), who had met Erasmus in Basel earlier in
1522 (Ep 1342:601–7), was an Augustinian whose services to the French crown
as adviser and diplomat were rewarded with rapid advancement in the
church. He acquired successively the sees of Embrun (1517), Bourges (1525),
Auch (1538), and Lyon (1551). In 1530 he became a cardinal, and in 1560 he rose
to be dean of the Sacred College. In 1552 he founded a college at Tournon
which subsequently flourished as a Jesuit academy.

ERASMUS OF ROTTERDAM TO FRANÇOIS, ARCHBISHOP OF
EMBRUN, GREETING
Not many days ago I sent letters[1] by Konrad the German bookseller,[2] who
has a house in Paris, both to you and to Budé[3] and Brie[4] and Bérault.[5] They
all claim the credit for securing a safe-conduct from the king,[6] which gave me   5
very great pleasure, to be sure, but it would have been greater had the king
signed it with his own hand.[7] Even so, they tell me, I cannot safely move to
your part of the world, for they say that ruffians are not much moved by
royal safe-conducts if one should chance to fall into their hands, while
among respectable folk I should have no need of one. But there is much that   10

* * * * *

1319
1 None of these letters survives, but Budé's reply, Ep 1328, does.
2 Konrad Resch (Ep 331:15n) had family links with the book industry of Basel
  and ran a bookstore in Paris.
3 Ep 403
4 Ep 1284 n13
5 Ep 1284
6 Cf Epp 1311:26–7, 1328:44–5, 1342:612–13.
7 In Ep 1375 Francis complied with this wish.

still detains me here. My health first of all, which gave me the greatest
trouble at Constance[8] – for I had betaken myself to Constance, meaning to
go on to Rome had I been allowed to; for many people assured me that it
might be to my advantage if I presented myself before the new pope. Then
fearsome reports began to arrive from that part of the world – war and   15
plague raging everywhere, and then that no journey was safe. Later on I
secured some wine from Burgundy and began to feel better;[9] so you can see
that by some fate or other France is good for me. All this time I am waiting for
some faint breath of peace from this pope, and as soon as we are clear of
midwinter I shall migrate bag and baggage to France.   20

On the question of my annuity from the emperor,[10] which is now
owing for the whole of this year, they keep on putting me off, and no one is
getting his annuity paid, so completely are we stripped to the bone by these
nabobs who love war so much more than peace. The safe-conduct I thought I
owed only to Budé and to you, and now Bérault and Brie are claiming a good   25
part of the credit for themselves. Last but not least, I find I am also indebted
to the cardinal of Lorraine;[11] and it is of course a pleasure to be indebted to
him, but most of all to the king, who told Budé, I hear, with great glee that
Erasmus would soon be in France. I hope I shall one day have the chance to
make clear in my turn what I feel for so generous a prince.   30

Your lordship's support of a poor mortal like myself is most gladly
accepted, and I will do all I can to avoid the risk of being thought ungrateful.
A letter reached me at the same time from Dionysius Coronius,[12] a recipient
of your bounty, and a very eloquent and polished letter it was too – one
could recognize the faithful follower of Budé. I have no time to answer him   35
just now, being kept busy by work of various kinds. My best wishes for your
lordship's prosperity, most excellent prelate.

Basel, St Martin's Eve 1522

* * * * *

8 See Ep 1316 introduction.
9 Cf Ep 1316 n7.
10 See Ep 1273 n4.
11 Jean de Lorraine (1498–1550), younger son of Duke René II of Lorraine. Jean
   was, from 1518, bishop of Metz and cardinal.
12 Dionysius Coronius (Denis Corron), fl 1518–51, of the diocese of Chartres, was
   a protégé of Tournon, who apparently financed his studies at Paris and later
   took him into his service. From c 1543 until after 1551 he was professor of Greek
   at the Collège de France. His letter to Erasmus is not extant.

1320 / From Herman Lethmaet　　　　　　　　Ghent, 12 November [1522]

The autograph of this letter, first published as Ep 5 in Enthoven, is MS Rehd
254.97 in the Rehdiger Collection of the University Library at Wrocław.

Herman Lethmaet of Gouda (c 1492–1555) had a brilliant career at the
University of Paris, where he stood first on the list of DDs in 1520. With the
help of letters of recommendation from Erasmus, he then joined the court
of Charles v at the invitation of Jean de Carondelet (lines 8–11). In September
1522 Adrian vi made him canon at St Mary's in Utrecht (Ep 1350). In 1530 he
became dean of St Mary's and in 1534 vicar-general of the diocese. In 1525
Erasmus wrote of having consulted him on theological questions (Allen Ep
1581:299–301) and praised him in the *Apologia adversus Petrum Sutorem* (LB IX
788D). But this brief series of letters in 1522–3 (the others are Epp 1345, 1350,
1359) is the only surviving trace of communication between them.

You would hardly believe, dear Erasmus, most eminent of men, what an
honour you have done me with your two letters of recommendation.[1] I will
do my best, after being thus as it were goaded by you into activity, to make it
clear one day to all men that you have spoken the truth at least to this extent,
if in the future I am known, not of course for the man of whom you speak so　5
very highly now, but for one who actively pursues that very same noble
ideal which you tell me I must somehow strive to reach. You will make me
entirely happy if you continue to honour me like this. It is to those same
letters that I think I ought to be grateful for my present position at the court,
which I was invited to accept in a most charming letter from the archbishop　10
of Palermo, head of the emperor's privy council. Do dedicate to him, I beg
you, either some production of your own which is due to make its first
appearance shortly or one of the ancient authors who are to be reborn in
your hands.[2] His name is Jean de Carondelet.[3] You are, I imagine, too
familiar both with his own distinction and with that of his ancestors to need　15
any details from me.[4] At all events he mentions you constantly in
complimentary terms – nothing could be more so, and so do almost all the
other courtiers, although in other respects they may be Philistines.

　　Into their society I have wormed my way, to tell the truth, readily

* * * * *

1320
1　Only one, Ep 1238, is extant.
2　This request was promptly granted; Ep 1334.
3　Ep 1334 introduction
4　Erasmus was, in fact, less well informed on this subject than Lethmaet
　imagined; Ep 1345:50–3.

enough; and do you know why? I have my eye, of course, on the main   20
chance; and if I can pick up something good, my idea is, dear Erasmus, to
return to the Muses – though even now, in the very midst of court life, the
Muses and I get on together very well. And if that hope of spoils deceives
me, at least I shall most truly have achieved the precise result which was my
second reason for following the court – to gain experience of the character,   25
the objects and the nature of a court, and of the actual arts of court life. To
such an extent am I really getting to know a great part of the world as well,
the very thing I thought and hoped it would be possible to aim at in the
court; for at court I thought one should be able – and one certainly is – to
survey the world from a kind of lofty watch-tower far and wide in all its   30
nations and its languages, great as it is. To such an extent do I also keep my
eye on outstanding examples of the way important business is conducted. A
single author, an Athenaeus or a Pliny, can supply a large proportion of a
complete knowledge of the arts; and if the assemblies of men are a kind of
books, living books, as indeed they are, a single court can furnish much the   35
largest part of the immense body of knowledge concerned with the conduct
of affairs. Breathes there the man who would not be attracted by such a
splendid prospect – especially if, in addition, one were invited, and invited
on complimentary terms, and invited by one who is a member of the
supreme council, and in fact the head of the entire imperial court?   40

But never mind: suppose I am done out of all the good things I speak
of. If only I can achieve thanks to the court one sole result, to be sent to
England to conduct the business of this government, I shall never have any
reason to regret what I have done; and in my opinion this should not prove
difficult to achieve. It is a project to which I am surprisingly attached, for I   45
wish to get to know the most cultivated court of a most cultivated king.[5]

Such, great Erasmus, is my plan. It is now your turn to consolidate my
slippery youth with good advice. To speak frankly, you have a duty to
perform for men of my age, for all of us I mean who have passed through the
stage of growing up and reached that part of Pythagoras' letter[6] where there   50
is a parting of the ways; and it is this. That is the stage at which you should
from time to time call out the rhythm for our oars, as Ulysses did[7] (for you are
the only true Ulysses of our time), this being by far the most perilous
moment in all the questions, so difficult and diverse and intertwined, which
face a man in the conduct of life – the moment when Lucian[8] was almost torn   55

* * * * *

5 Cf Ep 1313 n13.
6 The Greek Y (upsilon). See Persius 3.56; Lactantius *Institutiones divinae* 6.3;
  Ausonius *Technopaegnion* 13.9; Jerome *Letters* 66.11, 107.6.
7 Homer *Odyssey* 9:488–9
8 *De somnio sive vita Luciani*; Erasmus' translation is in ASD I-1 472–87.

in two by education and inclination and Hercules himself by virtue and vice, as Prodicus tells us in Cicero.[9] I have often greatly admired that story, and now for the first time I begin to understand it, now that I have left the university and the path marked out for me by my masters, and have come to a stop at the fork, abandoned to my own devices and surprisingly uncertain   60
which way to turn, until you give me some kind of indication which path I should now take. And this I beg and beseech you to do, as a suppliant before your sacred knees.

And so may Christ long preserve you unscathed for the benefit of us all and of all literature humane and sacred!   65

Ghent, 12 November
Herman Lethmaet of Gouda
Give my warmest greetings to Baer[10] and Beatus[11] and Glareanus.[12]
To Erasmus of Rotterdam, prince of the world of letters, in Basel

1321 / From Jan Becker of Borssele   Louvain, 23 November 1522

The autograph of this letter (=Förstemann/Günther Ep 11) was in the Burscher Collection at Leipzig (Ep 1254 introduction). Because the right-hand margin of the manuscript was badly worn, considerable restoration of the text was necessary in places.

Jan Becker (d 1536) was a native of Borssele, near Middelburg and Veere in Zeeland. He was educated at Louvain, where he taught for a time before departing in 1507 to spend most of the next decade as tutor to the nephews of Jérôme de Busleyden (Ep 205). Becker and Erasmus probably saw one another often at Louvain during Erasmus' residence there in 1502–3, and their acquaintance was renewed in 1517 (Ep 737). In 1518 Erasmus tried to secure Becker as the first professor of Latin for the Collegium Trilingue (Ep 805), but Becker chose instead to become dean of the chapter of Zanddijk or Zandenburg at Veere (Ep 849), a preferment he owed to the family of Adolph of Burgundy, heer van Beveren (Ep 93), who was now his patron.

Greeting. If you are well, best of teachers, I have every reason to rejoice, and so have thousands of other students who are most devoted to you. For my own part, I have been, rightly I think, intent upon my religious duties, and have refrained from interrupting you with a letter; for which there is no

* * * * *

9 *De officiis* 1.32.118
10 Ludwig Baer (Ep 488)
11 Ep 327
12 Epp 440, 1264 n2

stronger reason than my wish, knowing how you are burdened with work   5
that will benefit the whole world, not to break in upon you or disturb you
selfishly, as I can easily guess is done every day by many people who cannot
leave you alone. But my continual silence must not be taken as a sign of
ingratitude, and so I have now decided to have at least a few words with
you, that this letter may clear me of any suspicion of being ungrateful and   10
forgetful, and yet that being brief it may not be tiresome. But I would not
now dare to demand the book on the theory of preaching that you promised
three years ago,[1] since I see you beset on all sides by so many and such bitter
diatribes and critical comments that you are obliged to interrupt even the
most religious and most important labours of criticism and composition   15
which you had already undertaken. Let me however give you in a very few
words an account of my affairs.

I have lived hitherto in my parsonage at Veere, where last year I was
elected by the votes of all my colleagues to succeed the late dean of St Peter's
at Middelburg; though I almost fought against it and was reluctant to accept,   20
only that for good reasons the terms of that benefice appealed to me more.
When I followed up that election, I found the whole imperial court against
me, on account, they said, of an ancient privilege which empowers the
emperor to appoint deans and provosts to vacant positions as well as abbots.
And so with little difficulty, since I had no support – not even from my   25
patron,[2] who was reluctant to let me go except to the extent of allowing me to
take a small sum as an annuity – so being disappointed of that I stayed at
Veere and began eventually to take on the duties of a tutor by setting out to
teach the young son of the heer van Beveren.[3] When lo and behold, on the
advice of certain people he was sent to Louvain for the sake of his health   30
(which is very poor), not for the instruction, which he could get anywhere,
but for the climate, which is thought to be very healthy. So we moved here at
the end of September. We are Dorp's nearest neighbours,[4] for we live
opposite his house. I spend my time, so far as my tutorial duties allow, in
reading your most sacred expositions of the Scriptures and other religious   35
authors. Just recently the heer van Beveren conferred on me the living that

* * * * *

1321
1 See Ep 932:18–22. Erasmus made a beginning with the work in 1523 (Epp
  1332:41, 1341A:1334–8), but it was not to be published until 1535 as the
  Ecclesiastes sive de ratione concionandi.
2 Adolph of Burgundy; see introduction and line 29.
3 Philip, not Maximilian as asserted by Allen; de Vocht *Collegium Trilingue* I 264
  n5.
4 Ep 1266 n2

used to be held by Nicholas of Burgundy,[5] provost of Utrecht, called
Brouwershaven;[6] and he conferred it on me in my absence and with no
approaches made either by myself or anyone else on my behalf, rejecting
many other candidates for the benefice, so that my obligations to him   40
increase as his generosity towards me increases.

If you ever write to Dorp or your other friends, add a word of greeting,
if you can do no more, to an old friend who is most devoted to you. Farewell,
dear Erasmus, best of men and scholars, and go on doing to the last day of
your life what you have done for so many years now with great distinction to   45
yourself and even greater profit to the Christian religion. This is the true fruit
of the gospel, to do good to those who will not receive it and who even reply
with ill will and calumny and persecution. I pray you may enjoy long life and
most excellent health, and this not so much for your own sake (though it is
for your sake too) as for humane and sacred studies, to the advancement of   50
which you devote your whole life, attracted by no hope of reward except
what only Christ can give you. And so I wish you prosperity, now and for
very many years to come.

From Louvain, 23 November 1522
Your sincere friend Jan of Borssele   55
To the most eloquent and learned theologian of our age, Erasmus of
Rotterdam, his most respected and revered teacher. In Basel

1322 / From Jan Stercke   Louvain, 24 November 1522

The autograph of this letter (=Förstemann/Günther Ep 12) was in the Burscher
Collection at Leipzig (Ep 1254 introduction).

Jan Stercke (d 1536), of Meerbeke, near Brussels, was the first president of
the Collegium Trilingue at Louvain, an office he held until his retirement in
1526.

Greeting. Although your man Hilarius,[1] the bearer of this, could act as a
living letter from us to you and give you all our news, I hoped it would not be
unwelcome if I also sent you this note to report that we are all flourishing in

* * * * *

5 Adolph of Burgundy's uncle (Ep 144)
6 On the north coast of the island of Schouwen-Duiveland in Zeeland. This was
  Becker's compensation for the loss of the deanship at Middelburg (lines 22–8);
  de Vocht *Collegium Trilingue* I 266.

1322
1 Bertolph (Ep 1257 n10)

this our College – your college, rather – of the Three Tongues,[2] and that
everything about it grows more prosperous daily, so that there is nothing   5
more you could desire, except perhaps larger lecture-rooms. This college
will be honoured in the next few days by the arrival of two counts van
Egmond,[3] who are to lodge here; the business is all arranged. When this was
reported three or four days ago at some dinner where the theologians
customarily gorge themselves, there was a long silence as though they were   10
all astonished: this is how they congratulated us on such a success. There are
inquiries too from other nobles of the highest rank who want to come here,
but there is no room. All the same, if you decide to pay us a visit, we shall
easily find room for you; for master Conradus,[4] who now occupies the room
once designed for you,[5] will gladly move back to his ancient dungeon.[6]   15
Glapion,[7] about whom we were in doubt for a long time whether he were
alive or dead, has died in Spain; it is now definite. We hear of no moves
against you, but the attitude of the theologians towards you is haughty. The
rest Hilarius will tell you. Farewell, our glory and our great upholder. From
Louvain, 24 November 1522   20

Your humble servant and dependant Jan Stercke of Meerbeke
To the distinguished theologian Master Erasmus of Rotterdam, his
patron

1323 / To Archduke Ferdinand   Basel, 29 November 1522

First published in the *Opus epistolarum*, this letter is addressed to the brother of
Emperor Charles, Ferdinand of Hapsburg (1503–64), archduke of Austria and,
during his brother's prolonged absences from the empire, imperial viceroy. At
this time Ferdinand was in Nürnberg attending a meeting of the imperial diet
(November 1522–February 1523). Ferdinand's reply is Ep 1343.

The present letter had a dual purpose. First, and most obvious, it was a letter
of recommendation for an old friend, Jakob Spiegel (lines 34ff) of Sélestat.

* * * * *

2 On the current state of the young foundation, see Ep 1221.
3 Joris (d 1559) and Filips (d 1529) van Egmond, two of the younger sons of Count
 Jan III of Egmond (d 1516). The two young counts matriculated at the
 university on 6 December 1522 and stayed for some time at the Trilingue. Joris
 entered the church and eventually became bishop of Utrecht. Filips died while
 studying in Italy.
4 Evidently Goclenius (Ep 1257)
5 That is, a room at the Trilingue. As Ep 1296:17–18 shows, Erasmus preferred to
 retain his old lodgings at the College of the Lily.
6 The College of the Lily
7 Ep 1275

Spiegel (c 1483–after 30 June 1547), who was the nephew of Jakob Wimpfeling (Ep 224), had studied law, entered the imperial chancellery, and become one of Emperor Maximilian's secretaries. He sought Erasmus' friendship as early as 1515 (Ep 323) but the two did not meet until 1521 at Strasbourg (Ep 1342:232–4), by which time Maximilian had died (1519) and Spiegel had entered the service of Charles v. The warm praise bestowed by Erasmus in this letter helped Spiegel secure employment from Archduke Ferdinand, in whose service he remained until his retirement to private practice in Sélestat in 1526.

The second purpose of the letter is not so obvious. Although there is no mention of it in the text, it was evidently Erasmus' intention that Spiegel, in presenting the letter, should request from Ferdinand an imperial privilege for Froben (Epp 1344:123–46, 1353:253–65). For some reason, the letter did not reach Nürnberg until the beginning of February 1523 (Ep 1344:130–2 and notes), probably at the same time as Ep 1341, in which Erasmus solicited the aid of Pirckheimer in the matter of the privilege for Froben. Contrary to Erasmus' expectation (Ep 1341:21–2), Spiegel was not in Nürnberg (Ep 1344:132–3), so it was Pirckheimer who delivered the present letter to Ferdinand and who successfully presented Erasmus' petition on behalf of Froben.

ERASMUS OF ROTTERDAM TO FERDINAND,
BROTHER OF THE EMPEROR CHARLES

Respectful greeting, most serene Prince. I must not long delay your Highness when you are so fully occupied with so much important business; but you will remember, I suppose, that Erasmus whose book *De principe*[1]   5
you rendered more precious even to me as its author by deigning to read it.[2]
At the moment I ask nothing of you except that, if I deserve it, you should maintain your old good will towards me, especially in these days when all is in turmoil as never before. Nor do I ask this for any other purpose except that under your protection liberal studies and the gospel teaching in all its force   10
may daily grow in strength more and more among those who profess the name of Christians. For I have no wish for preferments or for stipends, being content with the humble position and the modest portion that are mine; but I do thirst for the glory of Christ, of which your Highness is no less a supporter than myself and can do far more to promote it. I at least, with   15

* * * * *

1323
1 The *Institutio principis christiani* of 1516. Erasmus described the second edition of 1518 as having been undertaken on behalf of Ferdinand, who at the age of fifteen was just entering upon his career in government; Epp 853:67–9, 1341A:1550–1.
2 Epp 943:23–4, 970:25–6, 1009:57–8

unsullied loyalty and a clear conscience, have laboured to promote it so far to the best of my ability.

In these last months I have dedicated to your brother, the invincible emperor Charles, a paraphrase on Matthew,[3] which I undertook on the insistence of Matthäus, cardinal of Sion,[4] and the emperor with his habitual kindness wrote most courteously to tell me that he highly approved of my work.[5] I now have in hand a paraphrase on John[6] which I have been encouraged by many people to attempt, but particularly by the cardinal of Mainz[7] and by that excellent prelate John, bishop of Rochester in England,[8] a man of incomparable holiness and learning, on the ground that this gospel contains more obscurities than the others, not only by reason of the sublime and heavenly themes of which it treats but also because the language is full of riddles which complicate the sense. This labour, such as it is, I have decided to dedicate to you; for you not only profess the teaching of the gospel, as we all do, but you have a great desire to understand it, and study to express it in your life and character. And the shining example which you set will, I hope, find more men to follow it, if your piety and your religious interest in Scripture become more universally known.

The bearer of this letter, Jakob Spiegel, was secretary to your paternal grandfather the emperor Maximilian, to whom he gave most loyal service which was highly valued. He is an elegant scholar with a felicitous style, and besides these gifts is a passionate and effective student of the Gospels. I would recommend him to your Highness, did I carry any weight myself or were he the sort of man to need any such recommendation; for I know that he will be most acceptable on account of his own merits, which have in fact already commended him to Maximilian, a prince who was a keen judge of men. Your serene Highness can promise yourself that your Erasmus will render any service which a lowly but loyal dependant can provide. May Jesus Christ the Almighty long preserve you in health and wealth, and may he prosper your counsels for the good estate of the commonwealth and for the glory of God.

Basel, 29 November 1522

* * * * *

3 Ep 1255
4 Ep 1255:27–31
5 Ep 1270
6 Ep 1333
7 Epp 1299 n10, 1308:23–4
8 Ep 1311 n9

1324 / From Adrian VI   Rome, 1 December 1522

For a year or more after Pope Adrian's election (9 January 1522), Erasmus anxiously sought some sign of the new pontiff's sentiments toward him, sending feelers via Barbier (Epp 1294, 1302) and approaching Adrian directly with the edition of Arnobius (Ep 1304) and its accompanying letter (Ep 1310). Despite their old friendship and Cardinal Adrian's encouragement of Erasmus' studies, Erasmus feared that his detractors in Rome and elsewhere might succeed in turning the essentially conservative, non-humanist Adrian against him (see Ep 1304 introduction). In the autumn of 1522 there were rumours that Adrian was dissatisfied with the Arnobius, that he had already pronounced Erasmus a heretic, and that he had publicly condemned Erasmus' books (Zw-Br Ep 246:19–20; Ep 1342:685–7, and Allen Ep 1518:24–9). It is not clear exactly when the present letter, with its unmistakable evidence of the pope's good will, reached Erasmus. It was sent to Brabant before being delivered to Basel (Allen Ep 1518:30–1). On 22 December Erasmus still had not received it (see Ep 1329 introduction). That it is mentioned in Ep 1341 but not in Ep 1337, both addressed to Willibald Pirckheimer, indicates that it reached Erasmus sometime between 8 and 28 January, perhaps delivered by Fabri (n13). Understandably, he was much relieved and greatly pleased (Epp 1341:30–2, 1345:17–20). Erasmus henceforth liked to call Adrian's letter the *Breve aureum*, boasted of it, and frequently cited it against his adversaries (see Aleandro's comments to this effect in Allen Ep 2638:34–5).

The basis of Allen's version was MS 1324 f 57 in the Librije (Town Library) at Gouda, a manuscript which, he conjectured, had been derived from the original letter received at Basel. The first printed edition, published with the *Exomologesis* in March 1524, contains numerous variants, some of which Allen incorporated into his text and all of which he appended in the notes. Far more significant are the numerous and lengthy variants in a draft of the letter in the Vatican archives (Cod Vat 3917 ff 16–17), which has corrections in what appears to be Aleandro's hand. The existence of this manuscript supports Aleandro's later claim (Allen Ep 2638:34–9) that the *Breve aureum* was his 'offspring' and that his draft was more generous in its praise of Erasmus than the version actually sent. Aleandro's claim in turn suggests that Adrian, finding the first draft by Hezius (see line 137 and Ep 1339) insufficiently warm (Ep 1342:698–704), may have dictated the substance of what he wished to say (Epp 1341:31–2, 1345:18–19) to both Hezius and Aleandro, charging each to draft a suitable breve, and finally accepting Hezius' second version. Allen included the most important variants in Aleandro's draft in his notes to the Hezius text. We have chosen rather to print Aleandro's entire draft as Ep 1324A (pages 209–14 below).

Pope Adrian VI
Ascribed to Bernart van Orley
Niedersächsisches Landesmuseum Hannover

POPE ADRIAN THE SIXTH TO HIS BELOVED SON ERASMUS OF
ROTTERDAM

Beloved son, greeting and apostolic benediction. We have read and reread
your letters with great satisfaction, one written to us in your own hand and
the other printed in front of the commentary of Arnobius in which you   5
dedicate your work to us. The letters delighted us, both because they came
from you, whom we have always valued highly for your outstanding
erudition, and because they gave evidence of exceptional devotion to
ourselves and to the religion we profess. As regards Arnobius, although the
press of serious business has not yet permitted us to read him, we are   10
convinced by the hasty soundings we have made in him so far, by his
venerable antiquity and the subject of which he treats, and last but not least
by your recommendation, that he cannot be other than a valuable author.
When you say in your letter[1] that you fear lest some men's enmity and
malicious gossip may have made us suspect you of a connection with the   15
party of Luther, we wish to put your mind at rest in this regard. For though,
to tell the truth, we have received reports on this subject from two or three
persons perhaps who are not very well disposed towards you,[2] yet by nature
and on principle, and also in accordance with the pastoral office which we
hold, we do not usually lend a ready ear to information reaching us to the   20
discredit of learned men who are noted for their holiness of life; for we
perceive that the more excellent the learning which we know to be theirs, the
more exposed they must be to the tooth of envy.

The affection however which we feel for you and the concern we have
for your reputation and true glory prompt us to urge you to employ in an   25
attack on these new heresies the literary skill with which a generous
providence has endowed you so effectually; for there are many reasons why
you ought properly to believe that the task has been reserved by God
especially for you. You have great intellectual powers, extensive learning,
and a readiness in writing such as in living memory has fallen to the lot of   30
few or none, and in addition the greatest influence and popularity among
those nations whence this evil took its rise; and these gifts you ought to use
for the honour of Christ, who in his most generous munificence endowed
you with them, and the defence of Holy Church and of the faith. And we
have this particular reason for desiring you to do so, that in this the best of all   35
ways you may silence those who try to fasten suspicion on you in connection

* * * * *

1324
1 Ep 1310:29–38
2 See Ep 1330:53–60.

with the business of Luther, and may crown the labours you have devoted
for so long to the assistance of the humanities and the correcting and
enriching of the Scriptures by this most sacred undertaking, than which
none can be more pleasing to God, more welcome to true Catholics, or more   40
worthy of you and of your gifts, your learning, and your eloquence.

Do not expect, moreover, that you will ever be given a more apt
opportunity of doing God a greater service or conferring a more fruitful
benefit on your own nation or indeed on the whole of Christendom than you
have now: you have only to take the heresies, as stupid and boorish as they   45
are godless, not so much invented by Martin Luther as inherited from
heresiarchs of former times (who have often been condemned by the
Catholic church and by the holy Fathers under the unquestionable inspiration of the Holy Spirit) and by him as it were newly unearthed from the
depths of hell, which daily, sad to say, subvert the souls of so many of your   50
brethren and fill the world with criminal confusion – these you must take
and, following the example and the praiseworthy zeal of your own master
Jerome and of Augustine and all the other holy Fathers, you must confound
them, abolish them, explode them by all the powers of reason and all the
authoritative texts of Holy Scripture. And indeed, Erasmus, you have many   55
publications to your credit hitherto, marked by admirable zeal and great
success; but however great the service they have rendered to the learned
world, when compared with the task to which we now invite you, and
which the agreement of all godly men urges you to undertake, they might
well seem of less immediate value. For they are useful to the learned only;   60
but this, with God's blessing, will redound to the general peace and
tranquillity of all Christian people, which is in our day almost the only
purpose of the teaching of the gospel.

This being so, Erasmus our beloved son, you, who from boyhood to
your present time of life have risen as it were through all the stages, and   65
have always made some advance for the better with all your powers in every
subject you have touched on by reasoning and by writing, must not hold
back any longer in this field, so uniquely adapted to your learning, your holy
calling, and your years; for while you have the same vivid energy as a writer,
your judgment is far more mature and the range of your knowledge far   70
wider. Nor could you reasonably decline this task by maintaining, perhaps
from some deeply ingrained modesty, that you are unequal to it. Apart from
the fact that this is contrary to common knowledge and to the truth of the
case, you will be supported in these efforts by God, whom you serve in so
doing, and by a most righteous cause, that of the faith, which has always   75
proved victorious over the craft and assaults of heretics, and will no doubt be
so again, although God in his most righteous judgment, on account of the

enormous crimes of men and especially of churchmen, allows the vessel of
his church to be somewhat hard put to it in these stormy waves.[3] Can we
suppose that this same God of ours will now desert his spouse the church,   80
which he purchased with his own precious blood[4] and promised that he
would be with her until the end of the world,[5] and will not confound instead
those men who are not afraid to set up their proud and perverse
understandings against the knowledge of God[6] and against the Catholic
truth? – for whom, as Peter the apostle says, 'judgment for long now does   85
not linger, and their destruction does not slumber.'[7] And the prophet says in
the psalm, 'I beheld the ungodly exalted above the cedars of Lebanon, and I
passed by, and behold, he was not; I sought him, and his place was not to be
found.'[8]

    And this, we have no doubt, will shortly befall Luther also and his   90
accomplices, unless they repent. Carnal men themselves and contemptuous
of authority, their aim is to make all others resemble them. Can you then
refuse to sharpen the weapon of your pen against the madness of these men,
whom it is clear that God had already driven out from before his face and
manifestly abandoned to a reprobate mind,[9] that they might say and teach   95
and do what is not right? By them the whole church of Christ is thrown into
confusion, and countless souls are involved together with them in the guilt
of eternal damnation. Arise therefore to bring aid to God's cause, and
employ your eminent intellectual gifts to his glory, as you have done down
to this day. Remember that you are placed in such a position that through   100
your labours and with God's help a great part of those who have been
subverted by Luther can return to the true path; those who have not yet
fallen may remain upright; and those who waver and are near to falling can
be preserved from giving way.

    How pleasing this will be to God, and what a joy to all true Catholics,   105
you can easily see for yourself. You ought also to bear in mind those words
of the apostle St James in which he declares that the man who turns back his
brother when he is wandering from the truth and recalls a sinner from the
error of his ways saves him from death, and for himself covers a multitude of

* * * * *

3 Ep 1344 n10
4 Acts 20:28
5 Matt 28:20
6 Cf 2 Cor 10:5.
7 2 Pet 2:3
8 Ps 37 (Vulg 36):35–6
9 Cf Rom 1:28.

sins.[10] For our part at least it cannot be expressed how welcome such a thing 11C would be, if as a result of your efforts those who are infected by that horrible heresy were to repent of their own accord, rather than wait to be smitten by the censor's rod of the church's canons and the laws of the Empire. How foreign this would be to our own nature you yourself, we are sure, know well enough from the time when we lived together in Louvain in the sweet 11! freedom of sacred studies and in what was still private life.[11]

Such is the urgent request we make of you in our great desire for the salvation of the flock entrusted to us and for the peace of Christendom; and if you are willing to increase its value by agreeing to something more, do, once the winter is past and the air of Rome, which has been suffering from 12C the plague for some months now,[12] is clear again, do come to us as soon as you can, but come in good health and spirits. Your arrival will give the greatest pleasure both to us and to all the friends whom you have here. You will be much helped also in this task, which you are as much bound as able to undertake, by the large supply of books in our possession and by frequent 12! discussion on these subjects with godly and learned men. We in our turn will do what we can and that soon, with Christ's blessing, to see that you have no reason to regret this journey and this most pious labour;[13] as our beloved son master Johannes Fabri,[14] a zealous man and a good scholar who is your very good friend and a great champion everywhere of your 13C reputation, will make clear to you at greater length by word of mouth or in writing; to whom we would ask you to give as much credence as you would to ourselves.

Given at Rome at St Peter's under the ring of the Fisherman in the

* * * * *

10 James 5:19-20
11 See Ep 1304 n2.
12 There was an outbreak of the plague in Rome in the period September–December 1522. Adrian, who insisted on staying in Rome, himself suffered an attack of fever in the third week of September. At the date of this letter, all but one of the cardinals had fled; Pastor IX 100–6.
13 Erasmus later stated (Ep 1341A:1681–3) that Adrian had offered him, doubtless orally through Fabri (see the following note), 'an honorific ecclesiastical preferment' (cf Ep 1345:19–20) and a gift of money, both of which he declined, apparently in the missing portion of Ep 1352.
14 See Ep 1260 n22. Fabri returned to Constance from Rome in the late autumn (end of November at the earliest) of 1522; see Ignaz Staub *Dr. Johann Fabri, Generalvikar von Konstanz, 1518–23* (Einsiedeln 1911) 177–8, n81; Rublack 212–13, n44. It is more than likely that when Fabri went to Zürich in January 1523 to attend the First Zürich Disputation, he included a visit to Erasmus at Basel on his itinerary; BAO no 142.

year of our Lord 1522, the first day of December, being the first year of our   135
pontificate
     T. Hezius[15]

1324A / From Adrian VI   Rome, c 1 December 1522

> This is Aleandro's draft of an alternative version of Ep 1324. For details, see Ep
> 1324 introduction.

Beloved son, etc. We have read and reread your letters with great
satisfaction, one written to us in your own hand and the other printed in
front of the commentary of Arnobius in which you dedicate your work to us.
The letters delighted us, both because they came from you, whom we have
always valued highly for your outstanding erudition, and because they gave   5
evidence of the highest devotion to ourselves and to the religion we profess.
As regards Arnobius, although the press of serious business has not yet
permitted us to read him through, we expect none the less that an author
cannot be other than excellent who is commended by his venerable
antiquity, by the subject of which he treats, and last but not least by   10
Erasmus. When you say in your letter that you fear lest some men's enmity
and malicious gossip may have made us suspect you of a connection with
the party of Luther, we wish to put your mind at rest on this score, not only
because your name has been reported to us in this regard less often perhaps
than you suspect, but also because by nature and on principle and, we might   15
add, in accordance with the office which we hold, we do not usually lend a
ready ear to information reaching us to the discredit of learned men; for we
perceive that the more excellent the learning which we know to be theirs, the
more exposed they must be to the tooth of envy.
     One thing we cannot possibly deny, that not only we ourselves but all   20
other men have long been greatly surprised that you have not yet brought
your fertile pen to attack these new heresies, since on many grounds there is
universal agreement that you are almost the one person for whom this task
seems to have been reserved by heaven. You have great intellectual powers,
extensive learning, and a readiness in writing such as no one else in living   25
memory has enjoyed; furthermore you have great influence and popularity
among those nations from which this evil took its rise. If you do not use
these gifts for the honour and defence of him who by his kindness alone
endowed you with them, take care lest by ingratitude towards your

        * * * * *

15 See introduction and Ep 1339.

Redeemer you do not both confirm the suspicion you so much resent, and   30
also waste the labours you have devoted so long to the enrichment of the
humanities and the correction of religious texts. For waste you undoubtedly
will the harvest of your intellectual gifts, if these rustic heresies are given a
footing. For how else are we to describe these monstrosities which Luther's
party after so many centuries unearths from hell, if not as damnable   35
delusions of Waldensian rustics?[1] These heresies are the more dangerous,
inasmuch as they are tricked out with the false colours of a meretricious kind
of style and filled with the corrosive poison of invective, and thus more
rapidly deceive simple minds, which have a natural bias in favour of
listening to calumny, and arouse them to the spreading of hatred and the   40
stirring up of sedition among the people of God, a situation which is all too
evident. Were these to remain unpunished, not only the humanities, for
which you have done so much, but all other sciences must inevitably either
perish altogether or suffer the most grievous loss; for the Doctors of the
church, the sacred councils, the laws both canon and civil, and the whole of   45
philosophy are by these profligate renegades despised and undermined.

It is true, Erasmus, that you have already many publications to your
credit, marked by admirable zeal and great success; but compared with
those which remain to be written and which are unanimously expected of
you, they are altogether of small account or at least are less necessary, as   50
being published for the benefit of the learned few. These other writings look
rather to the general peace and tranquillity of all Christian people, which is
in our day almost the only purpose of the teaching of the gospel. It is well

* * * * *

1324A
1 The Waldensians (also known as Vaudois) were followers of Peter Valdes
  (Waldo), a twelfth-century itinerant lay preacher from Lyon who denounced
  the wealth and worldliness of the church, preached poverty, simplicity, and
  strict morality, and undertook to make Scripture available to the public in
  vernacular translations. After Valdes was excommunicated in 1184, he and his
  followers organized a separate church which ordained its own priests, placed
  great emphasis on preaching, and rejected as unbiblical such things as
  purgatory, prayers for the dead, the veneration of saints and relics, several of
  the sacraments, and special status for the priesthood. Waldensian teachings
  spread throughout southern France and into Spain, northern Italy, Germany,
  Bohemia, Poland, and Hungary. As a result of fierce persecution beginning
  early in the thirteenth century, the Waldensians survived only in the mountain
  valleys of Savoy and Piedmont and in Germany and eastern Europe. In
  Bohemia, Waldensians were often mistaken for Hussites (see Ep 1260 n32). In
  the sixteenth century the Waldensians established friendly contact with Luther
  and other reformers. In 1532 those in the alpine valleys formally allied
  themselves with the Swiss reformed churches.

known that from boyhood to the present time, through all the stages of your
life, you have constantly enriched every subject you have touched on, both   55
by the arguments you have devised and the works you have written: what
do you suppose men will think and say about you if they now see you
holding back in a matter where you have an obligation to respond because of
your years and your holy calling, and especially since the vigour of your
writing remains as great as ever, your judgment has gained in maturity,   60
and, as one might expect, the range of your knowledge is much wider than
heretofore? Nor is there any reason for you to say that you are unequal to
this task or inferior to Luther; for the story that you said so, although in our
judgment false, and invented by very wicked men wishing to make their
cause respectable by the use of your name, is none the less circulating in   65
print. Apart from the fact that such a claim would be inconsistent with what
you and everyone else knows, and inconsistent too with the truth of the
case, you would also be showing yourself in some degree opposed to the
righteous cause of the faith, which elsewhere overcomes in the end all
attacks upon it open and secret. Could you ever think of any slanders with   70
which to assail the Christian religion more outrageously, or any greater
tribute with which to bolster up the false and self-destructive reasoning of
the heretics, than to confess yourself inferior to Luther's party in scholarship
or style? For many are convinced that once the rumour is put about of your
writing against them, they will collapse in a moment. As it is, they go about   75
proudly with their crests held high, some of them boasting of you as their
leader, maintaining that everything is done on your advice and in fact that
anything they have is drawn from you as the fountain-head; some saying
that you would never keep silence on these points, on which hinges a great
crisis in the church, unless you approved of what they write, seeing that   80
even the very smallest blemishes of language are more than you can tolerate
in Holy Scripture, though these at least have been made endurable by lapse
of time and force of habit in the church. But you will confront all these evils
with little effort, and will instantly dispel the cloud of suspicion that has
gathered in men's hearts as a result of your prolonged silence if, as soon as   85
possible and in all seriousness, you direct all the energy of your intellect and
of your pen against those who throw Christian charity into chaos and
equally cast a slur on your good name. Once you have done this, we do not
doubt that Luther's supporters will be moved by your honeyed eloquence,
by the sound and lively reasoning which you will bring into play, and most   90
of all by your authority, and will readily return to the flock of their
Redeemer, which they have basely deserted, led astray by an evil spirit, and
which they are trying with all the craft at their command to scatter and drive
over a precipice. You can readily see for yourself what a welcome

encouragement this would be to us and how preferable to correcting them   95
by the censor's rod of the laws. For remembering as you must how much
more inclined we were to mildness than to severity in the days when we
enjoyed the delightful freedom of study and what was still private life, you
ought to reckon that this merciful spirit of ours has not been weakened or
changed by increasing years and by our pastoral office, but increased. And   10
so it is with a great longing for the salvation of the sheep entrusted to us that
we urge you, beloved son, and beseech you in the Lord to undertake at last
this office, which is so acceptable to God and to men, so worthy of you as a
Christian and a theologian, and so welcome to us above all. For although
many distinguished minds have worked on this before now and not without   10
success, yet all consider that it is you who will, as they say, set the
coping-stone upon the work, if you once take it in hand. And if you are
anxious to increase the value of what we desire so much by adding
something more, do come to us as soon as you can, but come in good health
and spirits. And as for the task which we propose and which you are as   11
much bound as able to undertake, you will be much helped by the large
supply of books in our possession and by frequent discussion on these
subjects with us and with very many other godly and learned men. We for
our part will do what we can to ensure (and soon too, we hope) that you
have no reason to regret this journey and this most pious labour; for the   11
labourer, as the divine pronouncement runs, is worthy of his hire.[2] Given at
Rome.

1325 / To Duke George of Saxony   Basel, 5 December 1522

> The manuscript of this letter is in the same volume in the Staatsarchiv Dresden
> as that of Ep 1283 (Loc 10300) and was first published in the same place. On the
> background to the letter, see Ep 1313 introduction.

Greeting, most illustrious Prince. Since your Highness does not answer my
letter,[1] I suspect that it has never reached you. Were I inclined to suspect that
you were offended at the liberty I took in writing, your singular and
well-known kindness would make that impossible, especially since you
yourself invited me to write. This suspicion of mine is increased by Heinrich   5
Eppendorf,[2] who is afraid that the servant by whom he had sent it may have

* * * * *

2 Luke 10:7

1325
1 Ep 1313
2 See Ep 1283 n4.

been intercepted or some other misfortune may have befallen; which for his[3] sake I should much regret. For I find him a young man fully worthy of all the favours fortune can bestow, and he never tires of singing your praises. And so I send a copy of my earlier letter, in case it fell by the wayside.

I will add nothing at this time, except that I am with my whole heart your illustrious Highness' humble servant, whom I pray that Jesus Christ the Almighty may long preserve to us in health and wealth.

Basel, 5 December 1522

Erasmus of Rotterdam, your serene Highness' devoted servant, signed with my own hand

To the most illustrious Prince George, Duke of Saxony etc

1326 / To Heinrich Stromer   Basel, 5 December 1522

Heinrich Stromer (1482–1542) was a professor of medicine at Leipzig when he became personal physician to Albert of Brandenburg, archbishop of Mainz, in 1516 (Ep 578 introduction). In 1519 he entered the service of Duke George of Saxony and subsequently returned to Leipzig, where he became dean of the medical faculty in 1523. He was in Basel at the time of Erasmus' death, perhaps as attending physician.

This letter was first published in the *Opus epistolarum*.

ERASMUS OF ROTTERDAM TO HEINRICH STROMER
THE PHYSICIAN, GREETING

Honoured sir, 'many the friendships silence hath dissolved,'[1] so let me at least send these lines to greet my dear Stromer, and to assure you that your memory has not yet faded from my mind nor ever shall. What has happened to Petrus Mosellanus?[2] I long to know; for he had written to me at length about his coming here,[3] and since then I have not heard a word about him. He had also written to say that the most illustrious Duke George intended to give me a royal present[4] – that was the word he used. I certainly neither deserve nor expect a gift from that prince – not that I am a keen hunter of gifts from any quarter[5] – but if he has something in mind, I should be sorry if

* * * * *

3 Ie, Eppendorf's

1326
1 *Adagia* II i 26
2 Ep 1305
3 See Ep 1305 n1.
4 There is no mention of this in Ep 1305.
5 Cf Ep 1341A:1655–1774.

the generosity of that excellent prince were to come to naught, both for his sake and my own. Farewell.

Basel, 5 December 1522

1327 / To Huldrych Zwingli   Basel, 9 December 1522

This letter (=Zw-Br Ep 256) is Erasmus' reply to Zwingli's letter (now lost) replying to Ep 1315. The autograph is in the Staatsarchiv Zürich (E.II.339:88). It was first published by Hottinger (see Ep 1315 introduction).

Greeting. It is like your generous self, my dear Zwingli, to take my zeal for your welfare in good part. But the advice I give to many people is a waste of time. I could easily stomach other men's rashness if it did not weigh heavily on humane studies and on men of good will and on the cause of the gospel. In their misguided efforts to support it, they do it harm, so much so that   5
anyone who wished to snuff out Christ's teaching could not do more to help. Another piece of nonsense,[1] utter rubbish, has appeared about the pope. If the author had put his name to it, he would have been raving mad. As it is, he has put out his trash anonymously, which is as insipid as it is dangerous. If all Luther's party are like this, I wash my hands of the whole lot of them. I   10
never saw anything more mad than this foolish stuff. If the depths of winter did not tie me here, I would move anywhere rather than be forced to listen to such trumpery.[2] Farewell, my dear Zwingli, and maintain the cause of the gospel with prudence and with courage.

Basel, morrow of the Conception 1522   15
Your sincere friend Erasmus
To Huldrych Zwingli, parish priest of Zürich

1328 / From Guillaume Budé   Paris, 14 December [1522]

First published in *Budaei epistolae* I (Paris: Bade 1531), this letter is apparently an answer to the one of Erasmus mentioned in Ep 1319:2.

On Budé and his extensive correspondence with Erasmus, see Ep 403 introduction.

* * * * *

1327
1 Zwingli's anonymous *Suggestio deliberandi super propositione Hadriani pontificis Romani Nerobergae facta* ..., published at Zürich by Froschauer c November 1522; see Zw-Br Ep 256 n1. Erasmus' reference to the same work in Ep 1331:59–60 indicates that he had a good idea who its author was. Thus this letter in fact continues and reinforces the sharp criticism of Zwingli begun in Ep 1315.
2 See Ep 1319 introduction.

BUDÉ TO ERASMUS, GREETING

Thank you for your congratulations; your kindness ensured them a ready
welcome though not a cheerful one. You describe me as promoted to a most
honourable position[1] and speedily relieved at the same time of serious ill
health; but you must, I suppose, have derived this news from some rumour   5
which was as false as rumours usually are – as though it were possible that ill
health which has been chronic for eighteen years[2] and is now rooted, I might
say, in my vitals, could be finally cured in a man of studious habits, not to
say a man of my age. That I have been given a post which is honorific and
pretty lucrative I do not deny, for the king is really generous; and it is an   10
office which my friends and men of good will and lovers of the humanities
wanted for me and in some spirit of prophecy had earmarked for me long
ago, that humane studies might now be able to take a front seat and make
themselves heard from the platform both here and abroad, maintaining
their proper dignity as though from an exalted position. Such a thing it is to   15
deliver one's opinion in the city and in the highest courts of the land and to
show one's mettle in the councils of the court, and at the same time to be as
closely attached to so great a prince as one's gifts allow. For the duties of this
office have a wide scope and offer even more to me personally, inasmuch
as I already had the entrée to inner circles at court when an approach had   20
seemed desirable.

But to prevent me from making my mark in this position I have a new
form of ill health, offspring I suppose of that ancient trouble I have cursed so
often, for this year a kind of acrid phlegm mixed with bile has begun to
descend into my bowels, and there sets up such griping pains with severe   25
vomiting that no one would dare any more to promise me a life of some
length or at least make that seem likely now. And here you are, congratulating me on the departure of my illness when one like this has taken its place!
When I got your letter, I was well and truly on the rack, protesting loudly,
though I have as little self-pity as anyone. The next day I opened it and read   30
it with the greatest enjoyment, so far as my lamentable state permitted.
What I call the next day was today. So now what I want more than anything
else is to be allowed with the king's kind permission to live a city life in

* * * * *

1328
1 Budé had been a royal secretary since the 1490s, but during the years of his
   greatest scholarly productivity he had not actually functioned in that office. In
   1519, however, he returned to active service at court. In 1522 the king made
   him one of the eight 'masters of requests in the royal household,' ie, a
   magistrate of the Parlement. He was sworn in on 21 August. Budé provides a
   fuller account of the duties of a master of requests in Allen Ep 1370:57–103.
2 Budé's estimates of the duration of his illness tended to vary; cf Ep 1073:6–8.

future, which means making me my own master again, at least to some
extent. For this new office of mine is a half-and-half affair, the duties of   35
which oblige a pair of colleagues to be at court for a quarter of the year only.
Such conditions of work are just what I hope for, or rather, demand, for my
declining years and poor health, as a great kindness and a second
promotion. But I cannot really persuade the court to accept the reasons for
giving me leave of absence; for my outward appearance gives a highly   40
deceptive idea of my constitution and lends no support to my demands and
protests, which has always deprived my complaints and excuses of any
weight.

When you say in your letter that you have expressed your thanks for
the king's safe-conduct,[3] I have not yet discovered what this refers to. For a   45
second safe-conduct was sent you as well, and what happened after that I do
not know. Lately it so happened that I was on court duty in this city while
the king was here on a long visit,[4] and this I found very convenient. I hope
this activity will count as part of my official duties, just as though his retinue
were living abroad. The king is a supporter of your reputation, for he has   50
had some of your works translated into our vernacular, and reads them
often; he told me so himself the other day. Apart from that, what Konrad[5]
told you about the Greek lexicon[6] I myself neither accept nor deny. It had at
one time come into my mind, but the labour of the writing put me off. In the
way I had begun, it was an enormous task; not that the working up of the   55
material is more than I can now manage, but there is such a range of
subject-matter, at any rate after the labour of taking notes which I completed
long ago. For I have started on a great many things, up to the point where I
might perhaps not have to work very hard to finish them; but they are
scattered around in disorder all over the place, and after my death will be   60
very little comfort to my successors.

To ensure that I can find no spare time for this, on top of my duties at
court, I have been made provost of the merchants of this city,[7] an office

* * * * *

3 See Ep 1319 n6.
4 The court was at Paris from 29 November through 22 December 1522; see
  Catalogue des actes de François Ier ed Paul Marichal (Paris: Imprimerie Nationale
  1888–) VIII (1905) 438.
5 Probably Resch (Ep 1319 n2), who had published a Greek lexicon in July 1521
  (Bietenholz 348, no 3016), and who was perhaps now contemplating a new
  edition
6 Erasmus had urged Budé to produce a Greek lexicon; Ep 1233:179–85. Cf lines
  106–9 below.
7 The *prévot des marchands* of the city of Paris was supposedly the most important
  crown officer in the city government. Budé served one two-year term,

which suits me about as well as the army or business would go with a literary
life. For over four months this has already deprived me of reading time and   65
peace and cheerfulness, so that with the pressure and the fatigue of these
unaccustomed problems I have already had enough; and in the mean time
this city has been practically emptied by the exodus of citizens taking refuge
from the plague,[8] which rages here, while I and a few of my colleagues have
been obliged by the duties of our office to stay on here, so that on very few   70
days in the last three months, as opportunity offered, have I been able to
spend a night on my country estate at Saint-Maur, to which I had sent my
household. Besides which, the post of master of requests, which is the office
I have lately been given, after having previously been appointed prefect of
the royal library,[9] a position which has not much less in the way of   75
advantages (and I find that for me these two offices do not clash) – this post,
as I say, requires different interests, as foreign to those I started with as
litigation is to those who love a merry life and the books written by our
professors are to those with a love of good writing.

Both these offices were given me by the prince in my absence, so let no   80
man think me a successful place-hunter or greedy for power. The first of
them had summoned me from home and involved me after all in the retinue
of the court. But when I had seized an opportunity to return home and pay a
longed-for visit to my family,[10] the king sent me my letters of appointment to
the mastership from Lyon,[11] which is not only a pretty lucrative post but   85
very much sought after, and the lawyers at court actually intrigue for it,
though all this time I have had no one to put my claim either by arrangement
with me or of his own accord. With the appointment I got also a letter from
the prince addressed to me, which showed and set forth his real and true
generosity and his continued good will towards myself. Of the eight   90
members of the board, one, who also held a bishopric, had died at court
unexpectedly and on his return from an embassy.[12] After that, I went to

* * * * *

beginning on 16 August 1522. That he was seldom in Paris during that period
suggests that he was only a figurehead.

8 Cf Ep 1342:1128

9 The office of *maître de la librairie du roi* was created especially for Budé. Nothing
is known of the duties involved.

10 Early in June. Budé was still in Lyon on 3 June; Louis Delaruelle *Répertoire
analytique et chronologique de la correspondance de Guillaume Budé* (Toulouse 1907;
repr New York n d) nos 137–8.

11 The court was at Lyon most of the time throughout June and until 23 July; *Actes
de François ier* (see n4) VIII 437.

12 Jean Caluau, bishop of Senlis, who died at court in June, soon after returning
from an embassy to Switzerland

court to express my gratitude to the king (and the court meanwhile had moved nearer,[13] which saved me a long journey) and also to take the legal oath as is usually done (for until then the practice is that no pay is issued to new entrants on office), and then returned to the city to be admitted to a seat on the supreme court,[14] having first bound myself there too by the same oath; when, lo and behold, the day before my arrival news reached me of the offer of this position in the city,[15] which was made with public acclamation, though it was the last thing I expected, and I am not sure that it is a good idea. For there I discovered and ran head on into an Iliad, as they call it, of abuses and troubles.[16] But I could not refuse the honour, though it was an awkward and difficult moment, and I wanted to refuse, against the authority and orders of the prince, who arrived in the same city himself soon afterwards.[17]

So you cannot hope to get anything out of me for the common cause of good literature, much less for the compilation of a lexicon, though there is nothing anyhow that I would more cheerfully, willingly, and readily take on if I had the time.[18] Later on perhaps I shall see what it would be right for me to contribute, as best I can, if providence gives me rather more generous treatment, as I so much hope, and at the same time if this age we live in permits, which I fear will one day distinguish itself by a disastrous war. Please God I may be wrong! Farewell.

Paris, 14 December

Deloynes[19] came to see me, and he read your letter. He said he had had one from you on more or less the same subject,[20] to which he will soon send an answer. Farewell once more, O benefactor of good letters beyond precedent.

1329 / To Adrian VI   Basel, 22 December 1522

This letter was first published with the *Exomologesis* (see Ep 1310 introduction), where the editor noted that Erasmus had sent it before he received Ep 1324. Pope Adrian's reply is Ep 1338.

* * * * *

13 The court left Lyon on 23 July and proceded via Roanne (24 July) and Blois (4–15 August) to Paris (18 August); *Actes de François 1er* (see n4) VIII 437.
14 Ie, the Parlement of Paris; see n1 above.
15 See n7 above.
16 *Adagia* I iii 26
17 Ie, Paris, on 18 August; see n13 above.
18 In 1529 Budé did finally publish his *Commentarii linguae graecae* (Paris: Bade).
19 See Ep 494.
20 Not extant

TO HIS HOLINESS ADRIAN VI FROM ERASMUS OF
ROTTERDAM, GREETING

Most blessed Father, I send you for the second time, by the public courier of
the city of Basel, a token of my devotion to yourself and my active loyalty to
your see, in case the book I sent some time ago has not reached you.[1] At that   5
time I had nothing else in hand; should a more promising opportunity
present itself, I shall not fail to do my duty. Nothing can be more stormy
than the times we live in, in which it is most difficult to satisfy everyone. I at
least have satisfied my conscience hitherto, and hope to defend my record
even before Christ. Nor is the tempest of affairs always the same: conflicting   10
weapons, opinions, ambitions, factions, hatred tear everything to pieces.
The world looks to you alone to restore tranquillity to the affairs of men.

If your Holiness instructs me, I will make so bold as to give you an
outline in a secret letter of my own proposal,[2] unwise it may be but at least
loyal, for putting an end to this evil in such a way that it will not easily sprout   15
again. Not much is gained by suppressing it by brute force in such a way that
it soon breaks out again in more perilous form, like the scar of a wound that
has not healed. In a violent storm the master of a ship, however great his
experience, will listen to advice from anyone. Nor did Moses reject the
counsel of Jethro[3] – not that I am a Jethro, but Davus in Horace gives loyal   20
advice to his master.[4] If there is anything in it worth having, it can be made
use of; if there is nothing, it will be known only to us two, and there will be
no risk in suppressing it. We humble folk see and hear perhaps some things
that are not to be despised, which escape the notice of men in high places.

First then, my view is that we must not allow some men's private   25
resentment to bring public mischief on the world at large, and on Christ's
cause; and we must maintain the authority of men only so far as will not
compromise the authority of Jesus Christ, who alone is the same yesterday,
today, and for ever.[5] In my day I have written with some freedom,[6] for this
was then encouraged by the peaceful state of things, and I never suspected   30
the rise of times like these. But now – now that I see Christendom brought
into great peril, we must above all be on the look-out and allow absolutely no
scope to individual feelings. I have no desire to be a prophet of evil; but I see

* * * * *

1329
1 Arnobius; see Epp 1304, 1310. Ep 1338:3–6 indicates that both copies reached
  the pope.
2 See Ep 1352 introduction. For earlier ventures in the same vein, see Epp 1267 n6
  and 1275 n7.
3 Exodus 18
4 *Satires* 2.7
5 Heb 13:8
6 In the *Moria* and other satirical works. Cf Ep 1007:85–7.

more peril threatening than I could wish, and more than many men
perceive. May Christ turn it all to a happy outcome!   3

This city of Basel, so richly endowed and so flourishing, is drawn by a
special devotion to the Holy See for many reasons, but particularly on
account of the council that was held here long ago.[7] It therefore deserves, in
my opinion, to be favoured by your Holiness, especially as its request is
neither unfair nor burdensome.[8] I have been asked to add this, though it was   4
quite unnecessary. If your Holiness will deign to test my loyalty, give me
what task you will, and unless my obedience is prompt and cheerful, do not
count the name of Erasmus among your servants. May the spirit of the Lord
Jesus guide your heart and all your undertakings towards the salvation of
the world and the glory of God.   4

Basel, 22 December 1522

1330 / To Jakob Ziegler   Basel, 22 December 1522

This letter was first published in the *Opus epistolarum*. On Jakob Ziegler, see Ep
1260. On the intervening correspondence, see n5.

ERASMUS OF ROTTERDAM TO JAKOB OF LANDAU IN BAVARIA
Though always excessively busy, I have never been busier than I am now;
but none the less, when the magistrate of this republic told me that he would
be dispatching a special messenger to your part of the world,[1] I took your
preface,[2] which contains your skirmish with Zúñiga,[3] and read it through   5
without drawing breath. I will not thank you just now, dear Landau, for
your feelings towards me; I wish I could repay them. I salute, more than I
can say, your fertile and gifted mind and a vein of expression equal to your
gifts; and this makes me the more indignant with that noisy crew of
blockheads whose rascality means the dragging down into this sort of   10
quarreling of minds born for better things. What's more, though further
from envy than from any other fault, I am positively jealous of Zúñiga,

* * * * *

7 The Council of Basel, 1431–49
8 The purpose of the appeal to Rome is unknown.

1330
1 Cf Ep 1329:3–4.
2 The reference is to Ziegler's *Libellus* (Ep 1260 n50), which bears the subtitle *In
quatuor Evangeliorum perpetuam historiam prologus, cum Erasmianae traductionis
defensione*. The *Libellus* has no preface by Ziegler; it is itself a preface or prologue
to a continuous narrative of the Gospels intended for later publication.
3 Ep 1260 n36

believe it or not, for rousing your pen to write like this. Personally, I have
regretted over and over again that I ever touched that contagious wretch,
and I am resolved henceforward to put up with anything rather than give   15
tongue against him.[4]

Both your letters,[5] you must know, have reached me; if I did not
answer the second, there was no reason except my lack of leisure, which is
beyond belief. A good share of my time is claimed by my health, which lets
me down from time to time; and for the rest, the publishing of my books   20
means so much labour that Hercules twice over could hardly cope with it.[6]
On top of this there are so many letters from all directions that this business
by itself would be more than I could manage, however hard I try. Your
mistake was to me a very great blessing, since it produced such a long and
eloquent letter; for I was not consulting you whether Zúñiga should receive 25
a reply; I was dropping you a polite hint that you should write nothing in the
way of an attack on him, since this would merely stir up a hornets' nest. This
is just what that swashbuckler thirsts for: to be made famous, no matter
how, in what many people write; and he deserves much more to be
hounded by the doggerel of penny poets like a donkey in a swarm of bees.   30

What would you like to be done with your book? – you give no
indication. Nor could I make out from it whether you have read the defences
in which I have replied on two occasions to Zúñiga,[7] and shortly thereafter
to Carranza.[8] For I suppose they have been conveyed to your part of the
world by Claudio the bookseller.[9] I could not guess adequately what   35
arrangement you had followed in your book; for one thing, that brother[10] of
yours who copied it out made many mistakes in spelling. Whatever you may
decide about this piece, let me urge one thing: if you ever wish the work you
have started on the narrative of the four Gospels to see the light of day,[11] do
not let Zúñiga's name defile either that or any other work that you think will 40
live. What gain would there be in that? To make him ashamed of himself?

* * * * *

4 Cf Ep 1312 n5.
5 Ep 1260, Erasmus' answer to which is lost; and another letter, not extant, to
   which Erasmus had not yet replied
6 Erasmus was now working on a new edition of the *Adagia* (January 1523), the
   paraphrase on St John (Ep 1333), the edition of Hilary (Ep 1334), and the
   Catalogus lucubrationum (Ep 1341A).
7 See Epp 1277 n1, Ep 1260 n45.
8 See Ep 1277 n8.
9 Unidentified
10 Martin Richter of Redwitz, Ziegler's secretary and 'frater adoptatus'; see
   Schottenloher *Ziegler* 35, 62, 100, 102, 397.
11 See n2 above.

You could sooner make a boulder blush. To make him mend his ways? He is
past praying for. To show the world that a monster has been born? No result
could be more welcome to him, could this come his way.

And if it is Rome that has produced a lunatic to attack me openly, I   45
made a good guess at the standard of integrity of some men in that city, nor
is it concealed from me who put him up to do this, though libel comes to him
naturally and he was born to act this part. Moreover, if that elderly cardinal
called of Santa Croce, his fellow-countryman,[12] accepts the man and
honours him with his society, what can one say except that the cover is   50
worthy of the cup? From the high priest I like to hope for better things;[13] at
any rate, as far as I am concerned, I know that certain men who hate me have
been disappointed so far. There are three Furies among us who from hatred
of the humanities stir up all this sorry business, Jacob of Hoogstraten,[14] a
Dominican, Vincentius[15] of Alkmaar of the same society, and Nicolaas   55
Baechem,[16] a Carmelite. And there is a man one might well add to their
number, who is the more dangerous because he does everything in secret
and makes good use (very bad use, rather) of other men's lunacy.[17] Hateful
as they are to all men of good will, and daily becoming more so, these
characters have been a great help to Luther's faction.   60

* * * * *

12 Bernardino de Carvajal (Ep 239:55n)
13 Adrian VI. For Erasmus' apprehensions about the new pope, see Ep 1304
    introduction. Ep 1324, with its good news about Adrian's attitude, had not yet
    reached Erasmus; see the introduction to that letter.
14 Ep 1299 n25
15 Vincentius Theoderici; see Epp 1196 introduction and 1263:29–30.
16 Ep 1254 n6
17 Note the similarly worded references in Epp 1301:231, and 1302:83–8. Allen,
    citing Schottenloher Ziegler 62, suggested that the unnamed fourth Fury was
    perhaps Aleandro (Ep 1256 n11). The suggestion is plausible if one focuses
    solely on the passage in Ep 1302 describing the man in question as someone
    whose character, agreeable 'when he was still in a junior position,' had been
    deformed by greed and ambition. There are, however, at least two good
    reasons for thinking that Erasmus was referring to someone other than
    Aleandro. First, all three references in the letters strongly indicate that the
    unnamed adversary was someone present in Louvain, either a member of the
    theological faculty or someone closely associated with it. But by the time
    Erasmus wrote Ep 1301 he knew that Aleandro had long since departed for
    Spain (Ep 1271:68–71). Second, the present letter strongly implies that the
    unnamed ally of Baechem et al was an enemy of the humanities, which
    Aleandro certainly was not. There was, however, such a person in Louvain:
    Jacobus Latomus (Ep 934:4n), who fits Erasmus' description in all other
    respects as well. He and Erasmus had had friendly relations while Latomus
    was still a junior academic at Louvain (LB IX 79D, 82F), but in 1519 Latomus had

As to my coming to Rome, it is no use your putting forward reasons.
There is one counter-argument with more truth in it than I could wish: my
advancing years, my physical weakness, and on top of that stone in the
kidneys,[18] a fatal disease with which I am now all too familiar. What you tell
me to do with your letters I have always done hitherto, and will so   65
continue.[19] Athanasius in a Latin version by Reuchlin I will send you by this
courier if I can get a copy,[20] and also my *Apotheosis* of your friend Reuchlin.[21]
Johann Froben is devoted to you, and sends you his best wishes. Farewell.

Basel, 22 December 1522

1331 / To Johann von Botzheim   Basel, 25 December 1522

On Botzheim, see Ep 1285. This letter was first printed in the *Opus epistolarum*.
Botzheim's reply is Ep 1335.

ERASMUS OF ROTTERDAM TO JOHANN VON BOTZHEIM,
GREETING
Today your letter[1] of 14 November was delivered to me by the university
people. There was no need to take all that care in handing over so small a
present[2] to so great a prelate,[3] especially as there was nothing in it that   5

* * * * *

attacked the humanities and, by implication, Erasmus himself (so the latter
thought) in two published dialogues (see Ep 934 introduction). More recently,
Vives had reported that Latomus' success in his pursuit of the favour of the
Croy family had caused him to put on airs and made him unpopular with his
colleagues (Ep 1256:86–9). Vives also reported that Latomus and Baechem
were circulating 'wicked falsehoods' about Erasmus (ibidem lines 27–8).
Latomus' avoidance of Baechem-like public attacks on Erasmus would explain
the references to his dangerous habit of working in secret. Finally, Erasmus'
motive for suppressing Latomus' name would presumably have been his hope
for a détente in their relations; in both the *Catalogus lucubrationum* (Ep
1341A:831–8) and the *Spongia* (ASD IX-1 158:893–4), Erasmus states that he
had always tried to deal sparingly with Latomus in the hope that the latter
would desist from his attacks.

18 Ep 1267 n5
19 Ie, to burn them; see Ep 1260:307–9. But Erasmus had not burned Ep 1260.
20 Reuchlin had translated two of his works: *In librum Psalmorum* (Tübingen
   1515), and *De variis quaestionibus* (Haguenau 1519).
21 See Ep 1311 n15.

1331
1 Not extant
2 According to Allen, this apparently refers to the *divinatio* of Ep 1335:3, which
   Botzheim had evidently given to the bishop (see n3) on his own responsibility.
3 Hugo von Hohenlandenberg, bishop of Constance

properly concerned him. I will use other means, given the opportunity, of
showing my devotion to his Highness. Nor will this be a pretence; it will be
done from the heart, nor do I hope for anything out of him except good will
on both sides and a common enthusiasm for the gospel cause which is the
concern of all alike, and which that excellent bishop supports, I do not   10
doubt, as far as the state of things permits. My paraphrase on John I have
reserved for Ferdinand,[4] the emperor Charles having testified in a letter[5] he
actually wrote me how pleased he was with that on Matthew;[6] though I
learned that not only from him but from many other men's letters:
Gattinara,[7] his high chancellor; Glapion,[8] the Franciscan (who could do   15
whatever he pleased with the emperor while he lived); the bishop of
Palencia,[9] who has also died; Joris van Halewijn;[10] Antoon Sucket,[11] the
most fair-minded man of our generation; Jean de Carondelet,[12] archbishop
of Palermo – not to mention others who are private friends.

Those who expect to carry the same weight in Christ's business, which   20
is the concern of every nation and of every century, that they do in
theological wine-parties and petty scholastic disputations are very wide of
the mark. It is a mighty and unconquerable thing, is truth; but it must be
deployed with a wisdom learned of the gospel. Such is my hatred of
dissension and my love of concord that I fear, if it came to the point, I should 25
abandon some portion of the truth sooner than disturb the peace, always
assuming there is something I can do. That preacher of yours,[13] at any rate,
the worthy man, will prove to have done more for the gospel cause, of which
we are all supporters beyond a doubt, if he joins the wisdom of the serpent
in the gospel[14] to his dovelike innocence. Let him make the experiment, and   30
reject my advice unless he finds it true. What our deities are up to, whether

* * * * *

4 Ep 1333
5 Ep 1270
6 Ep 1255
7 Answering the letter mentioned in Ep 1281:2
8 Evidently in reply to Ep 1275
9 Evidently in answer to Ep 1273
10 Ep 1269
11 Not extant. Antoon (1) Sucket (d 1524) of Mechelen studied law and rose under
   the patronage of Jean Le Sauvage (Ep 301:38n) to be a member of Charles of
   Hapsburg's privy council in 1517. As one of the executors of Jérôme de
   Busleyden's estate (Ep 884:5n), he played an important role in the founding
   and management of the Collegium Trilingue. Erasmus' high opinion of him is
   expressed in Epp 1556 and 2191.
12 Answering Ep 1276
13 Johann Wanner (Ep 1335 n5)
14 Matt 10:16

the inner circle or the lesser fry – though of this too I get reports at length from various places – it is not for me, a member of the lowest walk of society, to pass judgment on. For myself, I shall play my part in this play, to be sure, with all my heart; the outcome must be left to Christ, who is our producer. 35

I am glad you found my letter[15] a pick-me-up; but it surprises me that you people in Constance can catch such a fell disease from so flimsy a rumour.[16] Were I of the same mind, who am a product of Holland[17] and not Constance and have falsehoods of this kind brought me every day, I should have expired long ago. Let me tell you this: those two theologians who used 40 to vent their private spite not on me, for I had never said a word against them, but on the humanities, which I had always defended, have never been better behaved than they are now.[18] In all this Pope Adrian was their last resort; and now that he has failed them, they are much cast down. They lay the blame for this on a certain theologian who is devoted to me,[19] though 45 we are quite unknown to one another, who can do what he likes (so they say) with the pope. A pope who from genuine principle forwards the business of Christ will have my support in every possible way, so far as my minuscule talent will reach. Nor have I any doubt that, being as he is an old man and a scholar and a man with great experience of affairs, he will answer 50 our expectations. If he should fail us at any point, I at least shall not go in search of strife.

Now for that last small question from your preacher: Must we abandon the whole gospel? In the first place, no one abandons it more thoroughly than its incompetent defenders. Then, think how slowly Christ revealed his 55 teaching! yet what could be more mad than some of those who now wish to be taken for champions of the gospel? I have warned a friend[20] not unknown to you about that letter of the bishop of Constance that is so much discussed;[21] and now there appears a piece of nonsense far more crazy than

* * * * *

15 Not extant
16 Perhaps the rumour that Adrian had declared Erasmus a heretic (Zw-Br Ep 246:20); cf Ep 1324 introduction.
17 Ie, thickheaded, dull; *Adagia* IV vi 35
18 An apparent reference to Zúñiga (Ep 1260 n36) and Carranza (Ep 1277 n8). The publication of Zúñiga's *Erasmi blasphemiae et impietates* had been banned by Leo x, by the college of cardinals, and by Adrian VI; Ep 1312 n4.
19 Apparently Hezius (Ep 1339), whose signature is appended to Epp 1324 and 1338
20 Zwingli
21 Zwingli's *Apologeticus Archeteles* (see Ep 1314 introduction) replies point by point to a letter addressed to the Zürich chapter by the bishop of Constance. Cf Ep 1315.

anything.[22] I cannot conceive what they have in mind or what they are   60
aiming at.

Cronberg has talked with me twice,[23] and I greatly liked his modesty
and good sense. Hutten I have not seen,[24] nor do I wish to see him just now.

* * * * *

22 See Ep 1327 n1.
23 Hartmuth von Cronberg (1488–1549), an imperial knight whose ancestral
   estate was at Kronberg im Taunus, northwest of Frankfurt am Main. An early
   convert to the Reformation, Cronberg wrote a number of pamphlets in support
   of it in the years 1521–3. In 1522 he made common cause with his father-in-law
   Franz von Sickingen (Ep 1342 n33) in the abortive Knight's Rebellion, as a
   result of which he was deprived of his property at Kronberg. In the autumn of
   that year he visited Basel, where he had two interviews with Erasmus (Ep
   1342:766–7), and in September 1523 he settled with his family in that city, his
   misfortunes having left him unperturbed in his loyalty to the Reformation.
24 Ulrich von Hutten (Ep 365), whose turbulent career as poet, pamphleteer,
   ardent German nationalist, hater of the papacy, champion of the free imperial
   knights, and violent supporter of the Reformation was drawing to a close.
   Forced to flee Germany because of his desperate 'war on the Romanists,' which
   involved a good deal of highway robbery and blackmail, Hutten, destitute and
   already terminally ill with syphilis, arrived in Basel toward the end of
   November 1522, departing again for Mulhouse (Mülhausen) on 18 January. In
   Basel, Hutten moved in the circle of reformers around Oecolampadius, who
   were annoyed by Erasmus' opposition to Zwingli and thus to the whole
   Reformation as they understood it (Epp 1314, 1327), an opposition that they
   attributed to cowardice and fear of the loss of income from Catholic patrons (cf
   Epp 1342:707–19, 799–806, 1348:34–40, and Allen Epp 1384:20, 1459:80).
   Meanwhile, Erasmus' affection for Hutten, for years his close friend and
   comrade in the battle against the enemies of languages and good literature
   (Epp 365, 611, 951, 986, 999), had since 1520 been increasingly strained by
   Hutten's persistent efforts, beginning with the unauthorized publication of Ep
   1033, to prod Erasmus into open support for Luther (Epp 1135, 1161). When
   Hutten arrived in Basel, Erasmus sent greetings and protestations of continued
   friendship, but declined to receive a visit from him. Of the several reasons
   which he later gave for this (Ep 1342:760–6, Allen Ep 1496:6–13, Spongia ASD
   IX-1 128–9), the most important was probably the fear that a visit from Hutten
   would have been misunderstood by Erasmus' Catholic patrons, including
   those at the imperial court, as a defection to the 'Lutheran' faction, something
   which would have deprived Erasmus of his unique mediating role in the
   religious conflict. Erasmus clearly expected that Hutten would, as a friend,
   understand the need for discretion, as did Melanchthon later in similar
   circumstances (Allen Epp 1452:16–18, 1466:20, 1496:3–5). He was thus
   genuinely surprised and hurt when Hutten, interpreting his action as a breach
   of friendship by someone who had already betrayed the Reformation for base
   reasons, launched a bitter attack upon him (see Epp 1341A:1019ff, 1356, 1378–9,
   1384, 1388–9). For a thorough analysis of the Basel incident and the subsequent
   controversy, see Kaegi 461–514.

I wish him well with all my heart, if he would give himself a chance. I have
other things to take my time. I wrote at the same time to you and to Fabri.[25]   65
Beatus is still away.[26] Eppendorf rarely comes to see me;[27] otherwise he is
much the same. Please give my greetings to all my friends, especially the
physician[28] (to whom I have never returned thanks although, as the Greeks
say, I have forgotten nothing), your preacher the Dominican,[29] and
Hummelberg.[30] I should be glad to know the names of the physician and the   70
preacher.[31] May your patronesses the Graces grace with success all that you
do or say. May you ever be a pleasure to your friends, and they to you, and
take your part with the Graces in the Muses' choir. This answers most of
your points, but I write soon after dinner, when Bacchus is my inspiration
rather than the Muses.   75

Christmas Day 1522

1332 / To Christoph von Utenheim   Basel, [early January?] 1523

Christoph von Utenheim (c 1450–1527), member of a noble family of Lower
Alsace, was educated at Erfurt and Basel (doctor of canon law, 1474). He
became a canon of the Basel chapter in 1475, coadjutor for the ageing bishop in
1499, and bishop in 1502. Although he proved to be an ineffective administrator
of his diocese, Christoph's genuine devotion to ecclesiastical reform and
humanist scholarship endeared him to the humanists of Alsace and Switzerland.
His generous hospitality to Erasmus during the latter's second visit to Basel
(1515–16) inaugurated a lifelong friendship (Epp 412–14), and Christoph's
influential presence at Basel was doubtless one factor in Erasmus' decision to
settle there in the autumn of 1521. Erasmus' *Epistola de esu carnium* (Ep 1293 n8)
was addressed to him, and the *De immensa Dei misericordia* (1524) was dedicated
to him.

   This letter was first published in the *Opus epistolarum*. The tentative nature of
the remarks concerning the new pope (lines 34ff, 69ff) indicates that Ep 1324 had
not yet arrived, hence the approximate month-date (cf Ep 1324 introduction).

* * * * *

25 See Epp 1260 n22, 1324 n14.
26 Beatus (Ep 327) was at Sélestat on business. Hutten had visited him there in
   November; ASD IX-1 130–1 (*Spongia*).
27 See Ep 1283 n4.
28 Johann Menlishofer (Ep 1335 n10)
29 Evidently Antonius Pyrata (Ep 1342 n97)
30 See Ep 1253 n6.
31 Botzheim misunderstood this request for the name of the Dominican preacher
   (see n29) and supplied the name of Wanner (n13 above) instead; see Ep
   1335:48–9. In Ep 1342:433–6, Erasmus evidently still did not know Pyrata's
   name.

ERASMUS OF ROTTERDAM TO CHRISTOPH, BISHOP OF BASEL

I have been toiling continuously at my researches,[1] from which, as you
know, I never take a holiday, and have been distracted by several other
pieces of business – not to renew just now my old complaints of ill health,[2]
and of the affliction which has now been my companion for too long.[3] All the   5
same, I wanted to comply with your request, for there is no man living
whom I would more readily gratify; and so I ran through the book you sent
me[4] – for I cannot say I read it properly. In the treatise on the position and
duties of bishops, many people will perhaps be put off by the simple style
and inelegant language; for in these days hardly anything is saleable unless   10
it also breathes all the perfume of the Muses. Apart from that, your
Carthusian author does not lack abilities, and his language, though not
entirely Latin, is clear. As far as the second work is concerned, however,
with such an abundance of subject-matter – for Gospels and Epistles,
prophets, every book in both Testaments in fact, have so much to say about   15
pastoral duties – I thought the author inadequate; and his obscurity too
would have interfered with the popularity of his book, even had he
somehow discovered a skill in handling to match the richness of the
material. In any case, many things which he repeats from the revelations of
St Bridget as though they could be taken seriously will raise a smile   20
nowadays, I am quite sure, with every educated reader; such are the
principles of human credulity.

The book by the bishop of Beirut,[5] whom I once knew,[6] is not
unscholarly, but smacks too much of canon law. On this ground I am sure
that nowadays at any rate it will be unpopular with the majority; though   25
apart from that it is thin and undistinguished. Consequently one is not likely
to find anyone ready to print it at his own risk. But if your lordship would

* * * * *

1332
1 See Ep 1330 n6.
2 See Ep 1256 n2.
3 See Ep 1267 n5.
4 According to Allen, this was apparently a volume, possibly in manuscript,
   containing two works by the Carthusian Dionysius Riker, also known as de
   Leeuwis (1402–71): *De vita et regimine praesulum*, and *De vita et regimine
   curatorum*. The revelations of St Bridget (line 20) are cited in both.
5 Jean Briselot (d 1520) of Valenciennes in Hainault, suffragan bishop of
   Cambrai, titular bishop of Beirut, prior of the Carmelite house near Valenciennes, and confessor to Prince Charles. He left numerous theological works in
   manuscript. The work in question appears to have been on the same subject as
   those by Dionysius Riker.
6 And did not like; Ep 597:2–16

prefer to take the risks of printing on yourself, it would not be a good plan for me to add a foreword to the work, on account of the various suspicions of both parties: Luther's people would grumble that I was supporting the cause 30 of the papacy, and the other side would suspect that I wished to criticize prelates and priests. In both factions passions run so high that I would not wish to be more deeply mixed up with a business that is sure to end in subversion. I wait to see which direction our new pope's energy and interests will take. If he appears to set Christ always before him, I shall back 35 him to the utmost of my power – if there is anything that can be done by a poor creature like myself.

I have decided to stay here until March,[7] for that is imperatively necessary; but I shall not be idle all that time. Besides other things, I have edited St Hilary's works at the cost of great efforts,[8] and if Christ grants me 40 the strength, I shall finish a book on the principles of preaching,[9] which I promised long ago and am frequently asked for in letters from that best of prelates, John, bishop of Rochester,[10] who appeals to our ancient friendship and his unfailing and continual support of me. There will be other things as well. 45

That repeated phrase in your letter, 'Your servant, who is not his own master,' made me very unhappy as I read it. I suspect that your lordship is tormented by ill health, and on this ground the thought of you truly becomes dearer to me, though I would rather it were more agreeable; for it is a true saying that mutual affection is sometimes roused by shared 50 misfortunes.[11] In any case, I am worthy of greater troubles than I suffer from, but a man of your high character deserved unbroken ease. But such is the law of our humanity: whether we will or no, our frail frame decays and this poor dwelling-place of ours must crumble. Though this is not so serious for men like you, my Lord Bishop, men whose holiness of life ensures that 55 their spirit is always strong in Christ, to whom Paul wishes to be more closely joined and to be freed from the burden of the flesh.[12] This life of ours, however agreeable our lot may be, what is it but a moment when compared to eternity? Though apart from that there is nothing in it that should make one wish it longer, except to prolong the chance to help as many people as 60 one can.

* * * * *

7 See Ep 1319 introduction.
8 Ep 1334
9 See Ep 1321 n1.
10 See Ep 1311:20 and n9 to that letter.
11 *Adagia* II i 71
12 Phil 1:23, Rom 7:24

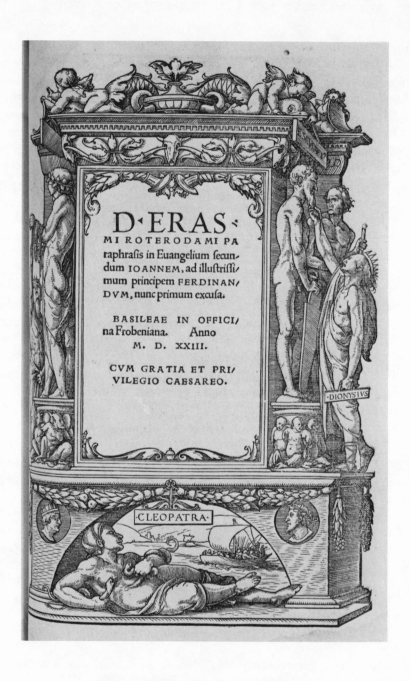

Erasmus *Paraphrasis in Ioannem* title-page
Basel: Froben 1523
Centre for Reformation and Renaissance Studies,
Victoria University, University of Toronto

I send your lordship a copy of Luther's book *De quatuordecim spectris*,[13] which has been very well received even by those who cannot stand his teaching at any price. He wrote it before things had reached their present pitch of lunacy. And I only wish that man could have been recalled to 65 moderate counsels by the advice of his friends as easily as he has been infuriated by their passions. But if there is anything evil in this too, you are wise enough to pick the gold out of the dunghill.

I know the new pope's character and qualities well, actually from personal acquaintance.[14] Nor do I doubt that he will set much to rights in the 70 way the church behaves, the excessive liberty in dispensations, and the vast accumulation of benefices. He will lay down rules for what clerics can properly wear, he will not stand those who are openly criminal, he will compel them to say mass frequently. All these things have their place as regards the outward appearance of religion; whether the force of true piety 75 is rooted in them, I am not sure. He will command universal obedience thanks to the authority of the emperor, whose interests will be the principle of his pontificate. The cardinals, even those who at heart wish him ill, will hide their feelings and put up with him until he has established the royal authority of the Roman see, which is now somewhat decayed. After that, he 80 cannot live long, and his successor will have things all his own way. I have of course no wish to abolish the primacy of the see of Rome; but I should wish to see it conducted on principles which will give a lead to all who strive after the religion of the gospel, just as for some centuries now the lessons to be learned openly from its example have been entirely contrary to the teaching 85 of Christ. Farewell, best of prelates.

From Basel, 1523

1333 / To Archduke Ferdinand   Basel, 5 January 1523

This is the preface to Erasmus' paraphrase on St John, first published by Froben in February 1523. An unbound copy was presented to Archduke Ferdinand at Innsbruck at the end of April (Allen Ep 1361:12–21). Erasmus later sent a properly bound copy (Allen Ep 1376:14–16). Ferdinand sent one hundred florins in acknowledgment (Ep 1341A:1738–41).

* * * * *

13 Ie, the *Tessaradecas consolatoria pro laborantis et onerantis* (1520); WA VI 104–34. The fourteen sections of the book are presented as 'images' (*spectra*), seven of evil and seven of good. Originally written to console Elector Frederick the Wise of Saxony during an illness, the *Tessaradecas consolatoria* was an appropriate gift for the ailing bishop. Erasmus mentions the work with approval once again in Ep 1341A:1231–2.
14 See Ep 1304:12–13.

TO THE MOST ILLUSTRIOUS PRINCE FERDINAND,
ARCHDUKE OF AUSTRIA, BROTHER TO THE EMPEROR CHARLES,
FROM ERASMUS OF ROTTERDAM, GREETING

When I undertook last year to make a paraphrase of St Matthew's Gospel,[1]
most honourable Prince Ferdinand, it was more on the authority of his   5
Eminence Matthew, cardinal of Sion,[2] than from any resolve of my own,
partly because the very grandeur of the work inspired a certain awe that
deterred my mind from approaching it, and partly because I was in any case
fully conscious of my own inadequacy, and there were many difficulties of
different kinds to dissuade me from the attempt. I then thought that in this   10
class of composition I had done all I ever should. And yet, I know not how,
the success of my earlier rash venture and the authority of great men,[3]
whose wishes it would be most discourteous in me not to comply with and
whose commands it would be wicked to disobey, have brought me once
again to the point of writing an exposition of the same sort on St John. I was   15
aware that his grand theme is even more majestic, being mainly concerned
as it is with the exposition of those hidden mysteries of the divine nature and
its marvellous association with our own. What human intellect can even
begin to encompass how God the Father without beginning and without
end eternally begets God the Son? – into whom in the act of generation he   20
pours the whole of himself, and yet loses nothing; and the Son is born from
him, yet never leaves the Father who brings him into life? Or again, how the
Holy Spirit proceeds from them both in such a way that there is a perfect
community of the same nature between them all, with no confusion
between the individuality of the three persons? Who can embrace in his   25
understanding the bond by which that supreme and ineffable nature bound
man unto itself, so that the same person who had eternally been very God of
very God was born very man of man?

In expounding subjects of this kind, in which sometimes the alteration
of a word might be an offence beyond expiation, what freedom can there be   30
for paraphrase? Besides which, I saw that my journey would lie through
country thickly beset with constant difficulties of every kind, interrupted by
precipices, impassable with forest and with bogs, and barred by floods and
whirlpools. No gospel has given rise to more numerous or more difficult
problems concerning the faith, none has been the object of more intense   35

* * * * *

1333
1 Ep 1255
2 See Ep 1255:27–31, 82–6.
3 The archbishop of Mainz and the bishop of Rochester had both encouraged
  Erasmus to undertake the paraphrase on John; Epp 1308:23–4, 1323:22–4.

efforts by the greatest intellects of antiquity, none has seen greater disagreement among its interpreters, and this I ascribe not to their stupidity or lack of experience, but either to the obscurity of the language or to the difficulty of the subject-matter. And there were those further problems in which this activity is specially involved: almost all of the language which the   40 evangelist puts into the mouth of the Lord Jesus is highly figurative and obscure. If one makes these figures clear in the paraphrase, there is no connection with the answers given to him by men who had failed to understand what he said. For the way in which our Lord says many things shows that he knew they could not be understood, and did not wish them to   45 be understood,[4] until the course of events should make his meaning plain.

And again, while it is the paraphrast's business to set forth at greater length what has been expressed concisely, it was equally impossible for me to observe the limits of time. Our Lord is said to have celebrated the Last Supper by night with his disciples, and while they were at dinner he washed   50 their feet; yet after supper he held that long discourse with them, until one wonders how there could have been time to say so much; especially since we know from the narrative of the other evangelists that much else was both said and done during that same night. This made it impossible for me to observe the limits of time, for I had to set out all these things at even greater   55 length.

Last but not least, John has a style of his own; he strings his words together as though they were links in a chain, held together sometimes by a balance of contraries, sometimes by linking like with like, sometimes by repeating the same thing several times, so that these elegances of style   60 cannot be reproduced in a paraphrase. For instance, 'In the beginning was the Word, and the Word was with God, and the Word was God.'[5] In these three phrases, 'Word' answers to 'Word' and 'God' to 'God'; and then he completes the circle by repeating his opening phrase, 'This was in the beginning with God.'[6] And again, 'All things were made by him, and   65 without him was nothing made. What was made in him was life, and the life was the light of men; and the light shines in darkness, and the darkness has

* * * * *

4 This sentence is the first of three passages in this letter (see also nn17 and 20 below) that were condemned, along with much else, in the *Annotationes* (1526) of the Paris theologian Noël Béda. In 1526-7, Erasmus replied in his *Divinationes, Elenchus,* and *Supputatio.* With respect to this passage, which Béda called impious, Erasmus replied in the *Supputatio* that the Doctors of the church had found this very quality of Jesus' teaching a mark of his mercy towards weak human understanding; LB IX 622A–E.
5 John 1:1
6 John 1:2

not understood it.'[7] In these it is clear that each limb of the sentence always picks up what preceded it, in such a way that the end of what precedes is the beginning of what follows, and one can recognize in this something like the   70
effect aimed at in the figure called *echo* in Greek. On all these questions I have said something in my introductions.[8] This particular elegance in the expression I could see that I should often have to jettison in a paraphrase.

Thus it came about that, although I foresaw these difficulties and many others like them, none the less I set about this task, for so many great men   75
urged me to undertake it by their encouragement or set me to it by their authority; and I was particularly encouraged by the success of the previous attempt, which was prompted by compliance rather than self-confidence. Nor was its success limited to the gratitude I received universally from fair-minded readers for the service I had done them. My work was   80
acceptable to Charles, of all the emperors whom the world has known in the last eight hundred years the greatest, if one looks at the breadth of his dominions, and the best, if one considers his other truly imperial virtues, and especially his zeal for religion and piety; and that he found these efforts of mine most acceptable (for I had dedicated them to him) he showed not   85
merely by his expression and by what he said, but in a letter which he wrote to me which was as complimentary as it was gracious.[9]

And so I thought it appropriate that, just as St Matthew had been dedicated to Charles, so St John should be dedicated to Ferdinand as Charles over again. Indeed, I flatter myself with the hope that this attempt will   90
achieve the same success with Ferdinand as its patron that the other achieved under the emperor Charles. Two names in this age of ours are supremely fortunate, and one pair of brothers in our time are pre-eminent in promise, nor need we doubt, I think, that the virtuous desires of truly religious princes are brought by the favour of God to good effect. For I   95
believe we can safely foresee a great future for those in whom, while they are still young men, a noble crop of virtues answers to the splendid hopes encouraged by the seed-time of their early years. Your spirit even in boyhood was something new and excellent, and displayed already the kindling sparks of such wisdom and temperance and gentleness, and such a   100

* * * * *

7 John 1:3–5
8 The phrase translated as 'in my introductions' is *in argumentis*. The stylistic feature to which Erasmus refers here is discussed in the *argumentum* which precedes the paraphrase on the First Epistle of John (LB VII 1141–2) and also in the annotation to John 1:3 (ibidem VI 339B–C). There is no *argumentum* in the paraphrase on John's Gospel.
9 Ep 1270

sense of honour, and such religion and piety, that everyone was confident
we should have an exceptional prince and one perfect at all points.

And if hitherto you have not betrayed the confidence placed in you by
the whole world, you now do something more: you make us believe that,
now you are grown up, you will fully satisfy what are no longer merely the   105
hopes but the prayers of us all. My book on the Christian prince,[10] such as it
is, you commended to all who care for such things long ago, while you were
yet a youth, by being so good as to read it.[11] And now this book, which is
expressly dedicated to you, you must be so good as to recommend, now that
you are a young man, the most successful of our age and for many reasons   110
the most universally popular. And the purpose is not that it may bring you
any credit or me some advantage, for your exalted position and your natural
modesty alike neither need nor wish for praise from ordinary men, and my
own spirit seeks nothing but Christ's approval, but rather that it may bear
more abundant fruit for those on whose behalf these efforts were expended   115
– and they were spent for the common good of all men. For things good in
themselves bring in great profit only when the moment comes that they
have conquered envy and achieved popular approval. To this it will be an
important contribution, if you make it clear that the gift of this work of mine
was not unwelcome.   120

For there is no fear, I imagine, that someone of your wisdom will give a
hearing to the people who will say perhaps, when they see a gospel
paraphrase dedicated to a Prince Ferdinand, 'What business has a lay
prince, what business has a young man, with the gospel?', and will take me
to task in the words of the old Greek proverb about serving wine to the   125
frogs.[12] As though the only men who give princes the right presents are the
authors who offer them books in some barbaric language on hunting and the
management of kennels, on the care of horses, on siege-engines, or perhaps
on games of chance.[13] My own opinion is the opposite: that the philosophy
of the gospel, fruitful as it is above everything for all men of high or low   130
degree or of the middle sort, is more needed by the world's most powerful
monarchs than by anyone. The greater the mass of business they must carry,
the more fraught with peril the tempest of affairs which they must control,
the more the opportunities offered them such as can often corrupt upright,

* * * * *

10 See Ep 1323 n1.
11 See Ep 1323 n2.
12 That is, giving someone something he does not need; *Adagia* II iii 20
13 Since Erasmus was by no means hostile to the vernacular tongues (see, for
   example, Ep 1126:105–9), this must be a slighting reference to the non-literary
   Latin used in books on the practical subjects listed.

well-born, well-educated natures, the more carefully ought they to be   135
equipped and armed beforehand with the purest and most unfailing
principles of gospel teaching; for if they go wrong, it is the whole world that
suffers. Bishops have a special duty to feed the people from the abundant
stores of gospel wisdom, and are therefore spoken of as shepherds; I quite
agree. But there is reason for the praise that Homer earns, even from men   140
who win high praise among Christians, for calling a king the shepherd of the
people.[14] How much more closely should this title fit a Christian prince! The
prince does not teach the gospel, he sets an example of it; and he who sets an
example teaches too. But how can he set an example of something he does
not know? And how will he come to know it, unless he grows familiar by   145
frequent and attentive reading, and by serious effort gives it deep root in his
own heart?

Who needs to be persuaded more than they that there is a king in
heaven who governs this world and whom nothing can escape, whose eye
no man can evade, whose power no man can resist, and who will judge each   150
man as he deserves – who needs this more than the sovereign princes, so
powerful that they fear no man and can deceive all men at will; who if they
do wrong are not merely free from the summons to any earthly tribunal but
are actually praised for their misdeeds? In whose minds should the
conviction be more firmly implanted that after this life, which even for kings   155
cannot be relied on to last longer than a single day and for no man can last
long, there follows a life which will never end, in which with no respect for
persons or positions (except that those who have enjoyed more power than
others here will have the heavier case to meet) each man will face the
inescapable sentence of an incorruptible judge and reap the crop he has   160
sown here, nor will anyone escape the alternative of receiving for his good
deeds a crown of eternal blessedness or for his evil deeds being handed over
to the eternal punishments of hell-fire? Who needs this conviction more
than those who are tempted by prosperity all around them and by the
approval of mankind to love the present and forget the future? Who need to   165
be more deeply impressed for their own good by Christ's denunciation 'Woe
to the rich and the powerful who have their reward in this world'[15] than
those who have an unlimited supply of all the things that can weaken mortal
resolution? Who should more properly have learned the lesson that each
man's talent is lent him for the advantage of the Lord, who will call on all   170
men to render their account, and should be laid out with care than they who,
because the Lord has given them power, have it in their hands to be a source

* * * * *

14 Eg, *Iliad* 1.263 and passim, especially in reference to Agamemnon
15 Luke 6:24

of much good or much evil in the affairs of men? Who have more need of the
sure conviction that men, however great and highly placed, can of
themselves do nothing; that for all of them anything that can truly be called a   175
blessing comes from Christ; that they must ask him for everything that can
be asked for in a Christian's prayers, and ascribe to him alone the glory for all
their achievements – who needs this more than those who, in return for
advantages which Christ taught us to despise, receive the plaudits of the
world as truly happy and who, because they enjoy some empty symbols of   180
felicity, are admired and reverenced by the common throng of men almost
like gods? Who ought to be more fully persuaded that brutality is hateful in
the Lord's eyes, and that one wrong must not be compensated by another,
that nothing is better than peace or more pleasing to God than mildness and
clemency – who more than those who have so many temptations every day   185
to violence and war and vengeance? Who should have more deeply
impressed upon their minds that neither desire of life nor fear of death ought
to deflect them from the path of duty and that no man ought to hope for the
reward of his good deeds in this life, while in the world to come no man can
fail of his deserts – who more than princes, whom so many temptations, so   190
many violent commotions, and so many opportunities continually encourage to do wrong? Surely a spirit like theirs, on which depends the public
happiness or misery of the world, ought to be fortified with serious and solid
principles of philosophy, that it may be able, upright and unshaken, to
withstand all the siege-engines that this world can bring against it.   195

But principles of this kind, which like the ballast in a ship do not allow
the mind to be tossed to and fro by the waves of fortune and events, cannot
be drawn from any better or more reliable or more effective source than the
study of the gospel. It may be that a secular prince, absorbed as he must be
for the most part in grosser business and in his duty to defend the public   200
peace, cannot always achieve the results which he clearly perceives to be the
most just; but if he has once drunk deep of the gospel philosophy, it will do
this for him at least, that so far as he can he will always strive for what is
nearest to the commands of Christ and will be deflected as little as possible
from his aim. This we wish we may find in all those who govern the affairs of   205
men upon earth; but in you, Ferdinand, we are confident that we shall: we
know that from your earliest years you were remarkably disposed to love the
reading of the Gospels, for it was not your habit to while away the time while
the priest was saying mass in muttering superstitious prayers or in frivolous
conversation, as most great men usually do, but to open the gospel-book   210
and reverently look to see what lesson was taught by the epistle or gospel for
the day. And I do not doubt that increasing years have much developed the
sample that you gave us in your boyhood; I have no ordinary hopes that we

shall see great crowds of mortals everywhere follow your example. For
while vice is an infection that spreads very easily to the multitude when it   21
starts from men in high place, the example of virtue in the same way is very
quick to find a welcome everywhere if it takes its rise from some
distinguished source.

With what solemnity the teaching of the gospel was clothed in former
times, the ceremonies handed down from antiquity which the church still   22
observes will suffice to show. The text in use is beautifully decorated with
gold and ivory and precious stones; it is scrupulously preserved among the
sacred treasures, and not laid down or taken in hand without signs of
reverence. Permission is asked from the priest to read it aloud; it is sanctified
by perfuming with frankincense and oil of myrrh, with balsam and with   22
spices; every brow, every bosom is signed with the sign of the cross; all bow
their heads and ascribe glory to the Lord; all rise to their feet and stand to
their full height, with bare head and attentive ear and downcast eye. At the
name of Jesus, every time it occurs, every knee is bowed; then the book is
carried round, held in deep reverence close to the bosom, that every man   23
may show his adoration with a kiss, until at length it is reverently replaced
among the sacred treasures. What is the message of these ceremonies, what
else have they to teach us, except that to Christians nothing ought to be so
important, so much beloved, so much respected as that heavenly philosophy which Christ himself delivered to us all, which for so many centuries   23
has enjoyed world-wide acceptance, and alone can make us impregnable
against this world and the prince of this world?

But think how rightly the Jews are criticized for empty superstition
which does not put first things first,[16] when they treat the book of their law
with such extraordinary veneration, laying clean linen cloths beneath it,   24
falling down before it and worshipping it, not touching it except with hands
that are ritually clean, while in their impiety they pay no attention to the
chief lessons of that very law; for in just the same way we must take care not
to be found as truly pagan in our neglect of the gospel as we are scrupulous
in our ceremonious respect for it. What purpose is served by a text adorned   24
with ivory and silver and gold, with silk and precious stones, if our way of
life is defiled with the taint of vices which are execrated by the gospel, if our
spirit lacks all the radiance of the gospel virtues? Of what use is it to press a
volume close to the heart, if that heart is far removed from what the volume
teaches, and what it condemns is sovereign in the heart? What does the   25

* * * * *

16 On Erasmus' attitude towards the Jews, see Ep 694 introduction. But see also
Heiko A. Oberman *The Roots of Anti-Semitism in the Age of Renaissance and
Reformation* trans James I. Porter (Philadelphia 1984) 38–40, 58–9.

fragrance of all this incense signify, if its teaching smells stale to us, while our way of life stinks like the grave? Of what use to bow the head before a gospel-book, if our lusts hold their head high and fight against its principles? What do we gain by rising from our seats and standing bareheaded, if our whole life is such as openly displays contempt for the lessons of the gospel? 255 How can a man find the face to kiss a volume of the Gospels who is a slave to lust and avarice, to ambition and gluttony and anger, and who treats its commands like dirt? How can he put to his lips a book which teaches nothing but peace, mildness, and charity when he despises Christ's teaching and is all corrupted with envy, besotted with hatred, aflame with 260 anger, and swept by an accelerating passion for revenge into mad rage against his neighbour, giving full rein to his appetites and plunging the world into the raging confusion of war? How dare a man embrace and venerate the gospel-volume, whose every motive allies him to this world and who is execrated as an enemy by the philosophy of that same gospel? 265

Can we handle the gospel-volume with clean hands and as godly men should, and yet with unclean hearts despise the precepts of the gospel? It is these, surely, that we should clasp to our bosoms, these that we should spiritually put to our lips, and before these that we should bow our heads. Some people even have part of St John's Gospel copied out and wear it 270 hanging round their necks to shield them from sickness or unhappy accidents of other kinds.[17] Surely it is the teaching of that gospel that we ought to wear next our hearts to be our shield against all the sickness of sin. I do not disapprove of ceremonies or criticize the religion of simple folk. But such things will never do us any good unless and until we carry out in 275 practice what we are called upon to do by these visible signs. If we are true Christians, which means that we profess the gospel teaching as its law directs, let us take all these external symbols and make them real in our hearts.

I hear there is a custom among certain peoples that the prince should 280 stand for the reading of the gospel holding in his hand a naked sword, and all the others with their hands on their sword-hilts. But how can a man use his sword to defend the gospel whose spirit is an enemy of the gospel, who breathes the spirit of the world entirely, who despises nothing so much as that pearl of great price which is the gospel and hates nothing so much as the 285 one thing which Christ taught us to seek, who preys upon his people, who oppresses the poor, who confounds all things human and divine by going to war, who provides so many evils with a starting-point and to glut his ambition sheds so much human blood? How can he brandish the sword in

* * * * *

17 Cf Ep 563:24–31 and the *Enchiridion* LB v 30F / CWE 66–70.

defence of the gospel of Christ? Let him first make his own peace with the   29
gospel, let him first use the sword of the gospel to cut back the evil desires in
his own heart, and then, if he likes, let him draw that sword to threaten the
enemies of the gospel.

Give me leave to say this, illustrious Prince, to establish the facts, with
no criticism of anyone. I simply exhibit the principle, and cast no slur on   29
individuals; and this I write with all the greater freedom because not the
slightest suspicion of these evils could touch a man of your high character.
To no one after the bishops is the religion of the gospel more appropriate
than it is to princes; but princes in their simplicity are often deceived by the
semblance of religion. Sometimes they are persuaded by men whose   30
credentials are the profession of a perfectly religious life, and suppose that
perfect piety consists in the performance of a daily stint of what they call the
hour-offices and in letting no day pass without hearing mass. In a prince
who is a layman and a young man too this would, I admit, be some evidence
of a religious disposition; but there are many other things more closely   30
related to the duty of a Christian prince. If he looks ahead to forestall the
storms of war before they rise, to prevent any violent assault on public
liberty, to see that humble folk are not forced to go hungry and corrupt men
not given office, in my opinion he will have offered God a more acceptable
sacrifice than if for six years he has told those beads we hear so much of. Yet I   31
commend this too, provided that what really matters goes with it.[18]

If however a prince were to suppose that he has met all the demands of
true godliness because he can rely on the observance of such things as this,
and were to neglect other things which are a proper part of his kingly office,
this is a real canker in religion and a deadly sickness in the body politic, and   31
those who make him think so are evil counsellors to both prince and people.
It is a godly action to hear mass, provided one attends with a pure heart. But
how can I approach with a pure heart the memorial of that true and supreme
prince who gave his life for the salvation of his people, if my anger, my
ambition, or my sloth bring misery or death to so many thousands of my   32
fellow men? To say nothing for the moment of the fact that princes have
scarcely any time of greater leisure and fewer anxieties than that which they
reserve for divine service; and yet why is it so important that the prince

* * * * *

18 This passage, beginning above at 'Sometimes they are persuaded' (line 300),
was also censured by Béda (see n4 above), who called it Lutheran. Erasmus
replied in the *Divinationes* (LB IX 481A–E), *Elenchus* (ibidem 499F–500A), and
finally at length in the *Supputatio* (ibidem 622E–624B), pointing out that he had
never rejected princes' attending mass or saying the offices; he had only said
that these are not the chief duties of princes, as the passage itself makes clear.

should say those prayers at regular hours, when he can never find all the
time he needs for the business of the commonwealth?   325

A prince will have uttered prayers in great plenty if he repeats every
day, and repeats from the bottom of his heart, the prayer of that young king
who was the wisest of mankind:[19] 'Lord, grant me wisdom and understanding, that I may go in and out before thy people.' Or one very close to that
which the same king, if I am not mistaken, recites in what is called the Book   330
of Wisdom: 'Give me Wisdom, that sitteth by thy throne, that she may be
present with me and may labour with me, that I may know what is pleasing
unto thee. For she knoweth and understandeth all things, and she shall lead
me soberly in my doings, and preserve me in her power, and my works shall
be acceptable, and I shall judge thy people righteously, and be worthy to sit   335
in my father's seat. But thy counsel who shall know, except thou hast given
wisdom, and hast sent thy Holy Spirit from the highest; and so the ways of
them which live on the earth have been reformed, and men have been
taught the things that are pleasing unto thee?'[20] And this wisdom, for which
that very wise young man prays, may be found above all in the text of the   340
Gospels, if a man searches for it wholeheartedly and with a pious desire to
find. Otherwise how has it come to pass that the moral standard of
Christians has partly sunk back into a way of life like that of gentiles but
worse, and partly has degenerated into a kind of Judaism, unless this comes
from neglect of the teaching of the gospel? Although, to speak openly, in no   345
centuries have men been lacking to pay the gospel the honour that is its due;
but all the same in these last four hundred years its energy in most hearts
had grown cold.[21] All the more then must we use every effort to rekindle to
the best of our power, each one of us, that spark of fire sent down to earth by
our Lord Jesus, the eternal Truth; nor has he any other wish except that it be   350
blown into a mighty flame, spread far and wide, and set all things on fire.

When the moral standards of the age are so much corrupted, and there
are these great dissensions in men's thinking that now reduce all things to
chaos, where can we better seek refuge than, as St Hilary rightly points out,

* * * * *

19 Solomon; see 2 Chron 1:10.
20 Wisd of Sol 9:4, 10–12, 17–18
21 This sentence was criticized not only by Béda (see n4 above) but also by the
   Paris faculty of theology (in a formal judgment adopted in 1527 but not
   published until 1531). Both read the sentence as a Lutheranizing assault on
   scholastic theology. Erasmus replied to Béda in the *Supputatio* (LB IX 624B–E)
   and to the faculty in the *Declarationes ad censuras Lutetiae vulgatas* of 1532 (ibidem
   910F–911C), arguing that he was not condemning scholastic theology or
   theologians out of hand but rather the excesses that had resulted from closer
   attention to intellectual systems than to the vigour of the gospel.

in the pure springs of Holy Scripture, of which the Gospels are the purest 35
and most unsullied part? Rulers ought not to suspect the gospel on the
ground that, as certain persons idly cry, it spreads subversion among those
whose duty it is to be obedient to princes. Not at all: what it does for princes
is to make them princes true to the name instead of tyrants, and what it does
for the people is to make them more willing to obey a good prince and more 36
patient in bearing one they do not like. And in the end of all it should not be
considered the fault of the gospel if someone makes a less than admirable
use of something admirable in itself. It is called the gospel of peace, first as
reconciling us to God and secondly as uniting us among ourselves in mutual
concord. The man who stumbles over this stone has only himself to thank 36
and not the gospel. There is no human violence, no cunning, no massing of
forces that can suppress the gospel truth, which shows its power most
clearly when it is most oppressed.

But on all this I fear I have already said more than enough. So, after a
few words on the author's purpose to increase the profit of reading him, I 37
will make an end. When our Lord Jesus Christ's life and teaching had
already been spread widely through the world by the preaching of the
apostles and the writings of the other evangelists, John, well known as he
whom Jesus loved, took in hand last of them all the writing of this gospel,
not so much to put together a gospel-history as to supply certain things that 37
the other evangelists had passed over, since they seemed not unworthy of
record. But the chief reason for his writing this gospel is thought to be the
desire to assert the divinity of Christ against the heresies which were already
like evil tares sprouting up in the good crop; in particular those of the
Cerinthians and the Ebionites,[22] who apart from other errors taught that 38
Christ had been nothing more than a man and had not existed at all before he
was born of Mary. It was however of the first importance that the world
should know and believe that Christ was at once true God and true man. Of
which the latter first makes a contribution towards arousing men's love
towards him (for we are more ready to love things which we know) and then 38
provides a keener incentive to imitate him. For who would try to emulate
what had been done by an angel in appearance only and not also in truth?

Furthermore, seeing that the difficulty of what he tells us to do is
matched by the splendour of the promises he makes us, it was right that his

* * * * *

22 The Cerinthians were the followers of Cerinthus, a Gnostic teacher in Asia
Minor c 100 AD who denied the virgin birth and the divinity of Christ. The
Ebionites were Jewish Christians who insisted on the observance of the whole
law, viewed Paul as a heretic, and agreed with Cerinthus on the person of
Jesus. Cf n24 below.

divine nature should not remain unknown, to give us confidence that he will 390
beyond question be the defender of his own people, whom he so dearly
loved, and that we can rely upon the promises of one whose lightest nod can
accomplish whatever he wishes. But the earlier evangelists had scarcely
touched on the divinity of the Lord Jesus. For this I take to be the wisdom of
which Paul used to speak 'among them that are perfect,' while professing in 395
front of everyone else 'not to know anything save Jesus Christ, and him
crucified.'[23] Perhaps the time was not yet ripe for such an ineffable mystery
to be made public in written form, for fear the godless might laugh to scorn
what they could neither believe nor understand. Though in other ways too
all the ancients are very reticent and use scrupulous language whenever 400
they speak of what relates to the deity, while using greater freedom in what
conduces more to living a godly life. Thus it was the foolhardiness of heretics
that drove the apostle into more openly claiming divine nature for Christ,[24]
just as the boldness of the Arians drove the orthodox Fathers to lay down
some more definite principles on the same subject when they would have 405
preferred to refrain from defining the kind of thing that far surpasses the
capacity of the human mind and cannot be defined without great peril. And
this province was rightly left for the blessed John, Jesus' beloved disciple; for
seeing that he who is the fountain of all wisdom loved John above the rest,
we may well believe that he inspired his favourite, if I may use the term, with 410
a fuller knowledge of certain mysteries. Let us all therefore drink deep of this
man whom Christ loved, that we in our turn may deserve to become lovers
of Christ.

There is one point only to which I wish to draw the reader's attention.
In this work I have followed the most approved Doctors of the church, but 415
not indiscriminately or at all points, for they too sometimes disagree among
themselves. But I always put forward in all honesty what seemed to me to be
the true meaning, although I could clearly see that ancient authorities
engaged in fighting the views of heretics distort the sense in places with
some force. I should be sorry however if anyone were to assign to this 420
paraphrase more authority than he would have assigned to a commentary, if
I had written one; not but what a paraphrase too is a kind of commentary.
Allegorical interpretations, to which I find some of the ancients devoted so
much space that it became a superstition, I have touched on sparingly, and
never more than I thought would suffice. Farewell, most honoured Prince; 425

* * * * *

23 1 Cor 2:6 and 2
24 In his *Adversus omnes haereses* 3.11.1, Irenaeus asserts that John wrote his
Gospel especially against the errors of Cerinthus (n22 above).

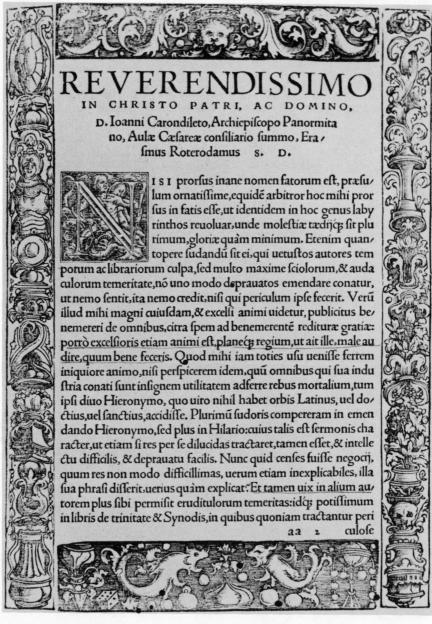

REVERENDISSIMO

IN CHRISTO PATRI, AC DOMINO,

D. Ioanni Carondileto, Archiepiscopo Panormita
no, Aulæ Cæsareæ consiliario summo, Era,
smus Roterodamus S. D.

ISI prorsus inane nomen fatorum est, præsu,
lum ornatissime, equidē arbitror hoc mihi pror
sus in fatis esse, ut identidem in hoc genus laby
rinthos reuoluar, unde molestiæ tædrjcȝ sit plu
rimum, gloriæ quàm minimum. Etenim quan,
topere sudandū sit ei, qui uetustos autores tem
porum ac librariorum culpa, sed multo maxime sciolorum, & auda
culorum temeritate, nó uno modo deprauatos emendare conatur,
ut nemo sentit, ita nemo credit, nisi qui periculum ipse fecerit. Verū
illud mihi magni cuiusdam, & excelsi animi uidetur, publicitus be
nemereri de omnibus, citra spem ad benemerentē redituræ gratiæ:
porrò excelsioris etiam animi est, planecȝ regium, ut ait ille, male au
dire, quum bene feceris. Quod mihi iam toties usu uenisse ferrem
iniquiore animo, nisi perspicerem idem, quū omnibus qui sua indu
stria conati sunt insignem utilitatem adferre rebus mortalium, tum
ipsi diuo Hieronymo, quo uiro nihil habet orbis Latinus, uel do,
ctius, uel sanctius, accidisse. Plurimū sudoris compereram in emen
dando Hieronymo, sed plus in Hilario: cuius talis est sermonis cha
racter, ut etiam si res per se dilucidas tractaret, tamen esset, & intelle
ctu difficilis, & deprauatu facilis. Nunc quid censes fuisse negocij,
quum res non modo difficillimas, uerum etiam inexplicabiles, illa
sua phrasi disserit, uerius quàm explicat? Et tamen uix in alium au,
torem plus sibi permisit eruditulorum temeritas: idcȝ potissimum
in libris de trinitate & Synodis, in quibus quoniam tractantur peri

aa 2   culose

First page of the dedicatory preface addressed to
Jean de Carondelet (Ep 1334) in Erasmus' edition of St Hilary of Poitiers
Basel: Froben 1523
Centre for Reformation and Renaissance Studies,
Victoria University, University of Toronto

with all your might strive for the glory of the gospel; and so may Christ the Almighty in return vouchsafe a favourable answer to your prayers.

Basel, 5 January 1523

1334 / To Jean de Carondelet   Basel, 5 January 1523

This is the preface to the edition of St Hilary (Basel: Froben, February 1523) which Erasmus undertook in order to correct the deficiencies in the earlier edition of Robert Fortuné (Paris: Bade 1511). Urbanus Rhegius had encouraged Erasmus to devote his talents to Hilary (Ep 1253:31–3); Maternus Hatten had furnished a manuscript (Ep 1289:17–19); and Herman Lethmaet had requested (Ep 1320:10–12) that Erasmus dedicate a work to Jean de Carondelet (Ep 1276).

Hilary (c 315–67), bishop of Poitiers, was the church Father who led the fight against the Arian heresy in the West. 'Most of his works were composed in the context of the Arian struggle, and Erasmus in his preface uses the example of St Hilary or at least the occasion of his role in that widespread controversy to draw certain lessons about doctrinal controversy in general and the recently arisen Lutheran controversy in particular ... Indeed it [the preface] contains some of Erasmus' most pungent comments on the nature of theology and on the baleful consequences of theological argument and contention' (John C. Olin *Six Essays* [see below] 93). As a result, this prefatory letter to Carondelet became one of Erasmus' more controversial writings. In 1526 the faculty of theology at Paris censured several passages. The *censurae*, with Erasmus' replies, are found in LB IX 920–1, 925–8. The following year, 1527, a conference of theologians at Valladolid in Spain vehemently attacked several other passages; see Bataillon 276–8 and Allen VI 471. The censured passages are indicated in the notes.

For analysis of this important letter, see John C. Olin 'Erasmus and his Edition of St Hilary' *Erasmus in English* 9 (1978) 8–11.

The translation used here, by John C. Olin and James F. Brady jr, was first published as an appendix to Olin's *Six Essays on Erasmus* (Fordham University Press 1979) 93–120. The translation has been slightly revised; two passages omitted from the text in *Six Essays* (lines 564–603, 881–926) have been newly translated by Olin and Brady; and the original notes have been revised and expanded by the CWE annotator.

TO THE MOST REVEREND FATHER IN CHRIST AND LORD,
JEAN CARONDELET, ARCHBISHOP OF PALERMO,
HIGHER COUNSELLOR OF THE IMPERIAL COURT IN BRABANT,
GREETINGS FROM ERASMUS OF ROTTERDAM
Unless the word 'destiny' is entirely meaningless, most illustrious prelate,   5

indeed I think I am destined to return again and again into labyrinths of the kind from which comes a great deal of vexation and weariness but the least possible measure of glory. In fact, without actual experience no one will believe, unless he personally has made the test, what effort he must expend who tries to emend the text of ancient authors which have been corrupted in   10 various ways through fault of the times and copyists but above all because of the rashness of half-learned and foolhardy men. But it seems to me to be a mark of a great and lofty spirit publicly to serve all well even without the expectation of receiving thanks for such service. Further, it is the mark of even a loftier spirit and one which is wholly regal, as the saying goes, to be ill   15 spoken of when one has done something worth while. And I would be more vexed that this has happened so often to me if I did not observe that the same thing has happened not only to all who have tried by their own industry to do something notably useful in the affairs of men, but even to St Jerome himself, whose learning or holiness is unsurpassed in the Latin world.   20

I had found the editing of Jerome's works a very arduous task,[1] but editing Hilary's text entailed even greater labour. The latter's style, even where the subject-matter itself is clear, is difficult to understand and susceptible to corruption. What, then, do you think was the nature of the task, when in that peculiar style of his he discusses rather than explains   25 matters which are not only very difficult but even inexplicable? Yet scarcely in the case of another author has the rashness of the half-learned allowed itself greater liberty, and that especially with regard to *De Trinitate* and *De synodis*. Because theological problems fraught with danger are treated in these works the greatest care must be taken, nor must the slightest change   30 be made. If we discover after comparing different copies that in some places prefatory remarks have been added to the beginning of chapters and also flourishes at the end and that in the middle patches have been sewn on, we are discovering that in some places someone with little learning has tried to explain more completely and clearly what Hilary in his own fashion had   35 said. On some pages twenty or thirty lines had been added.[2]

How often they excise passages which seemed at variance with the opinions accepted among the orthodox. Indeed in more than twenty places they had compounded a remedy, especially where he debates about the

* * * * *

1334
1 See Epp 308, 396.
2 Erasmus' complaints about the liberties taken by copyists and the corruption of Hilary's text are echoed in P. Smulders sj 'Remarks on the Manuscript Tradition of the *De Trinitate* of Saint Hilary of Poitiers' *Studia Patristica* 3-1 (Berlin 1961) 133–4.

pains and torments which affected the body and soul of our Lord Jesus   40
Christ. He does this in several places but chiefly in the tenth book of *De
Trinitate*, though so confusedly that sometimes he clearly seems to attribute
to Christ a body and soul subject to no troublesome conditions. When, to
illustrate this, he used the comparison of a weapon penetrating water or fire
by a violent thrust without the sign of a wound because the body attacked is   45
not susceptible of a wound, although it is the nature of a weapon to inflict a
wound,[3] someone took it upon himself to add the qualification 'if however
this comparison can aptly be made.'[4] Again when a little later he added that
'that body of the Lord may indeed have had pain similar in nature to ours, if
our body is so constituted that it treads upon the waves and walks upon the   50
waters,' etc, concluding from this difference undoubtedly that the body of
Jesus even in the sensation of pain was unlike our bodies, they had corrected
the text to read as follows: 'That body of the Lord may indeed have had
(because of sin) pain similar in nature to ours, if our body is so constituted
that it treads upon the waves (by its own nature or by the extraordinary help   55
of God) and walks upon the waters,' etc.[5]

A little later when St Hilary had written, 'And that man is from God,
having indeed a body to suffer, and he did suffer, but not having a nature to
feel pain,'[6] the passage was corrected, that is, corrupted, in this way: 'And
he did suffer, but not having a nature (weak because of sin like ours) to feel   60
pain.' Further on where Hilary had written, 'The opinion based on human
judgment therefore that he feels pain because he suffers is mistaken,' they
emended the wording thus: 'That he (as if in the flesh of sin) feels pain
because he suffers.'[7] Likewise at the end of the second book when it was
written as follows: 'Therefore we must seek this Holy Spirit, we must   65
deserve him, and then we must hold him by that faithfulness to and
observance of the commandments,' they had woven in, 'we must deserve
him, we must adore him.' They feared undoubtedly that someone might
suspect that he thought the Holy Spirit should not be adored when he
teaches in many ways that the Father and the Son should be adored but   70
makes no such pronouncement about the Spirit. Evidently this was because
it did not come to his mind or because at that time this had not yet been
precisely defined.

* * * * *

3 *De Trinitate* 10.23
4 The interpolations discussed in this passage are not found in any known
  manuscript.
5 *De Trinitate* 10.23
6 Ibidem 10.47
7 Cf Erasmus' dispute with Colet over the nature of Christ's agony in the garden
  of Gethsemane; Epp 108–9.

It is amazing, however, that the same individuals did not also corrupt
the end of this work, where consistently it is written: 'May I adore you, our   7!
Father, and your Son together with you, and may I be deserving of your
Holy Spirit who is from you through the only begotten Son.' For here also
when he declares that the Father and the Son 'should be adored,' he says
only that Holy Spirit 'should be deserved.' We have discovered such
additions in more than thirty places in Hilary, although we have cited no   8(
more than one or two passages as examples to avoid irritating the reader.
Again I am amazed that when he writes that the Holy Spirit is from the
Father through the Son and that he does not proceed from both, it was not
also corrected. Indeed in one particular text I discovered this correction:
through him was changed to *with him*.   8!

Now what is this rashness shown toward the writings of others,
especially those ancient authors whose memory, as it should be, is sacred to
us, I mean the readiness to erase, expunge, add to, delete, change, forge –
when there is no personal risk – any author at will? Is the object of this to
prevent anyone from thinking that there are any errors in the works of the   9(
ancients? Indeed whoever should try that would wash a brick, as they say.[8]
God has willed that the happy state of freedom from error be reserved for the
sacred books alone. Everyone else, however learned and keen-sighted he
may be, on occasion stumbles and gropes blindly. Obviously therefore all
remember that they are humans and as humans they are read by us, with   95
discrimination, with judgment, and at the same time with indulgence. But if
anything occurs in these writings which has the appearance of error, when
the author has a different opinion, the work must not be contaminated, but
scruples should be allayed by adding explanatory notes. Peter Lombard
attempts this in very many places, at the same time citing and explaining   10
several passages concerning the pain and fear of Christ in the third book of
the *Sentences*.[9]

That famous epigrammatic poet does not tolerate him who wishes to
show his cleverness in another's book.[10] But who would tolerate those who
arrogate so much to themselves that they sew on their own patches in place   10
of the genuine text wherever they please? It is a mark of courtesy to interpret
a work properly. To change arbitrarily the actual words in the works of the
ancients, however, is an act of rashness, not to say irreverence. And yet we
discover that this has been done even in the books of St Ambrose and in
more than one place. If the risk to the writer must be taken into account   11

* * * * *

8 Terence *Phormio* 186; *Adagia* i iv 48
9 3.15.5, where Lombard discusses certain passages from Hilary
10 Martial 1 praef

when a text is changed, it would be more fitting to do this in the books of modern authors, whom time has not yet placed outside the uncertainty of judgment or death thus far delivered from envy. Now almost too scrupulously fair toward the ancient writers, we distort certain passages which have nothing wrong with them in the authors of our own age and we   115
interpret everything improperly, just as if such an exegete would not be likely to find even in the Pauline Epistles something which he would be able to misrepresent as erroneous, as suspect of heresy, as scandalous, as irreverent.

But let us drop this subject. It is better that I briefly express my opinion   120
about each of Hilary's works individually. He wrote the twelve books of *De Trinitate* when an exile in Phrygia, where he had been banished by the faction of a certain Saturninus, bishop of Arles, which had circumvented the emperor. Indeed the Arian faction had sunk its roots so widely, had become so strong that the world for a long time wavered in doubt as to which cause it   125
would espouse, especially when the emperor Constantius by the use of exile, plundering, threats, and alarms forced men to go over to the side of the Arians. Wherefore Hilary complained to Caesar that it was shameful that men in an unprecedented fashion were being forced rather than persuaded to accept the faith, granting that the faith of the Arians was sincere. And   130
indeed he himself testifies in several places that for a long time he was silent. He observed this silence either because the soul even of that great man felt some doubt amid such widespread discord in the world or because when there was no hope that the better side could win he thought it preferable to adopt a calm silence rather than to exacerbate, not remove, the world's   135
general depravity by untimely boldness. He seems to have exerted all his energy, however, to manifest and put forth in this work whatever he could by his natural ability, by his eloquence, and by his knowledge of Holy Scripture. For we see that it was usually the ambition of distinguished writers as well as of outstanding painters and sculptors to leave in some one   140
work a finished and complete example of their art by which posterity might be able to evaluate what they would have been able to do if they had wished to exert their fullest powers. Virgil seems to have attempted this in the *Georgics*, Ovid in his *Medea*, Cicero in *De oratore*, Augustine in *De civitate Dei*, Jerome in his commentaries on the prophets, Thomas Aquinas on the   145
subject of the Eucharist,[11] Bernard on the Canticle.[12]

* * * * *

11 This is probably a reference to the *Summa theologiae* 3.73–83, though Aquinas dealt with the same topic in other works as well, including especially his commentary on the fourth book of the *Sentences* ('distinctiones' 8–13).
12 *Sermones in Cantica Canticorum*

We are stimulated more to this effort if there should come to hand a theme which is not only lofty and important but also new and accordingly not hackneyed. Indeed the grandeur of a subject, besides permitting a lofty treatment, also lends dignity of itself, and the newness adds to the charm. Moreover, the ancient authors philosophized very rarely about theological questions, and they did not dare to make any pronouncement about such matters which was not clearly set forth in those writings whose authority is inviolable to us. But the irreverent rashness of the Cerinthians and the Ebionites first drove John the Evangelist to commit to writing certain mysteries concerning the divine nature of Christ.[13] Later the elaborate subtlety of the Arians drove the orthodox to a greater necessity – namely, to discuss with great controversy the question of the extension of the divine nature, of the creation of the Son, of the adoption into the name of God, and then the matter of ὁμοούσιον and ὁμοιούσιον,[14] and finally to formulate definitions about these matters. Repeatedly the most saintly Hilary deplores this necessity, knowing full well how fraught with danger and how inimical to devotion it is to speak out on matters which are beyond discussion, to examine matters beyond understanding, to make pronouncements on matters beyond the grasp of the intelligence.[15] But St Augustine was carried still farther on this sea, evidently because the joy of inquiry like a favourable breeze lured the rich talent of the man from one realm of thought to another. More restraint is exercised by Peter Lombard, who when he cites another's views does not lightly add anything of his own, or if he adds anything, he offers it with diffidence. At length the matter advanced to the point of irreverent audacity.

But may the ancients gain the pardon besought by those whom necessity has driven to this pass. On what pretext will we ask pardon for ourselves, we who raise so many meddlesome, not to say irreverent, questions concerning matters very far removed from our nature, and who formulate so many definitions about matters which could have been either ignored without loss of salvation or left in doubt?[16] Or is he not destined to

* * * * *

13 See Ep 1333 nn22 and 24.
14 'Homoousion' and 'homoiousion' mean 'of the same substance' and 'of a similar substance,' respectively, and were terms used in the controversy in the fourth century over the divinity of Christ.
15 This is one of the passages censured by the Paris theologians in 1526. The *censura* declared that St Hilary did not think it dangerous to make pronouncements which conformed to the decisions of ecumenical councils; LB IX 925E–F.
16 This sentence and the one following it were censured by the Paris theologians on the ground that they were 'contumelious' towards general councils and the study of the Doctors of the church; LB IX 920E–921A.

have fellowship with the Father, Son, and Holy Spirit who cannot disentangle according to the method of philosophy what distinguishes the Father from the Son or the Holy Spirit from both or what the difference is between the generation of the Son from the Father and the procession of the Spirit? If I believe, as has been handed down, that the three are of one nature, what is the need of laboured disputation? If I do not believe, no human reasons will convince me. And such a dangerous inquisitiveness has generally arisen in us from the study of philosophy, a fact which the illustrious Tertullian, the most learned by far of all the Latin theologians, has asserted in several places,[17] although he himself was a philosopher of the first rank.

Socrates of Athens, to whom is attributed this famous axiom, 'What is above us is of no concern to us,'[18] brought down philosophy from the contemplation of natural phenomena into the midst of human life and frequently quoted that line from Homer: 'What evil and what good have been wrought in thy halls.'[19] Nevertheless, many things are apprehended with certainty concerning the nature of the stars, the motion of the celestial spheres, lightning, the winds, the rainbow, and similar phenomena, because either the bodily senses themselves or the observation of effects provide the beginnings of knowledge for matters of this nature, and the knowledge is especially pleasing and moves one at the same time to wonder and to love of the Maker. But yet because the wise man perceived that men sat idle all their lifetime in such study and neglected meanwhile what has greater relevance for us, he diverted all study from the contemplation of natural phenomena to the consideration of morals.[20] But those questions which we investigate and which we define sometimes have not been recorded in Holy Scripture, so that even if they cannot be understood they must at least be believed; nor can they, as they stand, be proved by any satisfactory arguments or grasped by the intellect or even vaguely conceived of by like means. And after the richest talents have applied all their energy for a long time to the investigation of them, this at last is the final result of their effort: they realize they know nothing; and what is more they contribute nothing to the devout life. Thus nowhere more does that well-known passage of Paul apply, 'Knowledge puffs up, charity builds up.'[21]

* * * * *

17 *De praescriptione* 7–14; *De anima* 2.7
18 See *Adagia* I vi 69, quoting Lactantius *Divinae institutiones* 3.20.
19 *Odyssey* 4.392
20 Socrates, as described by Cicero in the *Tusculanae disputationes* 5.4.10
21 1 Cor 8:1. The passage beginning 'But those questions' (line 202) was censured by the Paris theologians, who defended the definition of dogma

What arrogance, what contentions, what tumult, what discord in the world do we see gush forth from this kind of absurd learning! Although our life is so fleeting, we neglect meanwhile those things without which no one has any hope of attaining salvation. Unless I pardon my brother's sins against me, God will not pardon my transgressions against him. Unless I have a pure heart, I shall not see God. Therefore with all my energy I must aim, I must practise, I must strive to cleanse my soul of malice, envy, hatred, pride, avarice, and lust. You will not be damned if you do not know whether the Spirit proceeding from the Father and the Son has a single or a double principle, but you will not escape perdition unless you see to it in the mean time that you have the fruits of the Spirit, which are charity, joy, peace, patience, kindness, goodness, forbearance, gentleness, faith, moderation, self-control, and chastity.[22] Towards this end the chief concern of our study therefore must be focused and directed. Not that I think either that inquiry in the three divisions of philosophy[23] or that the investigation of phenomena beyond this world should be entirely condemned, provided that the inquirer is endowed with rich talent and is purged of rashness in defining, of obstinacy, and of the bane of harmony, the stubborn passion to get the upper hand.

The sum and substance of our religion is peace and concord.[24] This can hardly remain the case unless we define as few matters as possible and leave each individual's judgment free on many questions. This is because there is great uncertainty about very many issues, and the mind of man suffers from this deeply ingrained weakness, that it does not know how to give way when a question has been made a subject of contention. And after the debate has warmed up each one thinks that the side he has undertaken rashly to defend is absolute truth. In this regard certain men were so lacking in moderation that after defining everything in theology they contrived for those who are no more than men a new status of divinity,[25] and this has

* * * * *

about the Trinity and denied that this was 'knowledge that puffs up.' See LB IX 921E–F.
22 Gal 5:22. This sentence was censured by the Paris theologians; ibidem 920F–921A.
23 Ie, rational, natural, and moral
24 Censured by the Paris theologians; LB IX 926B–D
25 The Paris theologians censured this passage on the ground that it 'erroneously and rashly' slandered scholastic theology; LB IX 920C. In his reply (ibidem 920D) Erasmus stated that the passage was aimed not at scholastic theologians in general but rather at 'those who attribute too much to the Roman pontiff [and] whose adulation [of the Roman pontiff] ... is not approved even by theologians.' Cf LB VI 927D: 'Men are at least as busy arguing about the pope's

aroused more questions and greater commotion in the world than the
Arians in their foolishness once did. But certain pundits on some occasions
are ashamed to have no rejoinder to make.[26] On the contrary this is indeed
the mark of theological learning: to define nothing beyond what is recorded   245
in Holy Scripture, but to dispense in good faith what is there recorded.[27]
Many puzzling questions are now referred to an ecumenical council. It
would be much more fitting to defer such questions to that time when we
shall see God face to face without the mirror and without the mystery.[28]

But these matters will be discussed perhaps more appropriately   250
elsewhere.[29] I now return to our main theme. The subject of Hilary's *De
Trinitate* was especially magnificent and worthy of his lofty style, and it was
new because, unless I am mistaken, Hilary was the first of the Latins to draw
the sword of his eloquence against the Arians. That engagement also
brought a great deal of fame to him chiefly because the issue was joined with   255
a renowned foe. I do not doubt that several among the Greeks besides
Athanasius did the same. But it was a practice of that age to cite no one by
name with the exception of Holy Scripture, especially if the material was
drawn from Greek sources, for these they claimed for themselves as if they
had a right to them. In any case it seems to me to be the part of candour not to   260
conceal the names of those whom you have used to your advantage. Hilary
governs his expression throughout his work, however, as if he personally
had dug each of his ideas out of the sacred books. And although I might have
wished that such a talent, such an eloquence, such a mind might have richer
and more fruitful material, nevertheless the profit to the reader from this   265
work will also be not insignificant, because he explains with no less felicity
than accuracy, in my opinion, very many passages in John and Paul which
are quite obscure.

Furthermore Jerome in a certain letter to Paulinus, as he passes
judgment on the learned, writes that Hilary is distinguished by a lofty Gallic   270
style although in other respects his manner is marked by the embellish-

* * * * *

authority as about God's ... Whether he is a mere man or, as it were, a God, or
(with Christ) shares each nature.'

26 Censured by the Paris theologians; LB IX 928A–C. 'Pundits' (Erasmus actually
uses the term 'rabbis') was understood as an insulting reference to the
scholastic theologians who, according to the *censura*, were always ready with
an effective rejoinder to heretics.

27 The Paris theologians condemned this as an impious view worthy of Wycliffe
or Luther; LB IX 927A–D. Cf the *Ratio verae theologiae* (1518) LB V 83F–84A: 'The
chief aim of theologians is to interpret wisely Holy Scripture.'

28 1 Cor 13:12. This sentence was censured by the Paris theologians; LB IX 927D–E.

29 Possibly in the *De ratione concionandi*, which Erasmus had recently begun to
work on again; see Epp 1321 n1, 1332:36. See also lines 657–8 in this letter.

ments of the Greeks; he further says that he is read in vain by the more
ignorant because he sometimes uses long, involved periods.[30] Although
everywhere Hilary has his own characteristic style, it is especially present in
this work. For to the subject-matter which, as is probable, he borrowed from   27!
the Greeks he has added Gallic grandiloquence; for a learned simplicity is
characteristic of the Greeks, and a graceful and clear style is more to their
liking than a lofty and laboured one. And he often plays with standard
themes such as the following: it is very risky to discuss theological questions;
it is deplorable that a man, anxious lest he be embarrassed, should   28(
stubbornly defend a manifest error; Holy Scripture should not be twisted to
our inclinations, but our way of thinking should be corrected in accordance
with the norm of Scripture.[31] Moreover he frequently rises to what I might
call the grandeur of theatrical embellishments, especially in those parts
which easily lend themselves to brilliant expression, as for instance parts   28!
dealing with the structure of the universe, the nature of the heavenly bodies,
the harmonious discord of the elements, the gush of springs, the course of
rivers, the ebb and flow of the tides, and the various fruits of the earth. And
not infrequently he rises to the grandeur of tragic figures, personification
and apostrophe, by means of which he addresses either heretics or God   29(
himself.

Perhaps this grandiloquence is a characteristic of the Gallic genius.
Sulpicius Severus[32] possesses something of this sort, and Eucherius[33] also
has it; the latter's is a grandiloquence which is even more elaborate but
marked by a more felicitous care, if I am any judge. Nor does Guillaume   29!
Budé,[34] most renowned of the writers of this age, fail to reach the level of this
style. His style is so elevated that one imagines one hears a trumpet
sounding, not a man, and so felicitously finished that he never cloys the
learned reader and keeps at a distance those who have only a rudimentary
education. Furthermore, obscurity of expression results, albeit only in part,   30(
from the fact that Hilary often has difficulty rounding off a sentence
composed of various clauses. Clarity, however, is also hindered by the fact
that in handling a subject in itself involved and subtle he has also sought
applause for his acumen and sometimes for his richness of expression – a
mannerism which likewise marks the writing of Budé in his *De asse*. But this   305

* * * * *

30 *Letters* 58.10
31 *De Trinitate* 1.18
32 The historian and hagiographer Sulpicius Severus of Acquitaine (c 360–c 420)
   was the author of a life of St Martin of Tours and of a universal chronicle.
33 See Ep 676 introduction.
34 Ep 1328

disadvantage becomes easier to handle once you have become accustomed
to it. For as you may have difficulty understanding certain speakers unless
you hear them with some frequency, and as a type of music is less enjoyable
for the very reason that it is new and unusual, so because each author has his
own style that style becomes more familiar and therefore more pleasing by   310
our becoming accustomed to it. Indeed even Titus Livy, the most pleasing of
writers, is at first taste somewhat bitter. This happens, however, chiefly in
the case of those authors who, aside from what I might call their individual
flavour, bring to their work a capacity for taking pains and a striving for
subtlety. Among orators of this kind Quintilian especially ought to be   315
classed, and among poets, Horace.

It appears that St Jerome perceived this. He writes as follows in a letter
to a Roman orator: 'Hilary, a confessor of my times and a bishop, imitated
the twelve books of Quintilian both in style and in number.'[35] It is most
difficult, however, for the man who either teaches the rules of an art or offers   320
arguments on matters naturally subtle to combine a concern for polished
style with clear expression. In addition to these difficulties Quintilian also
strove for brevity. When I consider the varied diction of the ancient writers it
seems that hardly any provincials successfully reproduce the simplicity of
Roman speech except the few who were educated at Rome from boyhood.   325
For both Tertullian and Apuleius have a style of their own, and in the
decrees of the Africans, many of which Augustine refers to against
Petilianus and Cresconius,[36] you may observe an anxious striving for
eloquence, but such is their style that you recognize their African origin.
Augustine also sometimes is rather obscure and laboured, nor is Cyprian   330
entirely without African traits, although he is clearer than the others. Nor is
it strange if a Gaul reflects something Gallic or a Carthaginian something
Carthaginian when traces of Paduan idiom in Livy's Latin is offensive to
some. Generally, however, the striving is greater in one whose command of
a language is characteristic of provincials rather than citizens and who is a   335
foreigner rather than native-born. Undoubtedly this is why that old woman,
as the story goes, called Theophrastus a 'foreigner' because his language
was too Attic.[37]

Nevertheless, it seems to me indeed that St Jerome is misusing the
term 'imitated' for one who is like or resembles another. For the child is like   340

* * * * *

35 *Letters* 70.5. Like Hilary's *De Trinitate*, Quintilian's *Institutiones oratoriae* had
   twelve books.
36 *Contra litteras Petiliani libri tres; Contra Cresconium grammaticum et Donatistam
   libri iv*
37 Cicero *Brutus* 172; Quintilian 8.1.2

or resembles the parent rather than imitates him. But it is nature which in the production of offspring more truly imitates now the father, now the mother, now the grandfather or grandmother, now the aunt or uncle. Accordingly, imitation is a matter of effort, likeness is a result. Nor do we always resemble that which we imitate, and sometimes resemblance is unwitting. Moreover, 34 though perhaps it may not be improper to emulate Quintilian's style, yet it would rightly seem characteristic of what I might call an over-anxious scrupulosity even to have aimed at the same number of books, especially when the subject was different. For the rest, as Hilary is unlike Quintilian in the fullness of style (for he continually repeats and hammers home the same 35 idea in different words), so he is almost in distress in imitating a concern for order, spending no little time in promising what he is going to say and in repeating what he has said (in this indeed he is more like Aristotle than Quintilian), and spending much time in devising transitions to make neat connections between the various parts and much time apologizing when, as 35 the occasion arises, he touched on a topic which according to the division of contents he promised should have been treated in another place. In two respects he recalls Pliny, who wrote a history of the world, first because of a preface which is too elaborate, secondly because he intended the first book, which, it appears, he wrote last, to be a catalogue of the entire work.   36

And so much for the work bearing the title *De Trinitate*. *De synodis* follows it and treats the same subject in another way. For it reports on those assemblies of bishops in which the heresy of the Arians was condemned. He wrote this work for the bishops of Gaul, congratulating them for holding back from the Arian faction amid such great confusion in the world. He 36 translates it, as he himself testifies, from the Greek; he takes the liberty, however, of avoiding everywhere a word-for-word translation and only renders the thought, and where the opportunity presents itself he mixes in his own ingredients. He allows himself this liberty also in discussing the Psalms, as we shall soon explain in its proper place. Furthermore, although 37 this book restates the synodal decisions, he nevertheless seeks to avoid the risk of defending them, not so much, I think, because he lacked confidence in those for whom he was writing *De synodis* or because there were certain propositions of which he did not fully approve, but because of what I might call a scrupulous concern to avoid strong assertions, a concern which little 37 by little we have so forgotten that nothing causes shame. For thus generally in the affairs of men a situation from modest beginnings gains greater significance until it proliferates into something evil. St Hilary at the end of the twelfth book of *De Trinitate* does not dare to make any pronouncement about the Holy Spirit except that he is the Spirit of God – and it was unlikely 38 that he would have dared to say this unless he had read it in Paul: he does not dare to use the word 'creature' because he has not read it anywhere in Holy Scripture.[38]

This kind of profession would not be sufficient in this age because the needful diligence of the ancient Fathers has been very instructive for us, but   385 we are carried far beyond what is needful. Once faith was more a matter of a way of life than of a profession of articles. Soon necessity inspired the imposition of articles, but these were few, and apostolic in their moderation. Then the wickedness of the heretics made for a more precise examination of the sacred books, and intransigence necessitated the definition of certain   390 matters by the authority of synods. Finally faith began to reside in the written word rather than in the soul, and there were almost as many faiths as men.[39] Articles increased, but sincerity decreased: contention boiled over, charity grew cold. The teachings of Christ, which in former times were not touched by the clash of words, began to depend on the support of   395 philosophy: this was the first step of the church on the downward path. There was an increase of wealth and an accretion of power. Furthermore, the intervention of imperial authority in this situation did not improve much the purity of faith. At length the consequence of all this was sophistical controversy and the eruption of thousands of articles. And then it became a   400 matter of intimidation and threats. Although life may abandon us, although faith may be more on our lips than in our hearts, although that genuine understanding of Holy Scripture may fail us, yet we force men by intimidation to believe what they do not believe, to love what they do not love, and to understand what they do not understand. Compulsion is   405 incompatible with sincerity, and nothing is pleasing to Christ unless it is voluntary.[40] St Jerome calls to mind this work in a letter to Florentius, in these words: 'I ask that you send me the very comprehensive book *De synodis* of St Hilary, which I had copied with my own hand at Trier.'[41]

Coupled with this is the book he wrote against the emperor Constan-   410 tius, who favored the Arian faction,[42] but he wrote this book against him,

* * * * *

38 This last sentence was one of those criticized at the Valladolid conference in 1527; Bataillon 277.

39 An echo of Terence's 'Quot homines, tot sententiae' (*Phormio* 454)

40 In the copy of the Hilary edition which Erasmus sent to Jean de Carondelet (Houghton Library, Harvard University, *fNC5/Er153/523h/[A]), the entire passage beginning with the words 'The teachings of Christ' (line 394) was at one time obliterated. There is no reason to suppose that this was done by Carondelet himself, with whom Erasmus continued to have good relations.

41 *Letters* 5.2

42 *Contra Constantium imperatorem.* The emperor in question was Constantius II (d 361).

unless I am mistaken, after the emperor had died. For he is reproached in strong terms, whereas two other books addressed to the same man[43] – one written when he was alive; the other, it is believed, he also presented to him – are milder in tone. St Jerome recalls this in the *Catalogus* [*scriptorum* ecclesiasticorum]: 'Also there is that essay of his addressed to Constantius which he had presented to him when he was living in Constantinople. There is another one against Constantius which he wrote after his death.'[44] So much for Jerome. The harsher tone of the work against the deceased was due to religious devotion, the milder tone of his plea to the living was inspired by Christian prudence, which prefers to cure an evil, should the opportunity be offered, rather than to aggravate it. But none of these books in my opinion should be considered finished. For although they promise a piece of work complete and developed in detail they do not fulfill their promise, but suddenly as it were they fall silent. Because of the similarity of subject-matter there is joined to these an epistle written against Auxentius, whom he prosecuted for his involvement in the Arian heresy at Milan.[45] The epistle of Auxentius in which he offers a defence of himself to the emperors Valentinian and Valens accompanies it.

During my discussion of the foregoing the thought struck me in passing that perhaps some will be astonished that Hilary has scarcely anything to say about the Holy Spirit, although the aim of so many books and so much zeal and efforts and so many arguments, decisions, and anathemas is to make us believe that the Son is true God and of the same essence, or, as Hilary several times says, of the same genus and nature as the Father – the Greeks use the term ὁμοούσιον (that is, equal in power, wisdom, goodness, eternity, immortality, and all other attributes) – and although the entire controversy about the name of true God, about the term ὁμοούσιον, and about equality has no less a bearing on the Spirit than on the Son. Indeed nowhere does he write that the Holy Spirit must be adored and nowhere does he assign the word God to him, save that in one or two passages in *De synodis* he refers to those who dared to call the Father, Son, and Holy Spirit three Gods as condemned.[46] The reason was either that he thought at that time it was more important to defend the Son, whose human

* * * * *

43 *Ad Constantium Augustum liber primus; Ad Constantium Augustum liber secundus, quem Constantio ipse tradidit*

44 *De viris illustribus* 100

45 *Contra Arianos, vel Auxentium Mediolanensem, liber.* Appointed to the see of Milan by Emperor Constantius II in 355, Auxentius was a major supporter of Arianism in the West.

46 This sentence also came under attack at the Valladolid conference; Bataillon 277.

nature made it more difficult to win assent to the divinity of him who was   445
also human – and the Arians were trying to rob him of divinity, whereas the
question about the Holy Spirit had not yet been raised – or that it was the
scrupulous concern of the ancients that, although they worshipped God
devoutly, they nevertheless did not dare to make any pronouncements
about him which were not explicitly set forth in the sacred books. Though in   450
Scripture the name of God is several times assigned to the Son, yet nowhere
is it explicitly assigned to the Holy Spirit.[47] It should be acknowledged,
however, that the devout probing of the orthodox later ascertained with
sufficient proof from Holy Scripture that whatever was attributed to the Son
was appropriate to the Holy Spirit, except for the individuality of the person.   455
But because of the impenetrable obscurity of theological questions there
existed reverential reluctance in assigning names: they thought it was
wrong in theology to use words other than Holy Scripture used and the
general authority of the church handed down. They had read Holy Spirit,
they had read the Spirit of God, they had read the Spirit of Christ. They had   460
learned from the gospel that the Holy Spirit is not separated from the Father
and the Son. For the apostles are taught to baptize in the name of the Father
and of the Son and of the Holy Spirit. The fellowship of the three persons is
preserved in those short customary prayers left to us from the most ancient
usage of the church, at once brief and learned, in which the Father is   465
addressed in prayer through the Son in the unity of the Holy Spirit. The
Father is most frequently called God, the Son several times, the Holy Spirit
explicitly never.

  And these remarks of mine are not meant to call into question what has
been handed down to us from Holy Scripture by the authority of the   470
orthodox Fathers, but to show how much reverential reluctance the ancients
had in making pronouncements in theology, although they had a greater
devotion to theology than even we have – we who have rushed to such
extremes of boldness that we have no scruples about dictating to the Son
how he ought to have honoured his mother. We dare to call the Holy Spirit   475
true God, proceeding from the Father and the Son, which the ancients did
not dare to do, but on the other hand we have no scruples about driving him
repeatedly out of the temple of our soul by our evil deeds, just as if it were
our belief that the Holy Spirit is nothing more than a meaningless name.[48] By
the same token the majority of the ancients who revered the Son with the   480
greatest devotion nevertheless feared to use the term ὁμοούσιον because

* * * * *

47 Another sentence criticized at Valladolid; ibidem
48 The first part of this sentence and the last portion of the preceding one
   provoked heated objections at Valladolid; ibidem

that term is nowhere used in Holy Scripture. Indeed the progress of the church at first depended on purity of life rather than on an exact knowledge of the divine nature, and it has never sustained a greater loss than when it seemed to make the greatest possible advances in philosophical knowledge,   485 yes, and in the things of this world, not because they are evil in themselves but because they frequently involve man in the cares of this world.

Nor is learning evil in itself, but it often begets factions and dissension. The defence of the Catholic faith is put forward as a pretext, and in the mean time personal feelings become involved and the devil's business is pursued   490 in the name of Christ. I do not say this because I suspect anything of the sort about Hilary, which we certainly have found in the case of certain men of his age. Nevertheless, when he was alive he was a man; he did not lack human feelings; he could make mistakes, he could be misled. He had been banished and condemned by Saturninus;[49] he spent several years in exile among the   495 Phrygians, notorious for their uncivilized manners; he was hard-pressed in every way by the Arian faction. These influences and very many others could have played upon the feelings of even a good man under the guise of piety.

I do not deny that heretical intransigence must be abhorred, if   500 incurable. But meanwhile because of our hatred of one error we must beware of falling into another. Let us preserve that self-control, to prevent controversy from convincing us that the straight is crooked and the bitter sweet and vice versa. If this has happened to nearly all the ancients to some extent, then truly I shall not need to apologize for having spoken idly in   505 making these remarks. Tertullian, while he fought too aggressively against those who set a higher value on marriage than was reasonable, fell into another pit in condemning what Christ approved and demanding what he did not demand but only recommended.[50] Jerome fights with such excessive zeal against those who extolled marriage to the detriment of virginity[51] that   510 he himself with difficulty could defend his case in an unfriendly court if he should be charged with treating wedlock and a second marriage without enough respect. Montanus in opposing rather vigorously those who opened the doors of the church indiscriminately to the worthy and the unworthy at a time when there was an inordinate relaxation of church discipline fell into   515

* * * * *

49 Saturninus, bishop of Arles and an Arian, presided at the Council of Béziers (356), which condemned Hilary for having aroused public unrest. The order banishing Hilary to Asia Minor was issued by Emperor Constantius.
50 *Ad uxorem* 1.3; *De monogamia* 3; *De exhortatione castitatis* 1.4.5
51 *Adversus Helvidium de Mariae virginitate perpetua; Adversus Jovinianum;* and *Letters* 22, 130

the opposite error.[52] St Augustine in combating Pelagius with all his energy somewhere attributes less to free will than those who now reign in the theological schools think ought to be attributed.[53]

I could mention very many examples to illustrate this point even from modern authors, but it is better, I believe, not to be too wordy in dealing with   520
an unpleasant subject. We now turn to the subject of Hilary, who because of the sanctity of his life, because of his extraordinary learning, and because of his admirable eloquence was the light of his age. How great is the anger with which he attacks the Arians, again and again calling them impious, diabolic, blasphemous, devils, plagues, Antichrists! For already the label heretic is   525
too weak. And yet it is probable that there were men in the Arian faction who were convinced that their preaching about Christ was true and devout. Their doctrine rested on many and important authorities. Some passages in Holy Scripture gave the appearance of supporting it, and rational arguments were not lacking which displayed some semblance of truth. In addition   530
there was the authority of Caesar and beyond that the huge number of adherents, to which by right one ought to have yielded if the majority were always the better side. Finally, it was a controversy about matters far beyond human comprehension. I would have recommended that anyone in agreement with Arius be admonished and instructed, but I would not   535
immediately have called him Satan or Antichrist.

Indeed if these accusations must be hurled against anyone who errs on some point, what shall we do with our Hilary himself, not to mention so many outstanding Doctors of the church – Hilary who in so many passages seems to think that Christ had a body which was not susceptible to pain, that   540
hunger, thirst, weariness, and other states of this kind were not natural to it but were assumed? For he plainly wrote this in his exposition of Psalm 68, while in a council he pronounces an anathema against the man who would deny that the Father alone is called unborn God, as if the Holy Spirit either is not God or is also born himself of the Father. No one may plead that in   545
councils Hilary is simply repeating decisions already made and is not their author as well. For he makes the same statement in his own name in the twelfth book of *De Trinitate*, asserting that the Father alone is unborn God, that the Son alone is begotten, not created, that the Holy Spirit proceeds

* * * * *

52 Montanus of Phyrgia, founder of Montanism, a second-century apocalyptic and ascetic movement that condemned second marriages, found existing regulations on fasting too lax, and forbade flight from persecution. In about 206 the African church Father Tertullian became an adherent of the sect, which had already been condemned as heretical.
53 PL 44 has Augustine's voluminous writings against Pelagius.

from both in such a way that he can neither be said to be born nor yet be   550
admitted to share the name of creature, which some assign to the Son,
calling him a creature, for we utterly condemn the term creature no less in
the case of the Holy Spirit than in that of the Father and the Son. And both
elsewhere and in the eighth book of *De Trinitate* he maintains with great
vehemence that we also are one with the Father and the Son by nature and   555
not by adoption or by consensus only. Again in the third book of his work,
but more in the tenth book, he speaks in such a way about the body of Christ
that apparently he thinks that the Virgin Mary contributed nothing of her
own except the service of conception, pregnancy, and parturition, although
the orthodox believe that Christ was conceived by the agency of the Spirit, it   560
is true, but from the substance of the Virgin's body. And indeed there are
other passages which demand a courteous and proper interpreter. But what
law does he establish in his own case who becomes so furious with others?

But if anyone should take offence at the ascription of any feelings of
this sort to St Hilary, he ought to read the *Dialogus* Jerome wrote against the   565
Luciferians. He declares that Hilary had incurred a sentence of condemnation by the church because of his hatred of a faction which had been
harassing him for so long and against which he had waged war for so long.[54]
But it is better for Jerome's own words to enlighten us on this matter. 'If
heretics,' he says, 'do not have baptism and therefore must be rebaptized by   570
the church because they have not been in the church, Hilary himself also is
not a Christian: he was baptized in that church indeed which has always
accepted baptism by heretics. Before the Council of Rimini was held[55] and
before Lucifer was banished[56] Hilary, deacon of the Roman church, used to
admit those coming over from the heretics with that baptism which they had   575
previously received, unless perchance only Arians are considered heretics
and only their baptism may be rejected, not that of others. You were deacon,
Hilary, and you were wont to accept those baptized by the Manichaeans;
you were deacon, and you approved Ebionite baptism. Suddenly after Arius
appeared you began to be completely dissatisfied with yourself: with your   580
household slaves you stay apart, and you find a new bathing place.' Again
somewhat later he says: 'Let him also read the tracts of Hilary himself which

* * * * *

54 *Dialogus contra Luciferianos* 26. Here Erasmus mistakenly discusses a reference
    by Jerome to a different Hilary, deacon of Rome and a follower of the fiercely
    anti-Arian theologian Lucifer, bishop of Cagliari (d 370 or 371).
55 The Council of Rimini (359) was called by Emperor Constantius to deal with the
    Arian dispute. Under imperial pressure, the orthodox bishops submitted to an
    Arianizing creed.
56 To Palestine in 355

he published against us on the subject of rebaptizing heretics, and there he
will find that Hilary himself acknowledges that Julius, Malchus, Sylvester
and other bishops of early times admitted all heretics at once to do   585
penance.'[57] But if Jerome wrote these words against our Hilary, they clearly
reveal that out of hatred of the Arian faction he had fallen away from
Catholic belief and into heresy. For no one ever raved more impiously and
more insanely about Christ than the Manichaeans, and the blasphemy of the
Ebionites who taught that Christ was nothing more than man was so   590
obvious, and the Arians meanwhile acknowledged that he was God and
God Almighty though also a creature but one infinitely superior to all others,
a creature whom the Father had adopted into the dignity of the Son and the
divine name and through whom he had established all things both in
heaven and on earth. I admit that this does not measure up to the dignity of   595
Christ, but what is it compared to the blasphemy of the Ebionites? Yet he
who did not accept Arian baptism had accepted the baptism of the Ebionites.
To be perfectly frank, however, I am not certain whether Jerome makes
these remarks about our Hilary, especially since he fails to mention the
books he cites here in his *Catalogus scriptorum*. And Gennadius in his   600
Catalogus[58] lists a certain bishop of Arles named Hilary, although he makes
no mention of the tracts Jerome refers to. Therefore let this argument carry
only the weight of probability.[59]

   We say this by no means to dim the glory and damage the reputation of
a very holy and learned man, but to warn the bishops and theologians of our   605
day against allowing themselves to be caught unawares by the kind of thing
we see happen to so great a man. First, it is the part of evangelical honesty to
interpret fairly the deeds and writings of brothers. Then, if anyone has erred
whom we cannot ignore, he should not at once be subjected to our wrath,
since everyone errs, but an effort should be made to eliminate the error   610
without hurting the person concerned. Finally, a neighbour should be
admonished as we would wish to be admonished if we had fallen into
human error. Today we see some who falsely censure everything in the
books of others, who vent what I might call their rage against the good name
of a neighbour, although in their own books one finds clear blasphemies   615
against Christ. This would be an idle comment if I should not point out in

* * * * *

57 *Contra Luciferianos* 27
58 See Ep 676:21n.
59 By 1530 Erasmus had made up his mind that Hilary deacon of Rome and Hilary
   bishop of Poitiers were two different persons. As a consequence, this whole
   passage was omitted from the revised edition of Hilary which Froben
   published in 1535.

reality that in the books of certain men, which in great numbers now for the past several years have rushed forth from every quarter as champions of the majesty of the pope, there are notions openly insulting to Christ which at the same time give strong support to the dignity of a human being. If the actual   620
facts should not provide conclusive confirmation for this, I would be an unreliable witness.

I do not condemn the zeal of those who with moderation defend the authority of the pope against the seditious impudence of certain men; nevertheless I would prefer that the glory of Christ so flourish that it eclipse   625
the glory of all the world, even of Peter and Paul, should it be possible, not only of the Roman pontiff. For thus eclipsed we would truly be glorious, if we of ourselves were nothing, but Christ were all in all. However, I speak about a few who while they strive intemperately to claim for man his proper dignity have not been sufficiently mindful of the dignity of Christ, to whom   630
alone all dignity is owed. In matters like this, although a Maevius may excuse himself, towards others he is so fierce, so pitiless, and so unjust.[60] What judgment can there be in a matter in which hate is so unbridled? The sword of the gospel's word must always indeed be brandished against all wicked errors, and one should make every effort to combat heresies as they   635
spring up. But this must be our first concern: that what we rail at in others is not found in ourselves; and this must be our second: that we not be corrupted by our own personal feelings and call what is good evil, what is sweet bitter, what is clear obscure. For this is the mark of stubbornness implanted in the temperaments of the majority of men, that they never stop   640
defending a statement they have once made on some occasion or other, even if they discover that they have been wrong. First, shame stands in the way. Through contention it leads to stubbornness and at length stubbornness develops into a madness. As a consequence, while the dispute becomes violent on both sides, on both sides the truth is lost. The error is called a   645
schism if anyone diminishes the authority of the Roman pontiff. But why is no one disturbed when some men, extraordinarily impudent and basely servile, attribute too much to that authority? If falsehood causes displeasure, why does it not cause displeasure everywhere? Finally, why is the assertion that the Virgin Mother is free from original sin heretical among the   650
Dominicans, orthodox among the Scotists? Is this not tantamount to openly declaring that judgment has been corrupted? Is this 'cutting a straight furrow' for the word of God? We gladly use this Pauline word.[61] Therefore, let the eye of him who is ready to take the mote out of his brother's eye be

* * * * *

60 Maevius was a wretched Latin poet who attacked his contemporary, Virgil.
61 2 Tim 2:15

clear and unclouded.[62] Let us always keep before our eyes the gentleness of   655
him who, although he alone was free from all error, nevertheless did not
extinguish the smoking flax, or crush the bruised reed.[63] But these matters
also will be discussed more appropriately elsewhere.[64]

The *Commentaries on Matthew*, as Jerome calls them, come next. Others
have preferred to call them a catalogue because, I believe, he expounds some   660
headings separately. I do not doubt that he translated this work from
Origen; in fact it savours of both the genius and the style of Origen
throughout. For although Hilary's work imparts much excellent instruction
clearly revealing the author's expert knowledge of Holy Scripture, nevertheless his allegories are rather far-fetched in several instances and sometimes   665
rather harsh, and his excessive preoccupation with allegorizing results in
the loss of the historical sense. It is as if there is no place for allegorizing
without impairing the historical sense. Sometimes in joining the two (for he
also gives his attention to this) he has amused himself, it seems, with his
cleverness rather than treated a serious subject. We see, however, that   670
among his innumerable gifts this failing is peculiar to Origen in nearly all his
writings. I wish that the man had many imitators of his other qualities as he
had some followers even among Latin authors in this aspect of his work.
Furthermore Jerome declares that the commentaries which Hilary published
on the Psalms were more truly imitations of Origen's commentaries than   675
translations, especially since he himself had made some contributions of his
own.[65] What these are the experienced reader will have no difficulty
perceiving, for they are by and large the ideas which he had advanced in so
many books against the Arians. He himself does not indicate anywhere
whom he has followed; however, I think he did this not to conceal his   680
benefactor but to avoid the odium attaching to Origen's name. Ambrose
does the same thing everywhere.

Jerome mentions this work in the preface of the second book on
Micah.[66] He cites Hilary as having paraphrased nearly forty thousand lines
from Origen on the Psalms. One wonders, however, what Hilary's plan was   685
in selecting certain psalms for translation and passing over the rest, unless
by chance it was because he did not happen to come upon the complete

* * * * *

62 Matt 7:3–5; Luke 6:41–2
63 Isa 42:3, quoted in Matt 12:20. Although we have translated 'bruised reed,'
   which is the reading in both the Vulgate (*arundinem quassatum*) and the English
   Bible, Erasmus actually says 'broken staff' (*baculum fractum*); cf the Vulgate
   version of Isa 36:6.
64 See n29.
65 *De viris illustribus* 100
66 *Commentariorum in Michaem prophetam libri duo* 2 init

work of Origen. He wrote, as Jerome recounts, on Psalms 1 and 2, then on
Psalms 51 to 62, and again on Psalm 118 to the last. But we have more than
the number Jerome gives – namely, besides the first two we have   690
commentaries from Psalms 51 to 69 and again from Psalm 118 to the end,
except that the last part appears to be missing in the copies. This happened, I
suspect, because the final page of the manuscript codices either had been
torn off or had worn out. That page as a rule is lost, like the last bean plant in
the proverb.[67] It is inferred from this that Hilary's work on the Psalms did   695
not reach Jerome in its entirety. For he published the *Catalogus* of famous
writers[68] after the death of Hilary, so no one can claim that Hilary made
certain additions to his work after Jerome published his *Catalogus*. And he
testifies in this connection that he heard from some persons that Hilary had
written commentaries on the Song of Songs, but he denies that he had seen   700
the work.

Many works indeed have been lost to us, namely, letters which he
wrote to various persons and also a book of hymns. For an extant letter to his
daughter Apra has nothing of Hilary and a hymn has far less and not even
the character of a song, although Jerome testifies somewhere that he wrote   705
that song. Nevertheless, we have included both to provide a sample for
anyone who by chance might wish to make a judgment on these matters.
The literary style and composition of Hilary show that he was not
infelicitous in writing verse, and perhaps several hymns which the church
sings today, not without art but of uncertain authorship, are his, as for   710
example the hymn *De ligno crucis*, which begins 'Crux fidelis' and the hymn
De Ioanne Baptista, which begins 'Ut queant laxis.'[69] We also lack the
commentaries on Job which, as Jerome in the same work declares,[70] he
paraphrased from Origen. And indeed there is extant among the remains of
Origen a commentary on Job, the style of which has no affinity with Hilary's.   715
In fact the preface testifies that this same work had been translated by some
others but with neither accuracy nor learning. They made bad Latin out of
good Greek. Indeed, the author of the preface himself makes clear that he
was a man who neither knew Latin nor had talent or learning but whose
presumptuousness matched his ignorance. We are also lacking that book   720
which he wrote against the prefect Sallustius or against Dioscorus the

* * * * *

67 *Adagia* IV iv 72
68 Ie, *De viris illustribus* 100
69 The two hymns mentioned are, in fact, by Venantius Fortunatus (d after 600)
   and Paul the Deacon (d 799) respectively.
70 Ie, in *De viris illustribus* 100

physician.[71] In it he displayed, it seems, all the powers of his talent and eloquence. St Jerome makes this point in a letter to the orator Magnus: 'In a brief essay which he wrote against Dioscorus the physician he has shown his literary power.'[72] Also missing is a book against Valens and Ursacius which 725 contains a history of the Council of Rimini and the acts of the Council of Seleucia,[73] unless by chance this work was added to *De synodis.*

So much for the discussion of the individual works of our author. Now we shall offer a few remarks in general about the gifts of this most praiseworthy man. But first what point is there in speaking about the 730 sanctity of his life when ecclesiastical authority has long since inscribed his name in the catalogue of saints? In any event, however, all his books breathe what I might call a wonderful fervour of holiness. How great the authority attaching to his name was may be surmised even from the fact that St Jerome, who came close to belittling Augustine and who did not regard 735 Ambrose too highly, often cites Hilary with great veneration, calling him in one place 'the Deucalion of the world,'[74] in another 'a trumpet of the Latin language,'[75] and in another 'the Rhône of Latin eloquence.'[76] And in more than one passage Jerome made use of the example of that man like a shield against those who falsely charged him with consorting with the Origenists, 740 and he accorded him the fullest testimonial in a letter to Marcella, when he says: 'I do not dare criticize so great a man, the most eloquent of his day, who is praised for his meritorious service as a witness as well as for the industry which marked his life and the clarity which characterized his eloquence wherever the name of Rome has reached.'[77] What statement covers more 745 ground than this? And Jerome mentions him with no less respect in his commentary on Isaiah, when he says: 'Do not Cyprian, a holy and most eloquent martyr, and Hilary, a confessor of our time, seem to you to be like trees, lofty while they stood, in the building of the church of God?'[78] Indeed

* * * * *

71 Ibidem
72 *Letters* 70.5
73 Valens and Ursacius were fourth-century Arian leaders in the West. The Councils of Rimini and Seleucia (359) were dominated by the Arians. Parts of the book Erasmus refers to came to light later and were published in Paris in 1598; see PL 10 619.
74 *Contra Luciferianos* 26. This reference to Deucalion (a figure in Greek mythology analogous to Noah) actually applies to the other Hilary, deacon of Rome (n54 above), and thus should have been omitted from the revised version of the letter along with lines 564–603.
75 *Apologia adversus libros Rufini* 2.19
76 *Commentarii in Epistolam ad Galatas* 2 init
77 *Letters* 34.3
78 *Commentarii in Isaiam prophetam* 17, on Isa 60:13

St Augustine also with a laudatory introduction cites not without praise the   750
authority of Hilary in his *De Trinitate*.[79]

On the other hand, Hilary was entirely untrained in Hebrew. Hence if
he dealt with anything in this language either he used Origen as a source or
he handled it with little success. Indeed in explaining a Psalm he suggests
that *bresith* is more correctly rendered by *in filio* than by *in principio* – so   755
Jerome reports in his notes on the traditions of the Hebrews on Genesis[80] –
yet the authority of the Septuagint stands in clear opposition to this, as do
Symmachus and Theodotion, who fully concur in the translation ἐν ἀρχῇ.[81]
It is also at odds with the Hebrew text itself, which has *bresith* and which
Aquila takes to mean ἐν κεφαλίδι – that is, *in capitulo*. It does not have *babem*,   760
which is the translation of *in filio*. The word 'head,' however, is also used for
the beginning of anything. In this instance no one may rightly ask for
consistency in Hilary who, although he highly praises in more than one
passage the authority of the Septuagint, from which he thinks it wrong to
depart a hair's breadth, as it were, has not hesitated to disagree on this   765
word. I suspect that the passage which Jerome alludes to is in the
commentary which Hilary wrote on Psalm 2, for there he notes in passing
that *bresith* in Hebrew has three meanings: *in principio, in capite,* and *in filio*.[82]
Although this word has been rendered in different ways by translators
Jerome thinks that there must be no deviation from the authority of the   770
Septuagint. But Hilary made an even more extraordinary mistake with the
term *hosanna*. In his commentary on Matthew he states that the word in
Hebrew means *sanctificatio domus David*,[83] although there is nothing in this
term which has any affinity with such an interpretation. Indeed in Hebrew
redemptio is *pheduth*, and *domus* is *beth*. Moreover, it is self-evident to all that   775
David, since it is the same word in Latin, Greek, and Hebrew, was not
inserted here, as Jerome somewhere informs us.

Furthermore he had studied Greek literature superficially, if indeed we
believe Jerome, whose comment on this I quote from the letter to Marcella
wherein he explains Psalm 126: 'However, he should not be blamed,' he   780

* * * * *

79 6.10

80 *Liber hebraicarum quaestionum in Genesim*, on Gen 1:1. See lines 766–8. *Bresith* is
the Hebrew word with which the book of Genesis begins. In Latin it is
rendered as 'in principio' and in English as 'in the beginning.'

81 The Septuagint is the Greek version of the Old Testament produced by Jewish
translators in the third and second centuries BC. Symmachus and Theodotion
as well as Aquila of Pontus (line 760) made Greek translations of the Old
Testament in the second century of the Christian era.

82 The passage in question is found in section 2 of the commentary on Psalm 2.

83 21.3, 5

writes, 'ignorant of Hebrew as he was and with only a smattering of Greek, but the priest Heliodorus with whom he was intimately associated should be blamed. He used to ask him what Origen meant by those words he could not understand. Heliodorus, since he could not find Origen's commentary on this psalm, was not reluctant to insinuate his own opinion rather than to 785 admit his ignorance, and Hilary adopted it and discussed it in clear language and with some eloquence set forth the error of another.'[84] So far we have reviewed the words of Jerome in which while he zealously defends Hilary he treats Heliodorus with repugnance, especially since his explanation is only conjectural. But at this point to defend Hilary in passing: it is not likely, I 790 think, that such a great man was so credulous that in expounding Holy Scripture he placed his total reliance on the judgment of another or that he was so deficient in his knowledge of Greek literature that he could not of himself grasp the meaning of the original, especially in the case of Origen, whose language is admirably clear. This we can easily infer from those 795 works surviving in a Latin translation. Yet I do not quite see what caused the displeasure of St Jerome here. For the fact that he gives various translations from the Hebrew by ancient scholars has no bearing on Hilary, who admittedly always follows the Septuagint version, which in this passage[85] has the translation ἐκτετιναϲμένων. 800

Moreover, St Jerome asserts that Hilary interpreted the phrase 'the sons of those shaken off' to mean the apostles, because they were ordered to shake the dust off their feet with reference to those who had not accepted the gospel.[86] But if anyone should read with some attention Hilary's commentary on the psalm *Nisi Dominus aedificaverit domum*[87] he will find that the case 805 is somewhat different. For in my opinion Hilary calls those who through their own fault have been rejected by God and have been 'shaken off' as accursed because of their stubborn disbelief 'the apostles and prophets of

.* * * * *

84 *Letters* 34.3, a continuation of the passage cited in lines 742–5. This letter to Marcella is devoted to explaining certain passages in Psalm 127 (Vulg 126), *Nisi Dominus aedificavit domum* (Unless the Lord build the house).

85 The passage Erasmus refers to and which Jerome was trying to explain in his letter to Marcella is Psalm 127 (Vulg 126):4, which in the old Latin text used by Hilary and in the later Vulgate text (cf n96) contains the enigmatic phrase *filii excussorum*, 'the sons of those shaken off.' In the Septuagint the word for *excussorum* is ἐκτετιναϲμένων. Jerome criticizes Hilary's interpretation of this curious phrase, as Erasmus indicates at some length. (The new Latin version of the Psalms authorized by Pius XII reads *filii iuventutis* and the RSV has 'the sons of one's youth.')

86 Matt 10:14

87 Sections 18 and 19, on Psalm 127 (Vulg 126)

those shaken off' – that is, 'the sons of the wicked.' But his passing mention
in two words of the dust shaken from the feet means not that the apostles are   81(
said to be 'shaken off' but that the dust shaken off in the case of the
disbelieving Jews signifies that because of their stubborn rejection of the
grace of the gospel they themselves have been 'shaken off' for the falsity of
their understanding. This he also explains more clearly in his commentary
on Matthew in the words: 'And by the sign of the dust shaken off the feet let   81♦
an everlasting curse be left behind.'[88] I might also refer to the words of Hilary
himself from the Psalms except that it would be tedious and irksome for the
reader, especially in a preface. The fact is, then, that here Jerome either had a
lapse of memory or had not read Hilary's commentary with enough
attention. Now when Jerome approves the comment of Marcella, who wrote   82(
that the apostles were 'the sons of those shaking off' rather than 'of those
shaken off,'[89] I for my part do not see what he means, unless perhaps as the
Greeks speak of 'sons of doctors' for 'doctors' so the apostles were called 'the
sons of those shaken off' for 'the shaken off.' Otherwise the successors of the
apostles ought rather to have been called 'the sons of those shaken off,' if the   82♦
apostles are correctly known by the name of 'the shaken off.' Yet it is not
absurd for those who have shaken themselves off to be called 'the shaken
off,' just as those who have washed themselves are called washed and those
who have dined are called the dined. For so it is that both the dust has been
shaken off and the man or his foot shaken off, as we say something that   83(
stains has been spattered on a man and a man has been spattered by
something that stains.

It seemed appropriate to touch on these matters in passing not only to
defend Hilary, but also to show that at one time the holiest men had no
scruples about disagreeing with authors however great, and further that   83♦
even the greatest men sometimes nod, as did Jerome in this instance in
criticizing Hilary. Each man is a friend, but the truth ought to be the greater
friend for everyone.[90]

Let us now return to the original point. I would readily believe all the
same that Hilary did not have a complete knowledge of Greek literature. For   84(
as far as elegance of style is concerned he is more successful in what he
writes of and by himself than in what he translates, for his translations are
more concise and restrained in thought. I suspect that the cause of this was

* * * * *

88 10.10, on verse 14
89 *Letters* 34.3
90 This dictum is drawn from Aristotle's *Nicomachean Ethics* 1.6 (1096a) and was
given a wording and usage similar to Erasmus' by Petrarch in *On His Own
Ignorance*. See Ernst Cassirer et al eds *The Renaissance Philosophy of Man* (Chicago
1948) 111.

his practice not to undertake to translate anything unless he was free to use
his own discretion in rendering the meaning and to omit or add what he   845
thought proper. This is the safer course for anyone who does not have full
command of the language he is translating. Poggio availed himself of the
same privilege in translating Diodorus Siculus,[91] Rufinus did the same in
almost everything he translated, especially in the case of the books of Origen
and the history of Eusebius of Caesarea.[92] Even so this is not the liberty of the   850
translator but rather the licence which contaminates the writings of another.
Hilary, however, never professed to be a translator save in *De synodis*, any
more than did Ambrose, who for the most part drew upon the works of
Origen in his writings. It is my opinion that as the Greek text presented itself
to him Hilary erred when in assigning attributes to each person of the Trinity   855
he ascribes eternity to the Father, image to the Son, and use to the Holy
Spirit.[93] Perhaps he read in Greek τὸ χρῆστον or χρηστότητα, which is
derived from the Greek ἀπὸ τοῦ χρῆσθαι – that is, 'from using.' From this
εὔχρηστος means friendly and suitable to everyday life, and ἄχρηστος means
useless. But χρῆστον or χρηστότης in Greek has to do not with use or utility   860
so much as with goodness, friendliness, agreeableness, or, a frequent translation, kindness. Power is attributed to the Father, wisdom to the Son, and
goodness to the Holy Spirit. Augustine cites this passage in his *De Trinitate*,
going to some trouble in explaining what the term 'use' means.[94]

However this may be, although St Hilary did not have full command of   865
Greek, it is nevertheless worth while to see how carefully he philosophizes
about the usage of Greek words in his *Commentary on the Psalms*, now
diligently pointing out their aptness and significance, now seeking the
meaning of the Greek not rendered with requisite propriety by the Latin
translator, now removing the ambiguity from Latin words with the help of   870
the Greek. And where meanwhile are those who say that Greek literature is
of no value in the study of Holy Scripture? Where are those individuals –
camels[95] rather than men – who bleat that nothing comes out of Greek
literature except heresies? And though they keep shouting out these

* * * * *

91 Poggio's Latin translation of the first five books of Diodorus Siculus' *Bibliotheca
   historica* was printed at Bologna in 1472, and at Venice in 1476, 1481, 1493, and
   1496.
92 Rufinus of Aquileia (Tyrannius), a Roman ecclesiastical writer of the fourth
   century, translated the *Periarchon* of Origen and the *Historia ecclesiastica* of
   Eusebius.
93 *De Trinitate* 2.1
94 6.11, 15.5
95 A reference to the Louvain Carmelite Baechem (Ep 1254 n6), whom Erasmus
   often referred to scornfully as 'camelus' or 'camelita'

thoughts in public sermons, they are amazed if some persons think that they   87!
are in need of a dose of hellebore. Indeed the translation he uses is different
from the one which has now been commonly accepted![96] Moreover, since
Cyprian has his own translation, as do Augustine and Ambrose, and Hilary,
and Tertullian (his is different from all others), it is quite clear that at one
time there was no translation which everyone used.   88(

Perhaps it will seem too trivial to point out certain words and
expressions that are peculiar to Hilary but are contrary to the common usage
of those who speak Latin. For example, he repeatedly uses the pronouns *sui*
and *suus* rather awkwardly. Also he uses *tecum* and *cum illis* in place of *iuxta*
tuam and *iuxta illorum opinionem*. *Intimare* is also found in place of *significare*; it   88!
is found in other authors who are, however, later. He uses *disproficit* several
times in place of *degenerat* or *in peius proficit*. *Zabolus* instead of *diabolus*[97] is
found not only in Hilary, but one can see the beginning of its usage in
antiquity, which used ζὰ instead of διὰ not only in compound words but
also outside of composition. He uses several Greek or Hebrew words   89(
sometimes with a Latin inflexion, sometimes with a Greek. Somewhere he
uses *rheuman* instead of *rheuma*, as if one should decline *rheuma, rheumae* like
musa, musae. Somewhere he uses the forms *pascham* and *mannam*. Again
somewhere he uses *diapsalmam* and *diapsalmae* though in other places
diapsalma and *diapsalmatis* occur. These are cases in which you may find the   89!
obvious faults, but there is the kind that occasionally slips into the text of
even the most learned; indeed even in the works of Cicero you may find a
few. I say this so that no one will immediately conclude there is an error and
reach for an eraser.

I would give several examples of this had I not made notations in the   90(
margins where they occur; yet it would also not be difficult for anyone to
discover them by examining the index. In his commentary on Psalm 124
Hilary writes as follows: 'After the conversion of the prophet[98] took place,
praying that the Lord reward him who had stayed his hand from evil in
these words: "Do good, O Lord, to the good and upright of heart," signifying   90!
uprightness of will and deed in both.' For he has added *signifying* just as if
the words 'After the conversion of the prophet took place he prayed that
God reward ...' had preceded.[99] And for the most part the other solecisms
are of this type. Either this happens because of human error – the kind of

* * * * *

96 Numerous Latin translations of the Bible were in use until Jerome's version,
the Vulgate, became the commonly accepted one.
97 Cf Ep 1256 n26.
98 David
99 Ie, as if there had been a nominative case for *signifying* to agree with

lapse one finds even in Cicero – or he has imitated the Greeks, who use the   910
genitive case in this fashion as an absolute as we do the ablative and who
sometimes use the nominative instead of the genitive. This breach which the
Greeks call ἀναπόδοτον happens chiefly to those who in a lengthy period
hardly complete their sentence and whose attention is focused more on
content than on expression. For example, if anyone should say 'It was not   915
permitted to write to you' and at length add 'occupied with various matters'
after much has been inserted before it, just as if 'I was not able to write to
you' had preceded.[100] Without fault we copy a practice of the ancients when
we say *Non sum id nescius, Quoties eius diei mihi venit in mentem, Id anus mihi
indicium fecit*, just as if one had used *nescio* instead of *nescius sum, recordor*   920
instead of *venit in mentem, indicavit* instead of *indicium fecit*.[101] There is a
similar but a more obvious example in his commentary on Psalm 141, where
he writes: 'For beholding his body, which they had fastened to the cross, no
one looked for the power of the spirit, which had proved itself divine by
signs and deeds.' Here again *beholding* is used instead of *while they were*   925
beholding.[102] I trust that the citing of this example may suffice.

But indeed I am remarkably shameless in keeping the eager reader
from perusing the inspired work by so wordy a preface. I shall come to a
close, therefore, after I have made this one request of you, most gracious
prelate. I ask that you accept this work of mine, such as it is, dedicated to   930
your name, as a pledge and memorial of my devotion to you. Let others
judge what we have done. At least we have made a great effort to place
Hilary, that unique light of Gaul, into the hands of men in a considerably
more correct and refined form. The publication of his work will have even
greater appeal with the addition of your approval, since your influence is   935
foremost in the opinion of all and your sound and sincere judgments are
well known to everyone. Your outstanding abilities are one with the abilities
of the Carondelet family, which in its abundant fruitfulness has given us
many besides the distinguished chancellor of Burgundy.[103] I have known
five[104] of them, men of no less cultivation than integrity, loaded with every   940
kind of honour.

You understand therefore what I am seeking. I am of course seeking to

* * * * *

100 Ie, as if there had been the personal pronoun 'I' for *occupied* to modify
101 Ie, as if the personal pronouns were governed by the proper verbs
102 Ie, the nominative plural of the present participle is used instead of the correct
    verb form.
103 The archbishop's father; see introduction. The vagueness of this reference is
    intentional; see Ep 1345:50–3.
104 See Ep 1350 n7.

gain from the lustre of the Carondelet name some favour for Hilary, who ought to be held in the highest esteem by all students of theology. For I see that some, in view of the new books which are now springing forth from every quarter, are disdainful of the ancient authors, and to such an extent that they think that both Origen and Jerome, like sexagenarians in the proverb, must be driven from the bridge.[105] Just as men of genius in these times who either invent something new or restore something old should, I think, be above contempt, so it is characteristic of an inferior mind not to accord to old age the honour due it and characteristic also of an ungrateful mind to reject those to whose persevering efforts the Christian world owes so much. For what could we accomplish now in scriptural studies without the aid of the works left us by Origen, Tertullian, Chrysostom, Jerome, Hilary, and Augustine? I do not think that the works of either Thomas or Scotus should be rejected in their entirety. They wrote for their own age, and they passed on to us much that was drawn from the books of the ancient Fathers and examined with some discrimination. But I do not approve of the rudeness of those who ascribe so much to this kind of author that they believe they have the obligation to clamour against good literature happily springing up again everywhere. Diverse are the gifts of men of genius, and many are the different kinds of ages. Let each one reveal the scope of his competence, and let no one be envious of another who in keeping with his own ability and style tries to make a useful contribution to the education of all. Reverence is the due of ancient authors, especially those authors who are recommended by the sanctity of their lives in addition to their learning and eloquence; but this reverence does not exclude a critical reading of them. Fairness is the due of modern authors so that they may be read without ill will, though not without discrimination. Let the absence of furious contention, the bane of peace and concord, prevail everywhere. And let the Graces, whom the ancients not without good reason conceived as the companions of the Muses, attend upon our studies.

May he without whom there can be no salvation preserve your Excellency safe for us a long time, most illustrious prelate.

Basel, 5 January 1523

* * * * *

105 In ancient Rome sexagenarians, denied the right to vote, were driven from the bridge leading to the voting place; see *Adagia* I v 37.

1335 / From Johann von Botzheim   Constance, 7 January 1523

On Botzheim, see Ep 1285. This is Botzheim's reply to Ep 1331. The manuscript
of the letter, which was first published as Ep 20 in Enthoven, is in the Rehdiger
Collection of the University Library at Wrocław (MS Rehd 254.105).

I sent you a letter[1] a few days ago by a kinsman of Froben's,[2] the man you call
a most worthless fellow, and I a chatterbox and a lightweight, not without
reason. In the matter of your divination,[3] you need fear no danger; I shall be
too cautious to give you any cause for alarm on my account. I on the other
hand appeal to you as a good friend not to allow any trouble to arise out of   5
the letters I have sent you, for I often write to you carelessly and with too
much freedom. Your letter goes on record that you will support the pope to
the best of your power. There is nothing absurd about the policy, provided
the real truth is not suppressed. To hate dissension and love concord is
evidence of most genuine piety. But if the occasion should ever arise when   10
you would rather abandon the cause of truth than provoke a breach of that
concord, remember that truth must not be sacrificed to any and every
objective. Truth must sometimes be maintained in its rightful place and not
abandoned or hushed up in a way that might seem to be giving support to its
opposite; that is a thing I would think one ought not to do on any pretext   15
whatever. Nor does the truth ever come so close to subversion that, though
stated in the very moderate language which is habitual with you, it will be
judged revolutionary or subversive by any of those who are religious and

* * * * *

1335
1 Not extant, but see Ep 1342:685–6.
2 Perhaps Konrad Resch (Ep 1319 n2), whom Wolfgang Capito described as
  'Froben's kinsman' (Ep 1083:2); or Resch's uncle, Johann Schabler, called
  Wattenschnee, whose daughter Allen believed to have been the 'affinis mea
  charissima' in whose honour Froben reprinted Erasmus' *Encomium matrimonii*
  in 1518. Wattenschnee was a widely travelled book merchant who acted as a
  messenger for Froben. Bietenholz (29 n30) suggests as a third possibility
  another widely travelled book merchant, Benoît Vaugris (see Ep 1395), a close
  relative of Wattenschnee's wife.
3 Botzheim writes *divinatione tua*, the meaning of which is not clear. Allen
  thought that it might be a reference to Erasmus' *Consilium* on the Luther
  problem (Epp 1352 introduction and 1329 n3) or to an early draft of the
  Catalogus lucubrationum (Ep 1341A). According to information supplied by
  Craig R. Thompson, the late Preserved Smith made the more plausible
  suggestion that the *divinatio* in question was the colloquy *Exorcismus, sive
  Spectrum*, first published in the edition of August–September 1524 (ASD I-3
  417–23 / Thompson 230–7).

good Christians at heart. It is most difficult for you to write anything that will not be twisted into a calumny by someone, especially in such a complex business, which is already so highly inflamed. It is impossible for you to reconcile different convictions on the same subject, which are as violent and as controversial as they are on this topic, by peaceful agreement between the parties; I am much more afraid that if you support the papal case in your desire to maintain concord, you will be encouraging greater danger and confusion. It is right that truth should win the day, it is right to be on the side of truth, especially when conscience is at stake. I know your natural disposition in this regard. You would like to preserve truth entirely intact, if no one were hurt by it – which rarely or never happens. The position will be easier to defend if truth, however mild and peaceable in itself, earns some degree of ill will from certain people than if the truth, which means Christ, is deserted to please men. Suppose this path led to the extinction of truth on the ground that there are people who will find in it a pretext for subversion? Surely passions must give way on both sides, and we must fix our eyes on Christ, who is the just judge and will pass judgment on all things in truth and justice. I know you are marvellously skilled in this art, and our age has never seen anyone to match you, who know so well with what skill one must write on dangerous topics.

Fabri is acting vigorously against Luther,[4] but there are many grounds for suspecting that his unreasonable, or at least immoderate, savagery has been influenced by the benefices and gifts which he has received, though he is conciliatory enough in what he says and has all the fine words which we associate with Italians. In our day one must not attach too much importance to bishops and their tyranny, unless one is willing to contemplate the risk of bloodshed. This is a plague which spreads from the top downwards; and if some cure could be applied to the head, the body and limbs would easily be restored to health. Fabri preached for the second time in public in the absence of our own preacher Johann Wanner[5] (you expressed a wish to

*****

4 The vicar-general Johannes Fabri (Ep 1260 n22), recently back from Rome (Ep 1324 n14), where he had produced an *Opus adversus nova dogmata Lutheri* (M. Silber, August 1522)

5 Johann Wanner (d 1527) of Kaufbeuren studied theology at Basel and became preacher at the cathedral in Constance early in 1522. He associated with the humanist circle around Botzheim and Fabri and with the circle of reformers around Ambrosius Blarer (Ep 1341A n430). Wanner soon developed decidedly Protestant views, as a consequence of which he was dismissed from his preachership. But he soon secured permission to preach at St Stephen's church and remained a leader of the reformed party until his death. From 1525 he was paid by the city council.

know his name[6]). He urged the ordinary congregation and those who were
listening to him not to let themselves be carried away by new and outlandish   50
doctrines, but to cleave to the footsteps of the Fathers instead and follow
their opinions, which have been accepted from the time of the apostles until
now. He brought many persuasive arguments against Luther's teaching,
but did not mention him or anyone else by name. His charm and moderation
won over those who had been his opponents. Many of the arguments he put   55
forward could be refuted; but so conciliatory and persuasive a presentation
does have some effect on simple minds. I agree with Fabri at all points, with
one exception, his giving too much importance to tyrannical government in
the church. My own emotions are so constituted that they sometimes give
me more warmth and violence than I hoped or intended. I wish you would   60
write to him and speak well of me, on the basis that we are all three friends,
though he shows himself most friendly on the surface. I know he resents it if
anyone opposes his principles. Nobody shall say he was provoked by me
into subversion or given a reason for disturbing the peace. But I do wish the
two sides would listen to one another, for often a garden-boy can talk sound   65
sense.[7] Our preacher, Wanner, will either try to leave voluntarily – so they
tell me – or they will try to find some way to discharge him officially, so far as
I can make it out by guesswork.

If you did not let Hutten come and talk to you,[8] that disposes of the
suspicion that he is taking your advice, but only among those who know the   70
facts.

The rumour has been spreading openly of a great gathering in Basel of
men suspected of belonging to Luther's party, in order to draw up some sort
of plan.[9] Those monks who are your opponents deserve to be choked by
their own spite, now their designs against you come to nothing. Write as   75
you please without a second thought, for you can be sure that with me it will
be as secret as the grave; and you could do nothing to give me greater
pleasure. Farewell, my dear teacher, and mind you take care of your health.

From Constance, 7 January 1523

Your physician's name is Johann Menlishofer.[10]   80

* * * * *

6 Ep 1331:70–1 and n31 to that letter
7 *Adagia* I vi 1
8 Ep 1331:63
9 See Ep 1342:727–73, where Erasmus blames the rumour on his opponents.
Oecolampadius (Ep 1308 n7), Hartmuth von Cronberg (Ep 1331 n23), and
Hutten (Ep 1331 n24) had all recently arrived in Basel.
10 Cf Ep 1331:70–1. Johann Jakob Menlishofer (d 1548) of Überlingen became
town physician at Constance in 1516. Like Wanner (see n5 above), he belonged

1336 / To Francesco Chierigati   Basel, 8 January 1522/3

This letter first appeared in the *Opus epistolarum*. The contents of the letter require the interpretation of the year-date.

Francesco Chierigati of Vicenza (d 1539) was a papal diplomat who had become bishop of Teramo in 1522. He was now papal nuncio in Germany and had been in attendance at the Diet of Nürnberg since the end of September 1522.

ERASMUS OF ROTTERDAM TO FRANCESCO CHIERIGATI,
BISHOP OF TERAMO

Reverend Father. In the oration[1] which has reached us here in print, I recognized my dear Chierigati – for I still use the language of one old friend to another[2] – and rejoiced to find that the promotion you deserve has come   5
your way. I fancy it is the same see that Pius II conferred long ago on Giovanni Campano.[3] He himself sings the praises of the place in one of his letters;[4] it is called Interamna, I suppose, because the city intersects a river.[5] I am delighted too at your appointment to this mission, which is admirable and greatly to your credit. May you achieve your object, and having gone   10
out empty-handed may you return bearing your sheaves with you![6]

I would have written at greater length, but I was extremely busy[7] and was afraid that you might have left before this letter could reach you. I have not forgotten your affection for me, and wish I could make some return for all your kindness. There is a most admirable man where you are now, one   15

* * * * *

to both the humanist circle in Constance and to the circle of those who supported the Reformation.

1336
1 *Francisci Chaeregati electi Episcopi Aprunti, Principis Terami et Oratoris apostolici, Oratio habita Nurimbergae in senatu Principum Germaniae. xiii Cal. Decembris, m.d.xxii* (Nürnberg: F. Peyp). Addressed to King Louis of Hungary, the address appealed for the aid of Hungary against the Turks; see Pastor IX 128–9.
2 Erasmus and Chierigati may have met in Italy in 1506–9, or during Chierigati's nunciature in England in 1516 and 1517.
3 Giovanni Antonio Campano (1429–77), whose ready wit endeared him to Pope Pius II. Pius made him bishop of Teramo in 1463.
4 Ep 4 in Campano's *Opera* (Rome: E. Silber 1495; repr Farnborough, Hants 1969)
5 Teramo, in the Abruzzi, lies between the Tordino and Vezzola rivers at the point of their confluence.
6 Cf Ps 126 (Vulg 125):6.
7 Cf Ep 1337:10–11.

Willibald,[8] a member of the city council. You will rejoice to have made his acquaintance. Farewell.

Basel, 8 January 1522

1337 / To Willibald Pirckheimer   Basel, 8 January 1523

On Pirckheimer, see Ep 1259. This letter first appeared in the *Opus epistolarum.* Pirckheimer's reply is Ep 1344.

ERASMUS OF ROTTERDAM TO WILLIBALD, GREETING

I could have no misgivings about you, my dear Willibald, as a wise and prudent person, but some people wrote and suggested to me that I should make peace with you.[1] If only God would put into the minds of our princes some policy that might save the world! These commotions make me 5 ashamed. One might think that Phaethon had been put in charge of the chariot of the sun.[2] And all the time we consider ourselves Christians, and are concerned about Rhodes.[3] As for Zúñiga,[4] I have always despised him. But I could wish that certain of Luther's supporters showed more sense when treating of the gospel cause. I am in very great confusion just now,[5] 10 with the fair coming on;[6] once that is over I will write at greater length. Farewell for the moment. From Basel, 8 January 1522

Your sincere friend Erasmus

To the honourable Willibald Pirckheimer, senator[7] and counsellor to his Imperial Majesty. 15

* * * * *

8 Willibald Pirckheimer (Ep 1259), who formed a highly unfavourable opinion of Chierigati; Ep 1344:34–45

1337
1 Erasmus had shown publicly at the imperial court a private letter (not extant) from Pirckheimer and had been given to understand that Pirckheimer was offended; see Ep 1344:1–8.
2 Phaeton, son of Helios by Clymene, having received permission from his father to drive the chariot of the sun, lost control of the horses and nearly set the earth on fire.
3 Rhodes, invested by the Turks in June 1522, fell on 28 December. The news had not yet reached western Europe.
4 Ep 1260 n36
5 Cf Ep 1336:12.
6 Ie, the spring fair at Frankfurt; cf Ep 326A:16n.
7 Ie, town councilman in Nürnberg

1337A / To Silvester Prierias   Basel, [mid-January 1523?]

The only source for this letter is the *Opus epistolarum*, which gives a year-date
only, 1523 (line 72). Allen placed the letter at c January 1524 and published it as
Ep 1412. His case for this rests on 1/ the marked verbal resemblances (indicated
in his notes) to other letters written at about that time, 2/ the reference in lines
65–6 to dictation because of the effects of a recent attack of the stone (Christmas
1523; Allen Ep 1408:3n), and 3/ the fact that Erasmus dispatched a number of
other letters to Rome at that time. The problem with this is that the addressee,
Silvester Prierias (Ep 872:19n), had died at the beginning of 1523 as a result of
the plague that had raged at Rome in the period September–December 1522
and lingered into the first weeks of the new year; see J. Quétif and J. Echard,
Scriptores Ordinis Praedicatorum recensiti ... II (Paris 1721) 55a; cf Ep 1324 n12. It is
difficult to believe that Erasmus, with his excellent contacts in Rome, would
still have been ignorant of Prierias' death in January 1524. It is just as difficult to
believe that Erasmus would have replied to a letter that had to have been
written a year earlier without commenting on the delay. Indeed, the opening
lines of this letter were clearly written in response to a *recent* letter. The verbal
similarities between this letter and other letters of c January 1524 must
therefore be regarded as fortuitous. Allen's date is clearly untenable.

Unfortunately, it is easier to reject Allen's date than it is to find a new one.
The references in the letter are all so ambiguous that it could have been written
at almost any time during the period from early March 1522 until the time of
Prierias' death (or a few weeks thereafter). During those months, Zúñiga's
'raving,' Erasmus' frequent attacks of the stone, numerous invitations to
Rome, and anxiety about the attitude of the new pope, Adrian VI, were
recurring themes in Erasmus' correspondence; see especially Epp 1275, 1278,
1294, 1305, 1311, and 1330, all written in 1522. We know from Ep 1342:352–3
that before his visit to Constance in September 1522 Erasmus had received a
friendly letter from Prierias urging him to come to Rome. This letter could be a
response either to that letter or to a later one in which the invitation to Rome
was repeated. If the date 1523 is taken at face value – and it is by no means
certain that it should be – then the letter must have been written in the period
between Christmas 1522 and the receipt of the *Breve aureum* (Ep 1324), which
was delivered sometime between 8 and 28 January. After the receipt of that
letter, Erasmus would scarcely have expressed himself as cautiously on the
attitude of Adrian VI as he does in lines 68–9. Moreover, we can assume that
in January Erasmus was still ignorant of Prierias' death, and we know
that Zúñiga was on his mind at that time (Ep 1341A:868ff). There is no
independent documentation of an attack of the stone in the period from
Christmas 1522 to 28 January 1523. However, in view of the many documented

attacks throughout 1522 (Ep 1267 n5) and again in 1523 starting c February (Ep 1353:30–2), such an attack in January cannot be ruled out. We have therefore decided to place the letter conjecturally at 'mid-January 1523,' believing that it could not have been written any later than that but acknowledging that it might in fact have been written some weeks or even months earlier.

ERASMUS OF ROTTERDAM TO SILVESTER PRIERIAS,
GREETING

Your Reverence speaks of an unpleasant smell of smoke that hangs about my letter;[1] but what you mean I do not quite understand. To you at least I am grateful on many counts: because you tell me so openly and so kindly what it 5 was desirable I should know, and because you point out a way in which I can avoid the danger which you warn me of – I mean by explaining certain passages; and I should have owed you an even greater debt had you been so kind as to indicate which those places are. It would be nothing new, were some error to be found in my books, a thing that neither Jerome nor 10 Augustine was able to avoid, and especially when men's judgments differ so widely. But this at least has always been my intention, not knowingly to allow there to be anything in my books that could be at variance with orthodox doctrine. In Louvain I spent so many years, and no theologian either friend or enemy ever pointed out anything of the sort, though I often 15 asked them to tell me freely if there was any such thing. If Zúñiga[2] is openly raving like this in Rome, although I am not unaware who put him up to it, yet consider what a precedent he introduces. Suppose there are some indefensible things in my books; what precedent is there, may I ask, for issuing such insane pamphlets in order to mount an impudent and 20 scurrilous attack on a man who has at least never been condemned so far by any authority? In Louvain there is a Carmelite[3] who is plainly demented and insane and almost uneducated, and one Dominican[4] very like him. These are the only two who work against me and make me a Lutheran whether I will or no, though I was the first person ever to urge him not to act in hot 25 blood.[5]

What I say will sound somewhat arrogant, but it is true: had I been willing to write even one short letter professing some moderate support for

* * * * *

1337A
1 Perhaps *De esu carnium* (Ep 1274 n7), one of the works most hated by Erasmus' conservative critics
2 Ep 1260 n36
3 Baechem (Ep 1254 n6)
4 Vincentius Theoderici (Ep 1196)
5 See Ep 980:45–58.

Luther, you would have seen the whole of Germany in a state of exaltation – and that is at least a pretty wide area. Nor would the support of princes have been wanting. Assailed as I have been from so many quarters which I could name and wooed with honeyed words from many others, it has never been possible to detach me from my veneration for the church of Rome. Aleandro[6] does everything possible against Luther; but if you really knew the facts, I Erasmus by myself have done more to break the power and the spirit of that faction than all Aleandro's exertions. I have written so many letters both public and private which have discouraged Luther's supporters[7] –though Luther himself has taught us many lessons which were badly needed – but discord I simply cannot stand. Whether you and other people in your part of the world are convinced of this, I do not know; at any rate Luther's party here are fully aware of it, for they think their lack of success is due solely to me and are now in full cry against me in barbed pamphlets as an enemy to the cause. And such I really am; though I would rather see evil separated from good than good and evil alike consigned to perdition.

And now see the gratitude I get from those who attack me with such outrageous falsehoods, or rather, see how unwisely they conduct their own affairs. Luther's faction is not yet so near extinction as you people think, and I only wish it were, for it spells the death of all my literary work. There are countless thousands of men who give Luther a great measure of support because they hate the see of Rome, and they seek nothing but someone to lead them. As for me, neither angels nor men will make me a revolutionary, and yet these people try all they can to do so. I have the emperor's good will, and enjoy a salary from him as one of his councillors;[8] on him I can count. Here too I have several princes and kings who are my keen supporters, and several cardinals and bishops also. I wish the Zúñigas of this world and people like him with a zest for calumny would leave me to be orthodox in peace. You yourself have never caused me misgivings. Maybe in a letter to Hoogstraten I observed that in books written by you and Cardinal Cajetan there were some things which the Paris theologians disapproved of.[9] At that date he had written nothing except an attack on the Council of Pisa[10] –no more had you, except a little in opposition to Luther's first conclusions.[11] On

* * * * *

6 Ep 1256 n11
7 See Ep 1352:72–8.
8 See Ep 370:18n.
9 Ep 1006:153–6
10 See Ep 256:49n.
11 This is not true. Long before writing *In presumptuosas Martini Lutheri conclusiones de potestate papae dialogus* (June 1518) in response to Luther's Ninety-five Theses,

the writings of men like you two it is not for me to pass judgment; but the opinions of the learned are more accessible here than in your part of the world.

I have dictated this with difficulty to my secretary, in such a state with   65
calculus and digestive troubles that I was even tired of life. I should like to be in Rome even if it cost half my worldly goods, and I shall come if my health can stand it. The pope's attitude to me gives me no anxiety. He is not the man to listen habitually to such calumnies. I shall make sure that he has no fault to find with me as a man of good will. My best wishes to your   70
Reverence, to whom I profess myself entirely devoted.

Basel, 1523

1338 / From Adrian VI   Rome, 23 January 1523

First published in the *Exomologesis* (Basel: Froben 1524), this is Pope Adrian's reply to Ep 1329. It was delivered to Erasmus in Basel (c 11 March), after his return from a brief visit to Freiburg; see Ep 1353:249–50. Erasmus' reply is Ep 1352. On Pope Adrian himself, see Ep 1304.

FROM POPE ADRIAN VI

Beloved son, greeting and apostolic benediction. We received a few days ago the letter you wrote to us from Basel on 22 December together with a second copy, in an elegant and costly binding, of the text of Arnobius which you have revised and published with a dedication to ourselves, since you   5
had not yet ascertained whether the copy you sent at first had reached us safely. These two things filled us with heartfelt joy in the Lord almost passing belief. For your gift in itself, as we can well believe from the long letter which you have prefixed to your work,[1] and can detect from the little that our various occupations have hitherto left us time to read, is of a kind   10
that should give great satisfaction to all scholars on its own merits, apart from the fact that it has been put to the proof and published by you; and your letter[2] on the face of it gives such evidence of your sincerity, your piety, your zeal in God's service, your religious feeling, and your devoted obedience to us and to the see of St Peter which we hold that, had unfriendly report of   15
you, from which outstanding men are never free, caused any adverse

* * * * *

Prierias had published a number of works, beginning with a *Compendium dialectice* in 1496.

1338
1 Ep 1304
2 Ie, Ep 1329

suspicion of your integrity to enter our mind, it would have been removed entirely by this letter. We would therefore have you entirely believe that it has added very great weight to the good will with which we have always followed your progress, for the sake of our common country and of the studies and way of life which we both share,[3] and no less for the many and various gifts of mind and character which the giver of all good things has lodged within you.

But the most truly welcome thing in it was your promise of a policy by which the disorder and confusion of the times we live in might, as you say, be extinguished in such a way that it may never sprout again with any ease;[4] and we urge you in the Lord and require of you with all the weight at our command and in abundance of charity that you take steps to explain to us, so far as the Lord has so enabled you, the means and methods by which this terrible plague may be removed from the heart of our country while it can still be remedied, a thing which we should desire more ardently than anything else under the sun. The reason for this is not the threat which this fierce tempest seems to aim at our authority and power so far as we are particularly concerned, for neither of these did we ever desire and did indeed very greatly fear them both when they were offered to us not of our own seeking and would certainly (God is our witness) have refused them, had we not feared thereby to offend God and lay a weight upon our conscience. It is rather that we see so many thousands of souls, redeemed by the blood of Christ and entrusted to our pastoral care, who are moreover of our own native country in the flesh, being dragged straight to perdition in hope of the liberty of the gospel, but really it will be the tyranny of the evil one.

The greater the speed and secrecy with which you can expound to us your policy in this regard, the greater the service you will render to God and the more we shall be pleased. Speed is required by the common danger, secrecy by the danger to yourself, whose safety we value as we would our own. And although we believe that you must long ago have received a letter[5] from us in answer to your earlier letter with which you had sent the other copy of Arnobius, at the end of which letter we invited you to come to us once the winter is over and the air of Rome purged again of the present infection of the plague,[6] and this last letter of yours has given us great confidence that you will comply with our desire, yet we were unwilling to

* * * * *

3 Cf Ep 1304 n2.
4 Ep 1329:13–16
5 Ep 1324, in response to Ep 1310; see Ep 1324 introduction.
6 See Ep 1324 n12.

lose the opportunity of making the same request of you in this letter also
even more urgently, unless perchance you should be most clearly convinced
that if you stay where you are you are able to serve God and assist his church   55
more than by joining us. For in that case it would be contrary to our
principles and policy, by which we seek nothing but the honour of God and
his church in preference to our private feelings, if we were to recall you from
a more abundant harvest. Otherwise you should know for a truth that you
could do nothing more pleasing to us (so far as it can be done without   60
inconvenience to yourself) than to come to us and to come quickly, and that
we will take all possible steps to see that you have no reason to repent of
your journey and your toil, as we promised in our last letter; and we now
repeat the promise. Nor is there any reason why you should postpone your
coming for either of the two causes mentioned, for the winter has already   65
started to recede and the danger of infection from the plague has become so
slight that in so great a city it might seem almost non-existent.

The business[7] of your city is very near our hearts, both for its own
distinction and devotion to the Holy See and because you intercede for it;
and it will shortly be completed and returned direct to the city by the hand of   70
its own envoy. Given at Rome at St Peter's under the ring of the Fisherman
this twenty-third day of January 1523, being the first year of our pontificate.[8]

T. Hezius[9]

1339 / From Theodoricus Hezius   Rome, 25 January 1522/3

The manuscript of this letter (=Ep 11 in Enthoven), which is evidently
contemporary with Ep 1338, is in the Rehdiger Collection of the University
Library at Wrocław (MS Rehd 254.91). Erasmus apparently replied (Ep
1353:268), but the letter does not survive.

Dirk Adriaans (d 1555), who took the name Hezius from his birthplace,
Heeze, near Eindhoven in North Brabant, studied arts and theology at
Louvain. There he attracted the attention of Adrian of Utrecht, whom he
accompanied to Spain in 1515 as secretary. Hezius remained Adrian's
secretary after the latter's election to the papacy in 1522. But for Adrian's
unexpected death in 1523, Hezius would doubtless have been made a cardinal.
In 1525 he returned to the Netherlands and settled in Liège, where he was a
canon of St Lambert's. When he wrote this letter, Hezius was still an ardent

* * * * *

7 See Ep 1329:36–40.
8 Adrian evidently reckoned his pontificate not from his election on 9 January
  but from his coronation on 31 August 1522.
9 See Ep 1339.

admirer of Erasmus, who, in turn, was grateful for Hezius' support (Epp
1331:45, 1353:251–2). After his return to the north in 1525, however, Hezius'
admiration for Erasmus quickly cooled. He soon took sides with the Louvain
theologians against Erasmus and remained an anti-Erasmian for the rest of his
life.

Respectful greetings, reverend sir, my dear Erasmus. For many years now I
have regarded you with admiration and the deepest respect for the same
reasons, naturally, that have won you universal acclaim; and in these words
let there be no suspicion of flattery (which I particularly detest), for all your
talent you have derived, or rather you have received as a gift, from the Lord   5
who is the source of all good things. Added to which, the fact that we are
fellow-countrymen has somehow made me feel I have a share in your
esteemed endowments of intellect and personality, and the distinguished
reputation enjoyed by you and your works, and I feel I have a kind of right to
rejoice in them as though they were my own. Up till now, however,   10
embarrassment and the awareness of my lack of eloquence held me back, so
that I have never revealed these feelings and this bond of affection to you.[1]
But since reading those letters that you wrote to my sacred master after his
arrival in Rome,[2] and especially that of 22 December from Basel, with all
their deep religious feeling and unaffected piety, I was seized with such   15
enthusiasm, such heartfelt affection towards my Erasmus, that I have been
forced to make my passion known to you, however halting my language and
though it can be only in few words. And this I deeply regret; for I would
gladly do it at greater length.

But so many and so great are my duties in the papal service and in   20
public affairs that, even were they halved, they would be enough to claim
the whole of what brains I have. And so you must consider this a mere note,
written with the object of convincing you that Theodoricus Hezius,
secretary for what he is worth of our most Holy Father Adrian, has the
greatest respect, affection, veneration, admiration, and longing for you and   25
your virtues and your learning, and of persuading you to include him in the
list of those who are most devoted to you and always will be. If I am thought
worthy of that privilege, I shall think I have secured something greater than
if the Holy Father had actually given me a bishopric; and my conscience tells
me that I speak the truth.   30

* * * * *

1339
1 Cf Ep 1331:45.
2 Epp 1310, 1329. Adrian entered Rome on 29 August 1522; see Ep 1294
  introduction.

And since it is difficult, not to say impossible, to bend one's mind to embrace the unknown, if you wish to know who I am, Johannes Fabri, the vicar-general of Constance, who ought by now to have reached your part of the world long ago, will be able to inform you;[3] I lived with him here in close intimacy for some months, and often spoke with him very readily of the 35 Erasmus who is so dear to us both. I am greatly devoted to Fabri for his open and unselfish character and his varied learning and (a thing I value more than either) his zeal for the true faith and detestation of Luther's treachery – or should I say Luther's madness, perhaps the most ill-starred, most monstrous, most disastrous thing these many centuries have produced. For 40 this I can think of no other reason except that the God of justice allows this universal chaos because of the serious offences of men, and churchmen not less than the laity,[4] that from distress if nothing else they may learn their lesson and return to the Lord their God, all of them realizing what a bitter thing it is that they should have deserted that same Lord who is their God. 45 This is what I have always promised myself will happen in the end, as a result of this universal confusion in which everything, so to speak, is topsy-turvy, relying on God's infinite goodness and on numerous precedents in times gone by. Nor have I any doubt whatever that Martin Luther, who is now almost worshipped like a god and exalted above the cedars of 50 Lebanon,[5] and who seems to have drawn almost all things unto himself,[6] rejoicing in the perdition of so many souls, will soon,[7] he and all his flock of followers, be scattered abroad, unless he repents, like dust before the face of the wind,[8] and will be cast down into the depths of hell; for that is what we read has always happened to those (and there were many, as you know) 55 who have tried to assert and maintain these same doctrines or others like them, adapted to tickle the ears of the common herd. Can it be that light will not vanquish and overcome darkness, and truth falsehood, and wisdom wicked folly? Though in the mean while all those who can produce any remedy for this cancer that spreads so widely must do everything they can to 60 counter to the utmost of their power this most destructive and fell disease, which is no longer on its way to us but penetrates the inmost vitals of our nation. And you know well enough, if you are willing not to conceal the truth through modesty, what place you hold among such people and what armament you possess for fighting Christ's battles; and so I doubt not that 65

* * * * *

3 See Ep 1324 n14.
4 Cf Epp 1324:77–8 and 1344 n10.
5 Cf Ep 1324:87–9.
6 Cf John 12:32.
7 Cf Ep 1324:90.
8 Ps 35 (Vulg 34):5

you are already preparing some great, exceptional, effective stroke, which these longing eyes of mine will see, I hope, before many months are out.

But see how far my zeal has carried me away, when at the outset I had determined to write only a very short letter. Not but what this is nothing compared to what I should wish to say to my Erasmus face to face; and if, as I hope, I am fortunate enough to do so, I shall count it not the least among my blessings. But why do I speak of myself, when the Holy Father and all good men and good scholars here would say the same? However it may turn out, my beloved Erasmus can always count on me as entirely his, whether for friendship or service or the advancement of his fortunes. Long may he live, I pray, in health and wealth, to be a blessing to the human race.

Rome, 25 January 1522

Yours, for what little he is worth or ever will be, T. Hezius, secretary to our lord the pope

1340 / From Duke George of Saxony Dresden, 25 January 1523

This letter, Duke George's reply to Epp 1313 and 1325, was first published by J.K. Seidemann in *Die Reformation in Sachsen von 1517 bis 1539* II (Dresden 1847), using MS Loc 10300 in the Staatsarchiv Dresden (see Ep 1283 introduction). Like Ep 1313, this letter was intercepted, and Erasmus did not see it until more than a year later, when the duke enclosed a copy of it with Ep 1448. For details, see Ep 1313 introduction. Erasmus responded with Epp 1499 and 1526.

GEORGE, BY THE GRACE OF GOD DUKE OF SAXONY,
LANDGRAVE OF THURINGIA, AND MARGRAVE OF MEISSEN,
TO ERASMUS OF ROTTERDAM, THEOLOGIAN, GRACE AND FAVOUR
Your suspicion, most learned Erasmus, that the letter[1] of which you have sent a fresh copy[2] was intercepted, is correct. Previously it was not delivered; but what the reason was is not clear to us. As it is, that you should be so anxious to evade the task of writing against Luther and should decline to do so does not at all surprise us, now we have learned that you find so many good things in what he writes, for which you are anxious, and the main part of it moreover truly Christian, and that you think that to bring peace in this sad business there is no better way than silence. In consequence, and more especially since we too in particular have been

* * * * *

1340
1 Ep 1313
2 With Ep 1325

grossly insulted by him,[3] we shall cease in future to urge you to undertake
what you have so many reasons for declining; for we would not be thought
to be eager for revenge of some sort or to roll a stone against the torrent. We   15
should not have supposed, had we not been informed by yourself, that you,
who now reside, as you often have before, in Upper Germany, are ignorant
of the language,[4] and that therefore it served no purpose to send you the
pamphlets. We suspect however that you received them in the spirit in
which they were sent you.   20

Farewell. From our castle in Dresden, 25 January in the year of our
Lord 1523

To our trusty and well-beloved Erasmus of Rotterdam, the most
learned theologian

1341 / To Willibald Pirckheimer   Basel, 28 January 1522/3

On Pirckheimer, see Ep 1259. Like Ep 1259, this letter was first published in the
Pirckheimeri Opera. The year-date is indicated by the reference to the paraphrase on John. Pirckheimer's reply is Ep 1344.

Nothing could have given me more pleasure than your letter,[1] dear Willibald
my honourable friend. Just at this moment, being extremely busy,[2] I will tell
you briefly what I want. Everyone knows what a debt liberal studies owe to
Froben, the only man who is devoted to our interests at his own expense;
but, potters being what they are,[3] he has many hidden enemies, who   5

* * * * *

3 In his *Missive an Hartmut von Cronberg*, March 1522 (WA x-2 55), Luther called
   Duke George a *Wasserblase* (literally, 'water bubble'). This was a derogatory
   German rendering of the Latin *bulla*, which in established usage meant both
   'bubble' and '(papal) bull,' a double entendre which Luther delighted to exploit
   in his anti-papal polemics (as in the *Bulla Coena Domini* of 1522, WA VIII 712–13).
   In the case of Duke George and others, Luther used both *bulla* and *Wasserblase*
   in a derived sense for 'blusterers' or 'windbags' who supported the pope and
   his bulls. When the duke complained to Luther about his abusive language
   (WA-Br II 642), Luther answered defiantly, refusing to apologize and repeating
   the offensive epithet (ibidem III 4–5). Duke George's subsequent complaints to
   Luther's prince were in vain (ibidem 5–7).
4 See Ep 1313 n16.

1341
1 Not extant
2 Cf Epp 1336:12, 1337:10–11.
3 Ie, envious of one another and competitive; see *Adagia* I ii 25, and also Allen Ep
   1437:64–5, 222–3.

conspire almost on oath to ruin him. When anything in the way of a new work comes out which they think will be saleable, two or three of them soon purloin a copy from his printing-house, print it, and sell it cheap. All the time Froben is spending large sums on proofreaders and often too on buying copy from the author. This injustice can easily be remedied if there could be   10
an imperial prohibition on the printing of any book of which Froben has produced the first edition or one with some additions by the author within the space of two years.[4] It is not a long time; and the house of Froben deserves support for this reason if no other that nothing ever appears from it that is either worthless or subversive.   15

There is now at press a paraphrase on the Gospel of John dedicated to Ferdinand,[5] of which I send you part so that you can show it around if you think that a good plan. I do not doubt that the thing can easily be obtained; but it will make a difference if this could be done as soon as possible. If it is not convenient for this to be arranged through you, you will be able to   20
entrust it to someone else. There is with you at the moment, they tell me, one Jakob Spiegel,[6] a special friend of mine and a warmhearted person; or there is the prince-bishop of Teramo, the nuncio apostolic,[7] who with his habitual kindness has always supported me particularly. In this business, my dear Willibald, I have no axe to grind myself; and yet for the sake of   25
Froben and the humanities I shall cheerfully owe you a debt on this fresh head, though deeply indebted to you on many other grounds already. If an imperial privilege cannot be put through immediately, let me know at least that it has been granted, so that Froben can use the heading at the next fair.

The supreme pontiff has sent me an official letter[8] full of compliments   30

* * * * *

4 Froben had received privileges for five years from both Leo x and Maximilian I (Ep 802:11n) for the 1516 edition of Jerome (Ep 396). Maximilian had also granted a four-year privilege for the first edition of the New Testament (1516), where it was mentioned on the title-page but not printed. The pope granted a privilege for the editions of 1519 and 1522 (see the *Apologia contra Petrum Sutorem* LB IX 751E). The present request, which Erasmus had already attempted to present through Jakob Spiegel (Ep 1323 introduction), was quickly granted (Epp 1344:123–58, 1353:253–4). The privilege, drawn up in Emperor Charles' name, bore the date 14 February 1523, and granted Froben protection for all his books for two years from the date of publication. The privilege was printed at the beginning of Beatus Rhenanus' *Autores historiae ecclesiasticae* (August 1523). There may also have been an application for a papal privilege; see Allen Ep 1392:14–15.
5 Ep 1333
6 Spiegel was, in fact, not in Nürnberg; see Ep 1344:132–3.
7 Chierigati (Ep 1336)
8 Ep 1324

and good will. His secretary[9] swears that it is not common form, but that all of it was truly composed by the pope himself. Farewell, O credit to our generation.

Basel, 28 January 1522

To the honourable Willibald Pirckheimer, counsellor to his Imperial 35 Majesty.

1341A / To Johann von Botzheim   Basel, 30 January 1523

This very long letter is a document of capital importance for the study of Erasmus' life and works and of the controversies that they aroused. Written in response to the request of Johann von Botzheim (Ep 1285) for a catalogue of Erasmus' works, the letter is an expansion of the *Lucubrationum Erasmi Roterodami index* printed by Dirk Martens at Louvain in January 1519 and reprinted, with additions, by Froben at Basel in March of the same year. The letter, many times the length of the slender *Index*, was published by Froben in April 1523 under the title *Catalogus omnium Erasmi Roterodami lucubrationum*. A second, much expanded edition appeared from the same press in September 1524 under the title *Catalogus novus omnium lucubrationum Erasmi Roterodami*. The date of the letter (line 1844) was left unchanged despite the insertion into the text of dates which contradicted it. Many of the most important and lengthy of the apologetic passages appeared first in the edition of 1524, as did the scheme for the publication of Erasmus' works in ten volumes (lines 1500–1832). Following Erasmus' death, Froben issued a third, corrected edition (c February 1537). Finally, the *Catalogus*, again revised, was included among the introductory material in the first volume of the Basel *Opera omnia* (1540), an arrangement later duplicated in LB. Allen printed his edition of the text, with scant annotation, at the beginning of his first volume (pages 1–46), as a preface to the letters. Here, for the first time ever, the *Catalogus* is published and annotated as an integral part of the correspondence.

In our text, superscript letters 'a' through 'o' are used to mark the beginning and the end of the most important passsages inserted in 1524. Thus, for example: 'ᵃSo, for the benefit [line 297] ... [line 421] September 1524.ᵃ' The line numbers of the other insertions are as follows: b (434–40), c (493–5), d (499–568), e (633–49), f (747–9), g (760–73), h (776–87), i (789), j (890–9), k (912–27), l (955–1009), m (1019–1306), n (1394–1416), o (1500–1832). Small, insignificant changes in wording have not been noted.

* * * * *

9 This title should mean Hezius (Ep 1339), but in Ep 1345:15–17 Erasmus attributes the information to the papal chaplain, Pierre Barbier (Ep 1294), and Ep 1342:699–706 confirms the attribution.

Erasmus *Catologus lucubrationum* title-page
Basel: Froben 1523
Centre for Reformation and Renaissance Studies,
Victoria University, University of Toronto

ERASMUS OF ROTTERDAM TO THE LEARNED AND
REVEREND JOHANN VON BOTZHEIM, OTHERWISE ABSTEMIUS,[1]
DOCTOR OF CIVIL AND CANON LAW, AND CANON OF CONSTANCE

Unwilling as you are, dear Abstemius my most learned friend, to think that
any of my writings should be absent from your library, you complain that   5
from time to time you have to buy the same book twice, when it has been
either refurbished or enlarged or revised. You ask me therefore to make a list
for you of all the trifles I have published (for that is a truer word for them
than books) and to indicate which of them have received my final version, so
that nothing may escape you which you do not possess, and at the same   10
time you may buy nothing which you will soon be obliged to acquire in a
new form. I will do as you wish, and render a service at the same time by
your means, if I mistake not, to very many others. You love to add lustre to
your library, you say, with Erasmus' works. For my part, I think your library
adds lustre to my books, for it is one of the most illustrious I ever saw; one   15
might call it a veritable home of the Muses. And so I pride myself more on
your thinking my works good enough for a lodging in your library than I
should if they were laid up in caskets of cedar-wood in the temple of Apollo.
I do not suppose they will live; still less dare I hope they may be immortal;
but if they have the good fortune to survive their creator by some few years,   20
they will surely owe this to your library. Men will think there must be
something in books which that sober judge Abstemius thought good
enough for his shrine of the Muses. But in the mean time my own feelings
towards the progeny of my nightly toils are much like those of parents
towards their children when they have been unhappy in their offspring   25
because they are either misshapen and sickly or likely in other ways to bring
disgrace and disaster on their forebears. And in this regard I am the more
dissatisfied with my performance; for children's failings cannot always be
blamed upon their parents, but no one can answer for the faults of books
except their authors – unless perhaps I choose to say in my defence that time   30
and place have been unpropitious. When I was a boy, the humanities had
begun to put forth fresh shoots among the Italians; but because the printer's
art was either not yet invented or known to very few, nothing in the way of
books came through to us, and unbroken slumber graced the universal reign

* * * * *

1341A
1 From at least as early as 1507 Botzheim employed the byname Abstemius. This
   has been attributed to his admiration for the Italian humanist Lorenzo
   Astemio, but it is far more likely that he had acquired the name because of his
   noticeably temperate habits. As a student in Bologna he was described as
   'abstemius toto tempore vitae suae' (*Acta nationis Germanicae universitatis
   Bononiensis* ... ed E. Friedlander and C. Malagola [Berlin 1887] 257).

of those who taught ignorance in place of knowledge. Rodolfus Agricola   35
was the first to bring us a breath of more humane learning out of Italy;[2] in
Deventer, as a boy of twelve or so,[3] I was blessed with a sight of him, and
that was all. Then again, the generation and the country in which you write
make a great difference, the critical standards of your audience, and whom
you compete with: even an opponent of some distinction puts an edge on   40
your natural powers, and, as we all know, honour is the nursing mother of
the arts. None of all this was vouchsafed me, and yet a kind of secret natural
force swept me into liberal studies. My teachers might forbid it; even so, I
furtively drank in what I could from such books as I had managed to acquire;
I practised my pen, I used to challenge my companions to compete with me,   45
with nothing further from my thoughts than the publication of trifles of this
kind in print. These facts could not do away my responsibility, but they
might well make it less heavy. There are however some points on which I am
neither able nor desirous to defend myself. The chief thing is, that the man
who hopes to win a reputation by what he writes should choose a subject to   50
which he is by nature suited, and in which his powers chiefly lie; all themes
do not suit everyone. This I have never done; I have either stumbled on a
subject unadvisedly or chosen one to comply with my friends' feelings
rather than my own judgment. Next comes the importance, whatever you
have chosen, of taking pains in the treatment of it, of keeping it by you for   55
some time and often giving it further polish before it sees the light of day.
But for my part, once I have embarked on a subject I generally run through to
the finish without a break, and I have never been able to stomach the tedium
of revision. So my experience has usually been, as Plato puts it, that I go too
fast at the beginning, and am late in arriving at my goal.[4] I publish in a hurry,   60
and in the nature of things am sometimes obliged to refurbish the whole
thing from top to toe. It surprises me therefore to find people, especially in
so scholarly an age as ours, who read what I write. But they exist; if nothing
else, the way the printers reproduce my works so often proves it.
    But all this time you are waiting for a catalogue, not an apologia. So be   65
it! And first I will recount what I have written in verse, for in boyhood my
predilection for verse was such that it was with reluctance I turned to prose

* * * * *

2 The celebrated Frisian humanist (1444–85) and pioneer of the 'new learning' in
  the North (Ep 23:58n)
3 The probable date of Agricola's visit to the school at Deventer is April 1484
  (Allen I 581), in which case Erasmus would have been in his fifteenth or his
  eighteenth year, depending on whether one accepts 1469 or 1466 as the year of
  his birth.
4 This is apparently a negative form of the Platonic proverb 'The beginning is the
  most important part of every task'; see *Republic* 377A and *Laws* 753E.

composition. And in that field I strove for some time before succeeding, if one may use the word success. Nor is there any form of poetry which I did not attempt. The things that have fortunately perished or are unknown I   70 shall leave in obscurity and, as the Greek proverb has it, not rouse the ill that's safely hid.[5] It was in Paris that my indiscretions first began to be made known to the public,[6] for it was there that my friends published a heroic poem, with an admixture of tetrameters in the same style, addressed to Fausto Andrelini,[7] with whom I had lately made great friends. Then there   75 was another in hendecasyllables to Robert Gaguin,[8] whose opinion in Paris then carried no little weight. Then another, also addressed to him,[9] in a mixture of glyconics and asclepiads alternately. Besides these there was a poem on the hovel in which the child Jesus was born;[10] nor do I clearly recall if there was anything else. Again, on another occasion, I published Jesus'   80 appeal to a man who perishes by his own fault.[11] And many years before I had written a poem in sapphics on the archangel Michael,[12] not of my own choice, but driven to it by the appeals of a certain great man who presided over a church dedicated to St Michael.[13] I pitched this in such a low key that it

* * * * *

5 *Adagia* 1 i 62
6 Erasmus' first collection of verse was published in Paris by Ant. Denidel c January 1496. The volume took its title from the poem alluded to in line 79: *Carmen de casa natalitia Iesu*. Text and commentary in Reedijk 224–43.
7 *In Annales Gaguini et Eglogas Faustinas carmen ruri scriptum et autumno* (autumn 1495); Reedijk 240–43 (no 39). On Andrelini, see Ep 84.
8 *Ad Gaguinum nondum visum carmen hendecasyllabum alloquitur musas suas* (c September 1495); Reedijk 239–40 (no 38). On Gaguin, see Ep 43.
9 *Ad Robertum Gaguinum carmen de suis fatis* (spring? 1496); Reedijk 243–5 (no 40). Erasmus errs in placing this poem in the *Casa natalitia Iesu* collection along with the other poem addressed to Gaguin. It was first published in Willem Hermans' *Sylva odarum* (Paris: G. Marchand 20 January 1497).
10 *Carmen de casa natalitia Iesu ac paupere puerperio dive virginis Mariae lyricum, altero versu hexametro, altero iambico dimetro feliciter incipit* (autumn 1495); Reedijk 225–7 (no 33).
11 *Expostulatio Iesu cum homine suapte culpa pereunte* (1510?); Reedijk 294–6 (no 85). First published in the first edition of *De puero Iesu*, a rare quarto volume probably printed in Paris in September 1511 by Robert de Keyzere; Reedijk 291–2.
12 In fact, Erasmus had written, probably in the autumn of 1495 (Reedijk 227–8), not just one poem on the archangel Michael, but a series of four odes on Michael, Gabriel, Raphael, and all angels; Reedijk 229–36 (nos 34–7). Strangely, Erasmus had by 1523 forgotten that these poems had occupied a place of honour in the *Casa natalitia* collection.
13 Allen states that this was probably the priory church of St Michael's at Hem, near Schoonoven, with which the priory at Steyn had a close connection. But this is based on the questionable assumption that the odes were written in

might have been taken for prose; but he did not dare post it up, on the   85
ground that it was so poetical that, as he said himself, it might be thought
written in Greek. Such were the standards of those unhappy days! And
though I had spent so much labour on it, when I delivered my poem, my
generous patron gave me money to buy a pint of wine – which was about
what the poem was worth. I thanked him for his generosity, and refused the   90
gift on that ground, saying it was too much for a humble person like myself.
In no kind of verse have I had less practice than in epigrams; yet sometimes
while out walking, or even over the wine, I have at different times thrown
off a certain number, some of which have been put together by friends
over-zealous for my reputation, and published in Basel; and to make them   95
even more ridiculous, they appended them to the epigrams of Thomas
More, who is a master of the art.[14] A poem addressed to Guillaume Cop on
old age[15] I wrote in the Alps, when I first visited Italy. A bitter dispute had
arisen between a herald of the English king, who accompanied us as far as
Bologna to give us more safety on the journey, and the tutor of the young   100
men[16] whom I was then taking to Italy under the terms of an agreement in
which I was caught like a rat in a trap, not as their governor (for I had ruled
out any responsibility for their behaviour) nor to give them lessons, but to
keep an eye on them and steer them on a suitable course of study – my
destiny must needs be replete with every form of disaster, for it was the most   105
unpleasant year I ever spent. These two it was, then, between whom a
quarrel had broken out, so fierce that after violent insults swords were
drawn. At that stage I was angry with one of the two only; but when, after
such a tempest, I saw them reconciled of their own accord after downing a

* * * * *

1489, before Erasmus' departure for Paris. Reedijk, who places the composition of the poems in the autumn of 1495 (see n12), believes that the incident
took place at some church dedicated to St Michael in or near Paris (228).

14 The *Epigrammata* of Erasmus and More were published, together with More's
Utopia, by Froben in March 1518. As Reedijk points out (72, 91), Erasmus
certainly knew of Froben's plans and played a more active role in the
publication of the *Epigrammata* than he here admits. Most of the seventy-two
epigrams had already been published with earlier works (eg, the earliest
editions of the *Adagia*). See Reedijk 367 (no 164) for a guide to the location of
these poems in his edition.

15 *Ad Gulielmum Copum medicorum eruditissimum de senectute carmen* (the *Carmen
alpestre*), August 1506; Reedijk 283–90 (no 83). First published with the
Adagiorum collectanea (Paris: J. Petit and J. Bade 24 December 1506–8 January
1507). On Cop, see Ep 124:18n.

16 The young men were Giovanni and Bernardo Boerio, sons of Giovanni Battista
Boerio, physician to Henry vii; Epp 194:33n, and 267 introduction. Their tutor
was a man named Clyfton (or Clifton); Ep 194:36n.

stoup of wine, I was disgusted equally with both. Not only do I think men   110
must be mad to get so angry unless they have suffered some serious injury;
even more do I regard as quite untrustworthy those who make it up so
suddenly after being at each other's throats. And so, to relieve the tedium
while riding, I avoided any conversation with the two parties and finished
this poem, scribbling it down from time to time on a piece of paper on my   115
saddle-bow, so that I might not forget part of it while pursuing the rest;
when we reached an inn, I copied out from my notes what had come into
existence. Such is my equestrian, my nag-born and crag-born poem; and
yet, born as it was, good judges do not find it altogether a failure.

I have written at various times a number of epitaphs at the request of   120
friends, which it is needless to recount.[17] But some years before my visit to
Italy, in order to practise my Greek (for teachers were not to be had), I had
made a version of the *Hecuba* of Euripides; at the time,[18] I was living in
Louvain. This rash attempt was provoked by Francesco Filelfo,[19] who
translated the first scene of the play in a funeral oration,[20] without (as I then   125
thought) much success. After that, with encouragement from my then host,
Jean Desmarez,[21] public orator of the university and a very severe judge of
such things, I continued as I had begun. Then, when letters and promises
from my friends of the proverbial mountains of gold had persuaded me to
return to England,[22] I added a preface[23] and a poem in iambics,[24] very much   130
on the spur of the moment, to fill a chance space in my paper, and on the
advice of learned friends, and particularly of William Grocyn,[25] who was at
that time the most distinguished of the many scholars in England, I offered
the book with a dedication to William, archbishop of Canterbury,[26] primate
of all England and chancellor of the realm, which means the supreme judge.   135
This was then the happy opening of my acquaintance with him. Having
greeted me briefly before dinner (for I am a man of few words, and do not
push myself forward), he spoke with me again after dinner at no great
length, being himself a man of most congenial manners, and sent me away

* * * * *

17 Reedijk nos 12–13, 29–32, 41–2, 62–6, 73, 99, 104, 106–7
18 1503 and 1504
19 Ep 23:77n
20 The oration, delivered on 25 December 1461, includes a metrical translation of
    the speech of the spectre of Polydorus. For further details, see ASD I-1 196 n3.
21 Ep 180
22 Autumn 1505 to August 1506
23 Ep 188, 24 January 1506
24 January 1506; Reedijk 278 (no 80)
25 Ep 119:26n
26 Warham (Ep 188)

with a handsome present, which passed, as the custom is with him, in   140
private between the two of us, so as to spare the recipient any embarrassment or jealousy. This happened at Lambeth; and while we were returning
thence by boat, as the custom is there, Grocyn asked me as we sailed along
how big a present he had given me. I named a very large sum, by way of a
joke. He laughed, and I asked him why: Did he not think the archbishop was   145
the sort of man who would be ready to give so much? Was he too poor to
bear the expense of such generosity? Did my work not deserve some very
handsome present? At length I confessed the amount of the gift; and when I
asked him jokingly why he had given me so little, he replied under pressure
that it was nothing to do with any of my reasons; but the suspicion had told   150
against me that I might perhaps have dedicated the same work elsewhere to
someone else. This took me aback; and when I asked him what on earth
could have put that idea into his head, he laughed (and a mirthless laugh it
was) and said 'It is the sort of thing you people do,' suggesting that men like
myself make a habit of it. This barbed shaft remained fixed in my mind,   155
which was not used to such two-edged remarks. So as soon as I reached
Paris, intending to go on from there to Italy, I gave the book to Bade to be
printed,[27] adding the *Iphigeneia in Aulis*, which I had translated more fully
and freely while I was in England; and though I had offered the archbishop
only one play, I dedicated both to him. Thus I took the sting out of that   160
remark of Grocyn's, though at the time I had no intention to revisit England
and no thoughts of another approach to the archbishop; such was my pride
in those days, however empty my pocket. This work underwent two or
three revisions; and I have revised it finally this year.[28]

　　As a young man not yet eighteen, being weaker in elegiacs, I began to   165
write rhetorical pieces in that form against the vices – lechery, avarice, and
ambition.[29] These frivolous things were put out in print[30] by my friends

* * * * *

27 Euripides ... *Hecuba et Iphegenia; Latine factae Erasmo Roterodamo interprete* (Paris:
　 J. Bade 13 September 1506); critical edition by Jan Hendrik Waszink in ASD I-1
　 193–359
28 Dissatisfied with the Bade edition (n27), which contained a large number of
　 printer's errors and other mistakes, Erasmus entrusted the preparation of a
　 revised edition to Aldus in Venice (Epp 207, 209). It was published in
　 December 1507. Later editions published by Froben at Basel in February 1518
　 and February 1524 also contain improvements attributable to Erasmus himself
　 (ASD I-1 196–200). The edition published in 1524 is presumably the 'final' one
　 referred to here, ie, the revisions must have been done in 1523.
29 Reedijk 207–17 (nos 23–5). Reedijk places the date of composition at c 1489.
30 *Silva carminum* ed Reyner Snoy (Gouda: Allaerdus Gouter 18 May 1513). In
　 1521 Erasmus authorized Dirk Martens in Louvain to publish the *Progymnas-
　 mata* (Ep 1193), containing these three poems and two others.

when I was far away,[31] not without some damage to my reputation, and they would have published more had I not returned. A poem written entirely on the spur of the moment to greet Philip on his first return from Spain was published on my own responsibility,[32] some three and twenty years ago if I mistake not.[33] A long time before that, I had published some verses in a mixture of heroic hexameters and iambic trimeters in praise of King Henry VII and his children, and also of Britain itself.[34] This was three days' work; but work it really was, for it was now some years since I had either read or written anything in verse. It was extracted from me partly by embarrassment, partly by irritation. I had been carried off by Thomas More, who had come to pay me a visit on an estate of Mountjoy's[35] where I was then staying, to take a walk by way of diversion as far as the nearest town; for that was where all the royal children were being brought up, except only Arthur, who at that time was the eldest. When we reached the court, there was a solemn gathering not only of that household but of Mountjoy's as well. In the middle stood Henry, who was then nine years old[36] and already looked somehow like a natural king, displaying a noble spirit combined with peculiar courtesy. On his right was Margaret, then perhaps eleven, who afterwards married James, king of Scots. On the left was Mary, a playful child of four; Edmund was still a babe in arms. More and his friend Arnold[37] greeted the boy Henry, under whose rule England now flourishes, and gave him something he had written. I was expecting nothing of the kind and, having nothing to produce, I promised that some day I would prove my devotion to him somehow. At the time I was slightly indignant with More for not having warned me, all the more so as during dinner the boy sent me a

170

175

180

185

190

* * * * *

31 Erasmus was in England from the autumn of 1509 until July 1514.
32 On 6 January 1504, at the royal palace in Brussels, Erasmus presented to Archduke Philip the Handsome a panegyric celebrating the prince's return from a journey to Spain (see line 706 and nn169–70). At the end of the enlarged edition of the *Panegyricus* published the following month (Antwerp: Dirk Martens), Erasmus inserted, along with Ep 180, the *Carmen gratulatorium* ('Illustrissimo principi Philippo feliciter in patriam redeunti gratulatorium carmen Erasmi sub persona patriae'); Reedjik 272–6 (no 78).
33 Erasmus' memory erred by four years.
34 The *Prosopopoeia Britanniae* (autumn 1499), first printed in the *Adagia* (Paris: Jo. Philippi 1500) with Ep 104 as preface; Reedijk 248–53 (no 45). Cf line 607.
35 Ep 79
36 The ages assigned to Henry VIII and his sister Margaret (line 185) are off by one year. Henry, born 2 June 1491, was eight years old; and Margaret, born 29 November 1489, was ten. Mary (line 186) was born on 18 March 1495, and Edmund (line 187) on 21 February 1498.
37 See Ep 124:23n.

note, calling on me to write something. I went home, and even in despite of
the Muses, from whom I had lived apart so long, I finished a poem within
three days. Thus I got the better of my annoyance and cured my   195
embarrassment. There was published also a poem comprising elementary
instruction for the individual Christian.[38] This was written in a very simple
style; for those were my instructions from John Colet, who just then had
founded a new school at great expense, in which he meant the children to be
educated and brought up in religion as well as book-learning.[39] As a man of   200
exceptional wisdom, faced with the lamentable state of the times, he chose
out the younger generation, that he might pour Christ's new wine into new
bottles.

I had begun to translate *Podagra*, the first of Lucian's two pieces on the
gout, a most amusing work, but gave it up,[40] deterred mainly by the epithets   205
in which the choruses are so rich; for in them there was no hope of
reproducing in Latin the happy formation of compound words so noticeable
in the Greek vocabulary, while had I expressed each Greek word in several
Latin ones, the point of the whole poem would be lost. For religious hymns
often consist of such compound epithets of the gods put together in a   210
traditional way, especially in Greece. Of this kind are Homer's

> Ares all-power-surpassing, chariot-burdening, golden-helmed,
> Mighty-spirited, shield-uprearing, city-guardian, brazen-armed,[41]

or Lucian's

> Bandage-fancier bedward-sender   215
> Gait-obstructer joint-tormentor
> Ankle-burner tender-stepper
> Pestle-fearer knee-lamenting-sleep-destroyer
> Knuckle-chalkstone-devotee
> Knee-excruciator.[42]   220

* * * * *

38 The *Christiani hominis institutum*, 1513/14 (Reedijk 307–13, no 94), a translation
   into Latin verse of John Colet's English *Cathechizon*. It was included in the
   Opuscula aliquot Erasmo Roterodamo castigatore, the first edition of which was
   published by Dirk Martens at Louvain in September 1514. Dozens of editions
   from numerous presses followed in Erasmus' lifetime. Cf Ep 298 introduction.
39 At St Paul's Cathedral, London; it opened in 1510. Cf Ep 1211:370–90. On
   Colet, see Ep 106.
40 Nothing of this fragmentary translation seems to have survived.
41 *Homeric Hymns* 8.1–2
42 *Tragoedopodagra* 198–203

These words and others like them are most attractive in Greek because of the scope they give for humorous imitation, but the Latin language could not produce a pale reflection of them. Of Greek I had a taste as a boy, and returned to it when I was already grown up,[43] thirty years old in fact more or less, but at a time when we had no supply of Greek books and no less a 225 shortage of teachers. In Paris there was only one man, Georgius Hermonymus,[44] who had a smattering of Greek, and he was the sort of man who would not have known how to teach had he wanted to, nor wished to had he known how. Finding myself obliged therefore to be my own teacher, I translated many of Lucian's essays[45] to make myself at least read the Greek 230 with attention: *Saturnalia, Cronosolon, Epistolae Saturnales, De luctu,* the *Declamatio de abdicato, Icaromenippus, Toxaris, Pseudomantis, Gallus, Timon,* the *Declamatio pro tyrannicida, De his qui mercede vivunt in aulis principum;* besides these, a selection of eighteen from his shorter dialogues, and in addition the *Hercules Gallicus, Eunuchus, De sacrificiis, Convivium* and *De* 235 *astrologia.* Pieces of this kind I used at different times as a sort of modest new-year's present to greet my friends,[46] as the English custom is. I had also translated his *Longaevi,* only dictating a draft; but my amanuensis purloined it and published it at Paris with a dedication to Mountjoy as his own work.[47]

* * * * *

43 On Erasmus' progress in the study of Greek, see Erika Rummel *Erasmus as a Translator of the Classics* (Toronto, 1985) 3–19.

44 Georgius Hermonymus of Sparta, teacher of Greek at Paris from 1476 until at least 1505. Among his pupils were Reuchlin, Budé, and Beatus Rhenanus.

45 In 1505–6 Erasmus translated twenty-eight of Lucian's works. These, together with four dialogues translated by More as well as declamations by Erasmus and More answering the arguments in the *Tyrannicida* (line 233), were published as the *Luciani ... opuscula* (Paris: Josse Bade, November 1506). In June 1514 Bade published a revised edition with seven additional dialogues: *Luciani Erasmo interprete Dialogi;* critical edition by Christopher Robinson in ASD I-1 361–627. Translation of Erasmus' *Tyrannicida* by Erika Rummel in CWE 29.

46 See Ep 187, which is the only dedicatory letter dated at the new year (1 January 1506). All the rest (Epp 191–3, 197, 199, 205, 261, 267, 293) were written at other times of the year.

47 The amanuensis was Gervasius Amoenus of Dreux, Erasmus' servant-pupil in Paris in 1506 (cf Ep 209:63n). The information supplied by C.R. Thompson 'Erasmus' Translation of Lucian's *Longaevi'* *Classical Philology* 35 (1940) 397–415 indicates that Erasmus' charges may not be well founded. In 1513 or 1514 Amoenus did in fact publish a Latin translation of the *Longaevi* in his *Lucubratiunculae quaedam non invenustae* (text in Thompson ibidem 410–15 and ASD I-1 623–7). But in his dedicatory letter to Mountjoy (Thompson ibidem 405 / ASD I-1 373), Amoenus firmly denies authorship, states that he found the manuscript among Mountjoy's papers, and tentatively attributes the transla- tion to Erasmus. As Christopher Robinson, the ASD editor, points out, if

These trifles were snapped up at first by those who wished to learn, and   240
warmly welcomed;[48] but when the knowledge of Greek began to be widely
shared, as happened most successfully in our part of the world, they began
to fall into neglect,[49] which I knew of course would happen, and am very
glad it has happened. I attempted the same thing in the *Moralia* of Plutarch,[50]   245
whose style is somewhat more difficult, and there is more obscurity in this
matter, owing to his out-of-the-way learning. From Plutarch I translated an
essay called *Quomodo sit dignoscendus adulator ab amico*, which I dedicated to
the English king Henry,[51] eighth of that name. Besides that, one called *Quo*
pacto fieri possit ut utilitatem capias ex inimico; this I dedicated to the man who
is now cardinal-archbishop of York,[52] who at that time was lord high   250
almoner but was already destined for great things, so much so that before I
had an opportunity to present it to him, I had to change my preface three
times,[53] and even so, before it could be printed, he had already reached the
dignity of a cardinal.[54] Before those, I had translated Plutarch's *De tuenda*

* * * * *

Amoenus was telling the truth – and there is no good reason to assume that he
was not – then he cannot have been the secretary to whom the manuscript was
dictated, for he would surely have recognized his own handwriting. Moreover, the quality of the work, decidedly inferior to the translations published in
1516, suggests that it was a much earlier attempt. Robinson speculates that it
might have been completed in 1503 during a stay with Mountjoy at Hammes
and presented to him as a gift. Long afterwards, hearing of its publication but
not seeing the book with Amoenus' disclaimers of authorship, Erasmus
supposed that Amoenus had been his secretary at the time of dictation and
came to the conclusion that Amoenus had stolen the manuscript and put it out
as his own work.

48 For some examples of contemporary praise, see ASD I-1 367.
49 In fact, Erasmus' translations of Lucian remained popular, were much
    reprinted, and became standard texts for both Latin and Greek studies in
    schools; see ASD I-1 367–9.
50 In the autumn of 1512 Erasmus reported from London that he had translated
    'several works by Plutarch' (Ep 264:27–8). The *Opuscula Plutarchi nuper traducta*
    Erasmo Roterodamo interprete, containing the eight essays listed here (lines
    16–28), were published by Froben at Basel in August 1514; critical edition by
    A.J. Koster in ASD IV-2 101–62.
51 In July 1513 Erasmus sent a manuscript of *De discrimine adulatoris et amici* to
    Henry VIII with Ep 272, which became the preface to the essay in the *Opuscula*.
52 Wolsey
53 Two versions of the preface survive: Epp 284 and 297. The latter was the one
    included with *De utilitate capienda ex inimicis* in the *Opuscula*.
54 By the summer of 1514, when the *Opuscula* were printed, Wolsey had been
    designated archbishop of York, but he did not become a cardinal until 10
    September 1515.

valetudine,[55] *Quod in principe requiratur eruditio, Quod cum principibus maxime* 255
versari debeat philosophus, Utrum graviores sint animi morbi an corporis, Num
recte dictum sit, λάθε βιώσας, *De cupiditate divitiarum.* These exercises I
enjoyed all the more because they contributed substantially to the building
of character no less than to the learning of Greek; for I have read nothing
outside Scripture with such a high moral tone. There was this one 260
inconvenience, that Aldus printed Plutarch's work from a copy which was
corrupt in many places,[56] nor was there any supply of ancient copies within
my reach. I made a version of one declamation by Libanius, put in the mouth
of Menelaus, who is asking the Trojans to return his wife, and this was my
first experiment in translation. I also rendered some other short declama- 265
tions of uncertain authorship.[57]

I have written several things designed to be of use in education, among
which are two books *De copia verborum ac rerum*,[58] which I sketched long ago
as a pastime rather than started, to please John Colet, who with great
importunity forced rather than persuaded me to dedicate a new work to his 270
new school.[59] At his request I also corrected a small book by Lily,[60] whom he
had made high master of his school, on syntax; but I made so many changes
that Lily was unwilling to take responsibility for the work, nor could I do so.

* * * * *

55 Erasmus presented a manuscript copy of *De tuenda valetudine*, with Ep 268, to
John Yonge, master of the rolls, as a new-year's gift in 1513. The essay was
printed in July 1513 by Rych and Pynson in London, and the following
November by Dirk Martens in Louvain (with Ep 268 as preface), before it
appeared in the *Opuscula* of 1514.

56 The Aldine edition appeared in March 1509. Erasmus himself had helped with
the proofreading of the text (ASD IV-2 105).

57 In the autumn of 1503 Erasmus translated three declamations of Libanius into
Latin; see Epp 177–8. Besides the *Declamatio Menelai*, there were a *Declamatio
Medeae* and a *Declamatio Andromachae*. Modern scholars do not share Erasmus'
doubts about the latter two. The translation, together with the Greek originals,
were printed by Dirk Martens at Louvain in July 1519; critical edition by R.A.B.
Mynors in ASD I-1 175–92.

58 *De duplici copia verborum ac rerum commentarii duo*, begun at least as early as 1499
and finally published in 1512 (Paris: J. Bade) with a dedication to John Colet (Ep
260). Erasmus subsequently revised and enlarged the work three times (1514,
1526, 1534); see CWE 24 280–2. Text in LB I 3–110; Betty Knott's translation in
CWE 24 284–659.

59 See n39 above

60 William Lily (c 1468–1522); see Ep 341:21n. The book in question was *De octo
orationis partium constructione libellus*, first printed by Richard Pynson at
London in 1513. For more information on the genesis of the work and the
changes made by Erasmus, see Ep 341 (Erasmus' preface to the second edition,
published by Froben in 1515) and the literature there cited.

To please Pierre Vitré,[61] a friend out of the common albeit of lower degree, I
wrote the little book *De ratione studiorum et instituendi pueros*,[62] he having the   275
task of educating several well-born boys of great promise. To this class
perhaps belong the first two books of the grammar of Theodorus Gaza,[63]
which I turned into Latin in hopes of attracting more people to the study of
Greek, baiting the hook as it were by making it so easy; and the work I put
into it, such as it was, was so successful that it already seems unnecessary. I   280
had also made some notes, for the benefit of a certain Englishman, on the
theory of letter-writing, but with no thought of publication. After his death,
I saw the work, mutilated as it was and full of mistakes, published in
England, and so was obliged to waste a few days on trifles of that kind,[64]
which I really wished might be suppressed, had that been possible. There   285
had also appeared a small book of *Colloquia*,[65] pieced together partly from
familiar conversation and partly from my notes, but with a certain amount of
nonsense thrown in which was not only foolish but bad Latin and simply
packed with blunders; and this worthless piece was given a surprisingly
warm welcome – such a game does fortune play, here as everywhere. So   290
here was more nonsense to which I was obliged to devote some labour.[66] At

* * * * *

61 See Ep 66 introduction.
62 *De ratione studii*, the first authorized edition of which was published with *De
   copia* in July 1512 (Paris: Josse Bade) and dedicated to Vitré. Two earlier,
   unauthorized versions (1511, 1512) had preceded it; see Ep 66 introduction and
   CWE 24 665:1n. Critical edition by J.-C. Margolin in ASD I-2 83–151; Brian
   McGregor's translation of the ASD text in CWE 24 665–91.
63 Theodorus Gaza (d 1475) of Salonike taught Greek in Italy from c 1435 and
   translated a number of Greek authors, including Aristotle, into Latin. His
   Greek grammar was published by Aldus at Venice in 1495. Erasmus'
   translation of the first book of Gaza's *Grammaticae institutionis* was published
   by Dirk Martens at Louvain in July 1516 and by Froben at Basel the following
   November. In 1517 Erasmus translated the second book, which Martens and
   Froben published in March and May of 1518. See Epp 428, 771.
64 The original draft of *De conscribendis epistolis* was written c 1498 in Paris for the
   Englishman, Robert Fisher (Ep 62). The unauthorized publication of this draft
   at Cambridge in 1521 incited Erasmus to issue the greatly revised and enlarged
   Froben edition of 1522 (see the introductions to Epp 71 and 1284).
65 The *Familiarum colloquiorum formulae* (Basel: Froben, November 1518), an
   unauthorized edition undertaken by Beatus Rhenanus and based on materials
   which Erasmus had written in Paris for his pupils before the turn of the
   century. See Ep 130:108–9n; Thompson xxi–xxiii; ASD I-3 3–7.
66 The unauthorized edition sold well and within a few months had been
   reprinted in Paris and Antwerp as well as Basel. Erasmus overcame his initial
   indignation and wrote a preface (Ep 909) for the revised edition published at
   Louvain in March 1519 by Dirk Martens.

length, by taking more than ordinary pains, I added a good deal,[67] to bring it up to the right size for a book and make it at least seem to deserve the honour of a dedication to Johann Froben's son, Johannes Erasmius,[68] who was then a boy of six and astonishingly gifted. That was in the year 1522. However, a   295
book of this kind is naturally open to receive additions as often as one pleases. [a]So, for the benefit of those who wish to learn and of Johann Froben, I have frequently supplied further matter already,[69] always so managing my subjects that, besides agreeable reading and the advantage of improving the reader's style, there might be some contribution to the formation of   300
character as well.

And to be sure, as long as there was nothing in that book but the merest trifles, it found surprising favour on all sides. When it began to be useful in many ways, it could not escape the poison-fangs of slander. A certain divine in Louvain,[70] who is physically purblind and mentally even more so,   305
detected in it four passages that were heretical.[71] This book had another experience worthy of record. It was printed lately in Paris after the correction, which means of course the disfigurement, of several passages which were thought to glance at monks, vows, pilgrimages, indulgences, and other things of the kind which, if they were to have the greatest   310
influence with the public, would mean larger profits for that party.[72] Even in

* * * * *

67 Erasmus himself prepared the new, enlarged edition published by Froben in March 1522. It was twice as big as the first edition and the contents – real dialogues rather than sets of formulas – were far more interesting.

68 Ep 1262

69 By September 1524 (see lines 419–21) Froben had published four new editions of the *Colloquia* (c August 1522, August 1523, March 1524, August–September 1524), with new material added to each one. The process of growth continued through six more editions (February 1526–March 1533) until the work as we have it today was completed. Critical edition by L.-E. Halkin, F. Bierlaire, and R. Hoven in ASD I-3. Thompson's translation is based on the final edition.

70 Baechem (Ep 1254 n6)

71 See Epp 1299:59–79, 1300:3–157, 1301.

72 The adulterated version of the *Colloquia* described here was published in Paris towards the end of 1523 by Pierre Gromors (see Allen Ep 1581:414). It was the work of a German Dominican, Lambertus Campester (d post 1538), about whom little is known. He resided for some years at Lyon where, in the period 1516–20, he edited a number of works including the *Opera omnia* of St Bernard and the *Summa theologiae* of Thomas Aquinas. After some years in Paris, during which he published not only the corrupted *Colloquia* but also works against Luther (see n86 below), he returned to Lyon, where in 1525 he received papal permission to leave the Dominican order and join the Augustinian chapter of Saint-Amable at Riom in the Auvergne. There in 1538 he composed an *Oratio laudatoria* for King Francis I. No copy of Campester's edition of the *Colloquia* is

this he displayed such folly and such ignorance that you would swear it was
the work of some itinerant buffoon, though the author of this tedious
comedy is reported to be a theologian of the Dominican order, Saxon by
birth. There is little point in adding his name and designation, which he   315
himself makes no attempt to conceal. Such a monster does not know what it
is to be ashamed; he is more likely to expect credit for his misdemeanours.
This impostor added a new preface in my name, in which he pictures three
grown men toiling away at the education of a single child: Capito[73] to teach
him Hebrew, Beatus[74] Greek, and myself Latin. He ranks me lower than the   320
others both as a scholar and a Christian, detecting things scattered all
through the *Colloquia* which smack of the tenets of Luther. Some people will
laugh no doubt at this point, when they read the praises lavished on Capito
as an excellent man and a good scholar by that creature, who has such a
hatred of Luther. This and much like it he puts into my mouth, taking his cue 325
for this piece of effrontery from the letters of Jerome,[75] who complains that
his enemies have made up a letter in his name and circulated it in Africa in a
meeting of bishops, in which he is made to admit that certain Jews deceived
him into making mistakes in his version of the Old Testament from the
Hebrew. And they could have succeeded entirely in getting the letter   330
accepted as Jerome's, had they been able to some degree to achieve Jerome's
style. Though Jerome records their action as extremely and incurably
wicked, yet it was the one thing that appealed to that rascally Phormio,[76]
being more outrageous than any defamatory pamphlet; but his wish to do
wrong was not matched by the ability to carry out what he had intended.   335
The style of Erasmus, unpolished as it is, was beyond him; these are the
words with which he concludes his flowery preface: 'So does age warn me,
godliness instruct me, while life is yet vouchsafed me, bowed as I am with
eld, to purge what I have written, lest my spirit having reached retiring age
be laid in sad cypress by my aftermath.'   340

* * * * *

known to exist; see *Bibliotheca Erasmiana: Bibliographie des oeuvres d'Erasme* I
(Ghent 1903) 364–8. However, there is no reason to think that Erasmus
invented the story, and it is difficult to imagine that he could have described
the book in such detail without a copy of it in front of him. In the period
1525–32 there are numerous references to Campester and to his subsequent
career in Erasmus' letters; see Allen Epp 1581:410–18, 1591:15–24, 1598:8–11,
1603:32–3, 1655:13–17, 1686:52–6, 1697:84–6, 2728:8–21, 2780:57–72.
73 Epp 459 and 1290
74 Ep 327
75 In fact, Jerome tells this story not in a letter but in his *Apologia contra Rufinum*
2.24. Erasmus discusses it in the *Vita Hieronymi*; see Ferguson *Opuscula* 168.
76 Terence's Phormio (in the play of the same name) was a parasite, an inveterate
schemer, and an audacious impostor.

Although the man's whole style is like this, he had no misgivings as he
plaited his homespun blossoms into my garland; either he must be crazy
with self-satisfaction, or he has the lowest opinion of the theologians' critical
sense. It is for them he coins this base metal, supposing them all to be such
dullards that they will not instantly detect the patches he has cobbled onto   345
my work. He pays such grovelling homage everywhere to France, to Paris,
to theologians, to the Sorbonne, to the colleges that no beggar could be more
abject. So if he thinks something not complimentary enough to the French,
he transfers it to the English, or instead of Paris he puts London. He adds
some offensive remarks as though they were mine, in hopes of getting me   350
into trouble with people whose high opinion of me causes him pain. In
short, everywhere he cuts out, puts in, alters to suit himself, like an old sow
covered in mud and rolling in a stranger's garden; all is filth, confusion, and
upheaval, nor does he realize all the time that he is losing the point I was
aiming at. For when one character there says, 'From a Hollander[77] you're   355
turned into a Frenchman,' and the reply is 'Why? Was I a capon when I left
here?' he changed it to 'From a Hollander you're turned into an Englishman
… Why? Was I a Saxon when I left here?' And again where someone had
said, 'Your dress shows you've changed from a Dutchman to a Frenchman,'
he makes the Frenchman into an Englishman; and where he had replied,   360
'Better this change than turn into a hen,' alluding to the old joke about Gauls
and roosters, he changed the hen into a Bohemian.[78] Later on, when one
man says in jest that he pronounces Latin in the French manner, he put
English manner in place of French, and yet left untouched what follows:
'Then you'll never write good verses, because you have lost the quantity of   365
the syllables,' which does not make sense with respect to English. And
when some character says, 'What has happened to the French to make them
war with the eagle?'[79] he corrupts this into 'What has happened to the
leopards to make them war with the fleurs-de-lys?' as though lilies had a
habit of going to war. Sometimes he does not observe that what follows does   370
not hang together with the changes he has made, as in this same place. I had
written 'Is Paris free from plague?'[80] He alters this to 'Is London free from
plague?' In another place,[81] when someone says, 'Why do we shrink from

* * * * *

77 From the dialogue of Claudius and Balbus added to the *Colloquiorum formulae* in
   the Froben edition of March 1522 (ASD I-3 137 / Thompson 569–70).
78 Campester's version misses the point of Erasmus' pun on *Gallus* (Frenchman),
   gallus (cock), and *gallina* (hen).
79 Ie, the Holy Roman Empire
80 A play on the words *Lutetia* (Paris) and *lues* (plague)?
81 In the *Convivium profanum* (ASD I-3 198 / Thompson 594)

cutting up this rooster?' he changed rooster into hare, but did not alter the
following words: 'Which would you rather, wings or legs?' Again, though   37
he has such a soft spot in his heart for the Dominicans that he wished the
commissaries to sit under their roof, he takes a fierce attack on Scotus with
perfect equanimity; for he did not change the remark of someone: 'I would
much rather let all of Scotus perish than the books of a single Cicero.'[82]

Full of absurdity as all this is, there are a great many passages where   38
the absurdity is matched by equal malice. There is a place where one
character pokes fun at his companion for living a dissolute life and yet
putting his trust in bulls of indulgence.[83] Here the corrector makes him
confess that like his beloved Luther he believes that indulgences from the
pope are valueless, and further on without any authority he makes him   38
repent and express remorse for his past errors. And those he hopes to pass
off as my own corrections! What strange Atlas-figures support the tottering
faith! This is like a man who uses bloodstained clouts to counterfeit a wound
on the human body, and then heals the wound by removing his own
patches. Somewhere in the book a child says that the best confession is one   39
that is made to God.[84] The man has corrected this, declaring that confession
made to a priest is best. This is his way of helping the cause of confession
when it is in peril. I have given you only this by way of illustration, though in
this kind of falsehood he is most prolific. And all this, of course, represents
the recantation which he promises under my name in his forged preface, as   39
though anyone could publish a recantation of another man's errors, or as
though anything in that book put into the mouth of any character were my
personal conviction. It does not move me at all that he makes someone not
yet sixty into someone bowed with eld. It used to be a criminal offence to
publish anything in someone else's name, but now to publish such libels   40
widespread, forging the victim's own name, is child's play to our theologians. For he wishes to be taken for a theologian, though the facts cry aloud
that he does not know the first thing about theology. Nor do I doubt that this
rascal planted his falsehoods on a starveling printer; I do not think anyone
mad enough to be willing to print such ignorant rubbish with his eyes open. 40
The man's incurable audacity ceased to surprise me once I learned that he
was a chick who had at some time fallen out of that nest at Bern[85] – a real case

* * * * *

82 In the *Convivium religiosum* (ASD I-3 251–2 / Thompson 65)
83 In the *De votis temere susceptis* (ASD I-3 149–50 / Thompson 7)
84 In the *Confabulatio pia* (ASD I-3 178 / Thompson 38)
85 Erasmus seems to be saying, on the basis of hearsay, that Campester had at one
   time been a member of the Dominican community at Bern, perhaps as a novice

of the blackest crow laying the foulest eggs. One thing does surprise me, if the report is true that in Paris there are theologians who congratulate themselves on having at last found a man who can scatter Luther's entire 410 faction with the thunderbolts of his eloquence and restore the church to its primeval peace. For he has written, I am told, against Luther too.[86] And after this the theologians complain that I misrepresent them – I who help their studies so much by all my nightly toils, while they themselves readily embrace such monstrosities, which bring more disrepute upon the calling of 415 theologians, and even of monks, than the most malevolent enemy could do. He who has stomach for such a crime will not blench at arson or poisoning. And this stuff is printed in Paris, where it is a crime to print even the Gospels without a favourable verdict from the theologians! These *Colloquia* of mine made their latest appearance, provided with a supplement,[87] in September 420 1524.[a]

Apart from that, I perceived that many authors were either entirely neglected or read with very little profit because they were full of errors everywhere, and further, that some of them were in addition more defaced than expounded by the most witless commentaries. And so there too I set 425 myself to do what I could for the studies of the young and, following the Greek proverb,[88] did not try my prentice hand on potting a great jar but started with the school-book they call the *Cato*.[89] To this I added the *Mimi Publiani*, which are witty enough, to be sure, but were lying concealed among Seneca's works under a false title, and not only teeming with 430 corruptions but defiled by the admixture of many maxims which did not belong to the author. All these I provided with notes. I also added certain other pieces,[90] after revising them, too small to deserve record here if judged

* * * * *

('chick'), and that his behaviour reflected the standards of that community. This would be an allusion to the sensational events of 1507, when the Dominicans of Bern, in an attempt to discredit the doctrine of the Immaculate Conception of the Virgin and its Franciscan proponents, reportedly staged a series of fake apparitions in which the Virgin herself vigorously endorsed the Dominican view. In 1509 four Dominicans, including the prior, were burned at the stake. For other references to this 'villainy at Bern,' see Ep 1033:274–5 and the colloquy *Exequiae seraphicae* (ASD I-3 693 / Thompson 509).

86 In 1523 Campester published two works against Luther: *Heptacolon* and *Apologia in Martinum Lutherum* (Paris: Colinaeus).
87 See n69 above.
88 *Adagia* I vi 15
89 The *Catonis praecepta* and the *Mimi Publiani* (lines 428–9) were both published in the *Opuscula aliquot* (n38 above).
90 *Septem sapientum celebria dicta*, also in the *Opuscula aliquot*

by the labour I spent on them. ^bIn this class one should perhaps also place
Ovid's *Nux*, which I emended and explained in a brief commentary[91] for the 435
benefit of a young man of great promise, John More;[92] and to that I added
two hymns of Prudentius,[93] one celebrating the birth and the other the
epiphany of the child Jesus. These too I cleaned up and expounded in brief
notes to oblige an honourable young lady by name Margaret Roper.[94] This
was in 1524.^b I attempted something similar with Aldus, after the appear- 440
ance of my *Proverbia*,[95] on all the comedies of Terence and Plautus;[96] but here
my avowed purpose was no more than the rearrangement of the lines,
which were in great confusion, wherever it might have been possible. Then
the same on Seneca's tragedies, in which I felt I had made a few successful
corrections, but not without the help of ancient codices. The printer's copy I 445
deposited with Aldus, leaving it to him to decide what to do with it; except
that I made a fresh recension of Seneca's tragedies afterwards in England
and sent them to Bade, who thought fit[97] to mix my material with other
people's.[98] Then in Cambridge I came on several ancient codices, and set
about Seneca the rhetorician, with great efforts on my part, but the edition[99] 450
proved somewhat unfortunate. For being called back by business to my own
country,[100] I had entrusted to scholarly friends[101] the task of choosing out of
my marginal annotations what they thought worth using, and they –
generously, to be sure – undertook it. But I then learned for the first time
that even among those who are thought to be true as steel to anything they 455
have promised[102] there are some who cannot be relied on; and it was useless

* * * * *

91 *Commentarius in Nucem Ovidii*, published with the Prudentius (line 437) by
   Froben in 1524 (see Ep 1402); translations by A.G. Rigg in CWE 29.
92 John More (c 1509–47), the youngest child of Sir Thomas More
93 Printed with Ovid's *Nux* (n91); see Ep 1404.
94 Sir Thomas More's eldest and favourite daughter (c 1505–44), married to
   William Roper (1496–1578)
95 Ie, the Aldine *Adagiorum chiliades* of 1508
96 During his stay in Venice in 1507–8, Erasmus assisted Aldus in the preparation
   of the texts that became the basis for the Aldine edition of Terence (November
   1517) and Plautus (July 1522); see Ep 589:41–7.
97 Reading *cui visum est* for Allen's *qui visus est* (who appeared).
98 See Ep 263:13–21. Bade's edition was published at Paris on 5 December 1514.
   Erasmus' name appears on the title-page while the names of the other
   commentators are listed in the margins against their notes.
99 The *Senecae lucubrationes* (Basel: Froben, August 1515); see Ep 325.
100 Ie, his journey to England and back via the Netherlands in the spring and
   summer of 1515
101 Beatus Rhenanus (Ep 327) and Wilhelm Nesen (Ep 1257 n3); see Epp 328–30.
102 Ie, Germans; cf Epp 269:43, 305:45, 307:14, 334:9–10.

to regret that I had not followed the advice of the crested lark in the fable: Do
not wait for your friends to do what you can do yourself.[103] What was more,
that part of the copy which had the most notes went astray. Some people
suspected – and it was not unlikely – that the man who with a generous   460
show of promises had undertaken this task and shown a lack of honesty or
wisdom (I am not sure which) in performing it had secretly made away with
it for fear of being found out.[104] For some books I had no codices of any
antiquity to assist me, in the *Quaestiones naturales* for instance and the
Controversiae, and in these, in a few passages, I had added my conjecture   465
without changing the text. In other works where I was able to call on old
copies for assistance, I had filled the whole margins with notes; but these
notes needed a critical eye. Had I been at hand to help when this book was
printed, the unprejudiced reader would agree that any labour I devoted to
the text was not ill spent; as it is, I regret my misfortune as much as anyone,   470
and no man can accuse me of deceiving him. I hear that certain people in
Italy are working on a new edition of this author in reliance on very ancient
codices.[105] I shall support their enterprise to the best of my ability, and shall
be so far from supposing their success to reflect any discredit on me that I
even mean to collect some credit from it, inasmuch as my attempt, such as it   475
was, gave me a start and spurred them on to take up this most honourable
field of study.

After these preliminary exercises, I addressed myself to the New
Testament,[106] in which I had made up my mind to be so sparing of words
that my plan was to write notes in two or three words on every passage,   480
especially as I had already issued Lorenzo's critical work,[107] which seemed
to me more long-winded than the subject requires. None the less, when
Froben was already set to print my work, scholarly friends,[108] to whom I
sometimes defer more than I should, moved me actually to alter the Vulgate
text, and to be rather fuller in my annotations. This work of mine provoked a   485

* * * * *

103 Ennius, cited in Gellius 2.29.20
104 Cf n101. It is clear from later comments (Allen Epp 1479:86, 1804:72–3) that
Erasmus regarded Nesen as the chief culprit and that these remarks apply to
him.
105 Probably the *Tragoediae* published by Bernardus de Vianis (Venice 1522). There
was no complete edition of Seneca in Italy at this time.
106 On the genesis of the *Novum instrumentum* of 1516 and of the four revised
editions that followed (1519, 1522, 1527, 1535), see the introductions to Epp 373
and 384 in CWE and in Allen.
107 Lorenzo Valla's *Adnotationes* on the New Testament (Paris: Josse Bade 13 April
1505), the manuscript of which Erasmus had discovered near Louvain the
previous year. See Ep 182. On Valla himself, see Ep 20:100n.
108 Members of the Froben circle; see Ep 421:50–5.

great many men to the study either of Greek or of a purer form of theology; but at the same time the reputation it earned me was leavened with much ill will.[109] Here too I soon paid penalties that were by no means light, either for my audacity or for my undue readiness to follow my friends' wishes rather than my own judgment. With incredible labour I remade the whole work[110] and sent it again to the printer. Once again I have taken it in hand, for the third time, and supplemented it most carefully, in the year 1522, and this is the latest edition I have yet published. ᶜBut I have a fourth[111] ready, having discovered while writing the paraphrases[112] many things that had previously escaped me.ᶜ

Then again, I took Jerome's letters, which stand so high in both scholarship and style but were current in a most corrupt text, and corrected them with explanatory notes, separating what is spurious with critical comment.[113] This work I went over a second time in the year 1522, ᵈwith corrections or additions in not a few places where something had escaped me in the earlier edition. This was printed a second time in the year 1524. In this labour I acquitted myself so well that an attentive reader will easily see that in undertaking this revision my time was not wasted. In this I did not lack ancient codices, but they could not protect me in a number of places from the need to conjecture. These conjectures however I put forward with such moderation in my notes that no one could easily be led astray by them, but that the reader's interest might merely be aroused to pursue the trail. And I hope to see someone with the help of more correct copies restoring other passages which eluded me; I shall gladly pay their industry the tribute it deserves, and at the same time they will have no call to criticize my attempts for, though I made many successful restorations, I was obliged in certain passages to make my own the old Greek proverb, 'As best I could, not as I would.'[114]

For some men are disposed by nature, if they can add to the efforts of their predecessors, to claim the whole credit for themselves; and they pursue the other man with a torrent of abuse if they find him nodding or if in any place he has not achieved what he was trying to do. In such people I for

* * * * *

109 Some major examples of this ill will are discussed below in lines 811–1013.
110 Dissatisfied with the hastily prepared first edition, Erasmus set to work immediately on a new edition, which Froben published in 1519. See CWE 3 216.
111 The definitive version, not published until 1527
112 See lines 750–73 below.
113 Erasmus' edition of the letters of Jerome constituted the first four volumes of the Froben edition of the *Opera omnia*, published in 1516 in nine volumes. See Ep 396 introduction.
114 Not in the *Adagia*; source unidentified. An utterly banal sentiment in any case.

my part know not which to think more abominable, their unkindness or
their ingratitude. No one has stood in their way if they wish to produce
something nearer perfection. They maintain that nothing should be   520
published except what is quite perfect. Men who lay down this principle are
saying that nothing should be published at all, and that nothing of the kind
has yet been published by anyone. We used to concede this to the Dutch,
and to monks and theologians, who had as a rule no commerce with the
Muses; for the study of the humanities had not yet proceeded that far.   525
Anyone who bears this in mind will perceive that the task I have undertaken
is neither easy nor unrewarding. Will Italian critics[115] deny to the barbarians
the scope they are obliged willy-nilly to allow to their own fellow-
countrymen, Filelfo[116] and Ermolao[117] and the Vallas[118] – in a word, to all
those who within these sixty years have devoted their efforts to enlightening   530
the public either by translating Greek texts or by expounding and correcting
Latin ones? Those who publish nothing may avoid censure, but at the price
of earning no credit; or rather, while they try foolishly enough to avoid being
censured by men, they incur censure that is far more serious – or are we to
suppose a man less deserving of censure who has a full larder and gives   535
nothing to his starving friends than he who freely and openly brings out
what he has and would gladly give them better cheer if he could? Who
attacks Ermolao's notes on Pliny[119] on the ground that, deprived as he was of
the help of correct codices, a great many things escaped him, and in many
places too his conjectures were unhappy? Personally, I confess a great debt   540
to Beatus Rhenanus, who gave us a text of Tertullian[120] corrected in many

* * * * *

115 Ie, members of the so-called Roman Academy (cf Ep 1342 n90), who delighted
    in finding fault with Erasmus' editions and translations of classical and
    patristic authors and who dubbed him 'Errasmus.' They also found fault with
    his style and impugned his orthodoxy. See Allen Epp 1479:19–180, and
    1482:29–59, both written at about the same time as the 1524 edition of the
    Catalogus.
116 See lines 124–6 above.
117 See Ep 126:150n.
118 Reading *Valis* 'to the Vallas,' as in the original text, for Allen's *Vallae*, 'to Valla.'
    (Allen acknowledged his error in his note to Ep 1479:70.) One of the Vallas
    referred to was clearly the great Lorenzo, who had translated Herodotus and
    Thucydides, among others, and who, in Erasmus' words, had 'clearly made
    mistakes in a number of places' (Allen Ep 1479:69). The other(s) may have been
    either Niccolò Valla, who c 1471 had translated Hesiod 'with unhappy results'
    (Allen Ep 188:38n), or Giorgio Valla of Piacenza (c 1447–1500) who, according
    to Erasmus (Allen Ep 2422:48–9), had produced an infelicitous rendering of the
    Placita philosophorum, or both.
119 The *Castigationes Plinianae* (Rome 1492)
120 Basel: Froben, July 1521   See Ep

places, although what he gave us was incomplete and still beset by countless corruptions. A man is not defrauded of the credit he deserves who has done all he could in the circumstances and has opened the way for others to produce a more finished result. Nor do we find any critics more unfair than those who publish absolutely nothing themselves and do not even impart what they know, seeming to be jealous of public enlightenment, exactly as though whatever they find that they share with many others is lost to themselves. And if they catch one out in some human failing, oh, the cackling and the abusive language and the tragical scenes! Of all translators the most successful was Theodorus Gaza; and none the less in his books Trapezuntius[121] detected some mistakes, which he put right when they were pointed out. As for Ermolao, great man that he was, did he not make a childish blunder[122] at the outset of Themistius' preface to his commentary on Aristotle's *De anima*, meeting shipwreck (as they say) even before he had left harbour? Need I mention here Filippo Beroaldo,[123] Battista Pio[124] and their like, to whose errors the Italians turn a blind eye? Or almost all those who in the last eighty years have translated from the Greek Diodorus Siculus, Herodotus, Thucydides, Plutarch's *Vitae*, and even his *Moralia*? If we make allowance in their case for the fact that, with such a plentiful supply of good scholars and very ancient texts, they sometimes make astonishing mistakes, why must these people confound heaven and earth if in a mere Dutchman, deprived of all resources, they find things that need correction? Not but what I play the critic myself on my own writings, and have made many corrections in my versions from the Greek, as I mean to do while there is life left in me.

But I perceive, my dear Botzheim, that you have been recalling me for some time now to my catalogue.[d] Suetonius Tranquillus[125] I collated with a codex of astonishing antiquity, and restored with some success a number of passages which no one had previously noticed. I have done the same with

* * * * *

121 George of Trebizond (1395–c 1472), who translated many of the Greek fathers for Pope Nicholas v and also Plato's *Laws*
122 In the first and second editions (Treviso 1481 and Venice 1499), the first sentence of Barbaro's translation has *quo* or *quomodo* for *cum*; see Allen Ep 1479:68n.
123 Filippo Beroaldo the Elder (1453–1505), for many years professor of rhetoric at the University of Bologna, and editor of numerous Latin classics
124 Giambattista Pio (c 1460–1540), pupil of Beroaldo, taught at Bologna and elsewhere and edited a number of classical works
125 Included in the *Historiae Augustae scriptores* published by Froben in June 1518. See Ep 586.

the works of Cyprian.[126] I have also revised the commentary of Arnobius on
the Psalms, a work which I dedicated to Adrian VI,[127] who had then been
lately elected pope. I did the same for Hilary, who set me some surprising
problems; and these efforts I offered to Jean Carondelet,[128] archbishop of
Palermo and chancellor of the emperor Charles in Brabant. Besides these,   575
when I considered the important contribution made to elegance and
richness of style by brilliant aphorisms, apt metaphors, proverbs, and
similar figures of speech, I made up my mind to collect the largest possible
supply of such things from approved authors of every sort and arrange them
each in its appropriate class, to make them more accessible to those who   580
wish to practise composition with a view to securing a rich and ready
diction. In this field I made an experiment, if I mistake not, twenty-seven
years ago.[129] The occasion was this. On the beach at Dover, before going on
board ship, all my supply of money suffered shipwreck; this was in those
days small enough, but it meant a great deal to me, for it was all I had. The 585
agent in this was the officer (I almost said the pirate) in charge of the coast in
the king's name, though More and Mountjoy convinced me that there was
no risk unless I were exporting English coin; and I had no English currency
and no money either earned or given me in England. On the beach,
however, I learned that it was illegal to export any coin whatever, even iron   590
coin, to a higher value than six angels. Such was the price I paid for my first
and last lesson in English law.[130] When I had returned to Paris with an empty

* * * * *

126 Basel: Froben 1519. See Ep 1000.
127 Ep 1304
128 Ep 1334
129 Erasmus' memory is wrong by four years: the first edition of the *Adagiorum
    collectanea* was published at Paris in June 1500. This edition and all those which
    followed were dedicated to Mountjoy (Ep 79); see Epp 126 and 211, and lines
    1669–71 in this letter.
130 The 'English disaster' took place on 27 January 1500; see Ep 119 introduction
    and 9n. The gold angel-noble (5.157 grams fine gold each) still had a value of 6s
    8d sterling (a third of a pound); six were worth £2 sterling English, about £2 18s
    6d gros Flemish, and £18 6s tournois. Erasmus had run afoul of a peculiar
    English law that was evidently unique in western Europe. While virtually all
    countries had long forbidden the export of gold and silver bullion, most
    exempted legal tender coins, domestic and foreign, since the purpose of the
    ban was to direct uncoined precious metals (or metal in non-current coin) to the
    mint. But from 1364 (27 Edw III, statute 2, c 14), England had extended this
    export ban to include current legal tender coins, gold and silver, beyond the
    value of 40s, without a special royal licence. During the Anglo-Flemish
    commerical negotiations of 1499, Archduke Philip's ambassadors acidly
    reminded the English that 'theye do very moche for your subjectes to graunt

purse, I did not doubt that many people expected me to avenge this misfortune with my pen, as men of letters normally do, by writing something to arouse feeling either against the king or against England; and I feared at the same time that William Mountjoy, having brought about the situation in which I lost my money, might suspect that my feelings towards him were changing. I had to disappoint them, or rather, I had to show clearly that I was not so prejudiced as to blame my private mishap on a whole country or so thoughtless as for so small a loss to call down either on myself or on the friends I had left in England the resentment of so great a prince; at the same time I had to prove to my friend Mountjoy that my feelings of friendship towards him had not changed in the least. And so I decided to publish something forthwith. Having nothing ready at hand, I accumulated at random from a few days' reading some sort of a collection of adages, guessing that this book, such as it was, might find a welcome among those who wish to learn, at least for its utility. This I used as evidence that my friendship had not grown cold. Then I added the poem[131] I have already mentioned, to show that I bore no ill will against either the king or the country for the confiscation of my money; and this plan of mine was not unsuccessful, for such a moderate and fair-minded attitude won me many friends at the time in England, good scholars and men of high character and position. This slight work was printed a few years later by my friend Bade with a few additions and revisions by me mainly from Greek sources,[132] and later in Strasbourg by Matthias Schürer,[133] although I had meanwhile put together a more abundant supply for a Venice edition, which was published by the house of Aldus.[134] Moreover, as I saw that this work was so popular with keen students that it was clearly destined for a long life and was being published in competition by many printers, I enriched it repeatedly as either

* * * * *

them to conveigh oute of the archdukis landis all money current in thoos parties ... For the archdukis subjectes may not have like pryvylage to convey money nether plate oute of your realme of England' (Georg Schanz *Englische Handelspolitik gegen Ende des Mittelalters* II [Leipzig 1881] 196). That English export ban was rigorously enforced, with licensed exemptions rarely granted or sold, until 1663 (15 Car II, c 7), when Parliament removed the prohibition against exporting gold or silver bullion and foreign coins; but the ban on exporting English coin remained in force until 'Peel's Act' of July 1819 (59 Georg III, c 49).

131 See n34 above.
132 Twenty adages were added to Bade's edition of 1506.
133 1510
134 In the Aldine edition of 1508 (see Ep 211) the number of adages increased from 819 to 3260, the title was changed to *Adagiorum chiliades*, and the commentaries were far more extensive.

leisure or a larger supply of books became available. The latest revision was   620
published by Johann Froben in the year of our Lord 1523.[135] Besides which,
in rereading a number of authors in order to enrich my *Adagia*, I noted down
many parallels on the side, more pointing the way and setting others an
example of a work to come than finishing a book with the necessary care.
This makes one book of *Parabolae sive similia*,[136] addressed to Pieter Gillis,[137]   625
lawyer and citizen of Antwerp, who was once the companion of my studies.

Perhaps it will not be out of place if I subjoin to this class of work my
correspondence,[138] although in all my output there is nothing I like less. In
this department I have been over-responsive to the wishes of my friends,
particularly as with changing circumstances they often turn into their   630
opposites; but on this point I have already gone on record fully enough in
the first letter of the latest edition,[139] which appeared from Froben's press in
1521.[140] ^eWhat I then conjectured, I learned afterwards from actual experience only too well. The facts themselves testify that some men who were
once my sworn friends[141] – as true, I might have said, as any Pylades,[142] –   635
have become my bitterest enemies, combining deepest ingratitude with
deepest perfidy, for no other reason except that I would not lend my name to
a perilous enterprise, which I always foresaw would end in disastrous
discord. Yet I have never broken off a friendship with anyone because he
was either more inclined towards Luther or more against Luther than I was.   640
My disposition is naturally such that I could love even a Jew, provided he
were in other respects an agreeable person to live with and friendly, and

* * * * *

135 After the Aldine edition of 1508, there were eight more authorized editions in
     Erasmus' lifetime, each one enlarged, all published by Froben: 1515, 1517/18,
     1520, 1523, 1526, 1528, 1533, 1536. By 1536 the number of adages had grown to
     4,151. Critical edition by Felix Heinlimann and Emanuel Kienzle in ASD II-5 and
     II-6; English edition by M.M. Phillips and R.A.B. Mynors in CWE 31–36.
136 *Parabolae sive similia* (Strasbourg: Matthias Schürer, December 1514). Revised
     editions were published in June 1515 (Louvain: Dirk Martens), c December
     1516 (Paris: Josse Bade), and August 1522 (Basel: Froben). The last was
     enlarged by the addition of sixteen *similia*. Critical edition by J.-C. Margolin in
     ASD I-5 1–332; translation by R.A.B. Mynors in CWE 23 123–277.
137 Pieter Gillis (Ep 184). The dedicatory letter is Ep 312.
138 On the editions of Erasmus' correspondence up to 1524, see CWE 1 xx–xxi, CWE
     3 348–50, and Allen I 593–5.
139 Ep 1206
140 *Epistolae ad diversos* (Basel: Froben 31 August 1521), the first overtly authorized
     edition, containing 617 letters, 171 of which had not been included in earlier
     editions.
141 Especially Hutten; see lines 1019–1103.
142 The friendship between Orestes and Pylades was proverbial.

provided he did not vomit blasphemies against Christ in my hearing. And
this courteous approach can, I believe, do more towards ending strife. I am,
to be sure, only slightly moved when those who used to describe me in print   64
as the sun of Germany, the prince of true theology, and the champion of
sound learning now find me of less worth than seaweed; for those
pompous titles, which I always disliked, I gladly hand back to them. But the
ties of friendship I do not readily abandon to please anyone.[e]

I also tried my hand at the art of declamation, for which I was by nature   65
more fitted than for those collections of materials, although some inclination
urged me strongly in that direction. And so I amused myself in early days
with the panegyric on marriage and the attack on it[143] which now form part
of my work *De ratione conscribendi epistolas*.[144] This I did for the benefit of a
distinguished young man William Mountjoy, whom I was then grounding   65
in rhetoric. I asked him whether he liked what I had written. 'Yes,' he
merrily replied; 'I like it so much that you have quite persuaded me to get
married.' 'Do not make up your mind,' said I, 'till you have read the other
side.' 'You can keep that,' he said; 'the first half is the one for me.' He has
been married three times, and is now a widower; but perhaps will marry a   66
fourth time – so easy is it to push the wagon on the way it already wants to
go. But in very early youth, when hardly twenty, I had written in the same
style the *Laus vitae monasticae*,[145] which means the life of a hermit, to please a
friend who was laying traps for a nephew of his, whom he hoped to lure as a
proselyte into his net.[146] Three and twenty years ago I also wrote the   66
Encomium artis medicae[147] at the request of a friend who was lately physician
to the emperor Charles.[148] I have found among my papers the reply of a

* * * * *

143 Written for Mountjoy (Ep 79) when Erasmus was his tutor, probably in Paris c
   1497. The panegyric (without the attack) was first published as the *Encomium
   matrimonii* in Dirk Martens' edition of the *Querela pacis* (Louvain 1518). Critical
   edition by J.-C. Margolin in ASD I-5 333–416.
144 The panegyric and the attack were included in *De conscribendis epistolis* of 1522
   (see Ep 1284) as examples of *epistolae suasoriae* and *dissuasoriae*; ASD I-2 400–32 /
   CWE 25 129–48.
145 The *Laus vitae monasticae*, probably written c 1486 but first published in 1521,
   under the title *De contemptu mundi*, by Dirk Martens at Louvain; see Ep 1194. Cf
   lines 1447–9 below. Critical edition by S. Dresden in ASD V-1 1–86; translation
   by Erika Rummel in CWE 66 129–75.
146 See Ep 1194:13–15.
147 The *Encomium medicinae*, written c 1499 and first published in Dirk Martens'
   edition of the *Declamationes aliquot* in March 1530. See Ep 799. Translation by
   Brian McGregor in CWE 29.
148 Probably Ghisbert Hessels, town physician of Saint-Omer (Epp 95:13n and
   673:22n), who in 1513 was listed as surgeon to Prince Charles; see Allen Ep
   95:11n.

bishop[149] to an address of welcome from his people, and cannot rightly recall
the occasion on which I wrote it.[150] The address of condolence on a son's
untimely death, on the other hand,[151] I wrote in Siena, when Alexander,   670
archbishop of St Andrews,[152] son of James king of Scots, was my pupil. Long
before, in England, I had set down a declamation in reply to Lucian's attack
on tyrannicide,[153] being challenged to do this by Thomas More, who was
then the partner of my studies and is now treasurer to the English king.
Querimonia pacis[154] I wrote about seven years ago, when first invited to join   675
the prince's court.[155] Great efforts were being made to bring together a
conference at Cambrai of the world's most powerful princes, the emperor,
the king of France, the king of England, our own Charles, and there to
establish peace between them with adamantine chains, as the phrase
goes.[156] The chief agents in this were that distinguished man Guillaume de   680
Chièvres,[157] and Jean Le Sauvage,[158] lord high chancellor, a man born for
the public good. The plan was opposed by certain persons who have
nothing to gain from any peace, and who like Philoxenus (who said that
meat was most delicious which was not meat and fish which was not fish)[159]
much preferred peace that was no peace and war that was not quite war.   685

* * * * *

149 *Oratio episcopi respondentis iis qui sibi nomine populi gratulati essent et omnium
    nomine obedientiam quam vocant detulissent*, first published in Dirk Martens'
    edition of the *Querela pacis* (Louvain 1518)
150 Allen suggests that it may have been written for James Stewart (brother of
    James IV of Scotland) who in 1497 became archbishop of St Andrews; Allen Ep
    48:6n. R.R. Post has advanced the hypothesis that it was written for Philip of
    Burgundy, bishop of Utrecht (Ep 603); see *Archief voor de geschiednis van de
    Katholieke Kerk in Nederland* 9 (1967) 322–9.
151 *Declamatio de morte*, written in 1509 (see following note) and published with
    Froben's edition of the *Querela pacis* in December 1517; see Ep 604. Translation
    in CWE 25 156–64.
152 Alexander Stewart (d 1513), illegitimate son of James IV of Scotland. Stewart
    was Erasmus' pupil in Italy in 1509; see Epp 216 introduction and 604:4n.
153 See n45 above.
154 *Querela pacis* (Basel: Froben, December 1517; Louvain: Martens, March 1518).
    See Ep 603. Translation by Betty Radice in CWE 27 289–322.
155 The invitation to become councillor to Prince Charles was probably extended in
    May 1515, though the actual appointment apparently began in January 1516;
    see Allen Ep 370:18n.
156 On the circumstances in which the *Querela pacis* was written, see Ep 603
    introduction and line 28n. The conference at Cambrai took place in March 1517.
157 Ep 532:30n
158 Ep 301:38n
159 The authorship of this odd sentiment is a matter of controversy, but most
    modern scholars attribute it to Philoxenus Leucadius. See D.L. Page *Poetae
    Melici Graeci* (Oxford 1962) 441 (fragment 836).

And so on instructions from Jean Le Sauvage I wrote *Querela pacis*. By now things have come to such a pass that one ought to compose her epitaph, for there is no hope of her recovery.[160] Some of these trifling things 'to serious issues lead,' as Horace[161] says.

I wrote my light-hearted *Moria* while staying with Thomas More,[162] 69 being at that time returned from Italy – a work of which I thought so little that I did not even reckon it worth publication (for I was myself in Paris[163] when it was seen through the press by Richard Croke,[164] very badly printed and full of errors), in spite of which hardly anything of mine has had a more enthusiastic reception, especially among the great.[165] A few monks only, 69 and those the worst, together with some unusually squeamish theologians,[166] took offence at its freedom; but more were offended when Listrius added notes,[167] for before that moment it had gained from not being understood. I had at that time conceived the idea of three simultaneous declamations, in praise of Folly, Nature, and Grace; but some people I could 70

* * * * *

160 See Epp 1283 n3 and 1306 n22.
161 *Ars poetica* 451
162 On the genesis and history of the *Moriae encomium*, written in 1509, see Epp 222:1–26, 337:135–46, and *Adagia* II ii 40.
163 The first edition was published at Paris in 1511 by Gilles de Gourmont. Seven of the thirty-five subsequent editions were augmented and revised: 1512 (Paris: Bade); 1514 (Strasbourg: Schürer); 1515, 1516, 1521, 1522, and 1532 (Basel: Froben). Critical edition by Clarence Miller in ASD IV-3; translation by Betty Radice in CWE 27 77–153.
164 On Croke, see Ep 227:31n.
165 These included Pope Leo x (Epp 739:12–15, 749:16–17), Guillaume Budé (Ep 583:218–20), Jakob Wimpfeling (Ep 224:45–51), Ulrich von Hutten (Ep 611:10–12), and, of course, More himself (see *St Thomas More: Selected Letters* ed Elizabeth Frances Rogers [New Haven 1961] 6–64). See also Epp 450:15–21, 494:31–5, 561:63–72, 569:186–202.
166 Initially (1514) the Louvain theologians who made Maarten van Dorp their spokesman (Epp 304, 337); cf lines 811–17. Later theologian-critics were Edward Lee, 1518 (Ep 843:631–89), and Zúñiga, 1522, in his *Blasphemiae et impietates Erasmi* (Ep 1260 n45). *Folly*, of course, remained a favourite target of monks and theologians. In 1531 Maarten Lips described it as one of the three works most hated by Erasmus' enemies, the other two being the *Epistola de esu carnium* and the *Colloquia*; Allen Ep 2566:83–4.
167 Gerardus Listrius (Gerard Lister or Lyster), c 1492–after 1522, was rector of the school at Zwolle. With considerable help from Erasmus himself (see Allen Ep 2615:171–80), Listrius wrote a long, defensive commentary on the *Folly* which was printed with the Froben edition of 1515 and with most subsequent editions; see J. Austin Gavin and Thomas M. Walsh 'The *Praise of Folly* in Context: The Commentary of Girardus Listrius' *Renaissance Quarterly* 24 (1971) 193–209. See also Ep 641:3–6.

name proved so difficult that I changed my mind. It was as the merest youth
that I began the *Antibarbari*;[168] for this too belongs, I consider, to the class of
declamations. And although even among the works I have listed there are
several which relate to the theory of the good life, those I shall now mention
were written by me as a serious contribution to orderly and godly living.   705
Among these is the *Panegyricus*[169] which I offered to Prince Philip[170] on his
first return from Spain; for though I praised him, praise was combined with
the reminder of the objects to be observed by a good prince, as I showed
clearly enough in the letter to Jean Desmarez, which I then added to the
work.[171] Then there was the short book *De principe christiana*,[172] which I   710
offered to the emperor Charles (as he now is) when I had recently been
summoned to join the staff of the prince's court and serve as one of his
councillors.[173] So in this way I first entered on the duties of a trusty
councillor. 'Right trusty' is a conventional epithet of councillors, though
most princes like nothing less than those who are really trustworthy, and   715
most councillors do nothing to live up to their description. And yet none of
the great men took offence at the freedom of this book, small as it was. Good
princes tolerate freedom in their advisers; it is factious licence that they
cannot stand.

The *Enchiridion militis christiani*[174] I began about thirty years ago,[175]   720
when I was lodging in the castle of Tournehem, to which I had been driven
by the plague that was then raging in Paris. It started by accident. I had in the

* * * * *

168 See lines 1320–31 below.
169 *Panegyricus ad illustrissimum Principem Philippum, Archiducem Austriae* (Ant-
    werp: Dirk Martens, February 1504); see Ep 179 and n32 above. Critical edition
    by O. Herding in ASD IV-1 1–93; translation by Betty Radice in CWE 27 1–75.
170 Philip the Handsome (1478–1506), duke of Burgundy, archduke of Austria,
    and king of Castile, was the son of Emperor Maximilian I and Mary of
    Burgundy and the father of Emperor Charles V.
171 Ep 180
172 *Institutio principis christiani*, probably written in the summer of 1515 and first
    published c March of the following year by Froben (Ep 393). Critical edition by
    O. Herding in ASD IV-1 95–219; translation by Neil M. Cheshire and Michael J.
    Heath in CWE 27 199–288.
173 See n155.
174 First published in the *Lucubratiunculae* (Antwerp: Dirk Martens, February 1503;
    repr 1509). The next edition appeared in the *Lucubrationes* published by
    Matthias Schürer at Strasbourg in 1515. See also n180. Text in LB V 1–66, and in
    Desiderius Erasmus Roterodamus: Ausgewählte Schriften ed H. and A. Holborn
    (Munich 1933; repr 1964) 1–136; translation by Charles Fantazzi in CWE 66 1–127.
175 In 1501 (see Ep 164), which was twenty-two years earlier

castle a friend,[176] whom I shared with Batt.[177] He had a wife of a deeply religious turn of mind, while he himself was no man's enemy but his own – a spendthrift, plunged in fornication and adultery, but in other respects a pleasant companion in every way. For all theologians he had the greatest contempt, except for me. The wife was fearfully concerned for her husband's salvation, and she approached me through Batt to ask if I would write something that might get a little religion into the man; but on condition that he must not know that this was his wife's initiative, for he was cruel even to her, to the extent of beating her, as soldiers will. I did as she asked and jotted down something appropriate to the situation. This won the approval even of good scholars, particularly Jean Vitrier,[178] a Franciscan who was the great authority in those parts; and when the plague, which was raging everywhere, had again driven me from Paris, this time to Louvain,[179] I finished it at leisure. For some time my piece attracted no notice.[180] After that, it began to sell surprisingly well, thanks especially to the recommendation of certain Dominicans,[181] a number of whom have since been set against it by a preface which I added, addressed to Abbot Paul Volz,[182] a pure Christian character if ever there was one. I had attached to it[183] a letter of encouragement addressed to Adolf, lord of Veere,[184] who was then a mere boy; and besides that, two prayers to the Virgin Mother,[185] written to please the boy's mother Anna, lady of Veere,[186] in a childish style designed to suit her feelings rather than my judgment. Later I added a prayer addressed to Jesus,[187] which was more to my liking. With this was part of the extemporary

725

730

735

740

745

* * * * *

176 Identified as Johann Poppenruyter, a Nürnberger who established a gun foundry at Mechelen before 1510; see Ep 164 introduction.
177 See Epp 35 introduction, 163.
178 See Epp 163:5n.
179 Autumn 1502; see Ep 171 introduction.
180 Cf n174. Only after 1515 was the *Enchiridion* frequently reprinted and translated into nearly every European language; see *Bibliotheca Belgica: Bibliographie générale des Pays Bas* ed F. Vander Haeghen et al (Ghent: The Hague 1880–) nos E1000ff.
181 Unidentified
182 Ep 858, added to Froben's first edition (July 1518). The letter contains some harsh criticisms of contemporary monasticism.
183 Ie, to the *Lucubratiunculae* of 1503. See n174.
184 Ep 93
185 *Paean Virgini matri dicendus* LB V 1227–34 and *Obsecratio sive oratio ad Virginem Mariam in rebus adversis* ibidem 1233–40
186 Ep 145 introduction
187 *Precatio ad Virginis filium Iesum* LB V 1210–16

disputation I held long ago with John Colet on Jesus' despair,[188] if this can be allowed to belong with the formation of character. ᶠAnd this year, in 1524 that is, I have published my *Exomologesis*,[189] or On the principles of confessing offences to a priest.ᶠ

I also attempted greater things: I made an explanation by way of   750
paraphrase of Paul's Epistle to the Romans.[190] After this, encouraged to go progressively further by the success of my rash attempt and the urging of my friends,[191] I completed paraphrases on all the apostolic Epistles.[192] This work not being a continuous effort but finished at intervals, in such a way that as each section was completed I determined to refrain from more of the kind,   755
the result was that, contrary to my usual practice, the whole was not dedicated to any individual. Later, encouraged by Matthäus, the cardinal of Sion,[193] I attempted the same thing, not long ago, for Matthew. This piece of work I dedicated to the emperor Charles,[194] who was, I know, much pleased with the result of my efforts.[195] ᵍI had already ceased to think about making   760
paraphrases when, being unexpectedly recalled to this field by many friends,[196] I completed the paraphrase on John;[197] for John more than anyone makes many difficulties which hold up the reader. Nor was I allowed to stop there: there began to be a demand for Luke,[198] for there are many things in

* * * * *

188 *Disputatiuncula de tedio, pavore, tristicia Iesu, instante crucis hora, deque verbis visus est mortem deprecari: 'Pater, si fieri potest, transeat a me calix iste.'* See Epp 108–11. At the time of the publication of the *Lucubratiunculae* of 1503, Colet's replies to Erasmus' arguments were not available. These turned up later and were published in the Froben edition of 1518; see Ep 110 introduction.

189 *Exomologesis sive modus confitendi* (Basel: Froben 1524). See Allen Ep 1426. Several smaller works were printed with this work; see Epp 1310, 1324, 1329, 1347, 1427–8.

190 Louvain: Dirk Martens, [November] 1517. See Ep 710.

191 See Epp 755:4–7, 962.

192 Published in the period c January 1519–January 1521, in most cases by Martens at Louvain, though copies of these first editions, where they exist at all, are extremely rare. Froben's subsequent editions were printed in larger numbers and many more copies have survived. See Epp 916 (Corinthians), 956 (Galatians), 1062 (Ephesians, Philippians, Colossians, Thessalonians), 1043 (Timothy, Titus, Philemon), 1181 (Hebrews), 1171 (James), 1112 (Peter and Jude), and 1179 (John).

193 Matthäus Schiner; Ep 1295 introduction

194 Ep 1255

195 Epp 1270, 1342:273–81

196 Cf Ep 1333 n3.

197 Dedicated to Archduke Ferdinand; Ep 1333

198 Basel: Froben 30 August 1523

him which he shares with no other evangelist – so easy was it to find some 765
excuse for asking. This work was dedicated to the English king, Henry
VIII.[199] The addition of Mark[200] was then suggested to me by an eminent
friend,[201] that a gap in the middle of the work might not tempt someone to
interrupt its uniformity by adding something of his own. This was dedicated
to Francis I, king of France.[202] There remained the Acts of the Apostles,[203] 770
part of St Luke's Gospel, and those I dedicated to Pope Clement VII.[204] The
Apocalypse on no account admits of paraphrase. And so at this point my
paraphrases reached a fairly successful conclusion;[g] nor has any other work
of mine earned me less unpopularity than they have. I have also written a
commentary on two psalms,[205] being invited to undertake this by urgent 775
demands from certain quarters.[206] [h]Here, however, I am deterred not only
by the size and difficulty of the work but by the multitude of commentators,
such that there is a risk of their burying the message rather than explaining
it. The third psalm at any rate I expounded in paraphrase,[207] to please a
learned friend, Melchior Vianden.[208] I also wrote a paraphrase on the Lord's 780
Prayer,[209] at the request of Jost or Justus Weissenburg,[210] secretary of the

* * * * *

199 Ep 1381
200 Basel: Froben, December 1523
201 Unidentified
202 Ep 1400
203 Basel: Froben, February 1524
204 Ep 1414
205 The *Enarratio allegorica in primum psalmum* appeared in the *Lucubrationes* of 1515;
   Ep 327. A commentary on Psalm 2, with a preface in Froben's name, was
   appended to Erasmus' edition of Arnobius (Ep 1304), September 1522; see
   Allen V 100.
206 Henry VIII; see Allen Ep 2315:171–2.
207 *Paraphrasis in tertium psalmum*, first printed with the *Exomologesis* (n189); see Ep
   1427.
208 Ep 1257 n1
209 *Precatio dominica in septem portiones distributa* (Basel: Froben [1523]); Ep 1393.
210 Justus Ludovicus Decius (Jost Ludwig Dietz) of Weissenburg (Wissembourg)
   in Lower Alsace (c 1485–1545). C 1508 Decius, who had already acquired a
   thorough knowledge of commerce, finance, and mining in Moravia, Tyrol, and
   Hungary, settled in Cracow, where he joined the banking house of Jan Boner,
   an associate of the Fuggers. In May 1520 Decius became secretary to Sigismund
   I, king of Poland, whom he served as economic adviser and skilful diplomat. In
   1522, on one of his diplomatic journeys, Decius, who was also a bibliophile, an
   editor, and a patron of humanist scholars, visited Erasmus in Basel. In 1523 he
   arranged the reprinting of the *De conscribendis epistolis* in Cracow. Thereafter
   he corresponded with Erasmus and served as intermediary between Erasmus
   and other Polish admirers. Decius' own publications include a number of
   economic treatises and writings on Polish history.

king of Poland. I have lately finished the *Concio de misericordia Domini*,[211] for which I was asked by that saintly prelate Christopher, bishop of Basel, who had dedicated a chapel under that name;[212] and at the same time the *Comparatio virginitatis martyrii*,[213] asked for by a man of high character, Helias,   785
warden of the College of Maccabeites in Cologne.[214] The *Concio de puero Iesu*[215] I had written long before at the request of John Colet.[h 216] My *Methodus verae theologiae*, which had already gone through several editions,[217] I revised and enlarged in the year 1522,[218] [i]and again in the following year.[i 219]

For my part, I had formed the habit of boasting that, although I had   790
written so much, both light-hearted and serious, I had never yet attacked any mortal man in print by name; but some evil genius grudged me this enviable reputation. Not but what I have maintained my record of not writing to hurt to the extent of never drawing sword against anyone except under insufferable provocation; nor have I ever answered anyone without   795
overcoming by forbearance an adversary who had the advantage of me in scurrility. This is, I think, so clear from my publications that I have the right to claim this much credit without being criticized for boasting. At first it was my whole ambition to be attacked by no one and attack no one myself, and so ply my pen with a light heart without ever drawing blood. But in this I   800
was doubly disappointed: first because I was indeed attacked by many people most unpleasantly in published books, and even by those to whom I

* * * * *

211 *De immensa Dei misericordia concio* (Basel: Froben, September 1524); Epp 1456, 1464, 1474
212 The bishop Christoph von Utenheim (Ep 1332). For other references to the chapel, concerning which no information could be found, see Allen Epp 1456:9, 1474:1–2.
213 *Virginis et martyris comparatio*, first published in 1523 and then again, in enlarged form, in 1524; see Epp 1346, 1475.
214 Helias Marcaeus, warden of a convent of Benedictine nuns at Cologne that took its name from relics of the Maccabees possessed by the house; see Epp 842, 1475.
215 *Concio de puero Iesu a puero in schola Coletica nuper Londini instituta pronuncianda* (1511); Ep 175 introduction. Translation by Emily Kearns in CWE 29.
216 On Colet and his school, see n39 above.
217 A short *Methodus* was included among the introductory material in the *Novum instrumentum* of 1516. In the second edition, the *Novum Testamentum* of 1519, the *Methodus*, greatly amplified, appeared under the title *Ratio verae theologiae*. It was removed from subsequent editions of the New Testament since in November 1518 its long career as a separate work had already begun. See the introductions to Ep 745 and Allen Ep 1365. Cf lines 1579–80 of this letter.
218 Froben's edition of June 1522
219 The edition of 1523 had a new preface, Ep 1365. All earlier editions had had Ep 745 as preface.

had never given any cause; and secondly, because they were men whom I
could win no credit by defeating, while there was no honour – no profit,
even – in being matched against such creatures. Whenever therefore I am   805
driven to it, I remain laconic, I glance at the question in the fewest possible
words. Nor have I ever dedicated any such piece of mine to any fellow
creature: sometimes I neither expected nor wished them to survive,
sometimes I was unwilling to burden anyone with unpopularity, for I have
tried hard all my life to see that no trouble recoils from me onto my friends.   810
Maarten van Dorp, at the instigation of certain people I could name,[220]
opened the very first of these minor attacks on me;[221] and I replied to him as
one friend to another, defending my *Moria* and the New Testament together
in a single letter.[222] Nor did this cavalry skirmish cause any rift in our
friendship, for I knew that he did not stoop to this from any dislike of me,   815
but was young in those days and impressionable and was pushed into it by
others. He was followed by Jacques Lefèvre d'Etaples,[223] an honest man, a
good scholar, and an old friend of mine. In reply to him I took the line that I
preferred to suppose this a necessity, for which fate and not the individual
was responsible; and this incident, serious as it was, did not lead me to   820
renounce my friendship with him – even today the mutual good will
between us subsists unimpaired. Over this I lost twelve days' work. And not
long after, up jumped Edward Lee, a friend turned suddenly into an enemy,
whose attack on me showed by its form that he was not interested in taking
prisoners but wished to see Erasmus annihilated;[224] and him I answered in   825

* * * * *

220 Possibly Jan Briart (Epp 670 and 1299 n12) and Jacobus Latomus (Ep 934:4n)
221 Ep 304
222 Ep 337
223 See Ep 315 introduction. In his second edition of the Pauline Epistles (colophon
    date 1515, but see Ep 597:44n), Lefèvre criticized Erasmus' interpretation of
    Heb 2:7 (LB IX 68–80) in terms that Erasmus considered a charge of blasphemy.
    Erasmus replied with his *Apologia ad Jacobum Fabrum Stapulensem* (Louvain:
    Dirk Martens, August 1517 / LB IX 17–66). Cf Ep 597:37n.
224 On Lee, see Ep 765. His attacks upon Erasmus' annotations to the New
    Testament provoked an acrimonious controversy which lasted somewhat over
    two years (1518–20). More than seventy of Erasmus' letters in that period
    reflect his preoccupation with Lee's criticisms, which culminated in the
    printing at Paris (by Gilles de Gourmont for Konrad Resch) of the *Annotationes
    in Annotationes Novi Testamenti Desiderii Erasmi*, February 1520. Ep 1037 was
    Lee's preface; Ep 1061 and a letter addressed to the students at Louvain were
    also included. The controversy can be followed in detail in CWE 6 and 7, and a
    full account of it is found in A. Bludau *Die beiden ersten Erasmus Ausgaben des
    Neuen Testaments und ihre Gegner* (Freiburg 1902) 86–125.

three pamphlets,[225] though in the second edition[226] I left out the first of these
because it merely answered his poisonous, quarrelsome tirades, worthy of
any fishwife, from which the reader could derive neither profit nor pleasure.
On this, with the writing and the printing (for I corrected every page
myself), I wasted fifty days, as I have witnesses to prove. Then out crawled 830
Jacobus Latomus,[227] who was at the time a candidate for the highest honours
in theology,[228] which I know not how have for some years now been
awarded to hardly anyone in Louvain unless he has first published a sample
of his powers of malignant invention. To his book,[229] since in its twists and
turns it reflected its author's mind, I issued a more than laconic reply,[230] 835
refraining for the time being even from any expression of feeling, for in those
days I hoped that he would sometime adopt more straightforward behaviour. This meant a loss of three days, not counting the time taken to read his
pamphlets while I was travelling by carriage. They had also pressed
Atensis[231] to their cause; he was at that time vice-chancellor[232] of the 840
university there, an honourable man and in theology the best person they
had, a not uncivilized person and a fairly good friend of mine, but irascible
by nature. And there were experts there who, although capable of driving
the mildest nature into a frenzy, urged him at least on to his death; for his
age and state of health were not equal to the burden of such sorry business. 845
They had put him up, as I say, in a public lecture-room, on a solemn
university occasion,[233] to reflect on me with the most extraordinary
innuendo and indirect attacks, actually labelling me a heretic because (so he

* * * * *

225 The first, *Apologia qua respondet duabus invectivis E. Lei* (Antwerp: M. Hillen c
March 1520 / Ferguson *Opuscula* 236–303) took particular aim at Lee's version of
events in his prefatory epistles (see previous note). This was followed by two
long *Responsiones ad annotationes Ed. Lei* (Antwerp: M. Hillen, April and May
1520 / LB IX 123–284) in which Erasmus defended his edition of the New
Testament.
226 Ie, in the edition of Lee's *Annotationes*, together with Erasmus' two *Responsiones*, published by Froben in May 1520 at Erasmus' instigation. Ep 1100 was
Erasmus' preface.
227 Ep 934:4n. In 1519 Erasmus and Latomus quarrelled over the latter's
opposition to the teaching of Greek and Hebrew; see Ep 934 introduction.
228 Latomus received a doctorate in theology at Louvain in August 1519.
229 *De trium linguarum et studii theologici ratione* (Antwerp: M. Hillen 1519)
230 *Apologia contra Latomi dialogum* (Antwerp: J. Thibault, n d and Basel: Froben,
May 1519)
231 Jan Briart of Ath (Epp 670, 1299 n12)
232 See Ep 643:9n.
233 The circumstances are described in Ep 946 introduction.

said) I had spoken too highly of the estate of matrimony.[234] On this point he had already given me satisfaction, first by sending Maarten van Dorp and 850 Gillis van Delft to talk to me on the subject,[235] and then in friendly conversation with himself. Later on therefore, when I published a reply,[236] it was addressed not to Atensis but to the suspicions of men in general, and more in his interest than my own. And because there was a plot behind all this, one disturbance succeeded another;[237] for they thought that if they 855 could thus drive me out of the university, all the ancient languages and the humanities would be off too and never be heard of again. About the same time a clamour was raised against me by monks at London in England,[238] at Paris in France,[239] and at Brussels in Brabant,[240] and raised in sermons before crowded audiences, because I had put *In principio erat sermo* in my version 860 instead of *In principio erat verbum*. This disturbance too I suppressed with a pamphlet,[241] making it clear that the authors of the uproar were simply insane, though that was clear enough to educated people even before I uttered a word. The very first person to attack my version of the New Testament had been an obscure man[242] whom I thought sufficiently 865 answered in a letter which did not mention his name.[243]

And now it seemed that we should hear no more of this trouble, when

* * * * *

234 In the *Encomium matrimonii*; see lines 652–61 above.
235 See Ep 946 introduction.
236 *Apologia pro declamatione de laude matrimonii* (Basel: Froben 1519 / LB IX 105–12)
237 Briart's disciples renewed the attack in the aftermath of Erasmus' dispute with Latomus; see Ep 946.
238 The Franciscan Henry Standish (Ep 608:15n), bishop of St Asaph, who denounced Erasmus in a sermon in St Paul's churchyard; see LB IX 111E–112B and Ep 1126:21–98.
239 The identity of the Paris assailant is unknown; see LB IX 112D.
240 Erasmus' antagonist in Brussels was a young Carmelite and bachelor of theology egged on by his mentor to attack Erasmus in a sermon; LB IX 112C–D. The mentor was presumably Baechem (lines 928ff). The bachelor may have been Jan Robyns (Ep 946:4n).
241 *Apologia palam refellens quorundam seditiosos clamores apud populum ac magnates, quibus ut impie factum iactitant, quod in Evangelio Ioannis verterit, 'In principio erat sermo'* (Louvain: Dirk Martens, February 1520), with Ep 1072 as preface. An enlarged version, minus Ep 1072, was published by Froben in May 1520, along with the *Responsiones* to Lee (line 826 above) and the *Epistolae eruditorum virorum* (Ep 1083 introduction). LB IX 111–22 reprints the enlarged edition.
242 Perhaps Hieronymus Dungersheim, the Leipzig theologian whose criticisms of Erasmus' *Novum Testamentum* are found in Ep 554.
243 No answer in letter form survives. However, in the *Annotationes* Erasmus does reply to Dungersheim's arguments without naming the 'friend, versed in letters, who argues in his letter'; see LB VI 868C.

lo and behold in Spain, all of a sudden, up jumps Diego López Zúñiga[244] –
what sort of a man is clear from what he writes: boastful, shameless, stupid,
a great admirer of his own perfections, and a bitter controversialist, born,   870
one might think, for just such sorry business. Rumour of something
frightful had preceded, and the book[245] itself was full of extraordinary
delusions. I answered him briefly,[246] and never so much disliked answering
anyone. He proceeded to Rome to enjoy the triumphs of his exquisite
performance, and again put out an attack one me, which he entitled   875
Blasphemiae et impietates Erasmi[247] – the maddest thing that ever appeared.
As a result, the order of cardinals had forbidden its printing; and when none
the less it was printed secretly by certain monks, who regard the pope's
authority as sacrosanct when it happens to suit them, they again forbade the
sale.[248] Scarcely had I answered him,[249] briefly and with the contempt that he   880
deserved, when another pamphlet took the air, a forerunner of those three
in which, like a leading actor, he left no doubt of his prowess in scurrility.[250]
So I answered that one too,[251] by the oil of the same lamp, as the saying
goes.[252] A brother stood at his right hand, one Sancho Carranza,[253] a
theologian of Alcalá, to defend Zúñiga at least in the three passages which   885
he had chosen and, in the process of trying to make me out a heretic, to
advertise his own effrontery as a traducer. His pamphlet too I answered.
And Rome finds readers for such trash as this! Some people must read it, for
some buy it, though there is hardly anywhere there where you can find on
sale the works of the Fathers, which make for true religion. ʲIn fact, plenty of   890
people believe it right for the standing of the church to be defended by such
support as this; and though the chief point in their programme is that the
constitutions of the Roman pontiff should carry weight everywhere, he
shows in fact what respect they deserve from other nations by so often
making game of the edicts of popes and cardinals in Rome itself with   895

* * * * *

244 Ep 1260 n36
245 The *Annotationes contra Erasmum Roterodamum* of 1520; see Ep 1260 n36.
246 The *Apologia* of September 1521; see Ep 1277 n1.
247 See Ep 1260 n45.
248 See Ep 1302 n26. Cf lines 914–16.
249 With the *Apologia adversus libellum Stunicae* of August 1522; see Ep 1260 n45.
250 The *Libellus triorum illorum voluminum praecursor* of 1522; see Ep 1312 n4 and
     lines 901–2 of this letter.
251 In the *Apologia ad prodromon Stunicae*; see Ep 1312 n5.
252 An allusion, perhaps, to the adage 'oleum et operam perdere' (I iv 62), to spend
     one's time fruitlessly.
253 On Carranza, his pamphlet, and Erasmus' reply, see Ep 1277 n8.

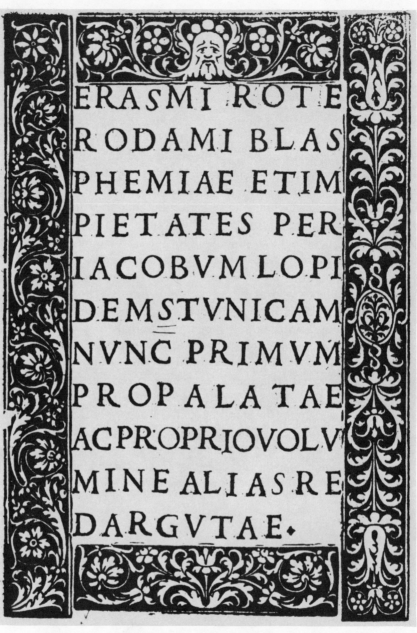

ERASMI ROTE
RODAMI BLAS
PHEMIAE ET IM
PIETATES PER
IACOBVM LOPI
DEM STVNICAM
NVNC PRIMVM
PROPALA TAE
AC PROPRIO VOLV
MINE ALIAS RE
DARGVTAE.

Diego López Zúñiga *Erasmi Roterodami blasphemiae et impietates*
title-page
Rome: A. Bladus 1522
Centre for Reformation and Renaissance Studies,
Victoria University, University of Toronto

impunity.[254] They tell you in reply that Zúñiga is tolerated in Rome as Pasquil is.[255] Pasquil is not so mad as that, and he performs only once a year. This man neglects everything else and makes this his sole business; and this he thinks a piece of rare good fortune.[j] Of Carranza I hear nothing, but Zúñiga is hard at work even now. He ranges up and down, collecting   900 support, and is pressing the pope for leave to publish those three famous pamphlets[256] with official approval. Personally I am astonished at some men's abandoned impudence: they take it upon themselves to attack with great virulence those who are working for the benefit of others, they are so often detected in barefaced errors, and yet, as though they had won the day,   905 they take the field again and deliberately challenge their opponents. They offer no excuses in the mean time; they continue to throw mud at other people. I myself at least, if anything of the sort had happened to me, should hide my head in solitude, and be ashamed to take the stage again before a learned audience. The man who errs while trying to be helpful secures our   910 forgiveness; but who can pardon those who make the most disgraceful errors in the course of an attack on a fellow creature? [k]Zúñiga had published the first fruits of his malevolence at Alcalá;[257] but when such a book found few buyers, he carried off his wares to Rome like any bagman. When Pope Leo refused him leave to publish the rest of his trumped-up accusations,[258]   915 he put out some things after the pope's death during the interregnum,[259] as I said, and would have published more, had not an edict of the cardinals[260] restricted him more than once; for Adrian hung about for several months in Spain before proceeding to Rome. Then, after a vain attempt to get leave,

* * * * *

254 See lines 914–26.
255 Pasquin or Pasquil (*Pasquino* or *Pasquillo* in Italian) was the name popularly given to a mutilated piece of ancient statuary unearthed in Rome in 1501 and set up near the Piazza Navona. It soon became the annual custom on St Mark's Day (25 April) to post on the statue anonymous satirical Latin verses, whether political, ecclesiastical, or personal. In the course of the sixteenth century it became common all over Europe for anonymous Pasquins to write satires and lampoons called pasquinades.
256 See n250 above.
257 Ie, the *Annotationes contra Erasmum*; see n245 above.
258 Ep 1213:37–41, Allen Epp 1581:191–6, 2385:69–72, and *Apologia ad Blasphemias Stunicae* LB IX 357B.
259 There was a lapse of nine months between the death of Leo x (1 December 1521) and the arrival of Adrian VI in Rome (28 August 1522) from Spain. Zúñiga's *Blasphemiae et impietates Erasmi* (line 876) and his *Libellus praecursor* (lines 881–2) were published at Rome in this period.
260 See line 877.

from Adrian this time,[261] to publish what he had written, as soon as the pope   920
was dead[262] he returned to his tricks and, while the cardinals were
incarcerated and fighting over the choice of a new pope, he issued a number
of conclusions which he had extracted from the whole range of my work,[263]
and was meanwhile getting ready to bring the rest before the public. And so
he would have done, had not the authority of Clement VII suppressed the   925
man,[264] who by this time was clearly raving mad. To this book likewise I
wrote a brief reply,[265] although I had already answered before.[k]

There is in Louvain in the theological faculty a certain Carmelite[266] who
has a habit of boasting that he uses his tongue rather than his pen; and a
tongue he most certainly has, though it is only fit for the purpose suggested   930
by Catullus.[267] This man's pastime, over his wine, in the theology
lecture-room and even in public sermons, is to call me a heretic; and he
makes such good progress that all sane men now despair of his sanity. His
example is followed by several others,[268] who think it is quite enough to give
them the air of eminent divines if they call anyone they please a heretic, a   935
schismatic, or a forger, as though any bargee could not do the same. This
man publicly, in his ordinary lectures, accused me of two trifling misdemeanours, heresy and falsification of the Scriptures, because in the First
Epistle to the Corinthians I translated only what I found in the Greek: 'We
shall not all sleep, but we shall all be changed.' This scurrilous attack with all   940
its impudence I rejected in a pamphlet,[269] but with no personal abuse and
even suppressing the man's name; and even so he is indignant. Very well: if
he himself thinks it fair that someone should be indignant with him for
wiping off mud thrown by anyone on his own clean white habit (the only
clean thing about him), I will agree that it is fair for him to be indignant with   945
me for rejecting such scurrilous impudence, even leaving his name out of it

* * * * *

261 See Ep 1331:40–3, Allen Ep 1415:13–17, and *Apologia ad Stunicae Conclusiones*
     LB IX 385A.
262 14 September 1523
263 *Conclusiones principaliter suspectae et scandalosae quae reperiuntur in libris Erasmi
     Roterodami* (Rome 1523)
264 Allen Epp 1432:35–9, 1433:13–15, 1438:14–16
265 *Apologia ad Stunicae Conclusiones*, the prefatory letter for which (Ep 1428) is
     dated 1 March 1524. It was published with the *Exomologesis* (Basel: Froben
     1524).
266 Baechem (Ep 1254 n6)
267 Ie, to lick the arse and the sandals of a peasant; Catullus 98.3–4
268 See Ep 1330:53–6.
269 *Apologia de loco taxato qui est in epistola Pauli ad Corinthios ... 'Omnes quidem
     resurgemus'* ... (Basel: Froben 1522). Text in LB IX 433–42

for the moment. And though his behaviour has earned him the disapproval
of all decent people, the one man whose support he can rely on is himself.
He declaims against scandalous pamphlets. No pamphlet is scandalous
which defends an innocent man against the inventions of a raving lunatic; it   950
is a scurrilous tongue that uses barefaced lies to bring such an atrocious
charge against a man who deserves none of it – who in fact deserves
gratitude. The same man lately had detected four heresies in my *Colloquia*,[270]
and on this score was triumphant everywhere; over the wine, in sermons
and conversation and lectures all his talk was of heresies. 'To this slander   955
also I replied briefly.[271] This man's outrageous utterances had been silenced
by Pope Adrian, who issued a diploma in which he gave strict instructions
that no one should vilify Erasmus.[272] He kept silence for a time, however
reluctantly. Soon after the pope's death[273] he returned to his old uproarious
behaviour, just as though orders rightly issued by the pope ought not to be   960
permanently binding. So he resumed his true self, and made amends for his
former silence by the energy of his vituperation. He was lecturing on St
Matthew's Gospel, and not seldom aimed a stone of some sort at me from his
rostrum in the school of theology, so brazenly that no hired buffoon could be
worse and so comically that a good part of those who attended his lectures   965
came solely for the entertainment; some think he plays the fool deliberately
in order to attract an audience. I had put out a defence of that passage in
Corinthians 'We shall all arise but we shall not all be changed.'[274] In this I had
disposed of his false accusations with arguments so solid that, as they say,
you could get your fingers round them; and yet, exactly as though I had not   970
said a word, he was not ashamed to speak like this in public. 'In this,' said
he, 'Erasmus has many supporters, but I will not conceal the truth. If
something is held by the church, whatever contradicts that is false and
heretical; what the church holds is in contradiction to Erasmus' reading;
therefore Erasmus' reading is false and heretical.' In the third chapter of   975
Matthew, for the old reading *Poenitentiam agite*, 'Repent ye,' my version had
Resipiscite. 'Here,' says our friend, 'Erasmus denies penitence,' as though
poenitentiam agere in Latin meant the same as to do penance enjoined on you
for your faults; or as though the word *poenitentia* came from *poena*,
punishment and not rather from *pone tenere*, grasping something from   980

* * * * *

270 See Epp 1299–1302.
271 In Ep 1301, which was printed with the first edition of the *Catalogus
   lucubrationum*
272 See Allen Epp 1481:62–4, 1359:2–3.
273 See n262 above.
274 See n269 above.

behind, understanding it (that is) in retrospect, as Greek uses *metanoia*; or as
though penance in the sense of making amends was done away with if the
word used to command a sinner is *resipiscere*. In chapter 6, his theology
positively blossomed. He declared that nothing could have been more
absurd than my introducing *remitte* and *remittimus* for forgiveness in place of   98
dimitte and *dimittimus*. *Remittere*, he said, means to send something back to
someone; and does anyone pray nowadays that God should send back to
him the sins that have been abolished by confession? It astonishes me that
he should not equally make fun of the Creed and even of the Gospels
themselves, for speaking so often of the 'remission' of sins; why does he not   99
insist that they should put 'dimission'? Why does he not turn his wit against
the seventh chapter of Luke, where *remitto* is used twice, in 'Her sins, which
are many, are forgiven her, for she loved much,' and then in 'Thy sins are
forgiven thee'? This Coroebus[275] of ours has failed to detect that the
nonsense he talked in vilifying my version applies equally to the standard   99
text of the church. In the second chapter of Matthew, for 'all Jerusalem' I had
put 'the whole city of Jerusalem,' not rejecting the familiar version but
expressing more exactly the translator's intention. On this he demonstrated,
starting from the substitutions in scholastic logic, that the same sense could
not be conveyed both by my words and by those of the translator, because   10(
my words do not admit of the substitution of the general for the particular or
of the particular for the general. This sort of rubbish is unloaded every day
by a man advanced in years who is the leading spirit of the Louvain
theologians; and then they wonder that the pope's policy makes so little
progress, when such are the men and methods used to carry it out! Men   10(
worthy indeed to be supported by the world of idleness! A theologian of
great authority, who well deserves that intelligent citizens should entrust
their children to him! For[276] he has taken upon himself the additional office
of protecting the multitudes from the humanities.[1] He has here a boon

* * * * *

275 See *Adagia* II ix 64: *Stultior Coroebo* (Sillier than Coroebus). Coroebus tried to
    number the waves of the sea although he could only count to five.
276 At this point, Allen, in his attempt to harmonize the texts of 1523 and 1524,
    committed a pair of blunders which the editors of LB had managed to avoid.
    First, he mistakenly repeated the sentence with which the inserted passage 'I'
    begins: 'Et huic calumniae paucis respondimus.' Second, he relegated to a
    footnote the sentence which is the real conclusion to insert 'I': 'Nam hanc
    quoque prouinciam suscipit, quo plures arceat a bonis literis.' We have
    eliminated the unwarranted repetition and put the banished sentence back in
    its rightful place.

companion, another man who has spent sleepless nights composing an 1010
attack on me,[277] which he means to publish, if he could find a vicar-general
of his order as mad as he is.[278] Nothing has done more to make Luther
acceptable to the world than the characters of such men as this.

I added moreover two or three defensive pieces to the New Testament
when it was about to appear, foreseeing that there would be no shortage of 1015
malicious attacks on it.[279] There are also letters mixed in with the others or
printed separately, which could be regarded as defences, for instance those
addressed to Marcus Laurinus and Jacob of Hoogstraten.[280] But it is a relief to
pass on from this record of controversy. [m]And it seemed already that
controversy was over, had not Ulrich von Hutten arisen, suddenly and quite 1020
unexpectedly, a friend turned all at once into an enemy;[281] such is the power
of malignant gossip over men who have no ballast.[282] No one ever attacked
me with more hostility than he;[283] and yet I intended not to answer, had not
influential friends judged that my reputation was at stake. And so I
published my *Spongia*,[284] the title of which already promised that I would 1025

* * * * *

277 Vincentius Theoderici (Ep 1196) was the driving spirit behind an *apologia*
   attacking Erasmus' *Exomologesis* (Ep 1426) and the *Epistola de esu carnium* (Ep
   1274 n7); Allen Ep 1571:65n. Owing to the reluctance of Theoderici's
   vicar-general (lines 1011–12, Allen Epp 1582:1–2, 1603:37–40), the work was
   not published until March 1525.
278 This sentence appears only in the first edition, 1523.
279 In the first edition of 1516, Erasmus included an *apologia* beginning with the
   words 'Iam ut paucis occurram Apologia' (LB VI **2r–**3r). To the second
   edition of 1519 he added an additional apology entitled *Capita argumentorum
   contra morosos quosdam ac indoctos* (ibidem **3v–***4r).
280 Epp 1342 (Laurinus) and 1006 (Hoogstraten)
281 See Ep 1331 n24.
282 See n297 below.
283 In the *Expostulatio cum Erasmo Roterodamo*, published during the summer at
   Strasbourg by Johann Schott; the text is in Böcking II 180–248, and an
   annotated English translation by Randolph J. Klawiter is in *The Polemics of
   Erasmus of Rotterdam and Ulrich von Hutten* (Notre Dame 1977) 59–138. Hutten
   wrote the *Expostulatio* in Mulhouse (Mülhausen) in the spring of 1523, after
   seeing Ep 1342 (published with the *Catalogus lucubrationum* in April), in which
   Erasmus repudiated all connection with Lutheranism.
284 *Spongia adversus aspergines Hutteni* (Basel: Froben, September 1523). Text in
   Böcking II 262–324; critical edition by C. Augustijn in ASD IX-1 91–210;
   annotated English translation in Klawiter *Polemics* (n283 above) 139–303. Ep
   1378 was the preface to the first edition, which was still at press when Hutten
   died in Zürich c 31 August. This circumstance, as Erasmus realized, robbed
   the *Spongia* of much of its welcome and caused him, first, to insert Ep 1389 as
   preface to the second edition (c October 1523) and, second, to insert this

write with moderation, though some people think I did nothing of the kind; while I can say with a clear conscience that I strove really hard to reflect on no one in passing while defending myself, and did my best to spare Hutten himself so far as the subject permitted. Those who wish Hutten's reputation to be universally watertight should reserve their indignation for the men whose falsehoods drove him into this position, and still more for those (but really they are the same people) who use all their endeavours to make me take pen in hand against a man even when he is dead. This however they shall never force me to; to be raving mad is not to my taste, and I perceive that this business has now issued in mere madness. And so I have no mind henceforward to take issue with prizefighting pamphlets of this kind.[285] My first effort shall be to keep my conscience clear in the sight of Christ, and I trust that the reasons behind my policy will be endorsed by all men of good will. As for those noisy ruffians who seem quite unaware of the difference between writing and raving, I for my part would rather do them a mischief in deeds than in words, if a Christian could wish to hurt anyone at all. Those who represent my *Spongia* as vindictive and insolent will please remember one thing: the special affection I had for Hutten's gifts, the generosity with which I recommended him to the public in so many of my publications when he was not yet well known, and all the letters in which I praised him to my friends,[286] and specially to the cardinal of Mainz.[287] In one particular letter[288] I compare him with Thomas More, the most upright, fair-minded, friendly, intelligent man on whom the sun has shone for many generations. How emphatically unlike him Hutten has shown himself, and falsified my praise of him! In my work on the New Testament, which is now in its third

* * * * *

apologetic passage into the 1524 edition of the *Catalogus*. In Allen Ep 1347:69–71, Erasmus names Froben and Beatus Rhenanus as the friends who instigated the publication of the *Spongia*.

285 Hutten's principal defender was Otto Brunfels (Allen Ep 1405 introduction), whose *Pro Vlricho Hutteno defuncto ad Erasmi Roterodami Spongiam responsio* was published by Johann Schott in Strasbourg early in 1524 (text in Böcking II 325–51). Some time later, possibly in the summer of 1524 (Allen Ep 1466:26–7) the *Judicium de Spongia Erasmi Roterodami* of Erasmus Alber (Allen Ep 1466:26n) was printed by Johann Setzer in Haguenau (text in Böcking II 373–8); see WA-Br III 158–9. For a time, Erasmus suspected that Hermannus Buschius (Ep 1291 n4) was the real author; Allen Epp 1466:26–8, 1523:102–4.

286 Epp 745:18–21, 778:53–5, 874:6, 967:115–21, 968:24–6, 1009:78–83, 1114:13–16, 1115:47–9

287 Albert of Brandenburg (Ep 661), to whom Epp 745, 968, and 1009 (see preceding note) had been addressed

288 Ep 999, written at Hutten's request, the earliest biography of More. See especially lines 5–11.

edition,[289] I sing his praises with no ordinary warmth.[290] Will they please remember something else: I never gave him any cause to withdraw from our friendship (and friendship ought not to be severed without very grave cause), and furthermore it was he who not only breached the laws of friendship but delivered the most bitter attacks out of a kind of ambush on 1055 the reputation and life of his friend. The facts absolutely speak for themselves: Hutten had no other purpose in writing against me as he did except to assassinate with his pen one whom his sword could not reach. Regarding himself as a man of valour, 'He is a poor old man,' he thought, 'he is an invalid, he is frightened and feeble; he will not be long for this world 1060 when he reads such a savage attack.' That those were his thoughts was shown by the vaunting words he used.

I will now appeal to the honest opinion of those who knew Hutten at close quarters, though even men who were unacquainted with him are aware that he always lived a soldier's life, to use no harsher term; and yet all 1065 through my Spongia I never cast in his teeth that lascivious living which not even his pitiful disease could teach him to abandon, nor the gaming and the wenching, the bankruptcy brought on by his extravagance, the massive debts, the disappointed creditors. And then the outrages he planned – the extortion of money from the Carthusians,[291] the mutilation of several 1070 monks,[292] the assaults on the public highway on three abbots[293] (a crime for which one of his servants was seized and beheaded by the count palatine[294]) – these, I say, and very many others of the sort are public knowledge everywhere; but I revive none of these old sores in the Spongia, nor do I answer an enemy's fire by charging him with true and notorious crimes 1075 though he has brazenly poured such a cesspit of utterly false accusations on

* * * * *

289 1522

290 In a note on Thess 1:2, also found in the editions of 1516 and 1519. The passage pertaining to Hutten is printed in Böcking I 103–4.

291 As part of his private 'war upon the Romanists,' Hutten in the autumn of 1522 declared a feud against the Carthusians of Strasbourg, who purchased peace at the cost of 2,000 Rhenish florins (with 2.53 grams fine gold each, then worth about £490 gros Flemish); Paul Kalkoff *Ulrich von Hutten und die Reformation* Quellen und Forschungen zur Reformationsgeschichte 4 (Leipzig 1920; repr New York 1971) 429–32. Cf Allen Ep 1445:40.

292 Cf Allen Ep 1445:40–1, where Erasmus states that Hutten had cut off the ears of two Dominicans. According to Kalkoff (see preceding note) 426, Erasmus is the only source for this incident.

293 This incident in Hutten's 'war on the Romanists' took place in 1522. Erasmus' information came from Eppendorf (Ep 1283 n4); see Allen Ep 1934:260–70. Cf Allen Epp 1356:51–4, 1445:41–3.

294 Ludwig v (1478–1544)

a friend, and one moreover who has done him service. In my whole *Spongia* no one is reviled as a robber or a ravisher, a highwayman or a bankrupt. What I say there in general terms aims not at the denigration of any single man but at the good of all. And some people find me savage in the *Spongia*!   10 What trivial things he protests against, what savage language he chooses to magnify them! For my part, with so much widely familiar material, how could I have failed to be eloquent, were I not by nature so violently opposed to speaking ill of anyone? I refer to the circulation of that letter to the cardinal of Mainz[295] in language which only the man himself is likely to understand.   10 Another thing he did that was even more treacherous[296] I do not touch on, for I had forgiven him both in the name of our friendship; and he thought it honourable, because I asked to be excused from a discussion with him, to rant like this against a friend. All this to give pleasure to two or three people[297] with whom he had struck up a new friendship which was not   10 destined to do him much good. If I had replied to his false accusations with falsehoods of my own, it would have been tit for tat, except that a man's case is the more likely to win sympathy who has suffered an injury before he enters the fray. And now I am thought vindictive, I, who after suffering injury from so many false accusations do not make use even of his real and   10

* * * * *

295 Ep 1033. Cf *Spongia* ASD IX-9 192–3.
296 Cf *Spongia* ASD IX-1 193–4. Hutten's 'other treachery' is identified in a letter of 8 May 1524 to Luther (Allen Ep 1445:49–52), where Erasmus alleges that in the spring of 1520 Hutten, already conspiring against the emperor, had 'extorted' from Erasmus several letters of recommendation to the imperial court (Epp 1114–5), his sole purpose being to exploit the emperor's name in the hunt for a wife. This version of events reads back into 1520 the hostility to Charles v which Hutten did not conceive until after the condemnation of Luther at the Diet of Worms in 1521. When he secured the letters of recommendation from Erasmus in Louvain, Hutten was on his way to the Hapsburg court at Brussels (Ep 1113:42), where he hoped to find employment and support for his great project of a united Germany, free of Rome, under the leadership of Charles v. It is possible that Erasmus was later reproached for having lent his support to someone already regarded at court as a dangerous man, but, at the time of his visit to Erasmus in Louvain, Hutten would not yet have known that he was so regarded (Kaegi 496 n3).
297 Although he believed that all his 'Lutheran' opponents had urged Hutten to write against him and that members of the reformed party in Basel had supplied Hutten with some of the information used in the *Expostulatio*, Erasmus' particular wrath fell upon Heinrich Eppendorf (Ep 1283 n4), who had been his intermediary with Hutten in Basel and Mulhouse, and who, Erasmus believed, had deliberately engineered the breach between him and Hutten; Allen Epp 1376:17–31, 1384:67–8, 1389:52–9, 1437:24ff, and *Spongia* ASD IX-1 172:130–3.

notorious crimes in my own defence. To get me into trouble they have
already published a letter from Martin Luther,[298] written privately to a
friend, about my *Spongia*. How much weight should be attached to this
opinion of Luther's I do not now inquire. I at least remain unmoved by it;
what I want to know is, why those who published this letter did not make   1100
public at the same time letters from Philippus Melanchthon, in which he
utterly rejects this attempt of Hutten's as pestilential to the cause of the
gospel, and more than once calls it madness. I have in my possession three
letters of his written to different friends in which he abominates the rabid
pamphlets to which this new gospel subjects us from time to time.[299] Not but   1105
what he has written at greater length to others. The cunning fellows keep
these pieces dark, venting their fury meanwhile in frenzied pamphlets with
no author's name or a fictitious one,[300] and then go on to boast that they are
ready to die ten deaths for the gospel's sake. Why then do they not make
their case in Rome? The spoken word carries great force. Why do they not   1110
vent their fury on the emperor no less than the pope? Because it is more
dangerous? What then has become of their readiness for martyrdom? They
ought at least to show him their case, even if they are reluctant to challenge
him. It has not escaped me that this was the strategy of some men I could
name who falsely boast themselves to be champions of the gospel – to   1115
overwhelm me with frenzied pamphlets to stop me from making any move
against Luther.[301] Let them suppose that I have been stoned to death: will
they at once be more successful? They do not stop to consider how much

* * * * *

298 Luther to Conradus Pellicanus (n309 below) in Basel, 1 October 1523;
published, without Pellicanus' name, with the *Judicium* of Erasmus Alber (n285
above). Text in Böcking II 379–80, WA-Br III 160–1.

299 Two of these letters can be identified with certainty: one to Oswald Ülin in
Ravensburg, 24 August 1523 (CR 1 627), a copy of which Botzheim sent to
Erasmus (Scheible I no 297); and the other to Johannes Oecolampadius in
Basel, 8 September 1523 (BAO no 173), in which Oecolampadius is asked to
convey the Wittenbergers' disapproval of Hutten's pamphlet to Erasmus.
Three other letters in which Melanchthon condemns the *Expostulatio* are
extant: two to Georgius Spalatinus (CR 1 nos 245, 253) and one to Joachim
Camerarius (ibidem no 254). One of these could have been the third letter in
Erasmus' possession.

300 See n285 above. Cf also lines 114–17.

301 Cf Allen Ep 1437:101–3, 2 April 1524, where Erasmus reports having learned
from Johannes Fabri (Ep 1260 n22) that the policy of Luther's followers was to
use threats to frighten him off from attacking Luther in print. In November
1523, Erasmus had informed Fabri that he was at work on the *De libero arbitrio*
(Allen Ep 1397:15), which is presumably the publication that the Lutherans
wished to prevent with their threats and 'frenzied pamphlets.' In this

harm I could have done, and still can do, to their cause if I had as great a
passion for vengeance as they have for violence. Who would not recognize
in this that spirit of the Gospels which the world has not seen for a thousand
years? Very well: let it be gospel teaching that we should pour frenzied
scurrilities upon the guilty. When it comes to discharging barefaced lies on
those who are quite innocent, does this too follow the gospel pattern? The
physician in the gospel pours wine into the wounds, but he pours in oil as
well, and it is wine not vinegar. Some of these men pour in not wine but
deadly poison. They kill no man with the sword, but more villainously with
tongue and pen.

And yet they have nothing they can bring against me except that I am
reluctant to risk my own neck by professing beliefs which I do not hold, or
regard as doubtful, or reject, and which would do no good if I did profess
them. Apart from that, has anyone been a more active opponent in print of
putting one's trust in ceremonies; of superstition concerning food and
liturgy and prayer; of those who give more weight to human inventions than
to Holy Scripture, who value the decrees of man more than the commandments of God, who put more trust in the saints than in Christ himself; of
academic theology, corrupted as it is by philosophic and scholastic
quibbling; of the rash practice of laying down rules for every mortal thing; of
the topsy-turvy judgments of the multitude? How far I am from flattery of
princes, even the greatest of them, my books are enough to show. This, and
very much else, which I have taught according to the measure of grace
accorded me, I have taught steadfastly, but never standing in the way of any
man who had something better to teach. And they say Erasmus has taught
nothing but rhetoric! I wish they would persuade my friends of that, the
foolish babblers, who steadfastly maintain that all Luther's teaching has
been drawn from what I have written. Not that I grudge Luther any credit on
that score; he is welcome to the whole of it, provided the gospel is glorified.
My misdeeds amount to this: I am all for moderation, and the reason why I
have a bad name with both sides is that I exhort both parties to adopt a more
peaceable policy. Freedom I have no objection to, if it is seasoned with
charity. But this mad-dog scurrility can produce nothing but sedition and
bloodshed. If we speak ill of the Roman church, and Rome in turn advertises
what we have done wrong, this will surely provide an agreeable spectacle

* * * * *

connection, Erasmus was, in the spring and summer of 1524, particularly
suspicious of Wolfgang Capito (Ep 1290), whom he believed to be an
accomplice of Eppendorf and also the moving spirit behind the publication of
Brunfels' *Responsio* to the *Spongia*; Allen Epp 1437:99–101, 1459:63–6, 1485,
1496:108–13.

for the enemies of our religion. Clement professes himself ready to heal the
corruption of the church; he dispatches a legate who is as fair-minded and
civilized as one could wish – and all they do is to abuse him,[302] as though
what they really enjoyed was universal chaos. On their head be it, if the
princes at length lose all patience and start venting their fury without
distinction on the livelihood and lives of most of us. If that happens, I fear
some people will approve my moderate policy, and it will be too late. Who
can endure certain men on that side whom I could name who, using the
gospel as a pretext, obey neither princes nor popes, and do not listen to
Luther himself except when it suits them?[303] On all other occasions they
regard even Luther as a mere man led by no inspiration, or consider that he
did not mean what he said. My offence is rank indeed if I merely wish to see
what is now done in a subversive spirit done without subversion and with
the consent of princes. But if the princes seem unlikely to act for the best,
what crime have I committed if I warn them? I do not restrain those who
wish to put out the fire; but I do condemn those who pour oil on the flames
and are in a great hurry to remove by violent drugs a disease which has by
now grown chronic over a thousand years and more, to the very great peril
of the whole body. The apostles showed toleration to the Jews, who could
not be weaned away from their ingrained taste for the Law; and the same, I
believe, they would rightly show to these men who for so many centuries
have accepted the authority of all those councils and popes and distinguished teachers, and find some difficulty in swallowing the new wine of
this modern teaching. And for the time being I assume that one party is
wrong and the other entirely right in what they maintain. Let both sides
pursue Christ's business on Christian principles, and they will see what I
have to contribute as my own humble share.

But I am carried away, and must return to Hutten. How I wish those
men who first aroused this tragic business and revive it now[304] would leave
Hutten's ghost in peace and not force me into a position where, as the saying
goes, I must do battle with the dead! I do not think, however, that it is
fighting with the dead to reply to a libellous book which someone has left

* * * * *

302 Lorenzo Cardinal Campeggi (Ep 961), to whom Erasmus had dedicated his
    paraphrase on Ephesians (Ep 1062). Appointed legate in January 1524,
    Campeggi was treated to a good deal of derision and abuse when he arrived in
    the Empire; Pastor x 111–12.
303 Erasmus was by this time (September 1524) thoroughly fed up with nearly all
    the leaders of the reform movement in Switzerland and Alsace, from Zwingli
    on down. His sentiments are expressed more fully in a letter to Melanchthon;
    Allen Ep 1496:67–166.
304 See nn285 and 297 above.

1155

1160

1165

1170

1175

1180

1185

behind him at his death like a poisoned javelin; but wantonly to accuse a
dead man who cannot reply – that would be to fight with the dead. When I
heard the news of Hutten's death, I prayed in a Christian spirit for God's
mercy on his soul; and I hear that on his deathbed he expressed regret that
he had been deceived by the cunning of certain persons into attacking a   1
friend.

I have, I perceive, wandered somewhat far from my theme; all the
same, I cannot refrain from pouring out in your friendly ear something I
have learned these last few days, to give you a clear idea how far from the
spirit of the gospel these men are, who seek out and invent causes of discord   1
and yet make such great play with the word 'gospel.' This is the story. The
person responsible[305] you will easily guess. It had often been reported to me
that he spoke of me in an unfriendly spirit, but I thought nothing of it, so
much so that I did not even protest in conversation. At length, when the
news reached me that he had described me in offensive terms as the prophet   1
Balaam,[306] as though I had been hired to curse God's people, I did not think
such a monstrous calumny could be overlooked. Meeting the man by
chance, I took him aside and asked him if what had been told me was true.
He shuffled, and said neither no nor yes. When pressed, he at length replied
that it had been said by a French merchant,[307] who by that time had left. And   1
it may be true that a merchant said it, but it was this man he learned it from.
When I insisted that he should give reasons why he thought I deserved such

* * * * *

305 Guillaume Farel (1489–1565), the future 'evangelist of French Switzerland.'
    Born in the Dauphiné, educated at Paris, and for a time member of the group of
    humanists and reformers at the court of bishop Guillaume Briçonnet at Meaux,
    Farel had by the end of 1521 embraced the Protestant faith. In the autumn of
    1523 he emigrated to Basel, where he joined Oecolampadius and other
    reformers, distinguishing himself by the intemperate zeal of his preaching.
    Irritated by Erasmus' growing aversion to the radicalism of the reformers and
    by rumours that Erasmus was conspiring with the pope to extinguish the
    Lutheran movement, Farel began to describe Erasmus as a 'Balaam,' thus
    precipitating the confrontation (May or June 1524) described here (lines
    1196–1215) and in Ep 1510. Farel reacted to that confrontation with pamphlets,
    now lost (Allen Ep 1496:131–40). Meanwhile, on about 9 July 1524 the Basel city
    council, doubtless encouraged by Erasmus, expelled Farel from the city.
    Subsequently Erasmus missed no opportunity to vilify Farel, whom he
    often called 'Phallicus'; Epp 1510, 1522, 1531, 1534, 1548. Cf the colloquy
    Ἰχθυοφαγία, 'A Fish Diet' of 1526 (ASD I-3 521 / Thompson 341), where he is
    called 'Pharetrius.'
306 The prophet whom the Moabite king, Balak, tried to bribe to curse the
    Israelites, but whom God compelled to bless them three times (Num 22–24)
307 Antoine Du Blet (d 1526), a Lyon banker who in the spring of 1524 accompanied
    Farel on a visit to Zwingli in Zürich. Cf Allen Ep 1510:18–19.

abuse, he replied that he had heard of my boasting that I had a plan by which this conflagration lit by Luther, that is to say, the gospel (for so he explained it), could be entirely extinguished. I answered (for I did not yet understand the source of the trouble) that I had promised the princes a plan for the settlement of this discord with the minimum of upheaval and without infringing the liberty of the gospel,[308] provided they were willing to have it conveyed to them in secret and under safeguards; but that my plan was such as I fear the princes will not accept.

A few days later, as luck would have it, I learned the source of the trouble from something my friend Pellicanus[309] said. He told me that a distinguished Polish nobleman Hieronim,[310] palatine of Sieradz, while he was here, threatened to take steps against the supporters of Luther on his return home. As he was known to be very friendly with me and had visited me frequently, some people thought that he had been aroused by something I said and was armed with some plan of mine. Now, my dear Botzheim, I will tell you the truth, and you shall see, as often happens, 'how long a tale from nothing takes its rise.'[311] After I had taken Hieronim into my library, he threw in some mention of Luther, and asked if he was a good scholar. I spoke well of his learning. What did I think of his opinions? I said the question was outside my cognizance, though it could not be denied that much of his teaching was excellent, his advice often sound, and that he had forcibly attacked certain abuses. He asked me which of his books I particularly approved of. I mentioned the commentary on twenty psalms[312] and the book on the fourteen images,[313] adding that these works were approved even by people who condemned the rest; 'although even in these,' I said, 'he brings in some of his peculiar doctrines.' He repeated the word 'peculiar,' and laughed. This was our first conversation about Luther,

1210

1215

1220

1225

1230

* * * * *

308 See Ep 1352 introduction.

309 Conradus Pellicanus (1478–1556), Franciscan, professor of theology and Hebrew at Basel until 1526, when he went to Zürich and joined the reformers

310 Hieronim Łaski (1496–1541), member of a distinguished Polish family with a record of public service. Often sent on diplomatic missions by the king of Poland, Łaski made the acquaintance of Erasmus in 1520 in Brussels and Cologne during such a mission to Charles v (lines 1274–6 of this letter). In 1523 he succeeded his father as palatine of Sieradz. In May 1524, on an embassy to Francis i, he again visited Erasmus, this time at Basel, and had the interviews recorded here (cf Allen Ep 1452:13–15). Erasmus dedicated the *Modus orandi Deum* to him; Ep 1502.

311 Propertius 2.1.16

312 The *Operationes in Psalmos*, published at Wittenberg in 1519–21 and reprinted by Adam Petri in Basel in 1521 (text in WA v). Cf Ep 980:59–61.

313 See Ep 1332 n13.

from which he got no clear idea of my feelings towards Luther, nor I of his. 1
Later, when he paid me a second visit, there happened to be lying on the
table among various papers a letter which Luther had recently written to
me.[314] Some words in this had somehow caught his eye, in which Luther
seemed to have a far from complimentary opinion of me. Soon, as we talked,
I got the impression that he wanted to purloin this letter, and without saying 1.
anything I got it back from him and put it in its place. After that we went into
my study, and conversed for some time on subjects that had nothing to do
with Luther. During this time I noticed that he again had the same letter in
his hand secretly. 'It looks to me,' I said with a smile, 'as though you had it in
mind to steal something.' He laughed, and admitted it. I asked him what his 1:
purpose was in taking it. 'I will tell you,' he replied. 'Many people have
actually tried to persuade our king that you are in a very close alliance with
Luther, and this letter will prove them wrong.' 'On that point,' I said, 'I will
make you rather better informed. I will give you the original of this letter as
soon as it has been copied, and with it two others in which he uses even 1
more offensive language about me, one of which had been printed in
Strasbourg[315] and the other was published lately by someone, I know not
who.[316] These,' I said, 'will enable you to prove, to the emperor if you like,'
for he was setting off there on a misson, 'that my relations with Luther are
not as close as many people maintain.' On another occasion, when he asked 1:
me in conversation whether I was writing anything against Luther, I told
him that I was so much distracted by essential work as to have no time for
anything else. He then explained to me how violently hostile the king of
Poland was towards Luther, describing how the entire fortune of one very
rich man had been confiscated for the king's treasury because one pamphlet 1:
of Luther's had been found in his house. On that I made it pretty clear that I
did not approve either the cruelty of it, or the precedent of seizing some
pretext to invade people's homes. Finally, as he was about to mount his
horses, he returned to me, and put a silver cup on the table. 'Please,' he said,
'let me leave this with you as a token of my sentiments.' When I refused it, 1:
on the ground that I had never done anything to deserve it, and that there
was no service I could possibly render him, 'I ask nothing of you,' he said,

* * * * *

314 Ep 1443, answered by Ep 1445
315 A letter addressed to 'X' in Leipzig, 28 May 1522 (WA-Br II 542–5), published by
     Hans Schott in 1523 under the title *Iudicium D. Martini Lutheri de Erasmo
     Roterodamo ad amicum*
316 Perhaps the letter of 20 June 1523 to Oecolampadius (WA-Br III 96–7 / BAO no
     157), though there is no record of its having been published at the time.

'except to be friends with the man who gave you this.' At length he gave it to me, with a proclamation by the king, in print.

This was the whole of our conversation about Luther. So he left me, 1270
better informed and embittered against Luther. This then, as I now see, was the man whom they cast for the part of Balak,[317] and supposed had hired me with a silver cup to curse the people of the gospel. And yet this friendship between us was none of Luther's making; three years before we had made each other's acquaintance,[318] first in Brussels and then in Cologne, when he 1275
was serving at the time as his king's envoy to the emperor. I found him a young man unusually well educated and possessed by a singular devotion, a sort of religious veneration, for the humanities. On this mission he had brought with him his two brothers, Jan,[319] who was somewhat younger, and Stanisław,[320] well read both of them and with the same feeling for humane 1280
studies that he has himself; and as it was generally believed that I was some good at them, their very eyes and their expression and, as the phrase goes, everything about them breathed a wonderful sort of affectionate good will towards me. It is not only that I accepted the good opinion of such men as they gladly enough; I rejoice to think that good literature begins to be 1285
respected by men even of the highest rank. Now, if he was unfair to Luther, he brought that attitude with him and did not imbibe it here. My influence made him milder, sooner than more indignant. Ought I to have refused to speak to him because he did not think highly of Luther? Why, at that same time I did not refuse to see men who had come from Wittenberg and were 1290
absolutely devoted to Luther, and would have been most eager to see Philippus Melanchthon himself had he come here. I have never rejected anyone's friendship either because he was too well disposed towards Luther or because he found him unsympathetic, provided he proves himself a loyal and agreeable friend. But those men you know of, ungrateful, treacherous, 1295
capricious, crazy, subversive, scurrilous, and false, the most dangerous enemies of the gospel and the humanities and the public peace – them I hate, on whichever side they may be. That present from Hieronim, which he meant to remain in my keeping as a memento of himself – ought I to have refused it like a rustic and a boor because he held the wrong views about 1300

* * * * *

317 See n306 above.
318 This must have been *four* years earlier, in 1520. Erasmus did not visit Cologne on his journey to Basel in 1521 (Ep 1342:180–1). But he was in both Brussels and Cologne (in the train of Charles v) in the autumn of 1520; Epp 1136, 1155.
319 Jan Łaski (1499–1560), who later became a famous Calvinist reformer
320 Like his brother Hieronim, whom he succeeded as palatine of Sieradz in 1543, Stanisław Łaski (c 1500–1550) had a career in public service.

Luther? At any rate, none of the princes has yet been able to plant anything on me on the understanding that I would write an attack on Luther, as some of these gospellers none the less maintain, lying most brazenly in defiance of their own consciences. So there is the whole foolish story.

I know what you will be saying already: What has this to do with the play? You are quite right; and I return to my catalogue.[m] In the class of defences may be included the letter which I lately wrote to that paragon of all the gifts proper to a prelate, Christopher, bishop of Basel,[321] on the eating of meat; which nevertheless I had not written with a view to publication. But when I found that it was in circulation and would infallibly be published by someone else, I preferred to revise it and publish it myself,[322] especially since I was recommended to do so by some of the leading men in this university.[323]

I will now indicate what has appeared in a mutilated state, and what is still in my hands and is not yet finished. My small work on abundance of style[324] lacks the example of a subject sketched with the greatest brevity and then treated a second time at full length. I had chosen a topic, the need to teach children their letters from the start, and I still have it by me, but two pages in the middle written in a very minute hand went astray in Rome through the carelessness of those who had copied out the text.[325] Of the Antibarbari[326] I had revised and enlarged two books in Bologna, and had a mass of material collected long ago for the remainder. This, and some other things with it, went astray through dishonesty, not on the part of Richard Pace, my most honourable friend, with whom I had left it in Ferrara on my departure for Rome, but thanks to another man,[327] who had too much of an

* * * * *

321 Christoph von Utenheim (Ep 1332)
322 *Epistola apologetica de interdictu esu carnium deque similibus hominum constitutionibus*, written in April 1522 and printed by Froben in August. See Epp 1274 n7 and 1353 n13.
323 In Allen Ep 1581:717–25, Erasmus states that the letter was published at the request of the bishop after it had been examined by Ludwig Baer (Ep 488), professor of theology at the University of Basel.
324 See n58 above.
325 This material eventually became *De pueris instituendis* (Basel: Froben and Episcopius, September 1529); Allen Ep 2189:24–34. Critical edition by Jean-Claude Margolin in ASD I-2 1–78; English translation by Beert C. Verstraete in CWE 26 291–346. *De pueris* opens with a 'declamatio, contracti thematis exemplum' (ASD I-2 23–4 / CWE 26 297–8), which is followed by 'idem argumentum locupletatum copia' (ASD I-2 25–78 / CWE 26 298–345).
326 On the genesis and subsequent history of the *Antibarbari*, which Erasmus began when he was about nineteen, see Ep 30:17n and CWE 23 2–15.
327 William Thale; see the references in the preceding note.

eye to his own interests to be true to those of any of his friends; though later, as luck would have it, I secured from England the beginning of the second book and in Bruges the end of it, with the loss of many pages in between. If only I could find the second book, I could easily finish the rest; and I have no doubt it is lurking in some thieves' kitchen or other, for I put two copies into safe keeping.[328]

I still have by me several things which I started long ago; among them is a commentary on Paul's Epistle to the Romans, of which I had finished four books, if I mistake not, twenty-two years ago.[329] For a work on the theory of preaching[330] I had only jotted down some divisions of the subject-matter. And yet, if Christ grants me life and tranquillity, I have a mind to finish a work on preaching, which may do some good, especially as I am urged to do so by men whose opinion carries great weight. Some time ago I began three dialogues in which I attempted a discussion rather than a confrontation on the question of Martin Luther,[331] but under altered names: Luther's part will be taken by Thrasymachus, the other side by Eubulus, and Philalethes will act as arbiter. The first dialogue investigates whether this approach would be expedient, even had every word Luther writes been true. The second will discuss some of his doctrines. The third will display a method of bringing this conflict to a peaceful end in such a way that it cannot easily break out again in future. The question will be discussed between the two of them without scurrilities, with no wrangling and no disguise; the bare truth only will be put forward, in a simple and countrified way, with such fairness and such moderation that there will be more danger, I think, from the indignation of the opposite party, who will interpret my mildness as collusion with the enemy, than from Luther himself, if he has any grain of the sense with which many people credit him – and I for one wish him joy of it if he has it, and hope he may acquire it if not. I perceive that certain people are more in favour of severity, and as far as I am concerned, every man is

* * * * *

328 Only the first book was published in Froben's edition of May 1520 (Ep 1110). Critical edition by Kazimierz Kumaniecki in ASD I-1 1–138; translation by Margaret Mann Phillips in CWE 23 16–122. Subsequent efforts to find book 2 (Ep 1210:18) failed.

329 The date is correct; see Epp 164:41–2, 181:36–8. The commentaries were never completed or published, despite the entry at line 1585. Cf lines 1638–9.

330 The *Ecclesiastes sive de ratio concionandi*, begun in 1523 (see Epp 1321 n1, 1332:36) but not published until 1535 (Basel: Froben)

331 Erasmus conceived the idea of 'a short treatise on how to end this business of Luther' sometime before April 1522; Epp 1268:86–8, 1275:23–5. By 17 March 1523 Jan de Fevijn (Ep 1317 n7) had heard of the three-dialogue format and wrote to Frans van Cranevelt (Ep 1317) about it; de Vocht *Literae ad Craneveldium* Ep 49:9–13.

welcome to enjoy his own opinion. To be severe is easier, but the other
seems to me the more profitable course. If some physical complaint is active
in one particular part of the body, cautery or amputation may prove to be the
answer; but when the trouble is diffused through the whole body, when it
permeates the inmost veins and tissues, we should perhaps need a second
Mercury to draw the poison by stages from our vitals, just as he relieved
Psyche's whole body from that deadly slumber.[332]

I undertook this work with encouragement from many sources. First
(for I cannot mention them all) there was Marino Caracciolo,[333] the papal
nuncio at the emperor's court; then that distinguished figure Girolamo
Aleandro,[334] unquestionably the best scholar of our age in the three tongues,
who likewise was serving at that time with the emperor Charles as papal
nuncio; then Jean Glapion,[335] the emperor's confessor, for he often wrote to
me on the subject at the emperor's wish in an earnest and warmhearted
way.[336] I was encouraged to it long ago by William Mountjoy,[337] and recently
by George, most illustrious duke of Saxony.[338] There have however been
many interruptions, which did not allow me to progress in the work I had
undertaken beyond two or three short pages, so that the work was not so
much undertaken as planned – though in other ways I am by nature greatly
disinclined to this sort of composition. Bloody disputes I hate, and am more
attracted by humour that hurts no one, as though I were born for that. And
then I am well aware how great a Hercules this project demands, and that I
myself am a mere pigmy. In fact I have simply not made up my mind as yet
whether I wish to finish what I have started.[339] Whatever happens will not
happen unadvisedly, nor will anything appear at all unless it has been read
in private and approved by those whose proper business it most is to uphold
Christ's glory; for that at least is the object I shall aim at as I beat it into shape

* * * * *

332 Actually, it was Eros/Cupid who awoke Psyche from her deadly slumber.
According to Apuleius, Venus sent Mercury in search of Psyche (6.7f) and it
was Mercury who led her to heaven (6.23). This may explain Erasmus' lapse of
memory.

333 Ep 1263 n1

334 Ep 1256 n11

335 Ep 1275

336 Cf Ep 1269:6–11.

337 Ep 1219:8–9

338 Ep 1298:30–40

339 For the reasons discussed here (down to line 36:17) and in the *Spongia* (ASD IX-1
164), the project was abandoned. It is possible that the *Inquisitio de fide*, first
published in the March 1524 edition of the *Colloquia*, is an abbreviated version
of the second of the projected dialogues; see *Inquisitio de fide* ed Craig R.
Thompson, 2nd ed (Hamden, Conn: Archon Books 1975) 37–8.

– if I ever do so, for I see that both parties are now inflamed to the point where each is set on either total victory or total destruction. In fact, the defeat of one of them will bring a great collapse of gospel truth and liberty in its train, while the other will not be put down except by a most destructive 1385 and world-wide catastrophe, which will engulf many innocent people as well. Personally I would rather see the question settled in such a way that each side yields the victory to truth and to Christ's glory. On this subject I have offered the monarchs a secret plan of my own,[340] if only they would instruct me to submit it; and so I would rather for the moment that in the 1390 light of this promise of mine no one should assume my support for one side or the other. Let there be no premature judgment; the verdict shall be based on my book when it appears.

"What I have recounted so far about this work was published in the first issue of this catalogue. In this there was nothing to upset any 1395 fair-minded person; and yet certain of these gospellers, as they love to be called, regardless of the teaching of the gospel, were driven nearly mad by it, as though it were a crime worthy of death by public stoning to hold any debate with Luther, even with the object of learning something. I will now reveal to my friends the secret purpose of this project, and especially to you, 1400 my dear Botzheim, for you rebuked me with a forbidding frown, which was most unlike you, because you thought I was showing levity on a serious matter. I would reluctantly admit that anyone was more devoted to the gospel than I am myself; but my hope was that this business might be handled with such moderation as would allow everyone to take part in it 1405 without civil strife. And so I wrote publicly, offering the prospect of something to this effect, angling for the result I so much desired, that both sides from a love of peace and concord should urge me to publish the volume I had promised; and some moves were made in this direction with the emperor. But when I perceived that neither party of itself offered any 1410 hope of laying this dispute to rest, I was unwilling to waste my labour and risk unpopularity from both sides for my efforts. Such were the cunning moves of which they spoke, and they had no source save a spirit that detests discord and has a passion for peace. As it is, I pray that the Lord Jesus, who alone has the power, may issue his commands to still these storms and calm 1415 this tempest in the church."

I also made an attempt to publish the entire works of St Augustine,[341] corrected by means of ancient copies and with added notes, identifying and separating out those which pass falsely under his name. The whole corpus

* * * * *

340 Ep 1352
341 See Ep 1309 introduction.

of his writings was divided into seven parts or volumes.[342] The first was destined for his practice-pieces, those which he wrote as a catechumen or about that time. The second for his letters, some of which he wrote as a young man. The third was reserved for what Greek calls his theoretical works, which we should call contemplative, in which class are his *Confessiones* and *Soliloquia* and others like them, to which it was my purpose to add the pieces concerned with the conduct of life. The fourth was appointed for the didactic works, those, that is, in which he gives instruction in theology; and this class includes the *De doctrina christiana* and the *De Trinitate*. The fifth should have had the polemical works, in which he does battle against the leaders of sundry poisonous heresies; under this heading he wrote a good deal, including the *De civitate Dei*. The sixth would have displayed the exegetical works, in which he expounds books of the Holy Scriptures. The seventh would have been for the spurious and doubtful pieces, those, that is, which are either wrongly attributed to him or of such a kind that one might well hesitate about the authorship. In the same volume would have been a table of those which have been lost with the passage of time. The size of the undertaking was a deterrent, but the learning and piety of the author were attractive, and the prospect of being useful urged me on. And so I divided the enormous task among several scholars,[343] in such a way that each should receive his share of the credit unimpaired. Such was the labour which I undertook without payment to assist the cause of public learning; and yet certain people set on me like barking dogs because I do not write, as they would prefer, about indulgences or collecting cheeses.[344]

As for correspondence, I have written so much,[345] and even today I write so much, that in future two wagons will scarcely suffice for the load. I myself acquired many by chance and burned them, for I observed that they were preserved by many people. In Bologna I had written a brief declamation of the hortatory kind, in which I discouraged a man from

* * * * *

342 The complete Augustine published by Froben in 1528/9 comprised ten volumes.
343 Vives assumed responsibility for *De civitate Dei*, which was published separately in September 1522 (Ep 1309) and later became volume 5 of the complete edition. In the end, Erasmus edited all the other volumes, though he had many helpers; see Allen Ep 2157 introduction.
344 Ep 1342:138–9
345 Six more or less official collections of Erasmus' letters had already been published (see CWE 3 348–50), and six more were to come before his death (see Allen 1 599–601).

adopting the religious life and then again urged him to adopt it.[346] In my
view it was worth printing, if anything of mine ever is; but the outside pages   1450
have been lost at either end, and what remains is still among my papers.
When I was living in Rome,[347] to please Raffaele, cardinal of San Giorgio,[348] I
wrote a speech against the proposal to declare war on Venice, for which he
asked me in Julius' name;[349] for the question was then under discussion in
the sacred college. I then put the opposite case; and the second speech won   1455
the day, although I had spent more effort on the first and written it more
from the heart; through the treachery of a man I could name,[350] the original
text was lost. I have begun again to jot down some of the heads of the
argument from memory, and I suppose that it is lurking somewhere among
my papers. Very many things have fallen by the way which I do not regret;   1460
but I could wish that some speeches in sermon form still survived which I
I delivered long ago in Paris,[351] when I was living in the Collège de
Montaigu.[352]

Such, my excellent Botzheim, is the list of my trifling productions, and
I hope it may arouse your acquisitive instinct. Now, when you complain that   1465
your purse is empty because you have to buy the same book so often, I
should like you to look at it like this. Suppose that my *Proverbia*[353] had just
appeared for the first time, and that the moment the book was published I
had died: would you have regretted your expenditure? I doubt it. Now
suppose something else, that after several years I came to life again and that   1470
at the same time the book revived with me, better and fuller, would you
regret what you had spent, or would you be delighted to see again both your
friend and his immortal work? Now I know what you will say: 'I should be
delighted to see you alive again; but none of this has really happened.'
Which then do you suppose to be the more blessed state, to rise again from   1475
the dead, or not to die? If you would be pleased to see me risen, you must be
much more pleased to see me still alive. Last but not least, if the later edition

* * * * *

346 Probably an amplified version of the *Laus vitae monasticae*; see line 663 and
n145 of this letter. Erasmus was in Bologna from November 1506 to November
1507.
347 Spring and early summer 1509
348 Raffaele Riario (Ep 333)
349 Ie, Pope Julius II
350 Doubtless William Thale; see Ep 30:17n and line 1325 of this letter.
351 Listed in the *Lucubrationum Erasmi Roterodami index* (see the introduction to this
letter) as 'Conciones aliquot olim habitae Lutetiae de laudibus divorum; sed
hae sunt ab amicis interceptae'
352 1495–6; see Epp 43–8.
353 Ie, the *Adagia*

contains nothing worth the extra money, you are free not to buy it; but if it does, you are making a gain and not a loss. If that earlier edition brought you good value for that small outlay, and if the later edition does the same,   148 surely you have made two good bargains, not suffered a loss. 'You might,' you will say, 'have given us a book that was perfect in the first edition.' But it is like life: as long as we live, we are always devoted to self-improvement, and we shall not cease to make our writings more polished and more complete until we cease to breathe. No one is so good a man that he could   148 not be made better; and no book has had so much work put into it that it cannot be made more perfect. Not but what I did myself openly admit long ago that on this point I take less trouble than I ought to; yet all the time other people make in my opinion a worse mistake who are far better scholars than I and yet, through some sort of religious scruple either publish nothing or   149 leave it till very late. Do not hope therefore that I of all people shall relieve you of this inconvenience, until I leave the stage and once and for all utter my 'So farewell and clap your hands' to the whole lot of you (and this, believe me, would have happened shortly, had not the wine of Burgundy come to my rescue like some god from the machine); so you must make up   149 your mind whether you would rather wish for that moment, or from time to time buy a book that has been enlarged and revised. In fact, if you recall what a lot of money you had spent on trash in the old days, you will not, I think, regret this expense quite so much.

°Already I hear some of my friends from time to time grumbling about   150 the division of my entire works into volumes. Whether there is anything in my writings that is worthy of posterity, be it for others to decide; at least, if they do descend to our successors, I could wish I had some loyal and scholarly Tiro[354] to do for me when I am dead what he did for Cicero his master. And yet, in case anyone thinks it worth trying, why, I will show him   150 the most convenient way to do it.

In the first volume can be put everything that concerns literature and education, for example:

De copia, two books
Ratio conscribendis epistolas   151
Ratio studiorum, addressed to Pierre Vitré
Theodorus' *Grammar*, two books, in my version
Syntaxis

* * * * *

354 Marcus Tullius Tiro was Cicero's freedman, secretary, and friend. He wrote a life of Cicero and, according to tradition, collected his speeches and letters for publication.

All my versions from Lucian, the titles of which are *Saturnalia*,
    Cronosolon or *Leges Saturnaliciae*, *Epistolae Saturnales*,   1515
    De luctu, *Icaromenippus*, *Toxaris*, *Pseudomantis*,
    Somnium sive Gallus, *Timon*, *Abdicatus*, *Tyrannicida*, *De mercede*
    conductis in aulis potentum, sundry dialogues (*Cnemonis et*
    Damippi, *Zenophantae et Callidemi[dae]*, *Menippi et Tantali*,
    Menippi et Mercurii, *Menippi et Amphilochi et Trophonii*,   1520
    Charontis et Menippi, *Cratetis ac Diogenis*, *Nirei ac Thersitae*,
    Diogenis ac Mausoli, *Simyli ac Polystrati*, *Veneris et Cupidinis*,
    Martis ac Mercurii, *Mercurii et Maiae*, *Veneris et Cupidinis*,
    Doridis et Galateae, *Diogenis et Alexandri*, *Menippi et Chironis*,
    Menippi et Cerberi), *Hercules Gallicus*, *Eunuchus*, *De*   1525
    sacrificiis, *Lapithae*, *De astrologia*. I should not wish the
    prefaces to these to be omitted, which make clear to whom each is
    dedicated.
A short declamation rendered from the Greek of Libanius, with several
    themes also translated   1530
A declamation against a tyrannicide, in answer to Lucian's
Laus medicinae
Similia, one book
Colloquia, one book
Euripides, version of *Hecuba* and *Iphigenia*   1535
Miscellaneous poems, on other than religious subjects, for those I have kept
    for their appropriate section
Commentarius in Nucem Ovidii
    The second volume can de dedicated to the *Adagia*, which make a
whole volume by themselves; and the subject-matter is not far from the main   1540
theme of volume one.
    The third should be allotted to my *Epistolae*, for in these too there is
much that is relevant to practice in composition; for most of them are trifles
which I wrote as an adolescent or at least as a young man. These I will revise,
and add a certain number, perhaps also removing some. To this class I   1545
should wish a number of preliminary dedications to be added, which
printers often either omit or alter according to their fancy. Such, for
example, are the prefaces to the works of St Hilary and St Cyprian, to the
Greek Lexicon, the letter to Jean Desmarez prefixed to my *Panegyricus ad*
Philippum, the preface added to my *De principe* intended for Charles' brother   1550
Ferdinand,[355] and anything else that may seem to deserve preservation.

* * * * *

355 Ep 853, an additional preface in the second edition

Volume four may be given to works which contribute to the building of character. To this class belong:

Most of the Lucian, though I have given it a place in the first volume

All my versions from Plutarch, the titles of which are *De discrimine adulatoris* 15 *et amici, Quo pacto possit utilitas capi ex inimico, De tuenda bona valetudine, Principi maxime philosophandum, An graviores sint animi morbi quam corporis, De cupiditate divitiarum, Num recte dictum ab Epicuro* λάθε βιώσας.

Moriae encomium, a small book full of humour, but it teaches serious lessons, 15 so do not be surprised to find it in this section.

Panegyricus, a speech of welcome to Philip, father of the emperor Charles, on his return from Spain

Institutio principis christiani, addressed to the emperor Charles

Isocrates de regno, addressed to him likewise 15

Consolatio de morte filii

Querimonia pacis

Dialogus Charontis et Alastoris

Carmen de senectute, addressed to Cop the physician

Paraenesis to Adolf, heer van Veere, who was then a child 15

De morte subita, to Joost Vroye

This is the place for Cicero's *Officia,* revised by me and supplied with summaries and notes. Why should one not also add the *Catunculus,* the *Mimi Publiani,* and other things of the sort?

The fifth volume can be allocated to works of religious instruction. 15 Among these are:

Enchiridion militis christiani

Letter to Paul Volz, abbot of Hugshofen

Methodus verae theologiae, from the edition of 1523 published by Michaël Hillen[356] 158

Paraclesis

Exomologesis

Commentarii in Psalmos primum et secundum

Paraphrasis in Psalmum tertium, dedicated to Vianden

Commentarius in Epistolam ad Romanos 158

Paraphrasis in Precationem dominicam

Commentarius in duos hynmnos Prudentii

Concio de puero Iesu

Concio de misericordia Domini

* * * * *

356 See Allen Ep 1365 introduction.

Comparatio virginitatis et martyrii, to the nuns of Cologne 1590
Expostulatio Iesu, in verse
Casa natalitia
Michaelis encomium
Liturgia virginis Lauretanae
Three prayers, two to the Virgin Mother and one to Jesus 1595
    The sixth volume shall be assigned to the New Testament as rendered by me, with my notes on it; a work which I have already revised and enriched for the fourth time. Anyone who does not like large books can divide this into two volumes.
    The seventh is for the paraphrases on the whole New Testament, 1600 exclusive of the Apocalypse. These too can be divided into two volumes, if anyone so pleases.
    Let the eighth volume be occupied by the defences. These too (alack the day!) will make a whole volume. Their titles are as follows, and I pray there may be nothing to add: 1605
Ad Iacobum Fabrum Stapulensem, one book
Ad Eduardum Leum, two books
Ad Iacobum Latomum de linguis
Adversus Nicolaum Ecmondanum de loco Pauli ad Corinthios: 'Omnes quidem
    resurgemus' 1610
Adversus quorundam clamores de hoc quod verteram: 'In principio erat sermo'
Ad Ioannem Briardum Atensem pro Encomio matrimonii
Ad taxationes Stunicae in Novum Testamentum
Adversus libellum Impietatum et blasphemiarum eiusdem, of which the first
    words are: *Vix mihi delitigata* 1615
Appendix adversus eiusdem libellum, entitled πρόδρομος. First words: *Dum*
    haec excuderentur
Adversus Conclusiones eiusdem. First words: *Reddidit mihi tuus*
Adversus Sanctium Caranzam theologum de tribus ab illo notatis. First words: *Post*
    longas et inutiles rixas. Here let my own words only be reprinted, 1620
    omitting what was included from Zúñiga and Carranza in the first
    edition.
Epistola ad R.P. Christophorum, episcopum Basiliensem, de delectu ciborum ac
    caeteris
Epistola ad Marcum Laurinum contra rumorem, of which the first words are: *Nae* 1625
    tu plurimum debes
Epistola ad Martinum Dorpium de Novo Testamento, which hitherto has been
    appended to the *Moria*
Apologiae, prefixed to the New Testament
Spongia adversus Ulricum Huttenum 1630

Liber antibarbarorum
De libero arbitrio διατριβή

Volume nine shall be dedicated to the *Letters* of Jerome, on which I have expended so much labour that I can without impudence add this work to my own list; though Hilary too cost me a lot of work, and so did Cyprian. Of Quintus Curtius I will say nothing; in Seneca I can claim nothing for myself, except that in that field I lost much labour by trusting to the promises of my friends. If Christ grants me life and strength enough to finish my commentaries on the Epistle to the Romans, they will occupy volume ten.[357]

I know that you have long found such a prolix reckoning tedious, but this is what it means to make a catalogue, and indeed if anyone wishes to do all that diligence can achieve in this department, he can add the first words of the individual works, as I did for one or two of the more obscure so that they might not be overlooked. I perceive that you wish to be released; and I will release you, once I have given a brief answer to those who keep saying that I draw ample profits from the dedications of my works because I have dedicated such a great number to men in high places.[358] Certain people use this as an excuse to charge me with fishing either for reputation or for money, possibly for both.[359] To the point about reputation I have already given the reply elsewhere, that I am more zealous for the good standing of these studies than for my own.[360] It is for their advancement that I have sought the favour of the great, nor has my policy been unsuccessful. And to some men who have been good to me I have offered this compliment, not to return their kindness but to show that I have not forgotten it.

Of the financial return you shall now have some account. With friends in more modest situations you know yourself how far I am from being mercenary, for after trying every means you have never been able to make me accept anything. In this context sincerity of feeling is of more value to me than any gift. In fact, while it is a question of skill either to accept gracefully or to give a courteous refusal, my friends know that it comes far more easily to me to express refusal than acceptance. And if they ever offer me anything in such a way that I cannot refuse it, I always recompense them to the utmost

* * * * *

357 In March 1530 Erasmus attached to Ep 2283 a catalogue of his works arranged into nine series or *ordines* rather than ten volumes. The ten-volume scheme of 1524 served as the basis for both the Basel and the Leiden editions of the *Opera omnia*.
358 A list of all Erasmus' dedicatory letters is found in Allen XII (indexes) 78–80.
359 Neither the annotator nor any of the eminent authorities whom he consulted has been able to identify the 'certain people' in question.
360 All the efforts of the annotator and his colleagues to locate the reply referred to here have been in vain.

of my power, and go further if I can. And so from the by no means scanty
offerings I have made to my more modest friends I derive the most ample
satisfaction of having given them pleasure, and having joined their memory   1665
with my own in a way that may perhaps survive to posterity. As for princes,
let me say at the outset that to some who have not rewarded me my debt is
no less than to those who have, and to those who have rewarded me I owe
the more because they did so unasked. William Mountjoy, the distinguished
English nobleman to whom I dedicated my *Proverbia* both when complete   1670
and in its many enlarged forms,[361] knows that I owe him a larger debt for
kindness than for coin.[362] His Grace William, archbishop of Canterbury,[363]
has shown the greatest readiness to help me;[364] yet even he will bear me
witness how often I have refused his proffered generosity on the ground
that I already had plenty of money.[365] Knowing that by the laws of   1675
friendship I shared all he had, I thought it safer to leave what I received in his
keeping.[366] From Leo x, to whom I dedicated the New Testament,[367] I neither
expected nor received a single ducat. The same from Adrian vi, to whom I
sent a book[368] the binding of which cost me four florins,[369] with another for
the courier on his outward journey and something too for his return. He   1680
accepted the volume with evident satisfaction,[370] and gave the bearer six
ducats in cash;[371] to me he offered a piece of preferment[372] of a fairly

* * * * *

361 See n129 above.
362 In the *Compendium vitae* Erasmus calls Mountjoy his 'Maecenas, though more
   of a friend than a benefactor' (CWE 4 408:129). For details see CEBR sv
   'Mountjoy.'
363 Warham (Ep 188)
364 Although Erasmus' first dedication of a work to Warham produced a
   disappointingly meagre reward (see lines 133–5 of this letter), the archbishop
   quickly became one of Erasmus' most generous patrons. In 1512 Warham
   bestowed upon Erasmus an annual pension from the revenues of the parish of
   Aldington in Kent (Ep 255 introduction).
365 One such refusal is recorded in Ep 457:51–3.
366 The payment of the pension from Warham remained a perpetual source of
   worry for Erasmus and of trouble for Warham.
367 Ep 384
368 The edition of Arnobius; see lines 571–3 of this letter and Epp 1304, 1310, 1329.
369 *Quatuor florenis*, not specified as gold coins and indeterminate in value;
   possibly the Florentine, Rhenish, or Hapsburg coin, possibly one of the related
   moneys-of-account. See CWE 1 316–18, 347.
370 Epp 1324, 1338
371 Six ducats (*ducatos sex*) were then officially worth 40s gros Flemish, 27s sterling,
   and £12 9s tournois. See Ep 1295 n1.
372 Epp 1324:117–28, 1338:47–64

honourable kind, which I refused[373] without more ado. I sent Clement VII his paraphrase[374] without a word, either from myself or through my friends, to suggest that I expected anything from him in the way of a present. So far was 168 I from expecting it that, when Adrian was preparing to send me a present that brought much honour with it, I wrote and asked him not to do so;[375] Clement however sent me two hundred florins,[376] the only ground being that I had dedicated to him my paraphrase on Acts,[377] for he knew I should refuse had it been sent on any other pretext. This I can prove from the actual 169 document itself. And yet some scandalmongering wretch,[378] who has learned Scripture only as material for his malignance, was found ready to say that Erasmus is our new Balaam.

Cardinal Grimani,[379] to whom I dedicated my paraphrase on the Epistle to the Romans,[380] did not send me a farthing, nor did I expect it. What 169 I was hoping for, he gave me – support and good will, not for myself but for the humanities, and for Reuchlin. Cardinal Campeggi[381] many years ago sent me a ring[382] from England as a token of friendship; and to him I later dedicated a paraphrase,[383] not asking for his generosity, but seeking to repay it. The cardinal of Sion[384] made me many offers on condition that I 170 came to Rome;[385] but through me he was not a farthing the poorer. Nor was I made a single drachma richer by the cardinal of the Santi Quattro,[386] to whom I dedicated my revision of Cyprian.[387] Jean de Carondelet,[388] archbishop of Palermo, found his purse not a halfpenny lighter as a result of my Hilary,[389] though I had sent my own servant to him with a copy. He gave 170

* * * * *

373 Ep 1352:136–67
374 On Acts; see lines 770–1 and 1688 of this letter and Allen Ep 1414.
375 See Ep 1324 n13.
376 *Florenos ducentos*, not specified as gold coins, but presumably Florentine or papal florins, then worth about £66 14s gros Flemish, £45 sterling, and £415 tournois. See Ep 1295 n1.
377 See Allen Epp 1438:16–23, 1466:3–7.
378 Farel; see nn305, 306 above.
379 Domenico Grimani, 1461–1523 (Ep 334)
380 Ep 710
381 See n302 above.
382 Epp 995–6
383 Ephesians; Ep 1062
384 Ep 1295
385 Epp 1299:49–50, 1300:66–8, 1302:71–4, 1305:5–6, 1311:23–4, 1342:346–52
386 Lorenzo Pucci (d 1531)
387 Ep 1000
388 Ep 1276
389 Ep 1334

me all I was fighting for, his support and his good will.[390] Philip of
Burgundy,[391] bishop of Utrecht, to whose diocese I belong, in return for the
dedication of the *Querimonia pacis*[392] offered me a prebend, and when I
refused it, he gave me a ring with a sapphire mounted in it, which had been
worn in old days by his brother David,[393] a former bishop of the see. This he   1710
sent me as a present, when I neither asked for it nor expected it. No less
unsought and unexpected was the loving-cup sent me by the cardinal of
Mainz.[394] To the cardinal of York, to whom I dedicated an essay of
Plutarch's,[395] I reckon I owe everything in return for the singular kindness
he has so long showed me; and yet hitherto his generosity has not made me   1715
one featherweight the richer. To the bishop of Liège,[396] who is now
cardinal, I dedicated the Epistles to the Corinthians,[397] sent him a copy with
gold ornament, and gave him two volumes of the New Testament on
parchment, elegantly illuminated and by no means cheap; I readily
acknowledge my indebtedness for the splendid promises he has made me   1720
more than once, but at the same time I have no reason to be grateful to him
for the present of a single farthing. He gave me as much as, if it should fall
into the most delicate eye, would cause no torment; and this he himself will
not deny. My own prince Charles had already summoned me to become a
member of his council and had presented me to a benefice[398] before I   1725
dedicated to him or even showed him my *De principe*;[399] so you can see this
was returning gratitude and not angling for spoils. I also sent him a
paraphrase[400] from Basel to Brussels by the hand of my own servant and at
my own expense. When the man set out to return he was given two
florins;[401] and yet the spirit in which the prince gladly accepted my gift[402]   1730

* * * * *

390 Ep 1342:283–4
391 Ep 603
392 Ibidem
393 Ep 603:14n
394 Epp 986:40–5, 1033:5–28
395 See lines 248–54 of this letter.
396 Erard de la Marck (Ep 738)
397 Ep 916
398 A bishopric in Sicily, which Erasmus refused; Epp 475:1–14, 476:12–33
399 See lines 710–13 of this letter.
400 Matthew; Ep 1255
401 Gold florins, probably Rhenish (then worth 4s 11d gros Flemish each) or
    Florentine (worth 6s 8d gros). Possibly, however, Erasmus meant the new
    Burgundian-Hapsburg carolus florins, named in honour of Charles v (worth 3s
    6d gros); but if so he would presumably have referred to them by that name.
    See CWE 8 350, Table B.
402 See n195 above.

gave me no less pleasure than if he had counted out a thousand gold pieces. Many years ago I had dedicated Plutarch's essay *De discrimine adulatoris et amici* to the king of England, Henry VIII.[403] I reckon my debt to him as great as the offer he made me, had I been willing to accept it; he offered me a position far greater than I deserved.[404] Long afterwards, in any case, when I had forgotten that dedication, he sent me sixty angels[405] on a suggestion or, more truly, a reminder from John Colet. Later, I dedicated to him my paraphrase on Luke.[406] Ferdinand, the emperor Charles' brother, with characteristic generosity accepted my paraphrase on St John[407] with the greatest readiness, and with his letter[408] sent me an honorarium of one hundred florins,[409] which was the last thing I expected. If I consider the attitude of the king of France towards me, and reckon what he has been willing to do for me, there is scarcely any prince to whom I owe more; but to my Hilarius,[410] who delivered a book to him, he gave thirty crowns[411] in cash by way of journey-money, and except for good will I myself got nothing; nor was I in hopes of anything else. Briefly, out of my paraphrases I did not get a

* * * * *

403 See n51 above.

404 Ep 296:120–7

405 Epp 816:8–10, 834. Sixty angel-nobles (*angelatos sexaginta*), or £20 English sterling, then worth about £29 gros Flemish, and £183 tournois. See Epp 1295 n1, and n130 above.

406 See lines 766–7 of this letter and Allen Ep 1381.

407 Ep 1333

408 Ep 1343

409 *Florenos centum*, not specified as gold coins, but cf Allen Ep 1376:14–16 (*centum florenos aureos*). This sum in Florentine coins would then have been officially worth £33 6s 8d gros Flemish (£22 10s sterling, or £207 10s tournois); Rhenish gold florins would have been worth about £24 10s 0d gros Flemish.

410 Hilarius Bertolph (Ep 1257 n10), who delivered the presentation copy of the paraphrase on Mark (Ep 1400) to King Francis

411 Presumably French *écus à la couronne*, struck from 1474 at 23 1/8 carats with 3.275 grams fine gold, but not minted during the first part of Francis I's reign, from 1515 to 1541. The only French gold coin then issued was the slightly heavier *écu au soleil* (originally also 23 1/8 carats, with 3.369 grams fine gold), whose obverse also contained a shield and crown, surmounted with a sun. In November 1516, both gold coins were raised in value in relation to the silver coinage: the *écu à la couronne* from 35s tournois to 39s, the *écu au soleil* from 36s 3d to 40s t; and in 1519 (May and July), the latter was slightly reduced in fineness and weight (23 carats, 3.300 grams fine gold), though not quite to the level of the *couronne*. Both gold *écus* then remained unchanged in value until March 1533, when their values were raised to 43s 6d and 45s t, respectively. At the time of this letter (1523), the official exchange rate for the *écu au soleil* was 76d gros Flemish in the Low Countries and 52d sterling in England; for the *écu à la couronne*, unofficially about 74d gros in the Low Countries and 50d sterling in

halfpenny, except from Ferdinand and Pope Clement. I had almost
forgotten Ferdinand's father, Philip;[412] he once gave me fifty philippics[413] in
cash when I showed him my *Panegyricus*.[414] The others gave me either
nothing or a sum too small to be worth remembering; I speak only of those to   1750
whom I have dedicated my work.

Now suppose a man surveyed the stately row of names and titles, and
believed me to resemble most other men, would he not suspect that my
dedications must have made me as rich as Midas? I do not recall this because
I have any complaints of the generosity of princes. I reckon any profit that   1755
accrues to humane studies as though it were money in my own purse; it is
for their sake that I have wooed the favour of princes. And indeed, that there
was nothing sordid in the way I wooed their generosity is clear from this if
nothing else, that so often it has been quite hard work to be able to refuse
their generosity towards me personally without hurting their feelings. My   1760
annual income is fixed at a little more than four hundred gold florins.[415] This
fortune is unequal, I confess, to the expenses demanded by my age and state
of health, by the assistance which my work must have in the way of servants
and transcribers, by my keeping a horse, by my constant journeys, and by a
spirit (to give it no other name) that will not tolerate meanness and squalor,   1765
that abhors bills unpaid, services unrequited, and friends neglected in their
distress. And so I have friends who make good the shortfall in my income by
their generosity, not so much giving me presents as forcing me to take them.
What they give me, they say they spend, not on Erasmus, but on the cause of
learning in general. They are men of such a position in the world that their   1770
fortunes do not feel this loss, and of such noble mind that they do not expect
their generosity to be made public or allow themselves to be thanked; and

* * * * *

England, so that 30 'crowns' would have been worth about £9 5s gros Flemish,
£6 5s sterling, and £60 tournois. See CWE 1 315, 342–3; CWE 8 350, Table B; Ep
1295 n1.

412 See n170 above.
413 Worth £10 8s 4d gros (1500–21), and about £65 12s 6d tournois (from 1516). The
philippus or florin of St Philip, first issued by Archduke Philip, had been the
chief gold coin of the Hapsburg Low Countries from 1496 to 1521; from 1500, it
was struck with 2.19 grams fine gold (15 carats 11 grains) and a value of 50d
gros Flemish. In February 1521, after Philip's son had become the Hapsburg
emperor Charles V, this coin was superseded by the carolus florin (14 carats,
with 1.70 grams fine gold), worth 40d, and raised to 42d gros in August 1521.
See CWE 1 318, 336–9; CWE 8 349–50, Tables A and B; Ep 1295 n1.
414 See lines 706–7 of this letter.
415 *Quadringenti floreni aurei*; presumably, from the context, Florentine florins,
worth about £133 6s 8d gros, £90 sterling, and £830 tournois. See Ep 1295 n1.

this makes it all the more unfair that their goodness should be unknown to posterity.

So much for the treasures I have accumulated by flying high in my 1771 dedications. The topic suggests that I should also throw a sop to certain trade rivals who get me a bad name among those who know no better for having reaped a generous harvest out of the munificence of Johann Froben[416] – a man of whom I think most highly, and for nothing more so than the zeal for promoting humane studies, in which he surpasses almost 1780 all other printers, and gets more reputation than profit for his pains. And I should at any rate have made no small gain out of him, had I accepted whatever he offered me; for he is most generous. As it is, he will himself bear me witness how small is the total I have let myself be forced to accept; nor would he have had even that much success, had he not explained that the 1785 money was put up by the partnership, so that the share which fell on him personally would be a very light burden. And yet, had he wished to do no more than pay for the work of my servants, he would have had to give me more than I received. Nor did I allow my meals at his table to cost me nothing. I lived in his house nearly ten months,[417] and for this I forced him to 1790 accept 150 gold florins,[418] against great reluctance; for he would rather have paid me as much again, but I forced him. And that no one may suppose me dependent on Froben's generosity, Froben himself can bear witness – for he received a good part of it in his own hands on my behalf in Frankfurt – that the sum of money, part of which I brought here with me two years ago and 1795 part I received by way of remittance from Brabant, exceeded 1,900 florins.[419] Of which sum not much is now left. And yet all the time my annuity from the emperor is postponed; but postponed on terms that it will be ready for me at once on my return.[420] This is promised in a letter to me by the Lady Margaret, illustrious aunt of the emperor Charles, to whom the emperor 1800 himself had lately written from Spain,[421] giving instructions for my annuity

* * * * *

416 Otto Brunfels (Allen Ep 1405) had made this charge in his *Responsio ad Erasmi Spongiam* (Böcking II 343:3–5). Cf n285 above and Allen Ep 1459:52–3.
417 See Ep 1289 n14.
418 Possibly Florentine florins, but, since Erasmus is discussing Froben's Basel residence, more likely Rhenish florins, and thus an amount then worth about £37 gros Flemish. But see n415 above.
419 *Mille nongentos florenos aureos.* These were probably Florentine florins, then officially worth £633 6s 8d gros Flemish (£427 10s sterling, or £3,942 10s tournois); if they were Rhenish gold florins, they were worth only about £465 gros. See Ep 1295 n1.
420 See Ep 1273 n4 and Allen Ep 1380 introduction.
421 Ep 1380

to be paid out of due turn, the annuities due in respect of all other offices
being suspended on account of the burdens of the war. And so anyone who
is jealous of Froben had better challenge him in a contest of generosity, and I
shall be on the winning side. At least there is no reason why anyone should   1805
grudge me his friendship. If thanks to him I can do learning some service, it
is without harming anyone else or standing in his way as he races to be rich;
nor have I any agreement with Froben, only good will mutual and
unfettered, in which I shall never endure to come second, challenge me who
will. I have presented my true account; it is reasonable that their criticisms   1810
should now cease. But this is the wretched constraint upon those of us who
publish books and begin to act our play before the public: we must satisfy
everyone, even the dregs.

Ennio, bishop of Veroli,[422] has written[423] to me to say that in your part
of the world there is a man who promises unfailing remedies for the stone[424]   1815
and has such confidence in his art that he will take no payment unless he has
driven away the disease. But who can he put up to guarantee that it will not
return when it has been driven away? In any case, who can assure us that in
expelling the disease he may not expel life itself at the same time? I do not
think it safe to entrust this frail body to a physician whom I do not know. I   1820
have made a friend here, a young man named Jan Antonin of Košice,[425] a
Hungarian by birth, of good education and open and most attractive
manners, who besides other remedies has given me an astrological lion,[426]
which I use to drink from. Whether things that smack of magic deserve any
credit, I do not know; but at any rate for some days now the stone has given   1825
me less trouble, whether I owe this to a change of wine, to other remedies, or
to my lion. I have not forgotten the old proverb 'Send for a young barber, but

* * * * *

422 Ennio Filonardi (Ep 1282)
423 Letter not extant
424 See Ep 1267 n5.
425 Antonin (c 1499–c 1549), from Kassa in North Hungary (now Košice in
    Czechoslovakia), studied medicine at Padua. In July 1524 he visited Basel and
    was welcomed into the circle of Erasmus, for whom he performed the medical
    services indicated here (cf AK Ep 2149:17–24 and Allen Epp 1512:44–6,
    1564:35–7). Though officially invited to settle and practice in Basel, Antonin
    left in November 1524, returning first to Hungary and then in 1525 settling in
    Cracow, where he became one of the most active protagonists of Erasmianism
    in Poland, winning Erasmus new patrons and maintaining friendly relations
    with him. Very few of the letters that they exchanged have survived. In 1526
    Erasmus dedicated some translations of Galen to Antonin (Ep 1698).
426 The Leo astrologicus was a coin minted in Padua in 1523 which, when dipped in
    wine, was believed to have magical properties as a remedy against gallstones.

an old physician';[427] but in my Antonin I find nothing young except his appearance – his character and scholarship have their own gray hairs, although he is not more than twenty-five, and he is a good Latin and Greek   183◦ scholar and so attentive to me that were he my own son he could not take more trouble.°

Mind you look after yourself properly, my most excellent Botzheim, with all your company, your Graces and your Muses; and long and happily may you be spared to live among them. Give my particular greetings to that   183 modest scholar Michael Hummelberg,[428] and at the same time to Johann Wanner,[429] your public preacher, and to those brethren born for virtue and piety, Ambrosius and Thomas Blarer,[430] and to the man to whom after the wine of Burgundy I owe my heaviest debt, Johann Menlishofer the physician,[431] a man in my opinion as civilized as he is learned. As for your   184◦ most honoured bishop,[432] do not cease to commend me to him, and I shall not cease to pray that all may go well with him, and all may be his that his outstanding character deserves.

Basel, 30 January 1523

1342 / To Marcus Laurinus   Basel, 1 February 1523

The addressee, Marcus Laurinus (1488–1546), was the second son of Hieronymus Lauwerijns, squire of Watervliet and treasurer to Philip the Handsome (Ep 1341A n170). Erasmus had met Marcus and his brothers in Bologna in 1506 (Ep 201). Marcus, who remained an intimate friend and correspondent of Erasmus for many years, became canon of St Donatian's at Bruges in 1512 and dean in 1519.

* * * * *

427 Not in the *Adagia*, but see *The Oxford Dictionary of English Proverbs* 3rd ed (Oxford 1970) 927.
428 Ep 1253 n6
429 Ep 1335 n5
430 Ambrosius and Thomas Blarer (or Blaurer) were sons of a town councillor of Constance. Thomas (d 1567) studied at Freiburg and (from 1520) at Wittenberg, whence he sent works of Luther and Melanchthon to Ambrosius (1492–1564), who was a Benedictine monk at Alpirsbach in the Black Forest. In the summer of 1522, Ambrosius abandoned the monastery to become the theological leader of the Reformation in Constance, to which he imparted a decidedly Zwinglian flavour. In 1523 Thomas returned to Constance to pursue a civic career. Erasmus probably met Ambrosius in the autumn of 1522 during his visit to Constance. In November 1523 he received a friendly letter from Thomas (Ep 1396).
431 Ep 1335 n10
432 Hugo von Hohenlandenberg (d 1532)

Erasmus himself counted this letter among his major apologetic writings (Ep 1341A:1016–18). Almost half of it (from line 650) is devoted to a detailed explanation of his much misunderstood attitude toward Luther. Much of the other half describes and justifies Erasmus' similarly misunderstood wanderings and his unexpectedly prolonged residence in Basel. The letter was published with the first edition of the *Catalogus lucubrationum* (Ep 1341A introduction) but omitted from the second. Beginning with the *Opus epistolarum* of 1529, it was published in all the major editions of his correspondence.

There are reasons, enumerated by Allen, for being suspicious of the date which Erasmus assigned to this letter. It seems unlikely, first of all, that Erasmus would have waited fourteen months before providing so intimate a friend as Laurinus with so lively and detailed an account of his journey to Basel in November 1521 (lines 98–242). Moreover, the references to the new pope succeeding Leo x (lines 631–2, 1000–4) and the brief echoes of Ep 1268 (lines 657–8, 1022–4) suggest a date somewhere in the period January–March 1522. On the other hand, the descriptions of Erasmus' visits to Sélestat and Constance in April and September 1522 (lines 333–8, 369–495), and certain references, such as that to the death of Hattstein in June 1522 (lines 206–7), could not have been written so early. Allen inferred from all this that Erasmus, wishing to publish an important letter clarifying his attitude toward Luther, combined it with an earlier letter, addressed to the same friend and full of vivid narrative, in order to produce a composition attractive to his reading public.

ERASMUS OF ROTTERDAM TO MARCUS LAURINUS, DEAN OF
THE COLLEGIATE CHURCH OF ST DONATIAN AT BRUGES, GREETING
I must say, you owe a great debt to our friend Hilarius,[1] who when you were quite dispirited by pitiless rumours,[2] as you say in your letter,[3] suddenly gave you back your spirits. But that there should be people who spread 5 rumours of this sort without a shadow of truth in them ought to surprise no one, for this reason if no other, that it is no longer new, especially since the world feeds so many idlers whose only object (and it comes easy to them, and is all they have left) is to pierce with tongues dipped in poison those who do their best to serve the cause of public enlightenment and the Christian 10

* * * * *

1342
1 Bertholf (Ep 1257 n10)
2 See lines 251–5, 564–7, 574–6, 590–1. See also Ep 1331 n16. According to Allen, who cites *Collectanea van Gerardus Geldenhauer Noviomagus* ed J. Prinsen (Amsterdam 1901) 74, Bertholf's arrival at Bruges with this letter dispelled a rumour of Erasmus' death.
3 Not extant

religion, that in this way at least they may cause temporary anguish to the spirits of those who rejoice in public progress and therefore support the men who devote their activities to the public good. What does surprise me is that people should be disturbed by rumours of this kind, especially when they have so often learned from experience how vain the outcome has shown them to be. But it ought not to seem surprising if men who have never known even in a dream what it means to be ashamed of oneself dare to tell lies about one who is so far away, when against their nearest neighbour they are wont to coin new fables all the time. There, I have produced a blank verse by accident![4] I think the subject deserved an iambic line, with some teeth in it.

I have spent so many years in Louvain.[5] Whenever I betook myself to Brussels or Mechelen, giving a good ten days notice of my departure before I left, these men, who have no sense of shame, used to put it about that I had run away. Then when I retired into the country for the sake of my health to Anderlecht,[6] which is a populous place and quite close to Brussels, where the emperor's palace is, though I rode into the city almost daily and returned from time to time to Louvain too, you may be sure they said I was taking cover. And often during the same period, so they said, I was ill of an untreatable fever in Louvain, and near Brussels I had fallen from my horse and nearly died of an apoplexy; though for many years, thanks be to Christ, I had not been in better health than I was at that time.[7] But within seven years I can't tell you how often they had buried me or brought me to death's door or laid me low with every kind of misfortune.

Could any Phalaris or Mezentius do worse?[8] Is it not enough to have killed my poor self once, but they must constantly torment me with unending troubles and snuff me out in repeated ruin? Nor can they sate their cruel appetites meanwhile with all these tortures and these endless deaths. What has become all this while of those words of the apostle John, 'Whosoever hateth his brother is a murderer?'[9] They make it pretty clear, I think, what they will do if they safely can, by killing me so often with their

* * * * *

4 The last four words of the previous sentence (*novas subinde comminisci fabulas*) form an iambic senarius. Iambics were traditionally the metre for invective.

5 1502–4, 1517–21

6 In the summer of 1521; see Ep 1271 n31.

7 Erasmus enjoyed better health at Anderlecht than he had for years; Epp 1208:1–2, 1223, 1238:12–15, and Allen 1518:20–4.

8 Phalaris, tyrant of Agrigentum in Sicily from c 570 to 554 BC, and Mezentius, king of the Tyrrheian Caere, later slain by Aeneas. Both were famous for their cruelty.

9 1 John 3:15

tongues because they cannot use cold steel. And yet the day cannot be far
distant when it will be true to say 'Erasmus is no more.' Of all the mischances
that may befall mankind, there is not one that I may not expect. Indeed it is
surprising that this poor body, feeble enough in itself, and now weaker still   45
from the onset of old age, should stand up to so much sickness, so much
misfortune, so much toil. And this I think I owe to their imprecations and
their vows, such being God's will, that they must wait for the fruition of their
cruel pleasure. Even now, when they have at last polished me off in these
horrible ways, they savagely attack my books, just as though they were my   50
beloved children, so that if I live again, as it were, in them – if I survive,
rather – I may die an even more cruel death. How often they have damned
these, branded with their theta,[10] how often consigned them to avenging
flames!

If I failed to attend the Diet of Worms or, as the learned have started   55
calling it, Berbethomagum,[11] to which I had indeed been invited, the reason
partly was that I did not wish to become involved with the Luther business,
which was then in a highly critical stage; in part because I could easily guess
that in such a gathering of princes and such a hotbed of humanity of every
sort, there would certainly be plague,[12] for Cologne had not been free of that 60
scourge when the emperor first lived there. After the death of the prince of
Chièvres[13] certain people I could name tried to bring some sort of charge
against me before the emperor;[14] but so outrageously that they convinced no
honourable and intelligent person. I myself was warned in letters from my
friends,[15] and by writing immediately to the chief figures at court[16] scattered 65
the whole nonsense so successfully that they all sent me answers which

* * * * *

10 That is, condemned; see *Adagia* I v 56: *Theta praefigere.*
11 'Borbetomagum' is the correct form.
12 The plague ravaged the imperial household during the Diet of Worms,
   carrying off Chièvres (Ep 532:30n), among others.
13 Cf n16 below.
14 The same incident is reported in the *Spongia* (ASD IX-1 150), where Erasmus
   identifies Aleandro (Ep 1256 n11) as the chief culprit, though there were surely
   others as well (see Ep 1195 introduction and Allen Ep 1482:11–13). The charge
   was that Erasmus was a supporter of Luther and the author of certain
   'scandalous pamphlets.' See Ep 1195.
15 One of these was Capito; Ep 1195 n1. None of the warning letters is extant.
16 Of the letters which Erasmus sent to court, the only one extant is Ep 1195,
   addressed to Luigi Marliano (d 1521), physician and councillor to Charles V and
   bishop of Tuy. If, as one assumes, all the other letters, including that to
   Aleandro, were written at the same time as Ep 1195 (25 March 1521), then
   Erasmus was mistaken in remembering (lines 61–2) that the move against him
   at court took place after the death of Chièvres, which occurred on 28 May.

were as cordial as they were complimentary. Among them[17] were that most
distinguished man Mercurio Gattinara, his Imperial Majesty's high chancellor, the cardinal of Sion, Marliano, bishop of Tuy, Girolamo Aleandro, who
was at that time apostolic nuncio – for others I purposely do not name. Only   70
the bishop of Liège[18] kept my messenger waiting for several days, and at
length being prevented by press of business sent me merely a verbal reply.

On the emperor's return to Brussels[19] scarcely a day passed when I did
not ride through the market-place and past the court, and I was often at
court myself, a thing not very habitual with me; in fact I lived almost more in   75
Brussels than at Anderlecht. Every day I was greeting bishops, though
normally I do not seek anything from such social duties; I dined with the
cardinal;[20] I had a talk with both nuncios;[21] I called on the envoys, and they
in turn came to see me at Anderlecht. Never in my life was I less concealed,
never lived more openly in the eyes of all men. And yet all this time there   80
were some of those voluble rascals who had described me as lying concealed
somewhere in Germany. Nor did I discover this fact before I had retired
here.

Again, when the emperor was living in Bruges,[22] together with the
king of Denmark,[23] and his eminence Thomas, the cardinal of York,[24] was   85
there at the time as envoy representing the English king, had I merely
confined myself to your house, you can say of your own knowledge what a
secret life I should have led, while you received everyone, or at least all the
chief figures at court, constantly at your table; and I sat among them and all, I
think, were pleased to see me there. As it is, think of the times I dined out or   90
supped with the nobility, and even with the king of Denmark, who actually
wished he could enjoy my society every day. Think how I rode out
frequently everywhere, and in your company. Was there any gathering of
magnates at which I was not present? – in the emperor's court one day,

* * * * *

17 Of the four answers listed here, two survive: Epp 1197 from Gattinara (Ep 1150)
and 1198 from Marliano (see the preceding note). Those from Aleandro and
Cardinal Schiner (Ep 1295) were presumably written at about the same time, ie,
early April 1521. According to the account in the *Spongia* (n14 above),
Aleandro's reply was conciliatory. Lines 78 and 120–5 below indicate that civil
relations were temporarily restored.
18 Erard de la Marck (Ep 1268 n9)
19 14 June 1521; Gachard II 30
20 Schiner (Ep 1295)
21 Aleandro and Caracciolo (Ep 1263 n1)
22 In August 1521; LP III 1458, Ep 1223 introduction
23 Ep 1263 n11
24 Wolsey

another in the household of the cardinal of York, and so on and so forth, 95
even though I was often invited and did not go. For I am a home-keeper by
nature, and that also is the manner of life demanded by my work.

And the way in which I then lay hidden is matched by the secrecy of
my departure later on. For six long months I had been preparing for my
journey to Basel,[25] and that too in the sight of all men; for this was the reason 100
why the treasurer[26] actually paid me my imperial annuity[27] in cash before the
due date, because I told him I had to go to Basel. Nor was there any secrecy
about the cause, which was of course the same that had made me pay so
many earlier visits to Basel, before I had any reason to fear these champions.
The first volume of my New Testament had been printed off,[28] and there 105
remained the annotations. I wanted to be there for them, not only that the
published text might be more correct but to be able little by little, as occasion
arose, to make changes or additions. For in this sort of work the author finds
his toil 'in ceaseless round returns, unsated ever.'[29] I hoped however to
finish my work in this final edition, which was the third. Do you find this a 110
frivolous excuse? Let it seem so, if you please, but only to those potbellies,[30]
who would not hesitate all the same to skip off all the way to Basel on foot for
the sake of a good dinner. I at least found the reason no less acceptable than
the king of France found his duchy of Milan.[31]

I was already booted and spurred, and there was no obstacle except the 115
risks of travel. I waited therefore for a safe escort. Meanwhile money was to
be got together from various places, and for this purpose I spent six days
actually in Louvain, in my usual concealment, of course, there too, in an inn
where nobody ever stays, so much so that frequently they cannot find room
for one. The sign of this populous hostelry is the Wild Man.[32] By pure luck 120
Girolamo Aleandro was there at that moment, and I spent a pleasant time in
his company, sometimes prolonging the conversation on literary topics until

* * * * *

25 Cf Ep 1242 introduction.
26 Ruffault (Ep 1287 n10)
27 Ep 1273 n4
28 The text of the third edition was sent to Froben at Basel sometime before 27
   May 1521; Ep 1206:72–3, and cf Ep 1174 n6. Text and annotations were
   published in February 1522.
29 Cf Virgil *Georgics* 2.401.
30 The Louvain theologians; cf Ep 1166:15–16.
31 Francis I won Milan at the battle of Marignano in 1515, lost it to Charles v in
   1521–2, took it again in 1524, and then lost it for good at the battle of Pavia the
   next year.
32 Ie, the *Homme Sauvage*, apparently the principal inn in Louvain at the time; cf
   Allen Ep 1244:3n.

midnight. We had agreed that if we had the chance of a safe journey we should set off together. When I returned there a few days later, I found Aleandro still mobilizing for departure, just as I was. In Brussels I had learned that the general Franz von Sickingen[33] was to be at Tienen the following day; at that time he was on excellent terms with the emperor, but what their relations are now, I do not know.[34]

That day was my birthday,[35] and also that of Sts Simon and Jude, and something happened appropriate to my birthday, by which I mean part of my fate. A certain Dominican,[36] I think the man who wrote notes on my *Moria*, had preached in the Sint Pieterskerk at seven o'clock. He is a cocksure fellow with a high opinion of himself – the type, you would say, of Phormio[37] in the play. He seemed to be not so much speaking from the sacred pulpit as thumping a tub. For a solid hour almost he held forth against me personally, joining in Luther's name from time to time, obviously to make his public suspect that there was much contact between him and me; but what particularly unleashed his ire was, as he said, my intention to correct the works of Augustine[38] as well, of which he said I understood nothing. He promised to preach at greater length on the same subject after dinner, for that is when inspiring tankards make these gentry more eloquent. Knowing nothing of this, when I went to church to attend high mass, I was greeted by Maquet,[39] a pleasant person and a former

* * * * *

33 Franz von Sickingen (1481–1523), a free imperial knight and soldier of fortune whose intelligence, military skill, income from the mines on his estates, and the scale of his activities as a 'robber baron' set him apart from the other members of the knightly class. Along with his fellow knight and friend, Ulrich von Hutten, Sickingen was an early and sincere, if violent and uncomprehending, supporter of Luther; see Ep 1308 n7. Here and in line 167 Erasmus refers to Sickingen as *dux* (duke), which must, under the circumstances, be construed as an indication of military leadership rather than of princely rank. To avoid confusion, we have translated *dux* as 'general.'

34 In July 1521 Sickingen entered the emperor's service in the war against France, but did poorly and fell into disfavour, losing his army and a great deal of money in the process. In the attempt to recoup his fortunes, to strike a blow for the Reformation, and to create the territorial basis for his elevation to princely rank, he launched an invasion of the archbishopric of Trier in August 1522. This led to his outlawry in October and to his defeat and death in May 1523.

35 Born during the night of 27–8 October, Erasmus celebrated the twenty-eighth, the feast of Sts Simon and Jude. See Allen 1, appendix 2, page 578.

36 Laurens Laurensen; see Ep 1166 n6.

37 See Ep 1341A n76.

38 Ep 1309 introduction

39 Jean Maquet (d 1535) of Binche in Hainault, since 1519 *syndicus* (legal agent) of the university, and before that twice *promotor* (a disciplinary official)

student of that university. He asked what had happened to make me be in
church so early, at seven o'clock in fact, and contrary to my usual habits.   145
'What do you mean, early?' I said. 'Yes,' he says, 'you were there in the
harangue.' I laughed, and gathered (which was no surprise to me) that some
noisy fellow had been prating to the congregation. He was a candidate for
the doctorate in theology, and in this way was giving a sample of his quality,
to show that he would not be unworthy of that honourable estate.   150

I went home and ate a brief dinner, intending soon to be on horseback,
for I had determined to leave at two o'clock. I found Aleandro pacing up and
down. I had often told him at length about the impudence of this sort of
noisy rascals, but he could never believe what I said. I advised him
therefore, if he wished to test my reliability, to send one of his people to the   155
Dominican church at one o'clock, when the last act of the ancient comedy
was due to be presented. He sent one of them to the Ploughboy,[40] the
biggest fool of all the theologians Louvain has had for fifty years; he's a real
Coroebus.[41] Aleandro told him formally (I quote almost verbatim) not to rant
against any man's reputation but to preach the gospel; and to frighten him   160
off more effectually brought in the authority of the supreme pontiff – for
which these men have a wonderful respect whenever it suits their book. I
suborned some people to listen, because I had to be off, as my companions
were all ready. They wrote me a full account afterwards, and said the man
complained that he was forbidden by certain persons to give free rein to his   165
inspiration.

When I reached Tienen, Franz the general was not there, nor was he
expected; but there was a large body of troops, some infantry, some cavalry,
some of the middle sort, who were removing their booty in carts together
with lame and wounded who had been careless on the battlefield. I had   170
these men as travelling-companions as far as Speyer; there I crossed the
Rhine and left them on my left. Being numerous, they secured me thus far a
very safe journey.

I had decided to incur the least possible expense on my way. It is a
German custom for local societies to meet in order to pay one their respects,   175
and nothing can be more enjoyable when one has the leisure; but when one
is hurried and exhausted and beset by the problems of travel, nothing is less
to the point. In the mean time, while we are exchanging greetings, the
horses are neglected, and pick up some disease or die of thirst. After the

* * * * *

40 Identified by Allen as Vincentius Theoderici (Ep 1196), but the reference to
   Aleandro's rebuke in lines 159–62 makes Laurensen (n36 above) the more
   likely candidate.
41 See Ep 1341A n275.

town of Düren therefore I went straight through Sickingen, leaving Cologne   18
on my left. That day we sat our horses, with no dinner, for nine solid hours,
riding steadily all the time, because the last part of the journey was longer
than we expected, and none too safe, as it wound through mountains and
hills.

Next day we got to Koblenz about ten o'clock. There too I longed to get   18
away without a word, but somehow that excellent man Matthias,[42] the
official of that city, who is entirely devoted to good literature and the good
life, got to know of it. As I had guessed would happen, he carried me off to
his house willy-nilly, and his friends came flocking in. There I learned for the
first time, and it was a very great surprise to me, that there were people in   19
Germany who feared that something might happen to me.[43] But I relieved
them of this baseless fear, actually laughed them out of it. They also told me
that the bishop[44] much wanted to meet me – in Cologne too he had invited
me to dinner,[45] but I used the pestilent and unseasonable weather as an
excuse, thinking it more important of course to mind my own health than to   19
comply with great men's wishes – but at this time he was away from home.
Furthermore, since it was clear that the friends who wished to greet me
would not allow me to detach myself that day, in order not to let a whole day
be lost without a line[46] I wrote several letters after dinner to various friends
for dispatch by that kindest of men, Karl Harst,[47] who had courteously   20
accompanied me thus far.

Before reaching Mainz I learned on the way that the cardinal of Mainz
was not at home;[48] so that left only Capito, whom I summoned for a talk. The
moment I heard that he too was away, I made ready to leave, and was
offered some of his household, armed, to go with me by that excellent young   20
man Marquard von Hattstein, a canon of Mainz cathedral, who has recently
died,[49] though in every way he richly deserved a long life. When I refused,
since such a thing often actually attracts the highwaymen, he gave me his
personal servant as a companion.

At Worms, while dinner was preparing, I summoned Hermannus   21

* * * * *

42 Matthias von Saarburg (Ep 867:64n)
43 Presumably because of his connections with Reuchlin and Luther
44 Richard von Greiffenklau, archbishop of Trier (d 1531)
45 In November 1520; see Epp 1155–60 and Allen Ep 1512:18–20.
46 Cf *Adagia* I iv 12.
47 Ep 1215
48 Archbishop Albert (Ep 661) and Capito (Ep 1290) were in Halle in November
   1521; see Ep 1241 introduction.
49 Hattstein, kinsman of Hutten and canon at Mainz (cf Ep 1109 n8), died on 13
   June 1522, aged nearly thirty-three.

Buschius,[50] a man of more than average learning and a very old friend of mine, for a talk. While a prolonged and fruitless search was failing to find him, I sat too long in a room with a stove and suffered severely;[51] for though up to now I had always been in capital health, at this point I began to feel sick, more from the stink than from the heat – so difficult do I find it to live   215
with German stoves, though I get on famously with the Germans themselves. I should think them much blessed with a thing in many ways so convenient, were I allowed to enjoy it with them. But this first physical setback was shaken off by the hard exercise of riding. We flew to Speyer rather than rode, and I had horses of the true Pegasus blood, who are eating   220
their master out of house and home even now.

When we arrived at Speyer – and our arrival was very late – I went straight with my horses to the house of Thomas Truchsess,[52] the dean of the cathedral, either because he had often written and told me to do so, or since I knew that all the inns on every side were stuffed full with soldiers, who   225
usually show more ferocity in the inn than on the battlefield, as a hero should. When I got there, I found some of the canons supping with him, and joined them at table. There too the stove was very hot, though there was an absence of stink. Immediately the same physical affliction returned that was already only too familiar. I therefore resolved to avoid this favourite German   230
device entirely. After two days there I recovered my health, and got to Strasbourg. Here too I had decided not to stay; but Jakob Spiegel,[53] the emperor's secretary, a good scholar and a man of spotless character, whom I dared not fail to greet in passing, made my presence known to the society,[54] which had a new recruit in Lucas Bathodius,[55] who has a more passionate   235
love of these things than any of them. I gave them one day, and then a second. From there I proceeded to Sélestat, escorted by several of them; among whom was Bartholomaeus Latomus of Trier,[56] a man unusually lively in both character and brain, who was master of a college of philosophy in Freiburg. From there some of the society[57] again gave me their company   240

* * * * *

50 See Epp 1291 n4.
51 See Ep 1258 n18.
52 See Ep 355:50n.
53 See Ep 1323 introduction.
54 See Epp 302 and 867:22–28.
55 See Ep 883:15n.
56 See Ep 1252 n3.
57 Ie, the literary society of Sélestat, whose founder and focal member was Jakob Wimpfeling; see Ep 323 introduction. For other members of the society, see BRE Ep 163 (page 221) and CEBR III 449.

as a compliment as far as Colmar, among them Beatus Rhenanus, who escorted me next day[58] as far as Basel.

Why need I at this point remind you, my dear Laurinus, of Thraso,[59] by recounting what warm congratulations I received on my return from that excellent and most saintly old man the bishop of Basel,[60] who even now 245 sends me presents and letters from time to time as evidence of his feelings towards me, and from the authorities of this city and all the other leading figures in the church and in higher education? And they would have displayed their enthusiasm at even greater length, did I not always make it clear from the outset that such formalities have absolutely no attractions for 250 me. And my presence was so far from escaping notice in Germany that according to the rumours which preceded me I had been there for several days before my arrival. Meanwhile these worthless fellows were triumphantly saying that I had decamped to Wittenberg. They really stick at nothing! 255

All this time in Basel my health was pretty good, until the rooms began to get cold. In any case, when I saw clearly that other people already found the cold unbearable, I allowed them two or three times to light up in moderation. But this unselfishness cost me dear: in no time I caught a pestilent cold. The cold was followed by an attack of the stone,[61] and the 260 trouble recurred so frequently that no day passed without my either conceiving or being in labour or bringing to birth or enduring postnatal convalescence, like women in childbed. Meanwhile my appetite collapsed so completely that no remedy could restore it. Fasting is by nature fatal to me; and during the birth-pangs of the stone, which often lasted two days, 265 food is the last thing one can face. As a result, though the pain was worse than any form of death, yet I was in no less danger from the complete loss of appetite. In short, I was in such straits that even Nicolaas Baechem[62] would have been satisfied.

But in the mean time, though I was in great trouble of body, my spirit 270 was unbroken and did not give in. Besides many other things I finished my annotations on the New Testament. I set about a paraphrase on Matthew, and finished it within about two months; when finished I sent it to the emperor,[63] and it was very well received by the whole court. Jean Glapion[64]

* * * * *

58 15 November; see Ep 1242 introduction.
59 The braggart soldier in Terence's *Eunuchus*
60 Christoph von Utenheim (Ep 1332)
61 See Ep 1267 n5.
62 Ep 1254 n6
63 Ep 1255
64 Ep 1275

showed it in his chapel in the presence of several court prelates, among 275
whom was the bishop of Palencia;[65] and he gave a most fair and friendly
report on my work which recommended it forcibly to the emperor.[66] His
Majesty at once recognized the Erasmus who had long ago dedicated the
Panegyricus to his father Philip[67] and to himself the previous book, *Institutio
principis christiani*,[68] and expressed his gratitude for the gift in a letter[69] which 280
was as kind as it was complimentary. Most obliging letters[70] to the same
effect arrived from many others, but particularly from Glapion himself, the
bishop of Palencia, the chancellor Mercurino, Joris van Halewijn, Jean de
Carondelet, archbishop of Palermo, Antoon Sucket, one of the councillors
who is specially influential, Maximilian, the most distinguished of the 285
secretaries.[71] When most people's pensions were either terminated or
reduced, they promised that mine would be untouched and paid in full, and
told me to hope in future for even greater evidence of the emperor's bounty.
Indeed his Majesty in person, when dining not long afterwards with the
king of England, went out of his way to speak highly of me,[72] and made it 290
quite clear what his feelings towards me were. This I learned for certain from
those who were in attendance at table.

I am sure you began to smile long ago at my showing off like this, but I
am driven to it by the impudence of those who accuse me falsely. Even so, I
tell rather less than the truth, so far am I from inventing any additions; for 295
you will have noticed, no doubt, how little appetite I have for these petty
distinctions. But they criticize me all this time for having stayed so long in
Basel and for not putting in an appearance before the emperor's departure,[73]
however often my friends wrote and told me to come.[74] On this point, my

* * * * *

65 Mota (Ep 1273)
66 See Ep 1269.
67 See Ep 179.
68 See Ep 393.
69 Ep 1270
70 For all the letters mentioned here, save the last, see Epp 1299:41–6,
1300:63–9, 1331:12–19.
71 Maximilianus Transsilvanus (Transsylvanus), d 1538, secretary to the imperial
chancellery under Maximilian I and Charles V. Erasmus apparently met him at
court in 1521. Transsilvanus made repeated attempts to secure the payment of
Erasmus' imperial annuity and also defended him in his conflicts with
conservative theologians, especially those at Louvain. See Allen Ep 1553
introduction.
72 Cf Ep 1302:64–6.
73 See Ep 1273 introduction for Erasmus' unsuccessful attempt to return to
Brabant in April 1522.
74 Cf Ep 1269:12–14.

most excellent Marcus, I could wish for my own sake that my case were less   30
strong than it is. In the emperor's circle there was no question at issue except
how to make the position which had fallen to my lot more permanent or
more distinguished; and personally I was completely satisfied with what I
had already, and in Basel was by no means unemployed – the facts speak
for themselves. Suppose I had attached more importance to this business,   30
which was of the nature of a service to the public, than to my personal
advantage, should I be taken to task for this? I was invited to accept very
high honours (so Glapion assured me in more than one letter), and there
was so much evidence to convince me of the emperor's good will – and it
was fear, if you please, that kept me away! Had any such risks been   31
displayed before these gentry who are dead to the world, how they would
have come scampering up with winged feet and open mouths!

As for me, if I feared anything in all this, it was simply that the task of
doing battle with Luther's party might be entrusted to me by a personage to
whom it would have been unlawful to say no – not that I am in favour of this   31
movement of rebellion, for nature has implanted in me such an abhorrence
of all strife that, if I had to undertake a lawsuit to secure great estates, I
would rather abandon the property than pursue my legal rights. I am in very
truth the vine and fig-tree of the parable in Judges,[75] which were invited by a
delegation from all the trees to reign over them and fight their battles and   32
replied that they could not leave the sweetness of their nature and plunge
into the confusion of war. The emperor had been persuaded by men in high
place, but wrongly, that I was above all the ideal person to undertake this
task, though no one less suitable could have been chosen. I saw many men
on all sides girding on their armour for this affair; I recognized how unequal I   32
was myself to such a responsibility, even had I been fitted by nature for such
unpleasant conflicts; I saw much else to dissuade me, on which I think it best
now to hold my peace.

And yet even these many considerations would not have deterred me
from returning, had not that vicious tyrant held me bound in chains. 'What   33
tyrant?' you will say; 'there are no tyrants in Switzerland.' I mean that
second Phalaris,[76] the stone;[77] and would that I could play the tyrannicide at
its expense! Even this however I ignored, and had got out as far as Sélestat;[78]
but I was in such a state from the journey that I had first to nurse my physical
weakness and reduce my fever by two days at Breisach with Heinrich   33

* * * * *

75 Judg 9:8–15
76 See n8 above.
77 See Ep 1267 n5.
78 See Ep 1273 introduction.

Gallinarius,[79] their parish priest, and then spend four days recovering with
Beatus,[80] the most open-hearted of all my friends, and thus managed to get
back to Basel, but only after staying again with Gallinarius to recover.
Meantime however I had resigned myself, if I should hear that Charles' stay
among us would be prolonged, to patch up my strength and make another   340
attempt at the journey. When I heard from the servant whom I had sent on
ahead for the purpose the definite date on which the emperor had decided to
set sail, it was the first of May, which was then imminent. Having lost all
hope of seeing him, I remained at Basel for some months, but gave myself by
no means an easy time.   345

Meanwhile I was invited to Rome in letters from learned men who
were not only numerous but such as I could safely trust, particularly from
the cardinal of Sion,[81] who pursued this idea frequently by way of third
parties and twice in warmhearted and enthusiastic letters from himself, in
which, over and above all the support and all the expectations, he promised 350
me on his own account five hundred ducats a year,[82] besides provision for
my journey by no means ungenerous. I was urged to the same course in a
most kind letter from that well-known figure Silvester Prierias.[83] Consequently I actually began to think of going to Rome, if only my domestic
tyrant[84] should issue me a passport. And there were many things besides to 355
make Rome attractive – the abundance of very good books and very good
scholars; all those old friends, among whom were Richard Pace,[85] who was
then living there, and Paolo Bombace[86] and Johannes Fabri[87] and Georg
Sauermann,[88] provost of Wrocław, a young man who is an accomplished

* * * * *

79 An example of Erasmus' frequent inaccuracy with first names. Gallinarius'
   name was Johannes; see Ep 1307 introduction.
80 Ep 327
81 See Ep 1299 n9.
82 See Ep 1299:49 and Ep 1295 n1.
83 Ep 872:19n. Prierias' letter is not extant.
84 See lines 330–3 of this letter.
85 See Ep 211:53n. Pace had been sent to Rome to work for the election of Wolsey
   to the papacy. He arrived on 27 January 1522 and by 4 August had retired to
   North Italy; LP III 1884, 1995, 2211, 2420. See also Ep 1294:15, and Allen Ep
   1360:11.
86 See Ep 1260 n43.
87 See Epp 1260 n22, 1324 n13.
88 Georg Sauermann (1492?–1527) of Wrocław studied law at Bologna, where he
   was rector of the university in 1513–14. In 1519 he entered the service of Leo x,
   who in 1520 sent him to greet Charles v in Spain, where he entered the
   emperor's service. Sauermann accompanied Charles back to the Netherlands,
   where his friendship with Erasmus presumably began. In the autumn of 1520

scholar and destined to do great things, and Herman[89] of Friesland, long
outstanding among the younger men and likely to make a name among the
learned; and all those new friends, among them Corycius,[90] most open-
hearted of men, and Landau,[91] who will one day be a well-known author
unless my forecast quite misleads me. I pass over for the moment all those
cardinals, of whom the greater part are my keen supporters, as I hear from
my friends' letters – and some of them have recorded their own feelings for
me in letters from themselves. If anyone wonders whether I can be trusted, I
can produce the letters, which will show that this is an understatement.

And so, although dissuaded by all my friends, I went to Constance,[92]
two of them offering to come with me, Heinrich Eppendorf,[93] who besides
his lineage and his learning is a most charming person, and Beatus
Rhenanus. We were all hospitably received by that distinguished man
Johann von Botzheim Abstemius,[94] one of the canons, who is as courteous
and as open-hearted as any man I ever met, born as one might say for the
Muses and the Graces. The house he lives in you would take to be a real
home of the Muses; no part of it but displays something in the way of polish
and elegance, no part without a voice – all speaks in paintings that attract
and retain the attention. In his summer hall, which (so he tells me) he had
fitted up for my benefit, nearest to the table stood Paul teaching the people;
on the other wall was Christ seated on the mount and teaching his disciples,
then the apostles setting off over the hills to preach the gospel. Next to the
fireplace stood the priests, Scribes, and Pharisees, conspiring with the
elders against the gospel, which was then raising its head. In another place
were the nine sisters of Apollo singing, elsewhere the naked Graces, a
symbol of simple good will and friendship without feigning. But why go on
trying to describe his whole house in a letter, when all the elegance and

* * * * *

Sauermann returned to Rome as imperial proctor at the papal court and c 1521
became provost of the cathedral in Wrocław. Among his works is the *De
religione ac communi concordia* (1524), a spirited defence of the church against
schism. He died of injuries received during the sack of Rome. None of his
correspondence with Erasmus survives.

89 See Ep 903:14n.
90 Johannes Corycius of Luxembourg (d 1527), cleric and jurist at the curia since at
least 1497. His house near Trajan's forum became the favourite resort of the
poets of the Roman Academy. Erasmus probably met him in Rome in 1509.
Like Sauermann (n88 above), he was badly handled during the sack of Rome
and died shortly thereafter. No correspondence with Erasmus survives.
91 Jakob Ziegler (Ep 1260)
92 See Ep 1316 introduction.
93 Ep 1283 n4
94 Ep 1285

charm of it one could scarcely survey in ten days? And in the whole house, exquisite as it is in every part, there is nothing more exquisite than our host himself. He keeps the Muses and the Graces more in his heart than in his pictures; they are more at home in his character than on his walls.   390

The moment of my arrival I had asked my host to invite no one to dinner, for by nature I enjoy a small party, and at that time I was so poorly that I was more likely to be a burden to others than to be able to recover my spirits in plenty of company. To begin with, I was weary after my journey, and then I was as far gone in pregnancy as any old sow, and very close   395 moreover to giving birth, for we can actually feel that coming on, just as pregnant women do. It was a sorry business, all this precaution! It so happened that Hugo, bishop of Constance,[95] was in town at the time, a man of heroic physical stature, singular grace of manner, straightforward and free from all pretence, free from pride too – no warrior like most of the   400 German bishops, but a real father in God. He heard at once of my arrival, and wished to invite me as a mark of esteem. Botzheim suggested, however, that he should have pity on my health, and promised to let him know when it would be convenient. In this matter the bishop deserves twofold credit for his courtesy. It was courteous to offer me hospitality, but still more   405 courteous to put up with a refusal. Some men resent it and think they are spurned unless you fall in with all their suggestions even at some cost to yourself. He sent his steward, however, to bring me some partridges as a present and offer me anything that a bishop's house could provide; and I made continuous use of the prelate's generosity. Some days later I was   410 brought to bed, but with more pain than ever before. I was very weak therefore after my birth-pangs, and in no state to be merry either for my own benefit or other people's; otherwise nothing was lacking to make one supremely happy. Immortal gods! what hospitality, what a host, what gentlemen! Everything so well found! The conversation, the reading, the   415 music! Truly they were repasts and suppers of the gods! I would not envy the poets' gods their nectar and ambrosia, had my health only been a little more propitious.

The situation of the place itself was full of charm too. Constance is dominated by a wonderful great lake, which stretches both far and wide for   420 many miles and at the same time loses none of its beauty. Its attractions are increased by the forest-clad hills prominent in all directions, some distant and some near at hand. For at that point, as though wearied by its rocky headlong passage through the Alps, the Rhine seems to have found an agreeable resting-place to recuperate in, through the middle of which it   425

* * * * *

95 Hugo von Hohenlandenberg (d 1532)

makes its gentle progress; at Constance it gathers again into its proper channel and therewith resumes its own name – though the lake as a whole has always preferred to take its name from the city, being the lake of Constance now but in the old days the lake of Bregenz, as long as Bregenz was the name of the city which is now called Constance.[96] It is said also to be full of fish and of almost incredible depth, such that in places there is a hundred and fifty feet of water between surface and bottom; for they say that vast mountain masses are hidden in its depths. The head of the Dominican society,[97] a man of the highest character and of solid learning, but with a remarkable turn of eloquence in his public sermons, presented me with an immense fish out of the lake, which they commonly call a trout – a gift fit for a king, had it been offered in our part of the world. Leaving the lake on its right, the Rhine glides for some little distance past the city of Constance, and then, as though not serious and merely indulging its fancy, it makes an island, which is occupied by a well-known house of nuns;[98] thereafter it runs together again and makes a smaller lake, which they call for some unknown reason the Venetian lake.[99] Thence it flows in a regular channel, full of whirlpools for the most part but navigable after a fashion, as far as a town, formerly an administrative centre under the Empire, called Schiffhausen,[100] I suppose because the river was crossed there by ship before there was a bridge. For not far below there are falls over which the Rhine hurls itself with a great roar; though in other places too it is frequently interrupted by cataracts and blocked with boulders, and so is scarcely fit for navigation as far as Basel.

But it is time for my story to return to Constance. The city has many claims to fame, not least the cathedral, which, though very ancient, is an elegant building, and the council once held there under the presidency of the emperor, and most particularly because that is where Jan Hus was burned.[101] Presents arrived for me from all directions, some from quite distant places. One man sent me some excellent wine, another a present of game, another fish; and so it went on. The city officers sent me their respects with a

* * * * *

96 Bregenz is, of course, a city at the other end of the lake.
97 Antonius Pyrata, called Guldenmünster (d 1534), preacher to the Dominicans of Constance and vicar of the provincial; see Rublack 248–50.
98 The only island between Constance and the Untersee is the Insel, with a Dominican friary but no nunnery.
99 The Untersee (Venetum)
100 Ie, Schaffhausen
101 The Council of Constance (1414–18), called at the insistence of Emperor Sigismund to end the papal schism, had the Bohemian heretic Jan Hus burned at the stake in 1415.

gift of wine, and for several days the town band played near by, for this is another mark of the respect they pay to selected visitors. If you also wish to know who dined with us, the regular guests beside Beatus and Eppendorf were a physician by the name of Johann,[102] a young man but distinguished for his wit and learning and no less for his good sense and modesty, and Michael Hummelberg,[103] who is (to give you a brief description of him) in good manners and scholarship and charm of character a second Rhenanus. Wanner,[104] their preacher, was there too, a man of true gospel integrity.

Once I had been brought to bed, when I had recovered a little strength, I used to devote an hour or so to the friends who came to greet me, but only a select group and those who had an introduction, for I was in no position to give everyone what he wanted. The bishop with his habitual kindness wished to do me such honour as he could; but my host warned him that I ate little, or rather nothing, and could not stand a crowded, noisy party, so would he please invite no one to meet me and make no special preparations beyond his daily style. He agreed, and invited nobody to dinner beyond that little society of ours. He took his leave of me with more respect, I am sure, than I deserved, and I went on to visit Ennio, bishop of Veroli,[105] who was there at the time as apostolic nuncio, for we had made friends already in an exchange of letters; and he came to meet me with as much alacrity as if someone really important had come to see him. We sat down, the two of us, and talked about all sorts of things; for he is a man of great wisdom, and long experience in the affairs of princes has given him exceptional judgment. The fact that we were of the same age and were sufferers from the same complaint increased the good will between us; for he too had been a victim to the stone, and had picked up the complaint from the same cause – the wine of those regions, which is thin and acid, rough and raw, both unkind and unpleasant.[106] On changing his wine, he had ceased to have any trouble, or at least had much less. He also gave me some other remedies which had been sent him from Milan. He too was making preparation for a journey to Italy, and nothing stood in the way except a papal brief, which he was hourly expecting; he wanted me to travel with him. For my part, I was much attracted, for Trent, they told me, was not more than six days' journey distant. We had to take that road because of the hostilities between the

460

465

470

475

480

485

490

* * * * *

102 Menlishofer (Ep 1335 n10)
103 Ep 1253 n6
104 Ep 1335 n5
105 Ep 1282
106 See Ep 1316 introduction.

imperial forces and the French.[107] Such are the monarchs with whom we are
now blessed! The Alpine meadows which smiled upon us from nearby were
attractive enough; but my friends were all against it – to no purpose, had not
the stone, that brutal counsellor, persuaded me to make for Basel again and
flutter back to my nest.   49

All this time, while Botzheim my host was finding a string of reasons to
delay me, and the boatmen were leading me a dance – for I had decided to
travel by boat downstream as far as Schiffhausen, having no confidence that
I could endure the bumping up and down on horseback, such was the state I
was in – I waited in Constance for nearly three weeks. At length, as the   50
sailors lied without ceasing, as is their privilege or at least their custom,
resentment gave me fresh strength: we mounted our horses at eight o'clock
and sped on wings to Schiffhausen before three in the afternoon. On
returning to Basel, it seemed a good plan to try some Burgundy[108] which had
been given me some days before in spite of my protest by that very generous   50
man Nikolaus von Diesbach,[109] dean and bishop-designate of Basel – what
they now call coadjutor. On first tasting it I did not much fancy it, but the
night following showed its true colours; my digestion was suddenly so
much mended that I seemed reborn – a new man. I had, to be sure, always
attributed this trouble to certain wines, most of which, though raw and acid   51
and therefore very bad for the digestion, yet make their way easily into the
kidneys and carry crude matter along with them. Besides which, as though
they had no curse on them already, people doctor them with disastrous
chemicals – lime, alum, resin, sulphur, salt – for the water which they add
so generously is the least of evils. In a word, most of them are only fit to be   51
drunk by heretics; for I should suppose these torments a sufficient
punishment for any misdemeanour. And yet men can be found willing to
get drunk on these dismal fluids!

I had previously tasted certain wines grown in Burgundy, but they
were fiery and dry. This one was of a most agreeable colour – you might call   52
it ruby-red, and the taste neither sweet nor dry but very pleasant; neither
cold nor fiery, but mellow and bland, so kind in fact to the digestion that
even when taken in some quantity it did very little harm; and, a rare quality
in wines on the red side, it had a mildly laxative effect, the result, I suppose,
of the natural mellowing power which it develops in the stomach. Happy   52
indeed is Burgundy on this count if no other, and well does she deserve to be

* * * * *

107 See Ep 1283 n3.
108 Ep 1316 n7
109 Ep 1258 n17

called a mother of men, now that she has such milk as this in her breasts! No wonder if the men of old worshipped as gods those whose efforts added some blessing to the life of mortals. Take this wine: the man who introduced me to it, who gave it to me though an introduction was sufficient, did he not 530 give me life rather than liquor? Another cask arrived not inferior to the first, except that the carrier had over-diluted it with water. The other had been sealed with plaster; one could draw out of it but not put anything in; and this one was different. Consequently the other when it arrived was not quite full, and this one full to the top; and that very fact which he intended should 535 prove him an honest carrier betrayed the wine-thief. And meanwhile, those who steal a coin are hanged: those who abstract at the same time one's property and one's life-blood play their pranks with impunity.

And so, my dear Laurinus, I could easily be induced to migrate bag and baggage into Burgundy. For the sake of the wine, you will ask? Why, I 540 would rather settle in an Irish bog than face even one attack of the stone. This at least I owe to all I have written, that whatever part of the world I turn to, I shall never lack friends. In the whole of Germany at any rate, wide as it is, I believe there is no city that will not be most ready to give my poor self a home, if I took a fancy to move somewhere else. Nor should I be very far 545 from the truth if I said the same thing of Italy and France. At least, I have had the kindest letters inviting me to visit some of them; and those I have visited hitherto on the way to or from Constance or Sélestat have made me welcome with a gift of wine, which is the traditional present made to visiting strangers as a mark of respect. This is a kind of distinction which I am so far from 550 enjoying that I have told my friends to arrange that nothing of the sort should happen, not solely because I think the honour should be reserved for others who are eminent men and not for someone in all respects so insignificant as myself, but also because, when one is tired or busy with other things, these compliments are sometimes more truly a hindrance than 555 a privilege.

And another thing, since I have begun to act the braggart soldier in the play.[110] Need I tell you of all the complimentary letters, either from scholars or from eminent men, which reach me here even from distant lands and bring gifts with them? Need I recount the learned men, some of them 560 actually in exalted positions, who have come to this place from distant parts with no purpose except to set eyes on Erasmus? I do not doubt that they experience what is described in the Greek proverb 'I found ashes where I hoped for gold.'[111] But whatever be my own merits, these things at least

* * * * *

110 Pyrgopolinices in Plautus' *Miles gloriosus*
111 *Adagia* I xi 30

expose the shameless inventions of these noisy rascals who, as you say in   56
your letter, had been putting it about in your part of the world that I could
find nowhere safe to live in Germany;[112] and therefore, I suppose, whenever
I go anywhere, I make a habit of asking for police protection! In any case,
what would prevent me from visiting many cities – a thing I would
sometimes have done for my own amusement – had my literary labours   57
allowed me the time for it – is the stoves,[113] which are going full blast here all
year round with scarcely three months off; and the lodging I have provided
myself in Basel I cannot take round with me.

Then there was an equally shameless lie: they put it about that I had
bought a house here in Basel and purchased rights of citizenship, presuma-   57
bly because I never meant to return to your part of the world. Supposing I
liked everything about Germany – and I do like a great deal – one thing at
least drives me away from here, and that is the universal use of stoves;
which means that I live by myself and cannot even visit other people without
risk to my health, nor can anyone else visit me without inconvenience, for   58
they dislike my cold house as much as I hate their hot ones. One thing is
perfectly true: there is a man in Basel who offered me as a present a house he
had bought for four hundred gold florins, in which I now live.[114] But I have
neither bought it nor accepted it as a gift. The idea of citizen rights has never
crossed my mind even in a dream. A man I know who is of some   58
considerable standing in Zürich[115] has proposed two or three times in letters
that I should accept citizenship there. His suggestion surprised me very
much, and I replied[116] that I wished to be a citizen of the whole world, and
not of one town in it.

As for my going to France,[117] and their saying this is practically the only   59
refuge I still have, this story is not wholly without foundation. I was
convinced that the wine I drank was the cause of my complaint, and had not
yet discovered that such good wine could be supplied from nearby in
Burgundy; and had it been possible, there were different rumours current
here at the time which inspired the fear that I might not be altogether safe   59
from war here in the future. Had anything of the sort happened, Burgundy

* * * * *

112 See lines 1–19 of this letter.
113 See lines 213–16, 577–8.
114 Presumably Rhenish florins, since the reference is to Froben's house in Basel,
     and therefore a sum worth about £98 gros Flemish; if Florentine florins, worth
     £133 6s 8d gros, or £90 sterling, or £830 tournois. See Ep 1295 n1. On the house,
     see Ep 1316 n10.
115 Zwingli
116 Ep 1314
117 See Ep 1319 introduction.

itself would not have been enough to quench my thirst. But since that was,
as I say, unknown to me, and rumours of this sort filled me with misgivings,
I began to think a little about going to France, with the idea that even with
wars all round it would provide me with a supply of wine. I mentioned the   600
subject to François,[118] archbishop of Embrun, who came to see me two or
three times, being here at that time on a mission; and he volunteered to
arrange for the issue of an official passport from the king which would make
it possible for me to perform the journey in greater safety, if I should decide
to do so.[119] This most obliging young man, quite delighted and boasting at   605
the king's table that in Basel he had seen Erasmus, put the matter of the
passport in train; the cardinal of Lorraine[120] was there at the moment. The
king agreed to his request, and gladly too. Then, the next time he saw Budé,
whom he has promoted to be one of the inner circle at court,[121] 'I say, Budé,'
he said, 'we shall soon have Lefèvre in this France of ours.' When Budé   610
replied that Lefèvre was in France all the time, the king realized he had got
the name wrong and said, 'Erasmus, it was Erasmus I meant to say. For the
passport is ready, so that he can get here safely.'

I was tempted by thoughts of my old sojourn in France, a country I
have always found delightful. I was tempted by the way he recalled me with   615
such munificent offers six years ago.[122] Had I accepted them then, I should at
least, to say no more, have escaped this prolonged contest with a number of
blockheads and vain babblers in Louvain, nor would my ears burn with this
sort of tragic bedlam, which keeps everything here at fever pitch. And my
finances would be somewhat more ample than they are now, or at least less   620
constrained; perhaps my health would be better too, for I have so often been
in mortal danger from the wine here and the stink of the stoves. I was
tempted also by the knowledge that if I lived in France, I should be much
nearer in future to Brabant, to which it would have been possible to slip
across even in wartime, thanks to my acquaintance and private friendships   625
with those who hold the cities near the border on both sides.[123] There was
one obstacle, war among the three kings.[124] To one of them, Charles, I am
actually bound by oath; with the second, the king of England, I have many

* * * * *

118 Tournon (Ep 1319)
119 See Ep 1319 n6.
120 Jean de Lorraine (1498–1550), son of Duke René II, bishop of Metz and
    cardinal, both since 1518
121 On Budé and his recent promotion, see Ep 1328.
122 See Ep 522 introduction.
123 Eg, with the family of Adolph of Burgundy, heer van Veere (Ep 93), whose
    principal residence was the castle at Tournehem; Ep 80 introduction
124 Epp 1283 n3 and 1306 n22

ties of obligation, as I have with the whole English people; the third, by
which I mean the king of France, I cannot fail to be warmly attached to for the   6
generous favour he has shown me. I hoped that the efforts of this new pope
at any rate would soon produce peace among them.[125] Not that the war
concerned me at all, for I was not approaching France at the head of an army
or in hopes of securing some high office in the king's household, but in order
to pass life more agreeably than I did here, in the pursuit of literature and the   6
Muses among my modest scholarly friends. And so the passport has now
been many months in my possession, and I have not used it.

You will say 'Why not come here instead?' Because in your part of the
world there were wars seething everywhere, and there was said to be an
immense shortage of everything, but specially of French wine – which is in   6
very short supply in your country even in peacetime, if one wants the real
thing. There were also certain madmen who had had a sword put into their
hands,[126] and it was no pleasure to be either their colleague or their
opponent. And I thought I had already fought long enough with certain
monsters who, having neither the will nor the ability to be of some use, yet   6
find time to spend their whole lives simply in harrassing those who pursue
the humanities, with their scurrilities if nothing else. Last but not least, from
France it would always have been a very short trip to join you, had anything
invited me.

That gives you the whole story, briefly but without concealment. As   6
for your saying in your letter that you have heard from several people of my
unpopularity even in Germany, this may perhaps be true; and it is no
surprise, for there are backbiters everywhere. For my part, I do all I can to
ensure that no man shall speak ill of me through my own fault. However, if I
were to hope for such good fortune as never yet befell anyone and think I   6
could contrive that absolutely no one should speak ill of me, it really would
be time to spit in my own bosom.[127] Rome has Zúñiga;[128] Germany too has
several men who do not know how to keep a civil tongue in their heads.
They tell me that some people who are passionate Lutherans, as they call
them, complain that I am milk and water, that I butter up the princes and am   6
too fond of peace. For my part, to tell the truth, I would rather err in that
direction, not merely because it is safer but because it is better morally. Let
every man enjoy his own opinion. There are some too on the other side who

* * * * *

125 See Epp 1304 n30 and 1353 n30.
126 Especially Baechem (Ep 1254 n6), who had been made an assistant inquisitor in
       1520. Cf Allen Ep 1358:36–7.
127 *Adagia* I vi 94
128 Ep 1260 n36

deliberately try to bring suspicion on me, as though I had some agreement
with the Lutherans. But rumours of this kind, which are purposely invented   665
by both sides, spring up at random and easily dissolve in the same way. And
certain people, to be sure, have to thank their old-fashioned characters for
the way they are surprisingly upset by worthless rumours of this kind.

There was a widespread yarn here lately that my books had been burned
in Brabant,[129] and that too on the authority of Father Jacob of Hoogstraten,[130]   670
an old acquaintance of mine at least, if not a friend, and this brazen
invention had actually been spread by educated men in letters full of
irresponsible gossip. I perceived at once that this was a trick, started by
certain people for whom I do not know what name I ought to use, but some
call them Lutherans – men whose object is to rouse a simple, easily deluded   675
character like myself to attack Jacob of Hoogstraten; because, if I should have
written anything at all outspoken against him, I should be obliged to change
sides and join their camp. A cunning plan, was it not! But the facts soon
showed that in my own country they had never even thought of such a
thing.   680

This was followed by another rumour even more outrageous, based on
a letter that purported to be sent from Rome. With this had been joined the
name of a man who commands great respect. The story was told as a known
fact, and with great feeling, in a letter to my friend Botzheim from a reliable
and scholarly man in Rome, whose name I knew. Botzheim wrote me a long   685
letter[131] almost in a state of panic, to report that my books had been publicly
condemned in Rome in the words of the pope himself.[132] I simply laughed; I
recognized another invention very like the last one. The purpose was, of
course, that a man like myself, innocent of the world and easily won over,
should be provoked by this to attack the pope both by word of mouth and in   690
writing, and should be obliged, having done that, to change sides and take
refuge with them. In any case, what a brazen invention it was was proved
not only by a number of letters written from Rome, but by a brief lately sent
me by the pope himself[133] – at least, I never yet received anything in all my
life more affectionate or more complimentary. Not but what, as far as praise   695
of myself is concerned, I understand this as an indication of the sort of man I
ought to be, not a picture of what I am. At any rate, approval or affection
from such a pope as this I find quite acceptable. And for fear I might pay

* * * * *

129 See Ep 1275 n16.
130 Ep 1299 n25
131 Perhaps that mentioned in Ep 1335:1
132 See Ep 1324 introduction.
133 Ep 1324

insufficient attention to the brief, someone I know in the papal household,[134]
and not its most junior member, wrote and told me that when the pope   700
found the wording of the diploma somewhat lukewarm, because the man
who had drafted it[135] is a friend of mine and had written about me with some
restraint on account of the special friendship between us, the Holy Father
himself dictated much of it in his own words. And in the same letter this
friend of mine offers me a benefice by no means to be despised, of which he   705
is now in possession, and he will resign from it whenever I wish.

Nor is there any basis in this for noisy protests that I have been
corrupted by a share in the spoils and am therefore a deserter from the cause
of truth.[136] I will admit that this is a true accusation if I have ever accepted
any gifts of this kind;[137] though if I were to accept one, there would be plenty 710
of precedent for my doing so. What little fortune I have was entirely mine
before Luther was known to the world at large, and came my way without
my seeking it. Half was forced upon me despite my protests by the
archbishop of Canterbury,[138] and half was generously offered me unsought
by the emperor Charles.[139] Even supposing I were to lose some of that, I shall 715
increase my income by reducing my expenses. If I could have been dragged
into this battle by rewards, that would have happened long ago. I was
deterred by thoughts of the size of the task on the one hand and my own
weakness on the other.

And now listen to a third invention, more brazen than either of the   720
other two. They had put it about that the supreme pontiff had written some
sort of an attack on me, and that many people had seen it. I scented their
game immediately. Of course the purpose of this imaginary pope is to
provoke me to write or say something unwise. But I have learned from the
apostolic Epistles[140] not to speak ill of my prince, but to revere a good one, 725
and endure a bad one if my protests prove ineffectual.

The other party too tell their own tales, for some of its members have
such an idea of the way to defend the see of Rome that if they were to

* * * * *

134 Barbier; see Ep 1345:17–19. His letter was presumably contemporary with Ep
    1324.
135 Hezius; see Epp 1324:137, 1339 introduction.
136 Cf Ep 1352:156–9. This became an especially hot issue during the controversy
    with Hutten; see Ep 1341A:1196ff, 1645ff. See also Allen Epp 1435:16–17,
    1437:172, 1459:54, 1477:7, and Böcking II 332:47–333:3 (Otto Brunfels' *Responsio
    ad Erasmi Spongiam*); cf Ep 1341A n285.
137 Cf Ep 1326:8–13.
138 Ep 1341A n364
139 Ep 1273 n4 and lines 100–1, 286–8 of this letter
140 Acts 23:5; Rom 13:1–6; 1 Pet 2:18–19; Tit 2:9, 3:1–2

attempt the most desperate measures they could not do more harm. These
men had lately spread a rumour that many of Luther's party were flocking to   730
Basel[141] for the sake of asking my opinion, and even that Luther himself was
in hiding here. This rumour was doing me absolutely no harm here, where
there are a great many people who know it is entirely false. I only wish it
were true that all the Lutherans and equally the anti-Lutherans were
flocking here to ask my advice, and would be willing to follow what advice I   735
give them! The affairs of men would be in slightly better case, I do believe.
Many men do foregather here in order to greet me,[142] and to set eyes on me,
sometimes in troops and most of them strangers. Not one of them has ever
declared in my hearing that he was a Lutheran, nor have I been given the job
of asking that question – and I am no diviner;[143] nor has anyone ever begun   740
to be acquainted with me or be recommended to me on the ground that he
was a Lutheran. Before this division reached its present bitterness I used to
enjoy literary friendships with nearly all the scholars in Germany and
greatly, to be sure, did I appreciate them. Several of them have now grown
cool towards me and some are entirely estranged; there are even those who   745
openly declare themselves my enemies and foretell my destruction. I also
enjoyed contacts with many who now take a more savage line against
Luther than I could wish, and indeed than is expedient for their own cause. I
dismiss no one from my friendship if he is a little over-inclined towards
Luther, nor do I renounce the friendship of anyone if he is more than   750
normally hostile to Luther, since each acts as he does from honest
conviction. For so I interpret the case, both in a friend and in an honourable
man.

There did come to Basel men whom they say are suspected of sharing
Luther's opinions, and I am ready to take all the responsibility for this if one   755
single one of them came here on an invitation from me and if I had not made
it abundantly clear to all my friends that I found this acutely embarrassing.
But if people find their way here who belong to one faction or the other, how
can they have the face to accuse me? I don't keep the gates of the city of Basel
or hold any public office. Hutten was here for a few days on a visit. During   760
that time he never visited me nor I him;[144] and yet, if he had come to me, I
should not have refused to see him, as an old friend and one whose

* * * * *

141 Cf Ep 1335 n9.
142 Cf lines 560–2 of this letter.
143 An apparent quotation from the *Hecuba* of Euripides; see *Adagia* I iii 36 (CWE 31
     265 13–16).
144 On Hutten, his visit to Basel, and Erasmus' failure to receive him, see Ep 1331
     n24.

wonderfully fertile and lively mind I cannot fail to find attractive even now. For if he has any business apart from that, it is nothing to do with me. Since however he was in poor health and could not leave his stove-heated room, nor could I endure it, the result was that we never met. Cronberg,[145] Franz's son-in-law, came to see me twice, and I found his character and conversation quite delightful. Here clearly was a straightforward person entirely free from guile, but much gifted intellectually. Our meeting, however, was of no great length and took place before witnesses. In fact, were Luther here in person, I would gladly have a talk with him, in hopes of giving him free and friendly advice on many points; although it may perhaps be too late now, except that, as Paul says, Christian charity hopeth all things.[146]

I hate discord as the worst of all evils, not only in accordance with Christ's teaching and example but from some deep-rooted impulse in my nature; and it torments me all the more when I consider how this world of ours is seething with both public and private hate, so that there is scarcely a vestige of true friendship left anywhere. It is not even permissible to love those who richly deserve our feelings for them, nor is any quarter of the world free from the contagion of this plague. One party it is impossible to despise and the other will not let us despise it; both seem to have in their hearts, if not on their lips, the old Homeric tag.[147] And I doubt whether either of them can be suppressed without the disastrous collapse of good causes at the same time. It cannot be denied that Luther has drawn attention to many abuses which it is in the interests of Christendom to rectify and which the world could endure no longer. And it is in this world-wide tempest in human affairs that my unhappy lot is cast, at a time of life when I should as it were have retired long ago to a well-earned leisure, to enjoy, as I justly might, the fruits of my laborious researches; or at least I might be allowed to be a spectator of this play, as I myself am so unfitted to be an actor and there are so many others on every side who crowd of their own accord upon the stage. Both sides, however, have taken special care to make this impossible; one party is eager to lure me on with their tricks until they can carry me off by force to join their camp, while in the other party there are some who strive by every means in their power to drive me into the ranks of the enemy, with no other motive except to use this way of destroying one who is a powerful supporter of the ancient tongues, of the humanities, and of classical theology, and whom they were not able to unseat from his

* * * * *

145 Ep 1331 n23
146 1 Cor 13:7
147 Perhaps *Iliad* 4.185–7, cited in *Adagia* III viii 21 (*Contemnentis dicterium*) as an example of the light-hearted dismissal of injuries

position. Thus it has come about, through no fault of my own but as a result
of the misguided zeal of certain individuals, that in both parties there are   800
certain people ill disposed towards me; on the one side there are those who
interpret my silence as support for the party they hate, while among those
who support Luther some are bitterly indignant because through cowardice,[148] as they term it, I desert the gospel cause, and not merely desert it but
even have some scheme on foot for bolstering up the papal (they would say,   805
the papist) cause.[149]

But the others have had their answer from me often. At this stage I
would gladly take on some supporter of Luther, but it must be one with a
sense of fairness. I believe I could make even him accept my case, on the
basis of points which he himself will concede me. First, I shall ask him what   810
he thinks of Luther. He is sure to reply that Luther is a saintly character, a
follower of the gospel, who has revived true Christian piety. Then I shall ask
the man whether Luther's devoted followers resemble him. He will confirm
that this is so without a doubt. I shall next enquire whether there is any
precedent in the Gospels for the use of chicanery and violence to force a man   815
into joining your own faction, especially as they well know that to profess
their views is no less perilous than it was once to be a professing Christian. It
was the Jewish practice to wander over sea and land in hopes of attracting
one proselyte into the meshes of the law.[150] The apostles never tried to win a
man by worldly artifice, and concealed those who had confessed Christ's   820
name until the moment of profession could not be deferred.

I could use these words if to profess oneself a member of the Lutheran
faction were no different from professing the teaching of the gospel, and if
any one of them had ever professed it in secret. As things are, I leave the
nature of that profession to be judged by others. In any case, be it what it   825
may, it came into existence without my knowledge and made progress in
spite of discouragement from me, even through all the stages during which
the world was still ready for the most part to applaud the play. During this
time there followed the *Captivitas babylonica*[151] and the *Abrogatio missae*, a
defence of the whole Hussite teaching,[152] not to mention other things which,   830

* * * * *

148 Cf Allen Epp 1384:20, 1459:80.
149 Epp 1352 introduction, 1341A:1208–13
150 Matt 23:15
151 Luther's *De captivitate babylonica* of October 1520 (WA VI 497–573), which was a
    brutal assault upon the Catholic sacraments
152 Luther's *De abroganda missa privata* of January 1522 (WA VIII 411–76) contains a
    passage (425:15–25) equating the church's condemnation of Hus with condem-
    nation of the gospel.

as they are written in German, I cannot even read.[153] And yet hitherto, for
many other reasons but above all because I perceived that the business was
beyond my understanding, I have made no public utterance on Luther's
opinions. I have only put on record in several published letters that I am
entirely opposed to the way the Lutherans band themselves together, and   835
that in such of his books as I happen to have read I find the modesty of a
Christian much to seek and could wish there were less bitterness.[154]

At this point I will appeal once again to that friend of Luther's. Is it his
view that this criminal purpose, which he pursues at great risk to his own life
and great risk to other people's, is a noble enterprise and worthy of all   840
praise? He will reply, I suppose, that it is entirely in the spirit of the apostles
and deserves undying fame. Very well, I will take him at his word. Who then
would have failed to reckon me the most arrogant of all men alive, had I
claimed so much credit for myself in a field where I did not deserve the
smallest scrap? Who in fact would not have thought me as crazy as any   845
Orestes,[155] if I had wished to purchase an entirely false reputation at the
price of great personal risk? Most monarchs and prelates were already
convinced that for the whole of Luther's teaching I was the source, the
authority, the champion, and the Atlas who bore it on my back – even that
the books which circulate under his name with Luther on the title-page are   850
really mine. Was it my duty to let such glory be ascribed to me, and say
nothing? John cried, 'I am not the Christ';[156] was it right for me to remain
silent? 'But you put this on record,' they say, 'in too many letters.' Not at all:
with all these letters I can still hardly convince certain people, so deeply has
this most brazen falsehood sunk into men's minds.   855

Then again, as regards his lack of modesty and his virulence, I will ask
my Lutheran another question. Is it expedient that Luther's teaching should
spread through the world as widely as possible and prove wholly acceptable
alike to high and low? He will of course reply, 'Nothing matters more.' Why
then are certain people so indignant with my humble self because I   860
expressed a wish to see Luther's books free from two features which do
more than anything to reduce their credibility and alienate all men of good
will, their arrogant air and their excessive virulence? And yet these faults are
so outstandingly obvious that even his most devoted supporters have no
excuse to put forward, except that our sins richly deserve to be chastised   865

* * * * *

153 Cf Ep 1313 n16.
154 See, for example, Epp 967, 1033. Erasmus himself did not publish Ep 939.
155 Orestes was driven mad by the Furies after murdering his mother, Clytemnestra.
156 John 1:20, 3:28

with scorpions by such a bitter critic. As far as I am concerned, at any rate, it was this ferocity of what he wrote and the flow of abuse that he has always ready that first made me have my suspicion of Luther's spirit. Nor do I doubt that a great many other people have had the same experience as myself. Suppose Luther's teaching is religious, how many men do you suppose 870 have been set against it by the book he wrote in answer to the king of England?[157] – a prince compared with whom there is hardly another alive today more richly endowed with every kingly virtue or further removed from tyranny or more popular with his own people or who sets a higher value on humane learning and outstanding excellence. Let there be no 875 suspicion of flattery if I pay this tribute to one from whom I receive nothing[158] and aspire to receive nothing.

This at least cannot be denied, that the king's intentions in writing were religious,[159] and that if he brought in some abuse of Luther, not only could he plead Luther's example as an excuse but he was attacking a man for 880 whom he was convinced that far stronger language was appropriate. And yet, if there is anything in that book which does not belong, I suspect it is certain unusually bitter remarks. And so, had Luther acknowledged the king's religious zeal and boldly brought the matter to a conclusion with solid arguments, without infringing the respect due to a king, he would, I believe, 885 have done his case far more good; and I will now assume, for the purpose of discussion with my Lutheran, that his case is excellent. What could be more unprofitable than abuse aimed at great princes? It is the easiest thing for them to pay no attention, and it is the work of a moment to answer the mockery if they so please. For my part, neither love nor hate for any mortal 890 man shall make me consciously a traitor to the truth of the gospel. Monarchs can tolerate free criticism, subversive impudence they cannot take. My only object in saying this is to make clear how little opportunity I have given the Lutherans themselves to be furious with me with good reason. Not that I am afraid of them, if it is their own warped minds and no fault of mine that 895 makes them attack me; but I should like my reasonableness to be known to all men. For several letters from different sources come flying on ahead like skirmishers, armed with threats of I know not what; and one among them[160] breathes very considerable venom, even before we come to close quarters.

* * * * *

157 See Ep 1308 n3.
158 Ie, no permanent income from pension or benefice; see Epp 296:117–27, 1341A:1732–7.
159 See Epp 1227–8.
160 Perhaps the *Iudicium D. Martini Lutheri de Erasmo Roterodamo ad amicum*; see Epp 1341A n315, 1348 n5.

At this point I should like to summon up once more the supporter of 900
Luther whom I have selected as a reasonably fair-minded judge of this case.
The reasons for their indignation are something like this. I was thought
somewhere in my letters to offer some degree of hope that, if I were given
leave and allowed the leisure, I would do what I could for the peace of
Christendom and the honour of the apostolic see.[161] How can this offer be 905
regarded as an attack on Luther? But let them suppose I have attacked him in
print, no matter how – which is untrue, to be sure, even now, when the
whole world of its own accord is sharpening its pen to attack him – why
must I be the only target for their indignation, if I were to rouse myself under
orders from those whom it is scarcely safe to disobey? One point, I think, my 910
judge must grant me: Luther's sense of fair play is not so much perverted
that, while he takes the liberty to differ not only from all the Doctors of the
church but from all the conciliar decrees as well, he is indignant if anyone
differs from him at any point and thinks himself affronted if anyone, while
abstaining from personal abuse, uses the testimony of Scripture, which he 915
thinks so important, and sound reasoning to pursue the truth. This is the
course he summons us all to take; and the Roman pontiff summons us to do
no more than put Luther to the test of sound reasoning and the testimony of
Scripture. And so it was hardly fair to threaten me, before having seen what
line my writing might have taken and with what moderation I had written. 920
    Many people were aroused by ridiculous suspicions which had led
them to believe that the attack on Luther published by the king of England
was the product of my bow and spear;[162] only that the king's name had been
put on the title-page to make it a heavier blow to Luther. For all the idiocy of
this, I had letters written in all seriousness from great princes and from 925
scholarly friends trying to elicit a confession of its truth.[163] Had this perfectly
idiotic suspicion won the day, Luther would, I suppose, have aimed the
same charming raillery on my luckless head as he now does on the king. Yet
all this time it was some years since I had set foot in England;[164] and when I
paid my respects to the king at Calais[165] in the presence of courtiers past 930
counting, a scheme of writing against Luther was not even thought of; all
thought was for the settlement of the dispute. For the *Captivitas babylonica*
had not yet appeared. In fact I did not know the book[166] had been written

* * * * *

161 See, for example, Epp 1144, 1167, 1195.
162 Cf Ep 1275:90–1. See also *Adagia* I vi 19.
163 Epp 1290:20–1, 1298:9–19, 1313:74–92
164 The last visit had been in April 1517; see Epp 566 and 577 introductions.
165 July 1520; Ep 1106 introduction
166 Ie, King Henry's *Assertio*; Ep 1275 n25

until I saw it in print; and that was in Bruges, when the cardinal of York[167]
was there for negotiations about a settlement between the emperor and the   935
king of France. I was waiting at the cardinal's door, talking to his principal
people and expecting to pay him my respects at the first opportunity. At
length out came Marino Caracciolo,[168] the apostolic nuncio, with a book in
his hands. I asked whether I might open it, and he said yes. I read nothing
but the title and the inscription that the king had written with his own hand   940
at the foot of the first page; and then, since at the moment there was no time
for more, I gave him back the book, saying with a smile 'I envy Luther such
an adversary.' He scowled in reply at first rather than smiled, but when I had
expressed the same meaning more clearly, he replied 'I too congratulate the
Holy Father on finding such a champion.'   945

Meanwhile, although I too had definitely been promised a copy of the
book several times, by some mischance it was never delivered to me, the
reason I suppose being the cardinal's unexpectedly early departure; for that
too is like a king. Yet a copy was meant for me, which the king had marked
with his own hand, 'For Master Erasmus.' This was dispatched in the month   950
of August in the year 1521, Roman style, and delivered to me in Basel in
February 1522. Nor did I ever have a chance to read the king's book, except
in a pitiful Strasbourg edition;[169] and after reading it through, I also read
Luther's reply shortly afterwards. That is all I know about the book, and not
a hair's breadth more than that. Nor could I ever detect whether the king had   955
had anyone's help in writing it. The style is clearly his own, and he has a
fertile and ready mind for every purpose; and yet, had he wished to use
scholarly help, he has a court overflowing with gifted authors and learned
men.[170] In any case, I praised nothing in my letter except the spirit shown by
the king;[171] and what else could I praise when I had not read the book? At   960
this point I await the verdict of my Lutheran: is it right that these suspicions
like an empty dream should count against me with these champions of the
gospel?

Now let me tell you another charge I have to meet. It is counted against
me that I did not retire from the stage with a final bow four years ago,[172]   965

* * * * *

167 Wolsey, whose visit to Bruges took place in August 1521; see Ep 1223
    introduction.
168 Ep 1263 n1
169 J. Grüninger published two editions at Strasbourg, on 9 August and 7
    September 1522.
170 See Ep 1313 n13.
171 Ep 1228:11–13
172 It is not known who had levelled this charge at this time. Luther expressed

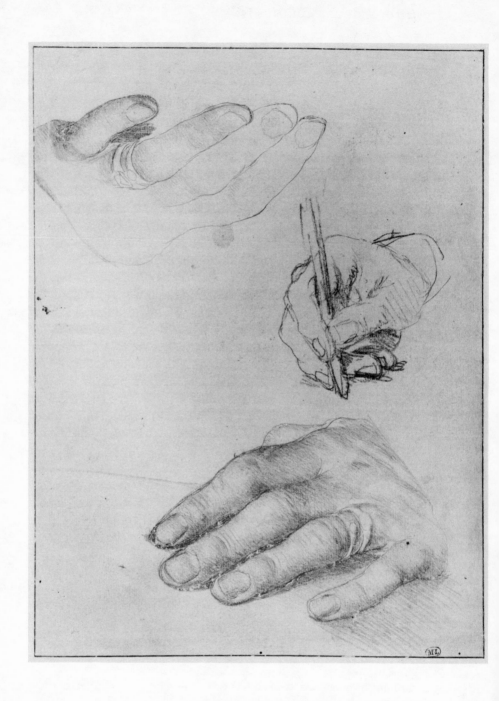

The hands of Erasmus
Hans Holbein the Younger, 1523
The Louvre, Paris

satisfied presumably with the reputation and reward I had earned by
devoting the ancient tongues to serve theology, by chasing the frogs of
sophistry from our universities, and by despising ceremonies and urging
men to return to the pure springs of Holy Scripture. On this head at least
they award me more credit than I am willing to accept. But I am not   970
permitted to leave this stage until my heavenly producer has given me my
orders. And yet I have played a part up to now on a level that means leaving
the grand scenes for the likes of Roscius and Aesopus;[173] and in the long run
I myself prefer to play in comedy rather than tragedy. I measure my capacity
according to my voice and physical strength and acting skill. 'But you stand 975
in the way,' they tell me, 'of those who will act out the rest of the play.' What
are they complaining of now? 'This man,' they say, 'still values highly and
acknowledges the church of Rome. He tells us the Roman pontiff is still to be
respected. He writes that no man of good will ever withdrew himself from
the pope's kingdom.'   980

All this and much more is to be found in what they write. The pope's
kingdom I have never mentioned. I have written somewhere or other that all
religious men everywhere support the authority of the pope.[174] Who would
not support the authority of a man who by his evangelical qualities gives us a
reflection of Christ in our midst? And this I always add, when I attach any 985
importance to papal authority. Wherein the true authority of the Roman
pontiff lies is a matter of common knowledge, and I have made it clear in
more than one passage in my works.[175] For my part, I have learned from the
writings of evangelists[176] and apostles,[177] and have discovered that some
importance is to be attached to heathen princes too, unless their commands 990
are plainly impious. Judged by this rule my opinion is that no bishop's
authority should be despised. Surely it is impious to despise a godly bishop?
But they give a picture of the kind whom they wish to be despised. 'And
who,' they say, 'is this Roman pontiff? Is he not one who puts the gospel in
the fire, God's enemy who leads astray all Christian people?' If such is the 995

* * * * *

similar sentiments in a letter of 20 June 1523 to Oecolampadius; WA-Br III 96–7
(=BAO no 157).

173 Q. Roscius, Rome's greatest comic actor, and his contemporary Claudius
Aesopus, Rome's greatest tragic actor, both friends of Cicero

174 See Epp 1144:9–10, 1167:386–7, 1195:47–8.

175 On Erasmus' recognition (in the *Annotationes* and the *Paraphrases*) of the biblical
basis of the Roman primacy, see Harry J. McSorley 'Erasmus and the Primacy
of the Roman Pontiff: Between Conciliarism and Papalism' *Archive for
Reformation History* 65 (1974) 37–54, especially 40–1.

176 Matt 22:17–21

177 See n140 above.

pope of whom they speak, no pope has ever had my approval. And yet, even were the pope like that, it is not my business to cast him down from his throne. Christ lives to this day, and he has in his hand a scourge with which to drive such characters from the temple.[178]

'But we cannot hope,' they say, 'that a better one than Leo will follow.' My first point is that I am not Leo's judge; he has his own judge, in whose eyes he stands or falls. If so many good ones have preceded, why have we no hope that he might have a successor like those early popes? On our present pope I express no opinion, for fear of seeming to curry favour.[179] Christ himself answered when urged to do so by a godless high priest, and did not remain completely silent when ordered to speak by Pilate. How does Paul argue his case before Festus and Felix and Agrippa? Naturally, of course, he calls them tyrants, slaves of the evil one, servants of sin, God's enemies who will shortly be consigned to eternal fire![180] And now consider how these men have replied to those who defend my own cautious language. 'This is how Erasmus should speak,' he says: 'Pope, you are Antichrist; you, bishops, are blind leaders; that Roman see of yours is an abomination in the sight of God' – with much else in the same vein, or even more disgusting. They do not approve the courteous language of a man like me unless they have first spoken in this manner – in good gospel style, of course. The first question I will ask my judge is, whether he thinks rules of this kind which he lays down for me are fair; and the second, whether he thinks they do any good to Luther's cause. If I were to write like that of good popes, should I not seem offensive? And if I were to rant in this strain against bad ones, the sole result would be to stir up a hornets' nest to the peril of myself and many others.

There still remains one charge against me, the most serious of all. In my paraphrase, where I explain the ninth chapter of Paul the Apostle to the Romans, I allot a very small share to freedom of the will,[181] for I was following in the steps of Origen and Jerome. To begin with, since a paraphrase is a kind of commentary, and since I state openly that on most points I follow accepted and ancient interpreters, what sacrilege have I committed if in some places I follow Origen and Jerome, who as authorities on Holy Scripture are, I take it, not to be despised? And this happened

* * * * *

178 John 2:15
179 Cf Ep 1304 introduction.
180 The words here attributed to Paul are not in the scriptural text, but some of the phrases occur in Erasmus' paraphrase on Acts 26:18, published the following year.
181 Cf Ep 1268:90–3.

before Luther put out his opinion, or rather Wycliffe's, that whatever we do,   1030
whether good or bad, is a matter of absolute necessity. For my paraphrase
was printed in Louvain in the year 1517,[182] and it had been written in
Antwerp some months before it was printed. And meanwhile someone I
could name[183] is called 'a complete Erasmian' because he agrees with me on
the freedom of the will and disagrees with Luther; yet he is forgiven for this,   1035
because he is a young man of promise and will soon change his mind.

At this point I appeal once again to my fair-minded judge. Seeing that I
wrote this before Luther's opinion was published, and seeing that all
theologians, ancient and modern, take the same view as mine – Origen,
Jerome, Chrysostom, Hilary, Arnobius, Scotus, Thomas – why am I put in   1040
the dock as though I had started it all? And why is a man who disagrees with
Luther called an Erasmian rather than a Hilarian or a Jeronymite? –
especially since I have not undertaken a full treatment of the question in my
paraphrase, but have touched on it in passing as did Paul himself, who does
not deign to reply on that point to a persistent inquirer. And yet observe,   1045
dear reader, how much smaller is the share I there allot to the freedom of the
will than is done either in the Fathers or in the lectures of more modern
scholars. For I suspect that the words at which they take offence are these in
chapter 9, for after setting out a captious question which is put to God in an
attempt to convict him of injustice, I go on: 'Not at all: something is seated in   1050
our own will and endeavour, although it may be so little that, compared
with God's goodness freely offered, it may look like nothing. No man is
condemned except by his own fault; no man is saved except by the goodness
of God. He judges worthy of this those whom he pleases, but in such a way
that while you may have cause for gratitude, you can have none for   1055
complaint.' I quote this from the paraphrase.[184]

I could see on one side the peril of Scylla, persuading us to put our trust
in good works, which I admit is the greatest threat to religion. On the other
side I could see Charybdis, a monster yet more terrible, by whom not a few
of them are now held fast, saying, 'Let us do as we please; for whether we   1060
torment ourselves or please ourselves, what God has once decided is sure to
happen.' I therefore controlled my language so as to allot a very small share
to freedom of the will, for fear of opening a window for such a mortal form of
sloth, which consists in everybody abandoning all efforts towards an

* * * * *

182 Ep 710
183 Mosellanus (Ep 560). See the *Iudicium de Erasmo Roterodamo* (n160 above);
    WA-Br II 544.
184 Erasmus here cites the 1517 edition. In the 1532 edition he altered the passage
    to eliminate the emphasis on free will, thus approximating the views of the
    Protestant reformers. See CWE 42 55, 153 n15, and cf ibidem xxxv.

improvement of life and doing just anything he takes a fancy to. And yet, when I wrote this, I had no idea that there had been anyone who entirely abolished all the force of free will, an opinion which, even though I were certain of its truth, I should be reluctant to spread abroad in so many words. As things are, everyone knows that philosophers were disputing about fate before the birth of Christ; and from them there have descended to us these insoluble problems about foreknowledge, about predestination by God, about human free will, about contingency of future events, in which I think it the best course not to spend too much anxious time, since this is an abyss no man can get to the bottom of. I would rather teach the doctrines that encourage us to try for the best in every way we can, while yet at the same time claiming no credit for ourselves, but leaving the judgment of everything to God, having developed perfect confidence in his goodness above all else.

Let that judge of mine therefore give his verdict at this point: should something be imputed to me as its author which no one, both of the ancients and the moderns, has failed to say? Is it fair to dispute on this question with me, when you ought rather to deal with all the authorities for this opinion who treat of this matter explicitly, while I have only touched on it briefly and in passing in my paraphrase? It is quite possible that, not being fully informed of all Luther's opinions, I may stumble unawares over some other stone; and if this should happen, are his friends instantly to raise a storm against me? There are so many people everywhere who discharge their hatred of Luther's teaching in loud clamour and a shower of pamphlets; and am I the one man who is not permitted to open his mouth if there is anything I do not much like? Let them at least make this concession to a man whom they rightly describe as cautious, whose knowledge is insufficient and who has no judgment in questions of this kind: allow him on some occasions to accept the verdict of so many recognized authorities, and in a time of such perilous upheavals silently to vote for the opinion of those whose authority has for so many centuries been followed by the Christian world.

Anyone who cannot love Erasmus as a Christian, though a feeble one, must adopt towards him what attitude he pleases; I for my part cannot be different from what I really am. If Christ has given anyone a grander measure of the gifts of the Spirit, and he has the self-confidence, let him use them for Christ's glory. I feel happier meanwhile in following a humbler but a safer course. I cannot fail to abominate discord, I cannot fail to love peace and concord. I see the great obscurity there is even in the affairs of men; I see how much easier it is to rouse an uproar than to pacify it, and I have learned how many are the tricks Satan can play. I would not dare trust my own spirit in everything; far less would I be able to give a reliable opinion on the spirit of other men. I could wish to see all men make a concerted effort to secure the victory of Christ and the establishment among all men of concord in the gospel, so that disorder might be ruled out in favour of sound reasoning, and measures might thus be taken to promote on the one side the authority of the priesthood and on the other the freedom of the people, whom the Lord Jesus wished to be free. Anyone embarked on this course can rely on me to the utmost of my power. But those who prefer to cause universal confusion will not have me, at any rate, as a leader or a colleague. They put forward as their excuse the working of the Spirit. Let them dance then among the prophets – and good luck to them – if they have been inspired by the Spirit of the Lord.[185] That spirit of theirs has not yet seized on me; and when it does so, they may well say, 'Is Saul also himself among the prophets?'[186]

I have no doubt you will have been saying for some time, 'What is the point of all this long and tedious stuff?' This, to be sure: I want you in future not to be shaken in the slightest by any vague rumours of this kind, even if there is no Hilarius[187] at hand to exhilarate you and restore your spirits. Pray give my warmest greetings to your two widow ladies[188] and to all my other friends. As soon as the winter relaxes, I shall take flight from the nest. 'And where will you go?' you ask. To visit you, if there is any gleam of peace and normality. If not, to any place where I can find a more ready supply of the wine that saves my life. For in Rome the plague[189] is playing its unpleasant tricks, and it is no less raging in Paris.[190] Farewell, my excellent friend.

From Basel, 1 February AD 1523

1343 / From Archduke Ferdinand Nürnberg, 15 February 1523

First published in the *Opus epistolarum*, this is Archduke Ferdinand's reply to Ep 1323.

FERDINAND BY THE GRACE OF GOD PRINCE AND
INFANTE OF THE TWO SPAINS, ARCHDUKE OF AUSTRIA,
DUKE OF BURGUNDY ETC, LIEUTENANT-GENERAL OF
THE EMPIRE, TO ERASMUS OF ROTTERDAM, GREETING
Honourable and learned sir and our sincerely beloved. We have received

* * * * *

185 An allusion to 1 Sam 10:5–6
186 1 Sam 10:11–12, 19:24
187 See n1 above.
188 Laurinus' two sisters
189 See Epp 1324 n12, 1338:66–7.
190 See Ep 1328:68–9.

your letter from Basel,[1] from which we duly learned what you had to say
about that admirable work of your composition, the paraphrase on John;
and this was most acceptable and gave us great pleasure. It is our wish, and
we warmly exhort you thereto, that you should persevere and continue in
such valuable activity, in these toilsome labours which deserve the highest   10
praise and commendation, and should take steps, as soon as time permits,
to send that paraphrase to the printer,[2] for the general advantage and benefit
of all learned and worthy men, and should send a copy thereof to us.[3] This
we shall endeavour to acknowledge and repay as opportunity offers,[4] with
all the generosity and indulgence at our command, in such ways as we can,   15
nor shall we be unmindful of your merits and your nightly toil.

Given in our imperial city of Nürnberg, the fifteenth day of the month
of February in the year 1523

1344 / From Willibald Pirckheimer   Nürnberg, 17 February 1523

This is Pirckheimer's reply to Epp 1337 and 1341. The original letter, no longer
extant, was published by Georg Theodor Strobel in his *Vermischte Beiträge zur
Geschichte der Litteratur* (Altdorf 1774). The autograph rough draft is in the
Stadtarchiv Nürnberg (MS PP.324). Ep 1353 is based on the news contained in
this letter.

It is no surprise, Erasmus my distinguished friend, if some people have
advised you to make your peace with me, although I was not in the least
offended, for there was no shortage of people to stir me up against you at
this end, on the ground that a letter from me written to you privately has
been published by you in the emperor's court.[1] Personally, having been   5
devoted to you always and more than commonly, and knowing as I do your
character and real integrity, I am sure there has been no hostility and no
deception on your side in all this. I also know what traps are laid by those
who are jealous of you, as much in Rome as in the emperor's court, but

* * * * *

1343
1 Ep 1333
2 The work was finished by early January (AK Ep 902:21–2) and was published in
February.
3 Cf Allen Epp 1357, 1361:12–21, 1376:13–14.
4 Ferdinand sent a gift of 100 gold florins; Ep 1341A:1740–1 and Allen Ep
1376:14–16.

1344
1 See Ep 1337 n1.

especially in Lower Germany; I know the strong feelings against you in   10
Luther's party; and I know from long experience how difficult and arduous
it is to resist all these insinuations and fight all these trumped-up charges –
and fight them in such a way as neither harms God's cause nor sets men
against you, to say nothing meanwhile of maintaining your proper
reputation. And so it did not hurt my feelings in the least if you gave my   15
letter to other people to read, for there is nothing in it that I might be
ashamed of or embarrassed by, and it is to your advantage to make other
people realize what a threat the two parties are and the sort of danger that
looms on either side. Goodbye therefore to those who try to set us one
against the other; I shall abide continually and sincerely in the affection that   20
already exists between us, and have not the least doubt that you will do the
same.

   In any case, when you say you could wish that some of Luther's people
would handle the gospel cause with more discretion, this is a desire you share
with many other men. If only the other side in their turn would act with   25
more circumspection and give more scope to reason than to their emotions!
Then we should not see so many outbreaks of serious unrest. It would have
been possible, and it might still be possible, if not to do away with this
business altogether, at least to pacify it to some extent, if it were treated with
self-restraint and with a sense of responsibility and with courtesy. But as   30
long as men who are beside themselves and whom God undoubtedly has
made unseeing strive to root out the whole thing by terror with threats and
despotic penalties and to end it root and branch, not only do they not put out
so great a fire, they steadily make it worse. The apostolic legate here[2] has
asked the princes that three preachers[3] in this city, admirable men, good   35
scholars, and extremely moderate, should be thrown into chains and sent to
Rome for punishment, in return for some statements which according to
him were perverse and heretical, when it was afterwards established that
they had said nothing of the kind.[4] He also accused one of them,[5] who is a
good Hebrew scholar, of being a Jew, when it is perfectly well known that he   40
is the son of Christian parents.

   * * * * *

2 Chierigati (Ep 1336)
3 In fact, four preachers were involved: Andreas Osiander (1498–1552) at St
   Lorenz, Domenicus Schleupner (d 1547) at St Sebald, Thomas Venatorius (c
   1488–1551) at the Hospital Church, and Karl Ress (d 1528) at the Augustinian
   convent (RTA III 411–12; Planitz 307).
4 The nuncio's demand, presented to the Estates on 3 January 1523, was
   indignantly rejected by both the diet and the Nürnberg city council (Planitz
   307–8, 310; RTA III 410–16, 428, 935–6).
5 Osiander (RTA III 935.23; Planitz 307)

You would hardly credit, my dear Erasmus, what a bad effect such brazen falsehoods and such outrageous actions have had on the authority of pope and legate equally, and what contempt this has earned them, not only among the citizens of Nürnberg but among the leading princes too, and it very nearly caused serious rioting with grave personal risk to the legate and some other people; the city council of Nürnberg were obliged to police the town by day and to mount nightly pickets to prevent anything so frightful. The legate has done several other things that were very foolish and most unpopular, from which he has earned such public contempt that he dare not show his face in public without embarrassment.[6] No one – I repeat, absolutely no one – pays him the slightest respect, and he is the laughing stock and butt of the whole population.

And all this has happened to him through the fraudulent inventions of the monks,[7] to which he has given more credit than he should have. For they have an intense hatred for the citizens of Nürnberg and call them Lutherans because this year they have abolished all beggars,[8] with such success that no one dares beg in public any more; they provide for them all, however, and generously too, in accordance with the circumstances of the individual. This pious activity is universally approved, and everyone contributes generously from what he has; but the monks think that whatever is given to the poor is thereby diverted from their own greed and gluttony. Hence all these tears and all this hellish uproar. I told the legate by way of mutual friends – for it was not possible for me to go and see him without undue risks – to beware of traps set by the monks, but they had made me too an object of suspicion to him; now he has begun to realize how honourably I dealt with him.

The pope has written to the city council of Nürnberg[9] and made certain

* * * * *

6 On the unrest in Nürnberg over the legate's behaviour, see the letter of the Regensburg delegate, Hans Portner, cited in RTA III 925n. Planitz 352 records the nuncio's private complaints about the general hostility towards him in Nürnberg.

7 In Nürnberg, as elsewhere, the regular clergy, especially the Dominicans and the Franciscans, were the principal opponents of the Reformation. By the end of 1524, they, together with a few conservative patricians (like Pirckheimer), were the only opposition left.

8 In the *Almosenordnung* adopted in outline by the city council on 23 July 1522 and printed in the summer of 1523; see *Die evangelischen Kirchenordnungen des XVI. Jahrhunderts* ed Emil Sehling et al XI (Tübingen 1961) 17–32. Protestant teaching and the example of Wittenberg were among the chief motives for the adoption of the ordinance.

9 See RTA III 404n. Breves dated 30 November, addressed to various German cities, were dispatched by the nuncio on 12 January 1523. The city councils were admonished to ban the printing and sale of Luther's works.

perfectly baseless accusations; this is all attributed to the legate, to whom the council have refused to reply though he presses very hard for an answer. He is also accused of some highly criminal conduct, I know not what. The pope 70
has also written to the princes, saying among other things that he freely admits that many scandalous crimes have been committed for some years now at the holy Roman see, and it is on account of these sins that the clergy are now scourged with the heresy of Luther.[10] We have all gone astray, he says; every man has turned to his own way,[11] and there is none found that 75
does good, no, not one.[12] At long last he makes many promises; and I only hope he means them, and if he means them, that he is able to perform them, and if he does perform them, that he achieves some real result! Many men find this impossible; but we must put everything into God's hands. The people of Nürnberg have a bad reputation in some quarters as supporters of 80
Luther because they give such an eager welcome to the teaching of the gospel. If only the Roman party had shown the same moderation and integrity as the Nürnbergers in the past, and still did so today! They would not see and hear and feel so much what they are obliged constantly to endure. 85

But enough of all this. I would tell you what resolutions were passed at the diet if I had them at hand.[13] Many subjects were brought up for discussion, relating particularly to the establishment of peace for the whole of Germany, but few reached any conclusion, except that the common people were burdened with fresh imposts – all merchandise, whether 90
imported into Germany or exported, is to pay four gold pieces on every hundred,[14] so that these 'kings who devour the common stock'[15] can finance their activities. Whether such an intolerable burden can be endured, the outcome will show. The representatives of the cities all left without taking leave of the princes, and were on no possible terms willing to agree.[16] This 95

* * * * *

10 See Pope Adrian's instructions to Chierigati (c 25 November 1522; RTA III 390–99) and the pope's breve to the German diet (ibidem 399–404), both read to the Estates by the nuncio on 3 January 1523. While Adrian sternly demanded strict enforcement of the Edict of Worms (May 1521), which had outlawed Luther and his followers and condemned his works, he also frankly admitted (as Pirckheimer notes) that the sins of the curia and the clergy were a major source of the current troubles, and he promised reforms.
11 Isa 53:6
12 Pss 14 (Vulg 13):3, 53 (52):3
13 The recess of the diet, adopted on 9 February 1523, is in RTA III 736–59.
14 The proposed *Reichszollordnung* of January/February 1523 is in RTA III 622–41.
15 Homer *Iliad* 1.231
16 The cities presented a formal complaint against the proposed customs levy (RTA III 641–4) and refused to sign the recess. For the rancorous negotiations

the princes very greatly resent, and if I am not mistaken there will be great upheavals over this. The princes are determined that this monstrous impost shall be ratified, and the cities resist absolutely and think anything more tolerable than such inhuman bondage.[17] And here we are, all the time, arming against the Turks, although on our side all is ablaze with discord and resentment, and promising assistance to others when we are destitute of all support ourselves. The princes can see their nobles everywhere preparing to revolt; they know that their subjects are crushed by very heavy burdens; and yet they are hastening to alienate the cities as well. Surely this could not possibly happen unless we were under the pressure of divine retribution. But I go on too long. May God show mercy on us!

When you say in your letter that the pope has sent you a letter full of good will,[18] I was delighted to hear it for the sake of your own reputation and no less for the benefit of your malicious enemies. He shows prudence enough, to be sure, if he mollifies you and other men of learning. For a fair number are irritated already; and Hoogstraten,[19] Eck,[20] Aleandro,[21] and the whole crowd of sophists will leave them absolutely no chance to settle down, unless the pope's authority steps in. The Roman party will discover eventually what a highly dangerous thing it is to put a sword into the hands of men who are crazy, drunken, headstrong, and filled with arrogance and pride, although they have had experience long since of the evils aroused on both sides by impetuosity and rashness that does not stop to think. Certain people keep silence though grossly ill-treated, under cover of papal authority; and they do more to maintain their cause by silence than some others who create an uproar and fill everything with noisy protestations – though when their time comes the quiet people too will perhaps begin to make themselves heard.

But to come after all this to Froben's business. Your last letter[22] arrived in the very nick of time, for it came when Ferdinand was about to depart[23]

* * * * *

between the princes and the cities on this and related issues, see ibidem 453–554.
17 The cities carried their case directly to the emperor in Spain. In this instance he sided with them; Karl Brandi, *Kaiser Karl v.* (Darmstadt 1961) 154–5. On the whole, however, his reign was one that saw the power of the cities vis-à-vis the princes decline sharply.
18 Ep 1324
19 Ep 1299 n25
20 Ep 769
21 Ep 1256 n11
22 Ep 1341
23 Ferdinand left Nürnberg on 16 February; Planitz 371.

next day and did not propose to attend the diet any further except to take 125
leave. I therefore set to work immediately, and that same night asked friends
of mine who now preside at the diet to take pains to see that we got what we
wanted. I entrusted the whole affair to the chancellor, as they call him, of the
imperial administration, a man no less well disposed to you than he is to me,
and I also handed over to him the letter you wrote to Ferdinand some time 130
ago.[24] Oecolampadius had given it to me[25] on the understanding that I
would not entrust it to anyone except your friend Spiegel;[26] but as there was
no sign of him, and Ferdinand was already preparing to depart, I did not like
to keep it any longer. And so the chancellor, Ulrich Varnbüler[27] or, as you
call him in one of your letters, Brackenbury,[28] immediately presented your 135
letter to Ferdinand as he was on his way to the diet, explaining at the same
time what it was we asked for and showing him copies of the books. The
prince seized your letter eagerly and read it, and immediately granted your
request. But since the matter is not entirely in his own hands, given the
opportunity he laid it before the princes himself, with some complimentary 140
remarks about you. All of them equally, including the delegates, decided to
comply with Erasmus' request, although the business was held up to some
extent by the views of those who thought that the privilege, as they call it,
ought not to apply to all your books but only to those of which you had
submitted copies. But the chancellor took trouble and your friends helped, 145
and we secured a general privilege.

Ferdinand told Ulrich of his own accord to get the letter[29] ready before
he left so that he could sign it in his own hand. So, although overwhelmed
with a mass of business, he obeyed and polished off the whole business
before Ferdinand's departure – and free, what is more, and no money 150
passing, a very great rarity in these parts – not so much for my sake as for
yours. So if things have gone as you wish, well and good, for I am ready at all
times and places to do what I can for you, and am not less anxious to oblige
Froben, because he does so much for the common cause of learning and is an

* * * * *

24 Ep 1323
25 This seems to imply that Oecolampadius (Ep 1258 n4) had visited Nürnberg
early in February, bearing Ep 1341. There is no trace of such a visit in
Oecolampadius' surviving letters.
26 Ep 1323:34ff
27 Ulrich Varnbüler of St Gallen (1474–1545), since 1507 protonotary in the
chancellery of the *Reichskammergericht* and since 1521 chancellor (ie, secretary)
to the *Reichsregiment*
28 *Varn* (or *Farn*) 'fern' or 'bracken' plus *Bühel* (*Hügel*) 'hill' or 'bury.' Cf Ep 867:39.
29 Ie, the privilege, dated 14 February, which was printed at the beginning of
Beatus Rhenanus' *Autores historiae ecclesiasticae* (Basel: Froben, August 1523).
Ep 1343 followed on the fifteenth.

excellent man. But you will do the right thing if you write Ulrich at least a   1₅
short letter of thanks and send him a copy in Froben's name in return for his
good will. For a document of this kind, especially one in general terms,
could not have been secured without twenty gold pieces.

For the rest, I would gladly poke a little fun at you for relying on certain
persons who made you worthless promises,[30] and not being ready to entrust   1₆
the whole affair to me. For indeed if they had been present in person, they
still would have needed my assistance. Ferdinand's secretaries do not carry
the same weight with him that Maximilian's used to, and so your business
came very close to being overlooked. And if you wish to reply that you did
not want to trouble me, especially as you had a man who could put the job   1₆
through admirably, I do not accept that as an excuse; for that man let you
down, and on my side hardly anything more agreeable could happen to me
than to do something to please you and show my feelings for you in action
rather than words. I therefore send you back your letter to him;[31] and I dare
say he will have a perfectly good excuse.   17

I send also a letter to you from the legate[32] and a certain number of
others, and I sent your letter[33] straight to him. He made no reply because he
was preparing for his journey and he did not dare leave except in company
with Ferdinand; so much has he exposed himself to danger and public
insult. He bears an answer from the princes to the pope such as perhaps no   17
man ever carried before,[34] though some of the bishops were against it. It is
written in courteous language, but it is so sharp that anything more severe
has scarcely ever been heard. Attached to it is a list of grievances of the
German nation, some seventy in number or a little more,[35] which our people
say they neither can nor will endure any longer; they think that up to now   18
they have had enough of words without deeds, and that now if ever is the
time to open their eyes. Where all this will lead, you must consider for
yourself.

But I must restrain my pen; for what else could I do at this season of
carnival?[36] And so farewell, my dear Erasmus, and remember that I am ever   18
yours; for that is how I think of you.

Nürnberg, 17 February 1523

* * * * *

30 Spiegel (Ep 1323)
31 Not extant
32 Not extant; presumably written before the receipt of Ep 1336
33 Ep 1336
34 Dated 5 February 1523. See RTA III 435–43 (text), 417–35, 443–7 (related documents).
35 There were seventy-four; RTA III 645–88.
36 17 February 1523 was Shrove Tuesday.

1345 / To Herman Lethmaet Basel, 21 February 1522/3

On Lethmaet, see Ep 1320, to which this is Erasmus' reply. According to Allen Ep 1383:17–21, this letter was circulating in print in August 1523, though Allen could find no copy extant. Erasmus, for obvious reasons (lines 46–7), never published it. The first known printing is an inaccurate text in Theodor J. van Almeloveen's *Amoenitates theologico-philologicae* (Amsterdam 1694). Allen's version is based on the autograph found in the Librije (Town Library) at Gouda (MS 959). The correct year-date is established by the reference to Ep 1324 (lines 17–19).

Lethmaet's response is Ep 1350.

Greeting. I had dedicated my Hilary to your Maecenas[1] already before your letter invited me to do so. I had intended it at first for the king of France; but though against the advice of my friends I changed my mind, on account of these upheavals in the state of things[2] which are so intensely adverse to all humane studies and to which I foresee no end unless there should arise 5 some god from the machine. And so I should be readier to congratulate you on a post at court if times were more peaceful. It is like your unselfish nature to say you are grateful to me, but it is you who secure your own promotion by your admirable qualities; and I am sure that you will use them to promote in turn the cause of Christ, to whom we owe everything. For you seem to me 10 most fortunate on many counts, were you to steer your course with prudence for the future, as I know you will without any outside advice. I only wish I could do something to promote your interests. I shall at least lose no opportunity. You speak of a mission to England, but I suppose with things in such great confusion nothing will come of it. If anything should 15 emerge, however, I will give you a share in all my friends.

The Roman pontiff has put his feelings towards me on record in a long diploma full of good will, which was written for the most part from his own dictation;[3] so Barbier tells me in a letter.[4] He also offers me a fairly distinguished deanery.[5] In my next letter to him I will mention your name.[6] 20

You need no advice from me. Above all things you should secure a position carrying some authority, to make men take you seriously; such is

* * * * *

1345
1 Ep 1334
2 The Hapsburg-Valois wars (Ep 1283 n3); see Ep 1342:590–649.
3 Ep 1324
4 Cf Epp 1341 n9, 1342:698–704.
5 See Ep 1324 n13.
6 Perhaps in the missing portion of Ep 1352

the spirit of the age. I have written a humorous letter on the way to live at court,[7] which introduces, however, more serious things; you will find it in my book on the theory of letter-writing. I know you will see to it that on all occasions you remain sober at a drinking-party; this will do much to earn you respect. The desire for distinction, even if you somehow find it tempting, must be completely kept under, equally in the way you dress and how you speak. The court is quick on the scent. In discussion be very careful never to get heated in scholastic fashion; and you should not enter into a dispute on every occasion or with everyone that offers or on any and every subject. You will thus be more highly thought of and will save yourself a lot of trouble. One should cultivate persons in high places, and those especially who have most influence. It is desirable to be polite to everyone, but not servile; remember the dignity proper to a theologian – but no hauteur. An air of piety too is well received. On business of the court you should not be too outspoken, and should not say forthwith what you think; and if you express an opinion, it should be fair and do as little harm to anyone as possible. Should you be obliged to join a party, always choose the more successful side. As for Luther's business, meddle with it as little as possible, if you can; and if you have to act, always remember to be fair. Be a bold champion of the ancient tongues and liberal studies generally, for Hulst and Baechem[8] persecute them worse than they do Luther. This will win you many friends and particularly among the generation now coming on. The present storm simply cannot last for long. Farewell.

I have written this with some freedom as you told me to; put it in the fire if you like, for I have kept no copy.

Basel, 21 February 1522

Sincerely yours, Erasmus

I was not sure about the archbishop's family[9] or I should have said more about it in my preface. I wasn't certain whether it was his father or grandfather who was chancellor, and no one here could even tell me his name. Farewell once more.

To the excellent theologian Herman Lethmaet of Gouda, in the imperial household

* * * * *

7 Printed in *De conscribendis epistolis* (ASD I-2 499–502 / CWE 25 195–7).
8 Frans van der Hulst was a lay jurist who in April 1522 had been named head of the Netherlands Inquisition (see Ep 1299 n22). Baechem (Ep 1254 n6) was one of his close collaborators. Hulst's indiscriminate zeal brought discredit and dismissal after about two years in office.
9 See Ep 1334 n103.

1346 / To the Nuns of Cologne   [Basel, c February] 1523

This letter comprises the opening and closing passages of the *Virginis et martyris comparatio*, written at the request of a convent of Benedictine nuns in Cologne with whose warden, Helias Marcaeus (Ep 842), Erasmus was on friendly terms (cf Ep 1341A: 785–6). The *Comparatio* was first published in 1523 with a new edition of the *Ratio verae theologiae* (Ep 1365). A second, much expanded version, prepared at Marcaeus' request, was published in September 1524 with the *De immensa Dei misericordia concio* (Ep 1475).

ERASMUS OF ROTTERDAM TO THE VENERABLE
COMMUNITY OF MACCHABEITE NUNS IN THE CITY OF COLOGNE,
GREETING IN CHRIST JESUS, WHO IS THE VIRGIN'S SON
AND THE CROWN OF ALL VIRGINS

More than once, most estimable virgin sisters, devoted as you are to your 5
profession, you have sent me titbits and sweetmeats to induce me to write
something in praise of the greatest treasure[1] you possess and make you
proud of your chosen way of life. You intend of course to make something
out of it. You have a target: in exchange for presents which beguile the sense
of taste, you hope to get something which will feed the mind. A virtuous 10
ambition this, a holy appetite, a prudent and profitable kind of exchange full
worthy of wise virgins, if only I were a man with the ability to reward you
with a spiritual harvest for the corporal seed that you have sown. Your
predilection is admirable; your selection is at fault. You set your heart on the
best; you do not set your hand on one capable of answering to your pious 15
wishes. But let me not be thought merely ungrateful. I congratulate you, O
saintly virgins, on this spirit that thirsts for nothing save the glory of your
bridegroom ...

Acknowledge then your own felicity, O virgin sisters, and you will not
envy this world its attractions; acknowledge your exalted station, and you 20
will not hanker for this world's sordid society. Cleave to your bridegroom,
for in him you have at once all that is joyful and splendid. Take courage to
persevere from the example in your own home set by those saintly young
men, whose joy is greater because the relics of their earthly bodies are
preserved in such a holy society. They chose to die rather than eat the flesh 25
of swine; and you too must treat as swine's flesh everything that is not
pleasing to your bridegroom. If you have tried to emulate the noble fight

* * * * *

1346
1 The relics of the Maccabees, then housed in the convent, now found in St Anthony's church, Cologne

they fought, you will be also partakers of their glory, with the aid of Jesus
your bridegroom, who liveth and reigneth for ever and ever. Amen
    In the year of the life-giving Incarnation 1523   3

1347 / To Joost Vroye   Basel, 1 March [1523]

> This letter, first printed with the *Exomologesis* (1524) and thereafter in all
> editions of the *Epistolae*, is also found in MS 1324 in the Librije (Town Library) at
> Gouda. Allen assigned priority to the manuscript despite his suspicion that it
> had been copied from the *Exomologesis*. All the sources give 1524 as the
> year-date. Allen, however, assigned the letter, in its original form, to the year
> 1523. His argument was as follows. The date of Jan de Neve's death, as
> established by Professor de Vocht (*Mélanges Charles Moeller* [Louvain 1914]),
> was 25 November 1522. It is hardly likely that Erasmus would have waited
> until 1 March 1524 to write so moving a lament on the death of a friend. There
> is, moreover, nothing in the letter to imply a date later than March 1523 save
> the solitary reference to Hutten (line 325), where the apparent implication is
> that he was already dead. This may well have been an interpolation at the time
> of printing, a supposition supported by the statement further on (lines 331–2)
> that Neve's death was the most recent of all. Finally, the echo, in the opening
> passage of Ep 1355, of the opening lines of this letter, indicates that Ep 1355
> may have been Vroye's reply, though the business portion of that letter has no
> counterpart here. Thus the year-date can be set at 1523 on the assumption that
> Erasmus revised and amplified the letter for publication, eliminating any
> business matter as irrelevant to what had become a literary composition. In the
> *Catalogus lucubrationum* (Ep 1341A:1571), this letter is listed, under the title *De
> morte subita*, among the 'works which contribute to the building of character.'
>   Joost Vroye of Gavere (d 1533) was a priest and an old friend of Erasmus (Ep
> 717:22). After taking his MA at Louvain in 1505, Vroye studied law while
> teaching languages, logic, and physics at the College of the Lily. He became a
> doctor of both laws in 1520 and subsequently held chairs of civil (1524) and
> canon law (1526). He was rector in 1521 and 1529, and held other administra-
> tive and honorific posts in the university as well. This letter and Ep 1355 are all
> that survive of the correspondence between Erasmus and Vroye.

ERASMUS OF ROTTERDAM TO JOOST VAN GAVERE,
A MAN OF WIDE LEARNING OUTSIDE HIS PROFESSION OF
THE LAW, GREETING
The news of the death of our common friend Jan de Neve[1] was a deep grief to

    * * * * *
    1347
  1 Ep 298 introduction

me, but it was also a salutary warning. I cannot fail to feel very severely the   5
loss of such a special friend, particularly since in himself he had many claims
on a long span of life. And again a death so sudden warns us all that no man
should wish to live in a state in which he would not wish to die. From my
friend's letters I gather that he had a cheerful and agreeable supper with
some friends and then, as he went upstairs – those stairs I have so often   10
climbed myself, for he had moved into my rooms[2] – he had a sudden seizure
about ten o'clock and survived this attack only six hours. However, his
death should perhaps not be considered sudden, since he had for so many
years been faced with paralysis. And in my view he was too much given to
physic, in which he himself was not unskilled. Is there in fact any   15
department of liberal knowledge in which he had not acquired some
experience to very good purpose? Such was his natural versatility.

And so in conversation I sometimes launch against him a favourite
quip, that Neve's gifts are very badly housed. That intellect of his was
indeed worthy of a happier dwelling-place. And again his mind was of a   20
quality that should not be infected by the humbler cares of life; yet once he
was entangled he could not shake himself free. How happy was his choice of
language, how fresh and ready his flow of words, if he had to speak on a
serious subject! What charm, what quickness if he had chosen a lighter vein
of wit and humour! And then his character: how ready he was to think well   25
of everyone, how delightful in society, what a good friend, how incapable of
betraying a secret, how free from selfishness! I had one fault to find in him,
for even Neve was not without a blemish: he would keep up a disagreement
longer than I thought desirable.[3] He did not easily fall out with anyone, but
when he did it was hard to make him give up his resentment. This was the   30
one point on which, in close agreement as we were, he and I sometimes had,
as you know, a difference of opinion. I could not make him understand how
often a serious dispute could be dissolved by a kind word, and how much
truth there is in the Greek proverb 'Many the friendships silence hath
dissolved.'[4]   35

I used often to remind him of an anecdote about John Colet,[5] a man
who deserves never to be forgotten. He got on very badly with his uncle, a
man of great age and very difficult character. The subject of the dispute was
no goat's wool or donkey's shadow, as the phrase goes,[6] but a great sum of

* * * * *

2 On the upper floor of the College of the Lily
3 See Epp 696, 838.
4 *Adagia* II i 26
5 Ep 106. Judging by the reference (line 43) to the *Enchiridion* (Ep 164), this
  episode can be dated no earlier than Erasmus' second visit to England, 1505–6.
6 *Adagia* I iii 52–3

money, so great that it might well induce a son to declare war on his father.   40
Colet was on his way to dine with that revered figure William, archbishop of
Canterbury,[7] and took me with him in the boat. On the way he was reading
the pages in my *Enchiridion* that suggest a remedy for anger, but did not tell
me why he was doing so. The arrangement at table when we sat down
meant, as it happened, that Colet sat opposite his uncle, with a long face,   45
saying nothing and eating nothing. Now the archbishop is exceptionally
clever in the way he ensures that no one at his table is not enjoying himself,
and matches his remarks to the mood of every individual. He therefore
started a conversation on the comparison between the various stages of life,
and those two, who had said nothing, began talking. At length the uncle   50
began to boast, as old men will, of the bodily vigour he retained in spite of
his years. After dinner they had a separate discussion between themselves
on some subject I know not what. When Colet and I had returned to our
boat, 'Erasmus,' he said, 'I see you are a lucky man.' I expressed surprise
that he should call a most unlucky man[8] lucky; and he then told me how   55
passionately hostile he was to his uncle, so much so that he had almost
decided to break the rules of Christian moderation, ignore the ties of
kinship, and openly declare war on him. That was why he had chosen to
read my *Enchiridion* in search of a remedy for anger, and he had been
successful. It was not long before that brief conversation started at the   60
dinner-table led to a lessening of the bitterness on both sides, with the result
that very soon the whole business between them was settled, the archbishop having acted as go-between. I used to recall such precedents as this
in talking with him,[9] and I never did much good. But think of the
outstanding qualities by which he made up for this one constitutional defect!   65

I will not continue at this point, my dear Joost, to console a man of your
wisdom and your wide reading for the loss of a friend. You knew that he was
mortal while you had him, like the pagan in the story who said of his son, 'I
knew I had not begotten an immortal';[10] and a man seems to me a stranger to
all philosophy who thinks it a sadder business for one who has been born to   70
die than for one who must die to be born at all, since both alike accord with
the nature of man. But it is strange to recount the abhorrence with which
ordinary people regard sudden death, to such an extent that there is nothing
they pray God and the saints to deliver them from more frequently or with

* * * * *

7 Warham (Ep 188)
8 Allen's note to Ep 1102:6 provides a long list of passages documenting
   Erasmus' conception of himself as habitually unfortunate.
9 Neve
10 Anaxagoras; see Valerius Maximus 5.10 ext 3.

more feeling than from death sudden and unforeseen. To die suddenly is   75
common to good men and bad alike. Herod suddenly perished when
smitten by an angel.[11] Eli the high priest, who was a good old man, died by a
fall from his chair.[12] The dreadful thing is not to die suddenly but to die the
death of the wicked. And this superstitious fear that mortals have invents
for itself vain remedies, an image of St Christopher, some particular brief   80
prayers to the blessed Virgin, certain words and signs akin to those used in
magic. How much better it would be if those who are so much frightened of
sudden death were to pray heaven for a good life! What could be more
foolish than to postpone amendment of life until one's deathbed! And how
few people are made better by a long illness! – if indeed anybody ever is.   85

One should never despair of anybody; but all the same he learns very
late to be a Christian who can no longer practise what he learns, and is very
late in applying the remedy of confession when his soul hovers already on
his lips. 'Grant me,' they pray, 'true repentance and a pure confession
before my death.' And this prayer they address sometimes to St Barbara or   90
St Erasmus. I ask you, what else does this request amount to except 'Let me
live in sin and kindly arrange for me to die in sanctity.' They are reluctant to
hate what they have done wrong except in the hour of death; they wish to
enjoy their sins as long as they enjoy good health. If it were not so, they
would say to Christ and not to St Barbara, 'Grant me now hatred of all my   95
sins, grant me for what I have done wrong the sorrow that brings salvation,
grant that remembrance of my former wrongs may always be bitter to me,
grant me while I am in good health a confession made once and for all that
will make confession in future unnecessary.' Some even tell God in detail in
their prayers by what kind of death they would like to die and how many   100
months they should spend in bed. How much more Christian it is to take
thought for nothing all the time except so to arrange one's life that whenever
that last day comes upon us it should never overwhelm us unprepared, and
leave the rest to the discretion of Almighty God! God knows what is best for
each of us. We are all born in the same way, but there are many different   105
ways of dying. Let him choose for us whatever he will. No one can die badly
who has lived well. And were it lawful for a religious man to choose the
manner of his death, none would I think be more desirable than a sudden
death to carry one off quickly heavenward in the middle, as it were, of a
career of virtuous acts. When one is sick already and willy-nilly the slave of   110
one's bodily ills, how much time is lost to one's religious duties! No
studying, no teaching, no preaching, no visiting of the sick, no labouring

* * * * *

11 Acts 12:23
12 1 Sam 4:18

with one's hands to obtain the wherewithal to help a brother in need; no, one is more likely all the time to be a burden to others whom charity would not wish to impose upon.

They say that Dietrich,[13] that Franciscan who died in Louvain and was, as you know, esteemed as a religious, honourable man, when he felt a burden of bodily weakness that he foresaw would lead to his death, used to express the wish among his brethren that God when he thought fit might take him hence suddenly, for fear a long illness might make him a burden to his brethren. So anxious is a good man to be no trouble to anyone in life that even in death he hopes not to be a burden. It happened as he had desired. On the day of his death he had preached twice, said mass, and assisted at the solemn liturgy. He sat down to dinner, and near the end of dinner asked permission to leave, saying he felt slightly sick. He went by himself to his cell, and they thought he was resting. When he did not appear for some time the brethren went in and found him lying on his bed fully clothed, dead, but with the air of one asleep. Who would not call such a death more blessed than a long illness?

'But there are no ceremonies, no holy water, no holy candle, no chrism, no sign of the cross, no crowd of mourners racked with sobs perhaps.' I will not observe at this point that these things sometimes do nothing but make death twice as disagreeable; I will merely reply that it was in such conditions that the eunuch of queen Candace was baptized.[14] It must have been much the same, I suppose, for those baptized by the Apostle Paul. Is baptism in our day a more blessed thing because performed with so many ceremonies? It is a wretched thing, they say, to die a solitary death. And yet the dead man is content if he has one angel to catch his poor parting soul and carry it to heaven. At the bedside there are sometimes those who can be a comfort to the dying man, but more often those who add to his grief and his despair: ill-tempered wife, disobedient children, companions from the gaming-table, the alehouse, or the brothel, a concubine, an enemy who has ruined him.

You know that councillor of Mechelen who was a friend and

* * * * *

13 Dietrich Kolde (Coelde, Dietrich von Münster), ca 1435–1515, of Münster in Westphalia. He studied in Cologne as an Augustinian Friar, but by 1479 he had become a Franciscan Observant, spending much of his career in the houses of that order in the Low Countries and gaining great fame as a preacher throughout the Rhineland and Westphalia. During an outbreak of the plague in Brussels in 1489 he selflessly tended the sick and the bereaved. Erasmus met him in Bergen around 1493 and admired him for the qualities described here and in Allen Ep 2700:124–50.
14 Acts 8:36–8

contemporary of Bogardus[15] the physician; for both of them lived to an   145
advanced age, and the Gronsellus[16] I speak of was even some years older, as
I learned from their conversation. I stayed with him once in Mechelen. I
learned there from his sons that when he had already taken to his bed (for he
died from old age rather than sickness) he told the relatives who were
proposing to sit up with him to go to bed. 'There is no need,' he said, 'for   150
anyone to put themselves out for my benefit. I can easily die by myself if
need be, for I am ready to go whenever God shall call me.' Those were words
really worthy of a Christian.

When I was living in Rome[17] they told a story of a certain man from
Saxony[18] who had arrived with several friends on pilgrimage. When he rose   155
and left the confessional of the priest before whom he had unburdened his
conscience, he knelt down before a neighbouring altar leaning on his staff,
and clasped his hands forcibly together and prayed. His companions, being
ready to leave, wondered why he spent so long in prayer, and when he
showed no sign of ending they plucked him by the sleeve to tell him it was   160
time to go. They found him dead, but exactly like a man in prayer.
Physicians also tell us that sudden and violent emotional changes can
produce death, as happened, they say, to a woman prostrated with grief
because she believed a false report that her son had been killed in battle;
when her son, who had survived unexpectedly, entered the house, she died   165
on the spot. The same thing must have happened to the man I spoke of. First
he had suffered intense remorse for what he had done wrong; then followed
intense joy from confidence in his absolution; and hence his sudden death.
'He died,' they say, 'with no light, no cross, no God.' But who would not
wish such a death as far the happiest?   170

None of the apostles or of those early disciples who were dear to Christ
above all other men died, we are told, of disease; all met a violent death, as
their lord, Christ himself, had done. And I for my part think that this kind of
death was granted them as a great privilege. Their whole life was spent upon
the gospel; their death of itself offered the greatest glory and the minimum   175
of torment. What could be more joyful and less to be lamented than a
martyr's death? And then how many diseases there are which are greater
torment than rods and hooks, than axe and cross! How many years of

* * * * *

15 Possibly Jacob Bogaert (d 1520), professor of medicine at Louvain, who entered
   holy orders after the death of his wife
16 Perhaps Gerard van Gronsselt (d 1514), who may have been the son of Jan van
   Gronsselt, professor of law at Louvain (d 1463)
17 Spring and summer of 1509; see Ep 216 introduction.
18 Unidentified

torture do men suffer from the gout, from excoriation of the kidneys and the
bladder, from my own executioner the stone![19] What cross can be compared   18
with the agonies of pleurisy? The law, at its most cruel, cuts a man alive into
four pieces before reaching his vital parts. But I believe a man would feel less
agony who was cut in pieces limb by limb than him who feels the fury of the
stone beneath his lower ribs and around what physicians call the mesaraic
veins – although the physicians of antiquity among the extreme forms of   18
anguish which bring sudden death assign the first place to calculus of the
bladder, which is perhaps more cruel for this reason that it is practically
untreatable (unless one can accept a remedy more cruel than death which
often means death itself). Next to this anyhow is calculus of the kidneys
when at its most painful. I for my part find it returns so often, and it attacks   19
me with such deadly force, that my worst enemy might rightly cease to hate
me, his hatred satisfied by such misfortunes. In fact so pitiless is the torment
caused by the stone that it sometimes kills the most robust and vigorous
body within three days; and if the pain lets up it does so simply that it may
return with greater violence. What else is this except to taste death over   19
again ever so often, and who would wish to be restored to life in order soon
to die once more?

Thus it is that great authorities not without reason have regarded
sudden death as life's greatest piece of good fortune. Many examples of this
are recorded by Pliny in his seventh book, chapter 53, and many more are   20
supplied by the experience of daily life. Although among these they seem
more fortunate who suddenly breathed their last from overwhelming joy.
Yet the most fortunate of all are those who after many years of happiness
met their end suddenly while engaged on some equally enjoyable and
honourable employment; we have all heard, for example, how death has   20
come suddenly to many people while saying mass or preaching or deep in
the contemplation of heavenly things. Some think a well-spent life is
happier than a long one; others again count length of life among the greatest
blessings. I cannot count myself among the fortunate, for I suppose that
scarcely any living man owes less to fortune;[20] although a great part of my   21
troubles, to speak frankly, I owe to my own thoughtlessness. But of the
length of my life I cannot complain, for I am now not far from my sixtieth
year. Had such a length of life been promised me by some astrologer or
palmist when I was young, I should never have believed him. And then too I
feel myself fairly long-lived when I compare myself with those who lived for   21
fewer years. I die before my time if I were to compare myself with St Jerome

* * * * *

19 See Ep 1267 n5.
20 See n8 above.

or with Varro, who was in his eightieth year when he wrote his work on agriculture, and wrote it with such spirit that after the labour of it he seems still to have been active in mind and to have taken delight in literary work. I compare myself for preference with those who, far more learned as they 220 were than I am, lived for proportionately fewer years. I will not mention such cases as Lucan and Persius.[21] Virgil died in his fifty-first year; Ovid was not much older;[22] Cicero in his sixty-fourth. Even these men of genius I number among mortal men.

But examples nearer our own time move us more strongly. Lorenzo 225 Valla I would put among those who have earned undying fame among posterity; he seems to have died before he reached old age.[23] Ermolao Barbaro, least barbarous of men, reached a fair age, but died long before his time came to decay.[24] Pico della Mirandola, Angelo Poliziano (what glories of their generation!) perished while still in the flower of their age.[25] Survey 230 the records of antiquity, and you will find many men of literary fame who lived to a great age; but within living memory you would discover very few, whether the reason for this is that the world itself is growing old or that nowadays a man must spend more of himself to acquire learning.

I come now to those whom I had the good fortune to see for myself not 235 many years ago. When I first went to Italy Filippo Beroaldo of Bologna was already dead.[26] He was then very famous and warmly remembered; and yet when he died he was younger than I am now.[27] His kinsman,[28] who recalled him by the same Christian name and surname, I saw in Rome, a young man of the highest character and in literary gifts and learning not inferior to the 240 elder Beroaldo and in many men's judgment (I too thought so myself) even superior. He was still young when fate snatched him away.

In Bologna for the first time I saw Scipione Fortiguerra,[29] a man of recondite and universal learning but so far from ostentation that unless you

* * * * *

21 Roman poets of the first century. Lucan died at twenty-five and Persius at twenty-seven.
22 Ovid died in his sixtieth year.
23 Ep 20:100n. Valla was about fifty-one when he died.
24 Ep 126:150n. He scarcely reached forty.
25 Pico (Ep 126:150n) died at thirty-one and Poliziano (Ep 61:154n) at forty.
26 Filippo Beroaldo the Elder (Ep 256:149n), who died in 1504 at age fifty-two.
27 By Erasmus' own reckoning in the *Compendium vitae* (CWE 4 403:4) he would have been fifty-six at this time.
28 Filippo Beroaldo the Younger (1472–1518) was a nephew of the elder Beroaldo. He taught at Bologna from 1499 to 1502, entered papal service under Julius II, and was appointed Vatican librarian by Leo X.
29 See Ep 217:4n. He was nearly fifty when he died, not forty-two as Erasmus here states (line 247).

drew him on you might have sworn he was illiterate. I got to know him 245
better afterwards in Rome. He too died when he was not much more than
forty-two years old.

In Padua I saw no famous men (I speak only of the dead) except
Raffaele Regio,[30] a man far advanced in years but 'fresh and green was his
old age.'[31] He was then I suppose not less than seventy, and yet no winter 250
was so severe that he did not attend at seven o'clock in the morning the
Greek lectures of Marcus Musurus,[32] who gave public lectures all round the
year with scarcely four days holiday. The young men could not face the
rigours of winter; but neither embarrassment nor winter kept that old man
from the lecture-room. 255

Musurus died before reaching old age, after he had begun to be an
archbishop by the favour of Pope Leo.[33] He was a Greek in origin, in fact a
Cretan, but such a good Latin scholar that it was quite extraordinary; few
other Greeks had this gift except Theodorus Gaza[34] and Janus Lascaris,[35]
who is still alive. And then for the whole of philosophy he had something 260
more than the greatest enthusiasm; he was a man born for the highest
things, had life been granted him. One day when I was to take supper with
him, and his little old father was there, who knew not a word of anything but
Greek, when it came to washing our hands, each of us made way for the
other as always happens; so to put an end to this pointless waste of time I 265
seized his father's hand and said in Greek, 'We're the two old men.' The old
man was perfectly delighted, and he and I washed our hands together;
although at that time I was not much older than Musurus.[36] Musurus,
however, put his arm round Zacharias,[37] a young man who was a very good
scholar, and said, also in Greek, 'And we're the two young ones.' 270

In Venice I saw Paolo Canal,[38] a patrician, a young man born for very

* * * * *

30 Ep 450:22n. He lived to be about eighty.
31 Virgil *Aeneid* 6.304
32 Epp 223:5n, 574 introduction
33 Musurus became archbishop of Monemvasia on 13 June 1516 (Ep 556:18n) and
   died on 9 August 1517 (Ep 729:60n), at about age forty-seven.
34 See Ep 1341A n63.
35 Ep 269:55n
36 The incident would have taken place in 1508, during Erasmus' residence in
   Venice. Musurus was about thirty-eight at the time, Erasmus forty-one.
37 Possibly Zacharius Calliergis (d 1524) of Crete, famous as a printer at Venice
   1499–1500 and 1509, and at Rome 1515–23
38 Paolo Canal of Venice (c 1481–1508), an accomplished Greek scholar and
   member of the circle around the publisher Aldo Manuzio. Erasmus and Canal
   probably met in the winter of 1507–8, during the first months of Erasmus'

great things had not death deprived the world of all those gifts. He died of consumption while I was still there. My host Aldo Manuzio died many years later, when he was not much less than seventy but wonderfully youthful in spirit in the field of literature.[39] Pietro Cotta[40] I only saw one day at dinner 275 and heard him talking; he was then in the flower of his age, a modest man and an equally good scholar.

In Rome I saw Pietro Marso,[41] who was aged rather than famous, for he was not far from eighty and was vigorous in mind and reasonably fit in body. He struck me as an honourable and upright man, and I could not fail 280 to admire his industry; at that advanced age he was writing notes on *De senectute* and other works by Cicero. It was possible to detect in him some traces of an older generation. In Rome I also got to know and made friends with Petrus Phaedrus,[42] who really won more fame with tongue than with pen, for he was a wonderfully copious and effective speaker. It is a great step 285 on the road to success to have made one's name in Rome. He first became known thanks to the *Hippolytus*, that tragedy of Seneca, in which he took the part of Phaedra, in the piazza in front of the palace of Cardinal Raffaele of San Giorgio.[43] So I was told by the cardinal himself, and that was how he got the nickname of Phaedrus. He was under fifty, I think, when he died, 290 having earned the name of the Cicero of his generation. Girolamo Donato[44] I saw on one occasion only, and had no later opportunity of meeting him. He

* * * * *

sojourn in Venice. Deeply interested in religious renewal as well as scholar-ship, Canal became a Camaldolese monk just three weeks before his death on 16 May 1508. Erasmus lamented his passing in *Adagia* II iii 48 (LB II 502A).
39 Ep 207 introduction. He died at about sixty-six.
40 Giovanni Cotta of Verona (c 1483–1509 or 1510), whom Erasmus incorrectly calls 'Pietro.' Both poet and mathematician, he became in 1503 the private secretary of the Venetian condottiere Bartolomeo d'Alviano. The dinner at which he and Erasmus had their only encounter probably took place in July 1508, during the celebration of d'Alviano's recent victory over the forces of Emperor Maximilian.
41 Ep 152:23n
42 Erasmus once again (cf n40) has the first name wrong. The reference is to Tommaso Inghirami, called Phaedrus, of Volterra (1470–1516), a learned ecclesiastic who spent his career at the curia in Rome. Famous as a preacher, he was by 1515 librarian of the Vatican and served as secretary to the Lateran Council in 1512. He died of a fall from his mule.
43 Ep 333 introduction
44 Donato (c 1457–1511), a Venetian diplomat who was an accomplished scholar and theologian as well. He translated a number of Greek patristic works and wrote treatises in defence of Roman doctrine against the Greeks.

was an old man but in excellent health,[45] fitted by his exceptional versatility not only for scholarship but for the performance of all sorts of public duties.

Britain is a far cry from Italy, but stands next it in the value of its learned men. How many of the circle of my old friends I have now lost! First Andrea Ammonio of Lucca,[46] a man, heaven knows, of great versatility, with a wonderful memory, and with all that lofty spirit so free from jealousy, so devoid of selfishness. Rising by his natural gifts and by the unbroken approval of princes, and destined for great things, he was carried off by sudden death when he was not yet forty. I for my part cannot refrain from grieving for his death as often as I remember how delightful I found his society. Of the same group was also Johannes Sixtinus from Friesland,[47] who died not long after him but was older than he. Even so, in body he might have lived to be as old as Nestor[48] had not some severe illness overtaken him; his mind was active in all fields and his memory prompt and tenacious. Besides the knowledge of canon and civil law which was his standby he had tried his hand successfully at every branch of knowledge. They were followed by John Colet,[49] dean of the cathedral church in London, who died perhaps in his fifty-third year. Of his outstanding gifts I need say nothing, for I have given an adequate picture of him in my letters,[50] and taken from life, for I knew the man intimately for many years. Not long after him we lost William Grocyn,[51] who to a professional knowledge of theology added a competence in every branch of learning that was precise to the edge of pedantry. Yet though he lived to a considerable age he left nothing behind him in writing.[52] After a stroke of paralysis he outlived his faculties for something like a year.

Of my German friends I have to mourn none but Johann Reuchlin,[53] who died in a flourishing old age that yet was not too much prolonged. In fact he might have been able to continue down to this day the support he so long gave to the public cause of learning, had it not pleased heaven to create certain creatures which do nothing but harm. The ox ploughs, the horse carries a man, and the sheep feeds him; of what value are hornets, gnats,

* * * * *

45 Donato was about fifty-two when Erasmus was in Rome (1509).

46 See Epp 218, 623–4.

47 Ep 112

48 Nestor, king of Pylos, ruled over three generations of men; *Adagia* I vi 66.

49 Ep 106

50 Ep 1211

51 Ep 118:26n

52 See Ep 540:88–104.

53 Epp 290, 1311 n15

vipers, and venomous beetles?[54] On top of them there is the general
catastrophe of war.[55] Would that it were possible to add Hutten to my list![56]   325

And now I have finished my circle and return to Louvain. There I
enjoyed for three days the society of Christophe de Longueil,[57] a native of
Brabant (for he was born, they say, in Mechelen). He died recently in
Venice[58] at the age of about thirty. A young man made for humane studies,
in which his schooling was precocious and successful, he would have made   330
a name for himself had he been allowed to live. And now last of all we have
lost Neve.

This is how soldiers tell over again the campaigns of famous generals
and from such precedents form for themselves a picture of what might
happen. And so we remain – remain, did I say? For my part, if I may speak of   335
myself, I have as they say outlived my vital thread,[59] happy could I but grow
young again and keep the memory of all I have experienced. But this is a
wish vain as the wind (I gladly use the Homeric phrase),[60] and does not
torment me in the least. I follow willingly the way I am summoned to take by
the common course of nature. On the length of my life I have no complaints.   340
I have had more than I hoped for, although I might have rested for some
years basking in the kindness of the friends whom the toil I put into my
books has won for me in such numbers all the world over, had I not, like the
mouse in the Greek proverb that fell into the pitch,[61] been born into this
tragic generation. The less felicity has fallen to my lot here, the greater my   345
confidence that it will be better for me in another world. But if I have been
unsuccessful, this has meant more to me than to other people. Some men are
born for themselves and for themselves they live. A nuisance to everyone
else, they keep their felicity to themselves, and do nothing to please other
people except by dying. Even then they have not lost their readiness to be a   350

* * * * *

54 Reuchlin's critics, especially Johann Pfefferkorn; see Ep 703:12–15, and cf Ep
   694:28–9, 88–90, 105.
55 See Ep 986:52–9, 68–72.
56 If the assumption is correct that this sentence was inserted at the time of
   printing in 1524 (see the introduction to this letter), after Hutten's death in
   August 1523, then Erasmus is saying that because of his bitter feud with
   Hutten (Epp 1331 n24, 1341A:1020–1191) the latter could no longer be
   numbered among his German friends.
57 Ep 914. The three-day visit with Erasmus took place in mid-October 1519; Epp
   1026:5–6, 1029:29.
58 Actually in Bologna, as Erasmus later reported in Allen Epp 1597:17 and
   1603:108
59 Cf *Adagia* I vi 67.
60 *Iliad* 4.355; cf *Adagia* III vii 21.
61 Theocritus 14.51; cf *Adagia* II iii 68.

nuisance: they burden posterity with memorial rites and prayer and sacrifice and ceremonies and vestments and the ringing of bells, so that even after death they are a trouble to the living. Personally I would rather be a Hercules and die amid my labours.

As for the manner of my death, the greatest torture that there is, I   355 console myself with the thought that there is absolutely nothing about it that can affect other people, while milder physical complaints like loss of sight or confused speech can actually be a trouble to anyone you live with. He who is troubled with the stone is the only sufferer, the only man who is at risk. And no torment is so great that human nature cannot bear it once it has grown   360 familiar, particularly with the help of courage. There is nothing womanish about those words of Electra in Euripides:

> There's nothing, so to say, so terrible,
> No suffering, no heaven-sent catastrophe,
> That human nature cannot bear the load.[62]   365

Indeed, as far as my spirit is concerned, it is not simply that I reckon an evil becomes less severe if one endures with resignation what cannot be avoided; I have to thank the philosophy of the gospel for something more. Once and for all I have put this wretched body of mine into the hands of Christ, just as a sick man in peril of his life puts himself into the hands of the   370 physician for gentle unguents and lotions or to be cut open and cauterized, in confidence that in whatever fashion he may treat this lodging of my soul, his only purpose will be my salvation. I lay down no conditions for him; let him be my saviour and he may do what he pleases. I know that he has no plans except what is best for me.   375

For the rest, I am almost free from those restraints which do not allow other men to say cheerfully to those who will outlive them 'And so farewell and give us your applause.' Even as a young man I never partook of food and drink except as a kind of medicine, and often regretted that it was not possible to live permanently without them. I was never a slave to venery,   380 and indeed had no time for it under the load of my researches. If I ever had a touch of that trouble, I was set free from that tyrant long ago by advancing years, to which on this account I am most grateful. Ambition I always abhorred, and now slightly regret this; one should accept in the way of office enough to prevent other men from looking down on one. But in those days I   385 could not imagine that such beasts in human shape existed as I now find

* * * * *

62 *Orestes* 1–3

existing; and now it is too late to look for honours which I could not support. Age often makes people careful about money. This is a disease which has never yet affected my spirit in the slightest. I wish I could control my expenses in such a way that when I die I may have no money of my own left   390 over and no debts; only what suffices to give my poor body a decent burial somewhere or other. As for the burden of reputation, I should be glad to be quit of it before I am quit of the body; so far am I from a concern for glory, if such a thing as glory really exists. I have no personal ties, such as love of children, parents or kinsfolk, to retain me in this life. I regard with equal   395 affection all who love Christ.

I have had something of a struggle with my spirit to make it adopt a truly Christian feeling towards those who knowingly and willingly and with deliberate spite like yelping curs defame a man who deserves none of it and has even served them well, and who even plan for my destruction. I have   400 achieved this too: not only do I have no thoughts of revenge, I do not even pray that evil may befall them. We find this gentleness even in soldiers when death stares them in the face; how much more ought we to be equipped with this feeling by the gospel philosophy! As it is, I find it something of a struggle to form in my mind a state of perfect confidence in my own   405 salvation, and on this subject I hold frequent debates within myself and sometimes share the problem with learned friends as well. Nor do I get any satisfaction so far either from Lutherans or from anti-Lutherans. And so the wisest course seems to me to be to seek security on this point in every way I can from Christ by prayers and by doing good up to the last day of my life,   410 and then to leave the decision on this point too to him, but with the feeling that just as I have the least possible hope from my own merits, so I have great confidence from his immense love towards us and his most generous promises.

This is the philosophy by which I now live, most learned van Gavere,   415 and I would exhort you to do the same, did I not know that a religious and learned man like yourself must have thought all this out long ago. You blame your indifferent health, and your complaints are justified. Those gifts of yours entirely deserved a better dwelling-place; but mind the trouble is not made much worse by imagining that you are ill. Physicians I approve of,   420 but giving them too much power I do not approve. Be sure to give my greetings to all our old companions, to Jean Desmarez,[63] to Dirk of Aalst,[64] to

* * * * *

63 Ep 180
64 Ie, the printer Dirk Martens (Ep 263:10n)

Jan of Armentières,[65] and to Pieter de Corte,[66] who have taken Neve's place, and besides them to the whole society of the Trilingue.

From Basel, 1 March 152[4] 425

1348 / To [Georgius Spalatinus] Basel, 11 March 1523

The only surviving version of this letter (Hauptstaatsarchiv Weimar Reg N.163) is a German translation in the hand of the Saxon court secretary Georgius Spalatinus (Ep 501), who probably prepared it for submission to Luther's prince, Elector Frederick the Wise of Saxony. The text was first printed in the *Zeitschrift für Kirchengeschichte* 2 (1878) 130. There seems to be no reason to doubt its authority.

The manuscript contains no specific indication that Spalatinus was the addressee. But his close relationship with both Luther and the elector, his friendly attitude towards Erasmus, and the fact that the manuscript is in his hand make the ascription highly probable. The extremely confidential nature of the remarks on Luther and King Henry explain why Erasmus never published the letter.

Greeting. Between you and me there is no disagreement. Rather, what has happened is pure mischance. Nor has it put our friendship under any form of constraint. At the same time this has done nothing for the gospel cause, which I try to promote in my own fashion according to my abilities more faithfully perhaps than some might think. You and I serve one purpose, but 5

* * * * *

65 Jan Heems (d 1560) of Armentières studied at Louvain. By 1521 he had obtained an MA and begun to study medicine. In 1521–2 he shared the regency of the College of the Lily with Jan de Neve, and from November 1522 to November 1525 with Pieter de Corte (see following note). For the remainder of his career he was professor of medicine and continued to serve the university in various administrative posts.

66 Pieter de Corte (Curtius) of Bruges (1491–1567) studied at Louvain and in 1515 became professor of eloquence at the College of the Lily, where Erasmus lived from 1517 to 1521. From 1522 de Corte was regent of the Lily, at first jointly with Jan Heems (see preceding note), then on his own (1525–45). In 1530, while serving the first of three terms as rector of the university, he was promoted to master of divinity, and the following year became professor of theology. In 1561 he became the first bishop of the newly created see of Bruges. Though a firm defender of Catholic orthodoxy and, later, of the Tridentine reforms, de Corte was also a warm supporter of Erasmus' Christian humanism, a protector of the Collegium Trilingue, and was close to many of Erasmus' good friends in the Netherlands.

what we do is not the same. Would God that Christ may turn it all to serve his glory, for therein lies our salvation!

On Luther's spirit I have never dared pass judgment; but I have often been concerned that the great impression he gives of arrogance and his great audacity in criticizing others may do harm to the gospel, which is so happily gaining strength. What purpose did it serve to use this kind of invective against the king of England,[1] the most religious prince of our generation? Far from me be any suspicion of flattery! I owe him nothing and want nothing from him.[2] He wrote under pressure, and he was convinced that his was a holy cause. It seemed to him that Luther was a most dangerous beast, and he was persuaded by men by whom it is no surprise to find a prince misled. For that he was misled I do admit. If only Luther had considered his intention, which is truly Christian; if only he had from the bottom of his heart forgiven the king's slanderous language, which was not directed against Luther but against the sort of man that, misled as he was, he took Luther to be; if only, without insulting the royal dignity, he had made a vigorous, disinterested reply based on solid arguments, he would neither have aroused so great a prince to be his enemy nor caused so many men to fall away from him.[3] Would God that even now he might learn meekness! But look at the preface in which he lauds Melanchthon's *Annotationes*![4] Was there ever such arrogance?

I am not worried about Luther, but two things concern me greatly. If Luther were to be overthrown, no god and no man would ever again be able to deal with the monks. And second, Luther cannot be made away with without the loss at the same time of a great deal of sincere zeal for the gospel. I have seen a letter he sent to one of his friends attacking me,[5] which is full of bitterness. I do know that there are a number of people who spur him on; but the wisdom of the gospel would have required him not to pass judgment on me or condemn me without first finding out the truth. If I sought only worldly advantage, there is nothing I could desire so much as that he and all his followers should attack me with all the venom at their command. But the

* * * * *

1348
1 Ep 1308 n3
2 Cf Ep 1342 n158.
3 Cf Ep 1342:870–2.
4 In his preface (WA x-2 309–10) to Melanchthon's *Annotationes in epistolas Pauli ad Romanos et Corinthios* (1522) Luther praises Melanchthon's work as far superior to that of Aquinas, Jerome, and Origen, and is especially contemptuous of the followers of Aquinas.
5 Probably the *Iudicium D. Martini Lutheri de Erasmo Roterodamo*; Epp 1341A n315, 1342 n160

outcome itself will show that nothing is further from my mind. Had I been willing to take a stand against the gospel, mountains of gold would have been my reward.[6] My refusal to do so has cost me all kinds of trouble and anxiety. Luther's friends on many occasions give too little thought to what needs to be done. Consequently they take no advice. I would gladly write to Luther himself, if the effort were not vain and likely at the same time to hurt myself and cause me more trouble. All I can do is to pray to Christ that he may deign to turn our rash and foolish actions to His praise. I would gladly also come and see you, were it not such a long way; for my poor health[7] permits me hardly any travel at all.

I beg you to commend me warmly to our gracious lord the most illustrious elector of Saxony, with whom I feel very great and sincere sympathy. And so farewell.

From Basel, eve of St Gregory 1523

Erasmus

1349 / To Gianfrancesco Torresani   Basel, 18 March 1523

Gianfrancesco Torresani of Asola (c 1481–1546) was the eldest son of Andrea Torresani (Ep 212:6 note), father-in-law and business partner of the famous Venetian printer Aldo Manuzio (Ep 207). After the death of Aldo in 1515, Francesco helped his father run the Aldine press, writing many of the prefaces to the books published.

Torresani's 'quarrelsome' letter and Erasmus' reply to it (lines 1–2) have been lost. But this second reply shows that Torresani's complaint had to do with the enlarged edition of the *Adagia* (ie, the *Proverbia* of line 10), the first edition of which had been published by the Aldine firm in 1508 while Erasmus was in Venice. Froben had reprinted it without authorization in 1513 (Ep 283:182–3), but since then there had been several Froben editions amplified and edited by Erasmus: 1515, 1517/18, October 1520 and, the latest, January 1523; see Ep 1341A n135. Without Erasmus' knowledge (line 16), the Torresani had reprinted the Froben edition of 1517/18 in September 1520, only to find it superseded by the Froben edition of October. Now they may have heard of the new edition just published. The essence of their complaint appears to have been that, as the publishers of the original edition, they were entitled to the chance at a subsequent edition that would not immediately be superseded by the product of a rival press. Since this was, broadly speaking, Erasmus' own

* * * * *

6 See Epp 1213:42–5, 1269:9–11, 1270, 1324, 1338, 1341A:1362–70. Cf also Ep 1352:131–2 and n20.
7 See Ep 1267 n5.

view of the matter (cf Ep 732:21 note), his reply was to offer Torresani the
chance to pirate the new edition with additions and revisions supplied by
himself. However, no such edition appeared from the Aldine firm.

The text is from Vatican MS Reg Lat 2023 f 160, first published by P. de
Nolhac, *Erasme en Italie* 2nd ed (Paris 1898).

Greeting, my dear Francesco. You have had by now, I expect, the letter in
which I reply to that rather quarrelsome one from you. I have certainly not
forgotten our original relationship, and if I wanted to forget it the stone in
my kidneys would not let me, which I first contracted when I was with you;[1]
and when it attacks me again, as it does from time to time, it reminds me of   5
Venice. I have no agreement with Froben or with any other printer, so far am
I from conspiring to injure you. And I admit that, when I left you,[2] your
father told me, if I had anything, to send it to him; but his expression, when
he said it, made me think it was a sardonic smile.[3]

Froben this past year[4] has printed my *Proverbia*, once again enlarged. I   10
have put my last touches to it, for I think I have already put enough effort
into that book, and I have made many additions from good authors. If yours
are sold out, I will send you a copy completed and revised, to which I will
give no one access in preference to you, provided you have in mind to print
within a year. If what you printed has not gone very well, you cannot blame   15
me, for I had no idea that you had done it. On this point therefore let me
know as soon as you can what your plans are. In publishing the Bible[5] you
admit yourself that you set up from uncorrected copy. I too have found
many mistakes, particularly in Proverbs, Ecclesiasticus, and books like
them. Your father will therefore do the right thing if he gives us the same   20
work again from copy that is more correct. If he were to print Chrysostom's
works in Greek, especially the things that have not been translated, they
should be highly saleable; or if there were anything of Origen's in Greek.[6]
The world has a passion for religious books, and there is no risk of any
competition with a big book.   25

* * * * *

1349
1 Cf *Adagia* II i 1 where, in a passage inserted in February 1526, Erasmus states
  that his first attack of the stone occurred when he was working on the *Adagia* at
  Venice; LB II 405C.
2 In December 1508; Ep 212
3 *Adagia* III v 1
4 Since the preface in Froben's name bears the date 1 January 1523, most of the
  printing had doubtless been done in 1522.
5 See Ep 770 introduction.
6 Nothing came of either of these suggestions.

The young man who brings this is keen to learn your profession.[7]
Please look into the question whether he can be any use to you, for he
begged me to recommend him to you with this in mind. Best wishes to you
and all yours, and pray give them my cordial greetings.

Basel, 18 March 1523   30

Your sincere friend Erasmus

To the learned Master Francesco Asola. In Venice

1350 / From Herman Lethmaet   Mechelen, 18 March [1523]

This is Lethmaet's response to Ep 1345. The manuscript of the letter (=Ep 14 in
Enthoven) is in the Rehdiger Collection of the University Library at Wrocław
(MS Rehd 254.96).

Greeting. All really good scholars without exception, dear Erasmus, are
passionately eager to see your Augustine,[1] and urge you with one voice not
to keep them waiting too long. Baechem[2] has openly listed me too among
Luther's supporters in a large convivial gathering of theologians, and has
easily brought several members of the same college[3] to share his opinion.   5
May I ask you another thing? Will you lay down for me the code at court
regarding presents and gifts, when to accept or refuse? When you commend
me to the pope, please do it in rather particular terms. He gave me in
September a prebend in St Mary's, Utrecht, and also excused me the
commission that would have come to him in accordance with the bulls. If I   10
am not mistaken, among all the men on whom he has conferred benefices I
stand first – and all this, as they call it, 'of his own mere motion.' Where this
may lead, I do not know. My uncle,[4] relying on an old friendship that began
when they were at the university, had written him a letter recommending
me, and that was how this good fortune first started.   15

My most reverend lord and master is always boasting of your having

* * * * *

7 Probably Johannes Hovius (documented 1518–27), who had been in Erasmus'
  service since 1518, primarily, it seems, as a copyist. This appears to be the point
  (cf Ep 867:189n) at which Hovius left Erasmus' employ to seek his fortune in
  Italy.

1350
1 See Ep 1309 introduction.
2 Ep 1254 n6
3 The faculty of theology at Louvain
4 Unidentified

dedicated Hilary[5] to him. A brother of his has arrived here lately from
Burgundy, who is among your warmest admirers. He is of a most generous
disposition, so that I have no doubt, if you paid him as great a compliment as
you have in this book to the archbishop of Palermo, you would find, and   20
find really and truly, that I am not romancing when I praise his liberality. My
master is of a different disposition. The brother's name, if you wish to know,
is Ferry de Carondelet.[6] He is the principal archdeacon of the cathedral of
Besançon, the city which is two days' journey away from Basel. He also has
countless other benefices, rich ones too, besides many annuities and an   25
abbey. Their father was chancellor. Five brothers[7] are still living, all very rich
and influential.

Please see to it, dearest Erasmus, that in future you do not torment me
with so many months' waiting for a letter from you as you have lately.[8]
Meanwhile our anti-Erasmians dream what they wish were true, and even   30
have the face to spread dreams of this kind among ordinary people as if they
were real. May their dreams always be false, and may you ever live safe,
vigorous, and happy!

Mechelen, 18 March

A most devoted recipient of your kindness, Herman Lethmaet of   35
Gouda

* * * * *

5 Ep 1334
6 Ferry (c 1473–1528), fifth son of the Jean de Carondelet (d 1501) who had been
   chancellor of Burgundy under Maximilian I, studied law. By 1508 he sat in the
   Grand Council of Mechelen and enjoyed the confidence of the regent Margaret
   of Austria. In 1509 Erasmus met him at Rome (Allen Ep 1359:11–13), where in
   1510 Ferry became legal agent for the Hapsburg and Burgundian lands at the
   papal court. Meanwhile, though never a priest, he became canon and
   archdeacon of the Besançon chapter (1504) and commendatory abbot of
   Montbenoît (1511). In 1520 he finally settled down in Burgundy to devote
   himself to the welfare of both chapter and abbey. In response to Lethmaet's
   suggestion that Ferry might be gained as a patron, Erasmus sent him a copy of
   the edition of Hilary (Ep 1334) that had been dedicated to his brother Jean
   (Allen Ep 1359:14–15). In 1524 Erasmus visited Ferry at Besançon (Ep 1610); in
   1526 he sought biblical manuscripts from him (Ep 1749); and just before his
   death dedicated to him an edition of Faustus of Riez (Ep 2002).
7 The eldest brother, Claude (1467–1518), head of the Council of Regency when
   Charles went to Spain in 1517, was now dead. Besides Jean (Ep 1276) and
   Ferry, three brothers were still living: Guillaume (d 1526), Charles (d 1529), and
   Philippe (d 1547).
8 Over three months between Epp 1320 and 1345. Erasmus answered this letter
   more promptly (Ep 1359, dated 17 April).

1351 / From Pieter Wichmans   Mechelen, 22 March 1522/3

The autograph of this letter (=Förstemann/Günther Ep 13) was in the Burscher Collection at Leipzig (Ep 1254 introduction). It is Wichmans' response to a letter that is no longer extant. Also lost are the letters (line 27) that caused Erasmus to doubt the loyalty of an old friend and host (Ep 1231). There is no other trace of this painful incident in the correspondence.

Greeting. I never would have feared that Fortune (though I have often felt her power) could ever be so cruel as to inflict on me the stigma with which you seem to brand me in your letter, a thing you would certainly never have done had you preserved any memory of the sort of man I am. For if you had, it would be clear that I am far too much moved by the solid devotion which 5 knows no disloyalty to be unfaithful and false and commit some offence against the very spirit of friendship. What, pray, could I, a mere country worm who counts for less than nothing, achieve, however deeply offended, against an Atlas like yourself? Was it for me to criticize the work in which, so as to leave no opening for any hostile critic, you express so briefly and clearly 10 what you think of Sancho Caranzanga?[1] Yet as your views become known to the world, the pope exalts them to the skies in an official letter,[2] resting upon your shoulders what remains of the church, whose tarnished reputation is now deplored. And in any case no other view of you can be taken by human judgment; for you and sound learning are synonymous. I have therefore no 15 fancy to explode such a notorious and shameless lie at greater length.

You wanted me to know this so that (as you put it) 'evil men would have no handle to take hold of.' To return the compliment, I should like you to know that in the case of Schrijver[3] and his colleague,[4] who are now in detention among the hooded brethren,[5] I have resisted the promptings of 20 charity a hundred times, hard though the struggle was, and have not even gone near the place, much less visited the prisoners, though I was invited time and again by the friars to do so and prodded by a certain alderman[6] to

* * * * *

1351
1 Ie, Carranza (Ep 1277 n8)
2 Ep 1324
3 Cornelis Schrijver (Ep 1299 n24)
4 Nicolaas van Broeckhoven (Ep 1299 n23)
5 Allen suggests, without citing his source, that the reference may be to the Franciscans of Brussels, who had been given charge of Jacob Proost (Ep 1254 n4), arrested at the same time.
6 Otto Clemen *Johann Pupper von Goch* (Leipzig 1896) 274–5, suggests that this was probably the 'consul Urselius' who helped Schrijver get permission to return to Antwerp after his release from custody.

help free the aforementioned colleague: I wanted to act honourably and
deny anyone that 'handle to take hold of.' 25

But it is your friends, you say, who pass on this information in their
letters. I freely admit, though you have deserved the gratitude of all men
past and present and future by the wonderful things you write, I know only
a few all the same who in this stormy time (I pass judgment on no man)
mention your name in public without reserve. Sucket[7] is one, and Adriaan 30
Wiele[8] the secretary, and (with his usual modesty) Maarten Davidts.[9] To
these I would add myself as a third or fourth, had not your 'friends' expelled
me from their number. Pieter Gillis[10] I have spoken to once, about your
books;[11] Goclenius[12] three times, hoping for news of you; Dorp,[13] at the time
of Jan Sucket's death;[14] that doctor who married poor Jan Sucket's 35
daughter,[15] who whenever he sees me starts a conversation about your
health; Herman,[16] a member of the household of my most generous lord the
archbishop of Palermo[17] – there is no one else with whom I have exchanged
a word, unless it be master Frans van der Hulst.[18] But, for pity's sake, it was
none of these, unless I am quite wrong, who wrote to you about me like this. 40

I keep my temper; but I have one thing more to say. Either strike me out
of the list of your friends or act as a man of your distinction ought to act and
give me some indication of who these 'friends' are, that I may show them,
whoever they are, to be either no friends, or liars. Whatever you do, I shall
not change, not because you deal out life and death with your pen as you 45

* * * * *

7 Antoon I Sucket (Ep 1331 n11)
8 Adriaan Wiele of Brussels (d post 1530), about whom little is known. In 1507 he
  was 'supervisor and tutor' to the future Charles V and his sisters. By 1523 he
  was secretary to Charles V in the Council of Brabant, in which capacity he
  attended the Diet of Augsburg in 1530 (Ep 2408).
9 Ep 1254
10 Ep 184
11 The books which Erasmus had left at the College of the Lily in the care of Jan de
  Neve; cf Ep 1355:20–1.
12 Ep 1257
13 Ep 1266 n2
14 Jan (I) Sucket (d 1522), brother of Antoon (n7 above), member of the Grand
  Council of Mechelen. Jan was clearly an old acquaintance of Erasmus, who
  addressed a letter to him in 1525 (Ep 1556), evidently forgetting that Wichmans
  had informed him of Jan's death two years earlier.
15 Jan's daughter Maria (d 1551) was married to Jan Vrancx (Van der Voirst),
  physician to Margaret of Austria. He is probably the physician referred to in Ep
  1355:12.
16 Lethmaet (Ep 1320)
17 Jean de Carondelet (Ep 1276)
18 Ep 1345 n8

think fit (be Erasmus by all means, as you have been or will be), but simply because of that deep devotion which I feel for you and which I shall continue to show with all affection and respect. Farewell.

Mechelen, this 22 March 1522 French style

Your most devoted Pieter Wichmans, priest, your host in the country, 50 who having done nothing to deserve this stigma[19] is paying a penalty he has not earned

I am delighted to hear of the pope's diploma.[20] Yet, if you were to number me among your friends, I should advise you to enjoy its external leaves and fruits to your heart's content, but without driving your teeth too 55 hard into the kernel.[21]

To the monarch of the world of letters, Master Erasmus of Rotterdam

1352 / To Adrian VI   [Basel, 22 March 1523]

This letter is what remains of the plan for dealing with the Lutheran trouble that Erasmus submitted to Pope Adrian. For Erasmus' offer to draft the plan and the pope's eager acceptance, see Epp 1329:13–16, and 1338:24–32. Despite the promise made in Allen Ep 1358:3 to publish 'shortly' a 'brief exhortation' to Christian concord, the letter was not published until 1529 in the *Opus epistolarum*. Moreover, the text breaks off abruptly soon after the beginning (line 168) of the section containing Erasmus' concrete proposals. The abridgment may have been intentional, reflecting a prudent decision not to publish a deliberately confidential communication (lines 26–7) in which Erasmus had expressed himself 'outspokenly,' even 'rashly' (Allen Ep 1358:42). Adrian never replied, which caused Erasmus to fear that the plan had given offence (Allen Epp 1384:25–6, 1496:55–8).

The date is assigned on the basis of Ep 1353:268.

TO ADRIAN VI FROM ERASMUS OF ROTTERDAM, GREETING

Most holy Father, the bearer[1] of this seemed to me more or less reliable, but he presented himself unexpectedly after dinner, with the intention of setting out at first light next day. I nearly decided therefore that it was wiser not to write at all to so great a prince on such a difficult subject than to write 5

* * * * *

19 See line 2.
20 Ep 1324
21 Cf Horace *Satires* 2.1.77–8.

1352
1 An unnamed canon of St Donatian's in Bruges; Allen Ep 1358:40–2

on the spur of the moment. None the less, since in both your official letters[2]
– and both have arrived safely – your Holiness urges me so strongly, and
appeals to me almost as a matter of obedience, to contribute to the best of my
ability any proposals I may have for bringing these disturbances to a
peaceful end, I bow before your authority and at the same time put my trust   10
in that mildness of yours which is so appropriate to your pontifical office,
and write even at short notice, in hopes of writing more fully when I have
more leisure and a more reliable bearer for my letter.

It would have been both safer and more convenient to treat of these
things face to face; such was definitely my intention, and your generous   15
invitation could not be more friendly. But I am forced to obey the edicts of a
most cruel tyrant. And who may that be? you will say. One far more cruel
than any Mezentius or Phalaris;[3] and its name is the stone.[4] In your city, it is
true, the plague has subsided and so has the winter; but it is a long journey,
even supposing it were safe, over the snow-covered Alps, by way of those   20
stove-heated rooms the very smell of which makes me feel faint,[5] as well as
dirty and uncomfortable inns, and acid wines of which the taste puts me in
instant peril.[6] If my health would support it, it would be safer to travel
through France; but this will come about in God's good time. Meanwhile I
call the Lord Jesus to witness to my conviction that whatever I write will be   25
written sincerely and in singleness of heart. No mortal man shall read this
letter except us two. If you approve it, it is at your service; if you disapprove
of any of it, suppose it was never written.

How I wish that I could command the resources which you attribute to
me to bring this discord to an end! I would not hesitate to heal the evils of the 30
time by the sacrifice of my own life. In the first place, many men write better
than I do, nor can this business be settled by pen and ink. My learning is well
below average, and such as I have is drawn from ancient authors and more
suitable to the pulpit than the battlefield. And then what weight can be
attached to a mere individual like myself? Will the authority of Erasmus have   35
any effect on people who give no weight to the authority of so many
universities, so many princes, and the supreme pontiff himself? My
popularity, if I had any, has either cooled off so far that it scarcely exists, or
has quite evaporated, or even has turned into hatred. Time was when
hundreds of letters described me as greatest of the great, prince of the world   40

* * * * *

2 Epp 1324 and 1338
3 See Ep 1342 n8.
4 See Ep 1267 n5.
5 Ep 1258 n18
6 Cf Ep 1316 n7.

of literature, bright star of Germany, luminary of learning, champion of humane studies, bulwark of a more genuine theology.[7] Now I am never mentioned, or am painted in far different colours.

I care nothing for these empty labels, which only laid a burden on me. But oh, the slanders which many madmen now pour on my defenceless head, the bitter pamphlets in which they attack me, the menaces with which they terrify me! For there was no lack of people who threatened to destroy me if I took any steps at all. But others complain loudly all the time that I have an understanding with Luther's party, and they complain that I never attack him in print; yet Luther's most violent supporters are saying indignantly that I attack Luther too often, and more bitterly than they think right. Luther makes just these protests in his letters to his friends.[8] Germany covers a wide area and is well supplied with able men; yet it is not only Germany that is in the grip of this movement. I would hardly dare to set down in how many regions and to what a depth the minds of ordinary people have been penetrated by support of Luther and hatred of the papacy. Indeed one would hardly credit the obstinacy of their minds; they themselves call it principle. And a good part of those who love the humanities are no strangers to this party.

It is with much grief and reluctance that I report this, most holy Father, and I wish it were not true. I had a most delightful relationship with all these scholars; in this possession alone I counted myself fortunate. I would have preferred death, almost, to the breaking of so many ties and drawing down the hatred of the world, I could almost say, on my own head. And yet I thought it better to do this than to seem a party man, nor do I yet regret the spirit in which I acted. I will not here recount what a tragic catastrophe, incurable perhaps, I could have started, had I let myself be exploited by some people's passions.[9] I would rather forego the gratitude I deserve for that than blurt out a secret. Nor do I look for gratitude if I refrained from doing wrong, however much the other side may call it true religion. If I had used ill health and old age as an excuse merely for taking no part in this business, I suppose I deserved some gratitude. But as it is, I have written so many letters[10] and published so many books that put on record how far I am from any understanding with Luther. I have deprived them all of any hope of my collaborating, and have not let them even use my name in public to

* * * * *

7 Allen's notes to lines 35–7 provide references to letters in which these flattering titles are used.
8 See Ep 1348 n5.
9 Perhaps, as Allen suggests, those who wished him to assume a leading role in the defence of Reuchlin; see Ep 1041.
10 See Ep 1275 n9. The most recent such letter was Ep 1342.

shelter under. I have urged them publicly[11] to give up their subversive policy, and in private[12] I have restrained or recalled anyone I could reach, or at least have made them less extreme. And I have had some effect; there are men who are grateful to me for my honest advice. Over and over again I have publicly expressed my dislike of Luther's intemperate language, nor   80 has anyone been more indignant than myself at the irreverence with which they have treated the name of the king of England.[13]

And all the time, while I am thus engaged in Germany, I am libelled in Rome[14] in crazy and worse than defamatory pamphlets. In Brabant it is no longer among sots and carters, it is in public sermons and in solemn lectures   85 that I am pronounced a heretic, a heresiarch, a schismatic, and a forger; this happens by no means rarely, and not with so little publicity that it can be ignored. If your Holiness could enquire of the common people, the first comer will giver you their names.[15] Luther's party has certain supporters who advance his cause under colour of having consigned themselves to   90 perdition unless they can overturn it by any means in their power. And these men[16] fancy that they carry the pope's cause on their shoulders. They put it about that there is nothing pestilential in Luther's books that is not also to be found in mine; nor have they yet been able to produce a single point in which I agree with Luther. But they put an interpretation on some things, it   95 is true, and in a most distorting way; they have their suspicions, and in a most hostile spirit. In the same way I could collect a hundred passages in the Pauline Epistles which agree with things that have been condemned in Luther's books. A sinister precedent for those who insist that we shall believe what they say in matters that concern the faith! For what result do   100 they achieve except that, while they are openly the slaves of their own private appetites, they undermine the cause of the faith, deprive themselves of all authority, and embitter the feelings of ordinary people towards the papacy.

I wrote a good deal before suspecting that Luther had come into   105 existence or before anyone dreamed of the rise of this generation. Almost all of it, I confess, has been done in a hurry, for this is a congenital fault of mine; but I have always submitted myself to the judgment of the learned, and

* * * * *

11 In the *Consilium* of 1520; Ep 1267 n6
12 See Ep 1275 n8.
13 Ep 1308 n3
14 By Zúñiga (Ep 1260 nn36, 45) and Carranza (Ep 1277 n8)
15 Baechem, Theoderici, Hoogstraten, and (possibly) Jacobus Latomus; see Ep 1330:53–8, and Epp 1299–1302.
16 Ie, the Louvain theologians; see the preceding note.

especially of the church. I have asked many people to point out to me if there
was anything in my work that needed alteration; and those who at that time   11
either said nothing or expressed their approval condemn what they
approved before now that Luther has appeared. They invent some reason to
complain of everything. There is a scorpion, as the saying goes, hidden
under every stone:[17] something dubious here, something scandalous there,
something irreverent somewhere else. And though no university and no   11
bishop has yet passed judgment on me, there are people who protest that I
am a heretic, a heresiarch, on their own private responsibility. Is there any
spirit so inflexibly loyal that these outrages would not drive it into rebellion?
But no force has yet been able to divert me from the true path. And yet this is
how Arius and Tertullian were first set in motion.[18]   12

Your Holiness must therefore discern whether you think this spirit
deserves to be abandoned to the unbridled enmity of certain persons, and
also whether that will be conducive to the business which you have in hand.
Those who wish well to the papal cause do their best to turn heretic into
orthodox, to recall those who have been estranged, and to strengthen the   12
waverers; and this is what your Holiness also urges with no less prudence
than true Christian spirit. But these Atlas-figures, who bear up the shaky
pillars of religion and the church, push the waverers off their balance,
estrange their friends, turn orthodox into heretic, and distort what has been
well and truly said. Am I not right to regret my old age, which has fallen in   13
this generation like the mouse in the proverb that fell into the pitch?[19] Many
owe promotion and wealth to Luther,[20] some have found it profitable to be
of his party. Could any position be more unhappy than my own? – I toil day
and night for the good of all men at my own costs and charges, and receive
no recompense except to be torn in pieces by both sides.   13

But your Holiness suggests a remedy for these misfortunes. 'Come to
Rome,' you say, 'or write some really savage attack on Luther. Declare war
on the whole of Luther's party.' In the first place, when I hear the words
'Come to Rome,' the effect is just like telling a crab to fly. The crab answered
'Give me wings,' and I shall reply 'Give me back my youth, give me back   14
good health.' How I wish my excuse on this point were not so un-
answerable! It would take too long to set down all the reasons which have
persuaded me to remain all this time in Basel. On one point I would dare to
take my oath: if I had seen any course more likely to be of service to

* * * * *

17 *Adagia* I iv 34
18 Cf Ep 1288:32–6.
19 *Adagia* II iii 68
20 Ie, his enemies; see Allen Epp 1397:27–9, 1408:25, 1417:13–15.

Christendom, I would have taken it even at the risk of my life. I never lacked   145
the will to achieve something, only the hope of making any progress. What
could be more foolish than to stir up trouble which is happily at peace, if you
have no hope but to make things much worse?

Let me beg you with all the force at my command: allow your humble
sheep for a few moments to speak freely to his shepherd. Supposing my   150
health permitted, what good should I do in Rome? Shall I be free from any
contact with Luther's party? I have no contact with them now, for there is no
communication between us. So that I for my part run no risk from them, as
far as my own attitude is concerned. As for correcting their errors, I shall
sooner do some good as their neighbour than if I am far away. What can a   155
physician do for his patients if he takes himself off a long way away? When a
rumour had got about here that I had been summoned to Rome, what a
hubbub instantly arose, with everyone saying that I was skipping off to your
part of the world for my share of the spoils![21] What weight then will anything
carry that I write when I am with you, and corrupted by rewards, as they are   160
quite convinced? If I join you, I shall perhaps live or write in greater safety;
but that is to think of myself and not of what is at stake. If I write against
Luther with some moderation and courtesy, it will look as though I am
trifling with him; and if I imitate his own style and challenge Luther's party
to a pitched battle, will this do anything but stir up a hornets' nest? Up to   165
now, I confess, I have kept alive my friendships with scholars by such means
as I could; for in this way I think I do more good.

Thus far, you will say, I hear nothing but complaints; what I am
waiting for is a plan. Yet even what I have said hitherto is part of a plan. In
any case, for a start, I perceive that many think this trouble should be healed   170
by severity; but I fear the outcome shows that this plan has long been a
mistake. For I see more danger than I could wish that this business will end
in appalling bloodshed. I am not discussing now what they deserve, but
what is best for the public peace. This cancer has gone too far to be curable by
the knife or cautery. In former times, I agree, that is how the Wycliffite party   175
was suppressed in England by the royal power; but it was suppressed rather
than extinguished.[22] And yet what could be done at that period in a kingdom

* * * * *

21 See Ep 1342 n136.
22 In 1401 Parliament inaugurated the suppression of the Lollards, as Wycliffe's
    followers were known, with the act *De haeretico comburendo*. Persons convicted
    of heretical views by diocesan courts were to be turned over to the secular
    courts to be burned. Despite active persecution (cf Allen Ep 1367:76–9), Lollardy
    persisted throughout the fifteenth century and into the sixteenth as an
    underground, largely proletarian, anti-clerical movement calling for a scriptur-
    al, non-sacramental, non-hierarchical, lay-dominated religion. In the 1530s the

which was subject entirely to the will of one individual is not practical here, I suspect, over such a vast area and cut up among so many princes. At any rate, if it has been decided to overwhelm this evil by imprisonment and scourging, by confiscation, exile, excommunication, and death, there will be no need of any plan from me. Not but what I see that a most humane nature like your own prefers a very different sort of plan, designed to heal the evils rather than to punish them. This will not be found abnormally difficult – if only all men were of the same nature as you, so that laying their private feelings on one side, to use your own words, they would wholeheartedly desire to promote Christ's glory and the salvation of Christian people. But if every man concentrates privately on his own advantage, if theologians insist that their own authority must be watertight at every point, if monks allow no reduction in their own privileges, if princes cling to all their own powers tooth and nail, it will be found very difficult to make any plan for the common good.

The first thing will be to investigate the sources from which this evil so often springs up afresh; for they must be set right before all else. And then it will not be found ineffective if once again a pardon is offered to those who have gone astray through the persuasion or influence of others; better still, an amnesty for all wrongs previously committed, which seem to have come about by some sort of destiny. If God deals with us on that principle every day, forgiving all our offences as often as the sinner shows himself penitent, is there any reason why God's vicegerent should not do the same? And yet for the present let the civil power and the princes restrain innovations which contribute very little to religion, and to subversion a great deal. I should also wish, if it could be arranged, for some limit on the liberty of printing pamphlets. Besides these measures, the world should be given some hope of changes in certain points where complaints of oppression are not unjustified. At the sweet name of liberty all men will breathe afresh. Every method should be used to promote this, so far as it can be done without imperilling religion; steps should be taken to relieve men's consciences of their burdens, but no less at the same time to safeguard the dignity of princes and of bishops. But this dignity should be measured by those things in which their true dignity really consists; and just the same is true of popular liberty.

Your Holiness will ask, 'What are these sources, or what are the points

* * * * *

old Lollard heresy gradually merged with the new Protestant heresy, so many of whose doctrines it had anticipated. See A.G. Dickens *The English Reformation* (London 1964) 22–37.

that need reform, of which you speak?' To evaluate these things my opinion
is that, region by region, men should be called together who are incorrupt-   215
ible, influential, humane, widely respected, and emotionally well-balanced,
whose opinion ...

1353 / To Udalricus Zasius   Basel, [23 March] 1523

This letter was first published in 1574 under the title *D. Erasmi Roterodami ad*
Vdalricum Zasium epistola de delectu ciborum in ieiuniis ab ecclesia catholica excusa,
edited by one Hilarius Pyrckmaier of Landshut. The volume is very rare: Allen
found only one copy, in the university library at Freiburg. No printer's name is
given. In his preface, Pyrckmaier states that the original, perhaps the letter
actually received by Zasius, had been supplied by Johann Hartung (1504–79),
professor of Greek at Freiburg. Allen's text includes some corrections and
insertions taken from a seventeenth-century manuscript (in the Stadtbibliothek Bern) which may also have been based on the original letter.

The month-date is assigned on the basis of the clear reference to the day after
Passion Sunday in line 179 (but see n12).

The letter was written shortly after Erasmus' return from a visit to Freiburg
in response to pressing invitations (Epp 1252:6–7, 1316:40). In the colloquy
Ἰχθυοφαγία, 'A Fish Diet,' first published in February 1526, he states that the
visit lasted only a few days and gives a light-hearted description, parallelling
the one here, of the excitement aroused when Zasius gave him chicken to eat
even though it was Lent: ASD I-3 529–30, Thompson 349–50. Erasmus was back
in Basel by 11 March (Ep 1348).

The freedom with which Erasmus expressed himself on highly controversial
subjects and his outspoken comments on the emperor (lines 117–24) doubtless
explain why Erasmus did not publish the letter himself.

ERASMUS OF ROTTERDAM TO HIS FRIEND ZASIUS
A light-winged breath of rumour (false, as I suppose) has reached us here to
the effect that you have been taken to court and obliged to defend yourself
on the charge that you had procured a roast chicken for my humble self and
that, although a lawyer of such eminence that you can act as counsel for the   5
defence in the most difficult cases, on this occasion you owed your acquittal
solely to the plea that this was authorized by a licence from the pope.[1] Of
course I want to know whether there is any truth in the story we heard, since

* * * * *

1353
1 Ie, the one granted to Erasmus; see line 65.

for my part I find it improbable. To begin with, I wonder what spy, what common informer could have reported the delicious odour of that chicken to the town council. Second, I do not believe any member of the council to be so uncivilized as to wish, after my making the journey to your city in order to show my respect for you, and my receiving more than one invitation in the name of the magistrates, to cast such aspersions on me and send me away with a black mark like this for my parting present. It was, I suppose, because you saw that I was in peril from the stone and therefore in a hurry to depart that secretly and without my knowledge you had provided a chicken for me in your house. This was a consummate example of your kindness, my dear Zasius, for which you are no less remarkable than for the learning which earns you a respect that few men share. I myself however, as you know, did not partake, and rebuked you for taking your kindness too far, and doing something for my benefit which might cause trouble. I felt that I was about to give birth to a stone,[2] and was absolutely determined to leave; and consequently, for fear that with the gathering of another large company I might be obliged to remain longer at table and shortly afterwards to ride my horse with a full stomach, I wanted to take an egg and a glass of wine in your house and get into the saddle immediately, that the birth-pangs might not come upon me while I was still with you. For we sufferers feel our travail in advance, just as much as women do in pregnancy.

Nor did my forebodings deceive. On the fourth day after my return I produced with acute pain an incredible quantity of stones and gravel and one stone of enormous size. Already when I went to stay with you I was still weak from a previous birth, and my only purpose in doing so was to see if the bodily motion would either kill or toughen me. As far as physical strength went, the motion did me good; but those longish walks before dinner and the protracted dinner and the change of wine brought back my trouble with the stone, and anyone who knows how close it is to death and what an agony it is would be a monster of cruelty if, for the sake of some superstition about diet, he expected anyone to plunge himself into such dreadful pain and put his life in obvious danger. For, to speak the truth, of all the practices that have wormed their way into the Christian life nothing contributes less to true personal religion, and nothing is so close to Judaism,[3] as this discrimination in what we eat. If it has the approval of certain bishops, its purpose is not to torture us with sickness and pain, but to moderate the heat of the body. It follows that the man who under pressure from some such great necessity eats food appropriate to his bodily condition

* * * * *

2 Ep 1267 n5
3 See Ep 1333 n14.

in moderation and with a thankful heart commits no sin by transgressing a decree of the bishops even if he has no licence; while he would sin against the divine law if through superstitious abstinence from food he were knowingly and deliberately to encompass his own death, no less than if on a fast day he were to starve himself to death for fear of transgressing a decree from the pope.

Would that person be thought to have the heart of a Christian who, though it was certain that someone, if he were to eat fish, would thereby run the risk of epilepsy or paralysis or apoplexy or the stone (which is more cruel than them all), yet forced the wretched man to eat fish? This is cruelty, not piety; its end is not Christian discipline but manslaughter; nor is this so much obedience to decrees made by bishops as to go against the intention of the bishops and be a slave to one's own superstition or other people's. The last thing the Roman pontiff wants is to see a man die for the sake of his decrees or be put in evident peril of his life; and even if he wanted such a thing, he has no legal power to make a decree which brings a man destruction and not well-being. In my case, the weakness of my wretched body has always made it dangerous to eat fish, and that is why I long ago secured a licence.[4] On top of that has come old age, which always takes something from one's bodily strength, and on top of that periodical attacks of the stone, a complaint more frightening than death itself. Add now my burden of work, even were it nothing but to answer all the letters that come pouring in from all parts of the world. And yet for the sake of weaker brethren I often put myself in danger, for fear that someone, using my example as an excuse, may do in self-indulgence what I am forced sometimes to concede to necessity. This indeed is carrying Christian charity to excessive and unnecessary lengths, to suffer yourself in order to avoid risk to a weaker neighbour. But what kind of charity is it to insist that for the sake of the weakness of two or three people their neighbour should be put in peril of his life? For my part, what I did not dare do in your house, my dear Zasius, I should have done without hesitation under the roof of the present pope, though he is not entirely exempt from superstition of the kind, but not to the extent of requiring abstinence from meat from Erasmus and others like him.

How much better they manage in Rome, and indeed in the whole of Italy![5] – and now in Basel too they are selling meat openly in the markets that

* * * * *

4 See Ep 1079 n1.
5 In the *Epistola de esu carnium* (LB IX 1206F) Erasmus notes with approval that in Italy meat is freely available, even in Lent, to those whose health would suffer without it. The same point is made in the colloquy Ἰχθυοφαγία, 'A Fish Diet' (ASD I-3 528 / Thompson 349).

those who need it may not go without. 'But,' you'll say, 'it is sometimes eaten by those who don't need it.' It is more tolerable for hundreds of people to eat meat who do not need it than for one man who deserves to live to die because there are rules about food. It is surprising how we choose this department by which to measure Christianity. If trouble is in store for those who do not abstain from meat, it is much fairer to punish those who do not abstain from supper.[6] But scandal they say, must be avoided. And a cruel scandal it is, if for the unjust superstition of a handful of men their neighbour must be forced to die. No, the public must continually be made to learn what the Apostle teaches,[7] that a man should not pass judgment on his brother in respect of food or drink, but put the best interpretation he can on anything that it is not wrong to do. 'But it is illegal without a licence.' No, an immediate emergency cannot wait for the protection of a licence. You are in the grip of a sickness that may kill you: are you to send to Rome for a licence that may protect you when you're dead? Though I do not approve of those who in a rash and subversive spirit condemn a public practice, whatever it may be.

I hear that your town council is over-superstitious in this regard. If this is true, I do not blame them so much as certain Pharisees who, having no true religion themselves, defend the semblance of religion with titles and colours and the shapes of vestments. In other ways you would find them entirely worldly. They love their comforts, nurse their resentment and satisfy it, are proud, brutal, self-satisfied, envious, greedy, devoid of any feeling of true charity, and the slaves of ambition and their bellies. What would these men have left in the way of piety if you removed their vestments and their discrimination between different foods? And of course this Pharisaical type insinuates this sort of superstition into the minds of princes, who are ignorant of the things of the spirit and take for holiness what they are taught by those who have the trappings of religion to recommend them. So the more inexperienced and ingenuous the prince, the less he knows how to suspect other people's deceptions, and so he is the more easily imposed on. Zeal is praiseworthy, even when not according to wisdom; but zeal without judgment must be corrected by the standards of true piety.

I cannot fail to approve the religious spirit of the emperor who, under

* * * * *

6 Erasmus thought that abstinence from food, ie, going without supper, had apostolic sanction, but that forbidding certain foods was an absurd human invention: see Ἰχθυοφαγία, 'A Fish Diet' ASD I-3 526 / Thompson 346 and *De esu carnium* LB IX 1202A–1203F. Cf Ep 916:164–9, 279–84.

7 Rom 14

the influence of Dominicasters[8] and Franciscans, believes that these things play an important part in the Christian religion. But he will think differently when years and experience have given him more judgment. And how I wish 120 that those who were able to implant this spark of religious feeling in his mind had given him other knowledge and other convictions conducive to the public good! He is a young man with plenty of brains and no doubt would have proved an apt pupil there too. Look at the universal corruption of magistrates, the uncontrolled brigandage, the disasters that befall 125 harmless country people, the cruel fleecing of the public, the impious upheavals of war, and the carnage! How can these be avoided? That is what they ought to have been taught by these men who mix earth and sky[9] over the eating of meat and make a grand tragic scene out of nothing at all. And so I cannot be induced to believe that men of any judgment with some wisdom 130 and knowledge of the world would cause trouble for anyone if on account of some unquestionable requirement of his body he were to eat in the privacy of his own house, no matter what the day, whatever should be demanded by his state of health. If, however, they have acquired something in the way of superstition from their pharisaical teachers, their intentions are to be 135 commended; but their judgment needs to be corrected by learned and honest men like yourself.

But if things have come to such a pass that we must be compelled by the civil magistrates to be religious, I wish people could be forcibly protected more than anything else from things which are a real menace to true 140 religion. Think of the evils of which drunkenness is mistress! But actually on Good Friday one is permitted to get so drunk that one vomits or has a fit, while for a sick man in peril of his life to eat chicken is a capital offence. In the old days, if the magistrates ever demeaned themselves to such humble cares, they made it their business to ensure that weights were not reduced 145 from their proper size to defraud the customer, that the vendor did not put up the price of things above a reasonable figure, that no monopoly was arranged between the sellers of anything, that wine was not adulterated, that no tainted or rotten meat or fish was sold, that dinners were not more expensive than was expedient, that nobody should spend more on building 150 a house or buying clothes than his means permitted. These are small things, but they contribute to the welfare of the citizens. And in any case, what a man should eat or drink in his own house to suit his bodily necessities is usually laid down by physicians rather than magistrates.

If, however, it is religious for the civil magistrates to take measures to 155

* * * * *

8 Ie, 'inferior Dominicans' (*dominicanus* plus the pejorative suffix *-aster*)
9 *Adagia* I iii 81

compel the public to observe the decrees laid down by men, much more was it right for this to be done in fields where God has laid down the rules. We commit fornication with impunity while we are in good health, and when we are sick we may not eat with impunity what may make us well. If a lay magistrate takes no notice of divine ordinances except when he so chooses, 160 why do they not maintain fair play in the ordinances of men? Or rather, why do they like things upside-down? One can sup as one likes with impunity, and one cannot eat an egg with impunity; and yet both are equally forbidden by the authority of the bishops. Wagoners and sailors openly carry things in and out on Sundays, and a cobbler is not allowed to sew a pair of shoes. 165 Horsemen go out riding on feast-days sometimes to hunt,[10] and we make a grand tragic scene if someone merely eats meat. No one gets into trouble because on a holy day he has failed to listen to a holy sermon; and yet this is a major contribution to Christian piety, and that was what the church set up basilicas and Sundays for in the first place. And it often happens that while 170 the priest is declaiming in church till he is hoarse, the gamesters in the brothel next door are making a rival hubbub with their drunken harangues; and this they can do with impunity by the good leave of the magistrates. What else does this prove, except that we have got our values upside-down, punishing actions forbidden by men more severely than what God forbids, 175 and clinging more tenaciously to things which have the minimum of influence on our religious life than to those which of their own nature are pious and honourable.

Yesterday, on the Sunday, that is, that they call Passion Sunday,[11] for the sake of my health I was going out for a ride with a friend before supper, 180 and we were beguiled by the wonderfully fine weather. There met us a great crowd of young men,[12] not one of whom was sober. Most of them were reeling as they walked, and some from time to time fell over and were then helped up by men as drunk as themselves, while others were dragged along, moving their feet with difficulty while the rest of their weight was 185 taken by the people who supported them. There was a little old man being carried high up on their shoulders like a parcel, his body folded over with his feet going first and his head hanging down behind their backs, and from time to time he vomited over the legs of those who were carrying him. In the

* * * * *

10 For Erasmus' views on the observance of feast-days, see Ep 1039:190–209, and the *De esu carnium* LB IX 1199F–1201A.
11 22 March 1523
12 This incident is also recounted in the colloquy Ἰχθυοφαγία, 'A Fish Diet' (ASD I-3 525–6 / Thompson 345–6), where it is said to have taken place on Palm Sunday rather than Passion Sunday (line 179). This letter, written the day after the event, is the better authority for the date.

old days, I imagine, that was how they were carried out to burial. Nor were   190
the carriers much more sober than the carried. They had been drinking, they
said, in a neighbouring village. God commanded that we should be sober,
and forbade that we should be drunk; men have laid it down that we should
observe a holy day. Here both laws were broken, and no one thinks any
offence has been committed. If one were actually to set eyes on a Carthusian   195
who had drunk more than was good for him, no one thinks that he has done
anything wrong. But if the same man has eaten meat, this is an offence
worthy of eternal imprisonment. What could be more hopelessly inverted
than this scale of values?

Meanwhile, as we were gazing at this astonishing spectacle, we found   200
ourselves within sight of the suburban property of that Sigismund[13] who
was so cruelly put to death a short time ago. This was the house in which,
just about this time a year ago, that disastrous dinner took place; and there
are people who reckon that action among the principal crimes for which the
wretched man paid such horrible penalties. For my part, I cannot possibly   205
refrain from condemnation of his headstrong folly, although those who
knew the man declare he was a lunatic and only at intervals in his right
mind. Such a remarkable coincidence brought that action back into my
mind, which aroused such a tragical uproar, and could not fail to be
contrasted with the scene before us. Since this happens frequently and as a   210
matter of course, no one thinks fit to take any measures against it, though at
the same moment it profanes a holy day, ignores divine service and the
word of God, and breaks the divine commandment. Drunkenness is the
mother of quarrelling, bloodshed, adultery, and almost every crime, and a
way of life so fraught with peril to the public good that at this day among the   215
Saracens drunkards are liable to capital punishment. But all this time we
priests cheerfully accept the support given by lay princes to our authority in
putting our decrees into effect, forgetting all the time the old saying that
mule scratches mule.[14] For we are obliged to support them in our turn when

* * * * *

13 Sigismund Steinschneider, a skilled surgeon, in whose house on Palm Sunday
(13 April 1522) a company of supporters of the Reformation openly defied the
Lenten fast by eating pork, thus setting off an uproar which lasted throughout
the summer (see Ep 1293 n8). Both the bishop and the town council issued
mandates against such flouting of custom and law. It was this incident which
moved Erasmus to address the *Epistola de esu carnium* to the bishop (Epp
1341A:1306–13, 1274 n7). Almost a year later (22 February 1523) Steinschneider,
a man given to rash utterances on many subjects, was executed at Ensisheim in
Alsace for blasphemies against the sacraments and the Virgin Mary. See the
scholia (1532) to the *Epistola de esu carnium* ASD IX-1 65–7.
14 *Adagia* I vii 96

they claim as their own our rights and our property, when they take away   220
our immunities, encroach on our benefices, and burden us with their
exactions; this is what it means to accept the support of princes in
ecclesiastical affairs. It is fair enough to boast that the Christian religion is at
last flourishing nicely if, while our whole way of life is filled with ambition,
brutality, avarice, disputing, fighting, manslaughter, warfare, plundering,   225
quarrelling, usury, simony, fraud, perjury, adultery, lasciviousness, and
theft, we are content to defend our reputation for piety by this criterion
above all others,[15] contempt for which was the first clear proof the apostles
gave that they had the courage to be Christians. Peter, before he had wholly
put away Judaism, abstained from food which had been forbidden by the   230
law of Moses; once he had had his lesson from heaven and developed the
courage proper to the gospel, he ate whatever food he pleased.

And I would say this, dear Zasius my most learned friend, with no idea
of encouraging those foolish people who think they show themselves men,
and worthy of the gospel, if when there is no necessity they eat meat in   235
defiance of the decrees or customs of the church, but to show how
upside-down the public's scale of values is. Not that I suppose your
magistrates, who are intelligent men with high standards, to be so
superstitious that they would wish to stir up trouble for a man who was
obliged by peremptory reasons of health to eat what he pleased, even if he   240
had no licence from the pope. So I shall consider this rumour absolutely
baseless until you write and tell me the facts. Apart from that, as far as my
own attitude is concerned, I am so little tempted by good living that I should
be glad to live perpetually on turnips and greens, provided such a diet
would maintain my wretched body in good health. My only regret is that in   245
this matter I have such a good excuse. I would rather pay the penalty ten
times to the bishops for eating meat than pay the penalty once to the stone
for eating fish.

The day I returned here a second diploma was delivered to me from the
pope,[16] much more complimentary and in much warmer language than the   250
first.[17] Besides which I send you a copy of a letter from a most open-minded
divine, Theodoricus Hezius, the pope's principal secretary, so that you may
know exactly how your friend Erasmus is placed.[18] Three days later I got a
privilege for Froben,[19] which I had secured by writing to Ferdinand.[20] My

* * * * *

15 Ie, abstinence from forbidden foods
16 Ep 1338
17 Ep 1324
18 Ep 1339
19 See Ep 1341 n4.
20 Ep 1323

letter arrived just in time,[21] for the next day he was preparing to leave. The   255
prince was not even coming to the diet, except to bid farewell to the top
people. He read my letter eagerly, recognizing at once the familiar name of
Erasmus. Next day he brought forward the same business at the meeting,
not without some complimentary remarks about myself. It was decided
unanimously that Erasmus should have what he wanted; and not content   260
with that, our excellent prince gave strict instructions to the chancellor to put
the document through that same day, so that he could sign it with his own
hand before he left. It was put through by Ulrich Varnbüler,[22] a man whom I
find frank and friendly, and what is more, free of charge, contrary to the
practice of these court officials. Shortly after, I received a letter from   265
Ferdinand,[23] in which he also thanked me, and promised that he would
reward my services. I suspect that the letter was composed by himself.

I answered[24] the pope and his secretaries yesterday by a safe hand[25]
(for the emperor's court has particular business with the pope, and the man
is genuinely friendly to me), but he was in a hurry; I took the risk however of   270
writing even on the spur of the moment, especially as he asked in his letter
for a speedy answer.[26] I have almost decided to stay here until next August,
and then to go either to Italy, where I have an invitation from the pope[27] and
several scholars,[28] or to France;[29] for something like the scent of peace
salutes my nostrils. I had guessed this might be so on my own account; and I   275
only hope my guess may not mislead me. The demands will be met, and an
agreement has been arrived at between the princes.[30] It is better to lose part

* * * * *

21 Here the narrative is clearly based on the information supplied by Pirckheimer
   in Ep 1344:123ff.
22 Ep 1344 n27
23 Ep 1343
24 Ep 1352
25 Ep 1352 n1
26 Ep 1338:43–5
27 In Epp 1324 and 1338
28 The letter answered by Ep 1349 may have included an invitation.
29 See Ep 1319 introduction.
30 Since the fall of Rhodes to the Turks on 21 December 1522, Pope Adrian VI had
   redoubled his efforts to mediate a peace or at least a truce between Francis I and
   Charles V in preparation for a united Christian effort against the Islamic foe. In
   February 1523 and again in March, Charles informed the pope of his readiness
   for an armistice, while Francis conveyed the impression of a similar readiness.
   Erasmus, with his many contacts at the imperial court and in other high places,
   seems to have heard reports of what was afoot and to have based his sanguine
   hopes for peace on them. Soon after this letter was written, however, Adrian's
   efforts at mediation were undermined by King Francis' demand that Emperor
   Charles restore Milan to him as the price of an agreement; Pastor IX 169–83.

of what you have than to fight a war and lose your life and your possessions.
I prefer peace at a price to war which will be more expensive still.

You will say at this point, I know, 'A genuine German[31] like you, what   28·
business have you with Frenchmen?' Not at all: I often have business with
capons and hens.[32] But, joking apart, I am driven from Germany by the
stoves and invited to France by the wine,[33] the supply of which here is
uncertain. And I should have left by now, had not that excellent man
Nikolaus,[34] the dean, who is the official of the bishop of Basel, given me now   28·
a third cask of Burgundy. And I did not understand his generosity. First of
all he himself sent me a cask, meaning it to be a present. I accepted that,
thinking I could either tolerate such great generosity or repay it. He ordered
a second to be delivered as though I were going to pay for it. When it arrived,
he refused the money. Another time, when he perceived that I was in   29·
danger, he arranged for them to bring a third. I offered his steward the
money for it before the messenger left, and he replied that that could be dealt
with when the wine came. When it arrived, I tried to make him accept
payment for the two; but I couldn't get him to agree to accept a farthing. So
this man's unheard-of and unlooked-for kindness to me who have done   29·
nothing to deserve it makes me most anxious to find some way of repaying
such generosity. And so, if you think it of any value to learning that Erasmus
should be still alive, and if my long stay among you is not unwelcome, you
too are in debt to the dean's liberality. My trouble is incurable, but gets
steadily worse as I get older. The physicians differ in their remedies. One   30·
lesson I learn from the facts, that my best defence against the trouble lies in
the wine; and in this respect France is more fortunate. I shall, however,
share myself between the two nations. My spirit will dwell in Germany and
my body in France. Neither party will be jealous of the other, because the
actual word[35] testifies that you are brothers.   30·

* * * * *

31 On Erasmus' notion of his German identity, see CWE 3 xii and the index to that
   volume under 'Germany, Germans.'
32 The old pun on *Gallus* (Frenchman), *gallus* (cock), and *gallina* (hen). Cf Ep
   1341A:355–62.
33 On the stoves, see Ep 1258 n18; on the wine, see Epp 1316 and 1319
   introductions. This determination to leave Germany was strengthened by the
   disorders attending the Reformation and by the attacks upon him from the
   reformers, which continued throughout the year; see Allen Epp 1359:16,
   1364:20–2, 1376:8–9, 1385:12, 1386:12–13, 1388:13. On 22 June 1523 Basilius
   Amerbach wrote to Bonifacius that Erasmus planned to migrate elsewhere 'sub
   Septembrem'; AK Ep 924:8–9.
34 Nikolaus von Diesbach; Epp 1258 n17, 1342:504–7.
35 Ie, *Germani*

When I was with you, you took an impression of my ring, which made me suspect that you meant to put up somewhere a representation of my emblem.[36] If I guess rightly, I do beg you, my dear Zasius, in the name of our friendship, let us have done with these vulgar practices, which are unworthy of educated men. If there is any point in personal emblems, enough of mine is already on record in my books. Besides which, you let fall once or twice words like 'chief' and 'hero.' I do not fail to see, dear Zasius, that this has no other source than your abundant affection for me. But that affection ought also to induce you to abstain from doing anything which will make your friend look ridiculous or involve him in ill will. Love for their children persuades parents to control that love and not give free rein to the affection they feel for a son, for fear of spoiling by indulgence one who ought to be corrected by severity. I have been laughed at for a long time and mocked by my clever critics as the 'thrice-greatest.' That is bad enough, without being laughed at in the future as 'great chief and hero of learning.'[37] For what little I am worth, I shall try very hard to do what I can. Those glorious names apply to you, who are so well equipped and polished and perfected with literary culture of every kind that I think you have everything needed for complete felicity except that it has not been your good fortune to live in some great city and famous university. Though wherever Zasius may be, it is his gifts that make him great. Even so, it makes a difference to one's fame, position, and chance of getting rich, whether one lives in Athens or Seriphus.[38]

Give my greetings to your esteemed rector[39] and with him to all the chief people and students of your university. I know how much I am indebted to them all. If I have no opportunity of repaying my thanks, at least I shall not lack opportunities to show that I have not forgotten. May Christ the Almighty long preserve your venerable years in health and wealth for the promotion of probity and humane studies. Farewell, from Basel, 20 [February] 1523.

It will be kind of you to let me know by letter if there is anything in which you think I could be of service to your magistrates. What they did for me[40] was far more than I deserved. The man who arranged that there should

* * * * *

36 Terminus; see Ep 604:4n.
37 See Ep 1352 n7.
38 An island in the Aegean, used by the Roman emperors as a place of exile for state criminals
39 Theobald Bapst (c 1497–1564) of Guebwiller in Alsace, professor of rhetoric and later (1535) of law
40 Evidently something more than the usual gift of wine (lines 342–3); cf Allen I 66:357–64.

be a proposal for a new present acted perhaps as one friend towards
another, but he did something I did not welcome. The same thing was going   340
to happen in Basel, when I lately returned here;[41] but I heard about it from
Baer,[42] and resisted tooth and nail anything beyond the usual present of
wine. Farewell once more.

1354 / From Claude Le Marlet   Dijon, [March 1523?]

The manuscript of this letter (=Enthoven Ep 160) is in the Rehdiger Collection
of the University Library at Wrocław (MS Rehd 254.103).
    Little is known about Claude Le Marlet (documented 1503–34), 'docteur ès
droits' and 'avocat' of the Parlement of Dijon. Two orations and some other
works are known to have been published. Allen assigned the date 'March
1523?' on the erroneous assumption that the Marletus of this letter was the
Morletus (Antoine Morelet du Museau) of Allen Ep 1370:5. Since, however,
there is no basis for assigning a more accurate date, the letter can be allowed to
remain where Allen placed it.

Greeting. You will wonder, perhaps, why a man you do not know should
write to you. But do not be surprised, he is no longer unknown, he is your
man; for long ago I devoted myself to you. As a result, I was consumed with
a very great longing to see you, and was even annoyed with my friend
Jussellus,[1] because he had met you when I was not here, for I felt he had   5
stolen a march on me in the joy of our meeting, which by mutual agreement
we were supposed to share. For we had arranged to visit you together; and
this I still greatly desire to do, nor shall I find the breezes blow favourably
until I have seen you, and you have had the opportunity of making my
acquaintance no less than I of making yours. Afterwards, however, since I   10
could not visit you at leisure, I longed very much to write; but fearing that
this might be thought impertinent, I restrained an eagerness you would
hardly credit.
    Overcome at length by this longing to know you, I could no longer
postpone writing to you forthwith, compelled to satisfy my desire even at   15
the price of my reputation. But so far am I from regretting what I have done,

* * * * *

41 In September 1522, after his visit to Botzheim at Constance; Ep 1316
   introduction
42 Ep 305:201n

1354
1 Possibly the 'Jussellus noster' of Allen Ep 1760:6; otherwise unknown

that I care nothing what anyone may say, compared with your friendship. In this there will be a very great strength to me, if you do not think me unworthy of it; and since I see that everyone else aspires to it, I must try all the more to be worthy of it, and to be admitted with others to that society, the honourable society of your friends. For this I have developed such a longing that everywhere I heard the name Erasmus, Erasmus, my most beloved Erasmus. And if Erasmus has had any devotees, I too am of their number; and this, it seems to me, is my one claim to be regarded as a very learned man – my delight in your writings and my great affection for yourself. And so it will be for the future: I shall love you always and, though your name is already well known of itself on account of your learning, I shall proclaim it everywhere and praise and magnify it.

Farewell, from Dijon, far into the night.

Your servant Claude Le Marlet, your most obedient disciple

To Desiderius Erasmus of Rotterdam, my revered master. In Basel

1355 / From Joost Vroye Louvain, 27 March 1523

The autograph of this letter (=Förstemann/Günther Ep 5) was in the Burscher Collection at Leipzig (Ep 1254 introduction). The letter is presumed to be Vroye's answer to Ep 1347: see the introduction to that letter.

Greeting. Sole glory of literature and leader of all learning, Neve's death – the saddest, most sorrowful, most heavy blow that could befall me – reminds me, since about eight years ago I suffered from a similar complaint, that I must do nothing and think of nothing of which I am not ready shortly to give an account to the most high God. As far as your business is concerned, our long-standing friendship requires that I should never fail to promote your interests, and so pray be quite convinced that it will be the greatest pleasure to me if I am ever blessed with an opportunity of doing anything for you. And so, as regards the request you make in your letter, I shall do my very best not to let you feel you lack the services of a man of good will and a friend. But the whole matter does not depend upon me, for others too are concerned in it, the physician[1] and the official of Bruges,[2] and other persons beside the heirs, who have in their hands the power to deprive us of all right to act, once they have agreed to accept the inheritance; from which, scenting danger, they have hitherto refrained, fearing that the debts may be heavier

* * * * *

1355
1 Ep 1351 n15
2 Identity uncertain. See Allen's note for two possibilities.

than the assets of the deceased. The family is not only not rich, but so poor that they have borrowed money on which they are living a pitiful life among us while they await the outcome; and so they are more greedy for the spoils and more impatient than is customary.

Concerning your library,[3] Neve had spoken vaguely about it in such a way that all his fellow-lodgers believed it to be his, except for a few papers which we discovered; but I hope, and at the same time I will do my best to see, that you are put to no inquiry on the subject. The cups I am quite convinced were yours; but how are you to persuade these very grasping characters that they are not covered by the agreement in which he puts on record that there is nothing left owing between you except mutual good will, or, if it does not cover them, that it equally does not cover the debt which they say you owe for your stay here, which in their opinion exceeds the value of the cups? So if you were to have some more definite evidence that you have paid for your stay here, I should advise you to produce that for preference. As for the wine, I am well aware that it was sent you as a present, for I have often heard that for the carriage alone you paid fourteen gold florins;[4] but if they say it has gone off (as they understood from the servants), how shall it be proved that it was the regent[5] let it go bad? We found the two chairs[6] of Brussels work, but they were both sold before your letter arrived. The litter of which you write I have not yet seen, but we have found the long table; and I only wish we could have found all these things (which we who are your friends here readily believe to be yours) in your possession rather than in his. I promise however to do all I can in this respect; but to enable us more easily to satisfy his friends, and the endless claims of these worthless people, if you have anything in your possession that might help to clear up this business, please send it either to me or to Goclenius[7] or to some other friend. Farewell, prince of scholars.

From Louvain, 27 March 152[2]

Your most devoted Joost of Gavere

To the prince not of theologians only but of all learned men, by me ever to be respected, Erasmus of Rotterdam. In Basel

* * * * *

3 Ep 1351 n11
4 If Florentine florins are meant, a sum then worth £4 13s 4d gros Flemish, or £3 3s sterling, or £29 1s tournois. See Ep 1295 n1.
5 Neve; Epp 298 introduction, 1347
6 See Epp 616:17–18, 637:13–14.
7 Ep 1209 introduction

Ep 1270A / From Battista Casali   Rome, spring (after 1 April) 1522

The manuscript of this letter, which was unknown to Allen, is in the Biblioteca
Ambrosiana in Milan (MS G 33 inf 1 ff 137–138r). It was first published
by Silvana Seidel Menchi as an appendix to her 'Alcuni atteggiamenti della
cultura italiana di fronte a Erasmo' in *Eresia e riforma nell'Italia del Cinquecento
Miscellanea* I (Florence and Chicago 1974) 69–133; see especially 94–7 and 129
(text of the letter). The letter has also been published in the French-language
edition of Erasmus' correspondence, *La Correspondance d'Erasme* ed Aloîs Gerlo
and Paul Foriers V (Brussels 1976). Although the existence of the letter was
known to the CWE editors (see CEBR I 276), it was unaccountably omitted from
the list of letters to be included in CWE 9. By the time the annotator discovered
the oversight, the volume had already gone to press and there was no option
but to insert the letter at the end of the volume. The translation is by Alexander
Dalzell.

Battista Casali of Rome (c 1473–1525), who held a prebend at St Peter's
basilica, was a poet, a participant in the Roman Academy (Ep 1341A n115), and
a professor of Latin at the Roman university, the Sapienza. Erasmus had not
met Casali when he visited Rome in 1509, but at some point had been made
aware of his existence. Sometime after the publication of the paraphrase on
Matthew (March 1522; Ep 1255), Erasmus sent a copy of the paraphrase to
Casali along with a letter, now lost, the aim of which was evidently (lines
7–9) to enlist Casali's aid against Zúñiga (Ep 1260 n36), who was also teaching
at the Sapienza (Ep 1260:191–2). Casali replied with this complimentary but
rather reserved letter. By 1524 Casali's reserve had turned into open hostility,
which he expressed in a brief but vitriolic 'Invectiva in Erasmum Roterodamum,' charging Erasmus with denigrating the Italian humanists and their
Ciceronianism, and also with undermining the Christian faith. In a letter of
31 August 1524 devoted to a response to his Italian critics, Erasmus denied that
he knew Casali and attributed the 'Invectiva' to Casali's friend Angelo Colocci
(1467–1549); see Allen Ep 1479:28–32 and the articles on Casali and Colocci in
CEBR I. Since Casali's letter has to have been written well before the 'Invectiva'
of 1524, Erasmus' denial that he knew Casali before August 1524 must be a
lapse of memory, which is easily understandable: Erasmus had never met the
man; writing to him might well have been someone else's idea (see n1); and it is
not even certain that Erasmus ever received Casali's letter.

Only an approximate date can be assigned. Line 2 indicates that the
paraphrase on Matthew, which came off the press sometime between 7 and 21
March 1522 (Epp 1264:19–20, 1267:32–?), had been published 'recently.' Even
if Casali's copy had been dispatched to Rome immediately upon publication, it
is difficult to imagine him having replied until sometime after the first of April;

the earliest surviving letters acknowledging receipt of the paraphrase (Epp 1269–70) were dated 31 March and 1 April in Brussels, which is much closer to Basel than is Rome. Moreover, lines 20–1 seem to indicate that Erasmus had made mention in his letter to Casali of his campaign in the spring of 1522 to win the support of important personages, especially those at the imperial court, against those who had charged him with being a supporter of Luther; see especially Epp 1267 (21 March), 1269 (31 March, 1273–6 (21–3 April). Under the circumstances, the decision of Gerlo and Foriers to adopted Seidel Menchi's date, 'spring 1522,' to add the qualification 'after 1 April,' and to assign the number Ep 1207A is as good a solution to the problem of dating as can be devised, so we have decided to adopt it.

Your servant brought me your letter together with the work on Matthew which you published recently; it is a gift both worthy of you and most welcome to me, first because it comes from one whose learning I have always greatly admired and whose mind I venerate for the rich and scholarly harvest which it never fails to yield; and secondly because I appreciate the   5
opportunity which it affords, and which I have long desired, to win your friendship, for you know the interest I take in your affairs. You say in your letter that you are harassed by people who treat you as a Lutheran and attack you with a cannonade of pamphlets.[1] In my opinion you have no cause to fear; for your life and character and writings will plead your case well   10
enough: they will provide everyone with ample evidence of the gulf which separates you from Luther.

As for Luther himself, whom you think we should treat gingerly for fear of making the fire blaze up more fiercely, I have always disagreed with those who took Luther more seriously than his effrontery justified. I have   15
come to the opinion that the best and most effective defence against him is silence. That surely is the proper way to deal with the matter: the whole business can easily be brought to a conclusion if, with no one to fight against, Luther becomes his own enemy and perishes on his own sword.

You plead for noble princes to help you against those who attack you as   20

* * * * *

1270A

1 Although it appears from this general phraseology that Erasmus had mentioned no one by name in his letter, it is clear that Zúñiga was the principal object of his concern. Jakob Ziegler had informed Erasmus in considerable detail about Zúñiga's anti-Erasmus campaign in Rome (Ep 1260:159ff), that Paolo Bombace's efforts at defence had been ineffective, and that 'things were going downhill' (ibidem 212–15). This would likely have convinced Erasmus of the urgency of seeking allies in Rome (cf Seidel Menchi 94–5), and it is conceivable that someone in Rome suggested Casali to him as a likely prospect.

a traitor and a follower of Luther.[2] Please be assured that I shall always be your most enthusiastic defender: in the past, before a full meeting of the senate,[3] I resolutely countered the Lutheran calumnies which were hurled against you. Whatever zeal and effort and industry can accomplish, I shall boldly accomplish on your behalf. My most earnest prayer is to be worthy of Erasmus' respect.

25

* * * * *

2 See Epp 1267, 1269, 1273–6, 1287, 1299, 1300.
3 Hardly the Roman senate, which was a judicial body with no interest in Erasmus' views or Casali's opinion of them; cf Seidel Menchi 87 n128. Possibly some sort of academic senate at the Sapienza, although the annotator could find no evidence that the Sapienza had such a body. It is most likely, therefore, that Casali is referring to the college of cardinals, which was frequently called a senatus (see, for example, LB IX 385B). In his 'Invectiva' (see introduction) Casali boasts that among those who have been an appreciative audience for his eloquence are 'pontifices universusque senatus' (Biblioteca Ambrosiana Milan, MS G33 inf part 2, f 84r).

TABLE OF CORRESPONDENTS

WORKS FREQUENTLY CITED

SHORT-TITLE FORMS

INDEX

TABLE OF CORRESPONDENTS

WORKS FREQUENTLY CITED

This list provides bibliographical information for works referred to in short-title form in this volume. For Erasmus' writings see the short-title list, pages 466–9. Editions of his letters are included in the list below.

AK   *Die Amerbachkorrespondenz* ed Alfred Hartmann and B.R. Jenny (Basel 1942–   )

Allen   *Opus epistolarum Des. Erasmi Roterodami* ed P.S. Allen, H.M. Allen, and H.W. Garrod (Oxford 1906–58) 11 vols and index

ASD   *Opera omnia Desiderii Erasmi Roterodami* (Amsterdam 1969–   )

BAO   *Briefe und Akten zum Leben Oekolampads* ed Ernst Staehelin 2 vols Quellen und Forschungen zur Reformationsgeschichte 10 and 19 (Leipzig 1927–34; repr New York-London 1971)

Bataillon   Marcel Bataillon *Erasme et l'Espagne* (Paris 1937)

Bietenholz   P.G. Bietenholz *Basle and France in the Sixteenth Century: The Basle Humanists and Printers in Their Contacts with Francophone Culture* (Geneva-Toronto 1971)

Böcking   Ulrich von Hutten *Opera quae reperiri potuerunt omnia* ed Eduard Böcking (Leipzig 1859–61; repr Aalen 1963) 5 vols

BRE   *Briefwechsel des Beatus Rhenanus* ed A. Horawitz and K. Hartfelder (Leipzig 1886; repr Hildesheim 1966)

CEBR   *Contemporaries of Erasmus: A Biographical Register of the Renaissance and Reformation* ed Peter G. Bietenholz and Thomas B. Deutscher (Toronto 1985–7) 3 vols

CR   *Philippi Melanchthonis opera quae supersunt omnia* ed C.G. Bretschneider et al *Corpus Reformatorum* 1–28 (Halle 1834–60; repr 1963)

CSEL   *Corpus scriptorum ecclesiasticorum latinorum* (Vienna-Leipzig 1866–   )

CWE   *Collected Works of Erasmus* (Toronto 1974–   )

Enthoven   *Briefe an Desiderius Erasmus von Rotterdam* ed L.K. Enthoven (Strasbourg 1906)

Epistolae ad diversos   *Epistolae D. Erasmi Roterodami ad diversos et aliquot aliorum ad illum* (Basel: Froben 31 August 1521)

Ferguson *Opuscula*   *Erasmi opuscula: A Supplement to the Opera Omnia* ed W.K. Ferguson (The Hague 1933)

Förstemann/Günther   *Briefe an Desiderius Erasmus von Rotterdam* ed J. Förstemann and O. Günther, XXVII. Beiheft zum *Zentralblatt für Bibliothekwesen* (Leipzig 1904)

Gachard — *Collections des voyages des souverains des Pays-Bas* ed L.P. Gachard and C. Piot (Brussels 1874–82) 4 vols

Holeczek — Heinz Holeczek *Erasmus Deutsch* I (Stuttgart-Bad Canstatt 1983)

Kaegi — Werner Kaegi 'Hutten und Erasmus: Ihre Freundschaft und ihr Streit' *Historische Vierteljahrschrift* 12 (1924–5) 200–78, 461–514

LB — *Desiderii Erasmi Roterodami opera omnia* ed J. Leclerc (Leiden 1703–6; repr 1961–2) 10 vols

LP — *Letters and Papers, Foreign and Domestic, of the Reign of Henry VIII* ed J.S. Brewer, J. Gairdner, and R.H. Brodie (London 1862–1932) 36 vols

Opus epistolarum — *Opus epistolarum Des. Erasmi Roterodami per autorem diligenter recognitum et adjectis innumeris novis fere ad trientem auctum* (Basel: Froben, Herwagen, and Episcopius 1529)

Pastor — Ludwig von Pastor *The History of the Popes from the Close of the Middle Ages* ed and trans R.F. Kerr et al, 6th ed (London 1938–53) 40 vols

Pirckheimeri opera — *Bilibaldi Pirckheimeri ... opera politica, historica, philologica, et epistolica* ed Melchior Goldast (Frankfurt 1610; repr Hildesheim-New York 1969)

PL — *Patrologiae cursus completus ... series latina* ed J.P. Migne (Paris 1844–1902) 221 vols

Planitz — Hans von der Planitz *Berichte aus dem Reichsregiment in Nürnberg 1521–3* assembled E. Wulcher ed H. Virck (Leipzig 1899)

Reedijk — *The Poems of Desiderius Erasmus* ed C. Reedijk (Leiden 1956)

RTA — *Deutsche Reichstagsakten, Jüngere Reihe* (Gotha, Stuttgart, Göttingen 1896–   )

Rublack — Hans-Christoph Rublack *Die Einführung der Reformation in Konstanz* (Gütersloh 1971)

Scheible — *Melanchthons Briefwechsel: Kritische und Kommentierte Gesamtausgabe* ed Heinz Scheible (Stuttgart-Bad Canstatt 1977–   )

Schottenloher *Ziegler* — Karl Schottenloher *Jakob Ziegler aus Landau an der Isar: Ein Gelehrtenleben aus der Zeit des Humanismus und der Reformation* (Münster/Westfalen 1910)

Thompson — *The Colloquies of Erasmus* ed and trans Craig R. Thompson (Chicago 1965)

de Vocht *Collegium Trilingue* — Henry de Vocht *History of the Foundation and Rise of the Collegium Trilingue Lovaniense 1517–1550* 4 vols Humanistica lovaniensia 10–13 (Louvain 1951–5) de Vocht *Literae ad Craneveldium* *Literae virorum eruditorum ad Franciscum Craneveldium 1522–1528* ed Henry de Vocht Humanistica lovaniensia 1 (Louvain 1928)

WA *D. Martin Luthers Werke, Kritische Gesamtausgabe* (Weimar 1883–   )

WA-Br *D. Martin Luthers Werke: Briefwechsel* (Weimar 1930–78) 15 vols

Zw-Br *Huldreich Zwinglis Sämtliche Werke 7–11: Zwinglis Briefwechsel* ed Emil Egli et al / *Corpus Reformatorum 94–8* (Leipzig 1911–35)

SHORT-TITLE FORMS FOR ERASMUS' WORKS

Titles following colons are longer versions of the same, or are alternative titles. Items entirely enclosed in square brackets are of doubtful authorship. For abbreviations, see Works Frequently Cited.

Adagia: Adagiorum chiliades 1508, etc (Adagiorum collectanea for the primitive form, when required) LB II / ASD II-4, 5, 6 / CWE 30–6
Admonitio adversus mendacium: Admonitio adversus mendacium et obtrectationem LB X
Annotationes in Novum Testamentum LB VI
Antibarbari LB X / ASD I-1 / CWE 23
Apologia ad Caranzam: Apologia ad Sanctium Caranzam, or Apologia de tribus locis, or Responsio ad annotationem Stunicae ... a Sanctio Caranza defensam LB IX
Apologia ad Fabrum: Apologia ad Iacobum Fabrum Stapulensem LB IX
Apologia adversus monachos: Apologia adversus monachos quosdam hispanos LB IX
Apologia adversus Petrum Sutorem: Apologia adversus debacchationes Petri Sutoris LB IX
Apologia adversus rhapsodias Alberti Pii: Apologia ad viginti et quattuor libros A. Pii LB IX
Apologia contra Latomi dialogum: Apologia contra Iacobi Latomi dialogum de tribus linguis LB IX
Apologiae contra Stunicam: Apologiae contra Lopidem Stunicam LB IX / ASD IX-2
Apologia de 'In principio erat sermo' LB IX
Apologia de laude matrimonii: Apologia pro declamatione de laude matrimonii LB IX
Apologia de loco 'Omnes quidem': Apologia de loco 'Omnes quidem resurgemus' LB IX
Apologia invectivis Lei: Apologia qua respondet duabus invectivis Eduardi Lei *Opuscula*
Apophthegmata LB IV
Appendix respondens ad Sutorem LB IX
Argumenta: Argumenta in omnes epistolas apostolicas nova (with Paraphrases)
Axiomata pro causa Lutheri: Axiomata pro causa Martini Lutheri *Opuscula*

Carmina varia LB VIII
Catalogus lucubrationum LB I
Christiani hominis institutum, carmen LB V
Ciceronianus: Dialogus Ciceronianus LB I / ASD I-2 / CWE 28
Colloquia LB I / ASD I-3
Compendium vitae Allen I / CWE 4
[Consilium: Consilium cuiusdam ex animo cupientis esse consultum] *Opuscula*

De concordia: De amabili ecclesiae concordia (in Psalmi)
De bello turcico: Consultatio de bello turcico (in Psalmi)
De civilitate: De civilitate morum puerilium LB I / CWE 25
Declamatio de morte LB IV
Declamatiuncula LB IV

Declarationes ad censuras Lutetiae vulgatas: Declarationes ad censuras Lutetiae vulgatas sub nomine facultatis theologiae Parisiensis LB IX

De conscribendis epistolis LB I / ASD I-2 / CWE 25

De constructione: De constructione octo partium orationis, or Syntaxis LB I / ASD I-4

De contemptu mundi: Epistola de contemptu mundi LB V / ASD V-1 / CWE 66

De copia: De duplici copia verborum ac rerum LB I / CWE 24

De immensa Dei misericordia: Concio de immensa Dei misericordia LB V

De libero arbitrio: De libero arbitrio diatribe LB IX

De praeparatione: De praeparatione ad mortem LB V / ASD V-1

De pueris instituendis: De pueris statim ac liberaliter instituendis LB I / ASD I-2 / CWE 26

De puero Iesu: Concio de puero Iesu LB V

De puritate tabernaculi: De puritate tabernaculi sive ecclesiae christianae (in Psalmi)

De ratione studii LB I / ASD I-2 / CWE 24

De recta pronuntiatione: De recta latini graecique sermonis pronuntiatione LB I / ASD I-4 / CWE 26

Detectio praestigiarum: Detectio praestigiarum cuiusdam libelli germanice scripti LB X / ASD IX-1

De tedio Iesu: Disputatiuncula de tedio, pavore, tristicia Iesu LB V

De vidua christiana LB V / CWE 66

De virtute amplectenda: Oratio de virtute amplectenda LB V

[Dialogus bilinguium ac trilinguium: Chonradi Nastadiensis dialogus bilinguium ac trilinguium] Opuscula / CWE 7

Dilutio: Dilutio eorum quae Iodocus Clithoveus scripsit adversus declamationem suasoriam matrimonii

Divinationes ad notata Bedae LB IX

Ecclesiastes: Ecclesiastes sive de ratione concionandi LB V

Elenchus in N. Bedae censuras LB IX

Enchiridion: Enchiridion militis christiani LB V / CWE 66

Encomium matrimonii (in De conscribendis epistolis)

Encomium medicinae: Declamatio in laudem artis medicae LB I / ASD I-4

Epigrammata LB I

Epistola ad Dorpium LB IX / CWE 3

Epistola ad fratres Inferioris Germaniae: Responsio ad fratres Germaniae Inferioris ad epistolam apologeticam incerto autore proditam LB X

Epistola ad graculos: Epistola ad quosdam imprudentissimos graculos LB X

Epistola apologetica de Termino LB X

Epistola consolatoria: Epistola consolatoria virginibus sacris LB V

Epistola contra pseudevangelicos: Epistola contra quosdam qui se falso iactant evangelicos LB X / ASD IX-1

Epistola de esu carnium: Epistola apologetica ad Christophorum episcopum Basiliensem de interdicto esu carnium LB IX / ASD IX-1

Exomologesis: Exomologesis sive modus confitendi LB V

Explanatio symboli: Explanatio symboli apostolorum sive catechismus LB V / ASD V-1

Expositio concionalis (in Psalmi)

Expostulatio Iesu LB V

Formula: Conficiendarum epistolarum formula (see De conscribendis epistolis)

Hymni varii LB V
Hyperaspistes LB X

Institutio christiani matrimonii LB V
Institutio principis christiani LB IV / ASD IV-1 / CWE 27

[Julius exclusus: Dialogus Julius exclusus e coelis] *Opuscula* / CWE 27

Lingua LB IV / ASD IV-1
Liturgia Virginis Matris: Virginis Matris apud Lauretum cultae liturgia LB V / ASD V-1

Methodus (see Ratio)
Modus orandi Deum LB V / ASD V-1
Moria: Moriae encomium LB IV / ASD IV-3 / CWE 27

Novum Testamentum: Novum Testamentum 1519 and later (Novum instrumentum
for the first edition, 1516, when required) LB VI

Obsecratio ad Virginem Mariam: Obsecratio sive oratio ad Virginem Mariam in rebus
adversis LB V
Oratio de pace: Oratio de pace et discordia LB VIII
Oratio funebris: Oratio funebris Berthae de Heyen LB VIII

Paean Virgini Matri: Paean Virgini Matri dicendus LB V
Panegyricus: Panegyricus ad Philippum Austriae ducem LB IV / ASD IV-1 / CWE 27
Parabolae: Parabolae sive similia LB I / ASD I-5 / CWE 23
Paraclesis LB V, VI
Paraphrasis in Elegantias Vallae: Paraphrasis in Elegantias Laurentii Vallae LB I / ASD
I-4
Paraphrasis in Matthaeum, etc (in Paraphrasis in Novum Testamentum)
Paraphrasis in Novum Testamentum LB VII / CWE 42–50
Peregrinatio apostolorum: Peregrinatio apostolorum Petri et Pauli LB VI, VII
Precatio ad Virginis filium Iesum LB V
Precatio dominica LB V
Precationes LB V
Precatio pro pace ecclesiae: Precatio ad Iesum pro pace ecclesiae LB IV, V
Progymnasmata: Progymnasmata quaedam primae adolescentiae Erasmi LB VIII
Psalmi: Psalmi, or Enarrationes sive commentarii in psalmos LB V / ASD V-2, 3
Purgatio adversus epistolam Lutheri: Purgatio adversus epistolam non sobriam
Lutheri LB IX

Querela pacis LB IV / ASD IV-2 / CWE 27

Ratio: Ratio seu Methodus compendio perveniendi ad veram theologiam (Methodus
for the shorter version originally published in the Novum instrumentum of
1516) LB V, VI

Responsio ad annotationes Lei: Liber quo respondet annotationibus Lei LB IX
Responsio ad collationes: Responsio ad collationes cuiusdam iuvenis gerontodidas-
cali LB IX
Responsio ad disputationem de divortio: Responsio ad disputationem cuiusdam
Phimostomi de divortio LB IX
Responsio ad epistolam Pii: Responsio ad epistolam paraeneticam Alberti Pii, or
Responsio ad exhortationem Pii LB IX
Responsio ad notulas Bedaicas LB X
Responsio ad Petri Cursii defensionem: Epistola de apologia Cursii LB X
Responsio adversus febricitantis libellum: Apologia monasticae religionis LB X

Spongia: Spongia adversus aspergines Hutteni LB X / ASD IX-1
Supputatio: Supputatio calumniarum Natalis Bedae LB IX

Virginis et martyris comparatio LB V
Vita Hieronymi: Vita divi Hieronymi Stridonensis *Opuscula*

Index

This book

was designed by

ANTJE LINGNER

based on the series design by

ALLAN FLEMING

and was printed by

University

of Toronto

Press